ATLANTIC REPUBLIC

1. *The Surrender of Lord Cornwallis at Yorktown, 19 October 1781*, by John Trumbull (*c*.1797). Cornwallis, pleading illness, declined to appear for the surrender ceremonies, and the English soldier offering his sword in the centre of the painting is Cornwallis's second in command, General O'Hara.

Atlantic Republic

The American Tradition in English Literature

PAUL GILES

OXFORD
UNIVERSITY PRESS

OXFORD

UNIVERSITY PRESS

Great Clarendon Street, Oxford OX2 6DP

Oxford University Press is a department of the University of Oxford.
It furthers the University's objective of excellence in research, scholarship,
and education by publishing worldwide in

Oxford New York

Auckland Cape Town Dar es Salaam Hong Kong Karachi
Kuala Lumpur Madrid Melbourne Mexico City Nairobi
New Delhi Shanghai Taipei Toronto

With offices in

Argentina Austria Brazil Chile Czech Republic France Greece
Guatemala Hungary Italy Japan Poland Portugal Singapore
South Korea Switzerland Thailand Turkey Ukraine Vietnam

Oxford is a registered trade mark of Oxford University Press
in the UK and in certain other countries

Published in the United States
by Oxford University Press Inc., New York

British Library Cataloguing in Publication Data

Data available

Library of Congress Cataloging in Publication Data

Data available

Typeset by Laserwords Private Limited, Chennai, India
Printed in Great Britain
on acid-free paper by
Biddles Ltd., King's Lynn, Norfolk

ISBN 0–19–920633–3 978–0–19–920633–9

1 3 5 7 9 10 8 6 4 2

To my American cats and my English parents
with affection, love, and thanks

Preface

Although they were not originally conceived as a trilogy, this is the third (and last) in a series of books exploring the interrelation between British and American literary cultures. Each volume has a different focal point: *Transatlantic Insurrections* (2001) considers how writers on both sides of the Atlantic engaged with the prospect of American political independence in the eighteenth century; *Virtual Americas* (2002) outlines alternative configurations for American studies in a transnational and digital era; *Atlantic Republic* switches the emphasis to ways in which the development of US society in the nineteenth and twentieth centuries served to create a potential space for dissent within modern English literature. The Anglo-American relationship is often understood today in characteristically conservative terms, the legacy of an American tradition of Anglophilia bound up with Brahmin gentility or, on the British side, with the political assumption since 1940 of a 'special relationship' between Churchill and Roosevelt, Thatcher and Reagan, Blair and Bush. As I hope to show in this book, the course of Anglo-American cultural relations over the past 230 years has, in fact, been far more complicated and historically variable than these emollient stereotypes would imply. Indeed, *Atlantic Republic* argues that the covertly disruptive influence of an American republican tradition has too often been overlooked in considerations of the ways in which English national identity has been formulated and consolidated over the past two centuries.

I should like to express my thanks to the Arts and Humanities Research Board and the University of Cambridge for allowing me two terms of sabbatical leave during the academic year 2001–2002, which helped towards the completion of this work. I would also like to acknowledge the assistance of the editorial staff of *PMLA* with two essays which comprised early versions of Chapters 3 and 8 respectively: 'Transnationalism and Classic American Literature', which appeared in *PMLA*, 118 (Jan. 2003), 62–77; and 'American Literature in English Translation: Denise Levertov and Others', *PMLA*, 119 (Jan. 2004), 31–41. Thanks also to Djelal Kadir and Martha Banta for the opportunity to contribute to these special issues.

An exploratory version of Chapter 1 was first presented at a symposium on the Atlantic Enlightenment at the Institute for Advanced Studies in the Humanities, University of Edinburgh, in May 2002. Thanks to Susan Manning for the invitation, and to Peter Onuf and Paul Gilje, among others, for constructive feedback. Other talks based on this material were given at the University of the West of England, Dartmouth College, Washington University in St Louis, Portland State University, the University of Mainz, and at the Congress of the International American Studies Association held at the University of Leiden in May 2003; at all of these events, members of the audience made helpful observations and comments. I am grateful also to J. G. Ballard and Caryl Phillips for answering specific questions about their writing careers, to Bénédicte Ledent for resolving a dating query, to Wai Chee Dimock and the other Oxford University Press readers of the manuscript for their very insightful comments, and to Andrew McNeillie at Oxford University Press for helping to ensure that the landing gear was locked tightly into place as the runway came into view after what seemed, at times, like an inordinately long and turbulent transatlantic passage.

PAUL GILES

Oxford, November 2005

Contents

List of Illustrations

Introduction: Reformation, Disestablishment, Transnationalism

Atlantic Republic is concerned with how the legacy of the American Revolution has manifested itself in English writing over the past two centuries, with ways in which the war of 1775–83 and the subsequent division into the two distinct nation-states created a schism in Anglophone culture that has crucially shaped ways in which English literature has conceived of itself. I shall argue that the United States has operated both literally and metaphorically for English writers as a locus of dissent, so that to read English literature transatlantically is to counterpoint its more traditional Anglican virtues by recovering the impetus of an English nonconformist tradition that can be traced back through the War of Independence as far as the Reformation. Part of this book, then, involves a consideration of ways in which particular forms of religious rhetoric have continued to reverberate in modern culture, albeit often in displaced, secularized, or figurative forms. I am not claiming that the Reformation functions as an all-encompassing topos for Anglo-American literary relations; I am suggesting, more modestly, that English writers who saw themselves as engaged with traditions of disestablishment and republicanism often looked back consciously to the sixteenth and seventeenth centuries as the era when these kinds of religious and political disputes first began to create ruptures within British society. The Reformation is used here retrospectively rather than prospectively, as a cultural scene to which modern writers keep returning, rather than as a source from which everything flows.

Any book with a title such as this can hardly avoid a nod to J. G. A. Pocock's magisterial work *The Machiavellian Moment: Florentine Political Thought and the Atlantic Republican Tradition* (1975). Without of course attempting to claim any kind of parity, *Atlantic Republic* might be seen on one level as an attempt to consider in relation to literature the kinds of question that Pocock addresses in the context of intellectual history, the ways in which the principles of revolution in America evolved out of, and were consistent with, radical traditions in Europe. But although I address Pocock's work later, my own emphasis is not so much on intellectual history for its own sake as on ways in which ideas were understood affectively and projected in aesthetic forms. In this wider public arena, the more rarefied, enlightened notion of a shared intellectual heritage—the significance of John Locke's influence on both sides of the Atlantic, for instance—has tended to carry less weight than the mutual suspicions and often brutal sense of antagonism that caused Dissenters and Anglicans, republicans and monarchists, to engage in cultural warfare with each other. In his historical account of the Reformation, Diarmaid MacCulloch takes issue with what he calls 'the complacent English boast of a national history of tolerance' by pointing out how the 'hard-line' attitude of Anglicans after the restoration of Charles II in 1660 served to create '"Dissent" out of those who had been part of the united pre-war Church of England'. MacCulloch goes on to describe how this reactionary force created lasting divisions within English society, even though today these 'partitions have been replaced and put up in different places', with the legacy of the Protestant Reformation now at its most overt and powerful in the United States.[1] The Puritan emigration from England to New England in the seventeenth century is an old story, of course: John Winthrop and his followers, including Anne Bradstreet, chose to flee from the royalist authoritarianism that prevailed in the years leading up to the English Civil War, while Edward Taylor left in 1668, shortly after the Restoration, because he would not sign an oath of loyalty to the Church of England. What has been much less considered, however, is the way in which this impulse of dissent develops subsequently into a counter-tradition within English literature, a form of resistance which has helped to demarcate the contours and define the internal assumptions of the subject. In this sense, *Atlantic Republic* is intended explicitly to involve a metacritical dimension, since it is concerned not just to describe an Atlantic tradition but also to extrapolate from this story various questions about how the institutional parameters of English literature have traditionally been codified, and why.

One aim of this book, then, is to redescribe English literature according to the logic of transnationalism, to suggest how this particular critical method can open up historical vistas that remain occluded when the field is understood according to older models of organic coherence and temporal continuity. Indeed, the historical legacies of the Reformation and schism might be seen as powerful precursors of transnationalism in their common emphasis on division and rupture. This consciousness of division would allow for a remapping of the genealogies for 'English Literature', as that domain was conventionally defined in the twentieth century. As Krishan Kumar has shown, English as an academic discipline was developed around the turn of the twentieth century, partly in reaction against the increasing prominence of Celtic (Welsh, Scottish, Irish) identities at that time. Oxford University established its Honours School in English in 1893, and Cambridge in 1917, while Sir Arthur Quiller-Couch's *Oxford Book of English Verse*, first published in 1900, had by 1939 been reprinted twenty times and sold

[1] Diarmaid MacCulloch, *Reformation: Europe's House Divided, 1490–1700* (London: Allen Lane, 2003), 531, 706.

half a million copies.[2] In his companion volume *The Oxford Book of English Prose* (1925), Quiller-Couch, by then Professor of English Literature at Cambridge, sought explicitly to bring together past and present so as to align English literary history with his sense of reverence for the country's national heritage. As he explained in his preface, the selections for this anthology were chosen

to make this book as representatively English as I might; with less thought of robust and resounding 'patriotism' than of that subdued and hallowed emotion which, for example, should possess any man's thoughts standing before the tomb of the Black Prince in Canterbury Cathedral: a sense of wonderful history written silently in books and buildings, all persuading that we are heirs of more spiritual wealth than, may be, we have surmised or hitherto begun to divine.[3]

Quiller-Couch's mystification of English cultural history might now seem to us merely pompous or absurd, but in fact it merely magnifies what John Lucas has described as the tendency throughout the study of English literature in the twentieth century to sanctify a spirit of place and the instinctive knowledge supposedly accumulated from an immersion within it.[4] For all of their ideological differences, both F. R. Leavis in *The Great Tradition* (1948) and Raymond Williams in *The Long Revolution* (1961) similarly sought to identify continuity and longevity as central characteristics of the English literary tradition. This is why what we might call the Wordsworthian impulse—the attempt creatively to imbue native landscapes with a sense of natural authority—is still a powerful force within the world of English studies. This synchronicity between the emergence of English literature as a professional field and the dissemination of popular forms of romanticism has served to canonize a particularly skewed version of English literary traditions, one that has marginalized metaphysical ideas and idioms as excessively recondite and chosen to glorify instead in the kind of raw domestic landscapes that we find in, say, Ted Hughes.

This partial version of the English heritage was complicated further in the twentieth century by the concern on the part of Quiller-Couch and others to deploy English language and literature as integral tools of a wider educational process. By a familiar bureaucratic pattern, the effort to disseminate English culture widely became interwoven systematically with an administrative, pedagogical concern for national standardization and cultural homogeneity. In 1921, for example, the president of the English Association, Henry Newbolt, published a report championing a prosaic orthodoxy in the uses of English and asserting that the function of the language should be to unify society into what he called

---

[2] Krishan Kumar, *The Making of English National Identity* (Cambridge: Cambridge University Press, 2003), 206–7, 220–2.
[3] Sir Arthur Quiller-Couch, ed., *The Oxford Book of English Prose* (London: Oxford University Press, 1925), p. xiii.
[4] John Lucas, *England and Englishness: Ideas of Nationhood in English Poetry* (London: Hogarth Press, 1990), 118.

'a national fellowship'.[5] From this perspective, the capacious structure of English language and literature was supposed to provide an architectonic framework within which fractious differences—particularly, by Newbolt's lights, differences of class—might be forgotten. The *Review of English Studies*, a journal based at Oxford University and dedicated to the 'English genius' and its 'continuity of spirit', was founded four years later, in 1925, and it is not difficult to see how this academic venture follows the same patriotic path as Newbolt, albeit on a more scholarly level. While the *Review of English Studies* did not propose a directly instrumental use of English, contributors to this journal, particularly in its early days, tended to adduce the same ethos of 'sanity and reasonableness' in every example of English literature from *Beowulf* to the twentieth-century novel, thus defining the national literary canon in terms of an unconscious Anglican ideology which would champion the virtues of moderation in all things.[6] In this sense, the diachronic view of English literary homogeneity propounded by the *Review of English Studies* can be seen as no less didactic than the synchronic view proposed by Newbolt; both were concerned to bind English culture into a communal sense of national fellowship.

The alternative tradition I go on to describe in this book is characteristically more fractious and edgy, less easy to assimilate within such comfortable pedagogical frameworks. Just as the short-lived English republic of the 1640s and 1650s positioned itself in theoretical opposition to the monarchy, and just as the American insurrectionists of the 1770s and 1780s chose on principle to dissociate themselves from the British realm, so a wide range of writers in the nineteenth and twentieth centuries sought to bring alternative philosophical and stylistic perspectives into the British cultural domain. The emphasis on freedom of worship and on the disestablishment of the church and the monarchy that impelled seventeenth-century reformers to seek havens in the New World was subsequently renegotiated metaphorically in a wide range of English writers, from Lord Byron and Arthur Hugh Clough through to George Gissing, W. H. Auden, Angela Carter, and others. I am attempting, then, to illuminate a tradition of transatlantic dissent within English literature, a tradition not to be identified solely with the Nonconformist Christian church—although a few of these figures, such as Donald Davie, were indeed practising Dissenters—but with a spirit of reformist iconoclasm more generally; these writers sought to achieve transposed perspectives on English literature and culture by repositioning their works within a transatlantic framework. I am not implying that the authors under discussion here comprise in any sense a homogeneous party, still less that they could be said to share a certain set of political or religious views;

    [5] Chris Baldick, *The Social Mission of English Criticism, 1848–1932* (Oxford: Clarendon Press, 1983), 104. On the relationship between the teaching of English and the promotion of national unity, see Stefan Collini, *Public Moralists: Political Thought and Intellectual Life in Britain, 1850–1930* (Oxford: Clarendon Press, 1991), 361.
    [6] Brian Doyle, *English and Englishness* (London: Routledge, 1989), 83.

what I do suggest is that this transatlantic dynamic, which has been crucial in the making of English literature, has too often been neglected because of the particular circumstances within which the process of canon formation has taken shape.

In the wake of the growth in postcolonial studies in the late-twentieth century, the realignment of English literary studies to accommodate spheres beyond the borders of the nation-state has, of course, been a project much discussed and debated. The final volume in the new *Oxford English Literary History*, published in 2004, is actually called *The Internationalization of English Literature*, though it takes as its chronological boundaries 1948–2000 and focuses mainly on the work of immigrants to Britain from Asia and the Caribbean.[7] My argument here is that such 'internationalization' is not simply a recent phenomenon but, rather, one that can be referred back on a transatlantic axis to the seventeenth and eighteenth centuries, so that the entire shape of English literary history appears different when it is viewed from a transnational critical perspective. In *Nations without Nationalism* (1993), Julia Kristeva distinguishes transnationalism from the idealization of *Volksgeist*, the spirit of the people, that became established in the nineteenth century through the romantic narratives of race and nation promulgated by Herder and Hegel. Instead, Kristeva relates transnationalism to Montesquieu's conception of an 'esprit général', with its Enlightenment attempt to reinscribe relations between the local and the universal, to see particular customs and manners as being linked systematically to a more cosmopolitan 'spirit of concord and economic development'.[8] But of course to look back now at this ideal of Enlightenment 'spirit' is inevitably to find its utopian dimensions crossed with the tangled wires of national self-interest, with the more material ways in which nationalism as a phenomenon became consolidated in the nineteenth and twentieth centuries. As Anthony D. Smith has observed, nationalism in the modern era has been driven not just by patriotic symbolism but also by the centralized state apparatus of administrative logic, educational bureaucracy, and military might. The idea of transnationalism, then, cannot mean a simple elimination of the more oppressive aspects of nationalism, as Montesquieu would ideally have preferred; instead, it involves, as Kristeva suggests, updating 'discussion on the meaning of the "national" today'. As a formal method of inquiry, transnationalism consequently serves to reveal the parameters of national systems and so to hollow out their pressing, peremptory claims to legitimacy. Transnationalism positions itself at a point of intersection—Kristeva talks about 'a transnational or international position situated at the crossing of boundaries'—where the coercive aspects of 'imagined communities' are turned

---

[7] Bruce King, *The Internationalization of English Literature*, Oxford English Literary History, xiii: 1948–2000 (Oxford: Oxford University Press, 2004).

[8] Julia Kristeva, *Nations without Nationalism* (1990), trans. Leon S. Roudiez (New York: Columbia University Press, 1993), 55.

back on themselves, reversed or mirrored, so that their covert presuppositions and ideological assumptions become apparent.[9]

One of the contentions of this book is that English literature, shaped in the nineteenth century by resistance to the emerging political landscape of republicanism in the United States and Europe, was similarly shaped in the twentieth century by resistance to the forces of fascism. Indeed, one of the curious aspects of English writing in the middle part of the twentieth century is how frequently it represents Nazi Germany and corporate America as uncomfortable mirror images of each other, alternative versions of a modernity which the insular British state would prefer to keep at bay. This is not to suggest, of course, that Germany and the United States were at this time in any sense political or moral equivalents; it is to suggest, though, as Paul Gilroy has recently observed, that the enduring post-1945 myth of a British triumph over an evil foe worked effectively to repress the various forms of 'racist violence' still embedded at the heart of 'British social and political life' in the late twentieth century.[10] Just as recovering the anti-republican agenda of Wordsworthian romanticism makes America central rather than marginal to the construction of nineteenth-century English literature, so recovering ways in which twentieth-century English literature has positioned itself in an uneasy, triangular relationship with both European fascism and American republicanism illuminates ways in which modern British culture has continued to negotiate uncomfortably with the spirit of reformation and modernity. A critical transnationalism, in this sense, is concerned not simply to transcend nationalism but to resituate it dialectically, to probe the significance of cultural jagged edges or other forms of apparent incoherence so as to illuminate our understanding of how local situations intersect with broader global currents.

We will see many examples throughout *Atlantic Republic* of this dialectic between local and global, attraction and repulsion, in the context of British and American cultures. When Winston Churchill was trying desperately in 1941 to bring the United States into the Second World War, he invented the legend of a 'special relationship' between the two countries, but there have been many other aspects to this dynamic since the seventeenth century which have been much more disturbing and unsettling for both parties.[11] To restore a transatlantic dimension to English literature is thus to problematize the nationalist teleologies which have encumbered the formation of both English and American literary canons, and which have often produced, in institutional terms, highly simplistic and at times

---

[9] Anthony D. Smith, *Nationalism and Modernism: A Critical Survey of Recent Theories of Nations and Nationalism* (London: Routledge, 1998); Kristeva, *Nations without Nationalism*, 50, 15. For the classic account of structural homologies between the development of print culture and national formations, see Benedict Anderson, *Imagined Communities: Reflections on the Origin and Spread of Nationalism* (London: Verso, 1983).

[10] Paul Gilroy, *After Empire: Melancholia or Convivial Culture?* (Abingdon: Routledge, 2004), 114.

[11] David Reynolds, *Rich Relations: The American Occupation of Britain, 1942–1945* (1996; repr. London: Phoenix Press, 2000), 144.

implicitly authoritarian assumptions about the ethical values of literary works.[12] Whether such assumptions might be conservative, liberal, or radical is hardly the point: the crucial question here concerns a tautology of response, the proclivity of educators simply to read back into any given texts the master narrative, the overall agenda, with which they started. This pattern goes back, of course, to Sir Arthur Quiller-Couch, and by now we are all familiar enough with political arguments about the nature of literary canon formation; but one of the problems with the academic study of US literature and culture in recent times is that it has tended merely to replicate the formation of these traditional canons from a different perspective. Rather than using American studies to interrogate and hollow out the whole question of national identity and its relation to cultural value, university courses in Britain and the rest of Europe during the second half of the twentieth century sought to establish parallel structures based upon the very same nationalist paradigm.

The historical evolution of this pedagogical formula and the impact of globalization upon traditional ways of organizing academic material in national terms was considered retrospectively in 2000 by Heinz Ickstadt, Professor of American Studies at the Kennedy Institute in Berlin. Ickstadt traced the institutional situation of American literature from the 1950s and early 1960s, when it generally held a minor status within English departments, through to the late 1960s and 1970s, when American studies often succeeded in breaking away and establishing itself as an interdisciplinary unit or autonomous department committed to the academic study of American national culture as a synchronic whole. 'Without undue exaggeration', wrote Ickstadt, 'one can say that during the seventies in places like West Berlin, "conservative" English departments and "progressive" American studies departments held each other mutually in contempt.' But contempt is, of course, a way of identifying oneself as well as one's enemy, and, as Ickstadt went on to observe, many American studies programmes in the early twenty-first century have been uncomfortable with the impact of globalization and the so-called transnational turn precisely because such developments would seem to undermine what he calls 'the homogeneity of the field, the solidity and coherence of knowledge and competences transmitted'.[13] This leads to an intellectual cul-de-sac where those professionally invested in the study of US culture, no less than those professionally invested in English literature, have a mutual interest in keeping these fields separate.

One common response to this trauma of academic disenfranchisement has been, predictably enough, replenishment, involving an attempt to shore up nationalist agendas by expanding the canon to embrace what had previously

---

[12] On this point, see Leo Bersani, *The Culture of Redemption* (Cambridge, Mass.: Harvard University Press, 1990).

[13] Heinz Ickstadt, 'Globalization and the National Paradigm; or, can English (and American) Studies be Globalised?', *European English Messenger*, 9/2 (Autumn 2000), 19, 21.

been omitted. Such a strategy is very evident on the part of *The Norton Anthology of English Literature*, whose seventh edition, published in 2000, finds room for authors such as Chinua Achebe, Anita Desai, V. S. Naipaul, J. M. Coetzee, and Salman Rushdie, in order to reflect how, as its editors explain, 'English literature, like so many other collective enterprises in our century, has ceased to be principally the product of the identity of a single nation; it is a global phenomenon.'[14] But the structure of the *Norton Anthology* fulfils this logic only partially, for, as a commercial publisher, Norton mirrors the traditional structure of university English departments in the way it retains a vested interest in organizing its materials on a nationalist basis. Consequently, Susanna Rowson and Denise Levertov are absent from this anthology but appear in its companion, *The Norton Anthology of American Literature*, while other writers with a transatlantic orientation tend to be marginalized: Clough is represented in the *Anthology of English Literature* only by three short poems, while Gissing, Davie, and Christopher Isherwood are not included at all. The achievement of the *Heath Anthology of American Literature* can similarly be seen as double-edged, in that it has made a deliberate and concerted attempt since the time when the 'canon wars' were at their most combustible in the late 1980s and early 1990s to introduce a much wider range of American authors. It is, of course, important to acknowledge the iconoclastic value of the *Heath Anthology* and its successors and the vital contribution they have made to the demystification of the old assumptions that framed the construction of American studies in the middle years of the twentieth century, when unexamined tenets of racism and patriarchy held sway. But it is also important to recognize that the principle of ever-increasing replenishment which impels this kind of anthology must, in the end, become self-defeating. Some of these recent anthologies aiming to incorporate 'the richness and diversity of American culture' are remarkable not just for their heftiness but for their apparent faith that such heft might, in itself, come closer to representing the heart of the national experience.[15] This suggests, ultimately, a politics of representation in its most restrictive form, predicated upon an ethical circumference of imaginary enclosure and an aesthetics of transparency. Like the Victorian novel piling up what Henry James called its 'treasure-house of details' in a vain attempt to approximate a condition of encyclopaedic inclusiveness, the new Americanist textbook would have us believe that these positive agendas of diversity and multiculturalism might in themselves allow access to a more complete version of the nation's cultural identity, wherein the negative polarities of exclusion are annealed and the

---

[14] M. H. Abrams and Stephen Greenblatt, preface to *The Norton Anthology of English Literature*, 7th edn., ii (New York: Norton, 2000), p. xxxv.

[15] Paul Lauter, 'To The Reader', preface to *The Heath Anthology of American Literature* (Lexington, Mass.: D. C. Heath, 1990), i, pp. xxxiii–xxxiv.

multiple languages of America are brought, either sentimentally or dialogically, into accord.[16]

The crucial point about the practice of transnationalism, by contrast, is that it involves not a filling up of partitioned spaces but an emptying out of them, not a recuperation of buried material but the deformation or dematerialization of cultural hierarchies and systems of authority that already obtain. Transnationalism in this sense is more of a Foucauldian exercise involving the renegotiation and redescription of power, not just the supplementation of power by parallel but fundamentally equivalent discourses of race, gender, and ethnicity. If, moreover, transnationalism necessarily involves a consideration of how power circulates, then the historical legacy of Britain as the former colonial proprietor of what is now the United States should open up all kinds of questions about the legacies of such imperial domination: the issue of who controls whom, who seeks to escape from whose jurisdiction, and the nexus of authority and emancipation that this entails. Back in 1778, in his *Tracts on Civil Liberty, the War with America, and the Debts and Finances of the Kingdom*, the Welsh Nonconformist clergyman and political philosopher Richard Price observed that the British war with America made no sense at all in terms of economic logic and was fuelled more by what he called the British aristocracy's 'spirit of domination' and their 'lust of power'; and it is an analysis of these kinds of power relationships and their modulation into symbolic forms, rather than any futile search for integral forms of identity, which underwrites the critical praxis of transnationalism.[17]

From an American critical point of view, it is perhaps true to say that a particular concentration on the Atlantic as a site of transnational exchange might seem to have something slightly retrogressive, even dated, about it. Much of the new work in international American studies concerns itself more with the borders between the United States and Latin America, partly in response to the increasing demographic presence of Hispanics within the USA itself, and with the development of transpacific currents linking America to Asia. From a British perspective, however, the power dynamics here work quite differently. Asia was the area of the globe that remained imperially subjugated until the Crown chose graciously to relinquish political control: over India and Burma in 1947, Malaya in 1957, and Singapore in 1963. The United States, by contrast, was a territory that the British peremptorily and unexpectedly lost, a country whose independent status was forced upon Britain rather than achieved through diplomatic agreement. The implications of this sudden reverse have continued to reverberate uneasily through English

---

[16] Henry James, 'Middlemarch', in *The Art of Criticism: Henry James on the Theory and Practice of Fiction*, ed. William Veeder and Susan M. Griffin (Chicago: University of Chicago Press, 1986), 48.

[17] Richard Price, *Two Tracts on Civil Liberty, the War with America, and the Debts and Finances of the Kingdom*, in *Political Writings*, ed. D. O. Thomas (Cambridge: Cambridge University Press, 1991), 46–7.

culture over the past two centuries, introducing into Britain's relationship with the United States a different kind of power structure from the one at work between Britain and her former colonies in Asia and Australasia. It is the refractory, two-way nature of this transatlantic exchange, rather than any simple notion of the passage westward across the ocean comprising a site of mythical transformation, which provides the impetus for many of the figures in *Atlantic Republic*.

Within this framework, to describe an American 'tradition' in English literature is to suggest something different from the solid parameters implied by customary uses of this term, both by contemporary anthologists and by critics in the high modernist period. When T. S. Eliot wrote 'Tradition and the Individual Talent' in 1919, he associated tradition with what he called a 'main current' of culture, through which an individual writer could become cognizant of 'the mind of his own country', something Eliot deemed 'much more important than his own private mind'. Although their ideological positions were very different, of course, F. R. Leavis in 1948 similarly understood tradition as a vehicle for canonization and discrimination, for the consolidation of moral value and aesthetic hierarchy: 'by "great tradition"', he wrote, 'I mean the tradition to which what is great in English fiction belongs'.[18] In *Atlantic Republic*, by contrast, tradition is represented as a form of intertextuality, a way of deliberately rearranging the components of the English cultural past so as to suggest ways in which its trajectory might be seen from an alternative angle. I am not claiming that Byron, Clough, and Gissing are 'greater' than Wordsworth, Arnold, and Hardy; nor am I arguing that a framework of transatlantic dissent is the only or even the most appropriate matrix through which the former writers might be interpreted. What I do suggest is that to read Byron, Clough, and Gissing—along with their twentieth-century counterparts such as Isherwood, Auden, Levertov, Carter, and Rushdie—alongside each other is to be made aware of a series of recurrent themes and patterns which, taken together, cumulatively form a counterpoint to the established national narratives of English literature. As I argue in the following pages, such concerns are often related in one way or another to questions of disestablishment, displacement, and individual liberty, which is one reason why the works of these writers are frequently haunted by cultural memories of Reformation and schism.

As noted in the Preface, *Atlantic Republic* has a loose relationship with my two previous books on Anglo-American literary relations, and one reason why I discuss Henry James only briefly here—in Chapter 6, in the context of canon formation—is because I considered at length his problematic relationship

---

[18] T. S. Eliot, 'Tradition and the Individual Talent' (1919), in *Selected Essays*, 3rd edn. (London: Faber, 1951), 16; F. R. Leavis, *The Great Tradition: George Eliot, Henry James, Joseph Conrad* (London: Chatto & Windus, 1948), 7.

with national identity and the aesthetics of surrealism in *Virtual Americas*.[19] Conversely, I am aware of many writers, particularly from the twentieth century, whose transatlantic affiliations might usefully have been studied within the framework of *Atlantic Republic* but whose work has been omitted altogether: Ezra Pound, Basil Bunting, Charles Tomlinson, J. H. Prynne, and others. (There is certainly a book to be written on 'The Poundian Tradition in English Literature', but, apart from my discussion of Donald Davie, I have not tried to write it here.) My choice of authors is intended ultimately not to install a different kind of transatlantic canon, but to propose a certain kind of methodological approach and thus to indicate, in a way that might be transferable to other situations, how various kinds of institutionalization have taken place. To reconstitute the genealogy of English literature in transnational terms is to elucidate the inevitably partial, politicized, and lopsided nature of all critical interpretations and also to highlight ways in which such established formations can sometimes appear at their most revealing when they are turned inside out.

---

[19] Paul Giles, *Transatlantic Insurrections: British Culture and the Formation of American Literature, 1730–1860* (Philadelphia: University of Pennsylvania Press, 2001), and *idem, Virtual Americas: Transnational Fictions and the Transatlantic Imaginary* (Durham, NC: Duke University Press, 2002), 88–126.

1

The American Revolution and the Rhetoric of Schism

SAMUEL JOHNSON AND THE LOSS OF AMERICA

To consider how the American Revolution is represented in English literature, in the writings of Samuel Johnson and Susanna Rowson and in the polemical essays of Richard Price, is to recognize how America in the eighteenth century was generally conceived to be, like Ireland or the Outer Hebrides, an offshore territory intertwined both politically and culturally with the British mainland. Somewhat misleadingly, the Revolution itself has by now achieved the status of a mythic event in the annals of US history, an original point of reference and definition for the nation. However, J. G. A. Pocock, among others, has argued that this War of Independence actually took its impetus not from a sudden irruption of nationalist separatism but from an idealized conception of more traditional British liberties. Pocock has written of the 'profoundly important sense in which the American Revolution can only be understood ... as one of a series of crises occasioned by the growth and change of English political institutions', and he goes on to describe 1776 as the last in a sequence of 'three British revolutions' after 1641 and 1688.[1] He accordingly aligns the English Civil War and the Glorious Revolution as direct precursors of the American Revolution in a broad Anglocentric movement for civil liberties, seeing John Locke as the crucial link between the revolutions of 1688 and 1776. Pocock's larger concern is with demystifying early American history, with seeing it as engaged in a 'dialectical process' striving towards the difficult political goal of constitutional liberty, and he consequently takes issue with the popular American view that the birth of the nation was a mythic advent of freedom brought about by 'the attempt to escape history and then regenerate it'. Instead, he understands the Revolution as participating in an ongoing transatlantic debate about virtue and corruption,

---

[1] J. G. A. Pocock, '1776: The Revolution Against Parliament', in *Three British Revolutions: 1641, 1688, 1776*, ed. J. G. A. Pocock (Princeton: Princeton University Press, 1980), 266.

within which the New World manifested itself as an ideological refraction and reconstitution of the Old.[2]

Pocock's genealogy of cultural and intellectual continuity, however, has been challenged by American scholars such as Ruth Bloch, who has emphasized instead how the millennial images associated with the idea of a new birth of freedom helped to galvanize the spirit of revolution among large sections of the American population. Rather than seeing this conflict as impelled by abstruse Augustan debates about the nature of liberty, Bloch focuses upon how ideas of apocalypse taken from evangelical Christianity came to be disseminated throughout the popular culture of the time, so that George Washington himself came to be cast in biblical terms as, in Ezra Stiles's phrase, the 'American Joshua' leading his people to victory.[3] Indeed, many of the historiographical questions around the American Revolution at the end of the twentieth century concerned the extent to which the synthetic accounts of liberty proposed by intellectual historians such as Pocock, Bernard Bailyn, and Gordon S. Wood tended to concentrate unduly on how ideas of freedom were understood by elite male politicians, and consequently to neglect ways in which 'African Americans, children, women, tenants, and other poor people' experienced the process of national independence very differently.[4]

Wherever the impetus behind the American Revolution came from, the point I wish to emphasize here is how suddenly it happened. There was not, as in most colonial situations, a protracted period of dissent and resentment against imperial masters; few in America dreamt of independence in the 1750s, while in 1763 John Adams was still describing the English constitution as 'the most perfect combination of human powers in society which finite wisdom has yet contrived and reduced to practice for the preservation of liberty and the production of happiness'.[5] To talk of the English constitution as designed specifically to ensure 'the production of happiness' might now seem strange, particularly in view of how the Declaration of Independence only thirteen years later, in condemning England, sought to requisition the idea of 'the pursuit of happiness' for itself. What such a sudden turnaround does suggest, though, is the dramatically foreshortened perspective within which the events of the American Revolution

[2] J. G. A. Pocock, *The Machiavellian Moment: Florentine Political Thought and the Atlantic Republican Tradition* (Princeton: Princeton University Press, 1975), 503, 545.

[3] Ruth H. Bloch, *Visionary Republic: Millennial Themes in American Thought, 1756–1800* (Cambridge: Cambridge University Press, 1985); Catherine L. Albanese, *Sons of the Fathers: The Civil Religion of the American Revolution* (Philadelphia: Temple University Press, 1976), 154.

[4] Barbara Clark Smith, 'The Adequate Revolution', *William and Mary Quarterly*, 3rd ser., 51 (1994), 691.

[5] Bernard Bailyn, *The Ideological Origins of the American Revolution* (Cambridge, Mass.: Harvard University Press, 1967), 67.

took place: one moment the colonists were looking back gratefully to Britain as the guarantor of their political heritage, the next they found they had delivered themselves into a perhaps unexpected condition of independence.

Virtual history is always a meretricious exercise, the province of God rather than man, since its possibilities are quite literally infinite.[6] Suppose, however, that the British forces had displayed a modicum of military competence at the Battle of Bunker Hill in 1775, so that this American uprising was remembered today as a minor skirmish. What would presumably have happened then is that the birth of American cultural nationalism would not have been contemporaneous with the romantic movement at the beginning of the nineteenth century, which worked in intellectual terms broadly to naturalize the relationship between peoples and their native lands. Rather than emerging, like post-Revolutionary France, out of this great era of nation building, America would have been positioned more like Ireland, as a western colony of Great Britain, so that pressure for Home Rule would probably have built up in America over the course of the nineteenth century, as indeed it did in Ireland. This would have meant that the gestation period for American political and cultural independence would have been longer, and that nineteenth-century American literature, in particular, would have been seen as involved in a more explicit dialogue with British imperial power. As I shall argue later, there is an important sense in which writers like Margaret Fuller and Henry David Thoreau were still driven implicitly by a politics of Anglophobic resistance, but this idiom of postcolonial struggle would have been much more obvious if historical events had taken a different turn. Writing of nineteenth-century Irish literature, from Lady Sydney Morgan to Oscar Wilde, Terry Eagleton saw it as engaged with an intertextual demystification of English hierarchical order: the parallel, sometimes parodic structures of Irish writing tended to create for their English overlords, argued Eagleton, an 'unthinkable conundrum of difference and identity, in which the British can never decide whether the Irish are their antithesis or mirror image, partner or parasite, abortive offspring or sympathetic sibling'.[7] The same thing is true, albeit less overtly, of relations between English and American literature in this period, since the formal legalization of independence could not altogether alleviate the dynamics of antagonism and oppression, dynamics which reflect the way in which transatlantic power struggles have continued to reverberate in British culture since the late eighteenth century.

In the wake of their sudden loss of America, a loss which took the English ruling classes largely by surprise, there was a determination in England at the turn of the nineteenth century not to make the same mistake twice. Linda Colley

---

[6] For examples of this hypothetical method, see Niall Ferguson, ed., *Virtual History: Alternatives and Counterfactuals* (London: Picador, 1997).

[7] Terry Eagleton, *Heathcliff and the Great Hunger: Studies in Irish Culture* (London: Verso, 1995), 127.

has described the American War as being for Britain like the Vietnam War was for the United States two centuries later: a David versus Goliath conflict which divided and demoralized the great power in question and which led, by way of reaction, to a sharp political swing towards the Right. Consequently, when a general rebellion broke out in Ireland in 1798, it was crushed harshly by British forces; George III strongly opposed any concessions to the Irish Catholics, and the Act of Union, passed in 1800, proclaimed that Ireland was henceforth to be tied indissolubly to Great Britain.[8] There was even a link between these American and Irish uprisings in terms of British military personnel, since General Charles Cornwallis, who had been forced to surrender to George Washington at Yorktown in 1781, was appointed Lord Lieutenant of Ireland in June 1798. Cornwallis, on hearing of the imminent arrival of French reinforcements to supplement the Irish insurgents, promptly assumed personal command of British forces in the field, and he was subsequently instrumental in constructing the political Act of Union, working under the 'conviction', as he put it in 1799, 'that an Union is absolutely necessary for the safety of the British Empire'.[9]

What all this indicates is that Britain was not altogether indifferent to the loss of America, as has sometimes been suggested, but was, rather, wary of the emergence of the United States as a significant presence on the world stage. Indeed, some of the more far-sighted public figures at the end of the eighteenth century expressed anxiety at how the American Revolution might eventually affect the global balance of power. In 1782, Prime Minister Shelburne was moved publicly to voice his concern in Parliament: 'The sun of Great Britain will set whenever she acknowledges the independence of America,' he said, and he admitted his apprehension that the 'independence of America would end in the ruin of England'. Simon Linguet, a French supporter of strong centralized monarchy who in 1777 started the journal *Annales politiques* from exile in London, similarly feared that the United States, by taking advantage of its rich natural resources, might grow and prosper to such an extent that it could put itself in a position to dominate world trade and to control the destiny of Europe.[10]

The first British responses to the prospect of the new United States, then, were worked out not so much on the level of philosophical abstraction or theoretical debates about how environment might shape character, but in terms of brute

---

[8] Linda Colley, *Britons: Forging the Nation, 1707–1837* (New Haven: Yale University Press, 1992), 144–5; Jacques Godechot, *France and the Atlantic Revolutions of the Eighteenth Century, 1770–1799*, trans. Herbert H. Rowen (New York: Free Press, 1965), 225.

[9] Franklin and Mary Wickwire, *Cornwallis: The Imperial Years* (Chapel Hill, NC: University of North Carolina Press, 1980), 244. It should be noted that Cornwallis favoured Catholic Emancipation as a measure to stabilize and strengthen the Union, arguing that 'some mode must be adopted to soften the hatred of the Catholics to our government'. However, this spirit of compromise was staunchly opposed by George III and Pitt's government.

[10] John Keane, *Tom Paine: A Political Life* (London: Bloomsbury, 1995), 233; Durand Echeverria, *Mirage in the West: A History of the French Image of American Society to 1815* (Princeton: Princeton University Press, 1957), 62–4.

political power. As Bernard Bailyn has observed, many pamphlets supporting the American patriot cause in the late eighteenth century argued on principle from the premisses of an Enlightenment reason that regarded liberty as indivisible and that tried to rise deliberately above the partiality of local sentiments. Advocates of the British cause, by contrast, tended to favour the more aggressive method of satire, which might be described as an attempt to exercise power in discursive form through its method of seeking not so much to address as to belittle or humiliate its object.[11] This suggests that the very idea of Enlightenment, with its hypothesis of universal reason, was itself an object of political dispute at this time, rather than being a framework that comprised the overall conceptual context within which such disputes occurred. As J. C. D. Clark has observed, the first use of the term 'Enlightenment' to denote a specific period of cultural history occurred in 1865; certainly nobody in the eighteenth century used the word in this way, though Kant in 1784 referred to 'enlightenment' to describe certain kinds of mental processes, 'a reform in ways of thinking'.[12] But the notion prevalent among some intellectual historians that the eighteenth-century Enlightenment formed a master narrative within which such progressive tendencies worked themselves out is a retrospective fiction; rather, the eighteenth century witnessed an intense series of internal ructions wherein the forces of enlightenment confronted the forces of reaction.

As if to exemplify this kind of conflict, the English writer charged by Lord North's ministry with producing a quasi-official reply to the Declaration of Rights by the first session of the American Continental Congress was none other than Samuel Johnson. In his 1759 novel *Rasselas* Johnson had ridiculed the human search for perfectibility, with all of the self-delusions such dreams of the 'happy valley' entail. In 1774 he turned his satirical disposition to political account in his pamphlet *The Patriot*, in which he mocks 'the ridiculous claims of American usurpation' against 'natural and lawful authority'.[13] One year later, in response to Sir Grey Cooper, the Secretary of the Treasury who acted as intermediary between Johnson and the North government, he produced *Taxation No Tyranny: An Answer to the Resolution and Address of the American Congress. Taxation No Tyranny* is in many ways a predictable enough document, which seeks to validate the position of the British government according to what Johnson calls 'the standing order of Nature', and which justifies taxation legally, as 'a payment exacted by authority from part of the community for the benefit of

[11] Bailyn, *Ideological Origins*, 18–19. On the conflict between Enlightenment radicalism and English nationalism, see also David Simpson, *Romanticism, Nationalism, and the Revolt against Theory* (Chicago: University of Chicago Press, 1993), 181.
[12] J. C. D. Clark, *The Language of Liberty, 1660–1832: Political Discourse and Social Dynamics in the Anglo-American World* (Cambridge: Cambridge University Press, 1984), 14; Emma Rothschild, *Economic Sentiments: Adam Smith, Condorcet, and the Enlightenment* (Cambridge, Mass.: Harvard University Press, 2001), 15.
[13] Samuel Johnson, *The Patriot*, in *Political Writings*, ed. Donald J. Greene (New Haven: Yale University Press, 1977), 396.

2. Samuel Johnson in old age. Portrait (1783–4) after John Opie.

the whole'.[14] There is, of course, an imperial logic at work here, whereby Britain is said to enjoy a 'natural' authority over America: 'A colony', writes Johnson, 'is to the mother-country as a member to the body, deriving its action and its strength from the general principle of vitality' (p. 425). He accordingly scorns the republican idea of freedom, seeing it as a 'delirious dream' (p. 428) which runs

[14] Johnson, *Taxation No Tyranny*, in *Political Writings*, 412, 417. Subsequent page references to this essay are cited in parentheses in the text.

contrary to the principles of centralized order and hierarchical subordination upon which his view of the world is predicated. One curious facet of this pamphlet is the intransigence of its rhetoric: the author ends up by advocating harsh punishments for the rebels, saying that 'erroneous clemency' in this case would be 'noxious to society', and recommending that when the Americans 'are reduced to obedience ... that obedience be secured by stricter laws and stronger obligations' (p. 453).

The thunderous tone of *Taxation No Tyranny* suggests the intensity of hatred in British conservative circles of this time for the very idea of insubordination which the American Revolution brought into view. James Boswell, in fact, reported in 1778 that Johnson used to dismiss Americans as 'a race of convicts', saying he would like to 'burn and destroy them'.[15] While the apparently hyperbolic nature of this antipathy might be seen as the reaction of an elderly man raging against a world that would no longer defer to his conception of it—Johnson died in 1784—it should also be understood more generally as indicative of the British government's anxieties about what kind of destabilizing properties might be unleashed if this open revolt against the legitimate order were to go unchecked, and it suggests also how the spectre of this American conflict helped to shape the direction of English culture towards the end of the eighteenth century. The North government watered down some of Johnson's most vitriolic language in *Taxation No Tyranny*, just as the American Congress in 1776 diplomatically toned down some of the purple passages in Thomas Jefferson's Declaration of Independence, but it is not difficult to see how these intellectual arguments over the meaning of liberty and authority at this time touched some raw nerves on both sides. While the Declaration of Independence is, of course, a foundational document in all senses within American culture, its position within this specifically transatlantic debate becomes clearer if it is set alongside a work like *Taxation No Tyranny*. Johnson's parallel narrative, in other words, works to recontextualize Jefferson, to translate his work from a mythic to a more historicist setting, and thus to suggest how the advent of American independence owed as much to contingency as to providence.

Another revealing aspect of *Taxation No Tyranny* is its geographic perspective, the way Johnson holds implicitly to an idea of London as the natural centre of the world and America as a subordinate territory on the margins, a 'parish in the kingdom', as he puts it (p. 436). In fact, the author mocks the idea of American independence by suggesting that it would be as absurd as if Cornwall were to secede by claiming for itself a separate history and language from the rest of Britain (p. 445). It is interesting that Johnson attempts to bolster the political power of the centre by testing it against what is most remote geographically

---

[15] James Boswell, *The Life of Johnson*, ed. Christopher Hibbert (Harmondsworth: Penguin, 1979), 176, 247.

from that centre, and this sense of inherent friction, of a social order pushing itself up against physical extremities, may help to explain some of the tortuous, excessive style of Johnson's pamphlets, whose vision of order turns more upon a struggle to force some kind of control upon a chaotic world than upon any polite assumptions about Augustan decorum. Just as Cornwall, at the southwest tip of England, brings America to Johnson's mind, so he constantly compares America to the barren landscapes of the far north of Britain in his *Journey to the Western Islands of Scotland*, which also appeared in 1775, the same year as *Taxation No Tyranny*.

Based upon a trip taken with Boswell in the autumn of 1773, and published at the very time when the British dispute with her American colonies was about to issue in war, Johnson's *Journey to the Western Islands* can be understood retrospectively in an elegiac light, as an intimation of the loss of that national coherence and administrative control after which his political pamphlets hanker. The narrator continually associates the 'uniformity of barrenness' he finds in Scotland with the 'desarts' and 'wastes of America', mocking this distant landscape as 'merely pastoral' and as altogether lacking in the commodious comforts of the metropolis.[16] Rather than acknowledging Scotland or America as locations with their own distinctive culture, as a nineteenth-century racialist might have done, Johnson simply chastises them as deficient in the properties of universal reason.[17] At the same time, he inveighs against 'the mischiefs of emigration' (p. 95), insisting that the loss of population weakens a country's defences, and he talks of how the owners of these islands deliberately spread stories of hardships in America in a vain attempt to keep the people content at home. Emigration, indeed, is a recurring theme in this narrative; Johnson writes of how those who fall for 'American seducements' (p. 132) become

as subjects lost to the British crown; for a nation scattered in the boundless regions of America resembles rays diverging from a focus. All the rays remain, but the heat is gone. Their power consisted in their concentration: when they are dispersed, they have no effect.

It may be thought that they are happier by the change; but they are not happy as a nation, for they are a nation no longer. (p. 131)

The metaphor of decentring and dissemination is especially apt here. Nostalgic and even at times maniacally desperate for the image of an authoritarian centre, Johnson also appears strangely compelled by these rituals of depopulation. (Boswell's *Journal* of the same expedition records how a dance on the Island of Skye was called 'America' after this pattern of communal emigration; the

---

[16] Samuel Johnson, *A Journey to the Western Islands of Scotland*, ed. Mary Lascelles (New Haven: Yale University Press, 1971), 40–1, 84, 37. Subsequent page references to this edition are cited in parentheses in the text.

[17] See Clement Hawes, 'Johnson and Imperialism', in *The Cambridge Companion to Samuel Johnson*, ed. Greg Clingham (Cambridge: Cambridge University Press, 1997), 114–15.

dance, he wrote, 'seems intended to show how emigration catches, till a whole neighbourhood is set afloat'.[18])

The colonizing mentality in Johnson's *Journey to the Western Islands* is obvious enough. As Katie Trumpener has observed, he altogether ignores the intellectual renaissance in Edinburgh at this time, and stereotypes the Scottish natural and cultural wilderness as a negative polarity to English civilized values.[19] This is also the basis for his analogies between Scotland and America as provincial territories, analogies which, as Robert Crawford and others have pointed out, were not uncommon in nationalist thinking around this time.[20] What makes Johnson's response unusual, though, is the darker, melancholic streak through which he seems at some level to recognize the demise of empire as fated. Politically, he advocates the kind of centralized authority of which Augustus Caesar would have been proud: 'As government advances towards perfection,' he writes, 'provincial judicature is perhaps in every empire gradually abolished' (p. 46). This is why the theorist of globalization Ian Baucom is not quite right, I think, to suggest that for Johnson the spectre of empire is inevitably a corrupting influence since it imprints 'spots of barbarism' in the native language, thereby undermining the integrity of English culture.[21] What it would be true to say, though, is that Johnson is always aware of the frustrating discrepancy between centre and province, civilization and 'barbarism', so that his works might be said to explore imaginatively the potential collapse of their own imperial designs. Johnson's poetic sensibility, in other words, often seems to be at odds with his political outlook: in *A Journey to the Western Islands of Scotland*, for instance, his theories of Augustan order come to be seen as merely hypothetical when set against the stark, mountainous landscape of rocks and thistles.

In this sense, Johnson the empirical observer unravels the more abstract projections of Johnson the imperial speculator, so that his texts are shot through with pessimistic intuitions about the vanity of human wishes. Regarding emigration from the Scottish islands to America, for example, he writes in a paradoxical, grimly comic vein about the self-defeating gestures of local chieftains: 'To hinder insurrection, by driving away the people, and to govern peaceably, by having no subjects, is an expedient that argues no great profundity of politicks' (p. 97). The remark is weighed down by Johnson's characteristic ballast of common sense, but it also suggests ways in which his account of the Scottish islands is shadowed by the spectre of America as alterity, imagined here as a negative

---

[18] James Boswell, *The Journal of a Tour to the Hebrides*, ed. Peter Levi (London: Penguin, 1984), 327.

[19] Katie Trumpener, *Bardic Nationalism: The Romantic Novel and the British Empire* (Princeton: Princeton University Press, 1997), 69.

[20] Robert Crawford, *Devolving English Literature* (Oxford: Oxford University Press, 1992), 185.

[21] Ian Baucom, *Out of Place: Englishness, Empire, and the Locations of Identity* (Princeton: Princeton University Press, 1999), 27.

force lying in wait to undermine the British Empire, a lurking shadow which throws a dark reflection upon the spectrum of national unity. Johnson's writing is simultaneously attracted to and repelled by this vision of disorder, which is why Boswell's popular version of him as a conservative, clubbable dispenser of *bons mots* can never be quite sufficient. What America brings to the surface in Johnson's writing, then, is the mixture of rational and irrational elements within his satirical polemics, the ways in which his fantasies of Augustan order are held in check by an implicit recognition of the impending collapse or inversion of that Anglocentric vision.

ENLIGHTENMENT LIBERTY: RICHARD PRICE AND SUSANNA ROWSON

As Lewis Namier noted long ago, British responses towards America at the end of the eighteenth century overlapped significantly with attitudes towards the Dissenting churches, with members of the Anglican establishment like Johnson seeking to consolidate the structural homology of church and state which Nonconformist thinkers such as Richard Price did their best to dissolve.[22] Price, whose pamphlets on the American question sold in huge numbers, was another exemplification of links at this time between America and the Celtic fringes, being a Welsh preacher steeped in the religious traditions of personal liberty and the philosophical doctrines of enlightenment. In his tracts on America, Price envisages the new country as a beacon of hope, an emblem of that 'spirit of illumination' which will, so he hopes, induce Britain to follow America's example by acknowledging the value of moral self-improvement. Perceiving power as a corrupting influence *per se*, Price in 1778 urged his fellow Britons to abjure their lust for dominion and to pursue instead more rational policies of equality and contractual partnership:

By exertions of authority which have alarmed [the Americans] they have been put upon examining into the grounds of all our claims and forced to give up their luxuries and to seek all their resources within themselves. And the issue is likely to prove the loss of all our authority over them and of all the advantages connected with it. So little do men in power sometimes know how to preserve power and so remarkably does the desire of extending dominion sometimes destroy it ... The people of America are no more the subjects of the people of Britain than the people of Yorkshire are the subjects of the people of Middlesex. They are your fellow-subjects.[23]

Like Joseph Priestley and other supporters of America among the Nonconformist clergy, Price became a frequent object of ridicule in Britain during the 1790s. In the midst of the British conflicts with America and France, Price's

---

[22] Sir Lewis Namier, *England in the Age of the American Revolution*, 2nd edn. (London: Macmillan, 1961), 38–9.   [23] Price, *Two Tracts on Civil Liberty*, 50, 70.

3. Richard Price, by Thomas Holloway, after Benjamin West (1793).

kind of middle-class radicalism became associated in the popular mind with eccentricity and neurosis, inclinations which reinvigorated the inherent anti-intellectualism of the British establishment.[24] Price's views on political liberty are characterized as absurdly abstract and hypothetical in Edmund Burke's *Reflections on the Revolution in France* (1790), while a James Gillray caricature in the same

---

[24] J. H. Plumb, 'British Attitudes to the American Revolution', in *The American Experience: The Collected Essays*, ii (New York: Harvester Wheatsheaf, 1989), 73.

year depicts a monarchical Burke looming over a cowering Price in the wake of the latter's last pamphlet, *A Discourse on the Love of our Country* (1789). Gillray's cartoon is entitled 'Smelling out a Rat; or, The Atheistical Revolutionist disturbed in his Midnight "Calculations"', and it lampoons as altogether too redolent of the inkhorn Price's final prophetic vision: 'Behold, the light you have struck out, after setting America free, reflected to France and there kindled into a blaze that lays despotism in ashes and warms and illuminates Europe!' Again, Price here conceives of the American Revolution as a model for subsequent reform movements closer to home, and in the final paragraph he specifically refers contemporary expressions of political dissent back to the spirit of the Protestant Reformation: 'Take warning all ye supporters of slavish governments and slavish hierarchies! Call no more (absurdly and wickedly) reformation, innovation.'[25]

In considering British reactions to American political independence, Price can be seen as a symptomatic figure in several significant ways. First, he places an extraordinarily high value on the importance of the American Revolution, declaring it in 1785 to be 'the most important step in the progressive course of improvement of mankind' since 'the introduction of Christianity'.[26] One of Price's prominent contemporaries who shared this view of America's significance was Adam Smith, who as a moral philosopher and an economist championed freedom from all kinds of institutional restraint. Smith was, of course, a staunch advocate of free trade, and in *The Wealth of Nations* (1776) he anticipated Price by suggesting iconoclastically that 'the discovery of America and that of a passage to the East Indies by the Cape of Good Hope', both of which facilitated economic exchange, should be seen as 'the two greatest and most important events recorded in the history of mankind'.[27] Second, Price thinks of America as linked intellectually with the Glorious Revolution of 1688, which introduced a form of constitutional government in Britain, and so he is a keen proselytizer for 'Mr Locke and all the writers on civil liberty who have been hitherto most admired in this country'. Third, Price understands the new United States to be an incarnation of what Britain could and should have been if it had followed Locke's principles to their logical conclusion: 'The liberty of America might have preserved our liberty', he says, 'and, under the direction of a patriot king or wise minister, proved the means of restoring to us our almost lost constitution.'[28]

Writing some 200 years later, Gillian Brown argued that the dissemination of Lockean liberalism in the eighteenth century 'crucially helped generate American identity', anticipating the model of consensual governance that has led towards more recent agendas of multiculturalism in the United States. Price would doubtless have approved of this institutionalization of American

---

[25] Richard Price, *A Discourse on the Love of Our Country*, in *Political Writings*, 196.

[26] Price, *Observations on the Importance of the American Revolution*, in *Political Writings*, 119.

[27] Adam Smith, *The Wealth of Nations*, Books IV–V, ed. Andrew Skinner (London: Penguin, 1999), 209.   [28] Price, *Two Tracts on Civil Liberty*, 20, 56.

liberal ideals, though he would also have wanted to consider their implications within a transatlantic context. Whereas Brown is concerned to formulate Locke's version of consent 'as the originary story of the American republic', Price is interested in how liberal America forms a distant mirror of England, its alter ego, that model 'city upon a hill' to be admired from across the water just as exiled Englishman John Winthrop had imagined 150 years earlier.[29] Brown, in other words, retrospectively appropriates pre-Revolutionary America from a specifically nationalist perspective, whereas Price wants to reconfigure America transnationally, even envisaging the possibility of what Richard Gravil has described as 'a united states of the British Empire', with sovereign governments in each nation but, as Price foresees it, 'a general confederacy ... formed by the appointment of a senate consisting of representatives from all the different states', to have 'the power of managing the common concerns of the united states, and of judging and deciding between them, as a common arbiter or umpire, in all disputes'.[30] Consequently, Price's writing conceives of the American Revolution not as an example of American exceptionalism, an event that could occur only in the special circumstances of the New World, but rather as an example of how the principles of the Reformation might be introduced into a benighted England. Like Winthrop, and like his friend Catherine Macaulay whose historical treatises of the 1760s and 1770s also traced the spirit of republicanism back to seventeenth-century regicide and schism, Price sought to reform English institutions and to purify what he saw as the corruption at the heart of the British social, political, and religious establishment. His 1759 sermon later published under the title *Britain's Happiness, and the Proper Improvement of it* assumes a direct teleological link between the Reformation and the Enlightenment by seeing them as both leading cumulatively towards an ethic of personal responsibility and individual salvation: 'The invention of printing followed by the reformation and the revival of Literature; the free communication which has been opened between the different parts of the world, and the late amazing improvements in knowledge of every kind, have remarkably prepared the way for this joyful period.'[31]

'[T]his joyful period': those are Price's words, and they demonstrate how for him the Enlightenment was a religious rather than a purely secular phenomenon. The general importance of the Reformation within British culture is, of course, a topic which has exercised historians for many years. Christopher Haigh, for

[29] Gillian Brown, *The Consent of the Governed: The Lockean Legacy in Early American Culture* (Cambridge, Mass.: Harvard University Press, 2001), 4, 23; John Winthrop, 'A Model of Christian Charity', in *The American Puritans: Their Prose and Poetry*, ed. Perry Miller (New York: Doubleday-Anchor, 1956), 83.

[30] Richard Gravil, *Romantic Dialogues: Anglo-American Continuities, 1776–1862* (Basingstoke: Macmillan, 2000), 15; Price, *Two Tracts on Civil Liberty*, 25.

[31] Price, *Political Writings*, 12. On Macaulay's opposition to the American War, see Kate Davies, *Catherine Macaulay and Mercy Otis Warren: The Revolutionary Atlantic and the Politics of Gender* (Oxford: Oxford University Press, 2005), 122--79. Macaulay wrote to Warren on 11 September 1774 of her hope that Americans 'will be the saviours and liberators of the whole British Empire' (p. 137).

example, has argued that the changes enforced by royal and parliamentary edict in the sixteenth century were a top-down, relatively superficial phenomenon, with the result that by 1600 England was 'a Protestant nation, but not a nation of Protestants'. Patrick Collinson, following Haigh's line, locates a 'second English Reformation' somewhat later, in the 1640s, when a mood of iconoclasm and anticlerical dissent began to become more widespread among the people.[32] I would not wish to argue here for a third or fourth reformation exactly, since in its more metaphorical forms this conception becomes too fluid and amorphous to be categorized in that way, but I would suggest that the arguments in Britain over American independence reintroduced many of the Reformation debates about freedom and authority in another guise. Following Price, I would also suggest that Britain's dialectical engagement with American culture over the course of the nineteenth and twentieth centuries witnessed the displacement of these Reformation theological disputes into more secular concerns, questions that were often related in one form or another to the accessibility of political and cultural representation, freedom of information, and disestablishmentarianism. The way in which for Price the religious conception of the Reformation becomes involved inextricably with political reform in the eighteenth century shows clearly how for him theological issues modulated almost indistinguishably into more worldly concerns.

One crucial question here involves the larger significance of the Enlightenment in Britain. Roy Porter argues that the 'English Enlightenment' has traditionally been seen as 'a scholarly black-hole' because of the insistence of scholars on trying to discover unifying ideas underpinning Enlightenment philosophy and to apply them to a British context. Porter's argument is that while the English Enlightenment may not have had the self-conscious style or avant-garde panache of Diderot and the *philosophes*, it nevertheless prided itself upon a more robust tradition of freedom and toleration, on creating conditions of possibility whereby 'individual and group fulfilment' could be achieved within 'the familiar social frame'. Porter's work on the English Enlightenment thus lays emphasis on its pragmatic virtues: on the achievements of science, on the cherished freedom of the press, and on the increasing importance of middle-class London, which took over control of cultural life at this time from the aristocratic court.[33] Paul Langford similarly finds in eighteenth-century England a general lack of interest in the monarchy, which had evolved by this time into a 'semi-republican' phenomenon 'suitable to the needs of a liberated society'.[34] The eighteenth-century English,

---

[32] Christopher Haigh, *English Reformations: Religion, Politics, and Society under the Tudors* (Oxford: Oxford University Press, 1993), 280; Patrick Collinson, 'From Iconoclasm to Iconophobia: The Cultural Impact of the Second English Reformation', in *The Impact of the English Reformation, 1500–1640*, ed. Peter Marshall (London: Arnold, 1997), 278–308.

[33] Roy Porter, 'The Enlightenment in England', in *The Enlightenment in National Context*, ed. Roy Porter and Mikuláš Teich (Cambridge: Cambridge University Press, 1981), 4, 16, and *idem*, *Enlightenment: Britain and the Creation of the Modern World* (London: Penguin, 2000).

[34] Paul Langford, *Englishness Identified: Manners and Character, 1650–1850* (Oxford: Oxford University Press, 2000), 274.

argues Langford, identified their national characteristics in terms of a dedication to freedom and the capacity to deal with a restless, unpredictable world. Gordon S. Wood, as a historian of the American Revolution, similarly claims that eighteenth-century Englishmen were thoroughly wrapped up in ideas of liberty: in the legal conceptions of habeas corpus and trial by jury, and in personal freedoms of speech and travel.[35]

There is, of course, a danger here of overgeneralizing about the characteristics of eighteenth-century Britain, and any equation between Enlightenment England and an essential spirit of 'liberty' would be as problematic as its identification with American culture, and for similar reasons: it risks overlooking the situations of people who were not part of this dynamic.[36] However, in England these excluded groups were defined more obviously by class than by race or gender. The African community living in London was often quite familiar with the perils and insecurities of travel, as we see from the careers and writings of Ignatius Sancho and Olaudah Equiano, while the sense of instability that was the concomitant to liberty is also readily apparent in the life and work of Susanna Rowson.[37] Rowson, born the daughter of a Royal Navy officer in Portsmouth in 1762, spent much of her

4. Portrait of Susanna Rowson, from Elias Nason's memoir published in 1870.

[35] Gordon S. Wood, *The Radicalism of the American Revolution* (New York: Knopf, 1992), 13.

[36] See, for instance, the critique of Michael Zuckerman, 'Rhetoric, Reality, and the Revolution: The Genteel Radicalism of Gordon Wood', *William and Mary Quarterly*, 3rd ser., 51 (1994), 693–702.

[37] On the significance of class in eighteenth-century English literature see John Barrell, *English Literature in History, 1730–80: An Equal, Wide Survey* (London: Hutchinson, 1983), and other works by Barrell. On Sancho and Equiano, see Giles, *Transatlantic Insurrections*, 112–13, 192–4.

childhood in America with her father, but their comforts were disturbed by the Revolutionary war, when the loyalist Rowsons were sent back penniless to England as part of a prisoner exchange. In 1793, after her marriage, Rowson returned to the United States, where she carved out for herself a successful career as a writer, though her narratives are frequently shadowed by the trials and tribulations of transatlantic displacement. In particular, *Reuben and Rachel* (1798) focuses upon the hazards associated with emigration, though its specifically transnational outlook makes for a rich and fascinating novel, one much more ambitious in its orientation than the author's more famous work, *Charlotte Temple* (1791).

In her important study of early American fiction, *Revolution and the Word*, Cathy N. Davidson attributes the enormous popularity of *Charlotte Temple* to its democratizing sensibility, the way its popular seduction narrative 'spoke to those not included in the established power structures of the early Republic'. Conversely, she mentions *Reuben and Rachel* only in passing, describing it as one of those novels 'which were set in Europe mostly, it seems, because the authors could not accommodate the requisite high-born villain to an American setting'.[38] But to promote Rowson as the forerunner of a tradition of sentimental women's writing that was to flower in the nineteenth century, in the work of novelists such as Susan Warner and Harriet Beecher Stowe, is to present only a partial account of Rowson's achievements, one that brings her into line with the nationalist orientation of nineteenth-century American literature at the expense of suppressing her eighteenth-century transnational provenance. It is also to underestimate ways in which Rowson's patriotic intent emerges not just from the advocacy of a community of feeling but from a more sweeping intellectual account of America's cultural history, such as we see in *Reuben and Rachel*. Davidson's argument about Rowson's status as an American novelist reinforces the allegorical designs commensurate with her thesis about 'the rise of the novel in America': that it was a sentimental genre, primarily female in its authorship and readership, which constructed a sphere of democratic sentiment standing in sharp contrast to the elitist, male world of abstract political philosophy that predominated in the new United States at the end of the eighteenth century. Like Ian Watt's thesis about the 'rise' of the novel in England, to which it bears some relation, Davidson's critical narrative is predicated implicitly on a teleology of social continuity, although a larger view of Rowson's transatlantic trajectory would suggest alternative ways of looking at her fiction, ways less subservient to such restrictive national designs.[39]

Reuben and Rachel's first volume starts in the early fifteenth century with the recently widowed Isabelle of Spain retiring with her daughter to Austenburg Castle, on the Welsh borders. There she peruses old letters from Christopher

---

[38] Cathy N. Davidson, *Revolution and the Word: The Rise of the Novel in America* (New York: Oxford University Press, 1986), 79, 228.

[39] Ian Watt, *The Rise of the Novel: Studies in Defoe, Richardson and Fielding* (London: Chatto & Windus, 1957). For critiques of Watt's thesis of organic continuity, see the special issue 'Reconsidering the Rise of the Novel', *Eighteenth-Century Fiction*, 12/2–3 (Jan.–April 2000).

Columbus, one of this book's tutelary spirits, who reminisces about the difficulties he experienced in combating 'received prejudice' when searching for a passage to the New World.[40] Isabelle's daughter, the aptly named Columbia, encounters similar hostility from the Catholic court of the English Queen Mary when she falls in love with a fellow Protestant 'heretic', Sir Egbert Gorges (p. 101). This first volume of *Reuben and Rachel*, then, works through the conflicts of the English Reformation—Isabelle herself is said to be 'convinced of the errors of the Catholic persuasion' (p. 98)—and, by chronicling the departure of Columbia's descendants for New England during the seventeenth century, it comes clearly to associate this Reformation spirit with America. Columbia's daughter, Elizabeth, named after England's Protestant queen, then marries Lord Henry Dudley, and the rest of Rowson's book charts the movements of this Dudley family between the Old and New Worlds in the seventeenth and eighteenth centuries. The plot involves a tangle of family property and finance as well as interludes of quest and adventure, in which the Indian wars feature prominently. Towards the end of the first volume, Arrabella Dudley arrives back in England in the spring of 1680, having been 'absent about thirty-four years', and she is said to be returning 'partly from the hope of her native air acting as a restorative to her health, and partly in the wish of securing to Reuben the estates of his great-grandfather, Sir Ferdinando Gorges' (p. 168).

This generic hybridity is, perhaps, why *Reuben and Rachel* does not fit into Davidson's scheme of early American fiction. Rowson combines the eighteenth-century English novel of property, family relations, and aristocratic society with a more recognizably American idiom of moral allegory and picaresque, thus creating a text which is peculiarly transatlantic in form and style as well as content. The twins of the novel's title are not born until the very end of the first volume, halfway through the story, and the second part of the novel revolves around the efforts of this new generation to leave their Lancashire home and establish themselves in Pennsylvania. America has now become for the Dudleys a kind of family mythology, with Reuben and Rachel as children asking their aunts and uncles to describe to them the 'boundless plains, majestic rivers and extensive lakes of that great continent' (p. 175); but the family's first plan to emigrate is thwarted when Reuben Dudley, the twins' father who has gone out to reconnoitre an estate on the banks of the Schuylkill, is shipwrecked on his passage back across the Atlantic. There follows a tangled web of adventure and deceit, with young Reuben arriving in America only to find that his father's overseer has appropriated the family property to himself, while Rachel remains in London to face all the English prejudices about America: ' "Dear me" ', says Mrs Varnice when she learns that Rachel's brother is in America, ' "what all amongst the blacks and the wild Indians? … what could tempt him to leave dear

---

[40] Susanna Rowson, *Reuben and Rachel; or, Tales of Old Times* (Boston, 1798), 15. Subsequent page references to this edition are cited in parentheses in the text.

little England?"' (p. 303). The formal intercutting of the narrative here, with one chapter being set in Pennsylvania, and the next in London, is particularly innovative; indeed, the transcontinental reach and scope that we see in *Reuben and Rachel* are more akin to the aesthetics of fissure and displacement in Salman Rushdie's work than to the emphasis on provincial locality that was to become prevalent in English Victorian fiction.

Rowson's novel ends happily enough, with Reuben proving his American credentials through bravery in the Indian wars, Rachel surviving another shipwreck to join him in Pennsylvania, and the twins vowing to reject the lucrative Lancashire estates and titles offered to them by a messenger from England at the end of the book. Reuben now says that such 'distinctions' are worth 'nothing': 'Our sons are true-born Americans, and while they strive to make that title respectable, we wish them to possess no other' (p. 363). The novel is thus an epic in the fullest sense of that word, a narrative encompassing 300 years which reworks its biblical prototype to chronicle the foundation of a society, binding together middle-class life in eighteenth-century Philadelphia with the voyages of Columbus and the English Reformation, so as to track historical developments which cumulate in the triumphant resolution of American independence. Such independence, however, is linked by Rowson not to the idea of a quest in any simple, purist sense, but rather to a narrative of transformation wherein identity is seen as mobile and so always remains potentially fractured. Carroll Smith-Rosenberg has talked about the difficulty that Rowson seems to experience in 'authorizing' the establishment of an American cultural identity in *Reuben and Rachel*, but such perplexities appertain only in the context of a critical attempt to position Rowson unilaterally, as an 'American' author engaged with 'American' themes.[41] As a transatlantic novelist, a writer herself displaced from England to America who grounds her vision of patriotic virtue upon acts of traversal, the texts of Rowson necessarily involve double perspectives whose subjects find themselves moving mentally as well as physically back and forth across the Atlantic.

Transatlantic displacement in the novel did not appear suddenly in the Revolutionary period—the heroine of Defoe's *Moll Flanders* (1722) is transported from low-life London to Virginia, where she becomes rich and successful—but my point is precisely that after 1783 this rhetoric of dislocation became more associated with American than with English literature and culture. The formalization of American independence created a schism within the British state, so that subsequently the characteristics of freedom, mobility, and republican iconoclasm, still common within Britain's conception of itself during the eighteenth century, were split off and came to be identified more specifically with the American party. The English who gave their allegiance to the new American state, whether through actual emigration like Rowson or not, identified themselves with a spirit

---

[41] Carroll Smith-Rosenberg, 'Subject Female: Authorizing American Identity', *American Literary History*, 5 (1993), 498–503.

of reformation and transformation; by contrast, the English who stayed literally and metaphorically at home retreated into more conservative postures and began increasingly to cherish the virtues of a settled, hierarchical society. Langford dates the word 'Englishness' from about 1805, suggesting that it came at this time to be linked more with notions of practicality, prudence, and stability, rather than with that natural sense of adventurousness which typified the Englishman's self-image in the previous century.[42] At the end of the eighteenth century, the notion of human behaviour moulding itself according to the contours of nature became increasingly equated intellectually with the experimental conditions of the New World—Crèvecoeur's *Letters from an American Farmer* (1782) is the most obvious example of this—with the result that Britain needed to define itself differently, to reposition itself not as nature's nation but as a country where more traditional social virtues still held sway.

Obviously the American Revolution was not the only reason for this new authoritarian mood in Britain at the end of the eighteenth century: the conflicts with France and various other social factors contributed to the general climate of reaction. Nevertheless, as Porter says, the war years up until 1815 were generally bleak times for the self-professed citizens of the British Enlightenment, who not only found themselves at odds with the nation and its government but who also, much to their dismay, found England now exulting in its role as the defender of Old World values.[43] When the American Declaration of Independence in 1776 accused the British Crown of exerting an 'absolute tyranny' over its subjects, this was the first time during the modern era that England had been forced into the position of an *ancien régime* oppressor, but it was a role to which the country was to become increasingly accustomed—indeed, increasingly partial—during the nineteenth century. After 1800, English poets like Wordsworth and Coleridge refurbished the idea of knowledge as a form of revelation, a gift from God, not something to be achieved through the powers of human innovation or reason. As Ludmilla Jordanova argues, this served indirectly to reunite religion and politics, since the Wordsworthian poetic belief in immanent value could readily be transferred to the conception that the English landscape itself embodied certain kinds of divine values: not so much a divine right of kings, perhaps, but certainly a divine right of country. When the American colonists in the 1760s and 1770s were first accused of stirring up revolution by promoting republican principles, they replied indignantly, with some justification, that the spirit of republicanism was the spirit of John Milton and the glory of the English constitution.[44] After the great schism of 1783, however, interest in upholding such republican liberties in Britain became much more of a marginal, minority concern.

---

[42] Langford, *Englishness Identified*, 1.   [43] Porter, *Enlightenment*, 474.
[44] Ludmilla Jordanova, 'The Authoritarian Response', in *The Enlightenment and Its Shadows*, ed. Peter Hulme and Ludmilla Jordanova (London: Routledge, 1990), 213; G. S. Wood, *Radicalism of the American Revolution*, 109–10.

2

Transatlantic Romanticism and Parliamentary Reform

WILLIAM WORDSWORTH, S. T. COLERIDGE, AND THE ANGLICAN ORDER

The purpose of this chapter is to consider ways in which the schism between Britain and America affected the construction of English romanticism in the early nineteenth century and how events across the Atlantic helped to shape social and political reforms in the 1820s and 1830s. By parliamentary reform, I mean not only the reform of Parliament itself, culminating in the Great Reform Act of 1832 which enfranchised about one-fifth of the adult male population, but also the other major reforms enacted by Parliament around this time: in 1828 the repeal of the Test and Corporation Laws, which had discriminated against Dissenters by making membership of the Church of England 'a Qualification for certain Offices and Employments', and in 1829 the introduction of the Roman Catholic Relief Act, which effectively granted Catholic Emancipation by enabling Daniel O'Connell to take up his seat as MP for County Clare, to which he had been elected the previous year.[1]

J. C. D. Clark has described these three structural changes—' "Repeal", "Emancipation", and "Reform" '—as signalling the collapse of the old constitutional order in English society. This was certainly how it appeared to conservatives at the time, for whom the establishment of the Church of England at the heart of the social fabric was essential for maintaining the authority of the state. 'Every national Constitution', wrote the bishop of Lincoln in 1812, 'with perhaps a single exception, has had its religious as well as its political part; and these parts are generally, if not always, so blended and entwined together, that the one cannot be destroyed without imminent danger to the other.'[2] The 'single exception' in the bishop's mind was the recently devised Constitution of the new United States, legally ratified in June 1788. Consequently, it is not surprising

---

[1] Norman Gash, ed., *Documents of Modern History: The Age of Peel* (London: Edward Arnold, 1968), 20.

[2] J. C. D. Clark, *English Society, 1660–1832: Religion, Ideology and Politics during the Ancien Regime*, 2nd edn. (Cambridge: Cambridge University Press, 2000), 434–5.

that many English radicals, as they sought to undermine the Anglican hegemony, perceived a direct correlation between the American war and their own campaign for parliamentary reform. In this sense, the aftermath of the American War of Independence crucially served to bring to the surface key constitutional questions in Britain; Thomas Paine's chapter 'Of Constitutions' in the second part of *Rights of Man* (1792), with its sharp differentiation between a monarchy based on precedent and a republic grounded on principle and its bald assertion that 'no such thing as a constitution exists in England', was but the most emphatic statement of a polemical position which was coming increasingly to unsettle the established order in the 1790s.[3] In a 1791 letter, Edmund Burke estimated that 90 per cent of English Dissenters wanted a republic, and the Pitt government responded peremptorily to the huge popular success of *Rights of Man* by trying Paine in his absence for seditious libel and banning him from ever returning to England.[4] Conversely, the reaction against schism manifested itself most clearly in Archdeacon Charles Daubeny's *Guide to the Church* (1798), which, in declaring the English constitution to be 'essentially and *exclusively Protestant*', deplored the 'wild sectarian spirit growing up in this country, which, if not properly counteracted, will work to the utter subversion of its constitution'. The foundation in March 1801 of *The Orthodox Churchman's Magazine*, a journal that conceived of itself as in the tradition of Lancelot Andrewes—the Elizabethan Anglican bishop whose version of reformed Catholicism was later to attract T. S. Eliot—suggests again the extent to which at the turn of the nineteenth century political divisions tended to manifest themselves in religious forms.[5]

For conservatives such as Daubeny, the constitutional questions that were surfacing in the 1790s could be understood as a direct legacy of the Reformation. As the leading theorist of the High Church movement, Daubeny was generally antipathetic towards the spirit of Reformation, preferring instead to stress England's apostolic succession from the medieval church and arguing that the Reformation itself was brought about by the mere corruption of the Roman Church, rather than by any fundamental doctrinal errors. In *Thoughts on the English Government* (1795), loyalist activist John Reeves similarly maintained that 'most of the errors and misconceptions relative to the nature of our Government, have taken their rise from those two great events, *The Reformation* and what is called *The Revolution*'.[6] Cromwell's brief regime was not playing just upon Reeves's mind, since the extent to which George III was active in promoting the war against America and later in refusing to sanction Catholic Emancipation—a refusal which led in 1801 to the resignation of his prime minister, William Pitt—indicates clearly enough the extent to which the role of

[3] Thomas Paine, *Rights of Man*, ed. Henry Collins (Harmondsworth: Penguin, 1969), 24.
[4] James J. Sack, *From Jacobite to Conservative: Reaction and Orthodoxy in Britain, c. 1760–1832* (Cambridge: Cambridge University Press, 1993), 199.
[5] Clark, *English Society*, 429–33; Sack, *From Jacobite to Conservative*, 193.
[6] Sack, *From Jacobite to Conservative*, 222.

the monarch within an English legislative framework was itself a fluid and highly controversial political question at this time.[7] What was at stake here was not simply the function of monarchy itself but the whole status of contract theory in a historical situation where the idea of natural deference to inherited authority was becoming increasingly problematical. As Paul Langford has observed, the unequivocal 'support which the Established Church gave to the war against the thirteen colonies is one of the clearer aspects of the British response to the American Revolution', and this makes particular sense in view of the fact that, as Clark remarks, the principal agency of the state at this time was not the 500 constituencies of Parliament but the 10,000 parishes of the Church. Any challenge to the principles of monarchical authority would therefore involve an attack on the hegemony of the Church of England, a fear that led the Reverend William Jones to condemn the American uprising as a 'Republican Revolution' against kingly government: 'This has been a Presbyterian war from the beginning,' he declared, 'as certainly as that of 1641.'[8]

English Romantic writing was heavily implicated and involved in these debates about the identity of the nation-state: the question of whether it might be understood as a natural organism where the bonds of affiliation drew the country together temporally and spatially, endowing it like an extended family with an immanent sense of its own past and future, or whether its political choices were more specifically volitional and contingent. The sense of division endemic to William Blake's poetry—'Without Contraries is no progression,' as Blake himself puts it in *The Marriage of Heaven and Hell*—betokens this condition of rupture in the state of England, with Blake's long poem *America* (1793) dramatizing a conflict between different interpretations of nationhood. The poem portrays Thomas Paine standing firm with luminaries of the American army against the 'thunderous command' of 'Albions Angel', a stand-off subsequently associated with the famous public arguments between Paine and Burke over the significance of the revolutions in France and America.[9] One of Blake's accompanying illustrations depicts the lumpish Albion's Angel as shackled, blinkered, and turned in upon itself, intent upon blocking a breach in a massive wall and unable to countenance within its line of vision the naked figure of one of the daughters of Beulah (Blake's mythical paradise), who shelters her two infant joys

---

[7] On this question, see Herbert Butterfield, *George III and the Historians* (London: Collins, 1957), 250–9.

[8] Paul Langford, 'The English Clergy and the American Revolution', in *The Transformation of Political Culture: England and Germany in the Late Eighteenth Century*, ed. Eckhart Hellmuth (Oxford and London: Oxford University Press and German Historical Institute, 1990), 275, 284; Clark, *English Society*, 320.

[9] William Blake, *The Marriage of Heaven and Hell*, in *The Complete Poems*, ed. Alicia Ostriker (Harmondsworth: Penguin, 1977), 181, and *America*, ibid. 218; William Richey, ' "The Lion & Wolf shall cease": Blake's *America* as a Critique of Counter-Revolutionary Violence', in *Blake, Politics, and History*, ed. Jackie DiSalvo, G. A. Rosso, and Christopher Z. Hobson (New York: Garland, 1998), 199.

(see Plate 5). Yet this apparent antinomy also involves a symbiotic relationship between these opposing forces; as Ronald Paulson has observed, Blake's poem is creative and destructive at the same time, paradoxically deriving its energy from restraint, from the way in which the rebellious impetus of Orc's 'fierce flames' breaks through the 'bolts and hinges' of Albion's established order. This means that Blake's central focus is not so much republican politics as apocalyptic

5. William Blake, frontispiece to *America a Prophecy* (1821 printing).

violence, the kind of millenarian vision that linked English radicals of the 1790s with American abolitionists of the 1840s, under whose aegis Blake's writing was first published in North America. In what Paulson calls Blake's 'mythic area of ambiguity and doubleness', America and Albion, like innocence and experience, revolve in a circle of mutually defining contraries.[10]

But if contradiction was for Blake a source of inspiration, for other English writers of this time it was a disturbing, disorienting phenomenon much better suppressed. *The Prelude*, begun by Wordsworth in 1798 and the first version of which was completed in 1805, is above all an epic narrative about recentring, about recovering the sources of personal integrity—'restorative delight', as he calls it—after the dislocation of being unhoused.[11] Wordsworth's strategy in this poem involves re-establishing the rooted and the commonplace at the centre of poetic consciousness—his own mind and memory, his home at Westmoreland, and, by extension, England itself—and thus consigning foreign objects to an extraneous vanishing point. This is not so much a specific politics of imperialism as a metaphorics of imperialism, where perspective is manipulated so as to magnify the familiar and make it appear synonymous, as if by a series of concentric circles, with the very origins of creative power and wisdom. In Book 8, accordingly, the narrator scorns a 'labyrinth of suburban villages' (p. 334) and celebrates instead 'that vast metropolis, / The fountain of my country's destiny / And of the destiny of earth itself' (p. 338). This nostalgic quest for a chimerical centre, something which runs all the way through *The Prelude*, ensures Wordsworth's hostility to Enlightenment principles of transnational interaction and exchange, and indeed in Book 12 he takes a swipe at Adam Smith, inveighing against 'The utter hollowness of what we name / The wealth of nations' (p. 492).

As every commentator has remarked, the revised 1850 version of *The Prelude* is more openly conservative in its orientation than the 1805 version. The Victorian Wordsworth upbraids the follies of the French Revolution, with all of its fanatical dedication to 'upstart Theory', and he salutes instead Edmund Burke's acquiescence in the wise practices of 'Custom' (p. 281). But while the 1805 *Prelude* may not be so overtly reactionary as the revised text, it is nevertheless seeking similarly to establish a poetics of retrospective domesticity, a counterbalance to the revolutionary traumas of the late eighteenth century. In this sense, all of Wordsworth's poetry is indeed a form of 'emotion recollected in tranquility', as he himself put it, an attempt to suture disruption and confusion by reconfiguring it within what Keats called his 'egotistical sublime'.[12] This ensures

[10] Ronald Paulson, *Representations of Revolution (1789–1820)* (New Haven: Yale University Press, 1983), 95, 110; Blake, *America*, 221. For Blake and the abolitionists, see Marcus Wood, *Slavery, Empathy, and Pornography* (Oxford: Oxford University Press, 2002), 193.

[11] William Wordsworth, *The Prelude: The Four Texts*, ed. Jonathan Wordsworth (London: Penguin, 1995), 458. Subsequent page references to this edition are cited in parentheses in the text.

[12] William Wordsworth, 'Preface to *Lyrical Ballads*' (1802), in *Selected Poems*, ed. John O. Hayden (London: Penguin, 1994), 449; Keats, letter to Richard Woodhouse, 27 Oct. 1818, in *The*

that the radical aspects of Wordsworth's politics—the interest in integrating common language within poetry and the concern for democratic accessibility, as expressed in the 1802 preface to the *Lyrical Ballads*—are always hedged around by a profoundly conservative ideology which seeks to justify the integrity of things as they are. There is an implicit correlation between Wordsworth's poetic representation of nature and what Alan Liu has called 'the majestic repose of the English Constitution', so that the variety and moderation of the English landscape are presented as a guarantee of the Englishman's constitutional rights and freedoms.[13] It is, consequently, no surprise to find Wordsworth's letters of the early 1830s expressing intense hostility towards parliamentary reform, which he associates with 'the dissolution of the present order of society', nor to find him writing to H. C. Robinson after the passage of the Great Reform Bill that he fears its effects will be to ensure that 'the ancient Constitution of England in Ch[urch] and State are destroyed'.[14] In line with conventional Tory wisdom of this era, he equates Lord John Russell with the regicides of the 1640s, declaring that the 'profligacy and folly' of this Whig administration were 'never surpassed since the parliament that overthrew the monarchy in Charles the First's time'. He also associates parliamentary reform specifically with the American example, citing in 1831 a piece by Edward Everett in the *North Atlantic Review* which argues that such an upheaval in the voting system will lead inevitably to universal suffrage—'Being a Republican and a professed Hater and Despiser of our modified feudal institutions,' says Wordsworth, 'he rejoices over the prospect'—and writing to Lord Lonsdale of his fears that the new electoral arrangements will 'convert the Representatives into mere slavish Delegates as they now are in America'.[15]

Great poets, as we know from numerous twentieth-century examples, do not readily conform to current norms of political correctness, and what is surprising in Wordsworth is not his arch-conservatism in itself but the ways in which this conservatism has subsequently been glossed over in an attempt sentimentally to read his work in a progressive light. Richard Gravil finds 'Romanticism' to be 'in large part the poetic compression of New World ideology', and he writes of intellectual 'continuities' between Wordsworth and the American Transcendentalists; but, despite Wordsworth's refusal even in 1833 to categorize himself as an 'Anti-Reformer'—'*that* I never was—but an Anti-Bill man'—it is difficult to see his commitment to a principle of emancipation as anything other than an abstract affair, one comfortably outweighed by his attachment to English

Letters of John Keats, 1814–1821, ed. Hyder Edward Rollins (Cambridge: Cambridge University Press, 1958), i. 387.

[13] Alan Liu, *Wordsworth: The Sense of History* (Stanford, Calif.: Stanford University Press, 1989), 164.

[14] *The Letters of William and Dorothy Wordsworth*, 2nd edn., v: *The Later Years. Part II: 1829–1834*, ed. Alan G. Hill (Oxford: Clarendon Press, 1979), 458, 748.

[15] Ibid. v. 530, 458, 468.

customs and traditions.[16] In his tract on the Convention of Cintra (1809), Wordsworth described the English wars against America and 'against the French people in the early stages of their Revolution' as 'two wars waged against Liberty', just as six years earlier he had published a sonnet, 'To Toussaint L'Ouverture', eulogizing the 'unconquerable mind' of one of the leaders of the slave uprising that took place in St Domingue in 1791.[17] Wordsworth himself, however, was reluctant to accept the idea of black equality, and in fact in 1833 he criticized the 'fanaticism' of those in Britain who were campaigning to bring about the abolition of the slave trade, so that what Wordsworth primarily admires about L'Ouverture is not his political activism but his heroic imagination, a quality perceived by the poet as analogous to his own explorations of the emancipation of selfhood.[18] By extension, Wordsworth was only ever interested in a distant, allegorical conception of American liberty, one that he was able to appropriate as a correlative to his own quest for individual freedom; consequently, he represses or excoriates ways in which the political facts of American independence might disturb and cloud the horizons of his own Anglocentric perspective. While he may admire in theory the spirit of Miltonic liberty, in practice his poetry resists any realignment of England's supposedly 'natural' situation at the centre of a world to which tribute flows and from which power radiates.[19] This also accounts for Wordsworth's extraordinary hostility in 1829 towards the prospect of Catholic Emancipation, which, like the Reform Bill, he fears will lead to the 'overthrow' of the Anglican establishment. He describes 'the Church of Rome' as the 'most pressing enemy' of the Church of England, talks of the 'wretched' and 'grossly uninformed' nature of the Irish 'swarms of degraded people', along with the 'peculiar and monstrous power' of their priesthood, and can comfort himself only by trusting that it is 'the intention of Providence that the Ch: of Rome should in due time disappear', leaving 'the United Church of England and Ireland as an Establishment' to diffuse and extend 'her spiritual influence, through these Islands and as the Head of the Protestant community, throughout the whole world'.[20]

We have, of course, become accustomed by now to seeing T. S. Eliot's anti-Semitism as a disturbing facet of his imaginative universe; but Wordsworth's anti-Catholicism was of a similar kind, and it developed for similar reasons.

---

[16] Gravil, *Romantic Dialogues*, 37, 43; *Letters of William and Dorothy Wordsworth*, v. 588.

[17] *The Prose Works of William Wordsworth*, ed. W. J. B. Owen and Jane Worthington Smyser (Oxford: Clarendon Press, 1974), i. 308; Wordsworth, *Selected Poems*, 172.

[18] Helen Thomas, *Romanticism and Slave Narratives: Transatlantic Testimonies* (Cambridge: Cambridge University Press, 2000), 114, 110.

[19] On the significance of Milton for English Romantic poets, see Robert M. Ryan, *The Romantic Reformation: Religious Politics in English Literature, 1789–1824* (Cambridge: Cambridge University Press, 1997), 13–18. Ryan treats the major English Romantic poets—Wordsworth, Blake, Shelley, Keats, Byron—and he also discusses Thomas Paine; but the absence from his analysis of any American dimension suggests the separatist, nationalist orientation of traditional literary scholarship. [20] *Letters of William and Dorothy Wordsworth*, v. 39–45, 64.

Because both Eliot and Wordsworth were emotionally and intellectually invested in a vision of Anglican order and hierarchy, they found it impossible to countenance forces that would threaten to undermine that sense of social harmony. This is the same kind of idealization of organic evolution, the commitment to a non-legalistic, non-republican version of human society, that we find in Samuel Taylor Coleridge's last published prose work, *On the Constitution of the Church and State, According to the Idea of Each* (1829). Whereas the American Constitution was predicated upon principles of religious freedom and a clear dissociation of church from state, Coleridge, like Wordsworth, attempts, by contrast, to bind church and state together in an organic synthesis. He does this by arguing that the original role of the national church was much broader than what came to be defined subsequently as religion, and he suggests that it should encompass all branches of knowledge and learning, both scientific and humanistic. For Coleridge, accordingly, English culture should be organized according to the logic of the symbol, creating what David Aram Kaiser has called a 'form of aesthetic statism', such that culture and aesthetics would be embedded organically within the national community.[21]

In terms of the larger trajectory of English romanticism, then, it could be argued that the vision of cultural integrity which inspired Wordsworth and Coleridge involved a conservative attempt to reinvigorate the ancient conception of a 'body politic', a notion that was waning in significance by the end of the eighteenth century as the diverging interests of social, political, and economic spheres brought about what Mary Poovey has described as a 'disaggregation of domains'. Adam Smith, for example, refers frequently in *The Wealth of Nations* to 'exchangeable value', indicating that value in his eyes arose not so much within the community but through the process of interaction and exchange with others.[22] This, of course, is one reason why Smith put such a high premium on the appearance of America as a counterbalance to the Old World of Europe, since trade always involves a process of reciprocity between alternative domains. For Wordsworth and Coleridge, though, the exchange principles of *The Wealth of Nations* were anathema, and indeed, Coleridge's conception of the state as what he calls 'a moral unit, an organic whole' might be understood in some ways as a specific reaction against the vectors of displacement involved in Smith's version of a transnational dynamic. Coleridge uses the phrase 'Body Politic' all the way through *On the Constitution of the Church and State*, arguing that the role of the state is to reconcile 'interests of permanence with that of progression—law with liberty', and he sees the monarchy as a centripetal force binding together these disparate interests: 'in

---

[21] David Aram Kaiser, *Romanticism, Aesthetics, and Nationalism* (Cambridge: Cambridge University Press, 1999), 68.

[22] Mary Poovey, *Making a Social Body: British Cultural Formation, 1830–1864* (Chicago: University of Chicago Press, 1995), 13; A. Smith, *Wealth of Nations*, 32.

the king the cohesion by interdependence, and the unity of the country, were established.'[23] Rosemary Ashton, in her biography of Coleridge, described the 'anti-democratic statements' of Coleridge in the early 1830s as seeming 'strange to us now'; but in fact they were not at all strange or anomalous in relation to his deliberately reactionary political agenda. Like Wordsworth, Coleridge was perturbed in 1831 by what he called a 'hellish Licence' in the country, and in April 1832 he described the Reform Bill as 'the ne plus ultra of that tendency of the public mind which substitutes its own undefined notions or passions for real objects and historical actualities'.[24] For Coleridge, as for T. S. Eliot 100 years later, the Anglican tradition constitutes something solid and 'real', against which individual 'passions' are thrown into relief as mere chimerical contingencies.

The structural conservatism of English society in the early nineteenth century has also been obscured by the broad support for abolitionism, exemplified by the parliamentary passage in 1807 of the Abolition of the Slave Trade Act, which prohibited Britain from further participating in the transatlantic slave trade. One problem here was that many of those who fervently opposed slavery also opposed American independence; again, the common thread for clergymen such as James Ramsay was an organic rather than a contractual vision of society, wherein relations between masters and vassals should occur naturally, so that the moral and financial iniquities of the slave trade merely clinched, in his eyes, the case against colonial self-government as a form of insubordination against legitimate authority. Marcus Wood has described British support for abolition in the early nineteenth century as frequently 'self-aggrandising', an attempt to displace the 'national guilt' associated with 200 years of British involvement in the slave trade; and indeed the duplicity of America in preaching liberty but practising slavery became a familiar refrain in English conservative discourse of this era.[25] 'If slavery be thus fatally contagious,' complains Johnson in *Taxation No Tyranny*, 'how is it that we hear the loudest yelps for liberty among the drivers of negroes?' (p. 454).

Given, however, the fact that the wealth of the British Empire at this time was inextricably linked to slavery in the Caribbean and elsewhere, it was not surprising that economic practices and ethical arguments began to pull in opposite directions. By overlooking its imperial dimensions and translating slavery into a fundamentally moral issue, a matter relating to Christian conscience or the

---

[23] Samuel Taylor Coleridge, *On the Constitution of the Church and State*, ed. John Colmer (Princeton: Princeton University Press, 1976), 44, 42.

[24] Rosemary Ashton, *The Life of Samuel Taylor Coleridge: A Critical Biography* (Oxford: Blackwell, 1996), 398–9.

[25] Christopher L. Brown, 'Empire without Slaves: British Concepts of Emancipation in the Age of the American Revolution', *William and Mary Quarterly*, 3rd ser., 56 (1999), 302–3; Marcus Wood, *Blind Memory: Visual Representations of Slavery in England and America, 1780–1865* (Manchester: Manchester University Press, 2000), 24.

creative imagination or both, poets like Wordsworth and Coleridge were able safely to circumscribe it as a domestic concern, a sordid affair which could be ameliorated by the assumption of a correct ethical posture towards one's native environment. In his 'Lecture on the Slave Trade' at Bristol in 1795, Coleridge placed less emphasis upon the practices of slavery themselves than on the iniquitous tendency of 'the Slave Trade & the West India Commerce' to create 'artificial Wants'.[26] For Coleridge, such a focus upon material commodities could only threaten the propensity of the human imagination to reach a state of 'exalted and self-satisfying Delight' (p. 235) beyond the confines of any worldly snare. Although Coleridge does have harsh words for the violence associated with slavery, which he calls 'a catalogue of crimes and miseries that will leave an indelible spot upon human nature' (p. 243), he is almost as scathing about abolitionists who actually perpetuate this trade by their consumption of its products: 'Had all the people who petitioned for the abolition of this execrable Commerce instead of bustling about and shewing off with all the vanity of pretended Sensibility, simply left off the use of Sugar and Rum, it is demonstrable that the Slave-merchants and Planters must either have applied to Parliament for the abolition of the Slave Trade or have suffered the West India Trade altogether to perish' (p. 246). In a roundabout way, therefore, Coleridge attributes the continuation of the slave trade to a want of independence and autonomy on the part of his own compatriots. As in his poems of this time such as 'This Lime Tree Bower, My Prison' (1797), Coleridge attempts in this lecture to remodel Protestant redemption narratives for his own singular purposes, so that what is saved, ultimately, is the subject of the narrative rather than its object, with the spirit of 'Creativeness' rising finally above the 'Vices' incumbent upon enslavement to any vulgar economic chattel (p. 235). Coleridge is hardly more concerned with slavery as a worldly phenomenon than he was interested in America as a geographical entity; just as his plan in 1793 to emigrate with Robert Southey to 'the banks of the Susquehannah' turned out to be more of a metaphysical than a material conception, so a few years later he shows himself to be concerned less with the physical power of the plantation owners to imprison slaves than with the paradoxical capacity of the slaves to drag the English mind into a state of bondage.[27] This is why, in 'This Lime Tree Bower, My Prison', the speaker counters this threat of imprisonment by fixing his gaze upon an English landscape which has been transformed by the mind of the poet into a rarefied symbolic design:

---

[26] Samuel Taylor Coleridge, 'Lecture on the Slave Trade', in *Lectures 1795: On Politics and Religion*, ed. Lewis Patton and Peter Mann (Princeton: Princeton University Press, 1971), 235–6. Subsequent page references are cited in parentheses in the text.

[27] The absurdity of this Pantisocracy scheme was revealed by Southey's prediction of their life in America: 'When Coleridge and I are sawing down a tree we shall discuss metaphysics; criticise poetry when hunting a buffalo, and write sonnets whilst following the plough.' Ashton, *Life of Samuel Taylor Coleridge*, 51.

Less gross than bodily: and of such hues
As veil the Almighty Spirit, when he makes
Spirits perceive his presence.[28]

Coleridge's tendency to apotheosize landscapes, writes Marilyn Butler, was driven by his 'current experience of fragmentation' in a world where the hegemonic power of the old order was crumbling rapidly, but it is precisely this sublimation of division into a state of spiritual unity that came to have most influence within nineteenth-century English culture.[29] The reasons for this are perhaps less directly attributable to Coleridge himself than to the ways in which he (and Wordsworth) were appropriated by what Duncan Forbes has described as the 'Liberal Anglican' intellectual tradition, something which became a massively influential force in English national life through the nineteenth and twentieth centuries. Under the pedagogical influence of Wordsworth's friend Thomas Arnold, Liberal Anglicanism promulgated the idea of a Broad Church, national unity, through its attempt to reconcile church and state within a framework of uniformity where differences of doctrinal emphasis could be accommodated. What was anathema to the Liberal Anglicans was the idea of schism; Arnold loathed the spirit of insubordination he associated with the American war and with the English Whigs of the latter part of the seventeenth century, and as a Victorian clergyman, he sought instead to consolidate, in Forbes's words, 'an organic conception of the State ... which was deeply religious'.[30] This led him to revere the spiritual propensities and Anglican ideologies of Wordsworth and Coleridge; it also led him to abhor materialism, scepticism, and the Utilitarian impulse that had helped to construct the American Constitution within a radically different legal framework.

It is clear in retrospect that there was a symbiotic relationship in the nineteenth century between Arnold's philosophical influence on the English public schools and Wordsworth's appeal to education as a remedy for what he took to be the pernicious effects of Emancipation and Reform on the spirit of England. In a letter of June 1829, in which Wordsworth expressed foreboding about the 'utter destruction' of English culture because of the impending Roman Catholic Relief Act, he said that he thought it 'next to impossible that the now existing order of Society can be preserved in Great Britain, unless our public Schools and Universities pursue a course of education more adopted to the exigencies of the times'.[31] Wordsworth, then, conceived of pedagogy as another version of 'restorative delight', an atonement for loss, just as Arnold sought to reconstitute

---

[28] Samuel Taylor Coleridge, *Poetical Works, I (Part One)*, ed. J. C. C. Mays (Princeton: Princeton University Press, 2001), 352–3.
[29] Marilyn Butler, *Romantics, Rebels and Reactionaries: English Literature and its Background, 1760–1830* (Oxford: Oxford University Press, 1981), 90.
[30] Duncan Forbes, *The Liberal Anglican Idea of History* (Cambridge: Cambridge University Press, 1952), 10. For Arnold's abhorrence of the American rebels, see Lytton Strachey, *Eminent Victorians* (London: Collins, 1959), 186.   [31] *Letters of William and Dorothy Wordsworth*, v. 88.

a spiritual ethic in education as recompense for what he took to be the materialist corruption of the times. Although their outlooks were not identical, they were mutually reinforcing, with Arnold helping to establish the Victorian tradition of English education as commensurate with a Wordsworthian idiom of nationalist apotheosis, thereby naturalizing to an extraordinarily successful degree what was a highly divisive and at times xenophobic mode of discourse. Henry Newbolt's assumption in 1921 about how the study of English should unify society into 'a national fellowship', as we saw in the Introduction, owes much to this Arnoldian and Wordsworthian legacy.[32]

What gets occluded from this narrative is not only class friction—another of those structural social divisions to which Arnold was antagonistic—but also the whole tradition of schism within the English-speaking world which had brought about the creation of an independent American state. In the 'Liberal Anglican' conception of English culture, American literature becomes categorized as a marginal and eccentric phenomenon, the province not of Anglophone dissenters but of renegades beyond the purview of the Broad Church. Arnold characteristically disapproved in principle of William Cobbett's *History of the Protestant Reformation in England and Ireland*, a publishing phenomenon in the 1820s which first appeared in parts between 1824 and 1826 and then in book form in 1826, and which by 1828 had sold an estimated 700,000 copies.[33] For Arnold, Cobbett's book was 'bad' in 'spirit', not because he disapproved of the philosophical basis of Cobbett's work—like Arnold, Cobbett expressed a nostalgia for national unity and deplored the momentum of schism and reformation—but because by tracing these conflicts within British history Cobbett was necessarily drawing attention to social divisions on which Arnold himself would have preferred not to lay so much stress. Arnold reluctantly admitted the pertinence of *A History of the Protestant Reformation* when he called it 'a queer compound of wickedness and ignorance with strong sense and the mention of divers truths which have been too much disguised or kept in the background, but which ought to be generally known'.[34] Cobbett's *History* adduces teleological continuities between the primary Reformation in the time of Henry VIII and Thomas Cranmer, 'Reformation the Second' of Cromwell and the seventeenth-century parliamentary reformers, the 'Glorious Revolution' which the author calls 'Reformation the Third', the American Revolution which he designates 'Reformation the Fourth', and the French Revolution, 'Reformation the Fifth'; all of these, argues Cobbett, have 'proceeded from Reformation the First, as naturally as the stem and the branches of the tree proceed from the root';

---

[32] Baldick, *Social Mission of English Criticism*, 104.

[33] George Spater, *William Cobbett: The Poor Man's Friend* (Cambridge: Cambridge University Press, 1982), ii. 443–5.

[34] Arthur Penrhyn Stanley, *The Life and Correspondence of Thomas Arnold, D.D.*, 6th edn. (London, 1846), 59. Arnold comments on Cobbett's *History* in a letter to John Tucker, 5 April 1825.

but he also suggests these multiple fissures have damaged 'the ease and happiness and harmony' within English society and have exacerbated a general spirit of intolerance.[35]

In this sense, Cobbett not only associates the recent American war with religious conflicts 200 years earlier but also identifies this state of internal strife as something endemic to British society. Cobbett himself, of course, oscillated during his career between sympathy for the Thomas Paine tradition of republicanism—he carried Paine's bones back to England from America in 1819—and hostility to what he saw as the hypocrisies of American claims for New World liberty, hostility which became particularly pronounced during his spell in Philadelphia during the 1790s as editor of *Porcupine's Gazette*. Yet, although welcomed back to England enthusiastically by the Tories in 1800 on account of his anti-American stance in the New World, Cobbett had by 1807 become an enthusiastic campaigner for parliamentary reform in Britain. Part of the explanation for this apparent inconsistency is that he always understands England and America in the light of each other, using the idea of American liberty to sustain him in his campaign for parliamentary reform just as he had used his English heritage to scourge American triumphalism. *Rural Rides* (1830), his portrait of social and political corruption in pre-Reform England, comprises a composite and frequently chimerical landscape that compares transatlantically everything from the salaries paid to ministers (low in the United States, high in England) to wood-fires in parlours ('fine and cheerful' in America, scarce in England because of the amount of 'wood suffered to rot every year ... round about almost every gentleman's or great farmer's house').[36]

In this sense, Cobbett's work is valuable not just for its critique of the new industrial civilization as 'unnatural', as Raymond Williams suggested in *Culture and Society*, but for its resituation of England within a wider transatlantic context.[37] His writing evokes most incisively not so much communitarian or nationalist nostalgia but a state of inherent disruption and division. If the thematic content of his work is an avowal of unity, the form of his writing—self-contradictory and at times self-reflexive—speaks more pointedly, even if less explicitly, to the fragmentation of the body politic in early nineteenth-century England. William Hazlitt complained in 1822 of Cobbett's 'outrageous inconsistency', observing: 'He writes better in favour of Reform than any body else; he used to write better against it'; but such inconsistency might be seen as

---

[35] William Cobbett, *A History of the Protestant Reformation in England and Ireland: Showing How That Event Has Impoverished the Main Body of the People in Those Countries* (London, 1857), i. 261, 290, 3.

[36] William Cobbett, *Rural Rides*, ed. Ian Dyck (London: Penguin, 2001), 378, 196. For the way in which scenes recollected from America function as 'an illusion' in *Rural Rides*, see John Whale, *Imagination under Pressure, 1789–1832: Aesthetics, Politics and Utility* (Cambridge: Cambridge University Press, 2000), 149.

[37] Raymond Williams, *Culture and Society, 1780–1950* (London: Chatto & Windus, 1958), 15.

an appropriate response to a country that was being pulled in violently different directions.[38] In his *History of the Protestant Reformation*, Cobbett remarks: 'It will be curious to behold the American and French Reformations, or revolutions, playing back the principles of the English Reformation-people upon themselves', and there is something in this conceit of 'playing back' which suggests how Cobbett was here consciously moving close to something Thomas Arnold said he would like to see, a history of England traced backwards.[39] Arnold and Cobbett, in other words, were both less interested in the inherent specificity and alien quality of the past than in mapping out imaginative continuities between past and present, and in Cobbett's narrative this retrospective projection of the Reformation takes on the qualities of 'self-conscious artifice', as he rhetorically manipulates the past so as to elucidate what he takes to be the social traumas of the present.[40] As a proselytizer for parliamentary reform in the 1820s, Cobbett also hankered after a state of social tranquility, a nostalgic reunification of national community, that the internal conflicts within his own writings implicitly acknowledge could never be fully embodied. In this sense, narrative instability and textual doubling become for Cobbett emblems of the fissures riving England itself, where the old order was losing its hegemonic authority and appearing increasingly fragmented.

Hazlitt's own endorsement of radical republicanism was less convoluted than Cobbett's. His early exposure to a culture of dissent derived partly from his father, the Reverend William Hazlitt, a friend of Richard Price and Joseph Priestley who enjoyed a modest career as an English Unitarian minister. As a keen supporter of the rebellious American colonists, Hazlitt senior himself actually spent four years in America, between 1783 and 1787, looking for a more congenial environment in which to express his views; his son therefore lived in New England between the ages of 5 and 9, and indeed towards the end of his life Hazlitt cited 'republicanism and puritanism' as the most indelible marks of his early education, even though he was himself in adult life not a religious believer. Nevertheless, as what his biographer describes as a 'relapsed Dissenter', Hazlitt followed in his father's footsteps by vigorously attacking the principle of 'Legitimacy', or the divine right of kings, in a series of essays written in the years immediately following the Napoleonic wars.[41] In 'What is the People?' (1817), Hazlitt impugns Legitimacy as a 'detestable fiction', commends the American War of Independence as 'the last successful example of a democratic rebellion', and, sounding like a good American federalist, deplores the 'insufficient checks and balances opposed to the

---

[38] William Hazlitt, 'Character of Cobbett', in *Selected Writings: Table Talk*, ed. Duncan Wu (London: Pickering & Chatto, 1998), 49.

[39] Cobbett, *History of the Protestant Reformation*, i. 226; Forbes, *Liberal Anglican Idea of History*, 89.

[40] Leonora Nattrass, *William Cobbett: The Politics of Style* (Cambridge: Cambridge University Press, 1995), 4.

[41] Herschel Baker, *William Hazlitt* (Cambridge, Mass.: Harvard University Press, 1962), 6, 30.

overbearing influence of hereditary rank and power' within the British system. 'On the Spirit of Monarchy' (1823) goes on to offer a subtle and compelling interpretation of monarchy as 'a false appetite in the popular feeling', suggesting that its allure arises from the way in which every individual would like to imagine himself or herself as a king, a queen, a god. In Hazlitt's view, the English enjoyment of pomp and pageantry stems from a kind of transferred narcissism, whereby the image of the monarch benefits from 'this reflex image of ... self-love'.[42] Hazlitt was, of course, vilified for these views by conservatives in the early nineteenth century, and the entire Tory press opposed the belated repeal of the Test and Corporation Acts in 1829, although by this time the older image of Dissent as a treasonous conspiracy to undermine the English Church and monarchy had to some degree abated.

P. B. SHELLEY, LORD BYRON, AND THE REPUBLICAN INHERITANCE

The extent of the general animosity between Britain and the United States in the generation after the War of Independence has been well documented by James Chandler and others.[43] Although overshadowed at the time by the French wars, the War of 1812 between Britain and the United States over trading rights and the question of whether or not the Royal Navy could legally 'impress' British-born sailors who had transferred their loyalty to the United States was a bitter and protracted conflict. British forces entered Washington in 1814 and set fire to the White House and the Capitol—hardly the stuff of a minor skirmish—and the war was concluded only by the uneasy compromises set forth in the Treaty of Ghent in December 1814. When the following year British troops began to return from the Napoleonic wars to an economically depressed country, there was a great deal of interest in the idea of emigration to America, with the Surrey farmer Morris Birkbeck becoming a well-known public figure after he described his economically advantageous move to the Illinois territory in *Notes on a Journey in America* (1817). While direct emigration to the United States was still legally proscribed at this time by a British government keen to keep its working population intact, there were well-known ways around this problem, with a detour through France being the most favoured route.

The affinities which developed in the first three decades of the nineteenth century between recognition of American culture and pressure for social reform

---

[42] William Hazlitt, 'What is the People?', in *The Fight and Other Writings*, ed. Tom Paulin and David Chandler (London: Penguin, 2000), 364, 371, 367; *idem*, 'On the Spirit of Monarchy', ibid. 339.

[43] James Chandler, *England in 1819: The Politics of Literary Culture and the Case of Romantic Historicism* (Chicago: University of Chicago Press, 1998), 441–80.

at home became, then, a source of particular concern to the British authorities. William Windham, a friend of Edmund Burke, argued in the House of Commons in 1809 that in its capacity to disturb the order of society 'Parliamentary Reform was of the same cast and character' as the American War. Because parliamentary reform was to become a 'shibboleth of Victorian society', as Clark observed, there was subsequently a tendency among Whig historians and their followers to sanitize the events of 1832, to regard the Reform Act as 'a wise and constructive achievement', rather than acknowledging how fundamentally shocking it appeared to established interests at the time. For the conservative daily newspaper the *Standard* in June 1827, such radical propensities could be traced back clearly to the pernicious influence of the American War and the new United States: it complained bitterly of how the liberally inclined cabinet minister William Huskisson wanted 'to change the nature of all our Institutions, to lower us to the similitude of trans-Atlantic democracy, and then to effect the ruin of all that moves above him, whether with relation to character or to birth'.[44]

Among Romantic writers, Percy Bysshe Shelley was one of many English intellectuals who correlated the political wind of change with transatlantic influences. Shelley's own grandfather had been born in Newark, New Jersey, in 1731, after the latter's own father, Timothy Shelley, had been forced temporarily to emigrate for economic reasons during the reign of George I.[45] In *A Philosophical View of Reform* (1819), Shelley himself applauds the American Revolution as 'just and successful', arguing that the US system of government had created 'a highly civilized community administered according to republican forms'.[46] Shelley again sees American independence as a continuation of the spirit of the religious Reformation, arguing that the 'great principle of reform consists in every individual of mature age and perfect understanding giving his consent to the institution' (p. 253) and excoriating those political rulers who, he thought, masked their own self-interest in assumptions of natural or divine authority. Although Shelley regards the American system as lacking the 'ideal excellence' (p. 234) that a more extended 'cultivation of the imagination' (p. 259) would lend it, he nevertheless acknowledges that the USA is 'scarcely less remote from the insolent and contaminating tyrannies under which, with some limitation of these terms as regards England, Europe groaned at the period of the successful rebellion of America' (p. 234). Most of this essay is devoted to a discussion of the practical politics of parliamentary reform in England, with the American republican model being always in the background as Shelley considers the prospect of extending the suffrage within Britain. His poetry of this period also addresses these issues of reform: 'To the Republicans of North America', written

[44] Sack, *From Jacobite to Conservative*, 148, 186; Clark, *English Society*, 548, 550.

[45] Richard Holmes, *Shelley: The Pursuit* (London: HarperCollins, 1994), 9–10.

[46] P. B. Shelley, *Shelley's Prose; or, The Trumpet of a Prophecy*, ed. David Lee Clark (London: Fourth Estate, 1988), 235, 234. Subsequent page references to this edition are cited in parentheses in the text.

in 1812, postulates a bond with American 'Brothers' seeking to 'fertilise the tree / Of new-bursting Liberty' and thus to oppose an 'unnatural tyrant-brood', while 'Ode to the West Wind' (1820) famously represents the wind of liberty blowing across the Atlantic from the west. In his long poem *Laon and Cythna* (1817), an enigmatic hermit similarly projects the New World in utopian terms as 'a home / For Freedom' and 'the dome / Of a new Heaven'. Shelley's imaginary America characteristically emerges here in primitivist, Neoplatonic terms, as a modern form of the classical Arcadia, an abstract scene of pastoral regeneration:

> There is a People mighty in its youth,
> A land beyond the Oceans of the West
> Where, though with rudest rites, Freedom and Truth
> Are worshipped. ...[47]

The English Romantic poet who has most to gain from being read in a transnational rather than a national framework, however, is Lord Byron. Unlike Wordsworth, Byron never sought to become a nationally representative writer in the sense of embodying the values and preconceptions of his native culture, and this has meant that his reputation in England has always been ambiguous. A concerted English campaign against Byron began in 1816, shortly after he had abandoned both his wife and his country. The attack, initiated by a Coleridge essay in *The Courier*, was continued by articles in various Tory journals, notably the *Quarterly Review* and *Blackwood's Magazine*: 'Most of the critics were active Anglicans,' noted Marilyn Butler, 'several were in orders.'[48] Blasphemy and obscenity were seen by conservatives at this time as key elements in the assault on the old order, and from this perspective it became easy for the Church of England to equate the sexual irregularities in Byron's life and work with his support for radical political causes. Whatever his status at home, though, Byron's international fame in his own time comfortably dwarfed that of the other English Romantic poets, and in the early nineteenth-century United States his only serious rival among the reading public was Walter Scott. As Chandler has noted, whereas the larger significance of Scott's corpus was brilliantly adumbrated by Lukács in *The Historical Novel*, Byron's *Don Juan* has 'not yet had its Georg Lukács' in the sense of having the wider cultural implications of its 'ambitious effort to modernize the epic after Waterloo' disentangled from popular legends about the author.[49] Indeed, Byron has remained relatively marginal to the canonical tradition of English Romanticism, partly because, as we saw in the Introduction, it has been so largely focused upon the identification and consolidation of a discrete literary nationalism, one that could be appropriated for pedagogical

---

[47] P. B. Shelley, *The Complete Poetical Works of Percy Bysshe Shelley*, ed. Neville Rogers, i (Oxford: Oxford University Press, 1972), 107, and ii (Oxford: Oxford University Press, 1975), 251–2.

[48] Marilyn Butler, 'Byron and the Empire in the East', in *Byron: Augustan and Romantic*, ed. Andrew Rutherford (Basingstoke: Macmillan and the British Council, 1990), 64.

[49] Chandler, *England in 1819*, 357.

6. Lord Byron, by Henry Hoppner Meyer, after George Henry Harlow (1816).

purposes. Byron in this sense is clearly not a comfortable fit: Wordsworth in 1812 denied both his 'style' and his 'moral qualities' to be 'English', while Walter Bagehot in 1864 deplored the absence in Byron's work of 'exquisite thought' and 'sublime feeling', his refusal of the notion 'that poetry is a deep thing, a teaching thing'. The American critic M. H. Abrams also positioned Wordsworth firmly at the centre of his influential book *Natural Supernaturalism* (1971): finding a religious intensity in Wordsworth's redemptive imagination, Abrams omitted Byron from his critical pantheon on the grounds that his 'ironic counter-voice' went against 'the vatic stance of his Romantic contemporaries'.[50]

---

[50] Andrew Rutherford, ed., *Lord Byron: The Critical Heritage* (London: Routledge, 1970), 37, 366–7; M. H. Abrams, *Natural Supernaturalism: Tradition and Revolution in Romantic Literature* (New York: Norton, 1971), 13.

The critical situation here is not unlike that associated with the institution-alization of Transcendentalism as a model for American literature as a whole. In his formative work *American Renaissance* (1941), F. O. Matthiessen excluded Edgar Allan Poe from his quintet of national writers—Emerson, Hawthorne, Whitman, Thoreau, and Melville—on the grounds that Poe's cynicism lacked 'moral depth' and made him 'bitterly hostile to democracy'; as with Abrams on Byron, an ethical judgement here became the basis for a literary one, and this in turn underwrote a critical politics of inclusion and exclusion.[51] For Byron himself, on the other hand, the very idea of knowledge was linked to the inherent curiosity that impelled him to cross frontiers, both geographic and moral. The libertine, in that word's original seventeenth-century meaning, was a freethinker, and Byron's work conflates intellectual and sexual transgression in order to pass beyond the hallowed boundaries of English custom. Whereas Wordsworth, the quintessential national poet, was intent upon apotheosizing a spirit of the local, Byron, the transnational poet, was always concerned to shed an ironic, alternate light on what he saw as these parochial fictions, taking a sportive delight in crushing their illusions of genteel religiosity with the harsher discipline of matter. If *The Prelude* is about recentring, *Don Juan* might be described as more about decentring: the hero goes through changes of country, changes of identity, even changes of gender, as if to delineate a universe that cannot, as the author remarks in Canto XI, be reduced to 'universal Egotism'.[52]

Byron in this sense is the English Romantic poet who inherits the eighteenth-century tradition of liberal reform, along with the cosmopolitan sensibility attached to it. He also inherits the republican sympathies that were prevalent in this Enlightenment era, since his interest in the USA stems from a desire acerbically to contrast American political designs of liberty and equality with the corrupt self-interest that he sees as characteristic of the English aristocracy. George Washington is honoured in 'Ode to Napoleon Buonaparte', where he is described as 'The Cincinnatus of the West', in *The Age of Bronze*, where he is cast as a 'tyrant-tamer', and in Canto VIII of *Don Juan*: 'such names will be / A watchword till the future shall be free' (v, 366).[53] In these hagiographies, it is noticeable that Byron, like the American patriots of the 1780s, validates Washington by depicting him as a character from ancient Rome, thus emphasizing how his stand for liberty represents a high classical virtue. *The Age of Bronze* also somewhat improbably characterizes Benjamin Franklin as a classical philosopher,

---

[51] F. O. Matthiessen, *American Renaissance: Art and Expression in the Age of Emerson and Whitman* (New York: Oxford University Press, 1941), p. xii.

[52] Lord Byron, *The Complete Poetical Works*, v, ed. Jerome J. McGann (Oxford: Oxford University Press, 1986), 465. Subsequent page references to *Don Juan* are cited from this edition in parentheses in the text.

[53] Lord Byron, 'Ode to Napoleon Buonaparte', in *The Complete Poetical Works*, iii, ed. Jerome J. McGann (Oxford: Oxford University Press, 1981), 266; *idem, The Age of Bronze*, in *The Complete Poetical Works*, vii, ed. Jerome J. McGann (Oxford: Oxford University Press, 1993), 13. Subsequent page references to *The Age of Bronze* are cited in parentheses in the text.

as it applauds 'stoic Franklin's energetic shade' (vii, 13), while *Don Juan* sings
the praises of Christopher Columbus and 'General Boon, back-woodsman of
Kentucky', who pursues a life of health and hunting in the 'free-born forest'
(v, 383, 385).

Despite expressing enthusiasm for the idea of visiting these forests, along with
the Niagara Falls and the Andes Mountains, Byron himself never travelled to
America. His sympathy for the United States did, however, become well known;
he told George Ticknor, an American who visited him in Venice in 1817, that
he had never envied any men more than Lewis and Clark, who had recently
discovered the overland route to the Pacific Ocean, while in an 1821 letter to
John Cam Hobhouse he reiterated his view that the USA was 'a model of force,
and freedom, and moderation'.[54] In his period of Venetian exile he wrote 'Venice.
An Ode' (1818), which makes explicit connections between Venetian struggles
for freedom and American naval victories over Britain during the war of 1812.
Byron consequently aligns American and European notions of republicanism
and places them both in direct opposition to the British monarchic system of
government:

> Still one great clime, in full and free defiance,
> Yet rears her crest, unconquer'd and sublime,
> Above the far Atlantic!—She has taught
> Her Esau-brethren that the haughty flag,
> The floating fence of Albion's feebler crag,
> May strike to those whose red right hands have bought
> Rights cheaply earn'd with blood.[55]

In 1822, the London *Times* reported that 'Lord Byron, who hates his own
countrymen and countrywomen, has a prodigious penchant for the men and
women of America.'[56] While this was true enough, Byron's 'penchant' involved
a refracted or inverted impression, idealizing a particular image of America as a
putative corrective to the ossified institutions of Britain. In this sense, Byron's
poetry tends always to deploy America as a reflexive mirror, a spectre of alterity.
As he puts it in *The Age of Bronze*:

> But lo! a Congress! What, that hallowed name
> Which freed the Atlantic? May we hope the same
> For outworn Europe?

(vii, 13)

Byron, then, uses an image of America to empty out the social and political
conventions of his native land. Like Hazlitt, he questions the institutional

---

[54] Paul R. Baker, 'Lord Byron and the Americans in Italy', *Keats–Shelley Journal*, 13 (1964),
62–3.
[55] Lord Byron, *The Complete Poetical Works*, iv, ed. Jerome J. McGann (Oxford: Oxford
University Press, 1986), 205. Subsequent page references to 'Venice: An Ode' are cited in
parentheses in the text.   [56] Baker, 'Lord Byron and the Americans in Italy', 67.

apparatus on which the British system is established, as when he addresses the Duke of Wellington in *Don Juan*:

> You have repaired Legitimacy's crutch,—
> A prop not quite so certain as before. ...
>
> (v, 409)

This goes along with an impulse to demystify the iconography of the British state. 'War's a brain-spattering, windpipe-slitting art', the narrator reminds us (v, 410), thereby subverting all the accoutrements of martial heroism which had surrounded Wellington since the Battle of Waterloo. *Don Juan* is often said to be written in a style of mock-epic, but the more appropriate category is perhaps high burlesque, since the poem is not so much concerned with a travesty of epic *per se* as with instituting the art of burlesque as a formal correlative to the poet's view of a world in which material interests and libidinal desires hold sway over more established ideals. *Don Juan* is, at heart, not so interested in mocking specific heroic conventions as in establishing buffoonery as a viable way of life. In this sense, Hazlitt's description in *The Spirit of the Age* of Byron's 'natural perversity' is exactly right, but it is, so to speak, a philosophical perversity, which works by demystifying cultural conventions and by iconoclastically exposing the hollowness of England's more sanctimonious political rituals, rituals which are targeted not merely for their stupidity but because of their hypocritical failure to acknowledge their own inherent baseness and corruption.[57] In this light, the Victorian view of Byron as lacking, in Matthew Arnold's words, 'patience, knowledge, self-discipline, virtue', and the twentieth-century complaint of T. S. Eliot about the 'imperceptiveness of Byron to the English word—so that he has to use a great many words before we become aware of him', were equally misplaced. Eliot, writing in 1937, was committed to a poetry that was 'concentrated' and 'distilled', and he consequently thought of Byron's use of English as incorrigibly vulgar, suggesting that he 'did for the language very much what the leader writers of our journals are doing day by day'.[58] But to traduce the high symbolic style with a rhetoric of garrulous popularizing was, ultimately, part of Byron's design, seeking as he did to disturb the pretensions of established culture to ideals of profundity and depth. In this sense, Byron's whole project, as he himself acknowledged, involved a self-conscious attempt to corrupt the language, although paradoxically he always sought to corrupt it for a moral, reformative purpose. Just as Byron's blasphemy and obscenity suggested a principled assault on the established order, so his aversion to a linguistic plain style was connected to a scepticism about the value of simple moralizing. For

---

[57] William Hazlitt, 'Lord Byron', in *The Spirit of the Age* (Oxford: Woodstock Books, 1989), 178.
[58] Matthew Arnold, 'Byron', in *English Literature and Irish Politics*, ed. R. H. Super (Ann Arbor: University of Michigan Press, 1973), 234; T. S. Eliot, 'Byron', in *On Poetry and Poets* (London: Faber, 1957), 201, 193.

Byron, poetic *sententiae* could not be dissociated from their rhetorical garb any more than, in a wider philosophical sense, spirit could be dissociated from matter.

The literary contemporary to whom Byron was stylistically most akin is not any of the English Romantic poets, but an American prose writer, Washington Irving. Irving was another legendary figure in his own time who spent many years living in exile and who used his experiential perspectives of estrangement to throw back a sceptical light upon the stiff principles and practices of his native country. Like Byron, Irving developed an ingenious, double-edged burlesque idiom whose valence involved not a simple parody of established customs but, more subtly, a parallel discourse enabling the narrative to move continually between recognition of familiar icons and their despoilment. In this way, Irving, like Byron, created a structural form of duplicity in which the text swerves away from its generic model, refusing to confine itself to a singular, univocal position. For Hazlitt, the 'perversity' of Byron consisted in his tendency to lapse into contradiction, his way of feigning enthusiasm for 'the principles of equality' while relying not infrequently upon the 'privilege of peerage'; but, like Irving, Byron actually embraces this principle of contradiction as an intrinsic component of his narratives, as if to signify how the construction of meaning is always a mobile, two-way process.[59] Byron himself was a great admirer of Irving's work, particularly the burlesque *History of New York* (1818), and in 1824 he gave a desire to 'see Irving' as one of five reasons for wanting to visit the United States (along with looking at the 'stupendous scenery', visiting Washington's grave, seeing 'the classic form of living freedom', and getting the American government to 'recognize Greece as an independent nation'). Irving in turn was very enthusiastic about Byron's poetry, writing in an appreciative essay of 1814 that it was the latter's fortunate alienation from English society which had 'provoked him to the exertion of full and masculine talent', and producing another piece in 1835 in which he commended Byron's capacity to interweave apparently conflicting categories within his narratives: 'the mystic, the misanthropic, the metaphysical, and the romantic'.[60]

If Byron's moral infractions riled his nineteenth-century Anglican readers, this idiom of multivalence or elusiveness in his poetry has also failed to endear him to some more recent English critics, who have rebuked him for not being more outspoken about political events of his own time: Byron had little to say about the Peterloo Massacre of 1819, for example, when eleven people were killed by heavy-handed authorities at a public meeting in Manchester to campaign for parliamentary reform. From this perspective, Malcolm Kelsall finds Byron's last great poem, *The Vision of Judgment* (1822), to be rather conservative and

[59] Hazlitt, *Spirit of the Age*, 179. On Irving and burlesque, see Giles, *Transatlantic Insurrections*, 142–63.

[60] Baker, 'Lord Byron and the Americans', 70; Washington Irving, 'Lord Byron', in *Miscellaneous Writings, 1803–1859*, ed. Wayne R. Kime (Boston: Twayne, 1981), i. 116, and *idem*, 'An Unwritten Drama of Lord Byron', in *Miscellaneous Writings, 1803–1859*, ii. 90.

old-fashioned in the way it sets about upbraiding the late King in a court of judgment, 'the celestial equivalent of either the House of Lords, or Westminster Hall where George III is impeached before the aristocracy of heaven and hell'.[61] *The Vision of Judgment* is, typically enough, another parallel narrative, a response to Robert Southey's poem of the same name which had depicted the King's triumphant ascent into heaven; but Kelsall's complaint is that Byron moves the debate on George III's political deficiencies back into the pre-1788 era, when the main concerns were American independence and freedom of the press. This suggests again the republican rather than democratic cast of Byron's political sympathies, a preference we see again in *Beppo* (1818), where he similarly expresses a particular interest in traditional Whig liberties: 'I like the freedom of the press and quill, / I like the Habeas Corpus (when we've got it)' (iv, 144). Just as the American Founding Fathers were alarmed in the 1820s to see the emergence of egalitarian impulses which their republican revolution had fostered, so Byron the patrician aristocrat was never entirely comfortable with the mass movements which gained in strength during the early decades of the nineteenth century.[62] This is also, of course, partly why Byron's poetry looks back stylistically to the more formal Augustan world of Pope, despising as vulgar and ramshackle the colloquial idiom of Wordsworth's verse.

The Vision of Judgment, then, suggests how Byron was attempting to preserve an old impulse of republicanism forty years after American independence had been won and lost. The poem expresses its approbation of Washington, Franklin, and John Horne Tooke, a British radical leader who was a keen advocate of a Bill of Rights and who was imprisoned for libel in 1775 after attacking the government's actions in America. Byron records how George III 'ever warr'd with freedom and the free', and he laments how England passed over its opportunity to rid itself of this royal tyranny earlier:

> The new world shook him off; the old yet groans
> Beneath what he and his prepared, if not
> Completed: he leaves heirs on many thrones
> To all his vices, without what begot
> Compassion for him—his tame virtues ... .[63]

Byron's complaints might by this time seem a little anachronistic, since the main focus of radical activity in the 1820s was not the monarchy *per se* but rather parliamentary reform, conservative opposition to which had become more entrenched and bitter after Peterloo. Nevertheless, the Crown had by no means become indifferent to such mockery, and in 1824 Byron's publisher was found

---

[61] Malcolm Kelsall, *Byron's Politics* (Brighton: Harvester Press, 1987), 128.
[62] 'This democratic society was not the society the revolutionary leaders had wanted or expected.' G. S. Wood, *Radicalism of the American Revolution*, 365.
[63] Lord Byron, *The Complete Poetical Works*, vi, ed. Jerome J. McGann and Barry Weller (Oxford: Oxford University Press, 1991), 326–7.

guilty of *lèse-majesté* in respect of *The Vision of Judgment* and compelled to pay damages of £100. It is probably true to say, though, that Byron was among the last generation of English writers for whom the American republic comprised not just a different but an alternative and potentially viable way of life. Byron was perhaps the last in a line of English Whigs looking back to the Glorious Revolution of 1688 and imagining America as an image of how England might be, conceiving in this distant mirror how principles of reform could be embodied within their native society. After Byron, the memory of this forked path faded, and English writers tended increasingly to view the United States as the cultural antithesis of Britain rather than what Byron called a 'living' republican alternative to it.[64]

There is no doubt that Byron was a political reformer of sorts: in 1812, he spoke in the House of Lords in favour of Catholic Emancipation and the Luddites, and he described the Luddites enthusiastically as 'the Lutherans of politics—the reformers'.[65] He was also sympathetic to the cause of Irish independence, influenced partly by his friendship with the Irish Catholic poet Thomas Moore. Yet, despite his reputation for being disrespectful towards the British Establishment, Byron's reputation fell away in the United States in the middle of the nineteenth century, just as it did in Victorian Britain. *Don Juan* was written off by Unitarians like Andrews Norton for its buffoonery and blasphemy against God and man; Ralph Waldo Emerson found the lack of any discernible aim to be a fundamental limitation in Byron's poetry and prophesied that 'posterity will assign him an obscure place'; Harriet Beecher Stowe produced in 1870 her 'True Story of Lady Byron's Life', deploring the poet's habit of 'plunging into every kind of vice and excess' and categorizing him as a 'man who skimmed over the deepest abysses with the lightest jests'. During the Civil War, it was the American South that tended to be more receptive to Byron's aristocratic scenarios, while northern and New England culture turned to Wordsworth as their intellectual precursor and patron.[66] In *Natural Supernaturalism*, Abrams links the radical novelty of *The Prelude* with what he calls an American literary notion of 'the fresh sensation of the child' being 'the norm for a valid relation to the universe', a link he makes by using Tony Tanner's *The Reign of Wonder* (1965) to establish a conceptual equation between Transcendental idealism and the spirit of 'American Literature' in general.[67] Such a teleology may be conventional enough, but my point is that it implicitly reinforces received ideas about the intertwining of literary and national narratives. An exclusivist design

[64] Baker, 'Lord Byron and the Americans', 70.

[65] Byron, letter to Thomas Moore, 24 Dec. 1816, in Byron, *Letters and Journals*, v, ed. Leslie A. Marchand (London: John Murray, 1976), 149.

[66] William Ellery Leonard, *Byron and Byronism in America* (Boston: Columbia University Studies in English, 1905), 103, 106; Harriet Beecher Stowe, 'The True Story of Lady Byron's Life', in *The Oxford Harriet Beecher Stowe Reader*, ed. Joan D. Hedrick (New York: Oxford University Press, 1999), 535, 549; Joel Pace, 'Wordsworth in America: Publication, Reception, and Literary Influence, 1802–1850' (D. Phil. thesis, University of Oxford, 1999), 237.

[67] Abrams, *Natural Supernaturalism*, 411.

promoting Wordsworth, Emerson, and Whitman as founders of their respective national literatures necessarily works to marginalize transnational literary figures like Byron, Irving, and Poe, who cannot so readily be fitted into this conceptual equation.

These issues of canonization and cultural legacy are particularly important to consider because, as Claude Rawson noted, they were of such crucial concern to Byron himself. At the beginning of *Don Juan*, the poet is clearly obsessed with Southey's status as Poet Laureate and Wordsworth's persona as poet of the people, while *The Vision of Judgment* is another work which specifically considers the relationship between poetic and national narratives.[68] Despising what he saw as the narrow provincialism of Wordsworth and the other 'pond' poets, Byron sought instead to realign English literature within a wider intellectual framework of republicanism deriving from the more cosmopolitan world of the Enlightenment. One belated transatlantic meditation upon Byron's position within English culture comes in the opera *Lord Byron*, with music by the American composer Virgil Thomson and a libretto by Jack Larson, which was premiered in 1972. The opera is set outside Westminster Abbey in 1824, on Byron's death, and the plot turns on whether or not the Anglican authorities will allow him to be buried in the Abbey. The statues of Spenser, Dryden, Milton, and Johnson in Poets' Corner have their say in song, and the action is intercut with scenes of Byron with his lovers. One theme of this opera is the relationship between past and present, in particular ways in which the identification of a continuous tradition is crucial to the formulation of English national identity, as we saw in the Introduction with Sir Arthur Quiller-Couch standing reverently before the tomb of the Black Prince at Canterbury Cathedral. Another theme, very much in the Virgil Thomson vein, is the discordance between high culture and low culture, with the musical interludes of hymns and folk songs in this work mimicking the hybrid, unstable nature of Byron's relationship to England's established institutions. In the end, the Dean of the Abbey refuses Byron a ceremonial interment, with the burlesque nature of Thomson's musical forms seeming to underscore Byron's ambivalent position on the various cultural boundaries which he traversed with such facility: between Enlightenment and romanticism, high culture and low culture, England and America.

REFORM AS APOCALYPSE: MARY SHELLEY AND THE NOVEL OF PURPOSE

Byron's republicanism, which envisaged British and American cultures as coterminous, is reflected also in what might be called the schismatic phase

---

[68] Claude Rawson, 'Byron Augustan: Mutations of the Mock-Heroic in *Don Juan* and Shelley's *Peter Bell the Third*', in *Byron: Augustan and Romantic*, ed. Rutherford, 84.

of the Anglo-American novel. This extends from the 1790s through until about the middle of the 1830s, when the passage of the Great Reform Bill in Britain and the emergence of Transcendentalism in the United States created new cultural conditions on both sides of the Atlantic. There is a whole cluster of transatlantic reciprocities and mutual influences surrounding the 'novel of purpose' pioneered by William Godwin in the wake of his *Enquiry concerning Political Justice and its Influence on Morals and Happiness*, published in 1793. Godwin was an admirer of Thomas Paine, a frequenter of Richard Price's sermons, as well as a friend of the American revolutionary poet Joel Barlow. His 'principles' of political justice, which Chandler sees as probably shaped by the American Constitution, place emphasis upon emancipation from subjection and on a 'rational system of government'.[69] For Godwin, in this more abstract mood, political justice is susceptible of being reduced to a science, and he optimistically envisages a time when 'the laws of morality shall be clearly understood, their excellence universally apprehended'.[70] However, Godwin's own novel published the following year, *Caleb Williams* (1794), by no means wholly subscribes to this Enlightenment doctrine, since it focuses upon the irrational compulsions of aristocratic authority, in particular the ways in which Squire Falkland wields 'arbitrary power' over the hapless rationalist of the novel's title, whom Falkland threatens at one point to 'crush ... with the same indifference that I would any other little insect that disturbed my serenity'.[71] In Godwin's novel, the ambitions of universal reason are set against the more atavistic traditions signalled by a Gothic mode, and the outcomes are correspondingly uncertain.

Godwin's exploration of contradictions between abstract, benevolent systems of philosophy or government on the one hand and the more erratic impulses of human behaviour on the other sets the tone for the development of the novel in these years of the early American republic. The American Founding Fathers did not at all care for novels, because their commitment to a rationalized scheme of political administration was based upon an elevated idea of the citizen as similarly motivated by enlightened concerns. By contrast, the novel at this time tended to look not forwards but back, to primitive fears or instincts which could not so easily be subsumed within a doctrine of human rights. The American novelist Charles Brockden Brown was a great admirer of *Caleb Williams*—in a letter to his brother, Brown spoke of the book's 'transcendent merits'—and Godwin's exposures of human and social self-contradiction anticipate the similarly Janus-faced structures of Brown's own novels a few years later.[72] Set in a post-Revolutionary United

[69] Chandler, *England in 1819*, 453.

[70] William Godwin, *Enquiry concerning Political Justice and its Influence on Morals and Happiness*, ed. F. E. L. Priestley (Toronto: University of Toronto Press, 1946), 169.

[71] William Godwin, *Things as They Are; or, The Adventures of Caleb Williams*, ed. Maurice Hindle (Harmondsworth: Penguin, 1988), 263, 159.

[72] Evert A. Duyckinck and George L. Duyckinck, *Cyclopaedia of American Literature* (New York: Scribner, 1855), i. 590.

States which is unsettled in every sense of that word, Brown's narratives straddle the dividing line between American independence and European custom, and they refract not only the anxieties suffered by the citizens of this new democratic state but also its inherent vulnerability to various forms of corruption and contamination. In *Edgar Huntly* (1799), the hero is described as an Irish emigrant who has, as he says, 'banished myself forever from my native soil', and whose understanding of American culture consequently involves recognition of it as a site for transmutation: 'Passage into new forms, overleaping the bars of time and space, reversal of the laws of inanimate and intelligent existence.' This is the dilemma faced by all of Brown's characters: the crisis of transformation, the allure of knowledge, the attraction of a new country or a new state, is balanced continually against a sense of their dangers. Towards the end of the novel, when talking about the possible interception of the malevolent Clithero, Edgar Huntly finds a phrase which seems to summarize the whole post-Revolutionary situation: 'It is', he admits uneasily, 'a visionary and fantastic base on which to rest our security'.[73]

This is partly why, as Ronald Paulson has remarked, post-Revolutionary Gothic tends to be a conservative literary form. In the fiction of Godwin and Brown, the Gothic style points to that which cannot be transcended, to the material constraints and primordial terrors which ironically circumscribe the possibilities of utopian regeneration. Robert S. Levine has observed how many of Brown's villains come from Europe: for instance, in *Wieland* (1798) the threat to American probity derives from the sinister European Catholicism of Carwin, who exercises an occult power over the novel's eponymous hero.[74] But it would also be true to say this transnational dynamic is endemic to the trajectory of Brown's fiction, so that it becomes a question not so much of American identity being undermined by European malfeasance as of the multiple confusions attendant upon the metamorphosis in national identity which took place in British North America towards the end of the eighteenth century. At the end of *Arthur Mervyn* (1799–1800), the hero opts finally to abandon plague-ridden Philadelphia and return to Europe with his new bride, Achsa Fielding, the daughter of a Portuguese Jew who changed her nationality to English and then to French, and who has only been in America for eighteen months. Identity in Brown's novels is thus a chameleonic, performative phenomenon, burdened by ancestral memories and threatened by the condition of post-Revolutionary insecurity; in Philadelphia, Mervyn comes across by chance a Mrs Villars, whom he had known in England, 'and', he says, 'the sight of my countrywoman, in a foreign land, awakened emotions, in the

[73] Charles Brockden Brown, *Edgar Huntly; or, Memoirs of a Sleepwalker*, ed. Norman S. Grabo (New York: Penguin, 1988), 83, 229, 281.

[74] Paulson, *Representations of Revolution*, 227; Robert S. Levine, *Conspiracy and Romance: Studies in Brockden Brown, Cooper, Hawthorne, and Melville* (Cambridge: Cambridge University Press, 1989), 16, 27.

indulgence of which I did not imagine there was either any guilt or any danger'. Inadvertent retrospection in Brown creates a mood of continual deliquescence, and consequently the plague in this novel seems not just an allegory of the civic ills and ungovernable state of America in the 1790s, but rather, a more amorphous image of the processes of decay that lurk as a negative potential within every rational form of organization, either social or psychological: the epidemic in Philadelphia, declares Mervyn, epitomizes 'the perverseness of nature'.[75]

This makes a clearer link between Brown and Godwin, where the disjunction between the kind of rationalism proposed in *Political Justice* and the irrationalism described in *Caleb Williams* denies his fiction the stability of a unified narrative point of view. Godwin acknowledged the influence of Brown's *Wieland* in his preface to *Mandeville* (1817), and the two authors not only admired each other's work but also responded in similar ways to the sundering of the English-speaking Old World from the New. Brown was also a favourite novelist of Godwin's daughter, Mary Shelley: she read all of his novels between 1814 and 1817, and wrote in a letter of 1826 that 'the Author of *Wieland*' was the one American 'whom I am sure I should have liked'.[76] Brown's work was also much admired by Mary Shelley's husband; indeed, Thomas Love Peacock wrote in his 'Memoirs of Percy Bysshe Shelley' that '[n]othing so blended itself with the structure of his interior mind as the creations of Brown'.[77] Although Brown died in 1810, there is an important sense in which his novels develop the myth of Prometheus that subsequently fascinated both Shelleys, so that Brown's novels can fairly be said to anticipate the mixture of abstract idealism and Gothic doom in the Shelleys' work. In the case of the Philadelphia writer, though, this Frankenstein myth operates specifically within a New World context, as his fictions investigate ways in which the quest for knowledge and independence, the rebellion against the shackles of the old order, becomes a hazardous and often self-defeating enterprise.

In *Frankenstein* itself, published by Mary Shelley in 1818, this dangerous Promethean tendency is associated indirectly with the New World. The novel turns upon Victor Frankenstein's departure from his tranquil family life in Switzerland and his ambitious resolve to seek out the scientific knowledge which will eventually destroy him: 'if no man allowed any pursuit whatsoever to interfere with the tranquillity of his domestic affections', he ruminates, 'Greece had not been enslaved; Caesar would have spared his country; America would have been discovered more gradually; and the empires of Mexico and Peru had

[75] Charles Brockden Brown, *Arthur Mervyn; or, Memoirs of the Year 1793*, ed. Warner Berthoff (New York: Holt, Rinehart and Winston, 1962), 351, 128.

[76] Mary Shelley, *The Letters of Mary Wollstonecraft Shelley*, iii, ed. Betty T. Bennett (Baltimore: Johns Hopkins University Press, 1988), 402.

[77] Thomas Love Peacock, *Memoirs, Essays, and Reviews*, ed. Howard Mills (London: Rupert Hart-Davis, 1970), 43.

not been destroyed.'[78] As Chris Baldick has noted, *Frankenstein* merges creation and transgression myths, and its opinion of the value of this new knowledge is generally contradictory—even, as George Levine suggests, schizophrenic—since the novel sympathizes with, but ultimately expels, the terrible creature it has raised: the monster volunteers finally to 'go to the vast wilds of South America' (p. 109) in order to put himself out of sight of the civilized world.[79] Edmund Burke in 1790 had talked of the new French political constitution as a 'monster', and there is something of Burke's spirit of reaction in Mary Shelley's implicit conservatism here, but the representation of America throughout the rest of her fiction makes it clear that she is concerned rather with establishing parallel universes, where her safe, existing world can be set alongside some alternative domain.[80]

   The Last Man (1826) is another example of the way in which Mary Shelley situates herself ambivalently between the old and the new. The novel features a plague sweeping across the world at the end of the twenty-first century, and it refers explicitly to 'the masterly delineations of the author of *Arthur Mervyn*', since, like Brown's narrative, this work links the advent of plague with the dissemination of a newfangled system of government.[81] In Shelley's futurist fantasy, England has transformed itself politically into a republic, but the question posed by the novel—'could England indeed doff her lordly trappings, and be content with the democratic style of America?' (p. 175)—is generally answered in the negative, since Adrian, the hereditary king now demoted to the role of Earl of Windsor, is portrayed here much more sympathetically than Ryland, the self-proclaimed man of the people. Ryland, formerly an 'ambassador to the Northern States of America' who had thought of settling in the west of America before being elected 'Lord Protector' of his native country (p. 190), turns out to be governed by demagogic self-interest, and a reference to *Macbeth* playing at the Drury Lane Theatre in London seems to point darkly to the dangers of regicide (p. 219). As Bill Christophersen has noted, there are also several references to *Macbeth* in Brown's *Wieland*, as if to remind American readers that killing a king is tantamount to upending nature.[82]

   [78] Mary Shelley, *Frankenstein, or The Modern Prometheus*, ed. Nora Crook (London: William Pickering, 1996), 38. Subsequent page references are cited in parentheses in the text.
   [79] Chris Baldick, *In Frankenstein's Shadow: Myth, Monstrosity, and Nineteenth-Century Writing* (Oxford: Clarendon Press, 1987), 40; George Levine, 'The Ambiguous Heritage of *Frankenstein*', in *The Endurance of* Frankenstein: *Essays on Mary Shelley's Novel*, ed. George Levine and U. C. Knoepflmacher (Berkeley: University of California Press, 1979), 15.
   [80] Edmund Burke, *Reflections on the Revolution in France*, ed. J. C. D. Clark (Stanford, Calif.: Stanford University Press, 2001), 364.
   [81] Mary Shelley, *The Last Man*, ed. Jane Blumberg and Nora Crook (London: William Pickering, 1996), 203. Subsequent page references are cited in parentheses in the text.
   [82] Bill Christophersen, 'Picking Up the Knife: A Psycho-Historical Reading of *Wieland*', *American Studies*, 27/1 (Spring 1986), 123. For a discussion of how Shelley in *The Last Man* 'rejects the meliorative political views of her parents' generation', see Lee Sterrenburg, '*The Last Man*: Anatomy of Failed Revolutions', *Nineteenth-Century Fiction*, 33 (1978), 328.

The Last Man lingers lovingly over well-known English landscapes and landmarks and, like *Frankenstein*, it seems to fear the threat of change and estrangement at the same time as openly canvassing it. Just as *Frankenstein* initially expresses impatience with 'that man ... who believes his native town to be the world' (p. 36), so *The Last Man* begins by subverting the idea of England being synonymous with 'the universe', a notion that becomes more pointedly satirical by the placement of the narrator's family home in the Lake District, at the heart of Wordsworth country: 'the earth's very centre was fixed for me in that spot' (p. 11). If Wordsworth's memories of the Lake District were about the recovery of a lost centre, Mary Shelley's digressive fictions, like Byron's, involve decentring: the tenor of her narrative is to wander, to resituate England within a larger context, both geographic and temporal, as if to admonish the more parochial perspectives of Wordsworthian poetics. At the same time, the novel puts a less than positive face upon this collapse of insular security, as it portrays plague-ridden Americans sailing east, ganging up with the Irish and then sweeping across England 'like a conquering army—burning—laying waste—murdering' (p. 232). Like some British science-fiction writers of the twentieth century— J. G. Ballard, for example—Shelley associates the apocalyptic impulse with a transatlantic dimension, linking her diagnosis of a 'dying England' (p. 259) with spectres of violent disturbance in the west.

The Shelleys, like Byron, were of that generation of English writers who viewed America primarily as a hypothetical alternative to English culture. Unlike Dickens or the Trollopes (both Fanny and Anthony) a few years later, they never actually set foot in the United States; instead, America is projected in their work as a repository of republican and pastoral values, a theoretical corrective to the conservative English state. By the time Mary Shelley was writing her major works in the 1820s and 1830s, republicanism as a political programme seemed to be more or less a spent force within British culture; as Fiona Stafford has observed, Napoleon's self-aggrandizing rise to power appeared to make a mockery of the old republican virtues, and the attention of radicals in Britain tended to shift towards more utilitarian, Benthamite concerns.[83] In a letter of 1826, Shelley signals both her ambivalence about and her mental distance from America, as she expostulates upon the American dramatist John Howard Payne's decision to return to his native land after living in London for twenty years:

Your last letter was very short & also melancholy—The idea of going to America may cause this—I should be *very* melancholy if I were going there—but I may be prejudiced, and ought to feel more kindly towards the overgrown daughter of England ... happy and prosperous as its natives are now they may well look on our starving population & deride our prejudices.—Yet prejudices & dislikes apart it is an awful thing to make so great a change—and to seek new ties & a new career in another hemisphere.[84]

---

[83] Fiona J. Stafford, *The Last of the Race: The Growth of a Myth from Milton to Darwin* (Oxford: Clarendon Press, 1994), 160.   [84] Mary Shelley, *Letters of Mary Wollstonecraft Shelley*, iii. 402.

While acknowledging that American citizens are 'happy and prosperous' while many of the English are 'starving', Shelley still cannot bring herself to contemplate an actual act of removal, since she is, as she admits, still bound emotionally to the country of her birth.

This kind of fissure between rational approval and irrational antagonism also manifests itself in *Lodore* (1835), where the aristocratic hero seeks refuge from his loveless marriage amidst the forests of Illinois. *Lodore* mentions the American War of Independence in its first chapter, and its theory of American pastoral involves a cerebral reversal of corrupt English conditions, for the hero as well as for the narrative in general. Lord Lodore's receptiveness to the American landscape is contrasted sharply with the opinion of his mother-in-law, Lady Santerre, who holds that Lodore's idea of 'quitting England and the civilized world for ever' is a simple act of 'barbarity'.[85] In a curiously circuitous way, Shelley's narrative partially validates this latter perspective, since it sets Lodore's 'abstracted, wounded, yet lofty spirit' (p. 107) against a more materialist doctrine which equates the condition of objectivity with a pre-existent world outside the purview of the romantic hero:

Our several minds, in reflecting to our judgments the occurrences of life, are like mirrors of various shapes and hues, so that we none of us perceive passing objects with exactly similar optics ... The chief task of the philosopher is to purify and correct the intellectual prism;—but Lodore was the reverse of a philosopher; and the more he gazed and considered, the more imperfect and distorted became his perception. (p. 62)

This is an illuminating passage, because it explicitly describes Lodore's utopian visions as 'imperfect and distorted'. *Contra* her late husband's proclamation that poets were the unacknowledged legislators of mankind, Mary Shelley here favours a more traditional, eighteenth-century understanding of common sense, where the reality of any given situation is determined by matter rather than spirit. This is consistent with *Lodore*'s emphasis upon a philosophy of sensibility, where feeling and sensation are said to have their roots in familial and national traditions: 'It is one of the necessary attributes of our nature,' declares the narrator, 'always to love what we have once loved; and though new objects and change in former ones may chill our affections for a time, we ... feel an impatient longing to return to the cherishing warmth of our early attachments' (p. 82). The novel, then, is deliberately bifocal, superimposing America upon England and viewing both countries simultaneously. This is why, despite growing 'to love his home in the wilderness' (p. 12), Lodore finds that England 'haunted his mind' (p. 69), and so eventually he feels the need 'to re-assert himself among his countrymen' (p. 77).

This, of course, is the reason why Mary Shelley's novels always look backwards as well as forwards, balancing off their view of transgression as adventurous advance against a regressive attachment to native sensibilities. *Lodore* has an

[85] Mary Shelley, *Lodore*, ed. Fiona Stafford (London: William Pickering, 1996), 56–7. Subsequent page references are cited in parentheses in the text.

7. Mary Wollstonecraft Shelley, by Richard Rothwell (1840).

interestingly recursive structure, moving backwards and forwards in time and space—we see Lord Lodore arriving as a stranger in Illinois, for example, before the narrative backtracks to consider his career in England—and this seems to fit with Shelley's intuitions about life being lived not sequentially but simultaneously, with the past and present converging into a single dynamic. This structural tribute to the power of ancestry and inheritance turns the representation of America in *Lodore* into something more like a moral exemplum, a pastoral allegory, a formal correlative to the classical authors that Lord Lodore himself peruses during his Illinois exile. America is here associated self-consciously with good feeling, but is also perceived, from a distinctly Anglocentric position, as a site for the construction of figurative fancies: Lodore's daughter, Ethel, is described as having imbibed a 'spirit of sympathy' not only from the 'white inhabitants of America' but also from the 'Red Indian and his squaw' (p. 257); yet Ethel's impoverished English suitor, Edward Villiers, describes her patronizingly as a 'little wild American', whose 'philosophy' is 'for the back-woods only' (p. 229). Towards the end of her writing career, Shelley herself came to seem somewhat old-fashioned in her loyalty to these classical forms of liberty, something which reveals itself in her preface to *Rambles in Germany and Italy* (1844), where she claims that 'Englishmen, in particular, ought to sympathize' with Italian struggles for republican independence because of their own ancestral legacy of freedom:

the aspiration for free institutions all over the world has its source in England. Our example first taught the French nobility to seek to raise themselves from courtiers into legislators. The American war of independence, it is true, quickened this impulse, by showing the way to a successful resistance to the undue exercise of authority; but the seed was all sown by us.[86]

What is most noticeable here is how Mary Shelley still adheres to the Whig line pursued by Byron twenty-five years earlier, about how America represents the culmination of British liberal values. By the 1840s, Britain and the United States were at each other's throats in many different ways—indeed, they were almost at war over the Oregon Country—but Shelley still continues here to promote the old idea of Britain as the cradle of republican liberties.

These myths of transgression and the defiance of supposedly natural boundaries, in which *Frankenstein* participates, can be seen as commensurate with the interest in border territories within many works of fiction during this period. By directing their attention towards border zones, authors like Walter Scott and James Fenimore Cooper positioned their narratives so as to consider how these borders came to be constructed and the various movements in different directions across them. This is why, as Katie Trumpener has written, Scott's novels, despite their often quite specific focus upon the borderlands between England and Scotland, speak implicitly to the expansive conditions of empire and the ways in which different national traditions are brought into conflict or reconciliation.[87] *Waverley* (1814) addresses the question of whether it is worth disturbing a settled government and plunging a kingdom 'into all the miseries of civil war' in order to satisfy some martial or political ideal, and the Anglo-Scottish relationship depicted here becomes analogous to other examples of civil war and imperial strife nearer to Scott's own historical era.[88] *Waverley* makes an explicit

---

[86] Mary Shelley, *Travel Writing*, ed. Jeanne Moskal (London: William Pickering, 1996), 67.
[87] Trumpener, *Bardic Nationalism*, 221–2.
[88] Walter Scott, *Waverley*, ed. Andrew Hook (London: Penguin, 1972), 222.

comparison between the Scottish Highlanders and American Indians, while *Guy Mannering* (1815), which is set in the period of the American Revolutionary war, includes an oblique tribute to Charles Brockden Brown in the form of a minor character actually called Arthur Mervyn, of Mervyn Hall on the Westmoreland border, who writes to Colonel Mannering about how he is entitled to defend himself against a highwayman 'as much as if I were a wild Indian, who owns neither law nor magistracy'.[89] Scott had all of Brockden Brown's novels in his library at Abbotsford, and *Guy Mannering* transposes Brown's figurative border between England and America into a geographical border between England and Scotland.[90] As Scott seems to have recognized, the issues in *Arthur Mervyn* and *Guy Mannering* are not dissimilar: Mrs McClandish in the latter work talks of how there is 'little money stirring in Scotland wi'' this weary American war' (p. 96), and the awkward relationship between established social authority and insurrectionary forms of freedom is crucial to both novels. In *Guy Mannering*, this desire for freedom is expressed metaphorically as an American phenomenon, with Dudley glorying in being 'as free as a wild Indian, enjoying myself at liberty amid the grandest scenes of nature' (p. 167). Indeed, the identification of such freedom both with American natural landscapes and with American Indians living amongst them was a familiar rhetorical strategy at this time on both sides of the Atlantic.

As an avowed political conservative, Scott himself was no great friend of the American Revolution. In his *Life of Napoleon Buonaparte* (1827), he attributes the success of the French Revolution to its leaders seeing 'in the success of the American insurgents, the total downfall of the English empire, or at least a far descent from that pinnacle of dignity which she had attained at the Peace of 1763'. He also describes disapprovingly how French auxiliaries fighting on behalf of the patriot cause 'brought with them to America minds apt to receive, if not already imbued with, those principles of freedom for which the colonies had taken up arms against the mother country'.[91] As Lukács noted long ago, however, the significance of Scott's writing cannot be confined to such narrow intentional categories, since it confronts wider questions about social divisions and antagonisms during the Revolutionary era. Lukács, in fact, perceived an organic symbiosis between the development of the historical novel and the emergence of national identity, finding 'the novel's return to true epic greatness' to consist in its capacity to encompass the whole of a society, to give synecdochic

[89] Walter Scott, *Guy Mannering* (London: Nelson, 1938), 97, 125. Subsequent page references are cited in parentheses in the text.

[90] J. G. Cochrane, *Catalogue of the Abbotsford Library* (Edinburgh, 1838), 114. Besides owning seven novels by Brockden Brown, Scott also owned William Dunlap's *Memoirs of C. B. Brown, the American Novelist* (London, 1822). His library copy of *Arthur Mervyn* was published in London in 1821, but it is likely that he would have known Brown's novel from an earlier American edition. The earliest Brockden Brown volume in Scott's library, *Edgar Huntly*, dates from 1803.

[91] Walter Scott, *The Life of Napoleon Buonaparte, Emperor of the French, with a Preliminary View of the French Revolution* (Paris, 1827), i. 79, 81.

expression to the 'popular life' of the community.[92] While any criticism of the novel in terms of its specific genre tends to rely upon idealist categories of one kind or another, it would nevertheless be true to say that Scott invites such an organicist approach by his predilection for typifying national identities. In *Ivanhoe* (1819), he describes the Normans as 'not, generally speaking, an intemperate race', while the figure of Garth is said to be endowed with 'all the characteristic terrors of a Saxon respecting fawns, forest-fiends, white women, and the whole of superstition which they brought with them from the wilds of Germany'.[93] Within this medieval world—the novel is set during Richard I's reign, in 1194—the Knights Templar are specifically excluded from the book's harmonious ending because their defiance of national authority means that they have no part to play in the developing nation-state. Scott, in other words, rewrites history in accordance with the ideological concerns of the early nineteenth century, seeking retrospectively to excavate that 'characteristic' Saxon quality which would justify the consolidation of discrete national identities in this post-Revolutionary era.

In *Life on the Mississippi* (1883), Mark Twain famously blamed Scott for helping to retard the progress of the American South, claiming that this region 'would be fully a generation further advanced than it is' were it not for their affliction by 'the Sir Walter disease', inducing a devotion to the 'jejune romanticism of an absurd past that is dead'.[94] It is possible, however, that Scott's appeal to the American South in the mid-nineteenth century may have been somewhat more subtle, turning not so much on his simple sentimentalization of a pre-industrial past but, rather, on his evocation of a world in a state of perpetual division, engaged in latent or actual civil war. Epigraphs from Scott frame some of the chapters in James Fenimore Cooper's early novel *The Spy* (1821), which similarly focuses upon a structural division within society, being set at the time of the American War of Independence, which, as the book acknowledges, 'had many of the features of a civil war'.[95] At the centre of the plot is one Harvey Birch, an American spy who infiltrates the British ranks and who, despite finding himself disturbed and harassed by the American army, is eventually congratulated by George Washington himself for acting 'with a strong attachment to the liberties of America' (p. 397). One interesting element here is how all the masks and disguises associated with Birch's chameleonic character seem to epitomize, on a more general level, the novel's contention that '[a]t the time of our tale, we were a divided people' (p. 150). We are told that 'British and American uniforms hung peaceably by the side of each other' in Birch's secret cavern where he keeps his

[92] Georg Lukács, *The Historical Novel*, trans. Hannah and Stanley Mitchell (London: Merlin Press, 1962), 349, 49.

[93] Walter Scott, *Ivanhoe: A Romance*, ed. Graham Tulloch (London: Penguin, 2000), 127, 100.

[94] Mark Twain, *Life on the Mississippi* (New York: Oxford University Press, 1996), 468–9.

[95] James Fenimore Cooper, *The Spy: A Tale of the Neutral Ground*, ed. Wayne Franklin (London: Penguin, 1997), 3. Subsequent page references are cited in parentheses in the text.

changes of costume (p. 356), and this image seems to betoken a larger structural ambiguity within the novel, where national identity is never quite as clear-cut as it seems. However, Cooper's expository method involves starting with these divisions and then dissolving them in the interests of moral unity and truth. In the concluding chapter, Birch is represented as a veteran fighting for the United States against Britain in the war of 1812, as if to exemplify his devotion to the cause of American independence, and the narrative seeks ultimately to validate this sense of patriotism by describing an environment underwritten by the imperatives of American exceptionalism: 'What a magnificent scene ... Such moments belong only to the climate of America' (p. 50).

Although clearly indebted stylistically to the British writer, Cooper hated to be called 'the American Scott', because his own epic enterprise involves the foundation of a quite different nation—indeed, a nation that won its independence precisely by rising up against the authority of Great Britain.[96] *The Pioneers* (1823) is also set in the aftermath of the American Revolution, but Cooper's concern in these Leatherstocking novels is to write specifically against models of European culture, to inscribe a pioneering, path-finding nation built upon personal merit rather than traditional social hierarchy, a world where Natty Bumpo in the role of nature's aristocrat becomes the exact converse of Scott's feudal barons. Clearly there is an intertextual element at work here: D. H. Lawrence, for instance, said that part of Cooper 'loved the genteel continent of Europe', just as the other half 'loved the tomahawking continent of America', and this kind of duplicity is manifested in the infinitely reflexive mirrors endemic to his style of picturesque, where the aptly named 'Glimmerglass', Cooper's fictional name for Lake Otsego, seems to refract the whole heritage of European romance in its lucid surface.[97] Whatever his attachments to European styles and customs, however, Cooper thoroughly disapproved of the avowed Anglophilia of his fellow American exponent of the picturesque, Washington Irving, and his own work became increasingly didactic on the subject of 'the national character' as his career progressed.

This phrase 'the national character' appears on the second page of the 'England' volume of Cooper's *Gleanings in Europe*, an account published in 1837 of a trip he had undertaken nine years earlier.[98] This 1828 expedition was Cooper's fourth visit to England; he came in 1806 and 1807 as a merchant seaman, and then again in 1826, so he was by this time fairly conversant with English manners. He also met various literary and intellectual figures in 1828, living

---

[96] George Dekker, *The American Historical Romance* (Cambridge: Cambridge University Press, 1987), 34.

[97] D. H. Lawrence, *Studies in Classic American Literature*, ed. Ezra Greenspan, Lindeth Vasey, and John Worthen (Cambridge: Cambridge University Press, 2003), 53–4.

[98] James Fenimore Cooper, *Gleanings in Europe: England*, ed. Donald A. Ringe and Kenneth W. Staggs (Albany, NY: State University of New York Press, 1982), 2. Subsequent page references are cited in parentheses in the text.

next to William Wilberforce in London, dining with Scott and Coleridge, and also meeting Godwin and Thomas Moore. But his primary focus in this 1837 book is not upon literary ideas as such, but upon the more general social and political differences between Britain and the United States. Whereas *The Spy* is predicated upon confusing similarities between these two countries, *Gleanings in Europe: England* prefers a distinct antithesis, and it is in fact not shy about stereotyping such differences in order to reinforce its points. Cooper suggests that the 'prejudices' in Scott's writing involve 'deference to hereditary rank', an idea which 'pervades his writings' (p. 121), and he extends this critique of the British ruling classes by arguing that colonial dependencies are essential to the maintenance of English authority—otherwise 'she would sink to a second-rate power in twenty years' (p. 257). He comments also on the general ignorance among the English population about American conditions; he recalls talking to a man who insists that 'the winters are too long in America to keep sheep', despite the fact that there are, he says, three and a half million sheep in New York state alone (p. 254). Paradoxically, though, such misunderstandings create breaches which Cooper welcomes, since his line here is to correct what he sees as the general American tendency to pay too much respect to English views. In this vein, he also applauds the Tory *Quarterly Review* for 'alienating the feelings of America from Great Britain' (p. 285). Seeking to free Americans from the 'mental dependence created by colonial subserviency' (p. 233), Cooper describes the British and American social systems not as branches of the same Anglo-Saxon family but as 'so completely the converse of each other, that it is matter of surprise, so many points of resemblance still remain' (p. 295).

In many ways, *Gleanings in Europe: England* could be seen as a counterpart to Ralph Waldo Emerson's famous lecture 'The American Scholar', which was also published in 1837, and which similarly demanded American cultural independence from the 'courtly muses of Europe'.[99] Emerson's essay, though, is characteristically abstract, representing freedom and self-determination as a philosophical, Neoplatonic necessity, whereas Cooper's treatise is more attuned to the material conditions which brought about increased tension between Britain and the United States in the 1830s. As we shall see in the next chapter, it was these conditions that furnished the (often overlooked) historical context for the rise of American Transcendentalism. Cooper mentions the war of 1812 as a lingering source of antipathy between the two countries, remarks upon English unease at the growing political power of the USA, and complains about the undue influence of British authors in America because of the absence of an international copyright law. He also talks about the necessity for electoral reform in England, pointing out in a footnote on one occasion that his words were 'actually written

---

[99] Ralph Waldo Emerson, 'The American Scholar', in *Nature, Addresses, and Lectures*, in *The Collected Works*, i, ed. Robert E. Spiller and Alfred R. Ferguson (Cambridge, Mass.: Harvard University Press, 1971), 69.

in 1828' (p. 59), before the passage in 1832 of the Great Reform Act, which did away with 'rotten' boroughs, introduced representation in Parliament for the industrial cities of the North and the Midlands, and extended the right to vote to any man owning a household worth £ 10, thereby enfranchising roughly 20 per cent of the adult male population.

This whole question of parliamentary democracy was one of the key issues of the 1830s, which brought latent antagonisms between Britain and America to the surface. Cooper's book is quite unequivocal on the matter: 'Reform must move fast in England,' he writes, 'or it will be overtaken by revolution' (p. 59). On the opposite side, Fanny Trollope's *Domestic Manners of the Americans*, with its negative, satirical account of America as a land of vulgarity and greed, was published on 19 March 1832, three days before the Reform Bill had its third and final reading in the House of Commons, leading the liberal *Edinburgh Review* to suggest that author and publisher had conspired to make her book 'an express advertisement against the Reform Bill'.[100] Such comments highlight not only how reform, in its various different aspects, has been crucial to the relationship between Britain and the United States since 1776, but also how this legacy of reform has often manifested itself in an oblique fashion. The Great Reform Act was not an American phenomenon in inspiration or execution, but attitudes towards it in Britain were crucially shaped, as through a triangulation process, by reaction in the country to the emerging democratic culture of the United States.

In his famous essay of 1952 on seventeenth-century American Puritans, 'Errand into the Wilderness', Perry Miller suggested that it was not until after the English Civil War ended in 1651 that the colonists finally realized that they were 'alone with America'. Expecting that their 'city upon a hill' would act as a beacon and a model to the corrupt Old World, particularly when Oliver Cromwell's anti-monarchist administration assumed power, the American exiles were disappointed to find themselves largely ignored.[101] The same kind of thing happened, if in a less dramatic way, two centuries later with British republicans and the Great Reform Act: radicals who had looked to America as their source of inspiration realized, after electoral reform had finally taken place in England, that the American republic they had always regarded as what Byron called a 'living' alternative to the British constitution was never going to materialize on their side of the Atlantic. The Reform Act of 1832 did not, of course, resolve all of their political grievances, but its passage signalled clearly enough how change in Britain was going to be a gradual, piecemeal, incremental process, a muddling through rather than a revolutionary renewal. Tory MP John Wilson Croker feared that the Reform Act was going to be 'a stepping stone in England to a

---

[100] Pamela Neville-Sington, Introduction, in *Domestic Manners of the Americans*, by Fanny Trollope (London: Penguin, 1997), p. xxix.

[101] Perry Miller, 'Errand into the Wilderness', in *Errand into the Wilderness* (Cambridge, Mass.: Harvard University Press, 1956), 15.

republic'—'The Bill once passed,' he declared, 'goodnight to the Monarchy, and the Lords, and the Church'—but this kind of forecast turned out to be a wild exaggeration; government in Great Britain continued to be largely aristocratic rather than populist.[102] In this sense, the Chartists and other oppositional groups were left alone with Britain, as Miller's Puritans had been left alone with America, and from the mid-1830s onwards the two countries began to assume distinctively different identities.

It was this sense of definitive separation that formed the conceptual rationale for the many travel books around this time which, in a reversal of Cooper's volume on England, purported to encapsulate American national identity. The fact that US political life also seemed to be developing in stridently anti-European, anti-aristocratic directions in the era of Andrew Jackson's presidency added to the mood of mutual repulsion. Trollope's *Domestic Manners of the Americans* (1832) and de Tocqueville's *Democracy in America* (1835) were two of the most famous examples of this genre, and the synchronizing impulses of the latter, in particular, came to be appropriated unproblematically as a manifesto for American studies programmes in the second half of the twentieth century, with too little sense of the contingent circumstances from which such reifications of national identity derived. One of the reasons why de Tocqueville's diagnosis of the national character became conflated so easily with the idea of American exceptionalism was the prevalence of the 'nation-building narrative' in the United States during the mid-nineteenth century, in the decades immediately before the Civil War; as Jonathan Arac has observed, George Bancroft, Nathaniel Hawthorne, and other writers sought self-consciously to outline scenarios of national unity in an attempt to anneal the divisions that were to become all too apparent just a few years later. According to Richard Pells, the term 'Americanization' originated in Britain during the 1830s before spreading more widely across Europe, and the timing of this phrase is revealing, because it was just at this point that Britain began to perceive America as a foreign entity, not merely a rebellious former colony but an independent foreign power capable of inflicting various forms of damage upon the English state.[103]

There is, then, a structural paradox associated with the significance of the Great Reform Act along a transatlantic axis. On the one hand, the legacy of dissent that helped to inaugurate the American republic helped also to pressurize the British state in the early nineteenth century into parliamentary reform. Poets such as Wordsworth, along with conservative politicians, saw a clear affinity between the new political framework of the United States and what they took to be the threat to the established constitution of Great Britain. Moreover, the

---

[102] Eric J. Evans, *The Great Reform Act of 1832*, 2nd edn. (London: Routledge, 1994), 66.
[103] Jonathan Arac, 'Narrative Forms', in *The Cambridge History of American Literature*, ii: *1820–1865*, ed. Sacvan Bercovitch (Cambridge: Cambridge University Press, 1995), 623; Richard Pells, *Not Like Us: How Europeans Loved, Hated, and Transformed American Culture since World War II* (New York: Basic Books, 1997), 7.

fact that this constitution, which prided itself on being so ancient as to be unwritten, was given the benefit of written justification by Burke, Coleridge, and others during this era introduced a note of self-contradiction into its claims for immemorial status; under the rhetorical assaults of Paine and the physical assaults of the American rebels, English defenders of the faith were compelled to commit the rationale for their system to words, and this by definition rendered the idea of the English constitution more open to scrutiny and interrogation.[104] On the other hand, the successful passage of the Great Reform Bill had the effect ultimately of driving a wedge between British radicals and their American counterparts, since it finally put paid to the dreams of old Dissenters such as Richard Price that there might some day be a revolutionary new United States of the British Empire. After 1832, the Atlantic republic was displaced from its status as a potential political entity, although it was subsequently to reconstitute itself as a metaphorical, imaginative conception.

[104] For the observation that in the early years of the nineteenth century 'essential to Conservative polemic is a theoretical reserve', see Paul Hamilton, *Metaromanticism: Aesthetics, Literature, Theory* (Chicago: University of Chicago Press, 2003), 156.

3

The First Cold War: Anglo-American Literature and the Oregon Question

MANIFEST DESTINY AND ANGLOPHOBIA

Relations between Britain and the United States in the middle years of the nineteenth century moved away from the accusations of sedition that had characterized the immediate aftermath of the Revolutionary war towards a situation in which transatlantic imperial rivalries began to come more sharply into focus. The 1830s and 1840s were marked by both political and geographical instability, since it was not until 1846 that Britain formally relinquished a claim to large areas of the Pacific Northwest that make up the present-day United States. The writing during the 1840s of English partisans such as Charles Dickens and George Ruxton reflects the international tension surrounding these disputed land claims, while the simultaneous emergence of American Transcendentalism was also impelled partly by a war climate. Kathleen Tillotson, whose classic study of the English novel in the 1840s relates the culture of this decade mainly to domestic contexts of industrialization and Chartism, suggested that British writers of this time tended to be 'patronizing, even contemptuous' about America; but this contempt was based not upon mere aloofness, but on suspicion, since Anglo-American travel writing of this era involves a sustained effort rhetorically to appropriate geographic territories whose proprietorship was becoming a matter of widespread anxiety.[1] Moreover, the resolution of this 'Oregon question', as it came to be called, was intricately tied up in Britain with the abolition in 1846 of the Corn Laws, a reform which undermined the protectionist interests of the landed classes by exposing agriculture to an influx of cheaper produce from abroad, notably from the United States. According to one historian, '[t]he repeal of the Corn Laws in 1846 was, in many ways, far more long-lasting in its political and economic implications than other supposedly pivotal events in nineteenth-century Britain, for example the Reform Acts of 1832 and 1867.'[2]

---

[1] Kathleen Tillotson, *Novels of the Eighteen-Forties*, 2nd edn. (Oxford: Clarendon Press, 1956), 6.
[2] Anthony Howe, *Free Trade and Liberal England, 1846–1946* (Oxford: Clarendon Press, 1997), 1.

The territorial instability that characterized the United States in the 1840s has often been overlooked by American scholars, who have chosen instead to concentrate on the country's own Civil War of the 1860s. This later sectional conflict obviously raises all kinds of issues linked to racial polarities and to the potential fracturing of US nationhood; yet, for all of its important challenges to the assumptions of white liberalism, such a focus on the 'house divided against itself', as Lincoln famously put it in 1858, has worked implicitly to shore up the nation-building agendas of the United States, with the political and geographical divisions of that internecine struggle always anticipating as their corollary a parallel state of unity and indivisible liberty.[3] To return so compulsively to the trauma of the Civil War, in other words, is an indirect way of asserting the primacy of traditional American ideals of federal unity and freedom. Far less prominent has been discussion of the international conflicts of the 1840s: the war with Mexico over Texas and the stand-off with Great Britain over the Oregon Country.[4] Whereas the Civil War turned upon a political effort to re-establish national boundaries that were represented as not only natural but divinely ordained, the earlier disputes raised the distinct possibility of the geography of the United States being organized quite differently from the 'sea to shining sea' model that later became established.

From this perspective, to reconsider the fraught state of cultural relations between Britain and America in the 1840s is to recover a sense of the contingent nature of national formations, of ways in which the geographic extent of their respective national domains might have been consolidated in radically different ways from what subsequently transpired. After the Louisiana Purchase of 1803, Thomas Jefferson had envisaged the Rocky Mountains comprising the western limit to the United States, while in 1839 Alexander Forbes, British vice-consul in Mexico, sought to take advantage of the political vacuum in the Far West by pleading with his government to appropriate California with all possible speed, emphasizing not only the natural abundance of that region but also its strategic usefulness as a gateway to the Pacific. Much twentieth-century Western history, influenced by the 'myth and symbol' assumptions of American national unity, imagined the 'reuniting of East and West', in Ray Allen Billington's phrase, to be somehow inevitable, a fitting restitution of some prior Edenic condition.[5] For example, in *The Year of Decision: 1846*, published in 1943, Bernard DeVoto

---

[3] Abraham Lincoln, ' "House Divided" Speech at Springfield, Illinois', in *The Portable Abraham Lincoln*, ed. Andrew Delbanco (New York: Viking Penguin, 1992), 89. On the significance of the American Civil War, see Philip Fisher, 'Introduction: The New American Studies', in *The New American Studies: Essays from* Representations (Berkeley: University of California Press, 1991), p. xv.

[4] For a discussion of this point, see Shelley Streeby, 'Joaquín Murrieta and the American 1848', in *Post-Nationalist American Studies*, ed. John Carlos Rowe (Berkeley: University of California Press, 2000), 166–7.

[5] Ray Allen Billington, *The Far Western Frontier, 1830–1860* (New York: Harper and Brothers, 1956), 147, 269.

worked with an assumption about the United States as a 'continental nation' and described the 'sense of incompletion' incumbent upon a disjunction of the Northwest Territory from the United States. Using as his 'invocation' Thoreau's injunction to himself, 'I must walk toward Oregon and not toward Europe,' DeVoto effectively replicated the nineteenth-century project of Manifest Destiny in his retrospective account of the events of 1846 forming 'a turning point in American destiny', 'a decisive turn in the history of the United States'.[6]

The purpose of this chapter, then, is to look specifically at the arguments between Britain and the USA over Oregon and other disputed boundaries in the first half of the nineteenth century, conflicts which came to a head and nearly resulted in war after James Polk was elected President in 1845. My concern will be with the ways in which these contentious issues permeated both English and American literature of the period, so that representations of the American West in the works of English writers such as Dickens and Ruxton might be understood as a textual refraction of these transatlantic disputes. This will suggest how English literature of this time needs to be understood as a transnational rather than a merely domestic phenomenon, just as the development of American Transcendentalism in the 1830s and 1840s should be seen as interwoven systematically with the belligerent Anglophobia of this era. In a curious foreshadowing of the 'Iron Curtain' rhetoric that became so widespread 100 years later, the ageng Andrew Jackson in 1844 warned that if Britain managed to establish a permanent foothold in the American Southwest, it could form an 'iron Hoop around the United States', with Britain being in a position to control Texas, Cuba, and Oregon as well as Canada. Stephen Douglas in 1845 similarly proclaimed: 'We want Texas to protect our commerce in the Gulf, and we want Oregon to protect our fisheries and our trade with China, and to put a stop to the unscrupulous aims of Great Britain at universal dominion.'[7] Whereas the war with Mexico never involved a threat of military reprisals on the US eastern seaboard, the idea of making war again with Britain was an altogether different proposition, involving a potential clash between two ambitious imperial

---

[6] Bernard DeVoto, *The Year of Decision: 1846* (Boston: Little, Brown and Company, 1943), 500, 9, 4. An indication of the extent to which the British dimension was erased from this generation of US Western history can be inferred from the fact that in his discussion of this process of 'decision' DeVoto mentions the Peel government only twice, briefly, near the beginning of his book. The British presence is equally excluded from the work of New Western Historians such as Patricia Nelson Limerick, who reads the American West in terms of capitalist exploitation and racial oppression but who nevertheless accepts 'the association of the region with a potent and persistent variety of nationalistic myth'. Limerick, *The Legacy of Conquest: The Unbroken Past of the American West* (New York: Norton, 1987), 30.

[7] Sam W. Haynes, 'Anglophobia and the Annexation of Texas: The Quest for National Security', in *Manifest Destiny and Empire: American Antebellum Expansionism*, ed. Sam W. Haynes and Christopher Morris (College Station, Tex.: University of Texas at Arlington–Texas A & M Press, 1997), 129; Thomas R. Hietala, ' "This Splendid Juggernaut": Westward a Nation and its People', in *Manifest Destiny and Empire*, ed. Haynes and Morris, 58–9.

powers which were at this time roughly equivalent in population and economic strength.[8] For the United States, then, such a clash with Britain would involve a real threat of subordination, and the opposition to the war with Mexico in American liberal circles, evident in the unease of Emerson, Thoreau, and their associates, turned to a much harder and more self-protective sense of antagonism in the face of this older enemy.

British interest in the Oregon Country had been developed over the years mainly by the Hudson's Bay Company, which had obtained from the Crown in 1670 a grant of land extending westward from the Rocky Mountains to embrace the greater part of what is now called Canada, as far north as today's Alaskan border. To the south, the area in question extended to the forty-second parallel, today's California–Oregon border, with shipping access to and control over the harbour of Puget Sound being the most important factor from an economic point of view. This royal grant included not merely rights of soil but exclusive rights of trade, and, as the fur trade flourished in the eighteenth and nineteenth centuries, the Hudson's Bay Company came to be seen as a crucial partner of the Crown in building up the British Empire in North America. The ensuing conflict between rival British and American claims to the Northwest Territory is foreshadowed in the *Journals of Lewis and Clark*, in which British commercial interests appear to form an impediment to the 'scenes of visionary enchantment' which enthral Jefferson's explorers on their journey west. Reaching the Marias River in present-day Montana on 8 June 1805, Meriwether Lewis describes it as

a noble river; one destined to become in my opinion an object of contention between the two great powers of America and Great Britain with respect to the adjustment of the Northwestwardly boundary of the former; and that it will become one of the most interesting branches of the Missouri in a commercial point of view, I have but little doubt, as it abounds with animals of the fur kind, and most probably furnishes a safe and direct communication to that productive country of valuable furs exclusively enjoyed at present by the subjects of his Britannic Majesty.[9]

There is a discursive as well as an embryonic political and commercial conflict here, for that note of sarcasm in Lewis's last sentence contrasts vividly with the tone of romantic exultation throughout other parts of his journal, where, as he gives names to the rivers and mountains, he mythologizes the West as a 'sublimely grand spectacle', a new Eden.[10] In this sense, the British presence in the Pacific Northwest became for Lewis analogous to the presence of Indian tribes, since they both embodied a prior, established culture liable to undermine his pioneering narrative's self-aggrandizing myth of origins.

---

[8] Christopher Mulvey, *Transatlantic Manners: Social Patterns in Nineteenth-Century Anglo-American Travel Literature* (Cambridge: Cambridge University Press, 1990), 166.
[9] Meriwether Lewis and William Clark, *The Journals of Lewis and Clark*, ed. Frank Bergeron (New York: Penguin, 1989), 144, 153.   [10] Ibid. 160.

The first symbol of this international dispute was Astoria, a small town at the mouth of the Columbia River built by the New York businessman John Jacob Astor, after he had obtained in 1809 a charter from the New York legislature for his 'American Fur Company' to rival the Hudson's Bay organization. During the war of 1812, the British captured Astoria and changed its name to Fort George, with the US government ignoring Astor's plea to send military forces to protect American interests in the West. In 1821, the British tried to consolidate their hold on the area by establishing through an Act of Parliament criminal and civic jurisdiction for certain parts of the Oregon Country. George Canning, British Foreign Secretary between 1822 and 1827, saw the retention, or at least the neutrality, of Oregon as essential to increasing British trade with the Orient, and he accordingly proposed incorporating the Pacific Northwest into what he called the 'New States of America', a territory legally separate from US jurisdiction. Tensions between the imperial powers which had been latent since the war of 1812 were exacerbated in 1838, when Congress produced a report praising Oregon in glowing terms and encouraging Americans to migrate there as rapidly as possible, and in January 1841 a resolution was introduced into Congress directing the President to serve notice to England of the termination of the convention of joint occupation of these Northwest territories.[11] It was at this point that diplomacy began in earnest, with British Prime Minister Robert Peel dispatching Lord Ashburton to lead negotiations not just about Oregon but also about the boundary between Maine and New Brunswick in Canada, another running sore between the two Atlantic powers. Ashburton was successful in negotiating a resolution of the Maine issue, with the Webster–Ashburton Treaty, signed on 9 August 1842, relinquishing four-fifths of the disputed territory to the Americans.

The Oregon problem, however, proved to be more intractable. After Polk's election victory in 1845, the rhetoric in Washington became ever more strident, with the new President in his inaugural address following up his 'invitation' to Texas to enter the Union with a round declaration that the American 'title to the country of the Oregon is "clear and unquestionable"'. John Quincy Adams, a veteran of earlier struggles with England, was moved to cite in Congress the Book of Genesis in an attempt to justify these American claims, prophesying that while the British intended to keep Oregon in a barbarous state for hunters, savages, and wild beasts, it was the destiny of Americans here to fulfil the divine injunction to 'be fruitful and multiply, and replenish the earth, and subdue it'.[12] In truth, Polk's Democratic Party was motivated not only by biblical injunctions of this kind but also by a domestic political need to expand its free

---

[11] Billington, *Far Western Frontier*, 84.
[12] Frederick Merk, *The Oregon Question: Essays in Anglo-American Diplomacy and Politics* (Cambridge, Mass.: Harvard University Press, 1967), 282–3, 228.

territory so as to counterbalance the growing influence of pro-slavery forces in the South. In the House of Commons, however, Peel retorted that the British also had 'clear and unquestionable' rights in Oregon, while the London *Times* also adopted a belligerent attitude, responding to Polk's inaugural address by declaring in March 1845: 'in spite of his marauders, and what he terms his constitutional rights, the territory of Oregon will never be wrested from the British Crown, to which it belongs, but by war.' There was for a while, then, a real prospect of all-out war between these old enemies, with the slogan 'Fifty-Four Forty or Fight' (referring to the latitude of the boundary demanded by the Americans) turning into a popular cry throughout the USA in January and February 1846.[13]

In early 1846, however, the British government decided to back away from confrontation, motivated mainly by a prudent recognition that, in the wake of the first failure of the Irish potato crop in 1845, Britain was henceforth going to be more dependent upon trade with the USA for its essential food supplies. Indirectly, then, the dispute with America over Oregon was instrumental in bringing about the demise of the Corn Laws, which had protected the established interests of English agriculture against the threat of foreign trade. Indeed, when Peel forced this reform through Parliament in January 1846, the Duke of Richmond was one of many in Peel's own Conservative Party who denounced any alteration in the Corn Laws as 'unconstitutional'. Conversely, however, Peel's Foreign Secretary, Lord Aberdeen, was the Prime Minister's staunchest supporter on repeal, since Aberdeen believed, as Charles Greville observed at the time, that nothing would 'tend so materially to the prevalence of pacific counsels' between Britain and America as 'an announcement that our Corn Laws are going to be repealed', with the consequent expectation of trade routes across the Atlantic being opened up.[14] In this sense, it could be argued that although the Oregon question did not result in outright war, it helped substantially to change the economic fabric of British society, since the second half of the nineteenth century saw a big fall in the price of grain and an ensuing depression in British agriculture as cheap imports from North and South America began to flood the market. The strategic retreat of the pragmatic Peel in 1846 was also influenced by two investigating commissions he had sent out to the Oregon Country, which reported back that such a distant outpost could never be defended successfully against American aggression, while the arrival in any case of migrants across the Rocky Mountains soon made the American settlement of this land a *fait accompli*. Peel's men left the ground grumbling about the absence of hot water and other civilized amenities, and the legend was put about in

[13] Ibid. 283, 302; David M. Pletcher, *The Diplomacy of Annexation: Texas, Oregon, and the Mexican War* (Columbia, Mo.: University of Missouri Press, 1973), 334.

[14] Cheryl Schonhardt-Bailey, ed., *Free Trade: The Repeal of the Corn Laws* (Bristol: Thoemmes Press, 1996), 104; Howe, *Free Trade and Liberal England*, 22.

England that the old fur trade was dying and that Oregon was merely, as Lord Aberdeen put it, a 'pine swamp' not worth fighting for.[15] By a treaty agreed in Washington on 15 June 1846, a compromise was reached placing the boundary at 49° latitude and allowing the Hudson's Bay Company to retain navigational rights in the Columbia River (rights that were subsequently terminated in 1859). A number of British subjects were, of course, forcibly expatriated by this 1846 treaty, while the Oregon Territory was formally brought into being as a constituent part of the USA by an Act of Congress passed on 14 August 1848.

So far from introducing immediately the spirit of life, liberty, and the pursuit of happiness, one of the Oregon legislature's first tasks was to pass in September 1849 a law consolidating previous exclusion clauses mandated by its provisional legislature so as to ban African-Americans from establishing permanent residence in the newly declared Oregon Territory. This legislative exclusion is symptomatic of American ante-bellum politics, since one thing suggested by these fierce transatlantic disputes is the extent to which the idea of a single Anglo-Saxon 'race' binding together English and American culture in the nineteenth century was part of what Reginald Horsman has called the 'romantic racial nationalism' of this time. Horsman points out the prevalence of racial thinking during this era: the influence of Herder, the myths of primitivism, and the proclivity of science to classify Anglo-Saxons, in the words of phrenologist Charles Caldwell, as 'the most endowed variety of the Caucasian race'.[16] All of this also fed into the debates surrounding slavery, with Southern apologist George Fitzhugh as keen to identify an Anglo-Saxon 'type' as he was negatively to describe the African race. While this myth of an Anglo-Saxon race may have been no less of a fiction than its African counterpart, it is nevertheless clear that this synoptic, dehistoricizing discourse of race was as powerful in the northern as the southern states of America during the nineteenth century. In its discussion of the Oregon question, for example, Congress tried to differentiate the British government, which it despised, from the English race, to which it felt attached. Looming over everything here, of course, was the impending conflict over slavery: when Massachusetts politician Daniel Webster, a prominent advocate of the Anglo-Saxon ideal, sought to reassure himself that Oregon, whether settled by Americans or English, would be populated by '*Anglo-Saxons* ... men educated in notions of independent government and all self-dependent', his implicit message was that at least Oregon would never become a slave state.[17] Webster's attempt to gloss over differences between Britain and America is commensurate with a tribute to the supposed Anglo-Saxon racial characteristic of 'aggressive freedom' from another

---

[15] Pletcher, *Diplomacy of Annexation*, 313; Billington, *Far Western Frontier*, 157; DeVoto, *Year of Decision*, 24.
[16] Reginald Horsman, *Race and Manifest Destiny: The Origins of American Racial Anglo-Saxonism* (Cambridge, Mass.: Harvard University Press, 1981), 158, 128.   [17] Ibid. 220, 251, 223.

New England source, Ralph Waldo Emerson, in his chapter on race in *English Traits* (1856).[18] Again, there is an indirect attempt in this period just before the Civil War, on Emerson's part as well as Webster's, to appropriate the idea of an Anglo-Saxon heritage and to align it with a spirit of emancipation in order to use this as an intellectual cudgel within the increasingly fractious world of American domestic politics.

It is also clear, however, that increasingly sharp political antagonisms ran alongside these old legends of tribal unity, and, as Robert W. Johannsen has noted, 'Anglophobia ... has been a missing ingredient in most discussions of Manifest Destiny.' The exigencies of historical confrontation tended to counteract these homogenizing fictions of Anglo-Saxon mythology: indeed, Sam W. Haynes concurs in the view that hatred of England was 'a shared experience for millions of Americans in the 1840s'.[19] Even though John L. O'Sullivan first referred to 'manifest destiny' in a commentary during the summer of 1845 on the annexation of Texas, his magic phrase did not attract widespread attention until he repeated it in an article for the *New York Morning News* on 27 December 1845 in relation to the Oregon affair:

Away, away with all these cobweb tissues of discovery, exploration, settlement, continuity, etc. ... were the respective cases and arguments of the two parties, as to all these points of history and law, reversed—had England all ours, and we nothing but hers—our claim to Oregon would still be best and strongest. And that claim is by the right of our manifest destiny to overspread and to possess the whole of the continent which Providence has given us for the development of the great experiment of Liberty and federated self-government entrusted to us.[20]

Coming as he did from an Irish Catholic family, and having alongside him in the Young America movement other Irish-American mavericks such as Samuel Langtree, O'Sullivan inherited what Edward L. Widmer calls 'a strong dislike of hegemonic Anglo-Saxon culture' and 'English imperialism'. This dislike was disseminated widely during the 1840s, and O'Sullivan played no small part in stirring it up. It was at this time that the notion of the United States justly extending 'from ocean to ocean' became naturalized: in an 1845 speech in the House of Representatives, Stephen Douglas, a politician influenced by the Young America movement who was particularly hostile to Britain, declared how he 'would make this an ocean-bound republic, and have no more disputes about boundaries or red lines upon the map'.[21] It was also around

---

[18] Ralph Waldo Emerson, *English Traits*, ed. Douglas Emory Wilson (Cambridge, Mass.: Harvard University Press, 1994), 28. Subsequent page references to this edition are cited in parentheses in the text.

[19] Robert W. Johannsen, 'Introduction', in *Manifest Destiny and Empire*, 5; Haynes, 'Anglophobia and the Annexation of Texas', 117.   [20] Pletcher, *Diplomacy of Annexation*, 320.

[21] Edward L. Widmer, *Young America: The Flowering of Democracy in New York City* (New York: Oxford University Press, 1999), 31, 195. O'Sullivan himself was actually an Episcopalian, though he converted to Catholicism later in his life.

this time (1846 and 1847) that Thoreau took himself off to conduct his experiment in living at Walden Pond, and all of the notions in *Walden* about transcending merely legal 'premises' and in establishing 'natural boundaries' for 'individuals' as well as 'nations' are involved at some level in the same discourse of Anglophobia.[22]

What we see here, then, is not just a binary relation between Old World and New, where the latter seeks to liberate itself from the crusty domination of the former. Instead, we find a much more complicated matrix wherein the British relationship with its former colonies, the United States, is shadowed and mirrored by its dealings with other colonial dependencies at this time. One of the reasons why Britain was willing ultimately to relinquish any claim to Oregon was that New Zealand had become a British colony in 1841 and had begun competing successfully with the Pacific Northwest for British settlers; the sea voyage from Britain to New Zealand at this time was several weeks shorter than the circuitous passage to the West Coast of America, and this contributed to a general preference for the Antipodes on the part of emigrants as well as the British government. Canada, of course, was a long-standing bone of contention between the British and American empires, with Lord Ashburton writing to Daniel Webster in 1846 that the real cause of the everlasting boundary squabbles here was simply the fact of British rule over a land 'which you begin to think should wholly belong to you'. For himself, Ashburton went on, he would be happy to be rid of Canada and hoped to find 'a decent Excuse to let the work of Annexation be completed'.[23] Ireland, though, was not a country that Britain would so willingly abandon, and the always difficult relationship here spilled over into transatlantic politics, with the British becoming increasingly suspicious of what they perceived as the growing Irish influence in the USA as the nineteenth century wore on. Herman Melville's older brother, Gansevoort, who was very active in Democratic Party circles before his early death in 1846, vociferously championed the cause of the immigrant Irish in America, and he campaigned for the repeal of the union between Great Britain and Ireland as vigorously as he supported the Young America policies of westward expansion and the annexation of Oregon.[24]

There were during this period, then, as Haynes says, 'many vectors of Anglophobia, all crossing the political axis at separate points, but never intersecting to generate a cohesive response'. Because the United States itself was still in a fairly fluid and inchoate shape, US reactions to the dangers posed by Great Britain were relatively amorphous when compared to 'the broad consensus that characterized US public opinion one hundred years later, when the nation perceived itself to be locked in another epochal contest for global economic and political hegemony

---

[22] Henry D. Thoreau, *Walden*, ed. J. Lyndon Shanley (Princeton: Princeton University Press, 1971), 81, 141. Subsequent page references to this edition are cited in parentheses in the text.

[23] Pletcher, *Diplomacy of Annexation*, 105, 338.

[24] Michael Paul Rogin, *Subversive Genealogy: The Politics and Art of Herman Melville* (New York: Knopf, 1983), 53–9; Widmer, *Young America*, 87.

with the Soviet Union'.[25] Perhaps the most significant aspect to this unevenness of response related to regional differences within the USA, with the increasing political power of the West beginning to manifest itself in more overt hostility towards British interests. As David Waldstreicher has shown, many of the Eastern Federalists, who were largely sympathetic to Britain, blamed the outbreak of war in 1812 on what they took to be their less sophisticated countrymen in the West, and they were no less contemptuous than Dickens in *Martin Chuzzlewit* of popular ideas about the West as a new Eden: 'However land-jobbers may try to prolong their credit by painting Kentucky and Tennessee as a new Arcadia,' said Fisher Ames in 1801, 'the evidence of facts will prevail.'[26] To the chagrin of Ames and his Federalist sympathizers, however, the rowdy patriotism engendered through the war of 1812 helped further to distance the influence of Britain on American affairs, while promoting a new version of American nationalism that was more populist and not so dependent upon Eurocentric Eastern values.

   In this sense, as Waldstreicher observes, the shift westward within American culture produced radically destabilizing effects in the early nineteenth century; only later did 'Western identity begin to be a unifying national force'.[27] This westward drift served not only to divide the American West from the American East, but also to drive a further wedge between the United States and Great Britain. In his *History of the Late War in the Western Country* (1816), Robert Breckinridge McAfee looks back scornfully at what he took to be British attempts to avenge defeat in the Revolutionary wars by infiltrating Indian settlements in Detroit, Kentucky, and other parts of the Midwest. He describes how Indians, who bore grudges against white Americans for taking away their lands, were 'secretly counselled' by the British, and how such 'unwarrantable interference with the Indians' became the prime source of 'that resentment against the British, which prevailed so strongly in the western states'. McAfee's book celebrates the recent American military triumphs, notably at the Battle of New Orleans in 1815, where, despite having administrative support in the form of a governor and civil magistrates all ready to swing into action, the British forces found themselves routed by General Jackson. It is important to emphasize, though, how easily the geography of the United States might have been different: the British, attacking northwards from their base in Jamaica, fully expected to take Louisiana, and, in the wake of the earlier Revolutionary wars, these kinds of conflict between Britain and the USA over the contours of the new nation continued well into the nineteenth century. Another significant factor here is the perceived association between British duplicity and the Indian 'savages', as the preface to McAfee's

[25] Haynes, 'Anglophobia and the Annexation of Texas', 141.

[26] William C. Dowling, *Literary Federalism in the Age of Jefferson: Joseph Dennie and* The Port Folio, *1801–1812* (Columbia, SC: University of South Carolina Press, 1999), 21.

[27] David Waldstreicher, *In the Midst of Perpetual Fêtes: The Making of American Nationalism, 1776–1820* (Williamsburg, Va.: Omohundro Institute of Early American History and Culture; Chapel Hill, NC: University of North Carolina Press, 1997), 274.

book calls them, an association that helped to justify subsequent draconian policies of Indian removal.[28] The 'Manifest Destiny' of westward expansion, in other words, was inspired not purely by romantic or commercial considerations but also by the desire politically and strategically to eradicate British interests from the US domain and thus to prevent the nation becoming enclosed within a dangerous 'iron Hoop'. Whatever the myths of Anglo-Saxon racial identity may have been, the more pressing facts of political confrontation between Britain and the USA at this time were pulling their relationship in quite another direction.

THE LAND POLITICS OF TRANSCENDENTALISM

Some of the clearest examples of this Anglophobia in American literature of the 1830s and 1840s manifested themselves in the writings of the Transcendentalists. Although Transcendentalism is usually thought to be a quintessentially American phenomenon having little impact on English culture, there is an important sense in which Dickens and (as we shall see in the next chapter) Arthur Hugh Clough were engaging consciously in dialogue with Transcendentalist assumptions.[29] In his 1844 essay 'The Poet', Emerson's choice of regions where the American creative spirit might flourish showed an astute awareness of international territorial disputes:

Our logrolling, our stumps and their politics, our fisheries, our Negroes, and Indians, our boasts, and our repudiations, the wrath of rogues, and the pusillanimity of honest men, the northern trade, the southern planting, the western clearing, Oregon, and Texas, are yet unsung. Yet America is a poem in our eyes; its ample geography dazzles the imagination, and it will not wait long for metres.[30]

The Transcendentalists are often considered primarily in relation to the abstract, philosophical terms within which they chose to frame their own discourse, with its emphasis upon a rejection of Locke and an aspiration instead towards a recuperative Neoplatonism.[31] As we see from this passage from 'The Poet', however, Emerson's move in 1844 specifically to nominate Oregon and Texas as appropriate candidates for American poetic treatment can be understood as a critical correlative to contemporary expansionist movements in the political sphere. Tony Tanner claimed that the Transcendentalists enjoyed an 'effortless

---

[28] Robert Breckinridge McAfee, *History of the Late War in the Western Country* (Lexington, Ky., 1816), pp. 2, v.

[29] Dickens had an 1841 edition of Emerson's *Essays* in his personal library. J. H. Stonehouse, *Catalogue of the Library of Charles Dickens from Gadshill* (London: Piccadilly Fountain Press, 1935), 42.

[30] Ralph Waldo Emerson, 'The Poet', in *Essays, Second Series*, ed. Alfred R. Ferguson and Jean Ferguson Carr (Cambridge, Mass.: Harvard University Press, 1983), 22.

[31] See e.g. Barbara L. Packer, 'The Transcendentalists', in *The Cambridge History of American Literature*, ii: *Prose Writing, 1820–1865*, ed. Sacvan Bercovitch (Cambridge: Cambridge University Press, 1995), 331–61.

confidence' in their intellectual conjunction of abstract and particular, but while Emerson's equation here of the circumference of the United States with the poetic imagination might seem 'effortless' enough, it is actually based upon a more severe sense of disjunction and conflict.[32] Emerson's stylistic genius involves eliding the contingent into the ideal so as seemingly to endow his idiosyncratic visions with an air of circular inevitability, but this rhetorical process cannot entirely suppress the embattled anti-English themes which they embody.

Emerson's political stance, however, was based not simply upon antipathy to Britain but on a sense that, as he put it in *English Traits* (1856), the British race had fragmented into two parts, with 'her liberals in America, and her conservatives at London' (p. 28). Like Richard Price, Emerson in this book advances a theory of schism in the British race, a schism which he traces through a tradition of liberal dissent going back as far as the Reformation. *English Traits*, based on a visit to England in 1847–8, critiques the dull-wittedness and sense of 'complacency' (p. 166) that the author finds in established figures like Wordsworth, and he suggests that 'the centre of the British race' has migrated to America (p. 155). In other works such as his 'Human Culture' lectures of 1837–8 on the 'historical progress of man', Emerson makes explicit the parallels he draws among the religious spirit of Luther, the American declaration of political independence from Britain, and the expansionist nature of American culture in the nineteenth century.[33] 'Man the Reformer' (1841) and 'New England Reformers' (1844) both pursue this equation of personal authenticity with a rejection of indolent conservatism; the latter essay aligns Byron with Rousseau, Napoleon, and Mirabeau as 'raging riders' prepared to shatter society's comfortable illusions, while the former piece argues that man is born only 'to be a Reformer, a Re-maker of what man has made; a renouncer of lies; a restorer of truth and good'.[34] In a journal entry for 1827, Emerson declared one of the 'Peculiarities of the present age' to be 'The reform of the Reformation', and his own subsequent work vigorously pursues this agenda, reforming the Reformation so that it becomes not just a theological concept, but a broader movement seeking to infuse what *English Traits* calls the 'old and exhausted' culture of Britain with new life (p. 155).[35]

---

[32] Tony Tanner, *The Reign of Wonder: Naivety and Reality in American Literature* (Cambridge: Cambridge University Press, 1965), 24.

[33] Ralph Waldo Emerson, 'Human Culture', in *The Early Lectures of Ralph Waldo Emerson*, ii: *1836–1838*, ed. Stephen E. Whicher *et al.* (Cambridge, Mass.: Harvard University Press, 1964), 213. See also Robert Milder, 'The Radical Emerson?', in *The Cambridge Companion to Emerson*, ed. Joel Porte (Cambridge: Cambridge University Press, 1999), 54.

[34] Ralph Waldo Emerson, 'New England Reformers', in *Essays: Second Series*, 161, and 'Man the Reformer', in *Nature, Addresses, and Lectures*, 156.

[35] Emerson, *The Journals and Miscellaneous Notebooks of Ralph Waldo Emerson*, iii: *1826–1832*, ed. William H. Gilpin and Alfred R. Ferguson (Cambridge, Mass.: Harvard University Press, 1963), 70.

Much of the work examining Emerson's relationship with nineteenth-century Britain has focused on his friendship with Thomas Carlyle, and it is true that they shared a romantic desire to overcome what they saw as the industrial dehumanization and social fragmentation pervading their respective societies. Any sense of a common idealistic purpose, however, was held firmly in check by their antithetical politics; their disagreement over the nature of American abolitionism, which Emerson enthusiastically supported but Carlyle abhorred, was merely a symptom of larger disagreements about the respective merits of conservatism and liberalism. During his 1848 trip to Britain, Emerson remarked that while the English continued in their characteristic disdain towards the New World, nevertheless 'they are Americanizing England as fast as they can'; he also acknowledged that one of the purposes of visiting Europe, so far as he was concerned, was 'to be Americanized', to reinforce his native understanding of American values as qualitatively different from those of the corrupt Old World.[36] In particular, Emerson's endorsement of free enterprise between 1842 and 1850, when he began to identify the creation of wealth with the growth of the new republic, suggests his complicity with a rhetoric of accumulation towards which Carlyle was decidedly antipathetic.[37] It was at this time that Emerson began to develop close links with the free trade campaigners in Britain: he shared a lecture platform with Richard Cobden at the Free-Trade Hall in Manchester in November 1847, and heard Cobden speak again at the free trade banquet in January 1848. Emerson described the latter event in a letter to Thoreau the following day, when he remarked on how he had 'heard the best man in England make perhaps his best speech'.[38] Emerson was characteristically vague on the 'confused appearances of the Free Trade facts', as he dismissively described them, but he did share at this time Cobden's higher vision of laissez-faire economics leading towards global peace and prosperity, to a world where, as Cobden put it, 'we will lay the Mississippi valley along side of Manchester' and enjoy a 'glorious trade' arising from the mutual reciprocities of these North Atlantic economies.[39] Cobden, who himself visited the United States in 1835 and 1859, was a great enthusiast for the social and economic principles of American society, claiming that in any direct comparison of 'class with class the people of the United States are raised to a much higher level than in any other country'.[40]

[36] Emerson, *The Journals and Miscellaneous Notebooks of Ralph Waldo Emerson*, x: *1847–1848*, ed. Merton M. Sealts jun. (Cambridge, Mass.: Harvard University Press, 1973), 434. See also Robert Weisbuch, 'Post-colonial Emerson and the Erasure of Europe', in *Cambridge Companion to Emerson*, 210, 202.

[37] Sacvan Bercovitch, *The Rites of Assent: Transformations in the Symbolic Construction of America* (New York: Routledge, 1993), 330.

[38] Emerson, *The Letters of Ralph Waldo Emerson*, viii: *1845–1859*, ed. Eleanor M. Tilton (New York: Columbia University Press, 1991), 144.

[39] Emerson, *Journals and Miscellaneous Notebooks*, x. 43; Schonhardt-Bailey, ed., *Free Trade*, 176–7.

[40] James Dunkerley, *Americana: The Americas in the World around 1850* (London: Verso, 2000), 332.

One of the difficulties in discussing Emerson's attitude towards national identity in general is that his conception of the nation-state tended to remain typically in a state of flux. In *English Traits*, he suggests at one point that the invention of new technology, such as steam-trains and the telegraph, are rendering national communities obsolete: 'Nations have lost their old omnipotence ... we go and live where we will' (p. 91). A deflection of the historical category of the nation into a more essentialized idiom of race, such as we see in *English Traits*, is one manifestation of this intellectual programme; yet it would also be true to say that here, as in 'The American Scholar' and so many of his other works, Emerson chooses to focus precisely upon national characteristics and their implications. This implicit dialectic of nation and race might perhaps be understood as commensurate with the dialectic of politics and fate at which Emerson worries away throughout his work. Discussing the American seizure of Texas in 1845, for example, he remarks in his *Journals* how 'it is quite necessary and true to our New England character that we should resist the annexation with tooth and nail', though he also goes on to observe: 'It is very certain that the strong British race which have now overrun so much of this continent, must also overrun that tract, & Mexico & Oregon also, and it will in the course of ages be of small import by what particular occasions & methods it was done.'[41] There is, of course, a certain irony in Emerson attributing the overthrow of the British government's interests in the Oregon Country to the advance of a 'strong British race' in North America, and this suggests how popular typological classifications of Anglo-Saxon racial characteristics in the mid-nineteenth century could not obviate the more immediate political antagonisms within this Anglo-Saxon world. But it also suggests how Emerson chose to justify Manifest Destiny by explaining it to himself as an inevitable phenomenon, a force of nature above the contingent values of political choice or historical circumstance.[42] In his eulogy for Thoreau in 1862, Emerson testified to his late friend's patriotic credentials by recollecting how 'he wished to go to Oregon, not to London'; and this movement west becomes, for the Transcendentalists, the guarantee of a symbolic rejection of England which they take to be their mythic destiny.[43]

The essay to which Emerson was referring in this eulogy was 'Walking', published posthumously in 1862. Here Thoreau maps out a geography of emancipation, casting the Atlantic Ocean as a 'Lethean stream, in our passage

[41] Emerson, *The Journals and Miscellaneous Notebooks of Ralph Waldo Emerson*, ix: *1843–1847*, eds. Ralph H. Orth and Alfred R. Ferguson (Cambridge, Mass.: Harvard University Press, 1971), 74. See also Len Gougeon, *Virtue's Hero: Emerson, Antislavery, and Reform* (Athens, Ga.: University of Georgia Press, 1990), 94.

[42] On ways in which scientific and philosophical theories of racial determinism in the 1840s influenced the composition of *English Traits*, see Philip L. Nicoloff, *Emerson on Race and History: An Examination of* English Traits (New York: Columbia University Press, 1961), 43–135.

[43] Ralph Waldo Emerson, 'Thoreau', in *Selected Essays*, ed. Larzer Ziff (New York: Viking Penguin, 1982), 399.

over which we have had an opportunity to forget the Old World and its institutions', and representing the 'subtile magnetism in Nature' as impelling him to 'walk toward Oregon, and not toward Europe'. Such a movement, of course, links American national destiny, from the Pilgrim Fathers onward, with a flight west: 'Eastward I go only by force; but westward I go free.'[44] Indeed, Thoreau's explicit hostility towards Britain and the concomitant symbolic flight west formed consistent strands throughout his career. They can be traced right back to his essay 'Advantages and Disadvantages of Foreign Influences on American Literature', written in April 1836 at the age of 18, where he describes the United States as mentally 'but colonies' and compares the American situation to that of subaltern though insurrectionary tribes in the ancient world: 'Every successive defeat afforded the Carthaginians new lessons in the art of war, till, at length, Rome herself trembled at their progress.'[45]

This perception of a continuing guerrilla 'war' between Britain and America is pursued in *A Week on the Concord and Merrimack Rivers* (1849), which starts off by paying tribute to Americans who fought in the wars of 1775 and 1812 before seeking to reconstitute an indigenous context for the native territory it describes. By emphasizing the Indian rather than the English provenance of names like 'Yankees', from the Indian 'Yengeese', Thoreau lays stress upon what he takes to be a nearer, more authentic matching of location to language.[46] This leads also to a tricky, double-edged quality to this river narrative, where the 'mirror-like surface of the water' (p. 48) twins together different names—'Hudson, once Nottingham' (p. 144)—as if to epitomize the natural evolution of the British heritage into an American landscape, 'New Angle-land' (p. 53), where things are necessarily seen in a 'new perspective' (p. 232). Thoreau tries here both to idealize and to naturalize the relationship between Americans and their environment, describing this as a matter not of 'the *annals* of the country, but the natural facts, or *perennials*, which are ever without date' (p. 219). Thoreau uses this phrase while describing Alexander Henry's adventures among the fur traders in the Pacific Northwest, as if to suggest that Henry's narrative is valuable not on account of 'the materials for the history of Pontiac, or Braddock, or the North West, which it furnishes' (p. 219), but rather for its mythic dimension. Thoreau's strategy, in other words, is to sublimate historical and political conflicts into a narrative conflating nation with nature, thereby making the American advance into the Oregon Country seem as natural as the flow of the Concord and

[44] Henry D. Thoreau, 'Walking', in *Collected Essays and Poems*, ed. Elizabeth Hall Witherell (New York: Library of America, 2001), 233–5.

[45] Henry D. Thoreau, 'Advantages and Disadvantages of Foreign Influences on American Literature', in *Early Essays and Miscellanies*, ed. Joseph J. Moldenhauer and Edwin Moser, with Alexander C. Kern (Princeton: Princeton University Press, 1975), 40.

[46] Henry D. Thoreau, *A Week on the Concord and Merrimack Rivers*, ed. Carl F. Hovde, William L. Howarth, and Elizabeth Hall Witherell (Princeton: Princeton University Press, 1980), 53. Subsequent page references to this edition are cited in parentheses in the text.

Merrimack rivers: 'we naturally look most into the west, as forward into the day'
(p. 320). Based on an expedition which took place in 1839, this book was written
at precisely the time when the international controversy over Oregon was coming
to a head, and, for all of its mythologization of a frontier spirit, the narrative also
represents an attempt by Thoreau to politicize the landscape and to throw in his
lot with the champions of Manifest Destiny. O'Sullivan himself met Thoreau
at Concord in 1843 and invited him to write for the *Democratic Review*, and
though Thoreau in fact managed to contribute only a couple of book reviews, he
subsequently expressed sympathy for O'Sullivan, describing him as 'at any rate
one of the not-bad'.[47]

In *A Week on the Concord and Merrimack Rivers*, Thoreau tries to represent the
frontier as an abstract, permeable entity: 'not east or west, north or south, but
wherever a man *fronts* a fact' (p. 304). However, the landscape of this book, which
endows the frontier with a more material and geographical substance, suggests
ways in which this mythological conception is necessarily intertwined with a
more specific political programme. Indeed, this elision of matter into spirit, the
dialectical process of converting a history which can never be entirely suppressed
into mythography, forms a recurrent pattern throughout Thoreau's writings. *The
Maine Woods*, published posthumously in 1864 but based upon an excursion
undertaken at the height of the boundary conflicts in 1846, tries again to project
itself as being 'concerned ... about natural, not political limits'.[48] Accordingly, it
represents its desire for primary 'contact' with the 'rocks, trees, wind' of 'the *solid
earth*' (p. 71) as being different in kind from 'the artificial forests of an English
king' (p. 80), from the merely hierarchical ordering of woodland according to
feudal customs. Thoreau castigates parks, gardens, and anything which threatens
to circumscribe or undermine the integrity of the natural world. He talks about
his distrust of maps, where the cartographic theory can never quite match the
plain fact, and at one point he dismisses the dispute between Britain and the
USA over the Canadian border as merely hypothetical, an abstract notion with
no significance within the larger world of nature:

I remembered hearing a good deal about the 'highlands' dividing the waters of the
Penobscot from those of the St. John, as well as the St. Lawrence, at the time of the
northeast boundary dispute, and I observed by my map, that the line claimed by Great
Britain as the boundary prior to 1842 passed between Umbazookskus Lake and Mud
Pond, so that we had either crossed or were then on it. These, then, according to *her*
interpretation of the treaty of '83, were the 'highlands which divide those rivers that
empty themselves into the St. Lawrence from those which fall into the Atlantic Ocean'.
Truly an interesting spot to stand on,—if that were it,—though you could not sit down
there. (p. 216)

---

[47] Widmer, *Young America*, 69.
[48] Henry D. Thoreau, *The Maine Woods*, ed. Joseph J. Moldenhauer (Princeton: Princeton
University Press, 1972), 66. Subsequent page references to this edition are cited in parentheses in
the text.

There is, however, a structural duplicity throughout this text, because Thoreau's conception of a 'natural' world transcending political boundaries is dependent on a suppression of the very nationalist force upon which his narrative impetus is predicated. Throughout the book, he associates the United States with a frontier spirit: 'We have advanced by leaps to the Pacific, and left many a lesser Oregon and California unexplored behind us' (p. 82); indeed, he specifically links the pioneer 'on this side of the country' with 'his brother in the West' (p. 124), thereby turning *The Maine Woods* into a text refracting not only the Maine boundary dispute but also the contemporaneous conflicts on the other side of the continent. As someone with, as he reminds us, 'a surveyor's eyes' (p. 252), Thoreau is quite aware of how his own desire to map out his American terrain goes against the geographical lineaments prescribed by the British monarchy; but he is also aware that the efficacy of his nationalist cause depends not upon pleading his political case but upon appearing to transcend it, as if the American relationship to the land were a purely natural phenomenon and the English claims merely distant and legalistic, the residue of a foreign culture that can no longer have any purchase upon this native American soil.

In this sense, Thoreau is the most thoroughgoing postcolonial writer in nineteenth-century US literature, the figure most consistently perturbed by what he sees as the unwelcome spectres of British rule. 'A Yankee in Canada' (1853) pursues the implications of the ambiguous boundary between New Brunswick and Maine by reporting back upon the disadvantageous conditions appertaining north of the border in what it calls 'British America'.[49] Like Emerson in *English Traits*, Thoreau in this travel narrative uses the condition of the 'foreign country' (p. 275) to reinforce by reversal his sense of the distinguishing characteristics of the United States. Thus, he comments adversely on the 'formality' of the British 'red-coats' (p. 260), spurns both aristocratic 'land titles' (p. 280) and the conformist influences of the Roman Catholic Church, and abhors the coercive powers of the 'colonial legislature' (p. 309), whose government conceives itself to be the master of the people rather than, as in the United States, their servant. *Walden* (1854), celebrated more frequently as a form of complex pastoral charting the dissolution of the familiar civilized world, is similarly charged with a rhetoric of Anglophobia and cultural reformation. Again, the narrator's sojourn in the woods, from 1845 until 1847, overlaps with the time of greatest hostility between Britain and America over the Oregon Country, and these parallels are marked by the way the Walden woods themselves are represented historically as disputed ground only a generation earlier. Thoreau recounts the story of Zilpha, a 'colored woman' whose house in the woods was set on fire by English soldiers during the war of 1812 (p. 257), while in an 'internecine war' between ants—'the red republicans on the one hand, and the black imperialists on the

---

[49] Henry D. Thoreau, 'A Yankee in Canada', in *Collected Essays and Poems*, 323. Subsequent page references to this edition are cited in parentheses in the text.

other' (p. 229)—the author finds an analogy to the Battle of Bunker Hill back in the War of Independence. This is, in other words, not an innocent landscape, but an environment replete with memories of transatlantic conflict. There is, moreover, a distinctly anti-royalist tone here—'We are amused at beholding the costume of Henry VIII., or Queen Elizabeth, as much as if it was that of the King and Queen of the Cannibal Islands' (p. 26)—while in the remark that 'the last significant scrap of news' from England 'was the revolution of 1649' (p. 95), Thoreau is implying that nothing of value has happened in that country since the conclusion of the English Civil War and the execution of King Charles I. *Walden* is a work dedicated to the possibilities of reform and renewal—'It is never too late to give up our prejudices' (p. 8)—but it is important to recognize how Thoreau, like Emerson, looks back specifically to the Reformation as a model for the cultural transformations he hopes to see within society.

The best-known account of the Oregon conflict by an American writer of this era, one that Thoreau's various naturalizations of the West were reacting against, was Washington Irving's *Astoria, or Anecdotes of an Enterprize beyond the Rocky Mountains*, published in 1836. Irving's historical narrative runs from 1810 to 1813, and his focus is on the struggles among the fur-traders for the town of Astoria during the war of 1812. Peter Antelyes finds in *Astoria* a commitment on Irving's part to the American 'principles of self-interest, national expansion, and manifest destiny', and he sees the author attempting here to re-establish his patriotic credentials after the years from 1815 to 1832 spent in European exile.[50] However, *Astoria* is much less straightforward than this, and the 'rambling anecdotes' of Irving's narrator testify not so much to a pioneering westward narrative as to a convoluted, slightly absurd style of rhetoric where every position becomes susceptible to reversal.[51] Irving, in fact, values the West not because it fulfils the country's expansionist logic but because it contradicts it; at the end of the book he talks of how, despite all traffic of British traders within the territories of the United States being outlawed by an 1815 Act of Congress, the British commercial companies nevertheless simply continued their operations, since this legal injunction 'in effect, was a dead letter beyond the Mountains' (p. 353). Here we see Irving's idiosyncratic style of burlesque, which takes delight in up-ending conventions and reversing the pompous rigmarole of officialdom. Irving admires the West precisely because of its elusive and uncharted characteristics, the way it fails to conform to the designs of either British imperialism or American Manifest Destiny. Characteristic of this delight in incongruity is the way he chronicles the capture of the fort at Astoria by the British naval officer Captain Black, who, from the big military build-up, had 'expected to find a fortress of some importance'

[50] Peter Antelyes, *Tales of Adventurous Enterprise: Washington Irving and the Poetics of Western Expansion* (New York: Columbia University Press, 1990), 150.

[51] Washington Irving, *Astoria, or Anecdotes of an Enterprize beyond the Rocky Mountains*, ed. Richard Dilworth Rust (Boston: Twayne, 1976), 193. Subsequent page references to this edition are cited in parentheses in the text.

and is thus bewildered to behold 'nothing but stockades and bastions, calculated for defence against naked savages'. Captain Black is said here to feel 'an emotion of indignant surprize, mingled with something of the ludicrous' (p. 348); and it is that sense of a farcical clash between self-important civilization and an uncooperative nature which runs all the way through this narrative.

Irving's West, then, is neither an empty landscape, as it was for Lewis and Clark, nor, as for Thoreau, a territory in which the British are perceived as squatters with no natural right to be there. Instead, Irving represents the American West in terms of a conflict between alternative possibilities and points of view, envisaging an arena where institutional meanings often contradict what the narrator reports as direct personal experience.[52] Irving's text thus mediates whimsically between English civility and American anarchy, taking delight in the seemingly absurd reversals of fortune which this landscape of duplicity brings about. Astoria is described as both an 'infant colony' (p. 67) and an 'embryo metropolis' (p. 61), and it is this faculty of perceiving the world through a bifocal lens, in terms of divergent perspectives, that distinguishes Irving's literary genius. To criticize Irving's style, as John Francis McDermott and many others have done, for its failure of directness and its relapse into the idiom of a 'self-conscious literary man' is completely to miss the point of his work, which involves not just the projection of 'a superficial European romanticism' upon the incongruous terrain of the American West but, rather, an assimilation of that terrain within a densely storied and politicized landscape where no object can retain its primordial innocence.[53] This is precisely how the American West appeared to English writers of the 1840s such as George Ruxton, as a landscape of constitutional doubleness.

This interest in doubleness also explains why Irving was so intrigued by incidents of espionage during the war of 1812. He recounts how the precipitate decision of an infamous character called M'Dougall to abandon Astoria and sell Astor's merchandise to the Northwest Company for a third of its real value awakened 'strong doubts' among the American party 'as to his loyal devotion to the cause'. M'Dougall is portrayed here as a turncoat: 'His old sympathies with the North West Company seemed to have revived. He had received M'Tavish and his party with uncalled for hospitality, as though they were friends and allies' (p. 323). Yet although M'Dougall is revealed clearly enough as betraying the American cause, he still conforms paradoxically to the topsy-turvy imperatives of nature, according to Irving's view of that domain, where reversals of position and the propensity to follow low instincts rather than abstract ideals are the way of the world. *Astoria* has a sharp eye for the double allegiances of the characters within its purview—the Indians 'talking with a "forked tongue"' (p. 219), the 'hybrid

---

[52] On this theme, see Bruce Greenfield, *Narrating Discovery: The Romantic Explorer in American Literature, 1790–1855* (New York: Columbia University Press, 1992), 133.

[53] Irving, *The Western Journals of Washington Irving*, ed. John Francis McDermott (Norman, Okla.: University of Oklahoma Press, 1944), 50.

interpreter' Pierre Dorion (p. 231)—and indeed Irving's narrative represents cultural hybridity as a natural condition within these western territories. There is also a larger sense in which the multiple exchanges of Astoria between British and American forces betoken in themselves a form of hybridity, so that this war of 1812 is depicted not as a clash of polar opposites but as one half of the English community turning against the other half in a kind of civil war. 'There is no enemy so implacable against a country or a community as one of its own people who has rendered himself an alien by his crimes,' comments Irving (p. 178), and one disconcerting aspect of this narrative is that the British and American parties seem to be so close together, in all senses, that it is difficult to recognize which is which; indeed, John Jacob Astor himself is portrayed here as having spent much of his business career in London. Irving, then, slyly undermines the categorical imperatives of national identity upon which the American westward movement in this Jacksonian era was founded, substituting instead a burlesque scenario whose governing features are betrayal and misrecognition, and whose ultimate trajectory is circuitous, the typically comic restoration of a prior condition. There is a brief sentence at the end of the book about how, at the conclusion of the war, Astoria 'reverted to the United States by the treaty of Ghent, on the principle of *status ante bellum*' (p. 353). Irving specializes not in epic transformation but in bathetic anticlimax, the collapse of grand ideals into less dignified modes of comic familiarity.

Astoria sold very well, and it helped to disseminate Irving's view of the West as a site of conflict between competing national interests to a wide audience, including many in Britain. Irving's popular account is, however, critiqued sharply in Margaret Fuller's *Summer on the Lakes* (1844), which, published in the midst of the Oregon crisis, stakes out clearly enough the mutual reciprocities between Transcendentalism and Anglophobia as well as showing how political attitudes in the 1840s were hardening. For Fuller, Irving's West is permeated with a 'stereotype, second-hand air', a remark which suggests how the Transcendentalists were directly taking issue with Irving's well-known narrative in their attempt to reconceptualize the West as an integral part of the natural US domain.[54] 'His scenery', Fuller goes on, 'is only fit to be glanced at from dioramic distance; his Indians are academic figures only' (p. 88). Fuller contrasts this 'distance' with her own discursive attitude towards the West, which she takes to be predicated upon an appreciation of native authenticity, particularly the authenticity of Indian culture, of which she finds 'traces' everywhere (p. 100). Indeed, Fuller presents this Indian culture as synecdochic of American independence from Europe more generally. Visiting a bluff called Eagle's Nest on the Fourth of July, she declares: 'certainly I think I had never felt so happy that I was born

---

[54] Margaret Fuller, *Summer on the Lakes*, in *The Portable Margaret Fuller*, ed. Mary Kelley (New York: Penguin, 1994), 88. Subsequent page references to this edition are cited in parentheses in the text.

in America' (p. 100); while later on she expresses her hope that there will be 'a national institute, containing all the remains of the Indians', established in Washington DC (p. 212). Fuller, then, seeks to institutionalize Indian culture at the heart of US federal politics. In her eyes, the liberation of the Indians—'a subjugated race' (p. 214)—becomes both a type and a mirror of the liberation of American culture more generally from the tyranny of British occupation and influence. Just as *Woman in the Nineteenth Century* (1845) proceeds by linking analogically the oppression of women and African Americans, so Fuller draws a theoretical parallel here between Indian recovery of their native territories and US occupation of its western domains. It is, of course, a rhetorical manoeuvre which again elides history into myth—the Indians are said to be in 'the captivity of Israel' (p. 214)—and which ignores both the tactical partnership between Indians and British in the West and also ways in which US forces engaged in indiscriminate acts of Indian removal as they cleared a path for themselves through the continent. Fuller, that is to say, attempts strategically to exculpate US oppression of the Native Americans by conscripting them as spiritual allies in a common campaign against the British tyrant.

Summer on the Lakes develops this form of resistance by arguing explicitly against the derogatory versions of the American West produced a few years earlier by Dickens and Fanny Trollope. Fuller deems 'Trollopian records' of the inhospitability of the country to be 'inventions of pure malice', and she mocks, for example, a woman who complains about the standard of the inns and who thereby 'showed herself to have been bathed in the Britannic fluid' (p. 93). Similarly, Fuller argues the need for local Western schools which enjoy a degree of pedagogical independence, asserting that 'methods copied from the education of some English Lady Augusta, are as ill suited to the daughter of an Illinois farmer, as satin shoes to climb the Indian mounds' (p. 107). At the same time, she is inextricably involved in a dialogue with England, even as she parodies and travesties English ways of thinking. When she claims that 'You may see a great deal of Life, in the London sense, if you know a few people' (p. 136), it is clear that Fuller is concerned to take English social assumptions and stand them on their head, thus turning her whole discourse into a rhetorical conflict which precisely parallels the political conflict with Britain over the Western territories in the 1840s. Although *Summer on the Lakes* chronicles a visit to what we would now call the American Midwest, the Illinois region, Fuller deliberately turns this country into a landscape that allegorically represents a wider Western domain, as when she arrives at a little town named Oregon in the heart of an Indian county and presents this as metonymical of the more extensive disputed territory of the same name further west. 'How could they let themselves be conquered, with such a country to fight for!' exclaims Fuller of the Indians here (p. 98), as if to criticize the Native American tribes for lending allegiance to a foreign enemy rather than acknowledging their historic association with 'this American continent' (p. 223). At Eagle's Nest, Oregon, she composes a poetic pastoral,

'Ganymede to his Eagle', which, with its diminutive 'rocky mountain' (p. 101) near 'a double log cabin' which 'was, to my eye, the model of a Western villa' (p. 104), becomes a kind of miniaturized and aestheticized replication of the Far West, as if to set the scene for another discursive battle with the old enemy. Her narrative also ends up contemplating relics from the war of 1812; in the last chapter she visits the old English fort at Point St Joseph's, and the work culminates with a meditation upon the failings of General Hull at the Battle of Detroit and the 'disgrace' he suffered at being surrounded by the Royal Navy. For Fuller, the events of 30 years earlier still rankle:

At Detroit we stopped for half a day. This place is famous in our history, and the unjust anger at its surrender is still expressed by almost every one who passes there. I had always shared the common feeling on this subject; for the indignation at a disgrace to our arms that seemed so unnecessary, has been handed down from father to child, and few of us have taken the pains to ascertain where the blame lay. But now, upon the spot, having read all the testimony, I felt convinced that it should rest solely with the government, which, by neglecting to sustain General Hull, as he had a right to expect they would, compelled him to take this step, or sacrifice many lives, and of the defenceless inhabitants, not of soldiers, to the cruelty of a savage foe, for the sake of his reputation. (p. 224)

It is not difficult to see how Fuller's attempt in this work to represent the American West as 'healthy and pure' (p. 145), with foreign influences eradicated, is fraught not just with racial but also with racist assumptions. In searching for a sense of national authenticity, she quarrels not only with the British but also takes exception to a woman 'whose growing complexion and dark mellow eye bespoke an origin in some climate more familiar with the sun' (p. 144). There is a similar kind of cultural xenophobia in Francis Parkman's *The Oregon Trail* (1849), an account of Parkman's trip a few years earlier to what is now eastern Wyoming, where again the narrator records proudly how within this indigenous landscape the 'scenery needed no foreign aid'. By rhetorically translating the actual location of Wyoming into a symbolic pathway towards the Far West, Parkman links his narrative with the spirit of Manifest Destiny and represents his journey as a recapitulation of the initial westward movement from Europe. In this sense, his narrative forms a deliberate attempt to move away from English law as embodied in 'the principles of Blackstone's Commentaries' and to map out an alternative version of natural law, a law which becomes firmly associated in his mind with the jurisdiction of the United States.[55] Parkman's version of the Far West, like Fuller's, thus represents a discursive annexation of this disputed territory in the interests of US nation building, and it attempts to mythologize the Oregon Trail not just as a mere rite of passage for Americans but as a means towards completing and making 'whole' the bi-coastal range of the country. The agenda of both Fuller and Parkman is thus to make the geographical boundaries of the

[55] Francis Parkman jun., *The Oregon Trail*, ed. David Levin (New York: Viking Penguin, 1982), 55, 63.

United States appear synonymous with the natural frontiers of the American continent, to embrace the nation within a self-enclosed circle from which foreign agency is excluded. This equation of cultural identity with the politics of land possession was to have important implications for both English and American literature in the mid-nineteenth century.

ENGLISH COUNTERFIRE: CHARLES DICKENS AND GEORGE RUXTON

When America was preparing in 1842 for the visit of the famous English author Charles Dickens, there was general anticipation that, as the *United States Magazine and Democratic Review* put it, his writings would 'hasten on the great crisis of the English Revolution'. Professing admiration for the author's 'popular tendencies', the magazine associated with the Young America movement expressed its opinion that Dickens's 'democratic genius' would turn the tide of reform 'far more effectively than any of the open assaults of Radicalism or Chartism'.[56] Similarly commending Dickens's 'singular freedom from aristocratic feeling', the *Boston Evening Gazette* intimated that it expected to find in this critic of English social institutions a republican fellow-traveller.[57] However, the anticipated sentiments of reciprocal good will never materialized, and Dickens's first visit to the United States ended with a strong sense of mutual antipathy. One reason for this was that the American expectation of Dickens as a republican radical was about twenty years out of date; as we have seen, Byron's generation in the first quarter of the nineteenth century was the last to treat the United States as a viable political alternative to Great Britain, in the sense of being a divergent branch from the same family tree, but by the 1840s these now distinctly separate countries had become political antagonists on the world stage.

Another compelling and perhaps more pressing reason for Dickens's impli‑cit—and, subsequently, explicit—hostility towards America was financial. During the US depression of the late 1830s, many British companies such as Baring Brothers which had invested heavily in America found the value of their state bonds collapsing. In August 1840, for example, Pennsylvania, whose securities were regarded as the best risk of all, was forced to postpone its semi-annual interest payment, with British investors learning to their cost that neither the American federal government nor taxpayers regarded themselves as responsible for the financial affairs of individual states.[58] One of Dickens's complaints about America in *Martin Chuzzlewit* (1843–4) is, as its hero tells

---

[56] Michael Slater, ed., *Dickens on America and the Americans* (Brighton: Harvester Press, 1979), 8.

[57] James C. Simmons, *Star-Spangled Eden: Nineteenth-Century America through the Eyes of Dickens, Wilde, Frances Trollope, Frank Harris, and Other British Travellers* (New York: Carroll and Graf, 2000), 99.   [58] Pletcher, *Diplomacy of Annexation*, 13–14.

Elijah Pogram, that, from 'disregarding small obligations', his countrymen 'come in regular course to disregard great ones; and so refuse to pay their debts'.[59] This double-dealing is associated by Dickens not just with a personal breach of trust but with the inherent financial instability of the country: one of Martin's English acquaintances tells the story of 'Lummy Ned', who emigrated to New York to make his fortune, but then 'lost it all the day after, in six-and-twenty banks as broke' (p. 214). This sense of the United States as a den of financial iniquity would have been conflated in Dickens's mind with his bitterness about the absence of an international copyright agreement, a situation which ensured that he received no royalties at all from his vast sales in the United States. He went to America partly to campaign for a change in the law, an issue on which he was supported by Washington Irving and other American authors; but, according to Jerome Meckier, he underestimated the ferocity of the American popular press in defending its territory against what they saw as unjustified levies, particularly levies imposed by the old tax tyrant, Great Britain.[60] Although the copyright question never surfaces overtly in *American Notes* (1842) or in *Martin Chuzzlewit*, this perception of the United States as a commercial predator is never far from the narrators' thoughts.[61]

It is appropriate that Dickens should have been welcomed to New York in 1842 by Irving—'*a great* fellow', remarked Dickens, and one of the few American authors he admired.[62] Indeed, when Dickens first broached in 1839 the project of travelling 'either to Ireland or to America' and writing 'a series of papers descriptive of the places and people I see', he told John Forster that he imagined this work being 'something after the plan of Washington Irving's *Alhambra*', the account of Spanish culture published by the American author in 1832.[63] *American Notes* is not unlike one of Irving's double-edged travel narratives in the way it describes the country, with a subtle emphasis upon scenes of international tension within Anglo-American relations. Just as for Irving in *Astoria* the practice of espionage becomes synecdochic of his text's tendency to face both ways, so Dickens in *American Notes* represents himself as a kind of spy, being on one level an honoured guest of the American nation but, on another

[59] Charles Dickens, *The Life and Adventures of Martin Chuzzlewit*, ed. Patricia Ingham (London: Penguin, 1999), 508. Subsequent page references to this edition are cited in parentheses in the text.

[60] Jerome Meckier, *Innocent Abroad: Charles Dickens's American Engagements* (Lexington, Ky.: University Press of Kentucky, 1990), 45–52.

[61] For a subtle analysis of how Pecksniff's 'architectural plagiarism' in his plans for the grammar school in *Martin Chuzzlewit* offer an oblique commentary on issues of originality, imitation, and copyright, see Gerhard Joseph, 'Construing the Inimitable's Silence: Pecksniff's Grammar School and International Copyright', *Dickens Studies Annual*, 22 (1993), 121–35.

[62] Dickens, *The Letters of Charles Dickens*, iii: *1842–1843*, ed. Madeline House and Graham Storey, and Kathleen Tillotson (Oxford: Clarendon Press, 1974), 96.

[63] Dickens, *The Letters of Charles Dickens*, i: *1820–1839*, ed. Madeline House and Graham Storey (Oxford: Clarendon Press, 1965), 564. Dickens owned many books by Irving, though the only copy of *Astoria* in the (incomplete) catalogue of his personal library is the volume included in Irving's *Complete Works* (1859). Stonehouse, *Catalogue of the Library of Charles Dickens*, 64.

level, an observer of what he takes to be the country's inherent defects as well as its hostility towards England, negative traits which he duly reports back to his loyal audience at home. In the introduction to *American Notes*, which he subsequently cancelled, Dickens claimed that the book was all about 'manners and customs', and he averred that it 'has not a grain of any political ingredient in its whole composition'.[64] This disclaimer, however, is somewhat disingenuous, as we see in this account of a visit to Cleveland, where he finds the issue of the boundary dispute with Maine featured in the local newspaper:

I entertained quite a curiosity in reference to this place, from having seen at Sandusky a specimen of its literature in the shape of a newspaper, which was very strong indeed upon the subject of Lord Ashburton's recent arrival at Washington, to adjust the points in dispute between the United States Government and Great Britain: informing its readers that as America had 'whipped' England in her infancy, and whipped her again in her youth, so it was clearly necessary that she must whip her once again in her maturity; and pledging its credit to all True Americans, that if Mr Webster did his duty in the approaching negotiations, and sent the English Lord home again in double quick time, they should, within two years, 'sing Yankee Doodle in Hyde Park, and Hail Columbia in the scarlet courts of Westminster!' (p. 241)

In the following chapter, Dickens crosses over to Canada and visits Niagara, where he comes across relics from the war of 1812. He observes how a monument to General Brock is now 'a melancholy ruin', having been blown up by some 'vagabond', and he suggests that this 'unpunished outrage ... is not very likely to soothe down border feelings among English subjects here, or compose their border quarrels and dislikes' (p. 246).

For all of its explicit protestations of political agnosticism, then, *American Notes* cannot avoid becoming implicated in the quarrel between Britain and America. At the mouth of the Niagara, Dickens sees the Stars and Stripes flying on one side and the Union Jack on the other, and he mentions with approbation the accommodation of 'our' soldiers, who are 'finely and airily situated'. He also comments on how, at 'any garrisoned point where the line of demarcation between one country and another is so very narrow as at Niagara, desertion from the ranks can scarcely fail to be of frequent occurrence' (p. 245). Again, there is a thin line, both geographically and metaphorically, between these two imperial countries, and Dickens, like Irving in *Astoria*, mentions the prevalence of military espionage during the 'Canadian Insurrection' of 1837 (p. 249), with the culture of spying again suggesting a chameleonic capacity to assume the characteristics of both nations simultaneously. Dickens, though, is at heart more of a univocal moralist than Irving, and he remarks censoriously on how 'it very rarely happens that the men who do desert, are happy or

[64] Charles Dickens, *American Notes for General Circulation*, ed. John S. Whitley and Arnold Goldman (London: Penguin, 1972), 298. Subsequent page references to this edition are cited in parentheses in the text.

contented afterwards; and many instances have been known in which they have confessed their grievous disappointment, and their earnest desire to return to their old service' (p. 245). Such caution is characteristic of both *American Notes* and *Martin Chuzzlewit*, where there is a flirtation with the possibility of a new land before a welcome retreat back into the familiar arms of the old. For Dickens, the sentimental comforts of home always outstrip the allure of the foreign, and so his warning against military treachery might be understood reflexively, as an implicit warning to himself, the author as spy, not to betray native values. This also helps to explain why Dickens in *American Notes* is most perturbed when he encounters English immigrants who appear to have betrayed their native land by assimilating themselves comfortably into their new circumstances. These 'countrymen of ours', declares Dickens, 'are often the most intolerable and most insufferable companions', because they 'display an amount of insolent conceit and cool assumption of superiority, quite monstrous to behold' (p. 159). It is, of course, both the similarity and the difference which disturbs Dickens's composure here; recognizing the native English characteristics of these immigrants, he also sees how such features have been traduced by exposure to this new land, so that the traditional categories and classifications of home no longer apply.

American Notes also maps its version of the United States by constant comparison to English affairs, discovering parallels between the two countries all over the East Coast—the effect of Yale, for example, being 'very like that of an old cathedral yard in England' (p. 125)—but finding the West much more difficult to fit into Anglocentric perspectives. The prairies, complains Dickens, don't give the same 'sense of freedom and exhilaration which a Scottish heath inspires, or even our English downs' because of their 'very flatness and extent, which left nothing to the imagination' (p. 226). Since the American West cannot be made to accord with Dickens's English perspective, he conceptualizes these untamed lands by relating them to the vulgar state of Ireland, another country to the west of England which is represented here as a parallel to the barbarous nature of these American frontier territories. On his journey to Cincinnati in the company of pioneers bound for the Far West, he comes across a village that is 'partly American and partly Irish' (p. 204), while in the heart of New York State he encounters 'an Irish colony', comprising '[h]ideously ugly old women and very buxom young ones, pigs, dogs, men, children, babies, pots, kettles, dunghills, vile refuse, rank straw, and standing water, all wallowing together in an inseparable heap' (p. 256). The jumble of disparate materials here has an affinity with the vast flatness of the prairies, in that both betoken a threat to the Dickensian predilection for an aesthetic frame interwoven with recognizable social and spatial hierarchies; the Irish, like the Americans, cannot be fitted into his sacrosanct domestic categories. On his second visit to the United States in 1867–8, Dickens expressed a more specific hostility to the 'enormous influence' of the 'Irish element' in urban centres like New York City, talking of the 'depraved condition' of their political culture and linking it with the Fenian explosion at Clerkenwell, near the City of London, in December 1867.[65]

The negative portrayal of the United States in *Martin Chuzzlewit* is well known, although it is sometimes suggested that Dickens chose to alter the scheme of the novel by sending his hero off on American adventures after disappointing sales in the early stages of the work's serialization.[66] However this may be, it is clear that *Martin Chuzzlewit* is dogmatically, compulsively anti-American in its overall style and structure as well as in those episodes actually set in the USA. The burden of the narrative is to expose what Dickens takes to be the hypocritical discrepancy between 'saintly semblances' (p. 198) and corrupt self-interest, a discrepancy which manifests itself on a personal level in the characterization of Pecksniff and on a national level through the inflated American conception of its own destiny in the 'Valley of Eden' (p. 347). With the relentless urge to crush self-aggrandizing delusions that typified the English Victorian moralist, Dickens seizes upon the fat target of slavery as a prime instance of the American tendency to preach liberty while practising oppression, mocking that 'air of Freedom which carries death to all tyrants, and can never (under any circumstances worth mentioning) be breathed by slaves' (pp. 247–8). This satirical overthrow of constitutional idealism is conceptualized by the author through iconoclastic imagery, as he describes how the 'great American Eagle, which is always airing itself sky-high in purest aether ... tumbles down, with draggled wings, into the mud' (p. 485). Associated with this sense of bathos is a thread running throughout the novel designed to interrogate the supposed primacy of 'mind over matter', as the author puts it (p. 566), and thus to elucidate what he takes to be the intellectual failure of dualism. Dickens's empiricist perspective ridicules the way 'Edeners were "going" to build a superb establishment for the transaction of their business, and had already got so far as to mark out the site: which is a great way in America' (p. 338); however, this indictment of an etiolated American spirit does not exist in isolation, but is of a piece with his critique of Pecksniff's 'mild abstraction from all sordid thoughts' (p. 519). Such forms of rarefaction are peremptorily contradicted by the dark, inchoate landscapes of the novel's urban London—'every house was in the brightest summer morning very gloomy' (p. 175)—landscapes which seem to run directly contrary to the American scenarios of disembodied allegory, where objects are always on the verge of being etherealized into theoretical shadows of themselves.

For Dickens, then, the American aspiration towards transcendence is accompanied by an aesthetics of abstraction and purification, whereas the British social scenes are immersed within a more heterodox and variegated materialism.

---

[65] Slater, ed., *Dickens on America and the Americans*, 230, 225.
[66] Malcolm Bradbury, *Dangerous Pilgrimages: Trans-Atlantic Mythologies and the Novel* (London: Secker & Warburg, 1995), 104.

Martin Chuzzlewit lampoons 'the two L.L.'s', American literary ladies, as 'Transcendental', and it also specifically satirizes Emersonian rhetoric—'Howls the sublime, and softly sleeps the calm Ideal, in the whispering chambers of Imagination'—which it identifies again with the dualistic representation of 'Mind and matter' (p. 512). The novel starts with an inquiry into the nature of kinship, tracing as it does 'the Pedigree of the Chuzzlewit Family' (p. 13), and this question also comes to have transatlantic implications, for, just as the Chuzzlewit family is riven by greed and murder, so the British and the Americans in this novel are revealed finally to be not so much kindred as mutual enemies. In this sense, old Martin's final opinion of Jonas Chuzzlewit—'I am not his friend, although I have the dishonour to be his relative' (p. 737)—might also stand as a summation for the transatlantic dimension of this book, written as it was in the early 1840s, when the idea of Britain and the USA as scions from the same stock was fading fast.[67] The financial swindling within the Chuzzlewit family is also mirrored in the way in which the gullible young Martin is enticed into land speculation in Eden, with the world of American capitalism being positioned here as a mercenary alternative to more substantial forms of virtue.

What *Martin Chuzzlewit* clearly reveals, then, is the limited nature of the affinity between Great Britain and the United States in the early 1840s. If the American assumption that Dickens would admire their country for its 'freedom from aristocratic feeling' was naïve, any expectation that the author's critiques of English society would cause him to champion alternative social structures is shown here to be equally unlikely. As George Orwell said many years ago, Dickens rapidly became such a national institution among the English that even those aspects of his writing which were critical of the status quo could readily be incorporated as part of an ethic of 'radiant idleness' locked in ultimately to the impossibility of change.[68] From this perspective, America in *Martin Chuzzlewit* represents a transgressive situation in all senses, a world which cannot be encompassed within the author's domestic circumference. During his sojourn in Eden, Martin encounters a member of the American military establishment, General Choke, who looks forward to making 'the British Lion put his tail between his legs, and howl with anguish' (p. 344), and there are also several mentions of conflict between Britain and America in Dickens's letters of this time. Writing to W. C. Macready from a steamboat en route from Pittsburgh to Cleveland in April 1842, he touches on the Maine boundary dispute as he refers derogatorily to 'the egotism [in America] which makes of Lord Ashburton's appointment, the conciliatory act of a frightened Government'; while in February

---

[67] For a discussion of this theme in *Martin Chuzzlewit*, see Dianne F. Sadoff, *Monsters of Affection: Dickens, Eliot, and Bronte on Fatherhood* (Baltimore: Johns Hopkins University Press, 1982), 10–11.

[68] George Orwell, 'Charles Dickens', in *The Collected Essays, Journalism and Letters of George Orwell*, i: *An Age Like This, 1920–1940*, ed. Sonia Orwell and Ian Angus (London: Secker & Warburg, 1968), 446.

1846, when the Oregon dispute was at its height and Dickens was safely back in England, he wrote to Emile de la Rue: 'The general impression here, is, that the Americans are Raving Mad. But it does not seem so probable today ... that they will force on a War, as it has done for some weeks past.'[69]

Dickens's scorn for American patriotic agitators also turned out to be strategically useful to the British authorities. When Lord Aberdeen and Robert Peel became convinced that some kind of compromise on the Oregon question would be prudent, they found themselves needing to conduct a skilful public relations exercise in order to appease the belligerent Palmerston faction in the Whig Party, which had attacked the Webster–Ashburton Treaty of 1842 to settle the Maine dispute as 'capitulation'. To this end, a series of articles portraying the Columbia River Valley as a valueless waste began appearing in prominent British journals: in the Whig-leaning *London Examiner* in April 1845, followed by the *Edinburgh Review* in July 1845, and *The Times* itself on 3 January 1846.[70] Although Dickens himself was not directly involved in this anti-American propaganda, there is no doubt that the recently published *American Notes* and *Martin Chuzzlewit* would have helped to pave the way for the British government's softening up of public opinion in relation to the Oregon question, or that Dickens's negative portrayals of the American West were ideologically complicit with the increasing hostility towards the United States in Britain during the 1840s.

As Dickens recognized at the time, these boundary disputes were involved in complex ways with the slavery issue, with the expansionist policies of the US government designed partly to provide a framework within which internal political divisions could be reconciled without the need for civil war. In a letter of 21 March 1842, Dickens reports to John Forster that a man in Richmond, Virginia, has been warning him of how the British should keep out of any American dealings with 'the niggers';[71] and it is of course a widespread indictment of slavery as 'the abuse of irresponsible power' that concludes *American Notes* (p. 271). After 1862, however, Dickens drifted towards support for the Confederate cause, and he was even moved, like Thomas Carlyle, to support Governor Eyre's violent suppression of a revolt by black plantation workers in Jamaica in 1865, as if to emphasize again the innate conservatism that framed and circumscribed his liberal rhetoric.[72] When Dickens returned to the United States for a second visit in 1868, he was full of praise for the 'amazing changes' in the country, and he talked in his farewell speech of the English and American people as 'essentially one', saying 'it rests with them jointly to uphold the great Anglo-Saxon race'.[73] This, however, was a sentimentalized conclusion to Dickens's dealings with America, a deliberate attempt to reach back to an earlier

---

[69] Dickens, *Letters of Charles Dickens*, iii, 176; *idem, The Letters of Charles Dickens*, iv: *1844–1846*, ed. Kathleen Tillotson (Oxford: Clarendon Press, 1977), 498.
[70] Billington, *Far Western Frontier*, 157–9.   [71] Dickens, *Letters of Charles Dickens*, iii, 141.
[72] Christine Bolt, *Victorian Attitudes to Race* (London: Routledge & Kegan Paul, 1971), 82.
[73] Slater, ed., *Dickens on America and the Americans*, 245.

era of mythic racial homogeneity before Britain and the USA had been divided by issues of politics, finance, and geography. As a skilled choreographer of public performances, Dickens in 1868 succeeded in projecting an ambience of bilateral harmony towards which the whole fabric of his earlier work had been severely antipathetic.

If the boundary disputes of the 1840s reveal Dickens's underlying hostility to the United States, they disclose a peculiarly double-edged conservatism in the work of a writer very popular in England during his own lifetime but much less well known today, George Ruxton. Ruxton was born in Oxfordshire in 1821 and educated at Tonbridge, an English public school, and then at Sandhurst military academy, from where he was expelled at the age of 15. He subsequently travelled widely in Spain and Africa as well as the Americas, and he pursued an adventurous military career which saw him posted in 1841 to the Detroit River in Canada, the scene of some of the most famous battles in the war of 1812. He spent most of the 1840s travelling through the American West and Mexico, publishing a novel, *Life in the Far West*, which appeared in serial form in *Blackwood's Edinburgh Magazine* in the summer of 1848. However, he died shortly afterwards, at the age of 27, having contracted dysentery in St Louis on his journey back to the Far West from England.

Ruxton is a very curious figure indeed, a writer whose success derived, according to Max Berger, from the way his works 'were the forerunners of the "Cowboy and Indian" story of a later period'.[74] While at Sandhurst, Ruxton read enthusiastically the novels of James Fenimore Cooper, and the few scholars who have paid him any attention have generally tried to conscript Ruxton into a tradition of American frontier writing mapped out by Cooper in the early nineteenth century. Thus, for example, Bruce Sutherland records the admiration for Ruxton expressed by Theodore Roosevelt, who said he 'did for the old time Rocky Mountain trappers, much what Hudson has done for the gaucho'.[75] Richard H. Cracroft, in a 1975 essay in *Western American Literature*, similarly contrasted favourably the authenticity of Ruxton's narratives with the sense given by Washington Irving of being merely a 'genteel and tophatted observer', rather than someone who is 'part and parcel of the mountain doings', and he concluded that 'Ruxton's spirit was a westering one, as was his whole life'. According to Cracroft, Ruxton's skill at the 'recording of mountain lingo'—'"gone under" for *dead*', for example—has 'permeated every Mountain Man novel written since *Life in the Far West*'.[76] James L. Simmons also remarked on the 'perfect insouciance' of Ruxton's temperament and argued that his sympathy for the

---

[74] Max Berger, *The British Traveller in America, 1836–1860* (New York: Columbia University Press, 1943), 213.
[75] Bruce Sutherland, 'George Frederick Ruxton in North America', *Southwest Review*, 30/1 (Autumn 1944), 86.
[76] Richard H. Cracroft, '"Half Froze for Mountain Doins": The Influence and Significance of George F. Ruxton's *Life in the Far West*', *Western American Literature*, 10 (1975), 38, 34.

8. Portrait of George Augustus Frederick Ruxton, from a miniature painted on ivory, mid-1840s.

American West transformed Ruxton into a man who 'had little in common any longer with the highly ordered and formal English society'.[77] This American view of Ruxton as epitomizing an indigenous 'westering' spirit certainly captures one aspect of his chameleonic character, the side that openly declared how 'the very happiest moments of my life have been spent in the wilderness of the far West'.[78] Impatient of the restrictions of English society, he enjoyed the solitude of the West, and in his non-fictional *Adventures in Mexico and the Rocky Mountains* (1847), he describes his delight at being 'paid the compliment of being more than once mistaken for an Indian chief'. Kitted out 'in all the pride of fringed deerskin and porcupine-quills', Ruxton succeeded in blending in perfectly with his new environment and in becoming part of the local scenery (p. 313).

One question passed over in silence by his American sympathizers, though, is Ruxton's ultimate rationale in thus seeking to accommodate himself to the Western landscape. There seems little doubt of his genuine attachment to the Far West or his sense of empathy with the American people, whose 'genuine spirit of kindness and affection' he salutes in his preface to *Adventures in Mexico* (p. iv); but it also seems likely that his motives were not so pure or romantic as is often imagined. Indeed, it appears highly probable that Ruxton was being employed in some capacity by the British authorities for diplomatic and espionage purposes, and that the government took grateful advantage of his position as an observer within this contentious terrain who could relay information back to London on matters relating to US involvement in Mexico and Oregon. Although we know that he had some links with the Colonial Office, the exact nature of Ruxton's undercover activities is, not surprisingly, difficult to determine: Frederic E. Voelker describes him as a 'roving commercial attaché of the British diplomatic service', though he argues that Ruxton was not 'a spy in the ordinary sense because he made no effort to conceal his identity'.[79] Lieutenant J. W. Abert of the US Army, for instance, describes Ruxton in November 1846 bringing 'a paper from the English minister, desiring all American officers to extend every facility to English traders on their route to Chihuahua'.[80] What we could infer from this is that Ruxton's role was in part simply that of a diplomatic facilitator, protecting British interests and assisting his countrymen in the practice of commerce within these remote and violent regions: at one point, he describes how, because of the war between the United States and Mexico, 'there was a very large amount of property belonging to English merchants and others of neutral nations, who were suffering enormous losses by the detention of their goods' (p. 157). Indeed,

[77] Simmons, *Star-Spangled Eden*, 174, 180.

[78] George F. Ruxton, *Adventures in Mexico and the Rocky Mountains* (London: John Murray, 1847), 280. Subsequent page references to this edition are cited in parentheses in the text.

[79] Frederic E. Voelker, 'Ruxton of the Rocky Mountains', *Missouri Historical Society Bulletin*, 5/2 (Jan. 1949), 84.

[80] Clyde and Mae Reed Porter, *Ruxton of the Rockies*, ed. LeRoy R. Hafen (Norman, Okla.: University of Oklahoma Press, 1950), 106.

the versatile Ruxton seems also to have acted in a similar capacity on behalf of the Mexican government at this time, as a commercial agent to promote and safeguard trade.[81] Yet there also seem to be more clandestine aspects to his activities: it is odd that he would choose freely to travel to and through Mexico at the height of that country's war with the United States, odder still that he would allude to this bruising conflict only right at the end of *Adventures in Mexico*, when he acknowledges how it is a subject 'which hitherto I have avoided mentioning in the body of this little narrative' (p. 322). In his preface, Ruxton remarks enigmatically: 'It is hardly necessary to explain the cause of my visiting Mexico at such an unsettled period; and I fear that circumstances will prevent my gratifying the curiosity of the reader, should he feel any on that point' (p. iii). As a fluent Spanish speaker, Ruxton appears to take a certain amount of pride in being generally assumed to be someone he is not, and he talks of how the Mexicans are puzzled by the 'mysterious fact of an Englishman travelling through the country at such a time' (p. 158). Just as Irving's *Astoria* presents espionage as in some ways a fitting response to the confused cultural conditions of the American West in the early nineteenth century, so Ruxton's chameleonic identity testifies to the way in which he understood the Western territories not simply as a raw, naturalistic phenomenon, but as a landscape that could be understood in many different ways simultaneously.

The strength of Ruxton's loyalty to and ties with England—he arrived back in Liverpool in August 1847, before setting out for the Far West again the following year—suggest a character who never intended to reinvent himself as a fully-fledged American. Indeed, the clearest intimations of Ruxton's double-dealing can be seen in the very conventional views of American degradation which emerge from his social commentaries in *Adventures in Mexico* and other works, observations which paint quite a different portrait from the romanticized image of the Rocky Mountain world that appears in *Life in the Far West*. For all of his maverick, rebellious impulses, Ruxton, even more than Dickens, always remained at heart an English gentleman. In October 1843, he notes disapprovingly 'the long-haired greasy countenances of rowdy Canadian and Yankee loafers ... lolling around the deck, chewing and spitting, and swearing in a most disgusting manner'; he also pours scorn on Americans near Buffalo, New York, who 'were bragging of what they had done in the last rebellion, or "Patriots' War," as they called it, and what they would do in the next, heaping imprecations on Britishers, whom they intended to "chaw up right off"'.[82] Like Dickens, Ruxton lambasts the American political system, inveighing against 'that liberty, which it is the theoretical boast of republican governments their system so largely deals in, but which, in reality, is a practical falsehood and delusion' (p. 107); and, as a military man, he remarks disapprovingly on how the lack

81 Voelker, 'Ruxton of the Rocky Mountains', 83.
82 Porter and Porter, *Ruxton of the Rockies*, 52–3.

of good order in the American army stems from the incompatibility of service 'discipline' with 'republican notions and the liberty of the citizen' (p. 177). As a skilled exponent of duplicity himself, Ruxton also has a keen eye for the deserters from the British army who people the US ranks, and in *Adventures in Mexico* he records an encounter with an American soldier named Herbert who used to be in his own regiment and who mistakenly imagines that Ruxton would fail to recognize him (p. 185). He is also fully aware of the impact of recent British travellers to the United States—he talks of how 'the Trollope and Boz castigations' have served to improve steamboat travel (p. 315)—and he follows Dickens in denouncing slavery as 'a foul blot upon humanity', upbraiding the 'moral cowardice of the American people' for failing to grapple with this issue (p. 317). In the Dickens manner again, Ruxton dismisses Chicago as 'the City of Magnificent Intentions' (p. 327), while *Adventures in Mexico and the Rocky Mountains* ends up with some snide remarks about the general intelligence of the natives. Hearing described as 'one of the smartest men in these parts' an American who vociferously anticipates a time when 'Liberty treads to the earth your aristocracy' and when 'the star-spangled banner waves over Windsor Palace', Ruxton comments wryly: 'This I easily believed' (p. 331).

Ruxton was, then, not just a loose cannon, but also a student of foreign cultures: he published various scholarly articles on ethnology, and in 1847 was elected a Fellow of the Royal Geographic and Ethnological Societies on the basis of his works on the American West.[83] Moreover, he was an astute, if highly partial, political observer who regarded both Mexico and the United States as postcolonial nations, maintaining that the separation of Mexico from Spain has been 'the ruin of the country', since it is 'incapable of *self*-government', a position which leads him to propose for Mexico 'the re-establishment of a monarchical system' (p. 106). He also interprets the war with Mexico as a trial run on America's part for the impending war with Britain over Oregon, arguing that Mexico was made the 'scapegoat' for American military preparations at a time when there seemed to be the 'certainty' of a more serious conflict ahead (pp. 323–4). He discusses how Polk successfully stirred up war fever throughout the United States, though he also suggests how it was the mixed success of this Mexican campaign that led the American President to seek a compromise with Britain on the Oregon question, on the grounds 'that, if such a *scrimmage* as the Mexican War gave him considerable trouble, an affair with such a respectable enemy as England was likely to be anything but an agreeable pastime' (p. 325). In 1846, the year before *Adventures in Mexico and the Rocky Mountains* appeared, Ruxton had published a short pamphlet entitled *The Oregon Question: A Glance at the Respective Claims of Great Britain and the United States to the Territory in Dispute*, which pursues a similarly belligerent line by arguing like a crusty Victorian pedagogue that it would work out for the

---

[83] Berger, *British Traveller in America*, 213.

benefit of both nations if Britain went to war to preserve its stake in the Oregon Country:

For us, because we shall thereby secure a firmer footing on the continent of America ... For them, because they will be taught a salutary though most severe lesson, in the castigation inflicted on their unprincipled and uncivilized institutions; as well as by their being brought to the conviction, that as the younger children of the civilized world, they must be taught to pay a proper deference to those principles recognized and enforced by other nations best qualified to set them an example of reason and humanity.[84]

These are more the words of an English Establishment figure than those of someone whose 'spirit was a westering one', and Ruxton's uncompromising attitude on the Oregon issue demonstrates clearly enough a man whose empathy with the western landscape has often masked his intense hostility towards the US political system.

It is, in fact, partly because of this empathy for the American West that Ruxton is so reluctant to cede Oregon to the United States. Echoing reports from the region carried out on behalf of the US government, he acknowledges in *The Oregon Question* that 'Few portions of the globe are to be found so rich in soil, so diversified in surface', and he also declares that for 'beauty of scenery and salubrity of climate, it is not to be surpassed' (p. 9). In the light of this area's commercial and geographical advantages, Ruxton attempts to trace the British claims back through the explorations of Francis Drake, who sailed along the Northwest coast between 1577 and 1581, and the voyages of Captain Cook at the end of the eighteenth century. He also cites Thomas Jefferson's view that the boundaries of the Louisiana Purchase did not extend to the territories west of the Rocky Mountains and asks why the United States should 'have a natural right to claim a tract of territory, hundreds of miles distant, simply because it lies on the same continent' (p. 22). In relinquishing the area around the Columbia River, argues Ruxton, Britain would not only 'virtually resign all sway on the western coast of America', but would also 'encourage the United States in their daring and unprincipled thirst for territorial aggrandizement' (p. 22). He points out that the Oregon Country had until recently been peopled almost entirely by the British, just as he takes pleasure elsewhere in noting how English settlers antedated the Mormons in Utah. Accusing the British government of indecision over this Oregon question, Ruxton suggests that the United States is set to 'repeat the unprincipled but artful *dodge*, which has already annexed Texas to the Union', by encouraging its 'refuse discontented population' to settle in the disputed territories (pp. 26–7). He specifically attacks 'the go-ahead principles of Young America' (p. 38) and tries to assume the moral high ground by claiming that a war against the United States would also become a crusade

---

[84] George F. Ruxton, *The Oregon Question: A Glance at the Respective Claims of Great Britain and the United States to the Territory in Dispute* (London: John Ollivier, 1846), 29–30. Subsequent page references to this edition are cited in parentheses in the text.

against slavery, 'the last "crying evil," the existing disgrace to the age in the civilized world' (p. 30).

Clearly enough, all this can be seen as a distinct antithesis to that frontier mythology which sought to validate the American pioneering spirit in terms of a geographical essentialism, its preordained 'reuniting of east and west'.[85] Ruxton cites *Martin Chuzzlewit* towards the end of his Oregon pamphlet—he says that the Honourable Caleb Cushing, a jingoistic American politician, reminds him of one of the characters in Dickens's novel (p. 40)—and Ruxton's own fictional narrative, *Life in the Far West*, has more in common ideologically with the works of Dickens than with the American 'mountain men' novels it is too frequently associated with. As cultural historian of the American West Tom Lynch remarked in 1997, Ruxton, as 'an Englishman writing about the Rockies', is someone who 'falls through the cracks of how we organize literary studies': he seems to fit comfortably neither with an English Victorian style of moral realism, nor with an American western idiom of epic adventure.[86]

Life in the Far West provides a distinctly transnational, non-US perspective on the peopling of the Western country. It chronicles the rapid rise of St Louis, described as 'the emporium of the fur trade, and the fast rising metropolis of the precocious settlements of the West', and it talks of how it was the 'trappers and hardy mountaineers' who 'opened to commerce and the plough the vast and fertile regions of the West'.[87] Rather than seeing these developments as a culmination of the US pioneering spirit, Ruxton reads them as a product of the early explorations undertaken by the Hudson's Bay Company. Ruxton here is not specifically describing the disputed territory in the Pacific Northwest but, rather, the country around the Black Hills, on the Colorado–Utah border. Nevertheless, Ruxton's version of American cultural nationalism runs directly contrary to Crèvecoeur's celebrated mythology of a melting pot, in which 'individuals of all nations are melted into a new race of men'.[88] Instead, Ruxton, in disarmingly non-legalistic fashion, envisages a country open to settlers of all nationalities without the threat of imperial incorporation by the United States: 'A curious assemblage did the rendezvous present, and representatives of many a land met there. A son of *La belle France* here lit his pipe from one proffered by a native of New Mexico. An Englishman and a Sandwich Islander cut a quid from the same plug of tobacco. A Swede and an "old Virginian" puffed together' (p. 78). The hero of *Life in the Far West*, La Bonté, is a Mississippi man whose

[85] Billington, *Far Western Frontier*, 269.

[86] Tom Lynch, 'Re: Rocky Mtn Writers', 19 May 1997, online: http://www.earthsystems.org/gopher/asle, accessed 22 Feb. 2001. Lynch is a Western ethnographer with a Ph.D. from the University of Oregon who currently teaches at New Mexico State University.

[87] George Frederick Ruxton, *Life in the Far West*, ed. LeRoy R. Hafen (Norman, Okla.: University of Oklahoma Press, 1951), 50–1. Subsequent page references to this edition are cited in parentheses in the text.

[88] J. Hector St John de Crèvecoeur, *Letters from an American Farmer and Sketches of Eighteenth-Century America*, ed. Albert E. Stone (New York: Viking Penguin, 1981), 70.

father was a French immigrant, and the novel is populated with representatives of many different nations. It includes a portrait of the 'hospitable Scotchman' (p. 137) William Drummond Stewart, a noted explorer of the Far West at this time, who is dressed in typical gentlemanly attire 'in a light shooting-jacket, of many pockets and dandy cut', as he rides along 'on an English saddle' (p. 133).

Rather than being a purist phenomenon, the landscape of this novel appears to be divided in a hybrid fashion between civilization and primitivism. Ruxton describes, for instance, a 'huge isolated mass of granitic rock', on which

are rudely carved the names and initials of traders, trappers, travellers and emigrants, who have here recorded the memorial of their sojourn in the remote wilderness of the Far West. The face of the rock is covered with names familiar to the mountaineers as those of the most renowned of their hardy brotherhood; while others again occur, better known to the science and literature of the Old World than to the unlearned trappers of the Rocky Mountains. (p. 130)

For Ruxton, then, the Far West is a dualistic, duplicitous landscape, a cross between the virgin territory cherished by Lewis and Clark and the corrupt, predatory world abhorred by Dickens. The tone of *Life in the Far West* is one of savage, sardonic demystification: Ruxton describes how 'the "lex talionis" ' (p. 82) of this region is a 'stoical indifference to pain and suffering' (p. 85), and he recounts vividly a grim story of Indian trappers reduced to the expedient of cannibalism, with the 'yet quivering' body of an Indian squaw being roasted in order to keep the others alive (p. 86). La Bonté himself is said to have a 'stoical indifference' to the prospect of this kind of atavistic reduction of 'civilised fastidiousness' to the bare necessities of human existence (p. 109): ' "Meat's meat" is a common saying on the mountains, and from the buffalo down to the rattlesnake, including every quadruped that runs, every fowl that flies, and every reptile that creeps, nothing comes amiss to the mountaineer' (p. 98). Ruxton's West thus serves to strip away the veneer of polite pretence from human society, with the caustic style of this English gentleman in exile becoming a formal correlative to the harsh nature of Rocky Mountain culture, which is admired here for its brutalizing qualities, its 'barbarism', as *Adventures in Mexico* calls it (p. 280), the way it systematically and at times sadistically hollows out the institutional illusions of gentility that prevail elsewhere. This is why *Life in the Far West* mercilessly mocks the expeditions westward in the 1840s of the Mormons, lampooning their founder, 'Joe Smith, on whom the mantle of Moses had so suddenly fallen' (p. 196). Ruxton opposes attempts to assimilate or domesticate the West, a land whose savagery he values and whose austere qualities he considers too valuable to relinquish to 'fanatic humbugs' (p. 195) intent upon appropriating it for their own parochial designs.

Ruxton's ideal of keeping the Oregon Country free from US control was an aim much discussed in Britain during the mid-1840s. Alexander Simpson, a former officer of the Hudson's Bay Company who also favoured a 'free and independent' Oregon, wrote in 1846 about how he feared that the incorporation of this territory as 'an appendage to the Atlantic States' would fatally alter the balance of global power and give the United States 'undue influence in the Pacific'.[89] A pamphlet published in the same year by Edward J. Wallace argued that the US claim to Oregon through a notion of 'contiguity' had no basis in international law, since the earth should be seen as the common inheritance of mankind, with each individual or nation acquiring a share only through actual occupancy and cultivation.[90] Gradually, however, despite the imprecations of Ruxton and others, public opinion in Britain came to acquiesce in the idea of US control over Oregon. Alexander Mackay, a Scottish journalist who wrote on political affairs in Washington DC for the *Morning Chronicle*, reported back to London on the expanding population of the American Western states and, as a natural consequence of this, 'the growing power of the West' in political terms.[91] Henry Warre, a member of the British force sent out by Peel in 1845 to fortify and reconnoitre the mouth of the Columbia River, described the Willamette Valley as a 'luxuriant' location of 'amazing fecundity', and he praised the 'magnificence of the rivers, the height and beauty of the distant mountains' as a 'wonderful' prospect; nevertheless, Warre also advised that from a military point of view the country was indefensible, especially since increasing numbers of American emigrants were pouring over the Rocky Mountains. In Warre's eyes, the Hudson's Bay Company had been outwitted: having received the first of these American emigrants in a 'kindly' fashion, the Company now found their local authority 'completely overruled by the number of Americans', so that they were obliged 'to subscribe to the laws of the very people whose settlement and occupation of the land they contributed so generously and largely to effect'. Although indicting the 'cupidity of our Transatlantic brethren' for taking advantage of British hospitality in this manner, Warre in 1849 clearly regards the settlement of Oregon by Americans as irreversible, and he contents himself with drawing pictures of this Western landscape—the Columbia River Valley, Cape Disappointment, Mount Hood—as if in elegiac recognition of its recent loss (see Plate 9).[92]

It is strange now to look at a map of North America in 1840, where California is part of Mexico and the Oregon Country subject to the jurisdiction of the Houses of Parliament in London. From the American point of view, the idealization of Oriental thought in Transcendentalist writings—by Emerson, Thoreau, Whitman, and others—was inextricably intertwined with the appropriation of

[89] Alexander Simpson, *The Oregon Territory: Claims Thereto of England and America Considered; Its Condition and Prospects* (London, 1846), 53–4.

[90] Edward J. Wallace, *The Oregon Question Determined by the Rule of International Law* (London, 1846), 4.

[91] Alexander Mackay, *The Western World; or, Travels in the United States in 1846–47* (London, 1849), i. 246.

[92] Captain H. Warre, *Sketches in North America and the Oregon Territory* (London, 1849), 2–3.

9. Captain Henry Warre, *Sketches in North America and the Oregon Territory* (1849).
Sketch no. 29: Valley of the Columbia River, August 1845.

the Western states of America as both a geographical bridge and a symbolic correlative to the abstract idea of transcendence which they promulgated. Thoreau's conception of the Orient, for example, was dependent implicitly upon a political erasure of British imperial interests from the Western territories, so that he could reimagine a symbiotic link between the cultures of matter and spirit, the American 'West' and the Asian 'East'.[93] It was the seizure of the West Coast, in other words, that enabled the United States to complete the circle of her domestic territorial ambitions and thus to reposition herself globally as an imperial force, with increasing sway over the Pacific as well as the Atlantic. This, of course, was precisely what British diplomats like Alexander Simpson had feared in the 1840s, when he wrote to the London *Times* cautioning the British government against taking the Oregon conflict too lightly and arguing that it involved not just a distant tract of land but, more crucially, the future balance of world power.

[93] On this point, see Rob Wilson, 'Exporting Christian Transcendentalism, Importing Hawaiian Sugar: The Trans-Americanization of Hawai'i', *American Literature*, 72 (2000), 540–1.

From a British point of view, then, the ultimate loss of the Oregon Territory was another significant stage in its gradual supersession by the United States as the leading world empire. In cultural terms, Ruxton also helped to popularize an image of the American West as a site of transfiguration, a landscape where genteel European codes of behaviour could be metamorphosed into something rougher and more authentic, an idea which was to attract and beguile subsequent British visitors, from Oscar Wilde to D. H. Lawrence and Christopher Isherwood. For Dickens, the barbarous nature of the American West also anticipated another strain in English literature, one more concerned with the circumscription of boundaries, both moral and geographic, and with the enclosure of more familiar domestic values. Whereas the previous generation of reformist British writers had been more influenced by the political institutions of the new United States, attention in the mid-nineteenth century turned more towards the open country of the American West and to a consideration of the significance of this space for the redefinition of British national interests. In this sense, the American westward movement in the 1840s, allied to portrayals of the West as alien country in Frances Trollope and Dickens, did not just influence the future shape of the United States; it also served effectively to reconfigure the parameters of British culture.

More generally, the abolition of the Corn Laws towards which Peel was finally driven by the need to settle this Oregon question had profound long-term consequences for the social and economic framework of the British state. Many of those who campaigned against the Corn Laws in the 1830s and 1840s were Dissenters who made quite overt links between the contemporary agitation for repeal and the old battles for religious and political liberty in the seventeenth century, what John Bright in 1845 called the constitutional struggle against a 'despotic and treacherous monarch'.[94] Dissenters regarded the Established Church as thoroughly complicit in the Corn Laws, because the economic system of protectionism effectively consolidated the rural organization of Anglican parishes: Cobden wrote to Bright in 1842 of how 'The Church clergy are almost to a man guilty of causing the present distress by upholding the Corn Law—*they having themselves an interest* in the high price of bread'.[95] Conversely, the sweeping away of these parochial fiefdoms was seen by Nonconformist preachers as analogous to the defiance of absolute monarchy, the promulgation of English liberties, and the reformist desire to spread an enlightened message of peace and prosperity across the globe. In this sense Cobden might be said to descend in a direct line from Richard Price; like Price, he looked upon America as his moral beacon, describing transatlantic commerce as 'to us, a vital matter' in the House of Commons in 1843, and predicting that the economic leadership

---

[94] Schonhardt-Bailey, ed., *Free Trade*, 161.
[95] Norman McCord, *The Anti-Corn Law League, 1838–1846* (London: Allen & Unwin, 1958), 26.

of the world would soon pass to the United States.[96] The ultimate significance of the Oregon question for Britain thus involved not so much the relinquishment of a distant territory as the displacement of fiscal autonomy closer to home, the reluctant recognition on the part of the Established Church and state that their nationalist instincts needed to enter into negotiation with the broader currents of the Atlantic world.

[96] Paul A. Pickering and Alex Tyrrell, *The People's Bread: A History of the Anti-Corn Law League* (London: Leicester University Press, 2000), 1; Schonhardt-Bailey, ed., *Free Trade*, 57; Howe, *Free Trade and Liberal England*, 304.

4

Arthur Hugh Clough and the Poetics
of Dissent

NEGATIVE TRANSCENDENTALISM: THE DIALOGUE
WITH R. W. EMERSON

After the fierce political disputes of the 1840s, the American shadow presence began to manifest itself increasingly in English literature of the mid-Victorian period as a disruptive influence, an alternative centre of gravity. The burgeoning culture of the United States threatened to disturb both the imperial geography that would place foreign cultures in subordinate relation to Britain and the moralized forms of aesthetics that sought to equate such cartographies with a just and accurate portrayal of the world. This chapter will suggest how the poetry of Arthur Hugh Clough reworks obliquely a version of American Transcendentalism and how these transatlantic dimensions effectively sever his work both from the Wordsworthian tradition of English and from the implicit institutional affiliation with the Church of England that underwrote that tradition. It will also consider how Clough looks forward to the Aesthetic Movement in England in the way he challenges the Establishment version of cultural tradition championed in their different ways by Thomas and Matthew Arnold, with both of whom he had been familiar since his days at Rugby School. By juxtaposing high and low cultures in parodic and unstable relationships, Clough translates national identity into a dialogical phenomenon, one predicated upon systems of alternation and interference rather than organic synthesis.

Although born in England in 1819, Clough spent six years of his childhood in Charleston, South Carolina, after his father took the family over to the United States in the winter of 1822–3. The plan of Clough's father was to circumvent the economic depression that had followed the Napoleonic Wars in Europe by tapping sources of raw cotton in the American South and exporting them back to England. The family did not settle back in England until 1836, and, though Clough himself was sent back to England to be educated at Rugby, he retained early memories of living by the harbour at Charleston—South Carolina was, of course, then still a slave state—as well as of three summers when the family sojourned in the milder climate of upstate New York. Clough was nicknamed

10. Arthur Hugh Clough, by Samuel Rowse (1860).

'Yankee' at Rugby, and in 1835 he wrote to a friend about the hardship of having to spend vacations on the school premises and 'the curse of being without a home'.[1] Curiosity about the circumstances in which his family was living impelled him to read de Tocqueville's *Democracy in America* as early as 1836, the year after it was first published, while the experiences of his childhood and youth

---

[1] Matthew Arnold, *The Letters of Matthew Arnold to Arthur Hugh Clough*, ed. Howard Foster Lowry (London: Oxford University Press, 1932), 48; Katharine Chorley, *Arthur Hugh Clough: The Uncommitted Mind, A Study of his Life and Poetry* (Oxford: Clarendon Press, 1962), 28.

also ensured that when he travelled to Boston as an adult in December 1852 Clough was aware in an important sense of returning to the United States, rather than encountering that country for the first time.[2] In one of his 'Parepidemus' letters, he addresses Americans about 'my early nurture under your "equal sky" and equitable polity', and though his identification with the United States is not without irony, it is also not without awareness of the particular qualities of US culture:

After an absence of twenty-five years I find myself again in America, and though not as yet invested with the privileges of a citizen, looking forward to a privileged residence ... I have lost perhaps during a long subjection to European forms of government that elastic principle of motion which my early education *should* at least have given me; having sunk into a sluggish unambitious indifference to that great fundamental American notion that since all men are equal therefore I have as good a right as any one to be superior to every body else ... .[3]

Clough is being sardonic here about the kinds of popular assumptions satirized in the late twentieth century by Garrison Keillor, in whose fabled Midwestern town of Lake Wobegon every child was said to be above average. Nevertheless, he is also responsive to the 'elastic principle' of the United States, which he contrasts favourably with the more hierarchical system that he associates with 'European forms of government'.

As is well known, Clough always enjoyed a tense relationship with the English cultural establishment. He felt a pull towards Nonconformism when he heard James Martineau (brother of Harriet) preach in the Liverpool Unitarian church in 1845, only two years after the award of an honorary degree at Oxford to the American ambassador had to be abandoned because of noisy protests about his Unitarianism.[4] Clough himself never formally became a Unitarian or anything else, but his manifest sense of religious unease came to a head in 1848 when he resigned his fellowship at Oriel College, Oxford, on the grounds that he felt himself unable in principle to subscribe to the Thirty-Nine Articles of the Church of England, a requirement at that time for all Oxford Fellows. He was then employed from 1849 to 1851 as Principal of University Hall, London, an academic institution more sympathetic to Dissenting ways; but Clough failed to impress the authorities there by his lack of entrepreneurial zeal in the recruitment of students, as well as by his reluctance 'to undertake the conduct or superintendence of any prayers'.[5] Clough had met and spent some considerable time with Emerson when the latter visited England in 1848—Emerson, the senior partner by sixteen years, noted in his private journal for December 1848:

---

[2] Anthony Kenny, *Arthur Hugh Clough: A Poet's Life* (London: Continuum, 2005), 24.
[3] Arthur Hugh Clough, *Selected Prose Works of Arthur Hugh Clough*, ed. Buckner B. Trawick (University, Ala.: University of Alabama Press, 1964), 249–50. Subsequent references to Clough's prose works are taken from this edition and are cited as *SP* in parentheses in the text.
[4] Kenny, *Arthur Hugh Clough*, 97, 74.   [5] Chorley, *Arthur Hugh Clough*, 171.

''Tis, I think, the most real benefit I have had from my English visit, this genius of Clough'—and, after Clough's trials and tribulations in English academe had led him to consider emigration, Emerson was quick to write encouraging him to come to America and assuring him of a plentiful supply of private tutorial work in Boston.[6] Emerson, who was a great admirer of Clough's first poem, *The Bothie of Tober-na-Vuolich* (1848), blamed the neglect of his friend on the narrow prejudices of English society, and he also hoped that Clough would assist him with 'a catechism of details touching England' in relation to his own work, *English Traits*, which he was then writing.[7]

At first, Clough was generally enthusiastic about America. He met James Russell Lowell and his wife on board the *Canada*, en route to the United States, and in New England he was welcomed into the Emersonian circle, becoming quickly acquainted with Longfellow, Hawthorne, Thoreau, Theodore Parker, Harriet Beecher Stowe, William Ellery Channing, and others; the Yankees, he wrote home in a letter of November 1852, are 'very kind'.[8] As someone with a lingering memory of a South Carolina childhood, Clough came to find himself rather uncomfortable with some of the more fervent New England abolitionists, and Parker in particular seems to have irritated him. Although progressive by temperament, Clough was also agnostic by inclination, and his scepticism about the efficacy of 'Liberty' as an abstract ideal is mirrored in his ambivalence about the emancipation of women, another burning issue in New England at this time.[9] Clough had seen 'a good deal' of Margaret Fuller in 1849 when they were both in Rome, and in Italy they shared republican sympathies, supporting Garibaldi and Mazzini while equally despising the papal resistance to such features of modernity as the railroad and the telegraph. But three years later in Boston, after being entertained to tea at Mrs Ward's, Clough was less than enamoured of what he called 'Margaret Fuller's set', which he described to his fiancée, Blanche Smith, as 'satirical', 'sarcastic', 'ill-natured', 'fastidious', and 'intellectual'; whereas you, he wrote home to the more conventional Blanche, 'are a very *good* girl I am sure'.[10]

This tension between what one might call intellectual adventure and social conditioning haunts all of Clough's American experiences in 1852 and 1853. One of his reasons for travelling to the United States was to earn enough money to marry his fiancée, whom he seems to have infantilized in a manner not untypical of an English Victorian gentleman—in his letters to her, he constantly uses endearments such as 'my dear good child'—and so it is hardly surprising

---

6 Ralph Waldo Emerson, *The Journals and Miscellaneous Notebooks of Ralph Waldo Emerson*, xi: *1848–1851*, ed. A. W. Plumstead and William H. Gilman (Cambridge, Mass.: Harvard University Press, 1975), 64.
7 Arthur Hugh Clough, *The Correspondence of Arthur Hugh Clough*, ed. Frederick L. Mulhauser (Oxford: Clarendon Press, 1957), i. 316.   8 Ibid. ii. 332.
9 On this topic, see Wendell V. Harris, *Arthur Hugh Clough* (New York: Twayne, 1970), 125. On Parker, see Clough, *Correspondence*, ii. 365.
10 Clough, *Correspondence*, i. 315; ii. 341–2.

that he was uncomfortable with Fuller's legacy among Bostonian feminists. Similarly, and rather absurdly, he complained of how 'domestic service' in the New World was 'evidently very imperfect', and he castigated in particular the 'dirty uninstructed Irish' who were 'very quick in learning to be independent and I'm-as-good-as-you in their manners'. Writing to Thomas Carlyle in 1853, Clough described Concord as 'rather a pokey sort of place', and he wrote dismissively of how 'a small literary reputation pays a large return in these savage regions'.[11] At the same time, however, Clough developed some important intellectual friendships in Massachusetts, particularly with Lowell and with Charles Eliot Norton, associations which were to have significant repercussions for his subsequent literary career.

Clough was indebted to James Russell Lowell, in particular, for the first publication of his best-known poem, *Amours de Voyage*, which was written in 1849 but suppressed by the author until Lowell persuaded him to allow it to be published in instalments in the new magazine he was editing, *Atlantic Monthly*, between February and May 1858. *Atlantic Monthly*'s first issue had appeared only in November 1857, so Clough was riding the first wave of publicity for a Boston periodical that featured on its cover an image of John Winthrop, founder of the Massachusetts Bay colony, and whose editorial policy, as stated on the inside cover of its first issue, sought to position the journal as an 'exponent of what its conductors believe to be the American idea'. Consequently, the editors declared, 'native writers will receive the most solid encouragement, and will be mainly relied upon to fill the pages of the *Atlantic*', so that by affiliating himself with Lowell's enterprise, Clough was reinforcing his status as an honorary New Englander.[12] Clough had earlier been dissuaded from publishing his long poem in England partly by the strictures of old friends such as John Campbell, later Professor of Poetry at Oxford, who found the work to be in 'bad taste' with 'nothing hearty and heart-whole in it', and who regarded *Amours de Voyage*, so he told the author, 'as your nature ridding itself of long-gathered bile'. Clough was also worried at this time about how the poem's impieties might offend what he called his 'Sadducees', the Management Committee of University Hall, a turn of events which would further have jeopardized Clough's fragile financial security; indeed, even when the poem appeared in *Atlantic Monthly*, Lowell cautiously omitted four verses for fear of what he called 'the so-called religious newspapers' charging his journal with publishing 'infidelities'.[13]

Unlike most English readers of the mid-nineteenth century, though, Lowell entertained a very high opinion of Clough's poetic capacities, arguing in 1871 that he 'will be thought a hundred years hence to have been the truest expression

[11] Clough, *Correspondence*, ii. 333, 360, 420, 398.
[12] Ellery Sedgwick, *The* Atlantic Monthly, *1857–1909: Yankee Humanism at High Tide and Ebb* (Amherst, Mass.: University of Massachusetts Press, 1994), 35.
[13] Michael Thorpe, ed., *Clough: The Critical Heritage* (London: Routledge & Kegan Paul, 1972), 122–3; Clough, *Correspondence*, ii. 537.

in verse of the moral and intellectual tendencies, the doubt and struggle towards settled convictions, of the period in which he lived'. The poem's publication in the United States seems to have caused little comment at the time in England, but Clough himself was grateful to receive from *Atlantic Monthly* some hard cash for his literary endeavours, and this encouraged him to think about the possibilities of further publication and perhaps to gather together a collection of his poems in book form.[14] It is important, then, to emphasize that, in terms of its conditions of production and dissemination, *Amours de Voyage* is an American rather than an English poem. As William C. Spengemann has pointed out, there is a certain meretricious quality in any attempt to classify the national identity of literary figures whose work consistently traverses national boundaries in both biographical and narrative terms, and any effort to incorporate Clough wholesale into an American literary tradition would be as pointless as to insist, conversely, upon the immutable nature of his inherited English assumptions.[15] What we can say with some certainty, though, is that Clough's work is torn between English and American influences, and that his poetry involves a shuttling between alternative, transatlantic points of view.

Amours de Voyage, which features a hero wandering forlornly through Europe who is unable to find within himself either human love or religious faith, might be described as a poem of negative Transcendentalism. There is a dialogue within this narrative between Neoplatonism and contingency, between idealist affinities and a more random sense of time and space. The shorthand term of the hero, Claude, for such postlapsarian contingency is 'juxtaposition'. After a self-consciously sublime opening invoking the grandeurs of the Western epic tradition, Clough's narrator parodically dissociates himself from those old romantic assumptions:

> Well, I know, after all, it is only juxtaposition, —
> Juxtaposition, in short; and what is juxtaposition?[16]

This intellectual dispute with Emerson is made more explicit in Claude's response in the third canto to Eustace, his epistolary sounding-board who remains silently off-stage throughout the entire poem:

> Juxtaposition is great, — but, you tell me, affinity greater.
> Ah, my friend, there are many affinities, greater and lesser,
> Stronger and weaker; and each, by the favour of juxtaposition,
> Potent, efficient, in force .... .

> (*P* 118)

[14] Chorley, *Arthur Hugh Clough*, 4, 200.

[15] See e.g. William C. Spengemann, 'American Writers and English Literature', *ELH*, 52 (1985), 209–38, and *idem, A Mirror for Americanists: Reflections on the Idea of American Literature* (Hanover, NH: Univ. Press of New England, 1989).

[16] Arthur Hugh Clough, *The Poems of Arthur Hugh Clough*, 2nd edn., ed. F. L. Mulhauser (Oxford: Clarendon Press, 1974), 101. Subsequent references to Clough's poetry are taken from this edition and are cited as *P* in parentheses in the text.

The dialectic here between 'juxtaposition' and 'affinity' bears a close resemblance to the transatlantic debate between Clough's sceptical materialism and Emerson's idealism. On the question of affinity, for instance, compare Emerson's *Nature* (1836): 'The perception of real affinities between events, (that is to say, of *ideal* affinities, for those only are real,) enables the poet thus to make free with the most imposing forms and phenomena of the world, and to assert the predominance of the soul.'[17] Claude develops his interrogation of this Neoplatonic conception of innate 'affinity' a few lines later, when he quizzically echoes the Emersonian image, in 'Circles' (1841), of nature itself as a series of concentric circles. Emerson's style is euphoric and dogmatic: 'The eye is the first circle; the horizon itself which it forms is the second; and throughout nature this primary figure is repeated without end.'[18] Clough's style, by contrast, is experiential and ruminative:

> *Vir sum, nihil fœminei,*—and e'en to the uttermost circle,
> All that is Nature's is I, and I all things that are Nature's.
> Yes, as I walk, I behold, in a luminous, large intuition,
> That I can be and become anything that I meet with or look at .... .
>
> (*P* 118–19)

Another way of explaining this negative or inverted Transcendentalism would be to emphasize how Clough's poetry reproduces as a kind of hypothetical experiment the idea of flexibility and multiple possibility that was endemic to Emerson's rhetoric of emancipation, its visionary belief in how the true poet 'unlocks our chains, and admits us to a new scene'.[19] However, Clough's perception of mutability is reliant more upon the processes of mere mechanical motion—'the movement still whirring and whirling within me: / Like a running-down watch', as he put it in cancelled lines to the fourth canto of *Amours de Voyage* (*P* 642)—and so his more mundane version of transformation and change altogether lacks the teleological purposes with which such powers of metamorphosis are endowed by his American idealist counterpart. This debate between idealism and materialism is worked through in formal as well as thematic terms, with Clough's garrulous, prosaic idiom implying an air of randomness and vagary, as opposed to the suggestions of vatic meaning in Emerson's taut, aphoristic prose style. Though he generally admired *Amours de Voyage*, Emerson himself disliked what he called 'the baulking end or no end' of the poem, its structural anticlimax whereby Claude and Mary Trevellyn miss each other on their travels, and he was appalled that Clough appeared to 'waste such power on a broken dream'; such a sense of let-down, declared the American orator, was 'bad enough in life, and inadmissible in poetry'. Clough answered indirectly

---

[17] Emerson, *Nature, Addresses, and Lectures*, 33.
[18] Ralph Waldo Emerson, *Essays, First Series*, ed. Alfred R. Ferguson and Jean Ferguson Carr (Cambridge, Mass.: Harvard University Press, 1979), 179.   [19] Emerson, 'The Poet', 19.

by writing to Norton that he had 'always meant' to organize the poem in this way, 'and began it with the full intention of its ending so'.[20] Clough's firm if not slightly antagonistic response here indicates how the English-born poet saw himself not as Emerson's acolyte or 'mere follower', but as his transatlantic rival and interlocutor.[21]

So intense does this intellectual exchange between Clough and Emerson seem to be throughout *Amours de Voyage* that one wonders if the initial letters of the fictional protagonists, Claude and Eustace, might bear any relation to these real-life prototypes. One obvious model here would have been Lowell's most famous poem 'A Fable for Critics' (1848), which similarly uses a comparison between 'C' and 'E', in this case Carlyle and Emerson, to draw out similarities and dissimilarities between English and American styles of thought: 'C.'s the Titan, as shaggy of mind as of limb,— / E. the clear-eyed Olympian, rapid and slim.' Indeed, the methodology of 'A Fable for Critics' explicitly draws into its orbit transatlantic writers who are 'fit for a parallel': William Cullen Bryant is placed alongside James Thomson and William Cowper, for instance.[22] *Amours de Voyage* is, of course, not so explicitly metacritical in its orientation as Lowell's poem, and to identify the fictional Claude exclusively with the figure of the author himself would be misleading. Anthony Kenny points out that Claude is deliberately presented as superior in wealth and social status to Clough: 'he is, indeed, Clough's *bête noire*, the gentleman.'[23] Nevertheless, Clough's work, like Lowell's, does deliberately incorporate a metacritical dimension, one that seeks to transliterate into aesthetic form the dialogue with Transcendentalism that was exercising the English poet's imagination in the late 1840s, and it is possible that in his portrayal of Claude the poet was offering not so much a self-portrait as a self-caricature, a heightened version of how he imagined his Oxford manners and style of empiricism would have appeared to the idealist temperament of Emerson.

Clough completed the first version of *Amours de Voyage* in November 1849, just a year after Emerson had visited him in Oxford, and after they had taken a trip together to Paris. Clough's diaries of this period are suffused with a Transcendentalist idiom as he seeks to explore theoretically the possibilities of interaction between material circumstances and ideal forms. Kenny, the editor of these diaries, found the poet's 'pseudo-biblical rhetoric' of this period to be 'puzzling, since it appears bombastic and bathetic by turns'. But although this

[20] Clough, *Correspondence*, ii. 548, 551.

[21] 'The best part of Emersonianism is, it breeds the giant that destroys itself. Who wants to be any man's mere follower? lurks behind every page.' Walt Whitman, 'Emerson's Books, (the Shadows of Them)', in *Complete Poetry and Collected Prose*, ed. Justin Kaplan (New York: Library of America, 1982), 1055.

[22] J. R. Lowell, *Poems of James Russell Lowell* (London: Oxford University Press, 1912), 173, 179.

[23] Kenny, *Arthur Hugh Clough*, 173. On the critical tendency to 'identify Claude too closely with Clough', see also Robert Micklus, 'A Voyage of Juxtapositions: The Dynamic World of *Amours de Voyage*', *Victorian Poetry*, 18 (1980), 407.

kind of bombast was unfamiliar within English Victorian poetics, it is clearly an Emersonian rhetoric which Clough was trying on for size. 'Even music whose fugitive quick evanescent & renascent & ever variant profusion most repudiates common sense ignores matter of fact, transcends the sphere of actuality', he writes; and again, sleep has 'renewed me, readjusted me, harmonized me that I seem to myself as it were some instrument of happiest unity, some harp of perfect concord'. 'Harp of perfect concord', of course, is pure pastiche Emerson. Such effusiveness is, to be sure, uncharacteristic of English Victorian literature, but one of the strengths of *Amours de Voyage* lies precisely in the way it tests the principles of Emersonianism against the more disillusioning sense of historical contingency that Claude experiences as he travels through Europe. Kenny is in fact probably right to suggest it was this 'embarrassing' performance in the diaries, as he calls it, that 'liberated ... Clough's muse', since the impetus for both *The Bothie* (also begun in 1848) and *Amours de Voyage* resides not just in philosophical or theological scepticism but in a willingness to entertain an imaginative spirit of Transcendentalism, to bring the ironic milieu of the Old World into collision with the spiritual optimism of the New.[24]

In this sense, the punning title of *Amours de Voyage* signifies not just Claude's love affairs on his travels but also his love of voyaging, his paradoxical delight in unstable situations and in playing different ideas and possibilities off against each other. Some of the most incisive critical commentary on Clough in the nineteenth century came from the Irish critic, Edward Dowden, in his 1877 essay 'The Transcendental Movement and Literature', in which he noted his important friendship with Emerson and argued that Clough's poetry was 'true, upon the whole, to the transcendental lobe of his brain', whereas his prose gives 'expression to his enquiring intellect'. It is arguable that this 'enquiring intellect' also works its way into Clough's poetic style, which itself tends not infrequently towards the condition of prose, but Dowden's general point about how Clough's strength emerges from his textual mediation (rather than reconciliation) of opposites is a powerful insight: 'This susceptibility to various cross and counter influences, which must have created some of the sorrow of Clough's life as a man, is the source of the special virtue of his work as a poet.'[25] *Amours de Voyage* is also linked to American cultural agendas by its generally positive representation of the republican movement in Italy—Garibaldi's political cause is described as being assisted by 'a man, you know, who came from America' (*P* 109)—as well as by its satirical reflections on the complacent nature of English society. These satirical observations were actually more barbed in Clough's first draft of the poem:

> O happy Englishmen we! that so truly can quote from Lucretius ...
> O blessed government ours, blessed Empire of Purse and Policeman.

---

[24] Arthur Hugh Clough, *The Oxford Diaries of Arthur Hugh Clough*, ed. Anthony Kenny (Oxford: Clarendon Press, 1990), pp. lx, 252–3, lx–lxi.
[25] Thorpe, ed., *Clough: The Critical Heritage*, 297.

Fortunate islands of Order, Utopia of—breeches-pockets,
O happy England, and oh great glory of self-laudation.

(*P* 631)

It is not surprising that John Campbell, when he read this first version of *Amours de Voyage* in 1849, should have criticized Clough as 'Beppoish or Don Juanish', since there is a Byronic aspect here not only to Clough's sardonic humour but also to his deliberate secession, through the medium of a travel narrative, from the domestic niceties of his homeland.[26]

At the same time, *Amours de Voyage* ultimately preserves a sense of detachment from the rhetoric of Italian nationalism, with Claude preferring to retain his state of disaffiliation from the claims of both republican national identity and marriage. In this sense, we can infer how Clough remained sceptical about the conception, espoused by Emerson as much as Mazzini, of poetry as a force for national integration and cohesion. Although Clough described himself in a letter of 1848 as being 'accounted the wildest and most écervelé republican going', *Amours de Voyage* uses the idea of republicanism to interrogate the parameters and ideological limitations of English society without itself endorsing any republican ideal.[27] In the light of the success of republican movements in mainland Europe at this time, Victorian Britain looked back with concern to its own seventeenth-century conflict between the defenders of monarchy and the advocates of republicanism, an issue that was addressed in particular by Walter Bagehot, whom Clough encountered during his years teaching in London. Bagehot completed an M.A. at University Hall in 1848 and subsequently served on the college's Council; Clough later described him as 'the only genius-like kind of man to be found there'.[28] Bagehot's famous work *The English Constitution*, which first appeared serially between May 1865 and January 1867, argued that, although Cromwell's republic had been peremptorily cast aside, 'the spirit which culminated in him never sank again, never ceased to be a potent, though often a latent and volcanic, force in the country'. In its constitutional emphasis on the supremacy of the House of Commons, suggested Bagehot, Britain was in fact 'a disguised republic', a 'republic [which] has insinuated itself beneath the folds of a monarchy', where 'certain ancient feelings of deference' towards the Crown merely served to obfuscate the fact that real power now lay in other hands.[29]

While Clough was of course never so directly involved in politics as Bagehot, his letters to *The Balance* in 1846 on political economy, which he called 'a science most needful for Christian men' (*SP* 211), indicate clearly enough his interest in

---

[26] Thorpe, ed., *Clough: The Critical Heritage*, 121.
[27] Matthew Reynolds, *The Realms of Verse: English Poetry in a Time of Nation-Building* (Oxford: Oxford University Press, 2001), 128; Clough, *Correspondence*, i. 216.
[28] Stefanie Markovits, 'Arthur Hugh Clough, *Amours de Voyage*, and the Victorian Crisis of Action', *Nineteenth-Century Literature*, 55 (2001), 456; Clough, *Correspondence*, ii. 559.
[29] Walter Bagehot, *The English Constitution 1865–1867*, ed. Paul Smith (Cambridge: Cambridge University Press, 2001), 178, 185, 44, 192.

the constitutional welfare of Great Britain. He writes in January 1846 of how the inevitable repeal of the Corn Laws will be 'economically beneficial' (*SP* 208), although he expresses concern about how this radical change will affect 'the body politic ... in a spiritual sense' (*SP* 209). Similarly, he supports the theory of 'our mercantile practice', believing that it works well in nine cases out of ten, but also that it is 'an instrument demanding perpetual superintendence; a sort of ruthless inanimate steam-engine, which must have its driver always with it to keep it from doing mischief untold' (*SP* 223–4). Clough described Britain in 1846 as 'on eve, I suppose, of a change, which will make us, more than ever, the traders of the world'; but, unlike the more radical free-trader Richard Cobden, he was anxious that this 'commercial spirit' should be harmonized with the 'ancestral feeling of service owed and duty to be done to the country', a quality he deemed characteristic of 'our great landholders' (*SP* 225). This concern to incorporate the new 'spirit of trade' (*SP* 225) within the traditional structures of English society suggests the way in which Clough's life and work were balanced precariously between the democratic, commercial instincts of American progressives like Emerson on the one hand and more conservative English social assumptions on the other. Although he was attracted towards the idea of an Atlantic republic, Clough tended to imagine this not so much in a positive as in a contradictory fashion, a form of double exposure, where the more elastic virtues of modernity superimposed themselves upon the established structures of the old order.

ANTI-ANGLICANISM: THE DIALOGUE WITH MATTHEW ARNOLD

The dynamic of estrangement that impels *Amours de Voyage* and Clough's later poetry effectively renders moot the received notion, promoted by Matthew Arnold and others, that Clough was ultimately a failure because he was too prickly and self-conscious to reconcile himself to the tranquil virtues of English culture. Clough was four years older than Arnold, but the two knew each other not only at Oxford but also at Rugby School, where Clough was also first exposed to the 'Broad Church' influences of the headmaster, Thomas Arnold. Dr Arnold's insistence on adducing historical analogies between classical civilization and nineteenth-century England was reworked by his eldest son, the first Professor of Poetry at Oxford to lecture in English rather than Latin, into an emphasis on the poetic continuities of Anglican culture; but these were both positions with which the more schismatically inclined Clough was later to take issue.[30] This makes it all the more unfortunate that, as Wendell V. Harris noted, Arnold's

---

[30] R. A. Forsyth, ' "The Buried Life"—The Contrasting Views of Arnold and Clough in the Context of Dr. Arnold's Historiography', *ELH*, 35 (1968), 221–2; Morris Dickstein, *Double Agent: The Critic and Society* (New York: Oxford University Press, 1992), 12.

elegy 'Thyrsis', written in 1866, has established the perspective from which this Arnold–Clough relationship has traditionally been seen.[31] 'Thyrsis' represents Clough as a congenital malcontent, a 'Too quick despairer', and it blends its classical motifs ('the Dorian strain') with a pastoral image of the countryside around Oxford, imagining Clough still sauntering in the narrator's company under 'the mild canopy of English air'. Arnold's poem consequently attempts to reincorporate Clough within this Oxford landscape he is depicted as having ill-advisedly abandoned:

> And this rude Cumner ground,
> Its fir-topped Hurst, its farms, its quiet fields,
> Here cam'st thou in thy jocund youthful time,
> Here was thine height of strength, thy golden prime!

Arnold associates Clough's 'golden prime' with the promise of his youth and perhaps with his early work *The Bothie*, which Clough subtitled 'a long-vacation pastoral' (*P* 44). Consequently, Arnold dismisses the poetry Clough later produced as wanting in sweetness and light:

> What though the music of thy rustic flute
> Kept not for long its happy, country tone;
>   Lost it too soon, and learnt a stormy note
> Of men contention-tossed, of men who groan,
>   Which tasked thy pipe too sore, and tired thy throat—
> It failed, and thou wast mute![32]

Clough, however, was not 'mute' after he left Oxford; he simply wrote poetry very different from the kind championed by Arnold. In a letter to Clough of February 1848, Arnold declared that he felt 'A growing sense of the deficiency of the *beautiful* in your poems, and of this alone as being properly *poetical* as distinguished from rhetorical, devotional or metaphysical'. This is the Arnoldian aesthetic in a nutshell: the formalist qualities of poetry are said to enjoy a symbiotic relationship with nature, while the excessively discursive qualities of allegory and other types of interpretative theory are said to lack 'sensuousness', so that Arnold can criticize Clough's poetry ultimately as 'not *natural*'. Arnold, of course, lamented the advent of modernity in general: he wrote to Clough in September 1849 about the deplorable proliferation of 'newspapers' and the growth of 'cities', and, as Morris Dickstein has observed, through his subsequent influence on F. R. Leavis in England and Lionel Trilling in the United States, Arnold 'did much to establish the modernist humanist critique of industrial society' that was a powerful force in twentieth-century literary criticism and

---

[31] Harris, *Arthur Hugh Clough*, 139.
[32] Matthew Arnold, *The Poems of Matthew Arnold*, ed. Kenneth Allott (London: Longmans, 1965), 498–508.

pedagogy.[33] Arnold's hostility towards American nonconformity emerged clearly in 1853, when he wrote to Clough in Massachusetts expressing his aversion to that 'brazen female' Margaret Fuller, to the 'woman Stowe' who 'by her picture must be a Gorgon', and to 'other female dogs of Boston'. In a phrase as notable for its assumptions about gender as for its conservatism, Arnold in this same letter deplored the 'absence of men of any culture in America'. Clough himself always remained ambivalent about the more progressive aspects of American culture, as we have seen, but whereas his works express that ambivalence by engaging in dialogue with scenes of modernity, Arnold's neoclassical poetry attempts to shut out contemporary landscapes altogether. Writing in 1848 of *The Bothie*, Arnold voiced antipathy to the expression of 'Zeit Geist' in Clough's poem, declaring that he did not want to 'be sucked for an hour even into the Time Stream', and remarking, perceptively, that Clough's work seemed 'more American than English'.[34] Clough, for his part, when he was in the United States wrote an acerbic critique of Arnold's poems for the *North American Review*, suggesting that Arnold needed to stop 'turning and twisting his eyes, in the hope of seeing things as Homer, Sophocles, Virgil, or Milton saw them', and that he should look instead at 'the object' itself (*SP* 160).

Such philosophical disagreements over the nature of art were not uncommon in the nineteenth century, of course, but because of the biographical associations and personal relationship between Arnold and Clough there has been a subsequent critical tendency to see these poets as occupying different positions along a continuous spectrum, though in fact from 1848 onwards they were more like intellectual enemies.[35] Whereas Arnold idealized the charms of neoclassical unity—praising Sophocles for the way he 'saw life steadily, and saw it whole'—the genius of Clough involved a more explicit focus upon the edgy characteristics of 'self-irony', the kind of ontological division and estrangement that, as Masao Miyoshi has noted, has attracted other poetic exiles from Byron to T. S. Eliot.[36] By contrast, Robindra Kumer Biswas, who argued that there is 'no real evidence to indicate that the New World made any decisive impact' on Clough, reproduced unconsciously the implicit cultural nationalism of Arnold's critical perspective by going on to indict Clough's poetry on the grounds that the

---

[33] Dickstein, *Double Agent*, 16.

[34] Arnold, *Letters of Matthew Arnold to Arthur Hugh Clough*, 66, 98–9, 111, 132–3, 95.

[35] On the 'sexual subtext' in the friendship between Arnold and Clough, see Joseph Bristow, ' "Love, let us be true to one another": Matthew Arnold, Arthur Hugh Clough, and "our Aqueous Ages" ', *Literature and History*, 3rd ser., 4/1 (Spring 1995), 27–49. Bristow notes that Arnold addressed Clough in a letter of 1848 as 'my love', and he argues convincingly that an intense 'same-sex comradeship', fuelled by emotional and sexual repression, governed the course of their ultimately antagonistic relationship. On the intellectual disagreements between Arnold and Clough, see E. Warwick Slinn, *Victorian Poetry as Cultural Critique: The Politics of Performative Language* (Charlottesville, Va.: University Press of Virginia, 2003), 96.

[36] 'To a Friend', in *Poems of Matthew Arnold*, 105; Masao Miyoshi, 'Clough's Poems of Self-Irony', *Studies in English Literature*, 5 (1965), 691–704.

reader finds in his work 'no clear metaphysic, no clear moral hierarchy'.[37] It is, however, precisely this absence of 'clear ... hierarchy' which attests to the American dimension within Clough's work, the dimension which Anglocentric critics of Biswas's kind have always sought to occlude. Clough, like Walt Whitman, was more interested in bringing together heterogeneous categories, in mixing things up; after Norton had sent him a copy of *Leaves of Grass* in 1856, Clough wrote to Emerson in 1856 that he found Whitman's book 'remarkable', though he added that he wondered if it were not 'a Waste of power and observation—The tree is tapped, and not left to bear flower and fruit in perfect form as it should'.[38] Clough's own work is positioned somewhere between what he saw as Whitman's original but amorphous qualities and Arnold's excessively hermetic version of formalism. In this light, it is not surprising that Arnold should have refused to write a prefatory memoir to the posthumous collection of Clough's poems, or that he should have tried to represent his old schoolfriend's death as somehow self-inflicted, a just recompense for infringing the native code of honour: 'I cannot say his death took me altogether by surprise,' Arnold wrote to Clough's widow in 1868, 'I had long a foreboding something was deeply wrong with him.'[39]

This conflict between what one might call the English Clough and the American Clough is mirrored in the struggle after his death between his widow, Blanche, and Charles Eliot Norton over editorial rights to Clough's poetry. As we have seen, James Russell Lowell was responsible for first publishing *Amours de Voyage* in the United States, and Norton subsequently suggested that a volume of Clough's poems should be edited jointly by himself and Lowell. Clough himself was keen on this idea, partly for financial reasons, the same motivation that had induced him to place a translation of Plutarch's *Lives* with the Boston company Little, Brown, who brought out the book in 1855; like many before and after him, Clough found that the commercial capacity of the United States to grease the wheels of art and scholarship was not something to be scorned too lightly. However, the outbreak of the American Civil War unavoidably delayed the plans of Lowell and Norton for an edition of Clough's poems, and after the latter's early death in 1861, Blanche became anxious to retain control over her husband's posthumous reputation. Clough's widow insisted that the American edition, now to be edited by Norton alone, be delayed until hers had appeared; consequently, the English version was published by Macmillan in July 1862, the American by Ticknor and Fields in September of that year. But, as P. G. Scott has argued, the edition produced by Norton is much the more reliable, having been prepared by a professional scholar rather than an amateur attempting to protect what she took to be Clough's conventional standing in Britain. Characteristically, Mrs Clough

---

[37] Robindra Kumar Biswas, *Arthur Hugh Clough: Towards a Reconsideration* (Oxford: Clarendon Press, 1972), 447, 381. See also Dorothy Deering, 'The Antithetical Poetics of Arnold and Clough', *Victorian Poetry*, 16 (1978), 16–31.   [38] Clough, *Correspondence*, ii. 520.
[39] Arnold, *Letters to Clough*, 163.

amended her husband's phrase 'stupid old England', in *Amours de Voyage*, to the more emollient 'poor foolish England'. She also omitted altogether 'In the Great Metropolis', with its suggestion that 'The devil take the hindmost' is the motto of English life, and she similarly chose to eliminate 'Natura Naturans', in which the narrator fantasizes about a female stranger in a railway car. Blanche left out the latter poem, she wrote to Norton, simply because it 'is abhorrent to me', and she persuaded Norton to do likewise.[40]

Part of the dissatisfaction with Clough in terms of his critical reputation in England can be attributed to (conscious or unconscious) reactions to his status as a schismatic poet, that is to say one who, *contra* Arnold, expressed little faith in the continuities of Anglican culture. Edmund Gosse's view in 1921 of Clough as 'a derelict schooner', someone for whom life 'all petered out', replicates this view of him as in some sense a self-indulgent sceptic whose failure to accommodate himself to the heartfelt genius of his native culture contributed to his own downfall.[41] One of the most interesting things about Clough's work, however, is precisely the way he uses the American dimensions of his experience to critique inherited assumptions. When he returned to London in July 1853, Clough wrote in a letter to Norton about his 'first *re*impression' of England, and indeed much of his poetry could be said to be about reimpressions, the art of doubling up, of reconceiving old ideas and situations within a new frame. In this 1853 letter, Clough observed that he liked 'America all the better for the comparison with England on my return', adding that he now believed that Norton was 'more right than I was willing to admit, about the position of the poorer classes here'.[42] This kind of 'comparison' between England and America also informs Clough's own critical work, going back to his lectures on English literature at University College, London, in the early 1850s, in which he criticized Wordsworth for his 'spirit of withdrawal and seclusion' (*SP* 119) and for his evasion of the modern industrial world. In another London lecture on the development of English literature, given in 1852, Clough specifically rejected the idea of appropriating a national literary tradition to inculcate a particular notion of moral character, arguing that the English literary heritage was made up of 'various and discordant voices', 'multifarious and contradictory impulses' (*SP* 141), and that to extrapolate from it a simple pedagogical directive would be drastically to homogenize and oversimplify. Such radical views on the restrictive nature and ideological blindspots of national literary canons are more characteristic of our own day than of mid-Victorian Britain. It was only a few years after Clough's lecture, in 1861, that Francis Palgrave's *Golden Treasury of Best Songs and Lyrical Poems in the English Language* appeared, with its explicit

---

[40] P. G. Scott, 'A. H. Clough's *Poems* (1862): The English and American Editions', *Harvard Library Bulletin*, 20/3 (July 1972), 328, 333; Chorley, *Arthur Hugh Clough*, 263.

[41] Edmund Gosse, *Books on the Table* (London: Heinemann, 1921), 132, 130.

[42] Clough, *Correspondence*, ii. 455.

ambition to produce 'a true national anthology' expressing a patriotic spirit of longevity across the centuries of English culture, and, as if to emphasize the institutional networks against which Clough was competing, it was Palgrave to whom Clough's widow turned for a prefatory memoir to her edition of her husband's poems after Arnold had declined to perform this service.[43]

There is an obvious correlation between Clough's sense of his own poetry as being in an interrogative relation to English literary traditions and what was in many ways the central philosophical dilemma of his life: the status of the Church of England, and the awkward relationship between this Established Church and individual conscience. Coming under the influence of German 'higher criticism' as expounded in the treatises of David Friedrich Strauss, Clough decided that Christianity embodied a mythic rather than a positivistic value, which was why he declined in 1848 to offer allegiance to the Articles of Faith.[44] At that time, of course, all dons at Oxford and Cambridge were obliged to be at least nominal members of the Church of England, so Clough's resignation of his Oxford fellowship also betokened a symbolic secession from the tenets of English national culture. In the wake of the 1832 Great Reform Bill, as Philip Davis has observed, the 1840s and 1850s in Britain were a time when the idea of reform seemed generally to be in the air, and the inevitable social conflicts that ensued were often played out with explicit reference back to the theological disputes of three centuries earlier. J. A. Froude, who like Clough was obliged to resign his Oxford fellowship after the publication of his book *The Nemesis of Faith* in 1849, subsequently produced the first great history of the English Reformation in twelve volumes between 1856 and 1870, as if to align his own personal history with a narrative of the English schismatic past.[45] As a veteran of Oxford doctrinal controversies, Clough corresponded with Froude when the latter resigned his post at Exeter College, Oxford; he also remarked in an 1858 letter to Charles Eliot Norton that he had been reading the third and fourth volumes of Froude's *History*, and of how they 'give one the sense of probable correctness'.[46]

National unity, whether of the religious or the literary kind, was, therefore, a deeply problematic category so far as Clough was concerned, particularly after his own explicit rejection of Anglican doctrine in 1848. Rather than acquiescing in any form of establishment or institutional settlement, Clough's imagination was inspired by the processes of secession and traversal, the movement from a known world to a more dangerous, unknown one. One of his shorter poems pays tribute to transatlantic explorers such as Columbus, Cabot, and Raleigh, acknowledging that it is hard enough to cross the Atlantic even when you are sure, as they heroically were not, that there is something on the other side (*P* 340–1). Another

[43] Collini, *Public Moralists*, 354.
[44] Anthony Kenny, *God and Two Poets: Arthur Hugh Clough and Gerard Manley Hopkins* (London: Sidgwick & Jackson, 1988), 74.
[45] Philip Davis, *The Victorians* (Oxford: Oxford University Press, 2002), 102.
[46] Clough, *Correspondence*, i. 246–7; ii. 547.

describes how human perceptions of time and space seem to alter as the narrator on board a boat in motion looks down at the water:

> Still as we go the things I see
> E'en as I see them, cease to be;
> Their angles swerve, and with the boat
> The whole perspective seems to float.

(P 354)

This is a poetry of radical mutability, where all stable assurances have been suspended. For Clough, it is the voyage, and in particular this process of transatlantic displacement, which reilluminates the inherently provisional quality of all fixed, habitual categories. In one of his 'Letters of Parepidemus', composed on board the *Canada* returning from America to England in 1853, Clough wrote: 'It is curious how soon and how completely I have become perfectly reconciled to the circumstances of this little life, this voyage. I could easily conceive that to the end of my threescore and ten I should go on day upon day traversing the salt water' *(SP 321)*. On the other side of the sheet on which this letter was written, Clough drafted the first stanza of 'Where lies the land to which the ship would go', one of the few poems he actually composed on his American expedition. With its emphasis upon mobility and traversal rather than any specific destination, this poem emphasizes again how the United States for Clough became associated with a site of alterity, a scene of figurative displacement.

As Clough himself noted in his Parepidemus letter, the metaphor of life as a voyage is, in itself, commonplace enough; but it is noticeable how in his poetry this idea is expanded to encompass motifs of hazard, chance meetings, and spatial dislocations. At the end of *The Bothie*, Philip and Elspie marry and emigrate—'they rounded the sphere to New Zealand' *(P 93)*—with their act of conscious exile acting as a thematic corollary to the formal structures of allegory which are also foregrounded in this poem. *The Bothie*, that is to say, rotates upon an axis of belatedness: it is a classical pastoral updated to nineteenth-century Scotland, couched in a style which deliberately cites intertextual antecedents—'One day sauntering "long and listless," as Tennyson has it' *(P 50)*—as if to emphasize its own lack of purchase upon a spirit of originality or authenticity. This is also why the framework of allegory—heavily discussed in the ninth section of the poem, in which all kinds of biblical parallels are adduced and commented upon—works in tandem with the discourse of emigration, since both processes are predicated upon the transference of a primary into a secondary object.[47] *The Bothie* also argues with the Coleridgean or Emersonian belief in analogical correspondences within nature—the idea of a 'wondrous Analogy' between a 'Woman' and 'a Cathedral' is openly questioned

---

[47] On allegory in *The Bothie*, see Isobel Armstrong, *Victorian Poetry: Poetry, Poetics and Politics* (London: Routledge, 1993), 187–92.

by Hobbes in section 5, for example (*P* 73)—so that the poem, rather than rendering objects and ideas synonymous with each other, finds its intellectual challenge in negotiating spaces between them. This is the basis of what Robert Crawford has called the poem's 'stylish irregularity', whose impetus derives, as the Tutor explains to Philip in section 4, from 'crossings and counter-crossings / Hard to connect with each other correctly, and hard to decipher' (*P* 69).[48] *The Bothie* was republished in Cambridge, Massachusetts, the year after its first English publication, and as Charles Eliot Norton wrote in 1862, 'it may be safely asserted that its merit was more deeply felt and more generously acknowledged by American than by English readers'.[49] Partly this was because, as Clough wrote to Emerson in February 1849, the English tended to find the work, with its oblique treatments of sexual desire and radical politics, to be 'indecent and profane, immoral and (!) Communistic!'; but it was also because English Victorians such as Charles Kingsley reacted against the intellectualized conception of the poetic act which this poem adumbrates.[50] *The Bothie* is concerned less with empirical narrative than with metanarrative, less with the telling of a story than with self-conscious reflections on how meaning and interpretation can be generated. Kingsley called *The Bothie* 'confused', but the poem was a great success among Emerson's circle in New England, where the intertwining of poetic forms with abstract discursive formations derived from religious or other theoretical sources was a more usual phenomenon.[51]

The figure of the voyage also dominates *Mari Magno, or Tales on Board*, Clough's last extended work, one which is surprisingly little known today, even though it was widely regarded in the nineteenth century as his most significant achievement. It appeared only posthumously, with Clough dictating parts of the poem to Blanche right up until the time of his death.[52] The title is taken from Lucretius, 'on a swelling sea', and the overall structure is not unlike that of *The Canterbury Tales* in that it comprises an interlinked series of narratives related by passengers on board a steamer over the six successive nights of an Atlantic crossing. Clough's voyagers are en route to the secular city of Boston rather than Chaucer's Canterbury, but there are similar elements of randomness in the organization of the poems, a randomness which Clough, like Chaucer, systematically plays off against the teleologies of epic quest and religious pilgrimage. For example, 'The American's Tale; or Juxtaposition' is set 'in a huge American hotel' (*P* 404), where a girl happens to end up by mistake in a man's bed, a chance encounter which leads ultimately to love and a happy marriage. There is an implicit philosophical dialogue here with the notion of

[48] Robert Crawford, *The Modern Poet: Poetry, Academia, and Knowledge since the 1750s* (Oxford: Oxford University Press, 2001), 130.
[49] Thorpe, ed., *Clough: The Critical Heritage*, 127. Norton's appraisal originally appeared in *Atlantic Monthly*, 9 (April 1862), 463–9.   [50] Clough, *Correspondence*, i. 240.
[51] Thorpe, ed., *Clough: The Critical Heritage*, 37.
[52] Biswas, *Arthur Hugh Clough*, 462; Kenny, *Arthur Hugh Clough*, 283.

love as an eternal Platonic category, a '*Superior Order*' (*P* 405), an idea that the author demystifies by stressing the ironic affiliation of romance with more mundane aspects of 'juxtaposition'. This latter conception he associates, here as elsewhere, with the profane world of American modernity. Many of these *Mari Magno* poems deal in edgy fashion with human sexuality, a topic which emerges in this sequence in tortuous rather than straightforwardly romantic ways. For instance, 'The Clergyman's Second Tale', which caused Clough to break down sobbing when he read it aloud to Tennyson, concerns an Oxford college fellow who seduces a Scottish orphan, plans to marry her, but then finds her family has sent her away to South Australia to bring up their child.[53]

It is easy enough from this example to see why Clough's widow was uncomfortable with the representations of amorphous, erratic sexuality in his poetry, but easy as well to see why John Addington Symonds admired it. Symonds's first article on Clough was published in *Cornhill Magazine* in October 1866, and he followed this up with another piece for the *Fortnightly Review* in December 1868. These essays helped set a tone for a general re-evaluation of Clough's work in the late nineteenth century, since Symonds was above all interested in valorizing Clough as a sceptical poet, one for whom sexual and religious doubts were at some level commensurate. Later, Symonds was to write a pioneering study of Whitman as a gay poet, but in 1868 he chose to focus on poems such as *Dipsychus* in order to praise the 'wholly undogmatic character' of Clough's religious attitude.[54] *Dipsychus* was first published posthumously in 1865; although it had been written in Venice back in the autumn of 1850, the hesitant Mrs Clough had hitherto regarded it as 'too unfinished to be published among his poems' (*P* 681). This work, which is twofold in form as well as in content, features a dialogue between 'Spirit' and Dipsychus, a word that Clough would doubtless have known from its use in the Epistle of St James in the New Testament: 'A double minded man is unstable in all his ways.'[55] In Clough's poem, this instability consists of religious anxieties as well as sexual insecurities, with the narrative eschewing the more comfortable conception of a conversation between two separate individuals in favour of a situation where the boundaries of identity itself become blurred.[56] This is partly why Clough chooses to set the poem in Venice, the traditional crossing point between East and West; as in *Mari Magno*, his poems are attracted compulsively to sites of transposition and exchange. Dealing as it does with Venetian prostitutes, *Dipsychus* also deliberately evokes again the ghost of the sexual rebel Byron, with the Venetian Lido being punningly described here as 'The ground which Byron used to ride on' (*P* 247).

---

[53] Biswas, *Arthur Hugh Clough*, 469.   [54] Thorpe, ed., *Clough: The Critical Heritage*, 224.
[55] Kenny, *God and Two Poets*, 139.
[56] On the way in which fragmentation in *Dipsychus* involves 'dialogism rather than dialogue', see Slinn, *Victorian Poetry as Cultural Critique*, 113.

Whereas Arnold cherished ideals of continuity and steadiness, then, Clough's work addresses a more divided state, both psychologically and politically. He mentioned in a diary entry for 1839 'my daily trespasses and double mindedness', but, as Charles Eliot Norton noted, it was this sense of inherent doubleness that allowed him in later life to avoid the English vices of 'insular narrowness' and 'hereditary prejudices'. The charges levelled against Clough of being self-indulgent and insufficiently 'manly', as Charles Kingsley complained in 1849, interestingly anticipate the kinds of criticism made against Decadent writers later in the nineteenth century, and in many ways it makes more sense to consider Clough within an intellectual framework of aestheticism than of Victorian moralism.[57] There are, in fact, various historical contexts linking Clough with aestheticism, broadly conceived. William M. Rossetti reviewed *The Bothie* in the first issue of *The Germ*, the Pre-Raphaelite magazine launched in January 1850, remarking in particular on Clough's ability to blend idiosyncratic 'individuality' with an air of classic, statuesque dignity by reviving the Homeric method of always defining a character in terms of the same attributes.[58] Clough himself mentioned the Pre-Raphaelite paintings at Oxford in a letter to Norton of 25 June 1858, and, writing again to Norton two years later, he admitted to being a 'little disappointed' with a picture of Holman Hunt, which he described as 'a marvellous piece of workmanship, but too much "modelled" I think'.[59]

There are, of course, obvious differences of emphasis between Clough and aestheticism; Swinburne, for example, dismissed Clough as a 'bad poet' on the grounds that his rhetoric was too prosaic and colloquial, insufficiently attentive to the more sensual qualities of language and imagery.[60] Nevertheless, it is equally plausible to suggest that had Clough lived out his three score years and ten and died in the 1890s, his intellectual affiliations with the Aesthetic Movement would have become more apparent. In 1908, Stopford A. Brooke published *Four Poets: A Study of Clough, Arnold, Rossetti and Morris*, which understood Clough's interest in paradox and antithesis to anticipate the stylistic characteristics of writers later in the nineteenth century, while what Anthony H. Harrison has called the 'dialectic of desire and renunciation' in the work of Christina Rossetti could apply equally to Clough, who frames his dramas of sexuality and loss in a less melodramatic but no less elegiac fashion.[61] Murray Pittock has also commented on the links between Clough and Ernest Dowson, seeing them as both devoted to an aesthetic of valediction, a melancholic loss of faith, while Tom Paulin has suggested that poems such as *Amours de Voyage* and *Dipsychus* anticipate the works of Oscar Wilde in their iconoclastic rejection of Victorian conceptions of morality and duty and their fascination instead with

[57] Clough, *Oxford Diaries*, 106; Thorpe, ed., *Clough: The Critical Heritage*, 129, 38.
[58] Chorley, *Arthur Hugh Clough*, 151–2.   [59] Clough, *Correspondence*, ii. 552, 576.
[60] Thorpe, ed., *Clough: The Critical Heritage*, 340.
[61] Anthony H. Harrison, *Christina Rossetti in Context* (Brighton: Harvester Press, 1988), 92.

a heterodox sexual underworld.[62] There are elements of truth in all of these interpretations, although it is important not to turn Clough into an excessively hermetic or precious poet of the Dowson kind. Indeed, one of the remarkable and innovative features of his work, particularly in *Amours de Voyage* and *Mari Magno*, is its capacity to bring together traditional epic forms with a more colloquial, conversational idiom, a stylistic innovation which is as radical, in its own way, as Whitman's popularization and democratization of the epic genre in *Leaves of Grass*.

In a revisionist account of late Victorian culture, Dennis Denisoff has suggested that the British Aesthetic Movement, which was at its most visible between 1880 and 1895, is normally understood too narrowly in critical terms. His argument is that the dimensions of this Aesthetic Movement should be extended both chronologically and conceptually, to embrace not only intellectual antecedents such as Swinburne and Tennyson, who were active in the 1860s, but also popular figures like W. S. Gilbert, who helped to bring Walter Pater's terminology of sexual 'deviance' more into the cultural mainstream. As Max Beerbohm observed, Gilbert and Sullivan's comic opera *Patience* (1881), with its caricature of Oscar Wilde as Bunthorne, offered a crucial public space for the burlesque representation of the Aesthetic Movement, belittling it but also, by bringing it to general notice, maintaining its public momentum. In this sense, according to Denisoff, parody became a crucial component of aestheticism in the last few decades of the nineteenth century, a way of opening out previously closeted questions of sexual ambiguity among the middle classes, so that these issues became more widely recognizable and 'were given room to develop'. Gilbert's own play *Topsyturvydom* (1874) similarly explored the malleability of gender roles and their potential reversibility within the formal charade of society.[63]

During the period between 1840 and 1870, as Howard J. Booth has emphasized, the notion that a person could be said to have a distinct 'sexuality' linked to his or her sense of integrity and identity was an unfamiliar idea; such distinct identifications were only to become consolidated psychoanalytically around the turn of the twentieth century.[64] But it is this conception of division that becomes the controlling force in Clough's work, a division that is expressed not just psychologically, in terms of a split personality, but also through his poetic conjunctions of epic and mock-epic, romance and burlesque. It is this kind of division, moreover, that allows space for the ironic reversals which characterize Clough's artistic style. *Amours de Voyage*, with its incongruous *mélange* of high

---

[62] Murray Pittock, 'Dowson and Clough', *Notes and Queries*, NS 34 (1987), 501–2; Tom Paulin, *Minotaur: Poetry and the Nation State* (London: Faber, 1992), 74.

[63] Dennis Denisoff, *Aestheticism and Sexual Parody, 1840–1940* (Cambridge: Cambridge University Press, 2001), 56–9, 9.

[64] Howard J. Booth, 'Male Sexuality, Religion and the Problem of Action: John Addington Symonds on Arthur Hugh Clough', in *Masculinity and Spirituality in Victorian Culture*, ed. Andrew Bradstock, Sean Gill, Anne Hogan, and Sue Morgan (Basingstoke: Macmillan, 2000), 116.

and low cultures, is not entirely unlike the early prototype of a Gilbert and Sullivan opera, and it is this idiom of hybridity that has also helped ensure the poem's marginal status within the canon of English literature. As an honorary 'Yankee' from first to last, Clough follows the American democratic principle of refusing to keep established aesthetic or social hierarchies in their place.

By the time of Clough's death in 1861, the notion of schism within a North American context had come to signify not the old rift between America and Britain but the American Civil War between its Northern and Southern states. Goldwin Smith, an enlightened liberal who was a university contemporary and friend of Clough's and Regius Professor of Modern History at Oxford before his move to Cornell in 1868, wrote a paper in 1887 on what he called 'The Schism in the Anglo-Saxon Race', suggesting that these two independent nations still comprised 'one people' in terms of 'blood and character, language, religion, institutions, laws and interests'. Smith liked to imagine the constitutional liberalism of the United States as a bulwark against the spread of aristocratic and Tory influences in England; but what he manifestly failed to recognize was how much the make-up of the United States itself had changed during the course of the nineteenth century. In particular, Smith became aggrieved at the extent of American sympathies for Irish nationalism, going so far as to urge Americans to 'give up gratifying their hatred of England by fomenting disorder in Ireland', and trying to draw attention instead to the Whig legacy of freedom which he believed England and America shared.[65] But immigration rates to America in the nineteenth century were much higher from Ireland than from Great Britain, with the result that political links between Ireland (and other European countries) and the USA grew stronger as those between Britain and the USA became more attenuated. In an 1883 letter to celebrate the 333rd anniversary of Santa Fé, Walt Whitman drew attention to the fact that the cultural inheritance of the United States had not been 'fashion'd from the British Islands only', and, in the light of this Whitmanian insistence on America as a mosaic of different languages and buried cultures, Smith's notion of Anglo-Saxon schism and of the United States as a republican alternative to British culture began to seem increasingly anachronistic.[66]

Clough's intellectual dialogue with Emerson, then, took place in the ante-bellum context of their mutual concerns about the problematic nature of transcendence and the status of religious freedom in what seemed to them like an increasingly materialistic age. These were concerns they shared with figures like

---

[65] Goldwin Smith, 'The Schism in the Anglo-Saxon Race', in *Canadian Leaves: History, Art, Science, Literature, Commerce. A Series of Papers Read before the Canadian Club of New York*, ed. G. M. Fairchild jun. (New York, 1887), 57, 54.

[66] Werner Sollors, 'Introduction: After the Culture Wars; or, From "English Only" to "English Plus"', in *Multilingual America: Transnationalism, Ethnicity, and the Languages of American Literature*, ed. Werner Sollors (New York: New York University Press–Longfellow Institute, 1998), 1.

Thomas Carlyle, anxieties which were characteristic of the mid-Victorian age on both sides of the Atlantic. Clough, however, died in the early months of a Civil War which was to reorient debates about freedom in a less abstract direction and which was to make Emerson's yearnings for spiritual independence seem less immediately pressing. After Clough's death, Emerson wrote to his widow recalling how on their first meeting in 1848 his 'intellectuality,—in my limited acquaintance in London, seemed so little English,—that I wrote home to my friends that I had found in London, the best American'.[67] What it meant to be an American in 1848, however, was not quite the same as what it meant in the years after 1862, when Clough died. By the end of the nineteenth century, Clough's American qualities appeared to reside less in his status as an honorary New England idealist than in his work's peculiar openness to the contingencies of mass culture, to the pressures of transatlantic commerce, through which disjunctive and delocalized versions of aestheticism began to invade the English cultural scene.

[67] Clough, *Correspondence*, ii. 611.

5

Aestheticism, Americanization, and Empire

THE AESTHETIC MOVEMENT'S TRANSATLANTIC HORIZONS

By the 1890s, the main focus of Atlantic republicanism in Britain had shifted, so that its front line was no longer a classical theory of democratic representation but the increasing power and importance of the transatlantic marketplace. This power threatened to usurp by more circuitous means the stable social hierarchies of Victorian Britain. In this sense, the interrelationship of the Aesthetic Movement with aspects of parody and burlesque, such as we see foreshadowed in Clough's work, brings into question the influence of America on *fin de siècle* English culture more generally. The idea of artistic 'decadence', which caused a moral panic in Britain at the end of the nineteenth century, has more traditionally been linked to the supposedly pernicious influence of France: the iconoclasm of poets such as Laforgue and Verlaine, the voyeuristic fascination with urban corruption in novelists such as Zola, the proximity of Paris itself as a scene of sexual licence for the English aristocracy. It is arguable, though, that a more widespread and ultimately more significant challenge to the organization of British society emanated from across the Atlantic, with the democratizing spectre of a 'low' popular idiom, of the kind that we see in embryonic form in Clough's colloquial style of verse, setting itself in opposition to more conservative patterns of culture. Although, as we have seen, the word 'Americanization' can be traced back to the 1830s, its first citation in the *Oxford English Dictionary* is taken from an issue of the London *Times* in April 1860, declaring how 'this Americanization is represented to us as the greatest of calamities'; another entry, from *Pall Mall* of 23 November 1882, talks sniffily about 'the partial Americanization of English journalism', suggesting how the term had become increasingly commonplace in London by the second half of the nineteenth century. Benjamin Disraeli in 1866 expressed his fear that 'if a dominant multitude were to succeed in bringing the land of England into the condition of the land of America ... England, from being a first-rate Kingdom, would become a third-rate Republic', and such anxieties epitomized the attitude at this time of the English Establishment, for whom the growing global influence of America represented a threat to their own privileged hold on the pyramidal structure of British life.[1]

Jennifer DeVere Brody has pointed out how the phrase 'splendid isolation' was in common political usage in England around the mid-1890s, when it was generally feared that hybridity in its various forms might bring about the fragmentation of a civilized English identity. As Brody remarked, the idea of race was closely linked to the idea of national identity in the minds of many Victorian intellectuals, and the increased presence of African Americans in Britain after the passage of the US Fugitive Slave Act in 1850 would have reinforced a reactive sense among many English communities that their security and cohesion depended upon a capacity to keep at bay American blacks no less than Irish Catholics.[2] The key imperative here was control over any alien force which was perceived as a threat to native authority. David Cannadine has argued that Britain conceived of its empire in the nineteenth century in terms of homogeneity and sameness, with the hierarchical class systems in overseas outposts such as India or Canada mirroring those in the domestic arena; the United States, however, manifestly did not fit into this imperial structure, as Anthony Trollope observed in 1873 when he contrasted the social organization of Britain with that of the more egalitarian United States and found, reassuringly, that 'the colonies are rather a repetition of England than an imitation of America'.[3]

Much British imperial discourse in the late nineteenth century involved an attempt to impose homogeneity and 'disciplined order' on widely disparate locations, a form of standardization which apologists for empire frequently associated with advances in travel and communication.[4] 'Our country is the British Empire,' wrote Royal Statistical Society fellow Ernest Williams in an 1898 issue of the imperialist weekly, *Outlook*: 'It is not fanciful to say that an Englishman, leaving Yorkshire for Ontario or New South Wales, does not abandon his own country more than he would by going from Yorkshire to Somersetshire.'[5] Indeed, as Clough's friend J. A. Froude observed, this 'feeling of identity', the sense of being linked by an indissoluble cord to the motherland,

---

[1] David Dimbleby and David Reynolds, *An Ocean Apart: The Relationship between Britain and America in the Twentieth Century* (London: Hodder & Stoughton–BBC, 1988), 20.

[2] Jennifer DeVere Brody, *Impossible Purities: Blackness, Femininity, and Victorian Culture* (Durham, NC: Duke University Press, 1998), 146, 103. Brody emphasizes the importance of Edward A. Freeman's *History of the Norman Conquest*, published in 6 vols. between 1870 and 1879, which produced an influential theory of 'an essential English type' and 'the purity of the English race' (ibid. 141).

[3] David Cannadine, *Ornamentalism: How the British Saw their Empire* (London: Allen Lane–Penguin, 2001), pp. xix, 39.

[4] Colonial Secretary Joseph Chamberlain laid emphasis on 'disciplined order' in a speech at the Royal Colonial Institute dinner in 1897. Elleke Boehmer, ed., *Empire Writing: An Anthology of Colonial Writing, 1870–1918* (Oxford: Oxford University Press, 1998), 213.

[5] Ernest Williams, 'Get Out!', *Outlook*, 19 Feb. 1898, 76.

was 'perhaps stronger in the colonies than at home'.[6] This colonial mentality was associated by politicians such as Joseph Chamberlain with a 'sentiment of kinship', the notion that the British Empire was one extended family, and by intellectuals such as John Seeley, Regius Professor of History at Cambridge, with the possibility of a future federation along American political lines. In *The Expansion of England* (1883), Seeley suggested that the future of the British Empire would depend upon England proving 'able to do what the United States does so easily, that is, hold together in a federal union countries very remote from each other'. Within this framework, the relationship between Britain and the United States was considered anomalous precisely because it lacked these imperial dimensions of familial authority and subordination. Seeley wrote of this Victorian domain as Britain's 'second Empire', referring back to 'the loss we suffered in the secession of the American colonies', and the policies he put forward were designed specifically to keep this new empire together as a single administrative unit.[7]

The identity of empire in the minds of British subjects also overlapped with conventional forms of gender identification. Audiences for whom the 'martyrdom' of General Gordon fighting the 'infidel' at Khartoum in 1885 and the exploits of Baden-Powell at the Siege of Mafeking in 1899 comprised the stuff of daily legend were naturally amenable to the glorification of masculine heroism in adventure stories of the kind written by H. Rider Haggard and G. A. Henty, whose books sold in vast numbers during the 1890s.[8] In a memoir of growing up in London during the first decade of the twentieth century, Frederick Willis recalled how the teaching of geography at his board school was 'confined to the British Empire' and of how the 'American War of Independence, indeed the existence of the United States of America, was hushed up'.[9] The most compelling reason for British distrust of America in the second half of the nineteenth century centred upon the ever-expanding commercial power of the United States. Alfred Lord Tennyson, in 'The Third of February, 1852', specifically disparaged the world of greedy profiteering, of Manchester 'cotton-spinners' and their free-trade associates, evoking instead a vision of empire that took as its source 'the manly strain of Runnymede', while his patriotic ballads of the 1870s and 1880s proceeded in the same vein to postulate a mythical Anglo-Saxondom as the

---

[6] Scott A. Cohen, ' "Get Out!": Empire Migration and Human Traffic in *Lord Jim*', *Novel*, 36 (2003), 383.   [7] Boehmer, ed., *Empire Writing*, 213, 78–9.

[8] Graham Dawson, *Soldier Heroes: British Adventure, Empire and the Imagining of Masculinity* (London: Routledge, 1994), 146. On the cult of masculinity, see also Patrick Brantlinger, *Rule of Darkness: British Literature and Imperialism, 1830–1914* (Ithaca, NY: Cornell University Press, 1988), 227–53.

[9] Frederick Willis, *101 Jubilee Road: A Book of London Yesterdays* (London: Phoenix House, 1948), 76–7. D. W. Griffiths's film *America* was banned in Britain as late as 1924 because its main theme, the American War of Independence, was considered offensive. See John M. Mackenzie, *Propaganda and Empire: The Manipulation of British Public Opinion, 1880–1960* (Manchester: Manchester University Press, 1984), 79.

historical progenitor of Queen Victoria's imperial family.[10] Henry Newbolt's martial ballads around the turn of the twentieth century performed a similar service, adducing parallels between a strong nerve on the school playing field and valour in battle, and installing old naval heroes such as Drake and Nelson in the forefront of the national pantheon. All of this served not only to consolidate an opposition between the courageous ethos of patriotism and the vulgarity of the market but also, implicitly, to reinforce affiliations between these categories and conventional types of sexuality. Whereas the empire was predicated upon the virtues of masculine vigour and self-discipline, complemented by a domesticated femininity, the fashionable world of the metropolis was thought to induce among men a fatal feminization and softness, a weakness for the fripperies of luxury and art.[11] Given the way in which the United States was popularly associated with this burgeoning consumerism, it is not difficult to see how America was widely suspected of introducing unwelcome ambiguities, particularly around the idea of masculinity, into an imperial culture grounded firmly upon more traditional notions of gender identity.

America, then, threatened to introduce various forms of confusion into the ordered domain of the British Empire during the last years of the Victorian era. One such disturbance involved its long-standing threat to established class hierarchies: as Lawrence Levine has noted, American culture in the nineteenth century, especially outside the WASP citadels of Boston and New York, tended to conceive of itself as a forum for participatory democracy, a place where highbrow and lowbrow cultures became intermingled. Whether in performances of Shakespeare rife with audience interruptions or in classical concerts punctuated by the airs of 'Yankee Doodle', American audiences in the Midwest and elsewhere resisted the reverential institutionalization of cultural monuments according to what they looked upon as merely ossified standards of social or professional taste.[12] But such social cross-overs might also be seen as analogous to traversals of traditional codes of masculinity, with the American scrambling of class barriers becoming akin, in British eyes, to the scrambling of sexual codes and restrictions. Walt Whitman, in particular, came to be read widely by various British intellectuals associated with Aestheticism, and they especially admired the way his poetry appeared to conflate challenges to established social, sexual, and artistic hierarchies.

Whitman operated at this time as a talismanic figure for English writers who were interested in the representation of sexual unorthodoxy, especially those

---

[10] Lord Alfred Tennyson, *The Poems of Tennyson*, ii, ed. Christopher Ricks, 2nd edn. (Harlow: Longman, 1987), 474–5. On Tennyson's anti-capitalism, see Deirdre David, *Rule Britannia: Women, Empire, and Victorian Writing* (Ithaca, NY: Cornell University Press, 1995), 167–8.

[11] On this theme, see Elaine Showalter, *Sexual Anarchy: Gender and Culture at the Fin de Siècle* (New York: Viking, 1990), 78–95, 169–87.

[12] Lawrence Levine, *Highbrow/Lowbrow: The Emergence of Cultural Hierarchy in America* (Cambridge, Mass.: Harvard University Press, 1988), 179.

who saw such heterodoxy as a deliberate subversion of the settled codes of Anglican order. In chapter 25 of Thomas Hardy's *Tess of the d'Urbervilles* (1891), Angel Clare justifies to himself his intellectual exogamy during his sojourn at Talbothay's Dairy by quoting to himself from 'Crossing Brooklyn Ferry': 'he could calmly view the absorbing world without, and apostrophizing it with Walt Whitman—"Crowds of men and women attired in the usual costumes, / How curious you are to me!"—resolve upon a plan for plunging into that world anew.'[13] Clare's pose here as a working-class dairyman soon turns out to be as insubstantial as his supposedly advanced views on sex outside marriage; having managed to exculpate his own previous transgression in Tess's eyes, he finds his old inherited prejudices rearing up again when she returns the compliment by recounting her own past history with Alec d'Urberville. Angel Clare, then, might be described as a pseudo-Whitmanian, and Bram Stoker, the author of *Dracula*, had a similarly ambivalent attitude towards Whitman's radicalism. Stoker admired the passionate aspects of the American writer's life and work—just as Whitman himself approved of Stoker's uninhibited qualities—but he was also made nervous by Whitman's overtly homosexual imagery, which Stoker, indeed, advised the American poet to censor.[14] Whitman's homoeroticism likewise troubled Gerard Manley Hopkins, who feared that his own poem 'Harry Ploughman', written in 1887, might be too Whitmanesque in its manner: 'I always knew in my heart Walt Whitman's mind to be more like my own than any other man's living,' wrote the Jesuit priest, adding that since he saw Whitman as 'a very great scoundrel', this was not a comfortable confession to make. Swinburne also includes distinct echoes of Whitman in *Songs before Sunrise* (1871), and he expressed interest at one point in bringing out an English edition of the American poet.[15]

English critical writing on Whitman at this time tended to stress his noncon- formist, transgressive qualities. John Addington Symonds in 1891 put forward a particularly innovative interpretation of Whitman—'a proto-queer reading', Robert Sulcer jun., calls it—where Symonds sought specifically to resist the pedagogical identification of great literature with a series of decent moral atti- tudes designed to reinforce racial purity and national identity. Symonds, in other words, used the example of Whitman in an attempt to illuminate the narrowness of the 'golden treasury' tradition of English literature that was being canonized and institutionalized around this time. There is a revealing contradiction here in the transatlantic reception of Whitman, for Symonds is especially interested in

---

[13] Thomas Hardy, *Tess of the D'Urbervilles* (London: Macmillan, 1974), 194.

[14] H. L. Malchow, *Gothic Images of Race in Nineteenth-Century Britain* (Stanford, Calif.: Stanford University Press, 1996), 133–4.

[15] Richard Dellamora, *Masculine Desire: The Sexual Politics of Victorian Aestheticism* (Chapel Hill, NC: University of North Carolina Press, 1990), 87–8; Robert Weisbuch, *Atlantic Double-Cross: American Literature and British Influence in the Age of Emerson* (Chicago: University of Chicago Press, 1986), 29.

what he sees as the pathological, deviant aspects of Whitman's verse, his ebullient infraction of generic and sexual norms, whereas Whitman himself wrote to Symonds in 1890 denying any reference to 'inversion' in the *Calamus* poems and saying that his work was 'only to be rightly construed by and within its own atmosphere and essential character'.[16] What this suggests, above all, is how Whitman was appropriated and, at times, creatively reimagined by British writers associated with the Aesthetic Movement in order to lend a sense of legitimacy to their own rebellious manifestos. Conversely, of course, Whitman also became a symbol of deviance in the eyes of conservative writers: Richard Dellamora cites an attack on Symonds by the Reverend St John Tyrwhitt in the *Contemporary Review* (1877), in which the clergyman used Whitman repeatedly as a code word for illicit desire. Whitman himself, on the other hand, understood his own work primarily in essentialist terms, casting himself as a spokesperson for his progressive race, a national laureate whose poetry could only be appreciated rightfully, as he put it, 'within its own atmosphere'. Whitman thus represented himself as an embodiment of American norms, an apologist for what 'Starting from Paumanok' calls the 'divine average', whereas Symonds preferred to think of Whitman's genius as an aberrant quality, a means of challenging the claustrophobic and allegedly organicist shape of English culture.[17]

This is not, of course, to suggest that Whitman's explicit intentions render Symonds's interpretations superfluous; indeed, recent queer theorists of Whitman, such as Robert K. Martin and Michael Moon, have been closer to Symonds in their readings of his poetry.[18] What it does indicate, though, is the extent to which the reception of Whitman on both sides of the Atlantic during the nineteenth century was inextricably involved with questions of political democracy and social legitimacy. Britain and the United States at this time conceived of their societies as rival cultural formations, alter egos, in the same way as the United States and the Soviet Union were to regard themselves as mutual antagonists 100 years later. Whitman's own essay 'Democratic Vistas' (1871), with its vindication of American political democracy as supplying 'a training school for making first-class men' and its celebration of the 'interminable swarms of alert, turbulent, good-natured, independent citizens' throughout 'the great cities' of America, can be seen as engaged in this war of words and, in particular, as a direct rejoinder to Arnold's more hierarchical assumptions in *Culture and Anarchy* (1869).[19] The latter work rigidly stratifies society into three distinctly demarcated classes: Barbarians, Philistines, and Populace, or aristocracy, middle classes, and working

[16] Robert Sulcer jun., 'Ten Percent: Poetry and Pathology', in *Victorian Sexual Dissidence*, ed. Richard Dellamora (Chicago: University of Chicago Press, 1999), 237, 245.

[17] Dellamora, *Masculine Desire*, 87; Whitman, *Complete Poetry and Collected Prose*, 182.

[18] See e.g. Robert K. Martin, *The Homosexual Tradition in American Poetry* (Austin, Tex.: University of Texas Press, 1979), 3–89, and Michael Moon, *Disseminating Whitman: Revision and Corporeality in* Leaves of Grass (Cambridge, Mass.: Harvard University Press, 1991).

[19] Whitman, *Complete Poetry and Collected Prose*, 952, 954; Weisbuch, *Atlantic Double-Cross*, 15.

classes. In typical neoclassical fashion, Arnold then goes on to idealize the idea of culture as a distant echo from a land that has all but passed away, 'the best which has been thought and said in the world.'[20] For Arnold, the 'best' is always in the past tense, equated elegiacally with traditions of classical learning that can be glimpsed only fitfully amidst the debased landscapes of industrial England.

While *Culture and Anarchy* is generally hostile to the conditions of modernity, the three essays on America which Arnold wrote in the last decade of his life are more interesting in the way they revisit the idea of an organicist utopia from a transatlantic perspective. Moving away from *Culture and Anarchy*'s emphasis on classical civilization and what Morris Dickstein described as a conception of 'the sacredness of state power', Arnold's late essays displace the idea of collectivity on to the more amorphous, emerging society of the United States.[21] 'A Word about America' (1882) quotes Edmund Burke's description of Americans as 'English people on the other side of the Atlantic', and it presents the unified culture of the United States as a good model for overcoming the class divisions which bedevil Britain, even though it also sees America as too much a 'paradise' for 'Dissenting ministers' and argues, along the lines of *Culture and Anarchy*, that a 'higher, larger cultivation, a finer lucidity, is what is needed'.[22] 'A Word More about America' (1885), written after Arnold's lecture tour of the United States in the winter of 1883–4, develops this organicist argument by maintaining that while America is assuredly made up of 'Philistines', it also comprises 'something besides': 'Until I went to the United States', writes Arnold, 'I had never seen a people with institutions which seemed expressly and thoroughly suited to it…As one watches the play of their institutions, the image suggests itself to one's mind of a man in a suit of clothes which fits him to perfection, leaving all his movements unimpeded and easy.' America, Arnold thus concludes, is a 'people homogeneous'. He goes on to contrast the country's 'soundness of health' and the capacity of its politicians to 'think straight and see clear' with the fractured state of Britain and, in particular, the 'anti-natural' condition of Ireland: 'Everything is unnatural there—the proceedings of the English who rule, the proceedings of the Irish who resist.'[23]

What is especially noticeable here is the ambivalence of Arnold's responses to America. While acknowledging that crusty Indian administrators such as Sir Lepel Griffin still abhor the United States for its populist and revolutionary tendencies, Arnold himself professes to admire it for its re-creation of a natural community, its overcoming of structural alienations and divisions within the

[20] Matthew Arnold, *Culture and Anarchy, with Friendship's Garland and Some Literary Essays*, ed. R. H. Super (Ann Arbor: Univ. of Michigan Press, 1965), 233.

[21] Dickstein, *Double Agent*, 28.

[22] Matthew Arnold, 'A Word about America', in *Philistinism in England and America*, ed. R. H. Super (Ann Arbor: University of Michigan Press, 1974), 2, 11, 22.

[23] Matthew Arnold, 'A Word More about America', in *Philistinism in England and America*, 195–7, 202, 203, 210, 205.

body politic. At the same time, however, he himself is enough of a traditional Englishman to remain perturbed by these levellings of social and cultural distinction, and in the last essay he ever wrote, 'Civilisation in the United States' (1888), he returns to these abiding preoccupations, arguing that the excessive glorification of 'the average man' leads to 'a great void' in American civilization, an absence of 'the discipline of awe and respect'.[24] It is easy enough to indict Arnold for this kind of innate conservatism, of course, and, as we have seen in his relationship with Clough, Arnold's assumptions about poetry could often seem prescriptive and narrow. But it is arguable that his social and cultural criticism is wider in its range, and there is a significant sense in which these American essays of the 1880s make a specific effort to entertain transatlantic comparisons in order to relativize and problematize the condition of England. It might be argued, in fact, that these pieces are more illuminating for the light they shed on British rather than American society. For example, the 1885 essay, taking its cue from the US Senate, denounces the whole notion of political appointments to the Houses of Parliament as 'fantastic' and argues that 'no scheme for a Second Chamber' at Westminster 'will be found solid unless it stands on a genuine basis of election and representation'.[25] It says something for Arnold's progressive credentials that this argument for a wholly elected House of Lords was still considered too dangerously radical by the Blair government when it embarked upon a programme of constitutional reform in Britain at the beginning of the twenty-first century. Amanda Anderson has suggested how Arnold's cosmopolitan interests impelled him to position himself at least partially in an estranged relation to his own heritage, pointing to his interest in Celtic literature as an avenue through which his essays on poetry diverge from the norms of formalist universalism.[26] What the Celtic tradition does for Arnold's literary criticism, the United States does for his social criticism: America provides Arnold with an alternative point of reference, a sense of estrangement that enables him to make unexpected connections and comparisons between British culture and foreign territories.

From this angle, Arnold's pursuit in the 1880s of a perspective of detachment places him, as Anderson observed, 'in a closer relation to Pater and Wilde' than is customarily imagined.[27] Whereas the conservative ethos at the end of the nineteenth century was all about separation—differentiating morality from immorality, heterosexuality from homosexuality, Great Britain from the

---

[24] Matthew Arnold, 'Civilisation in the United States', in *The Last Word*, ed. R. H. Super (Ann Arbor: University of Michigan Press, 1977), 360, 363.

[25] 'All schemes for forming a Second Chamber through nomination, whether by the Crown or any other voice, of picked noblemen, great officials, leading merchants and bankers, eminent men of letters and science, are fantastic. Probably they would not give us by any means a good Second Chamber. But certainly they would not satisfy the country or possess its confidence, and therefore they would be found futile and unworkable.' Arnold, 'A Word More about America', 212.

[26] Amanda Anderson, *The Powers of Distance: Cosmopolitanism and the Cultivation of Detachment* (Princeton: Princeton University Press, 2001), 98–9.   [27] Ibid. 22.

United States—writers such as Arnold and Oscar Wilde introduced apparently incongruous juxtapositions and paratactic associations which challenged the ruling order's natural sense of things. Dellamora has written of how the sexual scandals of the 1890s, culminating in the Wilde trial of 1895, 'provide a point at which gender roles are publicly, even spectacularly, encoded and enforced'; there was a need on the part of the British Establishment at this time 'to separate the gentlemen from the dandies', to quarantine the British Empire from threats of infiltration.[28] In this context, Jonathan Dollimore has argued that the popular

11. Oscar Wilde, posing in a cloak at the time of his arrival in America in 1882. Photograph by Napoleon Sarony.

[28] Dellamora, *Masculine Desire*, 194, 208.

notion of Wilde as a champion merely of art for art's sake is misconceived, since Wilde seeks rather to liberate art from its entanglement with conventional forms of morality, thereby challenging the habitual, unexamined folding together of aesthetic and ethical values. As Dollimore remarked, the dangerously subversive aspects of art, those that lie at the boundaries of the culture of decorum, involve disgust as well as desire, and this is why it is appropriate that part of Wilde's intellectual impetus should have been provided by America, a land beyond the bounds of British decency and a country which many English Victorians felt an intense attraction to and repulsion from simultaneously.[29] Travelling through the United States on his very successful lecture tour of 1882 (see Plate 11), Wilde found America sexier than Britain: it had, he wrote, 'the joy and power of Elizabeth's England about it', and his visit to Whitman at his home in Camden, New Jersey, seemed to symbolize this spirit of iconoclastic lustiness which both writers shared. In an essay on Whitman published in 1889, Wilde saluted Whitman as 'the herald to a new era', praising his 'new theme…the relation of the sexes, conceived in a natural, simple, and healthy form', and arguing that in Whitman's views 'there is a largeness of vision, a healthy sanity, and a fine ethical purpose'.[30]

It is interesting here that Wilde should so much emphasize the 'healthy' nature of Whitman's art, rather than, like John Addington Symonds, its heterodox qualities. Wilde, in other words, became enamoured with Whitman's own understanding of poetry as a means of utopian transformation—the value of Whitman's work, he wrote, 'is in its prophecy not its performance'—and he particularly commended Whitman's power to imagine a radically different future.[31] Of course, the threat of social instability was firmly associated in the minds of the ruling classes with sexual profligacy of one kind or another, and in this sense Wilde's engagement with Whitman, and with America, generally flaunts his status as an outsider to British culture: Wilde's work embodies a sinister capacity to pervert the purist lineaments of national respectability by smuggling in 'deviant' sexuality and other paradoxical values.[32] Terry Eagleton has written of how Wilde's Irish nationality was crucial to his oppositional stance towards England, how his theatrical poses appear to ape the manners of bourgeois society while emptying out their substantive content, and the same is true of Wilde's American affinities, which act as a reverse projection of English social formations, a way of mirroring and slyly parodying their inherent assumptions.

---

[29] Jonathan Dollimore, *Sex, Literature and Censorship* (Malden, Mass.: Polity, 2001), 98, 46.

[30] Simmons, *Star-Spangled Eden*, 302; Oscar Wilde, 'The Gospel According to Walt Whitman', in *The Artist as Critic: Critical Writings of Oscar Wilde*, ed. Richard Ellmann (London: W. H. Allen, 1970), 124–5.

[31] Wilde, 'Gospel According to Walt Whitman', 125.

[32] Eric Trudgill, *Madonnas and Magdalens: The Origins and Development of Victorian Sexual Attitudes* (London: Heinemann, 1976), 24–37, and George L. Mosse, *Nationalism and Sexuality: Respectability and Abnormal Sexuality in Modern Europe* (New York: Howard Fertig, 1985), 1–22.

In Wilde's dialogue 'The Decay of Lying' (1891), Vivian cites Emerson as a justification for his principled inconsistency—'Like Emerson, I write over the door of my library the word "Whim"'—and much of his work is concerned to internalize this Emersonian sense of provisionality and mutability so as to highlight, like Emerson himself, the artificial rather than natural constitution of British manners.[33]

In keeping with this calculated insubordination, Wilde empathizes more with mavericks and rebels in America than with the WASP establishment on the Eastern Seaboard. He expresses sympathy with Jefferson Davis, saying that the condition of the defeated South reminds him of equivalent, ongoing civil wars within British territories: 'We in Ireland are fighting for the principle of autonomy against empire, for independence against centralization, for the principles for which the South fought.' He also much admires the American West, describing San Francisco as 'a really beautiful city', with 'China Town, peopled by Chinese labourers ... the most artistic town I have ever come across', and finding in general Western people to be 'much more genial than those of the East'. America thus reveals Wilde, for all of his foppish and pseudo-aristocratic characteristics, to be at heart, like Whitman, a great democrat. In 'Impressions of America' (1883), he praises Americans for being 'exceedingly acceptive of new ideas', and he describes them, in an echo of Whitman's *Democratic Vistas*, as 'the best politically educated people in the world. It is', Wilde goes on, 'well worth one's while to go to a country which can teach us the beauty of the word FREEDOM and the value of the thing LIBERTY.' As with Whitman again, the aesthetic correlative to this celebration of political democracy is a valorization of the modern industrial world rather than, as with his English contemporaries such as Tennyson or Dante Gabriel Rossetti, a retreat back into rural idylls or medievalisms. Although American art itself often seems stilted, suggests Wilde, American citizens have nevertheless created a genuine sense of beauty within their everyday urban environment: 'I have always wished to believe that the line of strength and the line of beauty are one. That wish was realised when I contemplated American machinery. It was not until I had seen the water-works at Chicago that I realised the wonders of machinery; the rise and fall of the steel rods, the symmetrical motion of the great wheels is the most beautifully rhythmic thing I have ever seen.'[34] This, of course, is entirely Whitmanian in its artistic enfranchisement of a common culture, and it suggests how one of the disconcerting aspects of Wilde's particular version of aestheticism, so far as British traditionalists were concerned, was its willingness to embrace materials which the cultural conservatives would have deemed vulgar.

---

[33] Eagleton, *Heathcliff and the Great Hunger*, 326–41; Oscar Wilde, 'The Decay of Lying', in *The Artist as Critic*, 292.
[34] Simmons, *Star-Spangled Eden*, 325, 316; Oscar Wilde, 'Impressions of America', in *The Artist as Critic*, 9, 11–12, 7.

In 'The Decadent Movement in Literature' (1893), Arthur Symons made a connection between French Symbolism and the English school of Walter Pater, an equation that subsequently became something of a critical cliché, particularly in the more censorious climate after the Wilde trial, when supposedly effete English artists were linked through familiar national stereotypes to what George Moore in 1887 had called the French 'school of collapse'.[35] The more long-term threat to the stability of British cultural institutions, however, came not from a hedonistic French demi-monde but from a democratic, market-driven American society. As Regenia Gagnier has shown, Wilde was an expert manipulator of the mass market at the end of the nineteenth century, exploiting new processes of advertising and consumerism to construct a public persona for himself on both sides of the Atlantic. It was his American tour of 1882, according to Gagnier, that made Wilde 'hardened, commercial, responsible, and determined to be a dramatist', and his subsequent skill at manipulating audiences testifies to his willing engagement with the burgeoning commodity culture of his time.[36] This is not, of course, to suggest that Wilde was simply co-opted by the mass market; rather, like Whitman, he was concerned to choreograph popular culture into a series of aesthetic performances that would both reflect and refract the democratic values of his era. If Whitman translated urban scenes into the overt thematic content of his poems, we might say that Wilde translated this new environment into his work's formal constituents, framing his polite if ambiguous dramas within a glossy, attractive and commercial idiom that spoke eloquently to the popular assumptions permeating late Victorian England.

From this perspective, the real 'decadence' introduced into Britain by the Aesthetic Movement was not so much French oversophistication as American commercialization. By this time, Europeans had come to perceive the United States as the world's most advanced market society, and they feared the capacity of this new commercial world to undermine the more established parameters of national identity. Wilde, like Clough, threatened to disturb conventional social and artistic hierarchies by disseminating an idiom of travesty whose burlesque impetus was often associated with the democratizing spirit of American culture. Wilde was a keen supporter of James McNeill Whistler, an American painter working in London—indeed, according to Wilde, 'one of the very greatest masters of painting'—who in 1877 created a storm by suing John Ruskin for libel after the latter had excoriated the 'wilful imposture' and 'ill-educated conceit' informing Whistler's departure from realist modes of representation. Whistler described his works as 'nocturnes' or 'arrangements', rather than mere 'pictures,' but his abstract tendencies cut against the grain of Victorian literalism

---

[35] Suzanne Nalbantian, *Seeds of Decadence in the Late Nineteenth-Century Novel: A Crisis in Values* (New York: St Martin's Press, 1983), 7; Ian Fletcher and Malcolm Bradbury, preface, in Ian Fletcher, ed., *Decadence and the 1890s* (London: Edward Arnold, 1979), 11.

[36] Regenia Gagnier, *Idylls of the Marketplace: Oscar Wilde and the Victorian Public* (Stanford, Calif.: Stanford University Press, 1986), 56.

and also against the residual power of a cultural evangelism that demanded art be morally and aesthetically transparent. The libel trial that followed upon Whistler's suit perfectly dramatized this conflict between propriety and transgression, with Ruskin's counsel asking Whistler if his painting *Nocturne: Blue and Gold* could be described as 'a correct representation of Battersea Bridge?'[37] As Linda Dowling has observed, such a notion of correctness coincided with Ruskin's vision of art as the embodiment of a co-operative, meaningful spirit within an organic social whole. Whistler, by contrast, believed that such attitudes were simply philistine: he ridiculed the genteel amateurism whereby art was promoted only as an expression of good taste, and he deplored the stifling associations between artistic expression and social community that he saw being consolidated through such pedagogical processes as Ruskin's appointment to the Slade professorship of Art at Oxford. (In his autobiography, Whistler suggested that such lack of professionalism was akin to having a 'College of Physicians with Tennyson as President'.) Ruskin for his part denounced Whistler as a 'Social Monster', and it is true that they entertained very different conceptions of the relationship between the artist and society: Whistler, aggressive and self-advertising, thought of art primarily in terms of technical expertise; Ruskin, more proselytizing by temperament, looked to art as a manifestation of shared social values.[38] But one of the ramifications of the kind of transatlantic aestheticism developed by Whistler and Wilde was to interrogate the more restrictive, circumscribed conception of community upon which Ruskin's nostalgia for integrated meaning was predicated. The conflicting cross-currents that traverse the works of Wilde and Whistler set themselves in deliberate antagonism to Ruskin's organicist model, preferring instead to see art as a site for the mediation of paradox and contradiction.

In Wilde's play *Lady Windermere's Fan* (1892), the heroine in the first act describes herself as a 'Puritan' who has been brought up to know 'the difference that there is between what is right and what is wrong'. At the end of the play, however, she says to her husband: 'I don't think now that people can be divided into the good and the bad as though they were two separate races or creations.'[39] The racial analogy here is telling, for Wilde's paradoxical style is designed to yoke together unexpected things and categories in defiance of conventional logic. At the same time as Wilde was writing, the whole nature of racial classification was coming to be seen by many writers during the Reconstruction era in the United States as increasingly arbitrary and legalistic, as questions of race moved away from older, ante-bellum identities of white against black, freeman against

[37] Oscar Wilde, 'Mr. Whistler's Ten O'Clock', in *The Artist as Critic*, 16; James McNeill Whistler, *The Gentle Art of Making Enemies* (London: Heinemann, 1890), 1, 8.
[38] Linda Dowling, *The Vulgarization of Art: The Victorians and Aesthetic Democracy* (Charlottesville, Va.: University Press of Virginia, 1996), 25–45; Whistler, *Gentle Art of Making Enemies*, 33.
[39] Oscar Wilde, *The Complete Illustrated Stories, Plays and Poems* (London: Chancellor Press, 1986), 329, 362. See also Brody, *Impossible Purities*, 129.

slave. It is appropriate that Lady Windermere should eventually disavow her 'Puritan' upbringing, because the Puritan or Manichaean tendency to interpose a rigid dualism between good and evil, white and black, is what we find being problematized not only in Wilde's texts but also in the work of his American contemporaries concerned with the race issue. Mary Warner Blanchard has suggested, for example, an intellectual affinity between Wilde and Mark Twain, another devotee of glamorous white suits, who redescribes racial identity in terms of social conditioning in *Pudd'nhead Wilson* (1894).[40] Twain's narrative turns upon formulas of exchange, with white and black children being accidentally swapped at birth, and it suggests a Wilde-like disdain for the idea of deep, naturalized structures, a satirical dislocation of the supposedly atavistic principle of race into the more worldly domain of the law.

Similar dialectical interplays between racial purity and legal complexity are addressed in the work of several African-American writers of the 1890s. The plot of Francis E. W. Harper's *Iola Leroy* (1892) revolves around the legal complications arising out of racial hybridity and miscegenation, while in Charles W. Chesnutt's story 'A Matter of Principle' (1899) the identity of the 'light' negro Hamilton M. Brown is confused with that of the 'dark' negro, Henry M. Brown. In Chesnutt's tale, the Clayton family believe that the light negro would be acceptable as a suitor for their daughter whereas the dark negro would not: 'people will say we are prejudiced,' explains Mrs Clayton emolliently, 'when it is only a matter of principle with us.' Chesnutt's narrative, like Twain's, works through its structure of exchange comically to demystify the large abstract ideals mooted here: Cicero Clayton talks pompously about 'the brotherhood of man', for instance, but such principles are shown to be as hollow as the library book with nothing in it which fetches the highest price at auction in Chesnutt's later story, 'Baxter's *Procustes*' (1904).[41] Chesnutt, in other words, satirically transposes depth into surface, suggesting how supposedly 'deep' principles can be seen merely as extrapolations from worldly self-interest. It is one of the functions of the Aesthetic Movement in general to shift the register, as it were, to displace objects from naturalized to aestheticized phenomena by reconceptualizing them within an alternative framework of representation, and this is why there are important conceptual parallels between aestheticism and the denaturalization of racial identity. Through this process of denaturalization, as Russ Castronovo notes, abstract principles such as Clayton's 'brotherhood of man' are rendered material, so that this supposedly impersonal ideal becomes not neutral or disembodied but, rather, a marked and contested field.[42]

---

[40] Mary Warner Blanchard, *Oscar Wilde's America: Counterculture in the Gilded Age* (New Haven: Yale University Press, 1998), 19.

[41] Charles Waddell Chesnutt, *Tales of Conjure and the Color Line: Ten Stories*, ed. Joan R. Sherman (Mineola, NY: Dover Publications, 1998), 73, 79, 82, 108.

[42] Russ Castronovo, *Necro Citizenship: Death, Eroticism, and the Public Sphere in the Nineteenth-Century United States* (Durham, NC: Duke University Press, 2001), 224.

To aestheticize, then, is also to materialize, to dissolve rarefied abstractions by transferring them to a more secular, worldly context. While subverting the categories of racial purity that had been used to justify the institution of slavery, British aesthetes also undermined the tenets of the American abolitionist movement which had similarly established itself, initially at least, on the basis of an evangelical moral purity. Rossetti and others gleefully parodied *Uncle Tom's Cabin*, implying how Stowe's novel was badly constructed and had been written hypocritically for profit, while American slave narratives were pornographically travestied in England during the 1880s to flaunt the titillating nature of this material, particularly in relation to their depictions of flogging. Thus, Harriet Jacobs's *Incidents in the Life of a Slave Girl* was recast as 'The Secret Life of Linda Brent' and published in this revised form in an 1882 issue of *The Cremorne*, a magazine of dubious virtue that took its title from the Cremorne Gardens, a park on the Chelsea embankment frequented by London bohemians and prostitutes.[43] This parodic idiom suggests how the Decadent style actually saw itself as modernistic in its orientation because it was concerned to break down what it took to be the sanctimonious moral assumptions running through the Victorian cultural heritage. Rossetti, Aubrey Beardsley, and others prided themselves on their dissociation from the symbiotic unification of ethics and aesthetics within this tradition, and by giving epistemological priority instead to the aesthetic dimension, they rendered the inherited customs of the country fluid and therefore reversible.[44] It is not surprising that many of the artistic avant-garde in *fin-de-siècle* London were American by birth—Whistler, Henry James, editor of the *Yellow Book* Henry Harland—because the theoretical impetus for aestheticism involved an unravelling and transposition of categories that were related at many levels to processes of displacement and transnationalism. This also, of course, helps to explain why there were particular cultural tensions at this time between a transatlantic aestheticism and the British imperial ethos.

Decadence, then, paradoxically betokened a condition of modernity at the end of the nineteenth century, because it came to embody artistically the forces of dissolution and change. For all of the nostalgic medievalism shared by Charles Eliot Norton and his acolytes at Harvard, there was also in Boston at this time a receptivity to an emerging gay culture and an enthusiasm for parody in various forms, as we see, for example, in the popularity there of Gilbert and Sullivan's burlesque theatrical performances.[45] This kind of emphasis on parody and

[43] M. Wood, *Blind Memory*, 149; Collette Colligan, 'Anti-Abolition Writes Obscenity: The English Vice, Transatlantic Slavery, and England's Obscene Print Culture', *International Exposure: Perspectives on Modern European Pornography, 1800–2000*, ed. Lisa Z. Sigel (New Brunswick, NJ: Rutgers University Press, 2005), 74–82. The author of this parody of Harriet Jacobs was William Lazenby.

[44] On Beardsley, see Peter Michelson, *Speaking the Unspeakable: A Poetics of Obscenity* (Albany, NY: State University of New York Press, 1993), 72–3.

[45] Douglas Shand-Tucci, *Boston Bohemia, 1881–1900. Ralph Adams Cram: Life and Architecture* (Amherst, Mass.: University of Massachusetts Press, 1995), 13. On Decadence as modernity, see

performativity also runs through various facets of American medievalism, whose more iconoclastic aspects involved a readiness to transpose Dante and other religious icons into secular terms. Norton, who was a close friend of Ruskin and who founded the Dante Society at Harvard in 1881, became more conservative as he grew older and came to believe that the modern era was inescapably corrupt by comparison with this earlier time; but other medieval enthusiasts, such as the architect Ralph Adams Cram, were primarily concerned with the transvaluation of established cultural ideas, with rereading religious iconography for its purchase on extreme human conditions of love and beauty, rather than, in the way Ruskin would have preferred, as an integrated expression of humane social values. (Cram was also, not surprisingly, devoted to the medieval legends of Wagner.[46]) This, of course, is one reason for the difficulty in recognizing such a phenomenon as the Aesthetic Movement in the United States itself; the group around Norton, for example, is conventionally thought of as eccentric and elitist, because it tended to dissociate art from the more normal, domestic scenes of everyday American life.[47] As the sense of place is eviscerated, so narrative is displaced into a more theoretical domain whose purchase upon the observable world becomes increasingly hypothetical and tenuous.

In this way, the apparent threat to coherent liberal forms of national identity posed by aestheticism came to be associated with a threat to the realist modes of representation predominant throughout the Victorian period, modes which were predicated on an organicist method whereby the work of art came synecdochically to epitomize the social fabric of which it was a part. In the increasingly transnational marketplace at the end of the nineteenth century, it was becoming harder to identify exactly which properties were local and which were global, and this led to ambiguity and slippage within artistic works of all kinds, since it was no longer clear that any given form of representation could offer a transparent window upon the conditions of its own production. Systems of textual meaning, in other words, had become not localized and immanent but transnational and oblique. This is the crucial discursive dilemma which realist writers in both England and America faced at the end of the nineteenth century: the question of finding an aesthetic correlative to the processes of social and political change that were turning recognizably local environments into force fields of transnational evolution. In the novels of writers such as George Gissing, such realism emerges with difficulty not as an autochthonous reflection of native mores but as a mediation of the tensions between proximate circumstances and global displacements.

---

also Nalbantian, *Seeds of Decadence*, 116. For a contrasting view of this movement as primarily reactionary, see T. J. Jackson Lears, *No Place of Grace: Antimodernism and the Transformation of American Culture, 1880–1920* (New York: Pantheon Books, 1981).

[46] Lears, *No Place of Grace*, 204.

[47] For a discussion of the problematic relationship between Boston and US cultural nationalism at the end of the nineteenth century, see Martin Green, *The Problem of Boston: Some Readings in Cultural History* (New York: Norton, 1966), 203.

THE LOCAL AND THE GLOBAL: GEORGE GISSING

This tension between the local and the global also works its way through the aesthetics of realism and naturalism that developed towards the end of the nineteenth century, a tension that brought about internal contradictions in texts on both sides of the Atlantic. As Phillip Barrish has observed, American realism of this era claimed its intellectual prestige from the alleged authenticity of its representation, from its claim to show the most 'real' thing available.[48] By contrast, Leo Bersani has written of the genre of realism as involving a repression of alternative points of view, a compulsive need to achieve social and aesthetic consistency by proscribing alterity and desire: 'The ordered significances of realistic fiction are presented as immanent to society,' he argues, 'whereas in fact they are the mythical denial of that society's fragmented nature. In a sense, then, the realistic novelist desperately tries to hold together what he recognizes quite well is falling apart.'[49] Bersani consequently advocates a comparative study of literature in order to avoid a misleading process of naturalization whereby the aesthetic representation of any given scene is equated unproblematically with an environmental *donnée*. David Baguley has similarly stressed the need for more international studies of naturalism, a 'generic identity' that, as he says, is too often understood specifically in nationalist terms. As Baguley acknowledges, parody is important to the construction of realist and naturalist fiction, whose iconoclastic effects depend often upon a 'paratextual' demystification or recontextualization of the apparatus of romance.

Realism and naturalism consequently involve less a quest for pure 'accuracy of description', as Northrop Frye believed, than a series of provocations that are often associated with an impulse of deliberate obscenity or voyeurism.[50] The innovative and disconcerting effects of realism and naturalism involve an aestheticization of material conventionally excluded from the realms of art, a rendering of apparently ugly urban situations within a framework of the picturesque. In this sense, the formal dynamic of a work such as Stephen Crane's *Maggie: A Girl of the Streets* (1893), with its impressionistic evocation of Chicago slums, might be said to operate according to a logic of paradox, whose force derives from a decomposition of traditional romance and its reconstitution within apparently incongruous settings. Along parallel lines, Peter Brooks has argued that the narrator in Zola's fiction is positioned less as a scientist than

---

[48] Phillip Barrish, *American Literary Realism, Critical Theory, and Intellectual Prestige, 1880–1995* (Cambridge: Cambridge University Press, 2001), 3.
[49] Leo Bersani, *A Future for Astyanax: Character and Desire in Literature* (London: Marion and Boyars, 1978), 61.
[50] David Baguley, *Naturalist Fiction: The Entropic Vision* (Cambridge: Cambridge University Press, 1990), 7, 156, 184; Northrop Frye, *Anatomy of Criticism: Four Essays* (Princeton: Princeton University Press, 1957), 80.

as a voyeur who looks on as 'the material body', both human and social, is unveiled as the basis of all meaning.[51] This makes naturalism, for all its familiar reputation of home-grown authenticity, appear closer in spirit to the transgressive impetus of the Aesthetic Movement. As Jan B. Gordon has perceptively written: 'Naturalism is not often regarded as part of the "aesthetic" nineties...yet the scientific detachment that produced an allegedly "objective" vision can be seen as an authorial ruse enabling the naturalist to project himself onto nature while feigning the passivity of a naïve observer.'[52]

Put another way, it is the incompatibility between a desire for transparent representation and the projective slipperiness of an aesthetic model that creates some of the most interesting tensions in realism and naturalism towards the end of the nineteenth century. George Gissing's novels about life in London strive characteristically to elucidate the metropolitan environment by focusing upon the more mundane details of its social life, details which were customarily overlooked in more conventional, romantic treatments of the city; however, the mimetic difficulty faced by such a stylistic method is that London by the 1880s was, as Judith R. Walkowitz put it, 'an immense world-city, culturally and economically important, yet socially and geographically divided and politically incoherent'.[53] Gissing's novels attempt to read London according to the strategies of empirical observation, but the complexities of the metropolis at this time were bound up increasingly not just with domestic politics but also with international economic ties, particularly with Germany and the United States, ties which were rendering the infrastructure of the capital more expansive but also more opaque and unstable. London, in other words, was becoming in the late nineteenth century a world city whose labyrinthine networks could be rendered only partially legible within Gissing's style of realism, although it is precisely this contradiction between Gissing's aesthetic of local specificity and undercurrents of global displacement that makes for some of the most powerful, if unsettling, effects in his narratives.

For all of its rhetoric of brutal objective truth, then, the demystifications of naturalism typically involve a complicated process of transposition and transformation, whereby one conceptual space is folded back upon itself and refigured into its opposite. This again makes naturalism seem much closer in aesthetic practice to the Decadent style than is usually imagined. In Joris-Karl Huysmans's *Against Nature* (1884), a formative text of the Aesthetic Movement, the perverse and paradoxical supersession of reality by artifice is epitomized by the rearrangement of space within the narrator's apartment, where the reader

[51] Peter Brooks, *Body Work: Objects of Desire in Modern Narrative* (Cambridge, Mass.: Harvard University Press, 1993), 123.

[52] Jan B. Gordon, ' "Decadent Spaces": Notes for a Phenomenology of the *Fin de Siècle*', in *Decadence and the 1890s*, ed. Fletcher, 48.

[53] Judith R. Walkowitz, *City of Dreadful Delight: Narratives of Sexual Danger in Late-Victorian London* (London: Virago Press, 1994), 24.

finds the external world compressed and, as it were, magically inverted so that it comprises an alternative, autonomous universe. Deeming actual travel to be a waste of time, since the imagination provides a more than adequate substitute for the vulgarities of worldly contact, the narrator, Des Esseintes, opts instead to embark upon voyages of the imagination while sitting by his fire, and his living space consequently assumes a *trompe l'œil* effect, creating a mirrored illusion of perspective and depth: 'Like those Japanese boxes that fit one inside the other, this room had been inserted into a larger one.'[54] Walter Benn Michaels has written about 'the vogue for *trompe l'œil*' art during the 1890s, associating it with the 'illusionistic potential' offered by the circulation of corporate capital at this time, and this also implies the links between Decadent art and naturalist fiction of this period; the narratives of Frank Norris or Theodore Dreiser, for example, oscillate unstably between photographic realism and metaphorical conceptualization, between the phenomenological object and its displacement into allegory.[55] The transatlantic circulation of capital and commodities, in other words, creates internal or subtextual complications within the formal patterns of realism and naturalism, causing works that pride themselves on the authenticity of their local or national narratives to become uneasily aware of the inadequacy of empirical observation as a means of representation. By chronicling such disturbances, writers such as Gissing open out their texts, inadvertently or otherwise, to what appears to be an amorphous, illegible global domain. The problem for Gissing is that maps of London can no longer be read as clearly demarcated and bounded entities, but need to be understood in relation to larger transnational cartographies.

Gissing himself had first-hand experience of living and working in America, having arrived in Boston in October 1876, at the age of 19, after a scandal involving a prostitute had forced him to leave Manchester's Owens College. Initially he was very enthusiastic about the egalitarian society of the United States, singing the praises of American steam cars in a letter home to his brother William: 'There is only one class, and that very much better than 1st class in England. Our democratic notions do not allow of division into classes.'[56] It was in America also that Gissing began publishing articles in magazines, with his first piece, about two paintings on display in Boston, appearing in the *Boston Commonwealth* on 28 October 1876. After teaching for a while at a high school in Waltham, Massachusetts, Gissing headed west to Chicago, where he began publishing stories in the *Chicago Tribune*. The less scrupulous side of the American publishing world then became apparent to him when a New York journal, the *Troy Times*, took one of his pieces from the *Chicago Tribune* and

---

[54] J. K. Huysmans, *Against Nature*, trans. Robert Baldick (Harmondsworth: Penguin, 1959), 33.

[55] Walter Benn Michaels, *The Gold Standard and the Logic of Naturalism* (Berkeley: University of California Press, 1987), 161.

[56] George Gissing, *The Collected Letters of George Gissing*, i: *1863–1880*, ed. Paul F. Mattheisen, Arthur C. Young, and Pierre Coustillas (Athens, Oh.: Ohio University Press, 1990), 46.

reprinted it without payment. After a fruitless journey to New York in a quest for recompense, Gissing arrived back in England in October 1877.

None of the stories that Gissing published in America was actually set in the United States, but there is an important sense in which American culture comes to form a crucial alternative domain, even a latent infrastructure, throughout his subsequent English novels. Gissing's biographer John Halperin suggested that the novelist does not use American material very much in his books, and the eminent Gissing scholar Pierre Coustillas similarly argued that 'Gissing rarely looked back on his year of exile in America' and 'only once did he turn it to literary account', in his first novel, *Workers in the Dawn* (1880).[57] This is the novel in which Gissing addresses the theme of emigration most overtly, with the hero, Arthur Golding, abandoning England at the end of the narrative, and in 'a passionate desire for active exertion in an entirely new sphere' heading for 'the New World' (pp. 422–3). However, after an 'exuberance of health' on the stormy voyage over (p. 428), Golding gradually becomes disillusioned about the prospects of 'unrestricted liberty' (p. 432) in America and, regretting his new life as a 'wanderer', comes to feel increasingly nostalgic for the woman and the country he has left behind. By the end of the book, Golding believes that he has 'nothing in common' with Americans, whose taste seems 'hopelessly vulgar', and, finding himself 'a wrecked and ruined nature' (p. 430–1), he sees no option other than suicidally to plunge with a 'fierce joy of madness' into the 'roaring whirlpools' of the Niagara Falls (p. 436). Golding finds 'in the roar of the great cataract a ceaseless assertion that man is for ever dependent upon his fellows' (p. 432), while this image of a whirlpool, with its 'thousand conflicting currents', is also applied in this final chapter to the Atlantic Ocean itself (p. 429). There are, then, two distinct conceptions of human society here, and having exiled himself from the domestic comforts of Great Britain, with its emphasis on familiarity and community, Golding finds himself unable to come to terms with the individualistic, alienating climate of the United States. Despite his stringent critiques of English hypocrisy and complacency, Golding is unable finally to leave behind an emotional attachment to his native culture, and the 'perpetual indecision' (p. 431) he experiences in the United States results from a sense of being at home in neither place.

It is this kind of indecision which informs representations of America in Gissing's later works, where the transatlantic imaginary emerges as a site of contradiction, an invasion and displacement of organicist notions of English national identity. While Halperin and Coustillas are correct to say that Gissing does not actually set scenes in the United States or provide literal descriptions of its environment, it is important to recognize how America functions in these texts as a spectral realm, a potential reversal of traditional English cultural

---

[57] John Halperin, *Gissing: A Life in Books* (Oxford: Oxford University Press, 1982), 25; Pierre Coustillas, introduction, in *Workers in the Dawn*, by George Gissing (Brighton: Harvester Press, 1985), p. xxii. Subsequent page references to Gissing's novel are cited in parentheses in the text.

values. The dialectic in Gissing's most famous novel, *New Grub Street* (1891), is between classical tradition and new commercial systems: author Edwin Reardon, a devotee of ancient Greece and classical hexameters, finds it impossible to survive in the meretricious world of metropolitan journalism, whose provenance is clearly associated by Gissing with America. This link is made most obviously through the recollections of Whelpdale about his travels in the United States. Whelpdale recounts the story of how he crossed the Atlantic to see the Centennial Exhibition in Philadelphia in the hope of finding 'valuable literary material', and in an echo of Gissing's own experiences, he describes 'taking an emigrant ticket to Chicago' and publishing stories in that city before travelling back east to Troy, New York, in search of the editor who had copied one of his contributions without permission.[58] The structural importance of this episode in the context of *New Grub Street* lies in the way it magnifies and exemplifies those commercial pressures that have now begun to dictate the patterns of production and consumption in the English literary world. For example, the luckless Alfred Yule, a curmudgeonly littérateur from the age of Pope or Swift, finds himself superseded by Whelpdale's astute Americanisms and entrepreneurial values. Whelpdale, 'fertile in suggestions of literary enterprise', suggests renaming the journal *Chat* as *Chit-Chat*, on the grounds that '*Chat* doesn't attract any one, but *Chit-Chat* would sell like hot cakes, as they say in America' (pp. 495–6).

This new world of marketing is thus linked, as Simon Gatrell said, with an 'international economy'.[59] Consequently, it is appropriate within the framework of this novel that Denham is convinced he met Jasper Milvain in New York 'a year or two ago, under another name' (p. 200), because although this allegation is never substantiated, it functions symbolically to suggest Milvain's willing acceptance of his own impersonality and commodification, his relinquishment of authorial independence and reinvention of himself as an exemplar of market forces and exchange values. Milvain thus becomes an honorary American in a way that the other main character, Edwin Reardon, with his devotion to classical tradition, can never be. In May 1892, at the time he was planning *New Grub Street*, Gissing wrote a letter to Edward Bertz squarely laying the blame for the increasing vulgarization of English culture on America:

I want to deal with the flood of blackguardism which nowadays is pouring forth over the society which is raised by wealth above the lowest & yet is not sufficiently educated to rank with the highest. Impossible to take up a newspaper without being impressed with this fact of extending & deepening Vulgarity. It seems to be greatly due to American

[58] George Gissing, *New Grub Street*, ed. Bernard Bergonzi (Harmondsworth: Penguin, 1968), 427. Subsequent page references are cited in parentheses in the text. On Gissing's literary apprenticeship in America, see George Gissing, *Lost Stories from America: Five Signed Stories Never Before Reprinted, a Sixth Signed Story, and Seven Recent Attributions*, ed. Robert L. Selig (Lewiston, NY: Edwin Mellen Press, 1992).

[59] Simon Gatrell, 'England, Europe, and Empire: Hardy, Meredith, and Gissing', in *The Ends of the Earth*, ed. Simon Gatrell (London: Ashfield Press, 1992), 82.

influence, but there can be no doubt that the ground is prepared for it by the pretence of education afforded by our School-board system. Society is being *levelled down*, & with strange rapidity.[60]

A year earlier, Gissing had written in equally acerbic terms to Bertz and to his brother Algernon about the issue of American copyright, pointing out bitterly how 'Harper, & the rest of them, reprint almost every English novel simply because they can get them for a trifle & can publish them in pamphlet form'. He also expressed doubts about whether the new American copyright law (the Chace Act), passed in March 1891, would do very much to ameliorate this situation. As late as 1898, Gissing was still complaining about this 'thievish copyright law' in the United States, which demanded legally a simultaneous publication date on both sides of the Atlantic, but which in practice allowed American publishers to defer both publication and the payment of royalties to British authors.[61]

The obvious contradiction here is that Gissing is very much part of this commercial world of which he is so critical, and that he tries to take instant advantage of this new international copyright law at the same time as doubting its efficacy. It would be manifestly untrue to suggest that Gissing simply champions English values while excoriating American culture as irredeemably immoral; rather, like his first fictional hero Arthur Golding, his texts waver in 'perpetual indecision', both attracted and repelled by the idea of transatlantic mutability. In *New Grub Street*, for instance, Amy Reardon cites America as a place where 'people can get divorced if they don't suit each other—at all events in some of the States', and she goes on to ask rhetorically: 'does any harm come of it? Just the opposite I think' (p. 395). In this novel, Amy's willingness, indeed eagerness, to exchange the superannuated Reardon for the more worldly Milvain is represented as a form of selfishness; in other Gissing novels, though, the ready availability of divorce becomes a crucial issue, a concern that Gissing shared with other English writers of the late nineteenth century—George Meredith, Thomas Hardy—who protested against the nation's backward-looking divorce laws. (As Rachel Bowlby has remarked, Gissing tends to be more sympathetic to questions of male than female freedom, and he typically associates the independence of his men with a quest for authenticity, while his women are seen as having a more superficial and self-indulgent attraction to 'fashionable life', as with Amy Reardon in *New Grub Street*.[62]) Gissing was, therefore, welcoming in principle towards various aspects of American culture, and his letters reveal him to be also

[60] Gissing, *The Collected Letters of George Gissing*, v: *1892–1895*, ed. Paul F. Mattheisen, Arthur C. Young, and Pierre Coustillas (Athens, Oh.: Ohio University Press, 1994), 33.

[61] Gissing, *The Collected Letters of George Gissing*, iv: 1889–1891, ed. Paul F. Mattheisen, Arthur C. Young, and Pierre Coustillas (Athens, Oh.: Ohio University Press, 1993), 258, 276; Gissing, *The Collected Letters of George Gissing*, vii: *1897–1899*, ed. Paul F. Mattheisen, Arthur C. Young, and Pierre Coustillas (Athens, Oh.: Ohio University Press, 1995), 105.

[62] Rachel Bowlby, review of *The Whirlpool*, by George Gissing, ed. Patrick Parrinder, *Gissing Newsletter*, 21/2 (April 1985), 26.

a diligent and enthusiastic reader of American literature. He wrote to Algernon in August 1879, 'I have also bought Poe's Tales lately, admirable things'; he told his sister Ellen in March 1882 that he has been reading Henry James's 'life of Nathaniel Hawthorne (author of "Twice Told Tales"), very interesting indeed'; six years later, he went on to praise Hawthorne's 'exquisite style' and his 'independence of conventional views which makes his work very valuable to all who are reading for the maturing of their thought'. He also read Thoreau, Edward Bellamy, and, towards the end of his life, Stephen Crane (he wrote to Crane's widow commiserating with her on the 'untimely close' of her husband's 'happy & brilliant career'), and Henry James.[63]

The relationship with James is particularly interesting. Gissing was friendly with the American expatriate and spent a day at his house in Rye in 1901, although, according to the recollections of Gissing's final partner, Gabrielle Fleury, he subsequently talked of James 'as an example of the misfortune of a *déraciné* novelist', who had 'lost his Americanism, without ever acquiring as a novelist the Eng. Nationality, so that his novels have something *factice* [artificial], untrue, uncharacterized'. Gissing contrasted this with what he called his own 'direct & thorough knowledge, his true picture of Engl. Life', which came from 'his having so completely given himself to it'.[64] Gissing's emphasis here upon an authenticity that derives from 'observation' and from 'contact with English life' is commensurate with the views expressed in his short essay 'The Place of Realism in Fiction' (1895), where he describes realism as 'an attitude of revolt against insincerity in the art of fiction'. Priding himself upon 'artistic sincerity in the portrayal of contemporary life' and on a 'spirit of truthfulness', Gissing nevertheless believes that the novelist 'must recognise limits in every direction; that he will constantly reject material as unsuitable to the purposes of art; and that many features of life are so completely beyond his province that he cannot dream of representing them'.[65] David Trotter has suggested how this shows Gissing aligning himself with a tradition of 'English moralism' rather than French scientific method, Dickens rather than Zola, and in a certain limited sense this is no doubt true enough.[66] However, it is precisely this tension between what the novelist conceives as 'truthfulness' and what lies, in Gissing's revealing phrase,

---

[63] Gissing, *Collected Letters*, i. 197; *idem, The Collected Letters of George Gissing*, ii: *1881–1885*, ed. Paul F. Mattheisen, Arthur C. Young, and Pierre Coustillas (Athens, Oh.: Ohio University Press, 1991), 76; *idem, The Collected Letters of George Gissing*, iii: *1886–1888*, ed. Paul F. Mattheisen, Arthur C. Young, and Pierre Coustillas (Athens, Oh.: Ohio University Press, 1992), 236; *idem, The Collected Letters of George Gissing*, viii: *1900–1902*, ed. Paul F. Mattheisen, Arthur C. Young, and Pierre Coustillas (Athens, Oh.: Ohio University Press, 1996), 58.

[64] Gissing, *The Collected Letters of George Gissing*, ix: *1902–1903*, ed. Paul F. Mattheisen, Arthur C. Young, and Pierre Coustillas (Athens, Oh.: Ohio University Press, 1997), 276.

[65] A. C. Gissing, ed., *Selections, Autobiographical and Imaginative from the Works of George Gissing* (London: Cape, 1929), 217, 219–20.

[66] David Trotter, 'The Avoidance of Naturalism: Gissing, Moore, Grand, Bennett, and Others', in *The Columbia History of the British Novel*, ed. John Richetti (New York: Columbia University Press, 1994), 618, 623.

12. George Gissing, photographed by Messrs Elliott and Fry in H. G. Wells's house at Sandgate (1901). He was suffering at the time from emphysema, and a few weeks later was sent to a sanatorium in Suffolk.

'beyond his province' that provokes many of the most illuminating qualities in his narratives. Gissing's texts, in other words, are paradoxically as much about the limitations of realism, their generic failure to encompass or elucidate the world they describe, as they are about the transparent, moralistic re-creation of their native environment. This is one reason why the American dimension is crucial to Gissing's aesthetic perspective: it introduces, surreptitiously or otherwise, an alternative field of consciousness, the prospect of conceiving his home territory differently.

In this context, the American writer who most influenced and bothered Gissing was Walt Whitman. Morley Roberts, a friend of Gissing's who travelled extensively through and wrote about the United States, later tried to take credit for introducing Gissing to Whitman's work, though in fact the novelist was writing to Edward Bertz as early as September 1889 about what he considered to be the strengths and possible liabilities of Whitman's writing:

Now about Walt Whitman ... As you know, I myself have no genuine sympathy with his optimism, though I can take pleasure in it, as I can in any other manifestation of *strength* ... I do not go so far as the writer in the *Gentleman's*; these passages do not strike me as 'disgusting'; but, on the other hand, I am inclined to think that Bucke's enthusiasm makes him wilfully blind to this writer's meaning. In fact, the passages in which Whitman speaks in this way of male friendship awaken no sympathy in me; it is my habit to regard such language as a tender exaggeration.[67]

Despite his professed lack of interest in Whitman's unconventional representations of sexuality, Gissing reported to Bertz in May 1897 that he was reading John Addington Symonds's study of Whitman published four years earlier, which, as we have seen, made the case for Whitman as a specifically homosexual poet.[68]

Like other British writers associated with the Aesthetic Movement, then, Gissing was interested in Whitman's postulation of alternative vistas as a means to open out the restrictive domain of British society. While he was not so much of a proselytizer for Whitmanian largesse as Wilde or Swinburne, Gissing was concerned to establish a dialectical relationship between Whitman's spirit of emancipation and the rigid hierarchies of the English class system. The novel in which this dialectic is most fully worked out is *Thyrza* (1887), set in south London, where the idealist Walter Egremont, recently returned from America, attempts to further 'the spiritual education' of the people of Lambeth through a series of lectures on English literature.[69] Egremont also falls in love with Thyrza, a young Lambeth woman whom he charms by telling her how he 'dreaded the first sight' of the Niagara Falls (p. 235), although their relationship, predictably, ends in disaster, with the gulf in social background between these two people from opposite ends of the English class system proving ultimately too wide to bridge. In theory, though, Egremont has nothing but scorn for 'stiff, awkward, pretentious Anglicism' (p. 304), and believing that 'reform of institutions can only come as the natural result of a change in men's minds' (p. 92), he endeavours to make his followers more actively critical of the ossified social hierarchies that appertain in Britain. Like other Gissing characters, Egremont is thus represented as an internal exile who 'had unkind sentiments towards his native country, and asked himself how he was going to live in England henceforth' (p. 304).

As the plot of this novel unfolds, Egremont departs again for the United States and spends two years at 'a small manufacturing town in Pennsylvania' in an attempt to get Thyrza out of his system (p. 362). Here he comes to admire America's willing embrace of the business ethic with its reliance on industrial power to modernize and transform the country. He describes how Cornelius Vanderbilt was, personally, 'a disgusting brute', but also remarks

---

[67] Gissing, *Collected Letters*, iv. 110–11.   [68] Gissing, *Collected Letters*, vi. 286.
[69] George Gissing, *Thyrza: A Tale*, ed. Jacob Korg (Brighton: Harvester Press, 1974), 14. Subsequent page references to this edition are cited in parentheses in the text.

upon how he became 'a great philanthropist ... by the piling up of millions of dollars'. Egremont admires the way in which Vanderbilt's wealth enabled him to improve his countrymen's standard of living: 'He as good as created the steamship industry in America; he reorganized the railway system with admirable results; by adding so much to the circulating capital of the country, he provided well-paid employment for unnumbered men. Thousands of homes should bless the name of Vanderbilt' (p. 422). Acknowledging on his return to England that 'fifteen months of practical business life in America has swept my brain of much that was mere prejudice', Egremont is now more willing to countenance the 'goodliness' of a world whose spiritual efficacy arises out of, rather than in opposition to, its association with the materialistic world of commerce and industry (p. 424). This is, precisely, a Whitmanian vision: Egremont writes to Mrs Ormonde from America of how he has 'spent a good deal of time of late over Walt Whitman' (p. 420), whom he describes as 'a large, healthy, simple, powerful, full-developed man' (p. 423), and he says he wishes he had known about Whitman when lecturing in Lambeth. Egremont also defends Whitman strongly against the common English charge of vulgarity: 'I wonder whether you have read any of the twaddle that is written about Whitman's grossness, his materialism, and so forth? ... Is he not *all* spirit, rightly understood?' (p. 424).

In Gissing's divided narratives, however, such transcendental reconciliations of spirit and matter are never allowed to take root and flourish. Egremont finally returns to the more familiar landscapes of England, where he encounters, as he says, 'poetry of a different kind', moving 'from Whitman to Tennyson' (p. 439). And in *Thyrza* it is this Tennysonian impulse that ultimately prevails, as Egremont chooses to accommodate himself to marriage with the genteel Annabel Newthorpe, who in English terms is more his social equal. Annabel sympathetically tells Egremont at the end 'that you missed the great opportunity of your life when you abandoned Thyrza' (p. 490), and one clear implication here is that it is the divisive social system in England that finally makes the relationship between Egremont and Thyrza impossible. What is typical of Gissing, though, is the way in which this narrative explores other intellectual possibilities before pulling itself back into the safer realms of conventional domesticity. George Orwell admired Gissing as an honest chronicler of lower-middle-class 'vulgarity, squalor and failure', someone who showed characters 'acting on everyday motives and not merely undergoing strings of improbable adventures'; but there is a more radical side to Gissing, exemplified here by his interest in Whitman, a side that was attracted towards aestheticism and was more ambivalent about coercive pressures towards social and sexual propriety.[70]

---

[70] George Orwell, 'George Gissing', in *Collected Essays, Journalism and Letters*, iv: *In Front of Your Nose, 1945–1950*, ed. Sonia Orwell and Ian Angus (London: Secker & Warburg, 1968), 436, 433.

Gissing's relationship to the aberrant sexual mores commonly associated with the Aesthetic Movement, then, fluctuated as much as his attitude towards America, with which it was to some extent commensurate. Gissing complained to Gabrielle Fleury that his first wife had accused him of 'unspeakable' vices, of being a 'disciple of Oscar Wilde', and despite the evident uneasiness with homosexuality that runs through his letters and novels, Gissing was never less than ambiguous about the unorthodox world of aestheticism. He was, for example, an early enthusiast of Ruskin and attended the commemorative exhibition of Rossetti's work at the Royal Academy in 1882, though in 1895, in a letter to Morley Roberts, he described the 'Wilde business' as 'frightfully depressing', suggesting that Wilde had experimented with 'paederastic pleasures' more out of intellectual curiosity than from any 'natural tendency'.[71] Gissing also became interested a few years later in the works of Leopold von Sacher-Masoch, telling Gabrielle Fleury how much he liked Sacher-Masoch's *Contes Galiciens*: 'There is a strange wild flavour about the life they represent.' Sacher-Masoch's wife was a personal friend of Fleury's, and Gissing also met their son, Demetrius, in April 1900.[72] It was, of course, from the 1880s through to the turn of the twentieth century that sexual 'perversions' were first being categorized and codified, in the pioneering psychoanalytical work of Havelock Ellis, Richard Krafft-Ebing, and others, and Gissing's novels, for all of their protestations of empirical 'truthfulness', consistently flirt with various impulses of transgression that cannot so easily be contained within the normalizing realms of property and propriety. In *Adultery and the Novel*, Tony Tanner wrote of the symbiotic relationship between marriage and the Victorian bourgeois novel, and in these term Gissing deviates in both theme and genre, since many of his narratives fail to achieve the kind of closure endemic to the moral realism of middle-class English custom.[73]

In Gissing's second novel, *The Unclassed* (1884), the relationship between schoolteacher Osmond Waymark and chemist Julian Casti is specifically cast in quasi-erotic terms. Waymark meets Casti through advertising for 'companionship' in a lonely hearts column, and when he asks the latter if he has ever 'written verses', we are told that 'Julian reddened, like a girl'.[74] Later, Waymark even talks of how he feels 'quite ready' to marry Julian (p. 116). With women, conversely, Waymark finds himself unable to reconcile the intellectual and sensual aspects of his nature: while Maud Enderby is like a 'spirit' to him (p. 171), and while her ideas remind him of Schopenhauer's, he cannot experience with her the

---

[71] Diana Maltz, 'Bohemia's Bo(a)rders: Queer-Friendly Gissing', *Gissing Journal*, 37/4 (Oct. 2001), 12; *idem*, 'Practical Aesthetics and Decadent Rationale in George Gissing', *Victorian Literature and Culture*, 28 (2000), 55–7; Gissing, *Collected Letters*, v. 339.

[72] Gissing, *Collected Letters*, vii. 193; viii. 34–5.

[73] Tony Tanner, *Adultery in the Novel: Contract and Transgression* (Baltimore: Johns Hopkins University Press, 1979), 15.

[74] George Gissing, *The Unclassed*, ed. Jacob Korg (Brighton: Harvester Press, 1976), 39, 46. Subsequent page references to this edition are cited in parentheses in the text.

same sexual excitement that attracts him to Ida Starr, a product of London low life. Passion here betokens a sense of entrapment, the same kind of blind submission to 'the idea of Fate' (p. 225) which causes Waymark's own novel to be classed with 'the unsavoury productions of the so-called naturalist school' (p. 290). The subtext of *The Unclassed*, in other words, involves precisely the sense of displacement that Gissing himself referred to in an 1895 preface to the novel, where he insisted that the title did not signify '*déclassé*', but rather people who 'dwell in a limbo external to society' (p. v). Extending this metaphorical formulation further, we can say that Waymark seems to dwell in a world where the rationale for his own decisions is not entirely transparent to him, just as his own fiction suggests a form of dehumanization where the idea of free moral choice is illusory. In *The Unclassed*, much is left unsaid or takes place, as it were, in the wings—the Reverend Enderby flees to California after embezzling money, spiced beef in new American tins mysteriously appears in a shop window in Peckham—and all this gives readers a tantalizing sense that the scenes before them have been shaped by forces (economic, social, psychological) that remain obscure to the naked eye.

The Odd Women (1893), which was particularly admired by the New York journal the *Nation* for its quizzical scrutiny of the institution of marriage, is another Gissing novel whose 'oddness' lies not just in the socially eccentric behaviour of its fictional protagonists—in this case, two single women who eschew domestic life in order to work for the cause of 'female emancipation'—but also, more awkwardly, in the structural paradox whereby the behaviour of these characters becomes ultimately self-contradictory. Rhoda Nunn is, in fact, not so unconventional as she appears, and 'taking a morbid delight in self-torture', she finds herself torn between a quest for intellectual freedom and the more subliminal desire to relapse into marriage.[75] Gissing thus writes in *The Odd Women* a Victorian novel of romantic relationships that is also a critique of the assumptions upon which that genre is based. By following the Victorian presumption of resolution through marriage while simultaneously detaching his narrative from that trajectory, Gissing creates a doubleness or disjunction that opens up a parodic space within his text, so that his empirical realism comes reflexively to interrogate the grounds of its own representation.

It is this reluctant doubleness that projects Gissing's narratives into a world beyond their own domestic orbit. In an 1897 essay for *Harper's Weekly*, reviewing *The Whirlpool*, Henry James wrote of Gissing that it was 'mainly his saturation that makes him interesting'. While James claimed that he had 'a persistent taste' for Gissing's work and acknowledged him as 'the authority' on lower-middle-class life, he nevertheless felt that Gissing 'almost as persistently disappoints me. I fail as yet to make out why exactly it is that going so far he so sturdily refuses to

[75] George Gissing, *The Odd Women*, ed. Elaine Showalter (New York: New American Library–Penguin, 1983), 60, 322.

go further.'[76] But this precise quandary of whether or not to go 'further' is at the conceptual heart of *The Whirlpool* itself: the central characters, the Rolfes, are caught somewhere between the idealized stability and security of the Mortons, a family rooted in its house at Greystone, and the new world of global displacement and commercial exchange, facilitated by steamers and telegrams and exemplified by the way the Carnabys shuttle easily back and forth between hemispheres. Bound for Australia out of London, Sibyl Carnaby talks of wanting to visit Honolulu and asks her husband how to get there, to which he replies tersely: 'Across America, and then from San Francisco'.[77] The narrator then comments on the seeming dissolution of space associated with this projected voyage: 'A great atlas was opened, routes were fingered; half the earth's circumference vanished in a twinkling' (p. 59). It is this same sense of restlessness which impels Alma Frothingham to quit England and to pursue her musical ambitions in Germany, while in keeping with the tone of displacement that permeates the novel, we are told in passing about the peregrinations of a minor character, Mrs Fenimore, whose husband is busy in India, but who, because she cannot stand the Indian climate, has taken herself off instead to Stuttgart, to enable her children to learn German. On one level, this international perspective might seem to betoken simply an ebullient British imperialism: Rolfe is a great apologist for the empire, and believing that 'the future of England is beyond seas', he says he would have schoolchildren 'taught all about the Colonies before bothering them with histories of Greece and Rome' (p. 105). More insidiously, though, this erasure of domestic space introduces a sense of moral uncertainty and epistemological insecurity: deprived of a known and familiar environment, the inhabitants of *The Whirlpool* find themselves caught up within a kind of *mise-en-abîme* where character itself finally becomes illegible. 'I don't know you,' says Rolfe to his wife at one point: 'who knows any other human being?' (p. 116). The plot, turning on blackmail and betrayal, fits with what Mrs Abbott calls this 'whirlpool way of life' (p. 156), which has now seemingly become inevitable: 'It's the new world,' admits Rolfe, 'we live in it, and must make the best of it' (p. 215).

One consequence of this erosion of geographical limits, then, is an equivalent erosion of ethical demarcations, based as they are upon a secure circumscription of local values: 'There are plenty of good and honest people still,' says Hugh Carnaby, 'but they can't help getting mixed up among the vilest lot on the face of the earth' (p. 214). Another is the sense of living in a shadow world, where the main levers of power are operating elsewhere. This is one of the reasons why Gissing's novels frequently seem depressing, but also perhaps why the author failed, as James said, to go 'further'; he portrays in *The Whirlpool* a

---

[76] Pierre Coustillas and Colin Partridge, eds., *Gissing: The Critical Heritage* (London: Routledge & Kegan Paul, 1972), 290–1.
[77] George Gissing, *The Whirlpool*, ed. Patrick Parrinder (Brighton: Harvester Press, 1977), 58. Subsequent page references to this edition are cited in parentheses in the text.

world in which characters frequently attempt to act according to their best moral instincts, only to find that circumstances have dictated their choices without them realizing it. Gissing has no particular interest in analysing systematically the impersonal forces that loom over local situations; his emphasis is more firmly on individuals and their environments. But what we find in *The Whirlpool* is a disquieting sense of the epistemological grounds for moral realism sliding away from under the characters as they speak, so that *The Whirlpool* might ultimately be described as a novel about the failure of domestic agendas adequately to address transnational situations at the end of the nineteenth century. As we saw, Gissing employed the image of a whirlpool to describe the Atlantic Ocean in his first novel, *Workers in the Dawn*, and in this later work American terms such as 'boom' are used self-consciously, as if to indicate the inevitable incorporation of England into a world of multinational capitalism. (The narrator says in relation to Alma's musical career: 'Had she been able to use her opportunity to the utmost, doubtless something of a "boom"—the word then coming into fashion—might have resulted for her' (p. 372).)

This implicit dialectic between the local and the transnational in Gissing's novels leads him to return compulsively to scenarios where his method of representation fails. *In the Year of Jubilee*, published in 1895, is set in 1887, and it begins with scenes of crowds swarming through London to celebrate Queen Victoria's Golden Jubilee. In a gesture that mimetically recapitulates this imperial dynamic, Nancy Lord, in a 'conceit of self-importance', ascends to the top of the London Monument and looks out over the city's 'immensity': 'Here her senses seemed to make literal the assumption by which her mind had always been directed: that she—Nancy Lord—was the mid point of the universe.'[78] The overt narrative irony here is commensurate with the structural ironies running through the rest of the novel, which reveal the pretentious public rhetoric of empire—the lecture by Samuel Barmby on 'National Greatness: its Obligations and its Dangers', for example (p. 306)—but also demonstrate clearly enough how even this royal spectacle is immersed in a world of market commodities, as we see with the manufacturer of 'Jubilee Perfume' who nets a comfortable £100 per day (p. 64). John M. MacKenzie has described how in the last years of Victoria's reign the empire itself became heavily commercialized—through posters, cigarette cards, a vast expansion in popular publishing, and so on—and what we see in *In the Year of Jubilee* is something like an Americanization of the British Empire, with the old imperial capital being swamped by a welter of commercial traffic that it can neither order nor control.[79] King's Cross is described as a 'battle-ground of advertisements', with 'all the produce and refuse of civilisation announced in staring letters, in daubed effigies, base, paltry,

---

[78] George Gissing, *In the Year of Jubilee* (Brighton: Harvester Press, 1976), 104. Subsequent page references to this edition are cited in parentheses in the text.
[79] MacKenzie, *Propaganda and Empire*, 17–23.

grotesque' (p. 309), and it is the inexorable pressures of the international economy that drive the impoverished Lionel Tarrant to follow in the footsteps of an old college friend who has succeeded in making money out in the Bahamas. Tarrant thus goes off to Nassau, where 'a lot of Americans always spend the winter', thinking that this will be a 'useful step' towards 'preparing for the future' (p. 197), and from there he moves to Washington DC and New York, where he tries his hand at writing journalistic pieces such as 'A Reverie in Wall Street' and 'The Commercial Prospects of the Bahamas'. Though his friend Harvey Munden tells him that he has 'brought back a trans-Atlantic accent', the Oxford-educated Tarrant is by no means totally enamoured of the country of his exile, declaring that 'if I were condemned for life to the United States, I should go mad, and perish in an attempt to swim the Atlantic' (p. 334). Though forced to admit how 'in the United States he found so much to observe,—even to enjoy' (p. 339) that he was not so productive during his time there as he might have been, Tarrant is nevertheless the typical kind of vacillating Gissing hero who can never quite abjure an indebtedness to his native sensibility: 'Go and live for a month in a cheap New York boarding-house,' he tells Munden, 'and you'll come back with a wholesome taste for English refinement' (p. 336).

Tarrant's problem, of course, is that the 'English refinement' he has in mind is itself a nostalgic fiction. As we see from all the commercial enterprises that permeate London in this year of Jubilee, England itself has now become inextricably interwoven with America; even a dinner party in Kilburn, north London, is graced by 'an American joker, who, in return for a substantial cheque, provided amusement in fashionable gatherings' (p. 227). This is why Tarrant's style of 'pretty antithesis' and 'lively paradox' (p. 364) seems to cut little ice in the London of 1887; Gissing's novels are full of littérateurs who fail to achieve popular success, and this is not merely because of the vulgarizing tendencies of public taste but, more substantially, because there seems to be a structural disjunction between the genteel realms of literary art and the coercive economic forces that drive this modern world. Like Reardon and Biffen retreating into the charmed world of classical hexameters in *New Grub Street*, Tarrant finds that his foppish style does not speak to the conditions of 'trans-Atlantic' culture (p. 334). Yet Gissing continued to write about the failure of the artist even when his own career as a novelist was highly successful, and one reason for this apparent self-immolation is his intuitive awareness of what he sees as the necessary failure of all fictional representations to encompass the commercial cross-currents of this increasingly international world. Gissing consequently writes about an English society that has become, in his eyes, unknowable; neither realism nor naturalism, neither aestheticism nor epigrammatic wit, can do justice to the increasingly obscure nature of modernity. It is this philosophical pessimism, more than simply the pressures of the marketplace, that dictates why to be a writer in Gissing's world is to be doomed to failure.

Fredric Jameson has written about the 'crisis of narrative *totality*' in Gissing, the way in which his novels are riven by contradictions which make them unable to achieve the unifying vision which they seek.[80] However, the poignancy and ultimately the power of Gissing's work derive precisely from the frictions and frustrations involved in this attempt to achieve an Olympian narrative perspective. Nancy Lord's trip to the top of the London Monument in *In the Year of Jubilee*, for example, should allow her to map this imperial vortex in relation to a wider circumference—the issue of 'the emancipation of the niggers' in the Bahamas is mentioned briefly in the book (p. 55)—but the weakness of the novel, or perhaps its strength, lies precisely in the fact that these conceptual equations are not fully worked through; they remain peripheral events, on the edge of intellectual vision for both characters and readers. This is why alienation is for Gissing not just a psychological theme but also, in aesthetic terms, a structural compulsion. If Gissing's narratives are impelled by failure, one peculiarly revealing source of that failure is the erosion of the force of synecdoche. Local and global, image and abstraction, no longer coincide, so that Gissing's narratives chronicle the breakdown of an organic or 'natural' relationship between literature and its contextual environment.

Gissing's most extreme expression of this condition of inarticulacy is perhaps *The Nether World* (1889), which is often thought to be the most Zola-like of his novels in its swerve away from moral realism into urban naturalism, its flamboyant regression into a world of cruelty and the grotesque. The 'degradation' of violence is always a lurking threat here, a threat which makes itself manifest in the brutalized marriage between Bob Hewett and his wife Penelope, also known ingloriously as 'Pennyloaf'.[81] This kind of violence seems to arise partly out of an incapacity on the part of the characters to comprehend the social pressures that are hemming them in. John Hewett, for example, is motivated purely by an impulse of rudderless revolt: 'uncalculating, inarticulate, he fumed and fretted away his energies in a conflict with forces ludicrously personified' (p. 79). Because of this loss of intellectual vision, this inability to make a synecdochical connection between empirical object and abstract idea, Hewett radically misreads his environment, creating for himself a kind of crazy-mirror hall wherein London becomes merely the projection of his own pathological fantasies. Gissing's narrative wraps itself around these solipsistic perspectives by describing the city in anthropomorphic terms, so as to match the bizarre life with which it is endowed by its inhabitants: 'the shapes of poverty-eaten houses and grimy workshops stood huddling in the obscurity' (p. 32); 'the pest-stricken regions of East London, sweltering in sunshine which served only to reveal

---

[80] Fredric Jameson, *The Political Unconscious: Narrative as a Socially Symbolic Act* (Ithaca, NY: Cornell University Press, 1981), 190.

[81] George Gissing, *The Nether World*, ed. John Goode (Brighton: Harvester Press, 1974), 333. Subsequent page references to this edition are cited in parentheses in the text.

the intimacies of abomination … a city of the damned, such as thought never conceived before this age of ours' (p. 164). Such metaphorical projections are commensurate with the solipsism that also impels the actions of other characters, from Clara Hewett's masochistic attraction towards her own ruin—'as though by such act she could satiate her instincts of defiance' (p. 94)—to Michael Snowdon's obsessive idealism, which leads him to demand as a condition of inheriting his legacy that his granddaughter Jane should devote herself to the reform of the poor. Snowdon's scheme, says the narrator, has 'that horrible intensity of fanaticism which is so like the look of cruelty, of greed, of any passion originating in the baser self' (p. 308); and such oppressive 'dehumanisation' (p. 255), no less than the physical violence of Bob and Pennyloaf, turns Snowdon into an appropriate denizen of this nether world. These hellish incarcerations are epitomized, as Adrian Poole has noted, by the 'choric figure' of Mad Jack, whose overt craziness is lent 'oracular status' within this urban inferno.[82]

Like *In the Year of Jubilee*, *The Nether World* is a narrative of imperial circumference and spatial displacement, with the United States figuring again as a focal point of commercial instability. Michael Snowdon's estranged son, Joseph, is said to have made a lot of money in the States, partly through flirting with illegality in his trading, and on his return to England he enters the newfangled advertising business. At the end of the novel, after Joseph has returned to America, we are told that he has lost his wealth through commercial speculation: 'One of those financial crashes which are common in America caused his total ruin' (p. 389). Michael Snowdon's wealth, on the other hand, comes courtesy of his eldest son who emigrated to Australia and got rich from the sheep-farming industry, before dying young and leaving his fortune to his father, who had come out to join him in New South Wales. In this sense, the saturnalia of the black urban comedy that permeates *The Nether World* is mirrored in the novel's social and economic infrastructure, which also addresses a world of displacement and inversion: the 'nether world' is not just the 'city of the damned' in East London but also the world 'down under' in Australia, the location that provides the source of wealth for the plot of this novel. It is the nether world of Australia that provides the financial incentive for the manic behaviour of these characters in the London underworld; the spatial axis of this text is thus not only local but global. Just as John Hewett remains blind to the social forces enclosing him, so other characters in this book mistakenly believe that their 'nether world' is simply the landscape they see before them, whereas, through an elaborate *mise-en-abîme*, Gissing structures his narrative to elicit a dramatic irony whereby urban squalor and greed appear as the product of more distant, inscrutable forces. Raymond Williams saw Gissing as writing primarily about the mechanistic routines of the city and the forms of psychological alienation associated with them, while Adrian Poole similarly described the finest aspect of

---

[82] Adrian Poole, *Gissing in Context* (London: Macmillan, 1975), 92.

The Nether World as its understanding of what it feels like to be trapped 'inside' a particular enclosed space: a building, a slum, a class, a hell.[83] Neither emphasis seems quite right, however; more specifically, the trauma for the denizens of this novel involves not so much being trapped but being unable to identify what it is that is trapping them. Again, it is the illegibility of their environment that undermines the dignity of Gissing's characters, forcing them into crazed forms of personification and pathological vengeance which speak to the breakdown in teleology between local and global, cause and effect, object and meaning.

This loss of faith in a stable social body is placed by Gissing specifically within the historical context of the Reformation in *Born in Exile* (1892). The hero of this novel, Godwin Peak, is named by his radical Dissenting father after the author of *Political Justice*, while Godwin's younger brother, Oliver, is 'named after the Protector', Oliver Cromwell.[84] The book interrogates what it takes to be the intellectual complacency of the Church of England by the way in which Peak disguises himself as an Anglican clergyman in order to recommend himself to the conventionally minded family of Sidwell Warricombe and thus to further his own marriage prospects. Such 'simulated orthodoxy' (p. 215) particularly perturbs Sidwell's brother, Buckland, who associates the disruption of religious certainties with the destabilization of social positions, a state of uncertainty to which he is equally resistant. Anglicanism thus emerges here as a form of institutional hypocrisy, a social charade designed to prop up class hierarchies and old established social comforts. Peak's essay in *The Critical*, 'The New Sophistry', indicts 'English society at large' for the way it makes 'profession of a faith which in no sense whatever it could be said sincerely to hold', and in the tradition of English Dissent going back through William Godwin to the Church reformers of the seventeenth century, Peak declares how 'thousands of people keep up an ignoble formalism, because they feared the social results of declaring their severance from the religion of the churches' (p. 392). Meanwhile, Peak's old adversary from his school days, Bruno Chilvers, who goes on to enjoy a successful career in the Anglican Church, is shown ironically enough to be hardly less sceptical than Peak himself about conventional religious dogmas. However, whereas Peak is deliberately antagonistic and overtly provocative in his scepticism—going in for 'evolutionary speculations' in the wake of Darwin's *The Origins of the Species* (p. 123) and writing on progressive scientific topics for *The Liberator* as well as *The Critical*—Chilvers's sense of agnosticism is more emollient and socially palatable. It is this ingratiating style that enables Chilvers not to offend his ecclesiastical constituency as he attempts in a more gradualist manner to reconcile science and Christianity.

---

[83] Raymond Williams, *The English Novel from Dickens to Lawrence* (London: Chatto & Windus, 1970), 156–62; Poole, *Gissing in Context*, 101–2.

[84] George Gissing, *Born in Exile*, ed. Pierre Coustillas (Brighton: Harvester Press, 1978), 32. Subsequent page references to this edition are in parentheses in the text.

The difficulties experienced by Peak, in other words, emerge as much from his sense of social alienation as from his theories of intellectual dissent. Peak feels that he has no 'right of citizenship' within English society, where he is destined to be always 'a lodger' (pp. 298–9); but it is the quandary of his internal exile that he can neither abandon England altogether nor 'knit' himself into its 'social fabric' (p. 483). Peak's energy derives instead from being 'always a rebel' (p. 482); he seems to lack, as he himself puts it, 'the gift of pleasing—moral grace. My strongest emotions seem to be absorbed in revolt' (p. 404). This idea of revolt against English values is given literal expression by various figures who do indeed choose to move beyond the charmed circle of English society: Peak's friend Malkin goes off to Buenos Aires early in the novel, and when the latter's brother and sister-in-law subsequently set off for New Zealand on business, Malkin, not believing that he 'could ever make a solid home in England' (p. 423), thinks of following them. Similarly, one of the professors at Peak's Alma Mater, Whitelaw College, spends three years in the United States, before returning not only with advanced views on geology to unsettle further his British colleagues but also with a young American wife. But when Peak himself is freed economically at the end of the book to travel through Europe and pursue more cosmopolitan interests, he seems just to wither away. It is as if his sense of identity can emerge only from positioning himself in an iconoclastic, non-conformist relation to the society whose values he has at some level inescapably internalized.

In this sense, Godwin Peak's impersonation of an Anglican clergyman in this novel is not mere fraudulence, since it betokens the kind of split personality whereby Gissing's protagonist is both inside and outside English society at once. This kind of bifurcation also permeates Gissing's novels in a more structural sense: they describe English customs from a perspective of alienation, where national identity has become a condition to be scrutinized rather than an inherited ethos to be taken for granted. Poole has discussed the anxieties about temporality in late Victorian fiction, the increasing distrust of time as a continuous, teleological sequence, a distrust that helped to shape the fragmented patterns of fiction in the late nineteenth century.[85] In Gissing, however, such anxieties appertain even more noticeably to space: there is uncertainty about how British culture can be demarcated or circumscribed, and the extent to which domestic agendas are necessarily shaped and inflected by affairs beyond the native orbit. We know that Gissing read Clough in 1883, in a volume lent to him by his brother Algernon, and there are marked similarities between these two English authors both in their conceptions of internal exile and in their appropriation of the Reformation as a metaphorical rather than a theological means to highlight their sense of alienation from English society.[86] Gissing, like Clough, understood the long tradition of dissent in English society as an antecedent to his own sense of reimagining native culture on a transnational axis. Like Clough again, Gissing's secession from the

---

[85] Poole, *Gissing in Context*, 25–6.   [86] Gissing, *Collected Letters*, ii, 130–1.

values of the English *ecclesia*, both the Anglican Church itself and also the broader national community, led him to look towards a metaphorical exile as a means towards redescribing English culture from, as it were, the outside in, rather than from the inside out.

In the second half of the nineteenth century, then, the United States operated for British authors not so much as a prototype for political reform, as it had for writers of earlier generations, but as a reference point for philosophical dissent and an exemplification of the insufficiency of self-enclosed and self-defining national values. Clough's religious heterodoxy, like Wilde's sexual iconoclasm, looked 'westward', as Clough put it in 'Say Not the Struggle Nought Availeth', to 'where the land is bright' (p. 206), as if to find an alternative frame of reference for what each took to be the limited horizons of English culture. It is ironic that Churchill was to quote Clough's poem in an April 1941 radio broadcast as a tribute to the American spirit of democracy and a clarion call for the Anglo-American wartime alliance, since in the nineteenth century this spectre of an Atlantic republic was much more disturbing to the English political order.[87] In the final analysis, though, maverick writers like Clough and Gissing cannot imagine the idea of England without America or America without England. As a transnational poet, Clough disturbed the intellectual establishments on both sides of the Atlantic by redescribing them in a two-way mirror such that each party saw its own assumptions uncomfortably reversed, while Gissing's self-tormenting sense of the epistemological inadequacy of local mimesis and ethical circumference similarly led him to project a transatlantic world of dislocation and disjunction. Gissing, again like Clough, thoroughly revised the tenets of American Transcendentalism, admiring the ebullient optimism of writers like Whitman, but describing in his own work a scheme of alienation whose centre, to misquote Emerson's 'Circles', was nowhere and whose circumference was everywhere.[88] In this sense, the oblique involvement of Gissing with the Aesthetic Movement served to introduce into his works a transatlantic dimension which effectively countered nationalist suppositions in the nineteenth century about the responsibilities of literature to society. Rather than acquiescing in the British imperialist project, Clough and Gissing both deployed the hybridizing qualities of aestheticism to project a more complicated world in which the imperatives of centripetal order and the assumptions of ethical transparency were losing credibility.

[87] Roy Jenkins, *Churchill* (London: Macmillan, 2001), 652.

[88] 'The eye is the first circle; the horizon which it forms is the second; and throughout nature this primary figure is repeated without end ... St. Augustine described the nature of God as a circle whose centre was everywhere, and its circumference nowhere.' Ralph Waldo Emerson, 'Circles', in *Essays: First Series*, 179.

6

Great Traditions: Modernism, Canonization, Counter-Reformation

SPIRIT SUMMONED WEST: D. H. LAWRENCE

During the course of the nineteenth century, cultural relations between Britain and the United States were shaped by a number of conflicts in which the two countries were on opposite sides: the aftermath of the Revolutionary wars, the war of 1812, the dispute over Oregon. This was followed by the American Civil War, in which Britain was not directly involved, but whose outcome served to enhance federal power and thus to pose an increasing threat to British imperial dominion. In the twentieth century, by contrast, the defining event for Anglo-American relations was the Second World War, in which the United States and Britain fought on the same side. Because of the decisive way in which the United States intervened in the Allied cause in 1941 and the vigorous political promotion by Winston Churchill of a 'special relationship' between the two nations, there has, however, been a subsequent tendency to interpret the cultural development of this Anglo-American relationship in the middle of the twentieth century too simplistically.[1] I shall argue that Germany and America came to represent for Britain alternative versions of modernism, so that the country's moral agenda involved not just lining up the English-speaking world against the barbaric Hun but, more insidiously, considering how its own native domain might relate to the problematic dynamics of radical social transformation. Rather than a straightforward antithesis between the social democracies of Britain and the United States on the one hand and the totalitarianism of Nazi Germany on the other, there emerged a more complicated pattern of triangulation through which America articulated the aesthetics of modernism in what was, from the British point of view, a more emollient but no less alien and disturbing fashion. This chapter will focus specifically on D. H. Lawrence, born in Nottinghamshire in 1885, who had strong links with both Germany and America, and T. S. Eliot, born in Missouri in 1888, who first arrived in England in 1914 and went on to become a mainstay of the British Establishment.

---

[1] Reynolds, *Rich Relations*, 144.

One of the difficulties surrounding any general consideration of modernist writing at the beginning of the twenty-first century is that it does not yet seem sufficiently distant in time. We know that we need to make historical adjustments when reading, say, Alexander Pope or George Eliot, but there is still a misleading tendency to assume that the world of writers such as Lawrence and Eliot is recognizably our own. This dilemma is exacerbated in the case of Lawrence by his predilection for writing in the present tense, as if to convey the currency and urgency of his insights and thus to resist their relegation to the fossilized category of history; it is perpetuated as well by critics who continue to declare Lawrence's works 'many years ahead of their time'.[2] In fact, as Fredric Jameson has observed, the way in which the modernist canon has been constructed has been too much a product of the intellectual concern after the Second World War to distinguish sharply between high art and mass culture, with the result that the socially inclusive, utopian aspects of interwar modernism have largely been occluded in favour of concentration upon its aesthetic and technical aspects, the qualities that differentiated it from products of 'the television age'.[3] Yet, for all of their obvious differences, Lawrence and Eliot shared a commitment to the regeneration of the common weal, to imagining a community galvanized by the power of the word; consequently, they both envisaged aesthetics not as a retreat from broader social questions but as a way of giving their visionary consciousness a form of incarnate life. This kind of aestheticization of politics became very unfashionable after 1945, because the intercalation of aesthetic and political questions was by then seen as a practice associated specifically with fascist ideals, but it is crucial to acknowledge how modernist idealism was interwoven with the same utopian impulse that coincided with the rise of Fascist Italy and Nazi Germany. There were, of course, significant differences between these regimes: Italian fascism, strongly influenced by the Roman imperial past and by Roman Catholic doctrines of social hierarchy, sought to bind the different classes within a corporate model of state power, while National Socialism was more of a metapolitical movement which saw the state merely as a means towards empowering its people, for whom the mystical categories of race and nation would be the supreme value. Nevertheless, both parties were committed to deploying authoritarian instruments of power in the interests of furthering what was a broad and amorphous desire, particularly in a continent economically ravaged after the First World War, for social regeneration and the restitution of 'natural' order.

As Frank Kermode noted, however, these more 'apocalyptic aspects' of Lawrence's writing have largely been ignored as modernism has been safely

    [2] Mark Kincaid-Weekes, 'Decolonising Imagination: Lawrence in the 1920s', in *The Cambridge Companion to D. H. Lawrence*, ed. Anne Fernihough (Cambridge: Cambridge University Press, 2001), 83.
    [3] Fredric Jameson, *A Singular Modernity: Essay on the Ontology of the Present* (London: Verso, 2002), 177.

accommodated and given institutional status in university curricula in the post-1945 era.[4] Concomitant with this kind of critical sentimentality has been a tendency to domesticate Lawrence, to claim his work as an integral part of a specifically English cultural heritage. The most obvious example of this approach is the highly influential work of F. R. Leavis, whose 1955 book on Lawrence cites as an epigraph a letter written by the novelist in 1915, early in his career, in which he states: 'And I am English, and my Englishness is my very vision.'[5] At the beginning of *D. H. Lawrence*, Leavis specifically declares how '[t]his book carries on from *The Great Tradition*' and how he sees Lawrence as 'one of the major novelists of the English tradition', 'a great successor to George Eliot' as 'a recorder of essential English history'; in *The Great Tradition* itself, published seven years earlier, he similarly adduces George Eliot, Henry James, and Joseph Conrad as exemplars of 'the tradition to which what is great in English fiction belongs'.[6] Leavis goes on to explain here that by placing James 'in an English tradition I am not slighting the fact of his American origin', or seeking to ignore the fact that James might be said to represent 'a distinctively American tradition' if he were placed, contrariwise, alongside Hawthorne and Melville. Nevertheless, so he argues, it is through his relation to English social realism that James achieves his most fully embodied and 'mature' works: 'his debt to Dickens involves more than a mere manner; he was helped by him to see from the outside, and critically place, the life around him.'[7]

It was not, then, that Leavis was hostile in theory to the idea of a writer having multiple affiliations, many different intellectual traditions to which he or she was indebted. When it came to critical practice, though, he tended to insist dogmatically on what he took to be the supreme virtues of the English tradition, extolling 'the incomparably superior concreteness of *The Portrait of a Lady*' and writing off James's later novels, where he most diverges from the English Victorian style of moral realism, as exhibiting 'senility'.[8] Although friendly in principle to the idea of American literature, Leavis remained resolutely innocent of how ethnic and social diversity might enter into the making of literary texts so as to order their priorities differently; accordingly, he dismissed the German-American Catholic Theodore Dreiser as one who 'so clearly belongs to no tradition' except that of 'the culturally dispossessed', while deploring in the Irish-American Scott Fitzgerald the lack of those 'moral perceptions out of which a creative rendering of human life might come'.[9] All of these terms—'tradition',

---

[4] Frank Kermode, 'Apocalypse and the Modern', in *Visions of Apocalypse: End or Rebirth?*, ed. Saul Friedländer *et al.* (New York: Holmes and Meier, 1985), 98.

[5] F. R. Leavis, *D. H. Lawrence: Novelist* (London: Chatto & Windus, 1967), 8. Lawrence's letter, to Lady Cynthia Asquith, is dated 21 Oct. 1915.

[6] Ibid., 9, 17, 107; *idem, Great Tradition*, 7.   [7] Leavis, *Great Tradition*, 10, 129, 132–3.

[8] Ibid., 16, 126.

[9] F. R. Leavis, 'The Complex Fate', in *Anna Karenina and Other Essays* (London: Chatto & Windus, 1967), 155–6.

'dispossessed', 'moral', 'creative'—are ideologically loaded, of course; but their ideology operated for Leavis in an entirely unconscious way, so that he came to accept his own aesthetic values and critical touchstones as, absurdly enough, universal standards. Leavis uses as an epigraph to *Mass Civilisation and Minority Culture* (1930) a quotation from Arnold's *Culture and Anarchy*—'In any period it is upon a very small minority that the discerning appreciation of art and culture depends'—and it is a typically Arnoldian conflation of liberal humanism with universalism that leads Leavis later in this pamphlet to launch a jeremiad against the 'catastrophic' cultural standards of the American Midwest, as recently documented in *Middletown*, the 'remarkable work of anthropology' produced by Robert and Helen Lynd in 1929. For Leavis, the 'processes of mass production and standardization' chronicled by the Lynds in Muncie, Indiana, epitomize a 'levelling-down' which threatens English language and literature with the grim prospect of 'being Americanised'.[10]

It is important to recognize, then, that Leavis wants to claim Lawrence for English literature not out of bald nationalistic assumptions but out of an implicit conviction of the national culture's moral superiority: a great tradition for Great Britain. By contrast, Ezra Pound is described by Leavis as exemplifying 'the conditions in which the American writer works', a terrain of barbarism and rootlessness: 'no other civilization', he says, 'could have produced so robust a talent that had so little sense of what a living cultural tradition is, so little sense of the organic'.[11] It is, then, not difficult to see a parallel between Leavis's vision of a great tradition of writers forming an imaginative community extending over time and his equal reverence for the organic local community, the community extensive over space, which he sees it as Lawrence's genius to have embodied. For Leavis, the temporal and spatial organicism of the English tradition forms an ethical contrast to the raw state of America, and he consequently dismissed Harry T. Moore, Lawrence's American biographer, as 'a complete foreigner in regard to the England to which Lawrence ... so essentially belonged'.[12] Leavis's proprietorial air here was all the more marked because he felt himself self-consciously to be incorporating Nonconformist Dissent as a vital part of the English cultural heritage. His book on Lawrence specifically takes issue with T. S. Eliot's remark about the 'crippling effect upon a man of letters of not having been brought up in the environment of a living and central tradition', by which of course Eliot meant Anglicanism. Leavis quite justifiably points out that '[t]he Chapel, in the Lawrence circle, was the centre of a strong social life, and the focus of a still persistent cultural tradition'; but in his concern to displace Anglicanism as the default standard of the English cultural tradition,

---

[10] F. R. Leavis, *Mass Civilisation and Minority Culture* (Cambridge: Minority Press, 1930), 3, 6–8.
[11] F. R. Leavis, 'The Americanness of American Literature', in *Anna Karenina*, 150–1.
[12] F. R. Leavis, '"Lawrence Scholarship" and Lawrence', in *Anna Karenina*, 168.

he retreats into strategies of empathy and appropriation which verge at times on the xenophobic, as when he asserts: ' "*I* am a fellow-countryman of D. H. Lawrence." Mr. Eliot is not.'[13]

Leavis's nationalistic emphasis is in the end critically misleading, however, because Lawrence in fact spent a great deal of his life outside England, including two years in Germany and other parts of Europe after eloping with his German lover, Frieda Weekley, in 1912. Indeed, after November 1919, when Lawrence left England for Italy, he was in the UK for a total of only twenty-five weeks during the rest of his life, mainly on short visits to London or to his family in Nottinghamshire, until his death in France in March 1930. Developing alongside this personal exile was an increasing strain of abstraction in his writing, as his style moved away from the social realism of *Sons and Lovers* (1913) towards the modernist dislocations of *Women in Love* (1920) and the later works. Nevertheless, the legacy of Leavis's compulsion to anglicize him is still evident in the work of Raymond Williams, who in *Culture and Society* (1958) compared Lawrence's critique of industrialism to that of Thomas Carlyle and asserted how the 'tragedy of Lawrence, the working-class boy, is that he did not live to come home'. A few years later, in *The English Novel from Dickens to Lawrence* (1970), Williams categorically treated Lawrence, as his title suggests, 'as an English novelist', comparing his representation of 'living relationships' and working communities to that of Thomas Hardy and finding the 'abstract scheme' of *Women in Love* to be 'a radical *simplification* of the novel', a testament to the loss of the 'irreducible reality' of human life.[14] Graham Holderness in 1982 similarly emphasized 'the central and radical quality of the writer's social experience' in his analysis of how English class conflicts permeate Lawrence's work, an ideological perspective that led him to deplore what he saw as the displacement of historical realism into modernist myth in *The Rainbow*. For Holderness, the 'decisive confrontation' of Lawrence's later years was his trip to Nottinghamshire in September 1926 to stay with his sister, when he witnessed the General Strike at first hand. Holderness argues that it was this shock of recognition that inspired a belated return on Lawrence's part to social realism, evident particularly in the first version of *Lady Chatterley's Lover*, completed in December of that year and published posthumously as *The First Lady Chatterley*.[15]

Holderness's view of Nottinghamshire as a site of recuperation and recognition for Lawrence is, however, not borne out by the latter's untitled essay now known as 'Return to Bestwood', written shortly after his 1926 visit to Eastwood. On the contrary, he talks here of how '[i]t always depresses me to come to my native district', how he feels 'more alien, perhaps, in my home place than anywhere else

---

[13] Leavis, *D. H. Lawrence*, 104–5, 306–7.

[14] R. Williams, *Culture and Society*, 213; *idem, English Novel from Dickens to Lawrence*, 170–1, 179–82.

[15] Graham Holderness, *D. H. Lawrence: History, Ideology and Fiction* (Dublin: Gill and Macmillan, 1982), 2, 4.

in the world'. Although Lawrence does mention the strike in this piece, it is only to indict the coalminers for an excessively materialistic attitude: 'their pride is in their pocket', he claims, and he goes on to denigrate the 'class war' as being 'a fight for the ownership or non-ownership of property, pure and simple, and nothing beyond'. One of the subsequent attractions of National Socialism, particularly for the Hitler Youth movements, was the way it offered to eliminate existing class distinctions and snobberies by submerging them in a higher doctrine of race, and Lawrence's comments here suggest a similar kind of impatience with the great British discourse of class. Even less sympathy for his old habitat is manifested in his assertion at the end of this 1926 essay that a primary concern for 'the quality of life, not the quantity' should lead to '[h]opeless life' being 'put to sleep, the idiots and the hopeless sick and the true criminal'.[16] As early as 1908, Lawrence expressed his belief that the best way to deal with 'the sick, the halt, and the maimed' was to 'build a lethal chamber as big as the Crystal Palace' and 'lead them gently' into it, 'with a military band playing softly, and a Cinematograph working brightly'; and this kind of sentiment was later hardened into an official policy for producing a gifted race by the American Eugenics Society, founded in 1926.[17]

This is not, of course, to deny the general significance of English cultural landscapes for Lawrence's artistic imagination. It is, though, to suggest that his best work operates not through any kind of pastoral retreat into native territory, or through an innate sense of fellow feeling, but by means of an inscription of parallel, alternate worlds whereby the impetus of modernist defamiliarization is positioned alongside a nostalgia for communal belonging. It is, in fact, precisely this tension between recognition and defamiliarization that makes for Lawrence's most effective writing. He himself described *The Rainbow* to Edward Garnett as '*very* different from *Sons and Lovers*: written in another language almost'; and it is this discursive estrangement of convention, a desire to remodel familiar figures within new horizons, that creates the peculiarly transgressive quality of Lawrence's best works.[18]

Exile, then, furnishes Lawrence with an alternative realm through which he believes he can perceive English conditions more clearly. In his essay 'Which Class I Belong To' (1927), he acknowledges that it is only since returning to Europe from America that he has been able fully to appreciate the significance of class barriers. He subsequently maintained, though, that both middle classes and working classes in England are limited in different ways, the former 'shallow and passionless', the latter 'narrow in outlook, in prejudice, and narrow in

[16] D. H. Lawrence, *Late Essays and Articles*, ed. James T. Boulton (Cambridge: Cambridge University Press, 2004), 15, 16, 23, 24.

[17] D. H. Lawrence, letter to Blanche Jennings, 9 Oct. 1908, in *The Letters of D. H. Lawrence*, i, ed. James T. Boulton (Cambridge: Cambridge University Press, 1979), 81.

[18] D. H. Lawrence, letter to Edward Garnett, 30 Dec. 1913, in *The Letters of D. H. Lawrence*, ii, ed. George J. Zytaruk and James T. Boulton (Cambridge: Cambridge University Press, 1981), 132.

intelligence'; therefore, he concludes, '[o]ne can belong absolutely to no class.'[19] In another late piece, 'Hymns in a Man's Life' (1928), Lawrence pays tribute to his Congregationalist upbringing, noting how 'The congregationalists are the oldest nonconformists, descendants of the Oliver Cromwell Independents', and remarking how he learnt hymns as a child which he never forgot.[20] It is not difficult, of course, to see a correlation between this inheritance of Dissent and Lawrence's literary mode of iconoclasm, or to see how his intellectual turn to America in the 1920s aligns him with a tradition of English Nonconformist writers going back to Richard Price; indeed, in the first few pages of *Apocalypse* (1931) the author makes these analogies explicit by relating his current interest in the Book of Revelation to his own Sunday school background. The point remains, however, that the force of Lawrence's insights stems neither from his autobiographical fragments nor from his modernist archetypes in themselves, but rather from the points of intersection between these two categories, the 'living nodality', to use one of his own phrases, where human and mythological are conjoined.[21] The brilliantly prescient and uncanny quality of 'A Letter from Germany', written in 1924, lies in the way it intuits an 'ancient spirit of pre-historic Germany coming back', with the progressive movement of history being superseded by 'something primitive ... as if the years were wheeling swiftly backwards, no more onwards'. In this country which is transforming itself eerily from a quotidian environment to the world of fable, outsiders are confronted, as were the Roman soldiers of old, with the 'black, massive round hills' of the Black Forest, indicating 'that they were at their own limit'.[22]

The extent to which Lawrence himself was sympathetic to fascist ideals has become a common, even hackneyed question since Bertrand Russell remarked hyperbolically in 1953 that Lawrence's views on blood 'led straight to Auschwitz'.[23] (I use 'fascist' here in the lower-case sense to indicate the term's general currency as an idea in the interwar period, rather than specifying its relation to any particular political party.) Leavis in 1955 cited a comment by V. S. Pritchett on the alleged intellectual affinities between Lawrence and Hitler, though Leavis himself attributed this misunderstanding to 'the simple scheme of salvation adopted on the Left', while Williams in 1958 dismissed the 'public projection' that Lawrence was 'a precursor of the Fascist emphasis on blood' as a matter simply of 'ignorance'.[24] What is most noticeable here is the determination on the part of these British critics in the decade after the Second World War to disavow any kind of affiliation between English literature and the cultural

---

[19] D. H. Lawrence, 'Myself Revealed', in *Late Essays*, 180.
[20] Lawrence, 'Hymns in a Man's Life', in *Late Essays*, 133.
[21] On the 'nodality' of urban spaces, see D. H. Lawrence, 'Taos', in *Phoenix: The Posthumous Papers of D. H. Lawrence*, ed. Edward D. McDonald (London: Heinemann, 1936), 100.
[22] Lawrence, *Phoenix*, 108–10.
[23] Bertrand Russell, 'Portraits from Memory, III: D. H. Lawrence', *Harper's Magazine*, Feb. 1953, 95.   [24] Leavis, *D. H. Lawrence*, 20; R. Williams, *Culture and Society*, 199.

standards of a national enemy. With the benefit of greater historical hindsight, though, it is easier to acknowledge ways in which Lawrence shared intellectual roots with the fascist movement, notably in the romantic hostility to technology, the emphasis on rooted and organic societies, and the primitivist nostalgia for folk and fertility rituals. Anne Fernihough has observed how 'organicist metaphors and similes were two a penny' in Germany just after the First World War, and many of Lawrence's own personal interests and connections—in Nietzsche, Spengler, Wagner's Ring cycle—would have reinforced his interest in the ramifications of this Germanic tradition, as would his awareness of the anti-mechanistic philosophy espoused by Werner Sombart, a friend of Else Jaffe, the sister of Lawrence's own German wife, Frieda.[25]

Nor was Lawrence alone among English intellectuals of this period in his admiration for German culture. Lawrence was friendly with Rolf Gardiner, who read modern languages at Cambridge and who was to become an energetic proselytizer for the Nazis in the 1930s, after his editorship of *Youth* magazine had brought him into close contact with the German Youth Movement. In 1928, Lawrence enthusiastically expressed his embrace of a Teutonic ethos of 'song, dance and labour' in a letter to Gardiner: 'The German youth is almost ready to fuse into a new sort of unity, it seems to me, us against the world ... The Germans take their shirts off and work in the hay: they are still physical: the English are so woefully disembodied.'[26] Gardiner later extolled Lawrence as 'an old soul with an ancestral memory of earlier civilizations' and lectured on him at the University of Berlin in 1934, at a time when Lawrence's mystical prose pieces were particularly popular in Germany. He recorded shortly afterwards in a letter to the London *Observer* that although Lawrence 'looked upon fascism and Communism alike with a certain disgust', his 'views on leadership and the community, on discipline and power ... were remarkably akin to those exemplified by the German Buende' after the First World War. Gardiner, who also admired mining communities for preserving 'something of a religious attitude towards their work and towards the whole mysterious cycle of the seasons', added his opinion that 'National-Socialism in Germany is in very many respects the life of the Buende writ large, their spirit and forms amplified and translated into national terms'.[27] This kind of double movement on Gardiner's part is characteristic of the way in which Lawrence's political sensibilities have been handled: in the same breath as admitting Lawrence's sympathy with the intellectual 'spirit' of National Socialism, Gardiner rejects the notion that he could have had any truck with anything so

[25] Anne Fernihough, *D. H. Lawrence: Aesthetics and Ideology* (Oxford: Clarendon Press, 1993), 32, 22.

[26] Richard Griffiths, *Fellow Travellers of the Right: British Enthusiasts for Nazi Germany, 1933–9* (London: Constable, 1980), 143–4.

[27] W. J. Keith, 'Spirit of Place and *Genius Loci*: D. H. Lawrence and Rolf Gardiner', *D. H. Lawrence Review*, 7 (1974), 127–38; Emile Delavenay and W. J. Keith, 'Mr. Rolf Gardiner, "The English Neo-Nazi": An Exchange', *D. H. Lawrence Review*, 7 (1974), 291–4.

vulgar as a popular political movement. It is quite true that Lawrence wrote strongly and explicitly against the practice of fascism in the 1920s, dismissing 'Papa Mussolini' as 'a little harmless Glory in baggy trousers'; but it is also true that his sexual imagination, fermented around essentialist conceptions of gender and an eroticized principle of masculine mastery, inclined him naturally towards the visions of authoritarian order and apocalyptic purification that were not at all uncommon among intellectuals such as Gardiner during the interwar years.[28]

The central significance of America in Lawrence's writing lies in the way in which, like Germany, it appears to offer a primitivist alternative to the desiccated vistas of industrial England. Lawrence first visited the American Southwest in September 1922, ten years after his first trip to Germany, and he later declared that the 'magnificent fierce' landscape of New Mexico 'was the greatest experience from the outside world that I have ever had. It certainly changed me for ever.'[29] By contrast, as he wrote in his late essay 'Nottingham and the Mining Countryside' (1930), the 'paltry dwellings' of his home town seem 'so vile' that the only fitting response would be to raze them to the ground. 'Pull down my native village to the last brick,' he says: 'Plan a nucleus. Fix the towns. Make a handsome gesture of radiation from the focus. And then put up big buildings, handsome, that sweep to a civic centre. And furnish them with beauty. And make an absolute clean start. Do it place by place. Make a new England.'[30] In this sense, many of Lawrence's evocations of the old Aztec world in *Mornings in Mexico*, which conflates old Mexico and New Mexico as the 'solar plexus' of North America, should be understood not merely as an escape from the mining countryside but as its correlative. By describing 'the great living source of life' through rituals such as the Hopi snake dance, Lawrence seeks implicitly to regenerate the clutter and debris of English culture by infusing it with a spirit of primitive order.[31] It is not entirely coincidental that the swastika was originally a religious emblem representing the path of migration of Hopi clans, since the Nazis, like the Mexican Indians, used the intersecting crosses of the swastika to symbolize a junction of north–south and east–west axes. This is not, of course, to suggest that all Hopis were proto-Nazis, merely that they (and Lawrence) shared a philosophical interest in locating some magnetic centre of natural energy.[32] The same kind of emphasis is apparent in Lawrence's vision of urban renewal in

---

[28] D. H. Lawrence, 'Blessed Are the Powerful', in *Reflections on the Death of a Porcupine and Other Essays*, ed. Michael Herbert (Cambridge: Cambridge University Press, 1988), 323. For a discussion of associations between Lawrence's 'essentially sadomasochistic' view of sexuality and 'an erotic authoritarian politics', see Laura Frost, *Sex Drives: Fantasies of Fascism in Literary Modernism* (Ithaca, NY: Cornell University Press, 2002), 44.

[29] Lawrence, 'New Mexico', in *Phoenix*, 142.

[30] Lawrence, 'Nottingham and the Mining Countryside', in *Late Essays*, 293, 291, 294.

[31] D. H. Lawrence, 'Au Revoir, U.S.A.', in *Phoenix*, 104; D. H. Lawrence, *Mornings in Mexico and Etruscan Places* (London: Heinemann, 1956), 64.

[32] Frank Waters, *Book of the Hopi* (Harmondsworth: Penguin, 1977), 113–14. On ways in which 'ideals derived from images of primitive life were used by the Right' in the 1920s and 1930s,

'Nottingham and the Mining Countryside', in which he envisages the kind of 'handsome gesture of radiation from the focus' and grandiose 'big buildings' that were characteristic in the 1930s of fascist styles of architecture.

The work of fiction in which this contrast between England and America is worked out most explicitly is 'St Mawr' (1925). One of the interesting things about this short novel is the way in which national types are made to work synecdochically, so that characters personify elements supposedly characteristic of the land of their nativity. Thus, Mrs Witt, exiled in London, declares 'I'm an *American* woman, and I suppose I've got to remain one, no matter where I am'; while the character of Phoenix, three-quarters Indian and a quarter Mexican, can only be '*himself*', in Lawrence's emphatic mode, once he returns to the American West. To Mrs Witt's daughter Louise the 'hedged-and-fenced' landscape of England appears 'enclosed, to stifling', whereas she feels 'a certain latent holiness in the very atmosphere' of Arizona, a 'vast and living landscape' which enables her to reclaim her life 'straight from the source.'[33] In 'St Mawr', as in his travel essays of this period, Lawrence writes dismissively about California and the commercial culture of the East Coast of the United States: the skyscraper, he says, marks merely an 'interregnum', with the 'great cosmic source of vitality' that informs the American continent residing not in 'democracy and all its paraphernalia' but in the power of the culture of the Red Indians, 'the most deeply religious race still living'. San Francisco, he remarks, is one of those places that seems 'temporary on the face of the earth', whereas Taos appears 'final'.[34] Although Lawrence admitted his own sense of alienation as 'a bewildered straggler out of the far-flung British Empire' and acknowledged the difficulties he experienced in making a connection with the Apaches, he remained convinced that American civilization was interwoven fatally with the 'same old American dragon's blood', and that in order to retain her savage power, 'America must turn again to catch the spirit of her own dark, aboriginal continent'.[35]

On one level, Lawrence's idealization of Arizona and New Mexico is of the same order as George Ruxton's willing self-immersion in the mountainous landscapes of nineteenth-century Colorado, and it testifies to a similar kind of desire to withdraw from the claustrophobic confines of English gentility and hypocrisy. In 'Spirits Summoned West', a poem written in America in July 1923, Lawrence associates the loss of his mother with the more recent death of his old childhood friend, Sallie Hopkin, but he imagines himself as something like a god on Mount Olympus as he encourages their spirits across the Atlantic to be reunited with him:

---

see Marianna Torgovnick, *Gone Primitive: Savage Intellects, Modern Lives* (Chicago: University of Chicago Press, 1990), 9.

[33] D. H. Lawrence, 'St Mawr', in *The Short Novels*, ii (London: Heinemann, 1956), 40, 124, 84, 129, 137, 46.   [34] Lawrence, 'New Mexico', 146–7, 144; *idem*, 'Taos', 100.

[35] D. H. Lawrence, 'Indians and an Englishman', in *Phoenix*, 93; *idem*, 'Au Revoir, U.S.A.', 106; *idem*, 'America, Listen to Your Own', in *Phoenix*, 90.

England seems full of graves to me,
Full of graves …
And I, I sit on this high American desert
With dark-wrapped Rocky Mountains motionless squatting around in a ring,
Remembering I told them to die, to sink into the grave in England,
The gentle-kneed women.

So now I whisper: *Come away*
Come away from the place of graves, come west,
Women,
Women whom I loved and told to die.[36]

Aggrandizing himself into a figure with active power over life and death, Lawrence here compresses spatial perspectives in the same way as he conflates temporal perspectives through the apocalyptic premonition, in his essay 'New Mexico', of how the 'sky-scraper will scatter on the winds like thistledown'. Whereas the tension in Ruxton's narratives arises from the way in which the anarchic propensities of the Rocky Mountains complicate his political conservatism, the charm of Lawrence's 'fanged continent' lies in the way it mythologically renovates and refracts what he takes to be the tombstone-like condition of England.[37] Lawrence's American narratives, like those of Ruxton, are double, in the sense of evoking parallel worlds which intersect uneasily with each other. Apart from a few satirical barbs at a young New England couple in the short story 'Things' (1928), Lawrence generally has very little interest in the social climate or manners of the United States, preferring, as we see in 'St Mawr' and 'Spirits Summoned West', to juxtapose his mythical American dragons with the familial worlds of London and Nottinghamshire that he holds counterpoised in memory.

Lawrence was in the American Southwest between September 1922 and November 1923, and then again, after a brief trip back to Europe, from March 1924 until September 1925. His writing during these periods took on a more characteristically American idiom, with his poetry being influenced by Whitman's style of *vers libre*, just as the essays on American authors, which he revised in New Mexico and published in August 1923 as *Studies in Classic American Literature* became 'more personal, anecdotal as well as more abrupt and colloquial' in their forms of expression.[38] Lawrence's 1919 essay 'Democracy', which he originally intended to include in *Studies in Classic American Literature*, is relatively didactic and proselytizing in the way it dismisses Whitman's idea of the 'Average Man' as 'the reduction of the human being to a mathematical unit', something he takes to be 'a horrible nullification of true identity and being'.[39] In the final version

[36] D. H. Lawrence, *The Complete Poems*, ed. Vivian de Sola Pinto and Warren Roberts (London: Heinemann, 1964), i. 410–11.
[37] Lawrence, 'New Mexico', 147; *idem*, 'Au Revoir, U.S.A.', 104.
[38] David Ellis, *D. H. Lawrence: Dying Game, 1922–1930* (Cambridge: Cambridge University Press, 1998), 258.
[39] Lawrence, 'Democracy', in *Reflections on the Death of a Porcupine*, 63, 73.

of this book, however, Lawrence is more responsive to what he takes to be the enigmatic quality of the American continent, the 'spirit of place' which he says casts 'a powerful disintegrative influence' on the social and aesthetic construction of 'the white psyche'.[40] This creates within the field of American literature, he argues, a strand of 'double meaning', whereby authors signify one thing, but the continent which they describe signifies another: Hawthorne's 'inner diabolism', Poe's 'mechanical consciousness', and Melville's 'slithery' quality depend for their cathectic tension and force upon the author's failure precisely to encompass the destructive power of the homeland within their work. This, says Lawrence, is why American authors turn to Transcendentalism or to narratives about the sea: there is a conscious attempt on their part to avert their gaze from the corrosive impetus of the native soil, to avoid anything 'too specific, too particular'.[41]

This thematic tension between projection and embodiment which Lawrence attributes to American writing is commensurate with a series of illuminating contradictions within *Studies in Classic American Literature* itself. On one hand, Lawrence asserts that 'Men are free when they belong to a living, organic, *believing* community ... Not when they are escaping to some wild west', thus suggesting in a relatively orthodox way how American society lacks a sense of coherence. Yet his quest here to identify a 'classic' American literature which follows exactly this trajectory of deracination and flight, like Leavis's subsequent search for a 'great tradition' or Eliot's outline of 'tradition and the individual talent' four years earlier, suggests a typically modernist search for origins, for an architectonic structure within which national narratives might meaningfully emerge. All literary canonization is, of course, a form of retrospective projection, a way of realigning the narrative of history in order to elucidate the present, a strategy which seeks to explicate contemporary concerns by connecting them with a supposedly authentic past. On these terms, what unites these 'classic' American authors, according to Lawrence, is precisely that they don't form part of the 'living, organic, *believing* community' which he holds up as an ideal, but are instead forever 'straying and breaking away'.[42] It is, in other words, the rupture of social bonds and aesthetic conventions, the invasion of organic unity by ontological duality, that characterizes the American tradition in Lawrence's eyes. Its community might be classified paradoxically by the very absence of community, and this points to ways in which Lawrence's invocation of cultural tradition is less canonically constrained than that of his English cultural acolytes. Whereas for Leavis the organic community became an ethical imperative, Lawrence himself was equally attracted to the negative potential within communal spaces, the ways in which symbolic forms fail entirely to coincide with their social setting.

---

[40] Lawrence, *Studies in Classic American Literature*, 17, 55.
[41] Ibid., 12, 81, 77, 122, 106.   [42] Ibid., 17.

Lawrence called *The Plumed Serpent* (1926) his 'real novel of America', and it is in this book, set in Mexico, that we see his sensitivity to the dualities he associates with American culture, the cross-currents and contradictions whereby mythological forms of primitivism come into conflict with Western psychology.[43] The

13. D. H. Lawrence (*far right*) in front of a group of cacti, in Orizaba, Mexico, 1923. With him are (*from left to right*) Frieda Lawrence, Willard Johnson, and two unidentified Mexicans. Photograph by Witter Bynner.

[43] D. H. Lawrence, letter to Thomas Seltzer, 15 June 1923, in *The Letters of D. H. Lawrence,* iv, ed. Warren Roberts, James T. Boulton, and Elizabeth Mansfield (Cambridge: Cambridge University Press, 1987), 457.

language in this novel tends towards a kind of anthropological immobility—'the heavy reddish-and-yellow arches went round the courtyard with a warrior-like fatality'—and towards a concomitant transposition of individuals into types: Mrs Norris appears 'rather like a Conquistador', Don Rámon is 'the Living Quetzalcoatl', and so on.[44] Kate Leslie, an Irish woman educated in England, has similarly wearied of 'American automatism' (p. 93) and yearns amidst this archaic Mexican landscape 'for the unknown gods to put the magic back into her life, and to save her from the dry-rot of the world's sterility' (p. 103), a notion partially embodied through her relationship with Don Cipriano. All of this emphasis on 'blood-bondage' (p. 144), on the 'thud of the primeval world' (p. 333) and on the vision of 'some Saviour, some redeemer to drive a new way out, to the sun' (p. 136) points towards a mystical sublimation of mere politics, towards a fear and contempt of what Kate calls the English and Irish 'rabble', and towards the inference that 'democracy' is as stifling as 'a huge, huge cold centipede which, if you resisted it, would dig every claw into you' (p. 136). The actual forms that political allegiances take in *The Plumed Serpent* therefore appear relatively unimportant. Jesús wears a 'black Fascista shirt', though he is said to have 'the queer, animal jeering of the socialists, an instinct for pulling things down' (p. 144), while Kate herself feels profoundly uninterested in what she calls the 'stupid and *vieux jeu*' of Irish nationalism (p. 166), the cause for which her first husband died. But the point about what Jad Smith calls the kind of 'völkisch organicism' that permeates this novel is precisely that it aspires to transcend mere political partisanship by representing the country as a seat of ancient power.[45]

In this sense, to call *The Plumed Serpent* a novel of the fascist imaginary is not to suggest either that its author should be accused of support for Fascist political parties or that his narrative simply glosses over the multiple contradictions permeating fascism in the interwar period. We have become so accustomed after 1945 to associating fascism with the systematic elimination of contradiction and opposition that it can be disconcerting to realize the extent to which creative writers such as Lawrence entertained the idea as an intellectual hypothesis rather than as an explicit allegiance in the 1920s and 1930s. In *The Plumed Serpent*, we find Kate 'at once attracted and repelled' (p. 122) by Don Rámon's wisdom on the culture of blood and the substantiation of ancient mysteries, while the peculiar configuration of the relationship between subject and object—'The man had reached his strength again. He had broken the cords of the world, and was free in the other strength' (p. 169)—implies a situation where the quest for transformation always appears slightly askew, slightly surreal. The metamorphic impulse of the narrative does not always sit comfortably with its

---

[44] D. H. Lawrence, *The Plumed Serpent*, ed. L. D. Clark (Cambridge: Cambridge University Press, 1987), 32, 342. Subsequent page references to this edition are cited in parentheses in the text.
[45] Jad Smith, 'Völkisch Organicism and the Uses of Primitivism in Lawrence's *The Plumed Serpent*', *D. H. Lawrence Review*, 30/3 (2002), 7–24.

gorgeous evocations of local knowledge, as when the author describes exquisitely the aftermath of the rainy season, how 'the wonderful Mexican autumn, like a strange, inverted spring was upon the land' (p. 405). Lawrence, in other words, runs worlds in parallel with each other—the human and the archetypal, the natural and the mythological, Europe and America—without ever seeking fully to integrate or reconcile them; indeed, it is the figurative gap between conception and embodiment which seems to provide the impetus for Lawrence's imagination. He is inspired in *The Plumed Serpent* by a tantalizing image of the ancestral power that has been eviscerated from Kate Leslie's old homes of England and Ireland, just as his writing explores tentatively the ways in which human characters shadow, without ever fully incarnating, their primeval prototypes.

From this angle, the narrative of *The Plumed Serpent* might be said to internalize what it identifies as the negative force of America, 'the great death-continent' (p. 77), so as to unravel the anthropomorphic projections of the characters immersed within its landscape. Just as Lawrence in *Studies in Classic American Literature* finds the spirit of American culture generally to be infused with doubleness, turning as it does upon a discrepancy between 'white consciousness' and its dissolution, so *The Plumed Serpent* positions itself between an atavistic anthropomorphism and a destiny of disintegrative 'doom' (p. 24). Such equations are, of course, racially inflected and are associated, as always in Lawrence, with essentialized national types: *The Plumed Serpent* talks of a 'heavy, black Mexican fatality' (p. 24), while *Studies in Classic American Literature* contemplates how 'unappeased, aboriginal demons' play upon 'the white psyche'.[46] More extensively, though, we can see how the destructive power of America functions creatively for Lawrence as a site of regeneration, a place in which the exhausted conditions of European culture might undergo violent renewal.

In his 1921 school textbook *Movements in European History*, Lawrence writes with particular sympathy of the Reformation, calling it 'truly a people's movement' and describing how '[t]he Germanic temperament all through our course of history has reacted against the old social forms, gradually breaking them down and making room for a wider individual liberty'.[47] Lawrence's treatment of the Reformation actually drew criticism from one of the readers of the manuscript for Oxford University Press, who complained that the author had handled it 'in such a bigoted way that American Catholics would be outraged—and fairly outraged, I believe'; but it is one of the ironies of Lawrence's Protestant iconoclasm that it actually takes as one of its teleological ends the Counter-Reformation, the restoration of ritual and symbol to a world denuded of these

---

[46] Lawrence, *Studies in Classic American Literature*, 81, 55.
[47] D. H. Lawrence, *Movements in European History*, ed. Philip Crumpton (Cambridge: Cambridge University Press, 1989), 181, 173. This work was originally published under the pseudonym 'Lawrence H. Davison'.

sacramental properties.[48] The 'religious dance of the return of Quetzalcoatl' in *The Plumed Serpent* (p. 348) is one manifestation of this ceremonial impulse, while in *Apocalypse* Lawrence writes sympathetically of medieval Christendom, with its 'great natural cycle of church ritual and festival', contrasting this with how the 'cosmos became anathema to the Protestants after the Reformation'. In true modernist fashion, Lawrence seeks a genealogical precursor to the contemporary state of alienation: the post-Reformation Protestants, he says, 'substituted the non-vital universe of forces and mechanistic order, everything else became abstraction, and the long, slow death of the human being set in'.[49]

Later in *Apocalypse*, Lawrence proceeds to describe the nation, in Wagnerian fashion, as 'in a very old sense, a church, or a vast cult-unit'. Such dissociation of the mystical power of the nation from the merely legal apparatus of the state would allow its people, so he concludes, to 're-establish the living organic connections, with the cosmos, the sun and earth, with mankind and nation and family'.[50] In the twenty-first century, when national identity has become widely associated with more secular and instrumental agendas, such patriotic mysticism might seem a dangerous phenomenon; but in the interwar years such views did not appear at all exceptionable. In his positive review of William Carlos Williams's *In The American Grain*, Lawrence reiterated his belief that '[a]ll creative art must rise out of a specific soil and flicker with a spirit of place', and the ways in which even such an impeccable liberal as Williams could reproduce nativist ideologies throws light on one of the classic ideological contradictions of modernism in the earlier part of the twentieth century.[51] It is all too easy, as Jameson suggests, retrospectively to canonize writers for their literary works while dismissing as unwelcome baggage the utopian impulses that framed and informed their narratives. Such critical strategies work effectively to anaesthetize modernism, to dissociate its formal imagination from what seem now like its ultimately regressive investments in politics and philosophy, without considering more fully how, as an intellectual project, the reformist dimensions of modernism were inextricably interwoven with a totalizing logic.

THE CONSTITUTION OF SILENCE: T. S. ELIOT

Lawrence's early death in 1930 ensured that he avoided any taint of personal collusion with the momentum of fascism as it developed during the decade

---

[48] Philip Crumpton, introduction, in *Movements in European History*, by D. H. Lawrence, p. xxvii.

[49] D. H. Lawrence, *Apocalypse and the Writings on Revelation*, ed. Mara Kalnins (Cambridge: Cambridge University Press, 1980), 70, 79. [50] Ibid., 91, 149.

[51] Lawrence, *Phoenix*, 334. On the nativist impulse in *In The American Grain*, see Walter Benn Michaels, *Our America: Nativism, Modernism and Pluralism* (Durham, NC: Duke University Press, 1995), 74–85.

before the Second World War, but the position of T. S. Eliot in England was to become considerably more ambiguous. Whereas Lawrence's involvement with America came relatively late in his career, the American dimensions to Eliot's poetry were evident from the start, with initial British suspicion of his work after the First World War being associated with a wider concern about the supposedly baleful influence of popular culture from across the Atlantic. Eliot subsequently became established as such a pillar of English society—classicist, royalist, and Anglo-Catholic, as he announced in 1928—that it is hard to reconstitute his reception in London in the early 1920s, when the hybrid transatlantic dimensions of his work were often viewed with distaste and the ' "jazz" rhythms' of *The Waste Land* were thought to undermine the monuments of established British culture. There was an unsuccessful but symptomatic attempt in Britain to impose import quotas on American films in 1927, and Eliot's poetry of this period was seen also as implicated within this disconcerting American strategy of rendering more fluid the conventional boundaries—and, of course, the social barriers—between high and low art.[52]

Eliot's work, in other words, was never regarded in England purely as a technocratic phenomenon but as an art freighted with subversive social implications. The London scenes of *The Waste Land* are characteristically shot through with a second-hand irony which juxtaposes the banal contemporary scene with standard features from a heritage guidebook—Shakespeare's Elizabethan England, the fastidious Augustan world of Pope—in a way that superimposes the present upon the past, producing a phantasmic, distorted version of both. Twentieth-century London is consequently burlesqued in the light of its failure to live up to mythic expectations; sounding its 'Shakespeherian Rag', Eliot's jazzy comedy travesties the Old World, turning its established institutions into less elevated music-hall and vaudeville routines.[53] Moreover, as Eric Sigg has noted, the first draft of *The Waste Land* opened with a pack of four men cavorting around Boston to the strains of four contemporary songs, one of which, 'The Cubanola Glide' (1907), was a well-known example of ragtime.[54] Ezra Pound's editing of *The Waste Land* had the effect of turning it into a more oracular, impersonal poem, one with a neoclassical shape and a perspective centred more around the blind sage, Tiresias, than its worldly or satirical scenes; but, as David Chinitz has argued, '*The Waste Land* would have openly established popular culture as a major intertext of modernist poetry if Pound had not edited out most of Eliot's popular references.'[55]

---

[52] Peter Ackroyd, *T. S. Eliot* (London: Hamish Hamilton, 1984), 128; Ann Douglas, *Terrible Honesty: Mongrel Manhattan in the 1920s* (New York: Farrar, Straus & Giroux, 1995), 191.

[53] T. S. Eliot, *The Complete Poems and Plays* (London: Faber, 1969), 65. Subsequent page references to this edition are cited in parentheses in the text.

[54] Eric Sigg, 'Eliot as a Product of America', in *The Cambridge Companion to T. S. Eliot*, ed. A. David Moody (Cambridge: Cambridge University Press, 1994), 20–1. Sigg notes that a burlesque number entitled 'That Shakespearian Rag' was written for the Ziegfeld Follies in 1912.

[55] David Chinitz, 'T. S. Eliot and the Cultural Divide', *PMLA*, 110 (1995), 242.

It is, consequently, important to recognize how in its provenance *The Waste Land* was immersed in the world of low urban culture. Michael North has remarked on the significance of Eliot's poem being published in *The Dial* in November 1922 by Gilbert Seldes, who was to produce in 1924 one of this era's most influential intellectual defences of American popular culture, *The Seven Lively Arts*. It is also significant that English critics like Clive Bell chose particularly to attack the 'irreverent' and 'impudent' spirit of Eliot's poem, because its mongrel form threatened to unsettle the social and aesthetic hierarchies which English stalwarts such as Bell were intent upon upholding: rejecting Eliot's notion of jazz literature, Bell claimed that he wanted to protect Shakespeare and Milton from 'the coloured gentleman who leads the band at the Savoy'.[56] In this light, Geoff Ward's remark about Eliot's 'gloom over popular culture', though it speaks to received postmodern assumptions about the poet's inherent conservatism, could hardly be more wide of the mark.[57] Again, because Eliot has been canonically represented in the post-1945 era as a traditional formalist, the utopian impulses that led him in the interwar period to seek a wholesale transformation of social and cultural life have been generally disregarded, leaving us with an Eliot who appears aesthetically safer and politically less controversial, perhaps, but also considerably duller. Rather than anticipating the austere line promoted after the war by Theodor Adorno about the corrupt nature of popular culture, Eliot was in fact a fan of Marie Lloyd and music halls, an admirer of Charlie Chaplin, a friend of Groucho Marx. He also delighted in writing bawdy, lectured in America in 1933 on nonsense verse, cited *Alice in Wonderland* as one of the sources for 'Burnt Norton', and published in 1939 his brilliant *Old Possum's Book of Practical Cats*, on which, as Stephen Spender acutely observed, it is possible to detect the influence of Poe's popular ballads.[58]

The old question of whether Eliot should be classified as an 'English' or an 'American' poet is an imponderable and ultimately pointless one. Of more relevance are the ways in which Eliot disrupted both of these cultural traditions by cross-referencing them with each other. He specifically wrote against the New England inheritance of moral and transcendental idealism, suggesting in a 1919 review of the first *Cambridge History of American Literature* that the 'three important men in the book are Poe, Whitman and Hawthorne', a judgement endorsed in a talk on 'American Literature and the American Language' at Washington University in 1953, when he declared the most significant 'landmarks' to be Poe, Whitman, and Twain. Poe, of course, has

[56] Michael North, *Reading 1922: A Return to the Scene of the Modern* (New York: Oxford University Press, 1999), 140–6.

[57] Geoff Ward, *The Writing of America: Literature and Cultural Identity from the Puritans to the Present* (Cambridge: Polity, 2002), 3.

[58] Stephen Spender, 'Cats and Dog', in *T. S. Eliot: The Critical Heritage*, ed. Michael Grant (London: Routledge & Kegan Paul, 1982), ii. 407. On Eliot's immersion in popular culture, see Chinitz, 'T. S. Eliot and the Cultural Divide', 236–9, and Ronald Schuchard, *Eliot's Dark Angel: Intersections of Life and Art* (Oxford: Oxford University Press, 1999), 87–118.

always enjoyed a fractious relationship with the American literary canon, but in Eliot's eyes his 'intellectual abilities' made him 'the least pedantic, the least pedagogical of the critics writing in his time in either America or England'. Conversely, so Eliot claimed in 1919, a history of Puritan and transcendental writing 'would be a history not of American but of Boston literature'; just as *The Waste Land* subverts England's ossified class hierarchies, so Eliot chastises the Emersonian tradition for its parochialism, for the arrogant assumption of its own centrality to American intellectual life.[59]

It is, of course, true that Eliot never fully disengaged himself from his native past. Several of his poems, notably 'The Dry Salvages', reveal the nostalgic attractions of American landscapes, and, as Ronald Bush has suggested, for all of Eliot's antipathy towards Emerson, the dialogue with him never really came to an end: in 1959, Eliot said that the 'emotional springs' of his poetry were American, and one year later he declared that in the end he himself deserved the title of 'a New England poet'.[60] What is more interesting than any putative form of final identification, however, is the way in which Eliot sets up the English and American traditions as 'two literatures in the same language', arguing that they 'can help each other, and contribute towards the endless renovation of both'. There is a deeply embedded cultural paradox here, because Eliot's particular style of poetry and criticism thrives upon a metaphorical civil war whereby these different perspectives are brought into internecine conflict. Eliot in this sense is not so much an internationalist—he says in 1953 that he doesn't want 'one common international type' of Anglo-American literature—as a transnationalist, whose paradoxical pleasure derives from a reversal of inherited assumptions through bringing them into juxtaposition with their familial opposite.[61] By projecting contiguous contraries in this way, Eliot uses the weight of English cultural history to burlesque New England's claims to self-importance, just as he deploys the modernistic edge of the American lively arts to shake up what he sees as the moribund state of English letters.

This is one reason why the English Civil War plays such a crucial role in Eliot's writing, particularly in the work of his middle period, between about 1930 and 1950, a period which encompasses the rise of fascism and the Second World War as well as the publication of *Four Quartets*. In his first essay on Milton, published in 1936, Eliot said that he found Milton's theology 'in large part repellent'

---

[59] T. S. Eliot, review of *A History of American Literature*, ii, ed. William P. Trent, John Erskine, Stuart P. Sherman, and Carl van Doren, *Athenaeum*, 25 April 1919, 236; *idem*, 'American Literature and the American Language', in *To Criticize the Critic and Other Writings*, rev. edn. (London: Faber, 1978), 52. Poe was famously excluded from F. O. Matthiessen's literary canon on the grounds of not occupying a sufficiently 'serious domain'. Matthiessen, *American Renaissance*, 205.

[60] Ronald Bush, 'T. S. Eliot: Singing the Emerson Blues', in *Emerson: Prospect and Retrospect*, ed. Joel Porte (Cambridge, Mass.: Harvard University Press, 1982), 179–97; George Plimpton, ed., *Poets at Work: The* Paris Review *Interviews* (Harmondsworth: Penguin, 1989), 45; T. S. Eliot, 'The Influence of Landscape upon the Poet', *Daedalus*, 89 (Spring 1960), 421.

[61] Eliot, 'American Literature and the American Language', 51, 60.

and accused the English Puritan poet of not being 'balanced'; he attributed this lopsidedness to the way in which 'the living English which was Shakespeare's became split up into two components one of which was exploited by Milton and the other by Dryden'. This reworks the famous indictment of dualism in Eliot's 1921 essay 'The Metaphysical Poets': 'In the seventeenth century a dissociation of sensibility set in, from which we have never recovered; and this dissociation, as is natural, was aggravated by the influence of the two most powerful poets of the century, Milton and Dryden.' In his second essay on Milton, published in 1947, Eliot further asserted: 'the Civil War of the seventeenth century, in which Milton is a symbolic figure, has never been concluded. The Civil War is not ended: I question whether any serious civil war ever does end.'[62] Dryden, the Catholic and royalist cavalier, and Milton, the Protestant and republican Roundhead, epitomize for Eliot two distinct strands of English culture; but *Four Quartets* conceives one of its functions as to bring these opposing camps into some practical form of reconciliation. Hence, by a typical Eliot paradox, the *Quartets* attempts to reconstruct the Puritan migration in reverse: whereas Eliot's ancestor, Andrew Eliot, emigrated from East Coker in the west of England to Massachusetts Bay in the 1660s, his twentieth-century descendant journeys back aesthetically into this Somerset village with the aspiration of annealing the fissures and schisms which this seventeenth-century separatist movement created.

'East Coker' itself holds up the Elizabethan era as a time of 'concorde', citing a passage from Sir Thomas Elyot's *Boke Named the Gouvernor* (1531), where the image of dancing—'Two and two, necessarye coniunction'—comes to symbolize that integration of duality for which Eliot's poem strives (p. 178). 'Little Gidding', the last of the *Quartets* published in 1944, takes its title from Nicholas Ferrar's chapel in Huntingdonshire visited by King Charles I in 1633, 1642, and then again in May 1646.[63] On this latter occasion, the King, in a hopeless military position, came alone with his chaplain while journeying north to bring to an end the first phase of the English Civil War by surrendering himself to the Scots:

> If you came at night like a broken king,
> If you came by day not knowing what you came for,
> It would be the same, when you leave the rough road
> And turn behind the pig-sty to the dull façade
> And the tombstone.

> (pp. 191–2)

The third part of 'Little Gidding' picks up this theme by describing a 'people ... touched by a common genius', who are 'United in the strife which

---

[62] T. S. Eliot, 'Milton I', in *On Poetry and Poets* (London: Faber, 1957), 142–5; *idem*, 'The Metaphysical Poets', in *Selected Essays*, 3rd edn. (London: Faber, 1951), 288; *idem*, 'Milton II', in *On Poetry and Poets*, 148.

[63] Helen Gardner, *The Composition of* Four Quartets (London: Faber, 1978), 61–2.

divided them' (p. 195). Images of civil conflict, retribution and alleged traitors about to be executed on the scaffold are succeeded by an uneasy acquiescence in communality:

> We cannot revive old factions
> We cannot restore old policies
> Or follow an antique drum.
> These men, and those who opposed them
> And those whom they opposed
> Accept the constitution of silence
> And are folded in a single party.

(p. 196)

That phrase 'the constitution of silence' is both troublesome and, for 1944, resonant, implying a political settlement, a willingness to accept mutual coexistence, based upon something less than full candour.

In the late 1920s and 1930s, Eliot, like Lawrence and many other modernist writers, explored intellectually the possibilities of fascism, although ultimately he saw this movement as too populist and irreligious for his particular purposes. Nevertheless, Eliot's 1944 poem is deliberately invested in a language of public administration, with its studied neutrality offering a conciliatory counterpart to the patriotic hyperbole, the rhetoric of belonging and betrayal, which had characterized the earlier war years. This is, in itself, a brilliantly effective tone for the troubled times: in his poetic tribute 'To T. S. Eliot on his Sixtieth Birthday', W. H. Auden said that Eliot, in 'finding the right / language for thirst and fear, did much to / prevent a panic', and 'Little Gidding' is the work in which the poet casts himself as a voice of the nation most overtly.[64] *Four Quartets* thus judiciously blends historical perspective, metaphysical quizzicality, and a careful, anticlimactic sense of reassuring predictability to project a world in which the extremity of 'factions' will give way to a more peaceable landscape of quietist tranquility. The impersonal voice here is in some ways akin to that of an announcer on BBC radio, and it is no coincidence that Eliot himself made several broadcasts for the BBC during the 1930s, talking in 1932, for instance, on religious faith, and in February 1937 on 'The Christian Message to the World'. The idiom of the *Quartets* is ethereal and disembodied, a voice typically of the airwaves, seemingly removed from the domain of contingency and error. Eliot had originally intended to entitle this sequence of poems 'Kensington Quartets', but the eventual abstraction from place in the final published version fitted more aptly with the broadcasting tone projected here (see Plate 14).[65]

---

[64] W. H. Auden, *Collected Poems*, ed. Edward Mendelson (London: Faber, 1976), 440. For the poem's focus on an administered world, see John Xiros Cooper, *T. S. Eliot and the Ideology of* Four Quartets (Cambridge: Cambridge University Press, 1995).

[65] Gardner, *Composition of* Four Quartets, 26. For Eliot and the BBC, see Kate Whitehead, *The Third Programme: A Literary History* (Oxford: Clarendon Press, 1989), 220–5.

14. T. S. Eliot in a BBC Radio studio, October 1953.

This is not to argue that Eliot's texts achieve a full impersonal or communal authority, of the kind that he ascribes to Dante's poetry, where the work of art and the circumstances of its reception become mutually reinforcing.[66] It is, though, to suggest that the peculiar stress and aesthetic quality of Eliot's poetic language derive from its attempt to divest itself of personality, to heal the fractured places within the psyche, and within society, by aspiring towards a utopian scene of hierarchical stability. The stress points of Eliot's project are, of course, all too apparent: Franco Moretti has described how the desire for mythic homologies in *The Waste Land* is fractured into a series of merely surrealist analogies which seem to negate ideas of organic totality, while Andrew Ross has pointed to the persistence in Eliot's work of abject subtexts of subjectivity and sexuality that seem to undermine his quest for an integrated language.[67] All of this is true enough, but it is also true that Eliot's rhetoric of counter-reformation needs these civil wars thematically to react against; although his poetry sets itself in opposition to internecine strife, its conceptual impteus also relies upon it, so that the 'dissociation of sensibility' and the 'constitution of silence' become part of a single figure. Nor was Eliot's concern with civil war confined to his adopted country: he was as hostile to the American Civil War as to its English forerunner, describing the American conflict as 'the greatest disaster' in its history, a trauma from which the US nation has never recovered. In *After Strange Gods*, based on the Barbour Lectures at the University of Virginia in 1932, he declared that this war had actually ruined New England in much the same way as it had ruined the American South, creating a sectional, divided condition which denied to the North any ideology of conservatism or permanence.[68] Again, though, the emphasis on longevity in his American poems—notably in 'The Dry Salvages', where the Mississippi River becomes an emblem of spatial and temporal continuity—is designed deliberately to 'piece together the past and the future', to act in a counter-reformation manner as a bulwark to 'Years of living among the breakage' (p. 185).

One thing signalled by this revisionist version of English and American history is Eliot's interest in explicating cultures through theological frameworks. It is, of course, possible to argue that the English Civil War was more a constitutional and parliamentary struggle than a religious affair, but for Eliot, concerned as he was with the fortunes of the national church, doctrinal considerations—even if they manifested themselves in displaced or aestheticized forms, as in Milton or Dryden—were always paramount. Donald Davie, who spent much of the last twenty years of his life reinterpreting English literature in terms of a cultural

[66] T. S. Eliot, 'Dante', in *Selected Essays*, 237–77.

[67] Franco Moretti, *Signs Taken for Wonders: Essays in the Sociology of Literary Forms*, rev. edn., trans. Susan Fischer, David Forgacs, and David Miller (London: Verso, 1988), 228–31; Andrew Ross, *The Failure of Modernism: Symptoms of American Poetry* (New York: Columbia University Press, 1986), 86–9.

[68] T. S. Eliot, *After Strange Gods: A Primer of Modern Heresy* (London: Faber, 1934), 16.

tradition of dissent, acknowledged in 1976 that the 'last literary man to try to grapple with this awkward fact—that religious experience is a momentous and determining feature of culture—was T. S. Eliot'.[69] Whereas Davie refracted the English heritage through a Baptist and Episcopalian perspective, though, Eliot's viewpoint was decidedly Anglo-Catholic. In *After Strange Gods*, he says that it is 'impossible to separate the "poetry" in *Paradise Lost* from the peculiar doctrines that it enshrines', and he proceeds to criticize from a viewpoint of doctrinal 'orthodoxy' Milton's 'intellectual and moral aberrations'.[70] Conversely, in a talk the following year at an Anglo-Catholic summer school of theology on 'Catholicism and International Order', Eliot advocated the 'Catholic habit of thought' on the grounds that it allowed for distinctive regional variations while still preserving a universal order.[71] Again, schism is the great bugbear, and his interwar essays on specifically religious topics—'Lancelot Andrewes' (1926), 'John Bramhall' (1927), 'Thoughts after Lambeth' (1931)—emphasize the virtues of a *via media*, a Broad Church of humanistic culture and habitual common sense, rather than one too bound up either with philosophical rationalism (the way of Hobbes) or political radicalism (the way of Cromwell). The most awkward problem for Eliot in this context was the question of disestablishment, about which, as he admitted in 'Thoughts after Lambeth', he found it difficult to make up his mind. On the one hand, he acknowledged that the establishment of the Church had a certain pragmatic value: 'If England is ever to be in any appreciable degree converted to Christianity, it can only be through the Church of England.' On the other hand, he saw that such institutionalization tended to vitiate what he saw as the Church's spiritual force, turning it instead into a forum for petty party politics.[72]

Such conflations of religious idealism with social pragmatism bring to mind Eliot's work on F. H. Bradley, the subject of his doctoral dissertation at Harvard. Bradley's version of the organic society was inflected by what Eliot himself described as a 'practical metaphysic', glossed by Walter Benn Michaels as 'a pragmatism conceived in opposition to realism and idealism both'.[73] Coming out of a Harvard school of philosophy still dominated by William James, Eliot's view of a Christian society never entirely lost that sense of anti-foundationalism endemic to the American pragmatist tradition. This does not mean that Eliot's Anglicanism should be understood as mere 'mimicry' or vaudeville, as Hugh Kenner suggested, but it does imply that the dogmatically Christian interpretations of *Four Quartets*—from readers such as A. D. Moody,

---

[69] Donald Davie, *Essays in Dissent: Church, Chapel, and the Unitarian Conspiracy* (Manchester: Carcanet, 1995), 8.   [70] Eliot, *After Strange Gods*, 32–3.
[71] T. S. Eliot, 'Catholicism and International Order', *Christendom*, 3 (1933), 182.
[72] T. S. Eliot, 'Thoughts after Lambeth', in *Selected Essays*, 382–3.
[73] Walter Benn Michaels, 'Philosophy in Kinkanja: Eliot's Pragmatism', *Glyph*, 8 (1981), 174. On Eliot and pragmatism, see also Manju Jain, *T. S. Eliot and American Philosophy: The Harvard Years* (Cambridge: Cambridge University Press, 1992).

who thought that they demanded on the part of the reader 'a commitment to the unattainable absolute'—have tended towards critical tunnel vision and have in fact done Eliot's multilayered work a disservice by the narrow intransigence of their support for it.[74] Eliot said that starting to write drama in the 1930s helped him to engender a simpler language for *Four Quartets*, one more attuned to the public voice he was seeking, and this sequence of poems, with their stylistic irregularities, their mixture of prosaic and lyric idioms, and their passages of greater and lesser intensity, are designed formally to represent a world where the 'timeless' intersects casually, though not entirely randomly, with the circuitous pathways of time.[75] Anglicanism, in other words, becomes here something like an ideology, a means of bringing together disparate phenomena within a Broad Church of national unity, in a world where 'History is now and England' (p. 197). As Davie said, there is very little idea within the *Quartets* of what it is like to live in any particular place in England; there is, however, a strong sense of what it means to identify as English, and this again links Eliot's aesthetic ideology to the voice of the BBC, which was similarly concerned, particularly in wartime, to offer itself as an abstract point of identification for the nation. Eliot's talk 'Towards a Christian Britain' was broadcast on the radio on 2 April 1941, and the BBC, then as now, might be said to offer something very much like a secularized form of Anglicanism, since it has always traded off the supposed homogeneity of the nation and has sought to bind its diverse constituency into a unified field of consciousness.[76]

George Orwell wrote as early as 1942 of what he called 'the gloomy Pétainism' of the first three of the *Quartets*. Pétain was at this time head of the Vichy government in occupied France, so by his provocative phrase Orwell was suggesting not only a sense of 'resignation' and accommodation to the circumstances of the day but also 'a reactionary or austro-Fascist tendency', which, so he claimed, 'had always been apparent in [Eliot's] work, especially his prose writings'.[77] The question of Eliot's association with fascism is, however, a very complicated affair, even more so than that of Lawrence, since Eliot's career was unfolding contemporaneously with the wartime struggle. John Carey, in his swingeing attack on modernism in *The Intellectuals and the Masses*, castigated all the

---

[74] Hugh Kenner, *The Invisible Poet: T. S. Eliot* (London: Methuen, 1965), 251; A. D. Moody, *Tracing T. S. Eliot's Spirit: Essays on his Poetry and Thought* (Cambridge: Cambridge University Press, 1996), 180.　　[75] Plimpton, ed., *Poets at Work*, 40.

[76] Donald Davie, 'Anglican Eliot', *Southern Review*, NS 9, no. 1 (1973), 94; Roger Kojecký, *T. S. Eliot's Social Criticism* (London: Faber, 1971), 140. This emphasis on promoting 'a state of cultural homogeneity' rather than mere doctrinal 'orthodoxy' was one reason for the success of Eliot's critical work in establishing a largely consensual literary canon in the world of English letters during the middle part of the twentieth century. See John Guillory, *Cultural Capital: The Problem of Literary Canon Formation* (Chicago: University of Chicago Press, 1993), 138.

[77] George Orwell, review of *Burnt Norton, East Coker, The Dry Salvages*, by T. S. Eliot, in *The Collected Essays, Journalism and Letters of George Orwell*, ii: *My Country Right or Left, 1940–1943*, ed. Sonia Orwell and Ian Angus (London: Secker & Warburg, 1968), 240–1.

modernists equally for their supposedly elitist retreat into the opacities of art and their snobbish refusal to cater for a wider reading public, so that Lawrence's apocalyptic inclinations, Pound's conception of humanity as a 'mass of dolts', Yeats's feudalism, Wyndham Lewis's sympathy for Hitler, and Eliot's desire to return to the cloister are all tarred with the same dehumanizing brush. Such a clear-cut antithesis between reactionary and democratic writing, however, would appear drastically to oversimplify the situation of British culture on the eve of the Second World War. Philip Larkin, for instance, who is credited by Carey with being winningly accessible—'readily appreciated by schoolchildren'—came from a family in Coventry with explicitly pro-Nazi sympathies.[78] As late as 1939, Larkin's father used to decorate his office with Nazi regalia, while Larkin himself wrote to a friend in April 1942 praising 'the incredible daring recklessness of German troops' and declaring himself 'more than ever certain that England cannot win this war: there's absolutely no spirit in the country. I feel everything is in a mess, like the munition worker who won't go to work several days a week because he doesn't want to earn too much because of income tax.' Again, three months later, at the height of the war, Larkin wrote to J. B. Sutton: 'If there is any new life in the world today, it is Germany. True, it's a vicious and blood-brutal affair—the new shoots are rather like bayonets. It won't suit me. By "new" life I don't mean better life, but a change, a new direction. Germany has revolted back too far, into the other extreme. But I think they have many valuable new habits.' Given this kind of outlook, Larkin's poetry of the 1950s and 1960s might be said to speak literally as well as metaphorically to a defeated condition, plangently chronicling as it does a mediocre, suburbanized England out of which the spirit of high romanticism has been crushed.[79]

My point here is not to devalue Larkin's poetry, or to conduct a political witch-hunt against him, but just the opposite: to suggest how commonplace such attitudes were in Britain before and even during the Second World War, and how they became constitutive of English approaches to modernism around this time. Carey is right to say that Hitler's *Mein Kampf*, with its 'peasant ideal', is not so much 'a deviant work but one firmly rooted in European intellectual orthodoxy'; however, as we have seen from the mystic qualities of D. H. Lawrence's work, which Larkin revered, myths of primitivism and vitalist renewal were by no means confined to the privileged classes.[80] Eliot himself reviewed a number

[78] John Carey, *The Intellectuals and the Masses: Pride and Prejudice among the Literary Intelligentsia, 1880–1939* (London: Faber, 1992), 25, 214.

[79] Philip Larkin, *Selected Letters of Philip Larkin, 1940–1985*, ed. Anthony Thwaite (New York: Farrar, Straus & Giroux, 1993), 33–4, 36. For a perceptive positioning of Larkin 'on the more iconoclastic—even Romantic—wing of the European fascist tendency', see Christopher Hitchens, 'Something about the Poems: Larkin and Sensitivity', *New Left Review*, no. 200 (July–Aug. 1993), 168.

[80] Carey, *Intellectuals and the Masses*, 208. Larkin wrote in a letter to Norman Iles on 23 July 1941 of how he was 'reading Lawrence daily (like the Bible) with great devotion', and on 20 March 1942 he wrote to J. B. Sutton: 'I have been reading *Sons and Lovers* and feel ready to die. If Lawrence

of books on fascism for the *Criterion* in December 1928, declaring himself 'suspicious' of it because, although it extolled an 'order and authority' he believed in 'wholeheartedly', fascism nevertheless tended to vulgarize this phenomenon into a mere 'parroting' of political rhetoric, implying 'a craving for a regime which will relieve us of thought and at the same time give us excitement and military salutes'. Rather than fascism *per se*, Eliot extolled the Action Française movement led in France by Charles Maurras; in his theory of 'Integral Nationalism', Maurras chose to emphasize classical aesthetics and royalist order, which he developed into an organicist, decentralized version of society through which the will of the people was embodied locally within its native soil and incarnated symbolically in the figure of the monarch. This managed to avoid what Eliot saw as the chronic political problem of fascism, which is that it was necessarily mediated through a vulgarizing apparatus of dictatorship, with all of the performative rituals and social machinery of apparatchiks that implied. For Eliot, consequently, Maurras represented integral nationalism in what he called a 'more digestible form', though he ended his 1928 review by forecasting, not incorrectly, 'that the developments of fascism in Italy may produce very interesting results in ten or twenty years'.[81]

Hindsight is a fine thing, of course, and it would be easy to mock a prophecy which turned out to be true in more gruesome ways than Eliot envisaged. What is more difficult, though, is to reimagine the cultural context of the 1930s, when, as David Carroll says, fascism was still an idea offering attractions 'to vast numbers of intellectuals and writers' on account of its attempt symbiotically to fuse the modern alienated individual with a unified sense of national community and purpose.[82] As late as 1937, in reaction to the Spanish Civil War, Eliot was advising readers of the *Criterion* not to be frightened into supporting the Popular Front by the 'bogey of fascism', while the following year another *Criterion* piece, 'Christian Politics' by the Reverend Edward Quinn, averred: 'No matter how their popularity is acquired, no matter what propaganda and censorship is used, the fact is that these leaders [Hitler, Stalin, and Mussolini] really embody in themselves the soul of their people ... No one can deny that both leaders and people in every case have been united in a sincere desire to provide for the commonweal.'[83] Much of the discussion over recent years concerning Eliot's links with fascism has centred on the issue of his anti-Semitism—'the Jew squats

had been killed after writing that book he'd still be England's greatest novelist.' Larkin, *Selected Letters*, 19, 32.

[81] T. S. Eliot, 'The Literature of Fascism', *Criterion*, 8 (Dec. 1928), 287–8, 290.

[82] David Carroll, *French Literary Fascism: Nationalism, Anti-Semitism, and the Ideology of Culture* (Princeton: Princeton University Press, 1995), 15.

[83] Kenneth Asher, *T. S. Eliot and Ideology* (Cambridge: Cambridge University Press, 1995), 86; Revd Edward Quinn, 'Christian Politics', *Criterion*, 17 (July 1938), 626, 638. See also John D. Margolis, *T. S. Eliot's Intellectual Development, 1922–1939* (Chicago: University of Chicago Press, 1972), 200–1.

on the window sill', from 'Gerontion', has been much cited—but, as Christopher Ricks remarked, the whole question of racial prejudice is not incidental to Eliot's work but central to it.[84] The integrity of race and nation, and the significance of a religious structure such as Anglicanism which might encompass that integrity, are, finally, what his writings are about.

This is not, of course, to underestimate the noxious quality of both fascism and anti-Semitism, but it is to suggest that our view of English modernism both before and after the Second World War has been clouded by retrospective critical assumptions about a clear moral antithesis between good and evil, assumptions developed by liberal humanists in the post-1945 period which were not apparent to writers of the interwar years. Indeed, one of the major shifts in scholarship over the past decade or so has served to emphasize the contiguity of fascism and modernism rather than their absolute polarity; as Linda Mizejewski put it: 'It has taken forty years for some historians ... to begin to ask questions not about how different the Nazi is but how similar.'[85] One obvious reason for this intellectual evasiveness is the outcome of the war itself and the atrocities of the Holocaust, all of which necessarily transposed the global military struggle into something more like a Manichaean allegory, a conflict between good and evil. This worked against Eliot's representation of the enemy as an alter ego in a statement after the outbreak of war in 1939—'we cannot understand him unless we understand ourselves, and our own weaknesses and sins'—and also against the imagery of doubling in 'Little Gidding', where the 'pointed scrutiny' of a 'stranger' in wartime reveals not so much an alien as a doppelgänger, 'a familiar compound ghost/Both intimate and unidentifiable' (p. 193).[86] However, *Four Quartets* was completed well before the end of the war, and in the new post-1945 environment Eliot, like other fellow travellers of the Right, naturally looked towards self-preservation, towards avoiding any hint of collusion or sympathy with the enemy, so that the poet and his estate henceforth went out of their way to emphasize his anti-Fascist credentials. To reiterate, Eliot was technically correct in dissociating himself from the tenets of pre-war fascism, in so far as he always found its political organizations too profane and demotic for his tastes; but the larger conception of social order, involving the conception of an organic community inflected by religious hierarchies and systems, was something they had in common.

In his study *Fascist Modernism*, Andrew Hewitt described the 'reified harmony and ontologized violence' of fascist aesthetics as 'a perverted form of organicism, in which harmony has become the conceptual harmony of two antagonisms'. Fascist organicism, in other words, could be understood as a deliberate reaction

[84] Christopher Ricks, *T. S. Eliot and Prejudice* (London: Faber, 1988), 28–9. On this theme, see also Anthony Julius, *T. S. Eliot, Anti-Semitism, and Literary Form* (Cambridge: Cambridge University Press, 1995).
[85] Linda Mizejewski, *Divine Decadence: Fascism, Female Spectacle, and the Making of Sally Bowles* (Princeton: Princeton University Press, 1992), 32.   [86] Ricks, *T. S. Eliot and Prejudice*, 209.

against the mechanistic forces of rupture that threaten to tear apart its protected state, so that fascist modernism might more accurately be described as 'a totalized process of fragmentation and of the circulation of those fragments within an organized whole'.[87] By extension, the obsession with national identity and organic coherence in the 1930s developed partly because of the erosion of autonomy consequent upon increasingly transnational patterns of economic exchange. In a feature on British fascism in July 1939, for example, the popular magazine *Picture Post* included a profile of 'author-journalist-farmer Henry Williamson', who, from his vantage point in Norfolk, welcomed the Fascist political policy 'to ban all agricultural imports which can be grown at home'.[88] This kind of in-turned 'national allegory', in Fredric Jameson's terms, could therefore be seen as a back-formation against the threat of transnational displacement, involving what Jameson calls 'a formal attempt to bridge the increasing gap between the existential data of everyday life within a given nation-state and the structural tendency of monopoly capital to develop on a world-wide, essentially transnational scale'.[89] Thus, when Eliot concludes in 'Little Gidding' that 'History is now and England', his allegorical link between the 'secluded chapel' and a state of nationhood depends specifically upon an elision of the paradoxical contraries, the toings and froings, with which *Four Quartets* itself is permeated (p. 197). Eliot's symbol of nationalism, in other words, arises out of a reaction against the dualities of transnationalism and civil war; indeed, the very idea of reconciliation at the end of this poem—'When the tongues of flame are in-folded / Into the crowned knot of fire / And the fire and the rose are one' (p. 198)—involves not just the resolution of metaphysical or theological antitheses, but also a conjunction of political oppositions and geographical disparities. This is one reason why William V. Spanos and other critics have found it so easy to deconstruct the poem, to read it as a narrative of absence and deferral rather than 'the centred metaphysics of presence': in *Four Quartets*, as in fascist modernism generally, totality and fragment, like organicism and displacement, or nationalism and transnationalism, exist in complementary and mutually sustaining relationships.[90]

In this sense, the Atlantic republic of letters between the wars exposed Britain to an alternative domain of transatlantic modernism, a domain with which the home country entered into a sometimes reluctant dialogue. Lawrence and Eliot both sought to reconcile English culture with a mythological realm of primitivism (in Lawrence's case) or a historical back-projection of social and ecclesiastical

---

[87] Andrew Hewitt, *Fascist Modernism: Aesthetics, Politics, and the Avant-Garde* (Stanford, Calif.: Stanford University Press, 1993), 143, 41.

[88] 'Fascist Meeting', *Picture Post*, 29 July 1939, 34.

[89] Fredric Jameson, *Fables of Aggression: Wyndham Lewis, the Modernist as Fascist* (Berkeley: University of California Press, 1979), 103, 94.

[90] William V. Spanos, 'Hermeneutics and Meaning: Destroying T. S. Eliot's *Four Quartets*', *Genre*, 11 (1978), 571.

concord (in Eliot's). This made the reception of their work in Britain during the postwar years an oddly partial and blinkered affair. After 1945, Leavis attempted doggedly to recuperate an aesthetic version of modernism, proposing to salvage modernist writing from the wreckage of the Second World War by disentangling its imaginative genius from the fascist infrastructure which had underpinned its particular styles of utopia. Since fascism was of course positioned antithetically to British interests by wartime events and by the government propaganda surrounding them, what subsequently emerged in the postwar accounts of Leavis, Raymond Williams, and others was a curiously eviscerated reading of Lawrence, one which emphasized his commitment to domestic virtues while neglecting his interests in Germanic organicism, apocalyptic prophecy, and American primitivism. Hence, of course, the importance of Leavis's canonical strategy, which skirted around Lawrence's historical and political context by installing him as part of a 'great tradition' of English literature going back to George Eliot. For T. S. Eliot, similarly, the rupture of the Second World War cast a deep shadow upon his invocation of an organic and totalizing Anglican culture, although the recursive transatlantic dynamic of his work allowed for an alternative centre of gravity, an implicitly comparative consciousness, that served to ironize its own uncomfortable proximity to the rhetoric of fascist modernism. Haunted as it is by historical memories of the English Civil War, of flight and of exile, 'Little Gidding' seems resigned and stoical in the face of failure and the collapse of social ideals. The poem's enigmatic phrase 'the constitution of silence' also implies more generally, in relation to Eliot's later work, a knowingness about the perennially divided condition of the public domain, an acknowledgement, as he put it in 1947, of how civil wars never end.[91] Living on as he did until 1965, Eliot effectively became his own late modernist interpreter, doing what Leavis did for Lawrence: austerely stripping his work of its factional dimensions and attempting to present it instead as a gesture of transcendence.

[91] Eliot, 'Milton II', 148.

7

The Fascist Imaginary: Abstraction, Violence, and the Second World War

ARCADIA NOIR: P. G. WODEHOUSE

In 1964, the American journalist Martha Gellhorn was sent by the *Atlantic* to investigate postwar conditions in the Federal Republic of Germany. She reported back that German adults 'who knew Nazism and in their millions cheered and adored Hitler ... have performed a nationwide act of amnesia; no one individually had a thing to do with the Hitler regime and its horrors'. The reluctance of Germany to confront its own recent past was to become almost a routine observation over subsequent decades, but there has still been relatively little attention to ways in which this process of 'moral whitewashing', in Gellhorn's phrase, operated in postwar Britain as well.[1] The extent to which Establishment and other well-known public figures in Britain manifested Nazi sympathies in the 1930s is, even at the beginning of the twenty-first century, a subject too close for comfort, a story which has not yet been fully told.

Some British sympathizers with Germany in the interwar period were incited, like D. H. Lawrence and Philip Larkin, by racial romanticism. Edmund Blunden, subsequently to be honoured as a Companion of Literature at the Royal Society of Literature, described in a 1939 issue of the *Anglo-German Review* his recent visits to Hitler's Germany, where he was impressed by a 'prevailing sense ... of a great clearness and freshness of life, a pervading revival of national dignity and personal unselfishness', something he compared to Wordsworth's expression of national feeling in *The Prelude*. Others were motivated more by the apparent resistance offered by the Nazis to threats of Bolshevism: the middlebrow newspaper the *Daily Mail*, which had a circulation of about 1.5 million at this time, was a keen supporter of the Nazis all through the 1930s, with the paper's proprietor, Lord Rothermere, saluting Hitler in an editorial article of 10 July 1933 which appeared under the banner 'Youth Triumphant' and which was later deployed for Nazi propaganda purposes.[2] In 1938, the idea of Britain going to war

---

[1] Martha Gellhorn, 'Is There a New Germany?', *Atlantic*, 213/2 (Feb. 1964), 70.
[2] Edmund Blunden, 'Ourselves and Germany: A Retrospect', *Anglo-German Review*, 3/7 (July 1939), 210; Franklin Reid Gannon, *The British Press and Germany, 1936–1939* (Oxford: Clarendon Press, 1971), 32.

over Hitler's invasion of Czechoslovakia was opposed not only by the *Mail* and the *Daily Express*, which protested against any British involvement in the territorial disputes of Central Europe, but also by literary figures such as Vita Sackville-West, who argued that 'the Sudeten Germans [in Czechoslovakia] are justified in claiming self-determination'. Rather than engage in finger pointing, the important thing to acknowledge here is how this kind of outlook was not especially anomalous in the Britain of 1938. Many members of the British aristocracy and royalty—the Duke of Westminster, the Duke of Kent, the former King Edward VIII (who abdicated in 1936 and became Duke of Windsor)—were known to admire Nazi impositions of political order, while a more general admiration for the German cultural sensibility, along with a latent sympathy for its racial homogeneity, was also widely prevalent among the English middle classes. One of the contributors to the *Anglo-German Review* in 1937 estimated that 'over a quarter of a million British people travelled in Germany last year', and even if this was an exaggeration, it is clearly the case that British tourism to Germany flourished during the 1930s. Moreover, as this correspondent smugly noted, trips to sample the musical delights of Dresden or Heidelberg and the rural charms of the Rhineland were a 'middle class' phenomenon, 'since a holiday in Germany presupposes something more than a workman's income'.[3]

This kind of Germanophilia is reminiscent of the world of the Schlegel sisters in E. M. Forster's novel *Howards End*, for whom Germany represents a sentimental, bohemian alternative to the philistine empiricism of English culture. But there was also a brand of intellectual conservatism, encompassing Catholic writers such as Hilaire Belloc and G. K. Chesterton as well as the editor of the *English Review*, Douglas Jerrold, that scorned parliamentary democracy as an exhausted phenomenon bound up with the age of industrial revolution and looked back nostalgically to a time when the country's power was vested in the body of its people. There were, of course, elements of medieval fantasy involved in this position, but it is crucial historically to recognize how a work such as Eliot's *Idea of a Christian Society* (1939), with its attack on liberalism as leading inevitably towards an 'artificial, mechanised or brutal control' and its preference for traditional social hierarchies and parishes organized around a 'Community of Christians', was not only engaging antithetically with fascist ideals but also, to some degree, responding to a similar organicist agenda.[4] Eliot was attempting here to describe another kind of organic society, one more in accord with his religious beliefs, but the ambition to find a way out of the labyrinth of modern industrial and commercial society is one he shared with the ideology of fascist modernism.

---

[3] Griffiths, *Fellow Travellers of the Right*, 298–9, 45; M. H. Seldon, 'First Sight of Germany', *Anglo-German Review*, 1/4 (Feb. 1937), 192.
[4] T. S. Eliot, *The Idea of a Christian Society* (London: Faber, 1939), 16, 35.

None of these latter figures could be classified overtly as a Nazi sympathizer, and the point here is not to try to identify renegades but, more generally, to point out how quickly public narratives in England changed. Many prewar sympathies were not only suppressed but seemingly obliterated, with one obvious reason for the subsequent cultural amnesia in Britain being, as Richard Griffiths has suggested, the absence of a German invasion in the 1940s. Whereas the French were forced to decide whether to collaborate with the German regime or not, members of the British Establishment were never placed in the position of having to make such a choice.[5] This meant that after 1945 it became much easier for them to deny any such associations, to wipe the slate clean, to acquiesce in the postwar allegory of good against evil that pitted the monstrous Nazis against a democratic ethos of the common man. Without at all wishing to shy away from Nazi history, the fact that it is now a phenomenon of the last century may offer a more lucid perspective on ways in which this valorization of the common man helped to create its own distortions in the writing of postwar English literary history. This is particularly relevant in relation to the way in which an austere moral realism came to be pitted against the forces of dehumanization, forces that were, in this post-1945 era, still associated with the foreign bodies of modernism. Such an impulse of exclusion in the immediate aftermath of war resulted in what Malcolm Bradbury remembered as 'a notable and disturbing cult of Little Englandism, which seemed a deft way of shutting out the larger world'. In his 1946 essay 'The Decline of the English Murder', for example, George Orwell lamented the displacement of more genteel, decorous forms of English crime by the twisted scenarios of the American underworld, fuelled by 'the false values of the American film'. For Orwell, tolerance of this kind of violence could be attributed to the 'brutalising effects of war', and he argued that the aggressive, totalitarian characteristics of fascism had migrated west across the Atlantic, from where they offered a similarly insidious threat to the virtues of English decency.[6]

In an earlier essay, 'Raffles and Miss Blandish' (1944), Orwell had responded to the fact that Britain was now what he called an 'Occupied Territory'—a base for GI troops—by complaining how 'there are great numbers of English people who are partly Americanised in language and, one ought to add, in moral outlook'.[7] Discomfort with what was often thought of as the inhuman, coercive aspects of American military and economic power was, in fact, a pervasive theme in British culture during the 1940s. Ernest Bevin, Foreign Secretary in the postwar Labour

---

[5] Griffiths, *Fellow Travellers of the Right*, 373.

[6] Malcolm Bradbury, 'How I Invented America', *Journal of American Studies*, 14 (1980), 120; George Orwell, 'The Decline of the English Murder', in *Collected Essays, Journalism and Letters*, iv, 100–1.

[7] George Orwell, 'Raffles and Miss Blandish', in *Collected Essays, Journalism and Letters*, iii: *As I Please, 1943–1945*, ed. Sonia Orwell and Ian Angus (London: Secker & Warburg, 1968), 219; Reynolds, *Rich Relations*, 241.

government, described Britain in March 1946 as 'the last bastion of social democracy', the country whose humane social values formed a bulwark not only against
fascism and against 'the communist dictatorship of Soviet Russia' but also against
'the red tooth and claw of American capitalism'. During the war itself, according
to Orwell, any discussion of 'inter-allied relations' had been 'utterly taboo', and
of course the official government line in Britain still proclaimed the 'special
relationship' and the enduring bonds of transatlantic friendship. Nevertheless,
subterranean hostilities towards America continued to develop in Britain during
the late 1940s, fuelled partly by a recognition that the outcome of the war had
fundamentally realigned the global balance of power, so that the United States
was now a 'superpower', a term coined in 1944, while Britain manifestly was not.
By 1948, the US Ambassador in London was reporting back to his Secretary of
State on how anti-American sentiments in Britain 'border on the pathological'.[8]
Such sentiments were based not just upon a simple envy of American wealth
and power but upon an unease with the impact of modernism more generally.
Many in Britain shared Orwell's anxiety that the threat to individual personal-
ity posed by technological dehumanization, against which they had fought in
Europe for six years, might now infiltrate their island territory from across the
Atlantic.

The attempt to understand the Nazi regime within a larger cultural context
became quite a common occupation in the 1940s, as intellectuals sought to clear
space for postwar social and moral renewal by explaining why history had taken
such a wrong turning. One popular critical line during the late 1940s, developed
most forcefully by German exile Siegfried Kracauer in his book *From Caligari
to Hitler* (1947), drew structural parallels between the political emergence of
Nazism and the abstract dimensions of German Expressionist cinema. Kracauer
argued that the rise of Hitler was prefigured in the aesthetic innovations of
German films during the 1920s and 1930s, whose stylistic patterns revealed
in the German people their 'strange preparedness for the Nazi creed'. In Fritz
Lang's fascination with the hypnotic power of madmen in *The Last Will of Dr.
Mabuse* (1933), suggested Kracauer, or in Lang's mystical evocation of German
mythology in *Die Nibelungen* (1924), we see in embryonic form the 'spirit' of
Goebbels's propaganda, with the Nuremberg rallies incarnating the 'ornamental
pattern of *Nibelungen* ... on a gigantic scale'. It is in fact doubtful whether
these forms of Expressionism could validly be associated with 'deep psychological
dispositions predominant in Germany between 1918 and 1933' rather than
with a dynamic of modernity more generally; if the Nazi political movement
and German Expressionist cinema are acknowledged as different points along
the continuum of interwar modernism, then the causal relationship between

---

[8] D. Reynolds, *Rich Relations*, 436, 184, 438; Alfred Grosser, *The Western Alliance: European-
American Relations since 1945*, trans. Michael Shaw (London: Macmillan, 1980), 72.

them necessarily appears more tenuous.[9] Nevertheless, it is clearly the case that the memory of war haunts the narratives of American *film noir* as the genre developed in the late 1940s and early 1950s, when Kracauer's fellow German exiles in America—Lang, Billy Wilder, Josef von Sternberg, and others—were recasting the Bauhaus iconography of abstraction and estrangement within American urban settings. Lang's geometrical projections of New York in *Scarlet Street* (1945) and *While the City Sleeps* (1956) represent a cross between aesthetic pleasure in the avant-garde shapes of the metropolis and moral discomfort at the human costs wrought by alienation and anxiety, and in these postwar films American architectural modernity emerges as an alternative version of the German technological sublime.

American *film noir*, inflected as it was by European politics and stylistics, thus moved beyond its urban gangster origins to speak powerfully to a more disquieting sense that the political traumas of the past were not yet dead and buried. Orson Welles, who admitted to being fascinated by the power and 'showmanship' of fascism, deals overtly with the Nazi legacy in *The Stranger* (1946), where he plays a Nazi officer seeking to conceal himself after the war as a schoolmaster in Harper, Connecticut.[10] As part of this camouflage, he induces a local woman (Loretta Young) to fall in love with him, thereby setting up an ostensible antithesis between American innocence and Nazi corruption, an antithesis reinforced by the incorporation within the film of newsreel footage from the concentration camps. Yet the heroine is shown to be attracted subconsciously to the Welles character even after his gruesome past has been exposed, and their Wagnerian *liebestod*, erotically mingling love and death, exposes the psychological 'stranger' within the heroine's own personality. The effect of this disturbing film, 'noir' in all senses of the word, is to move beyond the tidy ethical conclusion to its narrative by implying how good and evil, the light and the dark, become paradoxically intertwined. One moment the Welles character is seen praying; the next he commits a brutal murder. Subsequently, he excites his lover by telling her he killed his victim with the same hands that are now holding her. The film thus refutes its opening hypothesis that 'in Harper there's nothing to be afraid of' by demonstrating how the sinister charms of corruption can infiltrate themselves into even the most socially respectable of American rural communities.

What James Naremore has called the 'discourse on noir', connoting a sense of moral ambiguity and stylistic abstraction bound up with a simultaneous attraction to and fear of new technology, became very popular in the United States after the war.[11] The genre's career in England, however, was much more chequered.

---

[9] Siegfried Kracauer, *From Caligari to Hitler: A Psychological History of the German Film*, rev. edn., ed. Leonardo Quaresima (Princeton: Princeton University Press, 2004), 204, 249, 272.

[10] Michael Denning, *The Cultural Front: The Laboring of American Culture in the Twentieth Century* (London: Verso, 1996), 378.

[11] James Naremore, *More Than Night: Film Noir in Its Contexts* (Berkeley: University of California Press, 1998), 12.

Various English films were made which focused on the social problems of maladjusted veterans and black marketeering, while there were also a number of *films noirs* involving culturally prestigious figures such as Carol Reed and Graham Greene, notably *Brighton Rock* (1948) and *The Third Man* (1949). Both of these films, however, were careful to preserve a sense of distance from contemporary England, the former being set, as the film's opening credits make clear, in the 'dark alleyways and festering slums' of a Brighton that existed only 'between the two wars' and is 'now happily no more', the latter in a crumbling, postwar Vienna. When St John L. Clowes directed a version of *No Orchids for Miss Blandish* in 1948, placing the gangster film with British actors in an American setting, the public reaction was one of outrage: Dilys Powell in the *Sunday Times* described the film as not 'fit for public exhibition', while Dr Edith Summerskill, Parliamentary Secretary to the Ministry of Food in the Labour government, declared that it would 'pervert the minds of the British people'. Harold Wilson, then President of the Board of Trade, roundly condemned 'gangster, sadistic and psychological films' and called for 'more films which genuinely show our way of life'. Some local authorities banned *No Orchids for Miss Blandish* altogether, and, as Andrew Spicer has observed, the generic problem in relation to English *film noir* of this period was its capacity to threaten the dominant 'consensual and co-operative model of post-war society' by presenting a harsher world based upon the peremptory demands of sex, power, and the survival of the fittest.[12]

For English audiences in the late 1940s, this nihilistic world seemed too close for comfort to the barbaric ghosts of prewar modernism. The collusion between film noir and modernism was safer if it was associated with enemy or alien territory, such as the Vienna portrayed in *The Third Man*, a city which was 'one of the cradles of both modernism and Hitlerian fascism'; it was a decidedly less comfortable prospect when brought home to the domestic context of postwar Britain.[13] The lingering fear of Nazi shadows in Britain after 1945 can be seen, for example, in the pedantic novels of C. P. Snow, which address in various ways the memory of war. In *The Light and the Dark* (1947), the mercurial but unstable Cambridge don, Roy Calvert, still excited by his wartime career as a fighter pilot, finds himself unwisely attracted to a Nietzschean irrationality; in *The Conscience of the Rich* (1958), Charles March is perturbed by the 'cruel glitter' of 'his sadic edge' which 'had to be watched and guarded against'; in *The Sleep of Reason* (1968)—whose title is taken from Goya's 1799 painting *The Sleep of Reason Produces Monsters*—there is a dwelling on the meaning of Auschwitz and a

---

[12] Andrew Spicer, 'The Emergence of the British Tough Guy: Stanley Baker, Masculinity and the Crime Thriller', in *British Crime Cinema*, ed. Steve Chibnall and Robert Murphy (London: Routledge, 1999), 82; Brian McFarlane, 'Outrage: *No Orchids for Miss Blandish*', in *British Crime Cinema*, 40; Steve Chibnall and Robert Murphy, 'Parole Overdue: Releasing the British Crime Film into the Critical Community', in *British Crime Cinema*, 1.

[13] Naremore, *More Than Night*, 77.

link postulated between the Nazi past and senseless murders in the present.[14] Nevertheless, the realistic, doggedly moralistic tone of Snow's fiction seeks to incorporate the values of middle England, formally as well as thematically, in order to stave off the threat of a violent modernism which is implicitly associated here with England's dark recent history. Perhaps the most explicit evocation of noir within English fiction manifests itself in Malcolm Lowry's *Under the Volcano* (1947), a work set in Mexico in 1938 which frames its scenes of looming social catastrophe against newsreels from the Spanish Civil War. Lowry, who was born in Cheshire but who spent most of his time in North America during the 1930s, rewrote his novel extensively between 1942 and 1944 to incorporate observations on Hitler's Germany, with the character of Hugh Firmin in *Under the Volcano* finding the 'Nazi system' to be symbolized by a dead shark, 'which, even though dead, continues to go on swallowing live struggling men and women!' The sense of vagrancy and exile in this novel ('the wrong place … so far away from home') is associated both with social dislocation and with a broader horizon of nihilism, 'the darkness of a world without meaning'.[15]

The writer whose troubled association with postwar England I wish to consider in more detail, however, is the more iconic, popular figure of P. G. Wodehouse. Precisely because his arcadian portraits of rural life in England were so popular both before and after the war, Wodehouse opens up some complicated questions about the relationship between culture and politics during this era. (Wodehouse wrote nearly 100 novels, but I shall focus here mainly on the best-known series featuring Jeeves and Wooster.) Born in Surrey in 1881 and educated in England, Wodehouse first visited the United States in 1909 and subsequently became popular on both sides of the Atlantic both for his fiction and for the Broadway musicals that he wrote in collaboration with George Gershwin, Jerome Kern, and others. Thanks to the money accumulated through these endeavours, he was able to divide his time between the wars among palatial establishments in England, France, and America, though after a series of murky wartime adventures in Europe he returned to Long Island, where he lived from 1947 until his death in 1975.

Despite his reputation as a lightweight author, Wodehouse has had many distinguished advocates. He was admired in his own time by literary connoisseurs such as T. S. Eliot, Rudyard Kipling, and H. G. Wells, and was saluted in 1999 by Joe Keenan, executive producer of the American television series *Frasier*, as 'the twentieth century's best comic writer', an author with a 'matchless command of comic tone and rhythm' and a 'superb ear for dialogue'. Moreover, unlike many English writers, his work is widely known throughout the world: Shashi Tharoor wrote in 2002 of how Wodehouse is 'by far the most popular English-language writer in India … sold on railway station platforms and airport bookstalls alongside the

---

[14] C. P. Snow, *The Conscience of the Rich* (London: Penguin, 1961), 125.
[15] Malcolm Lowry, *Under the Volcano* (London: Picador, 1993), 304, 321, 266.

15. Transatlantic traveller: P. G. Wodehouse leaves London, Waterloo, in 1930 on the boat train for New York, via Southampton. Wodehouse is accompanied by his stepdaughter, Leonora, while his wife Ethel stands on the platform.

latest bestsellers'.[16] At the same time, the critical writing on Wodehouse has been, by and large, quite dismal, consisting mainly of hagiographies by acolytes who not infrequently attempt to emphasize their devotion by breaking into a pastiche of the master's style. In part, this critical lacuna can be explained by the fact that literary scholarship has always found it more difficult to deal with comedy than with more 'serious' themes: as Wodehouse himself put it, humorists 'are looked down on by the intelligentsia, patronized by the critics and generally regarded as outside the pale of literature'.[17] But this critical neglect can also be traced to Wodehouse's uncomfortable relationship with English society, a relationship triangulated through Germany and the United States, which served to position him ultimately in an antagonistic attitude to the norms of English civic culture.

Part of the problem here is that Wodehouse got taken up early on by right-wing factionalists. When he was awarded the honorary degree of Doctor of

[16] Joe Keenan, introduction, in *The Code of the Woosters*, by P. G. Wodehouse (London: Penguin, 1999), pp. vi, xii; Shashi Tharoor, 'How the Woosters Captured Delhi', *Guardian Review*, 20 July 2002, 4.
[17] P. G. Wodehouse, 'A Note on Humour', in *Plum Pie* (London: Pan, 1968), 249.

Letters at Oxford University in 1939, Hilaire Belloc hyperbolically pronounced him the 'best writer of English now alive' and claimed that the figure of the manservant Jeeves epitomized 'what the English character in action may achieve', so that if over the course of the next fifty years his type 'shall have faded, then what we have so long called England will no longer be'.[18] Belloc's portentous association of Jeeves with his own lyrical understanding of the longevity and continuity of English culture was subsequently ridiculed by Hugh Kenner, who pointed out that Oxford never saw fit to give James Joyce an honorary doctorate and intimated that this was because Wodehouse fitted comfortably with a donnish version of high-table cosiness in a way that Joyce never could.[19] Another right-wing polemicist, Evelyn Waugh, equally misleadingly acclaimed his friend Wodehouse in 1961 for having created a 'timeless' world: 'The gardens of Blandings Castle are that original garden from which we are all exiled,' claimed Waugh, adding how Wodehouse had created an 'idyllic world' where 'there has been no Fall of Man'. Indeed, this notion of Wodehouse's atemporal quality became popular after the war, with W. H. Auden, in his 1948 essay 'Dingley Dell and the Fleet', declaring the 'four great English experts on Eden' to be 'Dickens, Oscar Wilde, Ronald Firbank and P. G. Wodehouse'.[20] The ultimate source of this idea was George Orwell's essay 'In Defence of P. G. Wodehouse' (1945), published shortly after the latter's infamous involvement in pro-German wartime propaganda, which sought to remove Wodehouse from the political domain by proclaiming: 'It is nonsense to talk of "Fascist tendencies" in his books. There are no post-1918 tendencies at all. Throughout his work there is a certain uneasy awareness of the problem of class distinctions, and scattered through it at various dates there are ignorant though not unfriendly references to Socialism.'[21]

This wish-fulfilment view of Wodehouse's fiction as inhabiting a protected realm of Eden, however, exemplifies English postwar cultural amnesia at its most blatant. Orwell's essay in fact represents a whitewashing job of the first order, for there are innumerable 'references to Socialism' and other aspects of modern society throughout Wodehouse's fiction, most of them very unfriendly indeed. These allusions, implicit in the earlier work, become more overt in the latter part of Wodehouse's career, most of them appearing in novels published after Orwell's death in 1950. For instance, in *Ring for Jeeves* (1953) the Earl

---

[18] Anthony Quinton, 'Wodehouse and the Tradition of Comedy', in *From Wodehouse to Wittgenstein: Essays* (Manchester: Carcanet, 1998), 320; Hilaire Belloc, introduction, in *Weekend Wodehouse*, by P. G. Wodehouse (London: Hutchinson, 1986), 5–7.
[19] Hugh Kenner, *A Sinking Island: The Modern English Writers* (London: Barrie & Jenkins, 1988), 34.
[20] Evelyn Waugh, 'An Act of Homage and Reparation to P. G. Wodehouse', in *The Essays, Articles and Reviews of Evelyn Waugh*, ed. Donat Gallagher (London: Methuen, 1983), 567–8; W. H. Auden, 'Dingley Dell and the Fleet', in *The Dyer's Hand and Other Essays* (London: Faber, 1975), 411.
[21] George Orwell, 'In Defence of P. G. Wodehouse', in *Collected Essays, Journalism and Letters*, iii. 352.

of Rowcester remarks on how in 'these disturbed post-war days, with the social revolution turning handsprings on every side ... it is still quite an advantage to be in big print in *Debrett's Peerage*', an observation with which the butler concurs: 'Unquestionably so, m'lord. It gives a gentleman a certain standing.' Jeeves later tells Captain Biggar that the earl's ancestral home, Rowcester Abbey, is now a financial liability: 'Socialistic legislation has sadly depleted the resources of England's hereditary aristocracy. We are living now in what is known as the Welfare State, which means—broadly—that everybody is completely destitute.' Despite the Earl of Rowcester's reminiscences about the 'Restoration gallantry' of his aristocratic ancestors, he fears that standards of 'domestic help' are fatally falling away, and so he finds himself compelled to sell his abbey to a rich American, Mrs Spottsworth, who plans to dismantle it 'stone by stone' and ship it to California, where she will reassemble it in the style made fashionable by the newspaper magnate William Randolph Hearst.[22] All of Wodehouse's postwar fiction, in fact, is charged with this querulous spirit of social discontent. In *The Mating Season* (1949), there are acerbic references to Labour politicians Ernest Bevin and Stafford Cripps—the latter likened in another story, 'Archibald and the Masses', to Stalin.[23] In 'Jeeves and the Greasy Bird' (1966), there is a gratuitous slap at modern English culture in the shape of Blair Eggleston, 'one of the angry young novelists', whose anger, says Jeeves, is directed at 'life'. In *Aunts Aren't Gentlemen* (1974), Bertie Wooster complains vociferously about student unrest, the frequency of protest marches, and government bureaucracy: if he wanted to keep pigs, he says, 'I should strongly resent not being allowed to give them a change of air and scenery without getting permission from a board of magistrates. Are we in Russia?' And in *Much Obliged, Jeeves* (1971) we find Jeeves and Wooster canvassing on behalf of the Conservative Party at a local by-election, where they come into conflict with a local newspaper which is, according to their preferred candidate, 'very far to the left', having 'had a cartoon of me last week showing me with my hands dripping with the blood of the martyred proletariat'.[24]

  Much Obliged, Jeeves in fact presents a comically miniaturized version of the French Revolution, with the struggle between the social classes played out here in the form of a local pageant. Bertie Wooster's former butler Bingley, who used to be, says Wooster, 'very gloomy' and 'sinister', as if he were always 'brooding silently on the coming revolution, when he would be at liberty to chase me down Park Lane with a dripping knife', now turns out to be merely a self-interested manipulator of events: his 'political views', says Jeeves, once 'very far to the left ... changed when he became a man of property'. In *Thank You, Jeeves* (1934),

---

[22] P. G. Wodehouse, *Ring for Jeeves* (London: Coronet, 1983), 79, 104, 133, 145, 184.
  [23] Owen Dudley Edwards, *P. G. Wodehouse: A Critical and Historical Essay* (London: Martin Brian and O'Keefe, 1977), 106.
  [24] P. G. Wodehouse, 'Jeeves and the Greasy Bird', in *Plum Pie*, 8; *idem, Aunts Aren't Gentlemen* (Harmondsworth: Penguin, 1977), 38; *idem, Much Obliged, Jeeves* (London: Sphere, 1972), 136.

Bingley was first presented as a 'bally Five-Year-Planner', but in Wodehouse's world radical politics appear always to emerge out of merely personal envy or malice, and Jeeves's citation in the later novel of Edmund Burke—'Custom reconciles us to everything'—makes clear where the ideological heart of the book lies. Wooster's comically endearing Aunt Dahlia is also described here as someone who can transform herself 'in a flash into a carbon copy of a Duchess of the old school', while Jeeves talks in an equally exclusive manner about how at the political meeting in the local town hall, 'together with the flower of Market Snodsbury's aristocracy', there was 'a rougher element in cloth caps and turtleneck sweaters who should never have been admitted'. The manifold references to social upheaval and insurrection are consolidated in this scene, with the throwing of turnips and tomatoes actually compared to violent 'passions which recalled the worst excesses of the French revolution'. Shortly afterwards, Aunt Dahlia herself is said to be 'like some aristocrat of the French Revolution on being informed that the tumbril waited'.[25]

All of this is brilliantly done, of course, and it is not at all my intention to suggest that Wodehouse's politically incorrect views in any way diminish his comic genius. To argue, however, that such events take place in a 'timeless' world or that Wodehouse can be seen as 'not unfriendly' to socialism is absurd. He was very keen on the history of his own English family which formed part of the East Anglian landed gentry—and, after 1797, the aristocracy—and he liked to point out how his ancestor John Wodehouse had fought at Agincourt, just as his fictional protagonist comically boasts of how 'There was a Wooster at the time of the Crusades who would have won the Battle of Joppa singlehanded, if he hadn't fallen off his horse'.[26] Wodehouse's letters are also scattered with derogatory references to the English working classes: Chingford, he tells his stepdaughter in 1920, 'isn't a bad place in itself but is too near the East End of London to be really nice'; a strike in 1921 'makes me spit'; England in 1959 is full of 'morons reading the *Express*', while to Guy Bolton in the same year he exclaims: 'Damn and blast the English working classes! ... What a curse these strikes are.'[27] Conversely, in a 1974 preface to *Joy in the Morning* he laments the loss of old social graces but sees 'signs of a coming renaissance' in the way 'the butler is creeping back ... in hundreds of homes there is buttling going on just as of yore'.[28] *Joy in the Morning* itself, completed when Wodehouse was a guest of the Nazis in Germany during the war and published in 1946, features a charade of English history, with the American businessman J. Chichester Clam attending a fancy-dress ball at

---

[25] Wodehouse, *Much Obliged, Jeeves*, 37, 73, 162, 171–2, 184; *idem, Thank You, Jeeves* (London: Penguin, 1999), 130.
[26] Barry Phelps, *P. G. Wodehouse: Man and Myth* (London: Constable, 1992), 27; Wodehouse, *Aunts Aren't Gentlemen*, 121.
[27] P. G. Wodehouse, *Yours, Plum: The Letters of P. G. Wodehouse*, ed. Frances Donaldson (London: Hutchinson, 1990), 11, 19, 234.
[28] P. G. Wodehouse, preface, in *Joy in the Morning* (London: Barrie and Jenkins, 1974), 4.

East Wibley town hall in the guise of Edward the Confessor, while the tissue of quotations and misquotations from Shakespeare, Gray, and other famous English writers that bestrews Wodehouse's fiction also furnishes these texts with a labyrinthine cultural memory, a depth of perspective, that implicitly links Bertie Wooster and his compatriots with a particular kind of cultural heritage. Similarly, Wooster's frequent recollections within his narratives of incidents from his own past—adventures generally related in other tales—create what might be called a synecdoche of this memory, since one of the charms of Wodehouse's world is how everything seems ultimately to be connected, historically through time and genealogically through familial relationships. This, of course, is one reason why Wodehouse hated the idea of social disruption so much: his work thrives on what Laura Mooneyham calls a 'recombinatory genius', where the same plots and characters recur again and again in slightly different forms.[29]

The farcical elements of these novels, which depend largely upon certain kinds of social stereotyping, are of course executed with consummate skill. It is important to recognize, though, that in terms of English class snobbery Wodehouse is the genuine article: not simply a clerk who was popular with suburbanites, as Carey oddly maintains, or an anarchic sentimentalist who prefers 'emotional affinities' to class politics, as the American critic Kirby Olson suggested.[30] It is true that Wodehouse's own family was always short of money in his youth, but this did not stop him from constructing an idealized version of English aristocratic traditions, and *Carry On, Jeeves* (1925) is dedicated to Bernard Le Strange, brother of Wodehouse's distant cousin Charles Le Strange, owner of Hunstanton Hall in Norfolk, a country seat which Wodehouse, who often stayed there in the interwar years, described as 'the most wonderful place of refuge'. The 1920s and 1930s were a time of clear and rigid class distinctions within English society, and this is an environment within which Wodehouse was entirely comfortable. If his world is 'timeless', as Evelyn Waugh and others have maintained, it can only be in that paradoxical way theorized by Roland Barthes, whereby the arcadian myth becomes a form of 'depoliticized speech', silently repressing the historical contingencies upon which its own claims to eternal wisdom are predicated.[31] Discussing 'the situation of the writer in 1947', Jean-Paul Sartre observed the following year how even authors who during the prewar period had prided themselves upon a position of detachment and transcendence now found themselves obliged reluctantly to acknowledge how 'history flowed in upon' them, and it would be true to say that the ironic discrepancies between

---

[29] Laura Mooneyham, 'Comedy among the Modernists: P. G. Wodehouse and the Anachronism of Comic Form', *Twentieth Century Literature*, 40 (1994), 127.

[30] Carey, *Intellectuals and the Masses*, 59; Kirby Olson, 'Bertie and Jeeves at the End of History: P. G. Wodehouse as Political Scientist', *Humor*, 9/1 (1996), 81.

[31] Robert McCrum, *Wodehouse: A Life* (London: Viking–Penguin, 2004), 164, 205; Roland Barthes, 'Myth Today', in *Mythologies* trans. Annette Lavers (St Albans, Herts.: Paladin-Granada, 1973), 142.

a fantasy condition of blissful atemporality and the entanglements of time, a conflict between myth and history, become more explicit (and cantankerous) in Wodehouse's later work.[32]

The covertly partisan nature of conditions that are presented by Wodehouse as self-evident can be elucidated by a closer inspection of *Types of Ethical Theory*, the book recommended to Wooster by his putative fiancée Florence Craye in 'Jeeves Takes Charge' (1925) and again in *Joy in the Morning*. The passage held up for ridicule in the latter work starts off: 'Of the two antithetic terms in the Greek philosophy one only was real and selfsubsisting: that is to say, Ideal Thought as opposed to that which it has to penetrate and mold. The other, corresponding to our Nature, was in itself phenomenal, unreal, without any permanent footing, having no predicates that held true for two moments together.'[33] One key word here is 'mold', which is what Florence Craye and various other women attempt to do to Bertie Wooster, who, by implication, rejects such moral idealism and prefers his own untutored state of 'Nature'. *Types of Ethical Theory* was in fact a work published in 1885 by James Martineau, a Victorian educator who became Professor of Moral Philosophy at Manchester New College. The brother of Harriet Martineau, who campaigned for the emancipation of slaves in the United States, he believed, *contra* Wooster, that man's nature had no substantive reality in itself but needed to be channelled in ethically appropriate directions. Later in *Types of Ethical Theory*, he writes: 'A country would not be a very promising school of patriotism in which there were no domestic traditions of heroism and faith, no hearth and altar, no parents, sons and daughters, but only public schools, and club-dinners, and shameless temples of Aphrodite to defend.'[34] By contrast, as Kathy MacDermott has noted, the predominant emphasis in Wodehouse's fiction on 'codes' of behaviour—external manners which enable Wooster to know instinctively whether someone is or is not a 'preux chevalier'—serve to displace the reader's attention from any kind of ethical question, since the latter would depend upon a sense of interiority rarely available in these narratives.[35]

The glancing references to Martineau in these texts enable us to position Wooster more precisely as a foe of the high liberalism that came out of the Victorian Whig tradition. This is the tradition represented by Wooster's nemesis, Aunt Agatha, and also in 'Jeeves and the Unbidden Guest' (1925) by a friend of Aunt Agatha, Lady Malvern, who has written a book on 'social conditions in India' and is now researching one on 'prison conditions in America'. Wooster's impatience with Martineau's anti-slavery politics also throws an illuminating light on the casually racist assumptions in *Thank You, Jeeves*, where a 'troupe of nigger minstrels' performs at an English seaside town, allowing Wooster and

---

[32] Jean-Paul Sartre, *What Is Literature?*, trans. Bernard Frechtman (London: Methuen, 1950), 157.
[33] Wodehouse, *Joy in the Morning*, 15.
[34] James Martineau, *Types of Ethical Theory* (Oxford: Clarendon Press, 1885), i. 108.
[35] Kathy MacDermott, 'Light Humor and the Dark Underside of Wish Fulfillment: Conservative Anti-realism', *Studies in Popular Culture*, 10/2 (1987), 47.

Sir Roderick Glossop to don black-face disguise in order to effect an escape from
J. Washburn Stoker's boat; the comic mechanism of this book depends precisely
upon the belief that a black visage is not acceptable in polite English society and
that anyone 'wandering around the country in a black face' would immediately
be classified as 'crazy'. This kind of assumption also accounts for the joke against
Harriet Beecher Stowe in *Much Obliged, Jeeves*, when Wooster asks Aunt Dahlia
how her husband is coping with a disruption to his reclusive lifestyle: ' "How,"
I asked, "is Uncle Tom bearing up under this invasion of his cabin?" ' To
which she replies: ' "Did you expect to find him here playing his banjo? My
poor halfwitted child, he was off to the south of France the moment he learned
that danger threatened." ' The worldliness and cosmopolitanism of the English
aristocracy is deliberately contrasted here with the alleged primitive simplicity of
Stowe's African-American characters.[36] (Wodehouse himself was always sensitive
about his lack of responsiveness to his adopted culture even after many years of
residence in the United States; when a publisher remarked disapprovingly on the
absence of authentic American characters and settings in his stories, he replied
dismissively: 'What did he expect from me? Thoughtful studies of sharecropper
life in the Deep South?'[37]) These oblique racist elements were matched by the
anti-Semitic observations strewn casually through his fiction and letters: in a
letter of 1931 to William Townend, to take one example, Wodehouse attributed
the current financial difficulties of the movie industry to the fact that 'all these
Jews out here have been having a gorgeous time for years, fooling about with
the shareholders' money and giving all their relations fat jobs'. As Owen Dudley
Edwards has noted, the Hollywood moguls in his stories tend to have Jewish
names—Isadore Levitsky, Jacob Z. Schnellenhauer, and so on—while in *Joy
in the Morning*, completed in Nazi Germany during the early 1940s, a Jewish
presence is confined to the world of drapery, with the Cohen Brothers being the
dispensers of fancy-dress costumes in London's Covent Garden.[38]

　　The extent to which Wodehouse actually collaborated with the Nazis during
the war remains unclear. Imprisoned after the German seizure of Le Touquet,
where he was living, the author agreed in 1940 to make five radio broadcasts
to America at the behest of the German Foreign Office, whose director, Paul
Schmidt, told Wodehouse that he was a great admirer of his writing, and
these talks were subsequently re-broadcast to Britain by Goebbels's Propaganda
Ministry. The programmes themselves, a mildly comic account of life in an
internment camp, were unexceptionable, though of course the mere presence

---

[36] P. G. Wodehouse, 'Jeeves and the Unbidden Guest', in *Carry On, Jeeves* (Harmondsworth:
Penguin, 1957), 53, 55; *idem, Thank You, Jeeves*, 15, 213; *idem, Much Obliged, Jeeves*, 54.

[37] Deepika Karle, 'A Reader's Guide to P. G. Wodehouse's America', *Studies in American Humor*,
NS 7 (1989), 43.

[38] Wodehouse, *Yours, Plum*, 129; Edwards, *P. G. Wodehouse*, 56. McCrum's view that Wodehouse's writing is 'strikingly free from either racist or anti-Semitic prejudice' is absurd. McCrum,
Wodehouse, 354.

of such an icon of Englishness on German radio alarmed the British wartime authorities, and they arranged for an attack to be made on BBC radio by the journalist William N. Connor, who duly denounced Wodehouse as an 'elderly playboy' who had chosen to betray his country for 'a soft bed in a luxury hotel'. There is no doubt that Wodehouse and his wife Ethel were treated favourably when they arrived in Berlin to make the notorious broadcasts, and indeed the Wodehouses subsequently spent more than two years living in Germany at the height of the war, staying part of the time with relatives of Major Eric Raven von Barnikow, whom Wodehouse had known in Hollywood as 'Eric Barnikow'. It has subsequently emerged, moreover, that Wodehouse was recommended to the German authorities as a possible collaborator by John Amery, who made virulent anti-Semitic, pro-Nazi speeches in occupied Europe, and who was hanged as a traitor by Britain after the war.[39] When they were in Berlin during the early 1940s, the Wodehouses often stayed at the Adlon Hotel, located in the immediate vicinity of various Reich ministries and a frequent meeting place for senior Nazi officials as well as for Amery and for William Joyce, 'Lord Haw-Haw', who was later also hanged as a traitor for his pro-Nazi radio broadcasts. Wodehouse by all accounts kept his distance from these political figures and preferred simply to get on with his writing, but the fact that he was welcome within this milieu clearly implies how the Nazis regarded him, potentially at least, as a fellow-traveller.

The question of whether or not Wodehouse was paid by the Nazis for his radio broadcasts has long been shrouded in uncertainty, though this now appears unlikely. It is clear that he was being remunerated by the German Foreign Office in 1943 and 1944, but Robert McCrum's biography states unequivocally that these were legitimate international royalties which needed at this time to be paid through the German authorities.[40] In general, though, the problem of Wodehouse's relationship to Nazi Germany has been framed much too narrowly, focusing on imponderable questions of personal motive and not enough on the broader context of English culture in this difficult era. It is clear that Wodehouse himself was, as he liked to portray himself, more of a hermit dedicated to his craft than an enthusiast for worldly politics, but it is also clear that the horizons of his work were generally compatible with those of the Nazi project, which is why the German propaganda machine had cannily identified him as a potential collaborator. Like the Nazis, he loathed what he took to be the degenerate spirit of the artistic avant-garde, with *Meet Mr Mulliner* (1927) containing a parody of T. S. Eliot's poetry entitled 'Darkling (A Threnody)', which evokes 'Chill winds, / Bitter like the tang of half-remembered sins', and casts the narrator as 'a worm that wriggles in a swamp of Disillusionment'. Conversely, he described to his German

---

[39] Frances Donaldson, *P. G. Wodehouse: A Biography* (London: Weidenfeld & Nicolson, 1982), 243; Iain Sproat, *Wodehouse at War* (London: Milner and Company, 1981), 135; Douglas Davis, 'MI5: Wodehouse was Nazi Collaborator', *Jerusalem Post*, 19 Sept. 1999; http://www.jpost.com/com/Archive/19.Sep.1999/News/Article/-9.html, accessed 28 July 2002.
[40] McCrum, *Wodehouse*, 342.

hosts in 1942 the period he spent in Degenershausen, a village on the edge of the Harz mountains, as 'the happiest time in all my life', and when the Wodehouses were allowed to move to Paris in 1943, he said that he was 'terribly sad about leaving Germany and all our friends'.[41] It was in Degenershausen that Wodehouse completed *Joy in the Morning*, though after his return to America at the end of the war he declined to renew any acquaintance with Anga von Bodenhausen and her daughter, who had been his close companions in Germany; because of the way in which the events of the war resolved themselves, Wodehouse was forced into a familiar stance of amnesia towards sympathies and affections of his former life. This is not to imply that Wodehouse was necessarily treacherous. He may not have been an active supporter of the Nazis, but he was one of that class of Englishmen—socially and politically conservative, mildly but instinctively racist, contemptuous of what he saw as the pretensions of modernism—who could probably have lived quite happily under Nazi rule. In this sense, the radio broadcasts from Germany were not merely 'a disastrous blunder' which had no connection with his fiction but, on the contrary, something fundamentally consonant with it.[42] Wodehouse's art, like that of all mythmakers, involved a systematic form of depoliticization, making strange, violent, or absurd events appear as if they were entirely humane and natural.

One general impression from this whole affair, then, is of Wodehouse trying to hedge his bets. He said that he had 'no interest' in wars, and as a writer who was by this time rich and internationally famous, one priority for him would have been to ensure that he could continue to flourish commercially after the war no matter what its outcome.[43] (He was, in 1940, notably pessimistic about the outlook for the Allies.) As David Damrosch has observed, Wodehouse began writing 'world literature' as early as 1915, with his primary loyalty being not to any particular community but to his international market; consequently, national characteristics were valuable primarily when they were recognizable enough to offer opportunities for comic stereotyping and mockery.[44] One of the things that Wodehouse feared above all was twentieth-century England changing so much that he would lose his readership; in an interview with the American correspondent Harry Flannery of the Columbia Broadcasting Company while he was in Berlin, Wodehouse stated: 'I'll tell you something about the war and my work that's been bothering me a good deal. I'm wondering whether the kind of people and the kind of England I write about will live after the war—whether England wins or not, I mean.'[45] Wodehouse here acknowledges the strong possibility of the war marking a final break with the old Edwardian world of aristocracy and servants, and this is one of the

[41] P. G. Wodehouse, *Meet Mr Mulliner* (London: Herbert Jenkins, 1927), 151–2; McCrum, *Wodehouse*, 232, 335, 339.
[42] McCrum, *Wodehouse*, 380, 417.
[43] Phelps, *P. G. Wodehouse*, 102; McCrum, *Wodehouse*, 268.
[44] David Damrosch, *What is World Literature?* (Princeton: Princeton University Press, 2003), 212.
[45] Donaldson, *P. G. Wodehouse*, 215.

reasons for the vehement attacks in his post-1945 books on what *Ring for Jeeves* terms 'Socialistic legislation': a socialist Britain threatened to be a more difficult market for Wodehouse to conquer. Conversely, if the Germans had invaded England and established some form of government there, it seems as probable that Wodehouse would have been fêted and institutionalized as a kind of laureate authorial voice for the country as that the Duke of Windsor, a neighbour of the Wodehouses on Paris's Boulevard Suchet in 1945 and 'Hitler's staunchest advocate in Britain' during his 1930s, would have been welcomed back upon the throne he had been forced to abdicate in 1936.[46] As Aldous Huxley remarked in 1935, the Nazi propaganda machine had grown considerably more sophisticated during the 1930s, and, rather than simply reproducing party slogans, it had become increasingly interested in disseminating 'decent' art commensurate with its fascist mythology in order to allow citizens 'to swallow their daily dose of propaganda without repugnance'. Wodehouse, with his arcadian idylls tinged with racist assumptions, would fit that bill perfectly, and indeed in 1942 he sold his novel *Heavy Weather* to a German film production company, on the understanding that the scene would be changed from Shropshire to Pomerania, that all the characters would become German, and that the film would be made only after the end of the war.[47]

So far from being the bumbling political innocent that he liked to pretend, then, Wodehouse was thinking ahead to a possible postwar situation in which a triumphant Germany would provide the mythological context for his idyllic stories, a context that Wodehouse feared was fast slipping away in Britain. It is true that Wodehouse overtly satirizes fascism in *The Code of the Woosters* (1938) through his representation of Roderick Spode, 'founder and head of the Saviours of Britain, a Fascist organization better known as the Black Shorts'; Spode is depicted as a bully with a hearty appetite for violence, who, says Wooster, hears crowds shouting 'Heil Spode' and imagines it to be 'the Voice of the People', whereas 'What the Voice of the People is saying is: "Look at that frightful ass Spode swanking about in footer bags!"' Spode is generally thought to be modelled on Sir Oswald Mosley, founder of the British Union of Fascists, and this satirical portrait is sometimes thought of as evidence of Wodehouse's anti-Fascist sympathies; however, when Spode reappears in *Much Obliged, Jeeves*, having succeeded to the title of Lord Sidcup, he has acquired a reputation as 'one of those silver-tongued orators you read about', and, like Jeeves and Wooster, he campaigns enthusiastically on behalf of the local Conservative candidate. The point here is that Spode, though personally unpleasant, is seen no less than Wodehouse's other aristocrats as a fixed part of the Establishment. There is some discussion in *Much Obliged, Jeeves* of Lord Sidcup relinquishing his title so as to allow him to stand for the

---

[46] Wodehouse, *Ring for Jeeves*, 104; *idem, Yours, Plum*, 101. On the Duke of Windsor's support for Hitler, see James Pool, *Hitler and his Secret Partners: Contributions, Loot and Rewards, 1933–1945* (New York: Pocket—Simon and Schuster, 1997), 89.
[47] Aldous Huxley, 'Ballyhoo for Nations', in *Complete Essays*, iii: *1930–1935*, ed. Robert S. Baker and James Sexton (Chicago: Dee, 2001), 434; Sproat, *Wodehouse at War*, 143–4.

House of Commons as an MP: 'He couldn't at one time,' says Aunt Dahlia, 'at least only by being guilty of treason, but they've changed the rules and apparently it is quite the posh thing to do nowadays.'[48] What might once have been treasonable is now considered orthodox behaviour; even the Fascist orator Spode has been folded back into the bosom of Wodehouse's social establishment.

With his massive successes on Broadway in the 1920s and his spell in Hollywood during the 1930s, Wodehouse had already spent a considerable amount of time in the United States between the wars, and in 1947 he and his wife returned to America for good. He never set foot in England again, taking American citizenship in 1955, although his wife did return across the Atlantic for a few short solo visits. Wodehouse was shrewd enough to realize that if he returned to Britain he might be arrested and tried for treason, since the judge in the William Joyce case in 1945 had ruled that the motive for broadcasting on enemy radio was immaterial. If this strict interpretation of the law had been upheld, the familiar defence of Wodehouse as what Anthony Quinton calls a 'genial and indulgent' buffoon could not have carried any judicial weight.[49] However, the report into Wodehouse's wartime activities prepared by Major Cussen of the British security services in 1944 accurately observed that 'the question of prosecuting Wodehouse raises matters of policy in addition to, and apart from, the questions of law involved', and one reason why the British government would have been a reluctant party to this case is the affection in which Wodehouse was held by large sections of the British population. (Orwell, for example, recalled how he had been reading him 'fairly closely since 1911, when I was eight years old'.)[50] To prosecute Wodehouse would thus have been to risk opening up ideological fissures within postwar British culture, to divide the country between those still attached to the supposedly timeless idyll of Edwardian manners and those committed to the bureaucratic reconstruction of the postwar state, and this was a policy that the government was not unwise enough to pursue. Given the lack of a German invasion and the relative absence of collaboration from within domestic territory, Britain after 1945 was blessed with the appearance, at least, of being a relatively homogeneous people, and it made much more sense to gloss over Wodehouse's alleged infractions than to attempt to hunt down any possible links with the Nazis, particularly as he planned henceforth to live in the United States. Major Cussen astutely advised Wodehouse henceforth to stay 'out of the Jurisdiction', and one of the reasons why he took American citizenship in 1955 was to protect himself against the possibility of arrest if he were ever to return to Britain.[51]

The more general point here is one made frequently in relation to the English and American Civil Wars, that it was clearly in the interests of the British

48 Wodehouse, *Code of the Woosters*, 49, 113; *idem, Much Obliged, Jeeves*, 52, 142.
49 Quinton, 'Wodehouse and the Tradition of Comedy', 333.
50 Sproat, *Wodehouse at War*, 166; Orwell, 'In Defence of P. G. Wodehouse', 345.
51 McCrum, *Wodehouse*, 390, 392.

16. American pastoral: P.G. Wodehouse at his home in Remsenburg, Long Island, mid-1960s.

authorities, after having made examples of some of the more flamboyant traitors, to seek a renewed social stability by binding opposing factions together, so that, as Eliot's 'Little Gidding' puts it, they 'Accept the constitution of silence/And are folded in a single party' (p.196). This is one reason for the invisibility of fascist modernism in Britain after the mid-1940s, despite its widespread popularity during the previous decade: by refusing vindictively to hound or suppress it, the British authorities cannily sought to minimize the space for its oppositional energies to function. It is also why Evelyn Waugh's 1961 'Act of Homage and Reparation to P. G. Wodehouse', although theoretically wrong-headed, was disconcertingly perceptive in the way it identified hostility to Wodehouse with British wartime government propaganda—what Waugh calls the 'conspiracy to identify aristocracy with treason'. By critically impugning the supposed impartiality and beneficence of the British state apparatus, the maverick Waugh opened up sores which the authorities would have preferred to keep soothingly covered: 'Our rulers at the time,' Waugh insisted, 'like our enemies, were dedicated to fomenting hate. They would have had us believe that the whole German nation comprised a different order of creation from ourselves.'[52] In attempting to exculpate Wodehouse from the charge of political

[52] Waugh, 'An Act of Homage and Reparation', 563.

involvement, Waugh in fact unwittingly drew attention to the ways in which he had become an important political figure in the post-1945 period.

By migrating to America, however, Wodehouse established for himself just the kind of oppositional perspective that enabled him to view these developments in postwar British society askance. The more inhumane aspects of Wodehouse's compulsively ordered world are displaced from an imaginary arcadian pastoral to a context of hard American violence, violence which is used to hollow out what the author sees as the hypocritical pretensions of the genteel, liberal humanist British environment. *The Mating Season*, published in 1949, is the most obvious example of this transatlantic displacement, as it systematically reinscribes the rural village of King's Deverill within the imaginative framework of Hollywood. Some of the characters in this story actually live in America: Corky Pirbright, a film actress, says that she has become 'the scarlet woman' to her English aunts—'They've lived all their lives at that mouldering old Hall ... They judge everybody by the county standard. If you aren't county, you don't exist'—while her brother, Claude, is said to be 'more like Groucho Marx than anything human'. The story also features a dog named after the Hollywood mogul Sam Goldwyn—'A South London dog, belonging to the lower middle classes or, rather, definitely of the people'—as well as a plot which is outlined in cinematic terms, with its denouement described as a 'good third-reel situation'.[53] Christopher Isherwood, when he visited England in 1947 after eight years away, wrote of an English village church as 'so absurdly authentic that it might have been lifted bodily off a movie-lot at MGM', and *The Mating Season* does something similar, describing King's Deverill as 'one of those villages where picturesque cottages breed like rabbits'. But this rural milieu is metamorphosed into a sinister *film noir* setting, an 'abode of thugs and ghouls', with Aunt Agatha's son Thomas represented as 'one of those tough, hardboiled striplings, a sort of juvenile James Cagney with a touch of Edward G. Robinson'. The *film noir* theme is also heightened by the sadistic extremities of the plot, with Bertie Wooster being surprised at one point to discover a 'deeper coshing side' to Jeeves, as the valet forcibly eliminates one of their adversaries.[54]

Although, as we have seen, Orwell defended Wodehouse in 1945 as a 'harmless old-fashioned' jester, he also complained the following year about the 'false values' and 'brutalising' effects of American gangster films.[55] In fact, though, Wodehouse's 1949 novel deliberately rejects such an antithesis, reconceptualizing English arcadia within a framework of American *film noir*. For the gleeful Wodehouse, such ruthlessness works as a rebuke to the more sentimental,

[53] P. G. Wodehouse, *The Mating Season*, introd. Christopher Hitchens (London: Penguin, 1999), 21, 8, 36, 212.

[54] Christopher Isherwood, 'Coming to London', in *Exhumations: Stories, Articles, Verse* (London: Methuen, 1966), 154; Wodehouse, *Mating Season*, 155, 139, 190.

[55] Orwell, 'In Defence of P. G. Wodehouse', 349, and *idem*, 'The Decline of the English Murder', 100–1.

complacent side of British culture; indeed, part of the author's plan in *The Mating Season* is to suggest how King's Deverill, with its twee village concert and constables, is as much a scene of dangerous violence and social indignity as any American urban jungle. Wodehouse's acerbic view of postwar England from the safe haven of Long Island produces an angry as well as a funny book, with the most obvious expression of this resentment being the vengeful targeting of those in Britain who had criticized its author during the Second World War. Wodehouse pays back A. A. Milne, who had attacked him in a letter to the *Daily Telegraph*, by depicting the character of Gussie Fink-Nottle being forced to recite Christopher Robin poems—'nauseous productions', Fink-Nottle calls them—at the village concert; he avenges himself on Alfred Duff Cooper, the politician responsible for setting up William Connor's hostile BBC broadcasts, by having the same character use Cooper's name as an alias when he is arrested; he also attributes an inept violin solo at the village concert to 'Miss Eustacia Pulbrook', in a mocking allusion to Sir Eustace Pulbrook, a fellow alumnus of Dulwich College who had denounced Wodehouse in the national press.[56] The concert itself, by Wodehouse's familiar method of parodic miniaturism, reinscribes the Fascist rally within an alternative, apparently incongruous domain: Esmond Haddock, previously too timid to declare his love for Corky Pirbright, finds that the experience of performing in public, 'swaying a fairly vast audience ... does something to you. It fills you with a sense of power'; and, fortified by the 'cheers of the multitude', he duly succeeds in carrying Corky back to Hollywood. Wodehouse, then, delights in paradoxically portraying King's Deverill as a site of Fascist rallies, *film noir* violence, and an American criminal mentality: Aunt Charlotte, one of the bastions of the English county set, voices her approval of the longer prison sentences that she hears are becoming standard in the United States, 'going on to say that the whole trend of modern life in England was towards a planned Americanization and that she, for one, approved of this, feeling that we had much to learn from our cousins across the sea'.[57]

The Mating Season is accordingly a novel which uses the harsh edges of American popular culture to problematize the comfortable distinction between fascist amorality and English sentimentalism, a moralizing assumption that had become commonplace in the country in the immediate aftermath of the Second World War. Like so many of Wodehouse's novels, it refracts traditional English settings through Americanized formal structures, transforming a familiar world of aristocratic manners into what the author called a 'musical comedy without music', a lowbrow lampooning of highbrow assumptions.[58] There are fleeting

[56] Wodehouse, *Mating Season*, 82, 27, 167; Robert F. Kiernan, *Frivolity Unbound: Six Masters of the Camp Novel* (New York: Continuum—Frederick Ungar, 1990), 112.

[57] Wodehouse, *Mating Season*, 197, 211.

[58] Roger Kimball, 'The Genius of Wodehouse', *New Criterion*, 19/2 (Oct. 2000), 12. On the use of stage techniques in Wodehouse's fiction, see Robert A. Hall jun., *The Comic Style of P. G. Wodehouse* (Hamden, Conn.: Archon, 1974).

references in *The Mating Season* to Thomas Paine—Esmond Haddock talks of
'the times that try men's souls'—while Constable Dobbs, known in the village
as 'an atheist' and a disruptive influence generally, is a devotee of the works
of the nineteenth-century American freethinker Robert Ingersoll.[59] Christopher
Hitchens considers that Wodehouse, like Oscar Wilde, mocks the English class
system here, depicting its assumptions of hierarchy as 'an absolute scream', but
this view is perhaps too simplistic. It is true that Wodehouse himself talked in
1966 about how a 'humorist' such as himself sees 'the world out of focus', in
a 'slightly cockeyed' fashion, a strategy that leads the comic author 'to ridicule
established institutions', thus earning the disapproval of 'most people' who
'want to keep their faith in established institutions intact'.[60] There is, indeed, a
subversive potential in Wodehouse, a sense of the bogus, self-serving aspects of
English manners. But what his highly wrought narratives offer above all is not
a negative critique or satire of these gentlemanly charades but, rather, a sense of
their absurd or farcical nature, a quality linked through Wodehouse's polished
style to the comic pleasures of dehumanization. The frequent violence in *The
Mating Season*, with its references to 'disembowelling with a blunt bread-knife'
and so on, can be seen as a heightened version of the manic, playfully sadistic
demeanour which permeates much of his other work. One might, in fact, suggest that the idiosyncratic nature of Wodehouse's metaphoric style, transposing
characters into objects to be hurled around linguistically—'There was a flash of
pink, and Esmond Haddock curvetted in'—has significant ideological affinities
with the brutal nature of the scenes described.[61] This kind of dehumanization
is associated with the compulsion for uniformity, the drive to return ritualist-
ically to a state of sameness, which impels his quasi-arcadian fictions, and it
highlights the inhumane edges of the fantasy world that Wodehouse projects so
effectively.

Robert F. Kiernan finds all this aggression to be 'amoral good fun' which
'affords the audience a holiday from conscience', while Robert McCrum has also
written about Wodehouse's 'gentle satire' and 'distaste for violence', thereby indicating the cocoon of critical sentimentality in which the author continues to be
immersed.[62] However, representations of violent conflict in Wodehouse—which
are linked frequently to the miniature pageants such as the spoof Fascist rally
in *The Mating Season* and the re-enactment of the French Revolution in *Much
Obliged, Jeeves*—delineate a world into which various forms of coercion are
systematically integrated. More usefully, Susan Sontag, in her 1974 essay 'Fascinating Fascism', talked of the 'utopian aesthetics' of fascist art, its skill at 'the
turning of people into things', such as we see, for example, in the cinematic

[59] Wodehouse, *Mating Season*, 45, 60.
[60] Hitchens, introduction, in *Mating Season*, pp. ix–x; Wodehouse, 'A Note on Humour', 248.
[61] Wodehouse, *Mating Season*, 75, 195.
[62] Kiernan, *Frivolity Unbound*, 108–9; McCrum, *Wodehouse*, 87–8.

pageants of Busby Berkeley, one of Hitler's favourite film-makers.[63] The Nazi aesthetic of a human figure abstracted into a vast symmetrical design has a structural equivalence to Busby Berkeley's elaborate set pieces, and there is a similar 'turning of people into things' in Wodehouse's fiction, a flattening out of characters—most obvious in the case of relatively minor figures such as Aunt Agatha—so that they are always identified by particular tics and become grotesque distortions of fully rounded human beings. Wodehouse's comic idiom thus exemplifies a delight in dehumanization, whose discomfiting allure, as Sontag observed of this kind of art, is precisely that it is so 'fascinating'. Wodehouse created scenarios of farcical encounter and stylistic finesse whose appeal ranged far and wide across the twentieth century, but it is precisely the allure and brilliance of these fake utopias that makes them so hysterically disconcerting. Ultimately, the effect of their incongruous reversals and transatlantic displacements is to indicate the uncomfortable proximity between scenes of conventional country life and forces of amoral brutality, to suggest that there was never so much of a polarity between the code of the Woosters and the attractions of fascist uniformity as retrospective mythologies of the postwar period liked to imagine.

THROUGH THE LOOKING GLASS: ALDOUS HUXLEY AND CHRISTOPHER ISHERWOOD

The triangulations among England, Germany, and the United States that were, to some extent, forced upon Wodehouse are foregrounded in more self-conscious, metaphorical ways in the prose writings of two other English natives of this period, Aldous Huxley and Christopher Isherwood. Both Huxley and Isherwood have become controversial figures in the annals of English literature because they chose to move to California at the midpoint of their careers: Huxley in 1937, at the age of 43, Isherwood in 1939, when he was 34. Both writers were products in different ways of the English Establishment: Huxley, who was the grandson of Victorian scientist T. H. Huxley and whose mother was the niece of Matthew Arnold, came from a blue-blooded intellectual family, while Isherwood, 'socially by far the grandest' of English writers at this time, hailed from a family of landed gentry which had its 'seat' in Cheshire. (When he became an American citizen in 1946, Isherwood took the opportunity officially to change his name from the hyphenated Bradshaw-Isherwood.[64]) Both writers also had positive reasons for feeling at home in the American West: in a 1964 memorial essay for Huxley, Isherwood recalled how he 'was attached to California by a love for the terrain

---

[63] Susan Sontag, 'Fascinating Fascism', in *A Susan Sontag Reader* (New York: Random House–Vintage, 1983), 316. For Hitler's fascination with Busby Berkeley's idyllic 'By a Waterfall' number in Lloyd Bacon's film *Footlight Parade* (1933), see Mizejewski, *Divine Decadence*, 192.

[64] Peter Parker, *Isherwood: A Life* (London: Picador, 2004), 5, 554.

itself', particularly for the desert; while Isherwood explained his own decision in April 1939 to leave his travelling companion W. H. Auden back in New York by saying: 'the real America, for me, was the Far West. All my daydreams were based on D. H. Lawrence's *St. Mawr*.'⁶⁵ Both Huxley and Isherwood greatly admired Lawrence, whom Huxley knew personally in the 1920s and about whom he wrote a brilliantly sympathetic essay in 1936, comparing him to Pascal as someone who was always aware 'of the otherness that lies beyond the boundaries of man's conscious mind'.⁶⁶ Huxley and Isherwood first met socially in California in the summer of 1939, subsequently collaborating on a number of film scripts and other projects, and they remained friends until Huxley's death in 1963.

In Britain, however, their emigration was particularly contentious because of its timing. A question was asked in Parliament in 1940 about 'British citizens of military age, such as Mr. W. H. Auden and Mr. Christopher Isherwood, who have gone to the United States and expressed their determination not to return to this country until the war is over', while Harold Nicolson wrote an article in the *Spectator* lambasting Huxley's 'spiritual arrogance'.⁶⁷ This charge was directed specifically against the pacifism embraced by Huxley in the mid-1930s and by Isherwood after his move to America, a pacifism that developed alongside their immersion in Eastern religion, with its philosophy of sublimation and detachment; in 1947, Huxley wrote an introduction to a translation of the *Bhagavad gītā* by Isherwood and their mutual patron, Swami Prabhavanandra. Pursuant to, but fundamentally concomitant with, the political hostility directed towards Huxley and Isherwood in the 1940s has been the subsequent critical attempt to suggest that the work of both writers lost focus after their move to California, that the writings of their English period retain more sharpness. Evelyn Waugh felt that Huxley 'never wrote a good novel after *Antic Hay*' (1923) and that he was a cautionary example of how 'even the most bookish and meditative minds ... decay in exile'; Orwell in 1946 described Huxley's American novels as 'much inferior to his earlier ones'; George Woodcock, who placed Huxley's early satirical work within a 'tradition of radical political dissent that stemmed in England from Godwin, the Chartists and the largely pacifist British socialist movement', found 'the views of art and the artist's function which Huxley developed after 1936' to be 'not only false in themselves, but also unfortunate in their effect on his work'. Conversely, Isherwood himself in his memorial tribute maintained stoutly 'that nearly all of Huxley's best work was done in the latter, American half of his life'.⁶⁸

⁶⁵ Julian Huxley, ed., *Aldous Huxley, 1894–1963: A Memorial Volume* (London: Chatto & Windus, 1965), 156; Christopher Isherwood, *Diaries*, i: *1939–1960*, ed. Katherine Bucknell (London: Random House–Vintage, 1997), 14.
⁶⁶ Aldous Huxley, 'D. H. Lawrence', in *The Complete Essays*, iv: *1936–1938*, ed. Robert S. Baker and James Sexton (Chicago: Dee, 2001), 80, 73.   ⁶⁷ Parker, *Isherwood*, 469, 466.
⁶⁸ Evelyn Waugh, letter to Nancy Mitford, 24 Oct. 1946, in *The Letters of Evelyn Waugh*, ed. Mark Amory (London: Weidenfeld & Nicolson, 1980), 237; Orwell, 'As I Please' (6 Dec. 1946), in *Collected Essays*, iv. 253; George Woodcock, *Dawn and the Darkest Hour: A Study of Aldous Huxley* (London: Faber, 1972), 15, 25; Julian Huxley, ed., *Aldous Huxley*, 154.

Isherwood had his own axe to grind, of course, no less than Waugh or Orwell, and the question of whether Huxley's English or American works are categorically superior is, finally, an imponderable one. What it would be true to say, though, is that Huxley's later career comprises a logical extension of his earlier writing, in that his primary concern was always with an intertextual renegotiation of his English literary and cultural heritage. Situated in an inexorably belated position by his distinguished ancestry, Huxley found himself needing constantly to argue with the values of the English intellectual establishment as they were handed down from the Victorian era. His 1929 essay 'Wordsworth in the Tropics' draws upon his own childhood memories of Sunday walks in the Surrey hills ('For good Wordsworthians ... a walk in the country is the equivalent of going to church') as it takes issue with the Wordsworthian assumption that nature is essentially benevolent: a 'voyage through the tropics', suggests Huxley, 'would have cured [Wordsworth] of his too easy and comfortable pantheism.' Like Byron 100 years earlier, Huxley specifically rejects here the moralizing dimensions of Wordsworth's poetry, the ways in which his 'god of Anglicanism' was requisitioned simply to sanctify the 'reassuringly familiar'.[69]

This impulse quizzically to redraw the map of the English cultural tradition was a concern of Huxley's right through his intellectual life. In an interview at the end of his career, in 1961, he defined 'the natural in our Western tradition [as] *in fact* our projection of concepts upon the world'; and in this sense his work can be seen consistently to interrogate familiar distinctions between the abstract and the natural, the mediated and the instinctive.[70] In *Literature and Science* (1963), he demolishes the binary opposition between a scientific 'world of abstractions and inferences' and the artistic domain of the 'ineffable' by showing how literary works, by seeking to re-create subjective experience in all their 'unrepeatable uniqueness', necessarily displace themselves on to a 'symbolic level' in order to become 'public and communicable'. Thus, he concludes, language and literature are abstractions to start with, so that the traditional romantic antithesis between form and feeling is without merit. This serves implicitly to justify Huxley's own idiosyncratic literary idiom, a hybrid concoction of novel and essay against which the standard complaint of more plodding English critics, that the author 'is concerned with ideas and not with persons', is rendered theoretically null and void.[71] It also effectively underwrites his own method of intertextual transposition, which involves not any 'creative' or 'original' representation—since such categories cannot be said rationally to exist—but rather an argument with ways in which the world has been

---

[69] Aldous Huxley, 'Wordsworth in the Tropics', in *Complete Essays*, ii: *1926–1929*, ed. Robert S. Baker and James Sexton (Chicago: Dee, 2000), 334, 342, 338, 336.

[70] Robert S. Baker, introduction, in Huxley, *Complete Essays*, vi: *1956–1963*, ed. Robert S. Baker and James Sexton (Chicago: Dee, 2002), p. xvi.

[71] Aldous Huxley, *Literature and Science* (London: Chatto & Windus, 1963), 11–13; J. B. Priestley, *Literature and Western Man* (New York: Harper & Row, 1960), 427.

understood and internalized. For instance, *After Many a Summer* (1939) takes
its title and its epigraph from Tennyson's 'Tithonus' and proceeds to reconsider
the implications of the Victorian poet's humanist treatment of the unwelcome
immortality enjoyed by the Greek classical hero amidst the futuristic landscapes
of California, where the processes of ageing and death have become susceptible
to scientific control.

Huxley's American work, then, functions as a mirror, a looking glass, in
which inherited English assumptions are held up for scrutiny. Just as his early
English satire comically traduces Victorian values, so his later American writings
meditatively traverse and refract the 'great tradition' of English culture. In *Jesting
Pilate* (1926), a travel book written before his permanent move across the
Atlantic, Huxley maintains a detached, satirical perspective towards America,
chastising it for living out the 'democratic hypothesis ... that all men are equal
and that I am just as good as you are', an idea that he says leads to the perversion
of standards and 'progressive falsification of values'. He also has a passage in this
book mocking morticians in Chicago who offer to 'lay the Loved Ones to rest', a
scene which anticipates the patronizing tone of Evelyn Waugh's *The Loved One*
(1948), set among the mortuaries of California, which similarly mocks American
vulgarity as from a great height.[72] However, by the time he publishes *Brave New
World* in 1932 much of the supercilious distance in Huxley's attitude towards
America has disappeared, since this novel moves beyond mere pointed satire to
outline the vision of a world where new technology engineers a 'rich and living
peace', a balmy sea of tranquility. The allusion to *The Tempest* in the book's title
is of course ironic, and the utopias described here are associated with a fatal loss
of human freedom, with the representation of life in Malpais, a community in
the American Southwest, being a specific slap at D. H. Lawrence's idealization
of primitivist vitalism in his New Mexico writings of a few years earlier. But the
all-encompassing Americanization of *Brave New World*—the refurbishment of
Our Lord as 'Our Ford', the translation of the Christian sign of the cross into
'the sign of the T', in homage to the automobile manufacturer's most famous
model—project a scenario wherein the ubiquity of American mass culture has
taken on an air of apparent inevitability.[73] Huxley himself stated in a 1927 essay
that the 'future of America is the future of the world', since '[f]or good or for
evil, it seems that the world must be Americanized'.[74]

As a political or philosophical statement this is, of course, open to dispute,
and Theodor W. Adorno's complaint about *Brave New World* was that its
author 'makes a fetish of the fetishism of commodities', seeing them as 'ontic

[72] Aldous Huxley, *Jesting Pilate* (London: Chatto & Windus, 1930), 276, 279, 272.

[73] Aldous Huxley, *Brave New World* (London: Grafton, 1977), 76, 36, 123; Jerome Meckier,
'Aldous Huxley's Americanization of the *Brave New World* Typescript', *Twentieth Century Literature*,
48 (2002), 436–7.

[74] Aldous Huxley, 'The Outlook for American Culture', in *Complete Essays*, iii: *1930–1935*, ed.
Robert S. Baker and James Sexton (Chicago: Dee, 2001), 185.

and self-subsistent', so that 'he capitulates to this apparition instead of seeing through it as a mere form of consciousness, false consciousness, which would dissolve with the elimination of its economic basis'. Adorno is correct to point out how Huxley in this novel elides politics into ontology, diminishing the space for active human 'praxis' by presenting his technological utopia in the form of 'entropy'. But he is probably mistaken to assume that Huxley was ever as interested in protesting 'zealously' against this administered society as was Adorno himself, in *Dialectic of Enlightenment* and his other critical works of the late 1940s.[75] Whereas Adorno sought consistently to distance himself from the Californian commodity culture into which his flight from the Nazis had thrown him, Huxley's own relationship to what was to become his new home was much more ambiguous. In the foreword to the American edition of *Brave New World* which he wrote in 1946, after his own move to the United States, Huxley claimed as the ancestor of the principle of structural interchangeability that governs his imagined universe the 'revolution' prophesied by the Marquis de Sade in the eighteenth century, with its vision of how 'bodies were henceforward to become the common sexual property of all and … minds were to be purged of all the natural decencies'.[76] Although Huxley never abandoned an attachment to the idea of freedom, the way he understood this concept differed markedly from that which inspired his Victorian forebears; indeed, a systematic elimination of the illusory 'natural decencies' of Anglican humanism is the project that runs through Huxley's American writing.

This means that for Huxley the American West Coast becomes a site of symbolic transformation, as he uses the figure of America rationally to demystify both Wordsworthian sentimentalizations of the local and liberal assumptions about the autonomy of human character. This ensures that Huxley becomes simultaneously attracted to, as well as repelled by, his abstract landscapes of technological futurism; aesthetically and indeed libidinally he comes to have an investment in scenarios of creative destruction, taking pleasure in gouging out the illusions of English cultural tradition and in turning established customs on their head. W. B. Yeats said in 1936 that he sympathized with Huxley's 'sadistic hatred of life', although Orwell in 1949 was not so friendly towards *Ape and Essence*, describing Huxley's new Hollywood novel in a letter as 'awful. And', he continued, 'do you notice that the more holy he gets, the more his books stink with sex. He cannot get off the subject of flagellating women.' *Ape and Essence* typically involves both a fear of technology and a surreptitious delight in its anti-humanist potential, an impulse that correlated with Huxley's experiments with mescaline and states of altered consciousness in the 1950s. All of this, however, was clearly out of kilter with the robust moral realism that was coming

---

[75] Theodor W. Adorno, 'Aldous Huxley and Utopia', in *Prisms*, trans. Samuel and Shierry Weber (Cambridge, Mass.: MIT Press, 1981), 113, 117, 114.
[76] Huxley, foreword, in *Brave New World*, 10.

to dominate English writing during this period, with Kingsley Amis, energized as he was by the first flush of the 'Movement', dismissing the deracinated Huxley in 1956 as merely a 'crank'.[77]

What Huxley's marginal situation did enable him to do, however, was astutely to perceive structural parallels between cultural and intellectual traditions that were normally thought of as quite distinct, thereby problematizing the ethical oppositions on which postwar English society had grounded its social and aesthetic values. Thus, *After Many a Summer* does not simply mock the empty pretensions of the West Coast 'New Civilization'; through the *mise-en-abîme* of its plot, which involves an English scholar working through the Hauberk Papers purchased by Mr Stoyte and shipped over to his Californian castle, it also allows Huxley to re-create an aesthetic simulation of the world of eighteenth-century England. Jeremy Pordage, the English scholar who in the first paragraph of the novel is described as 'carrying the Poetical Works of Wordsworth', soon discovers that the archives of English history, with all of their material about aristocratic violence and the slave trade, do not present such a sublime view of Anglican ideals as did the revered Lake poet. George Woodcock described *After Many a Summer* as 'perverted Peacock, *Nightmare Abbey* revised by the Marquis de Sade'; but the effect of this revision is disconcertingly to adduce analogies between the American castle and its English prototype, not satirically to suggest—as Evelyn Waugh would have done—that one is merely a decayed replica of the other.[78] Instead, Huxley implies how the values of the English ruling class are no more or less meretricious than those of their Californian counterparts. Mr Propter, the *eminence grise* of this novel, makes a sardonic remark to Pordage about Matthew Arnold's reverence for '[th]e best that has been thought and said'—'very nice', counters Propter. 'But best in what way? Alas, only in form. The content is generally deplorable'—and the trajectory of this novel, under Propter's guidance, proceeds to divest Victorian liberal nostrums of their credibility, disavowing equally 'the ferocious lunacies of nationalism' and a 'Humanism' which 'affirms that good can be achieved on a level where it doesn't exist and denies the fact of eternity'. It is significant that Propter is presented here as the author of a book entitled *Short Studies in the Counter Reformation*, since Huxley's own interest in baroque art and music increasingly drew him during his residence in the United States to what he called an 'amphibian' perspective, half worldly experience and half timeless abstraction, from which vantage point worldly conceits and categories appeared increasingly tendentious.[79]

[77] Donald Watt, ed., *Aldous Huxley: The Critical Heritage* (London: Routledge & Kegan Paul, 1975), 282, 334, 28.

[78] Aldous Huxley, *After Many a Summer* (London: Chatto & Windus, 1962), 3; Woodcock, *Dawn and the Darkest Hour*, 220.

[79] Huxley, *After Many a Summer*, 157, 247; Huxley, 'The Education of an Amphibian', in *Complete Essays*, v: *1939–1956*, ed. Robert S. Baker and James Sexton (Chicago: Dee, 2002), 191–209.

It is this kind of 'paradoxical, antithetical' style, a style he associates in a 1956 essay with the madrigals of the sixteenth-century Italian composer Carlo Gesualdo, that helps to shape the metaphysical dimensions of Huxley's American writing. Gesualdo's dissonant harmonies of 'psychological disintegration', the 'strange products of a Counter-Reformation psychosis working upon a late medieval art form', clearly echo Huxley's own concern to disrupt the tones and modulations of humanism.[80] He also wrote in 1941 about his admiration for the 'fanatically marginal' seventeenth-century Dissenter George Fox, whose 'intransigent theocentrism' would not allow him to risk any kind of worldly compromise by accepting an invitation to dine with Oliver Cromwell, a spirit of estrangement that Huxley's own late writings also seek to imitate.[81] Although sardonic in *After Many a Summer* about Arnold's liberal humanism, he presents it more positively in a 1956 discussion of John Dewey's theories of 'learning through doing' and 'education as life adjustment', where he castigates American pedagogy for teaching 'only conformity to current conventions of personal and collective behavior. There is', Huxley continues severely, 'no substitute for correct knowledge.'[82] He was, then, prepared to turn English intellectual traditions against the American democratic collective, just as he deployed American simulacra to demystify English claims to moral authority and legitimacy. This is the 'paradoxical, antithetical' mode he attributes to Gesualdo, which refuses to assume specific positions and takes its impetus instead from an aesthetic of traducement.

It is this kind of traducement that was, of course, so unwelcome to the general British public in the context of the Second World War, when it was construed simply as patriotic betrayal. Yet it is precisely this dangerous border between conformity and contumacy that Huxley's art works most effectively to illuminate. In *Brave New World Revisited* (1959), he describes how Hitler manipulated techniques of mass media and advertising to gain power in the 1930s, but he also comments in his wartime letters on what seems like a similarly oppressive regime in England: 'Government tyranny is complete,' he writes in 1944. 'There is no Habeas Corpus and people can be, and are, sent to prison indefinitely without trial—or even *after* trial and acquittal, by government fiat.' For Huxley, the most significant effect of the war in Britain was to eliminate space for intellectual dissent and to inure the people to the kind of authoritarian central control which had, so they were assured, brought about their military victory; Huxley described Attlee's postwar Labour administration as 'eager Totalitarians—because they're convinced that they can Do Good, that fatal illusion which justifies every form of wickedness, oppression and tyranny'.[83]

---

[80] Huxley, 'Gesualdo: Variations on a Musical Theme', in *Complete Essays*, v. 449, and *idem*, 'The Doors of Perception', in *Complete Essays*, v. 177.

[81] Huxley, 'Politics and Religion', in *Complete Essays*, v. 21.

[82] Huxley, 'Knowledge and Understanding', in *Complete Essays*, v. 213.

[83] Aldous Huxley, letter to Frieda Lawrence, 10 April 1944, in *Letters of Aldous Huxley*, ed. Grover Smith (London: Chatto & Windus, 1969), 503–4.

There is, of course, a significant class issue involved here, and it is easy to see why a rich Hollywood screenwriter staying at Claridge's Hotel in London in 1948 would not have been welcomed with open arms by the impoverished compatriots he was indicting for a passive acquiescence to bureaucratic authority. But it would also be true to say that the circumstances of the Second World War had the effect of rendering English institutional life blind for many years to the intellectual complexities of modernism, as well as hostile in principle to any implication that its own national culture might be insufficient or that it might have shared certain kinds of values with Nazi Germany. The disturbing quality of Wodehouse, Huxley, and Isherwood in British eyes derived ultimately not from their personal American wealth but from their disruption of the fixed moral antithesis, the mythology of virtue, which sustained the country during the hard postwar years of social and economic reconstruction.

In a diary entry for December 1939, Isherwood records a visit to California by the scientist Julian Huxley, brother of Aldous, whom Isherwood calls 'very much the official representative of England at war. Behind his sternness, I thought I could detect a certain puritanical sadism—a satisfaction that the lax peace-days were over, and that we'd all got to suffer.'[84] Like Huxley, Isherwood took a sardonic pleasure in demystifying pompous English claims to familial and communal responsibility, in exposing the latent forms of self-gratification that frequently underpinned assertions of moral altruism. It is a theme of escape from the stuffy, repressive confines of English life that drives his first novel, *All the Conspirators* (1928), whose hero, a would-be writer heavily under the influence of Joyce's *Portrait of the Artist as a Young Man*, seeks to get away from both his mundane office job and his claustrophobic upbringing. Even at this early stage of Isherwood's career the vision of flight is associated with a symbolic journey west: in the first chapter, a cormorant vanishes 'into the empty gulf of light westward, like an absurd impulse of desperation, towards America'.[85] This metaphorical treatment of England as an extended family, whose genealogical relationships are as smothering as they are comforting, recurs frequently in Isherwood's later narratives, notably in *Down there on a Visit* (1962), where the narrator recalls approaching Dover harbour in 1938 and being aghast at 'the staring, unblinking, uncompromising familiarity of it all'. Written many years after his move to California, *Down there on a Visit* reacts violently against what it calls the sense of 'chilly decay' in England, with its genteel round of 'Dainty Teas' and its insular 'absorption in cricket, football pools, the pictorial press'; by contrast, the novel holds up Byron and Wilde as two heroic literary figures who succeeded in charting a path away from this 'utterly self-satisfied' atmosphere of English culture. Isherwood's persona here finds his ancestral home not just dull but psychologically threatening: 'The Past seemed to take me by the throat, with

[84] Isherwood, *Diaries*, 58.
[85] Christopher Isherwood, *All the Conspirators* (London: Random House–Vintage, 2000), 20.

its disgusting claw, and choke me; I shuddered to feel its power, even now ... I wanted to go to America and change my family name and forget that I had any ancestors.'[86]

Part of Isherwood's project, then, involves a principled, existentialist search for freedom. George, the protagonist of *A Single Man* (1964), advises his fellow exile Charlotte not to return to Britain, not to fall back into the mire of living there with her sister: 'The Past is just something that's over,' he insists. But Charlotte's response is that even if she is miserable in England, 'At least, when I'm there, I shall know *where I am*'; for her, the comforts of social and familial placement outweigh the dangerous insecurity of alienation, to such an extent that she wonders if 'masochism's our way of being patriotic'.[87] Isherwood's work itself is caught between these two conflicting positions, with his family memoir *Kathleen and Frank* (1971), a reconstruction of his parents' lives based on their diaries and letters which he spent time researching back in Cheshire, forming what Rita Delfiner described as Isherwood's ultimate 'reconciliation with his family'.[88] Technically a *tour de force*, *Kathleen and Frank* uses the putatively transparent medium of family archives to present the lives of his parents in their own words, thereby creating the illusion of a narrative unfolding in the present tense, an illusion which is periodically disrupted by the narrator intervening to put events into perspective. This creates within the book a kind of double time scheme, through which the death of his father in the First World War becomes both suspenseful and fated, as the boundaries of past and present become blurred. This complex narrative structure also shows these family members merging psychologically into each other, with Isherwood himself becoming more closely related to his mother than his brazen declaration of himself as a 'born existentialist' would have us believe. Such relationships again suggest how the links between England and America in Isherwood's work are complex and paradoxical, not unilinear. Despite describing himself as 'not by temperament a backward-looker', his works circle back perpetually into the past, striving to reconcile his experiences on either side of the Atlantic within a personal and philosophical continuum.[89]

Isherwood said in the 1970s that he felt 'entirely British in a certain sense, but not nationalistically British', and that when he was in England 'my American half—after all, I have lived here more than half my life—comes out; but while I'm here [in America], my English half comes out'.[90] National identity in his work thus tends to appear as an arbitrary and reversible phenomenon, an

---

[86] Christopher Isherwood, *Down there on a Visit* (London: White Lion, 1974), 151, 190, 175.

[87] Christopher Isherwood, *A Single Man* (London: Methuen, 1964), 118–19.

[88] Rita Delfiner, 'The Camera Speaks', *New York Post*, 17 Feb. 1972, n.p.

[89] Anne Taylor Fleming, 'Christopher Isherwood: He Is a Camera', in *Conversations with Christopher Isherwood*, ed. James J. Berg and Chris Freeman (Jackson, Miss.: University Press of Mississippi, 2001), 94; Isherwood, foreword, in *All the Conspirators*, 7.

[90] Len Webster, 'A Very Individualistic Old Liberal', in *Conversations with Christopher Isherwood*, 66, and Studs Terkel, 'Christopher Isherwood', *Conversations with Christopher Isherwood*, 167.

assumption prefigured in *On the Frontier*, a play he wrote in England with W. H. Auden in 1938, which represents 'country' and 'frontier' as 'old-fashioned words that don't mean anything now'.[91] With a stage divided between the territories of 'Ostnia' and 'Westland', *On the Frontier* suggests how the mass culture, slogans, and propaganda of each country succeed only in mirroring those of its rival. T. S. Eliot, who attended the first night of the production in Cambridge, subsequently wrote: 'I am afraid that Hitler is not the simpleton that the authors make him out to be'; but the burden of this drama, which offered an uncomfortable message to England in 1938 and would have been quite unacceptable a couple of years later, was that the supposed antithesis between English probity and German corruption was much less clear-cut than official government rhetoric—what Isherwood in the summer of 1939 called 'the whole hate-Hitler racket'—liked to make it appear.[92] As we have seen, when Isherwood and Auden left Britain for the United States in January 1939, they were widely accused of defection; but Isherwood later wrote that it was not so much the bombs he feared as 'the atmosphere of the war, the power which it gives to all of the things I hate—the newspapers, the politicians, the puritans, the scoutmasters, the middle-aged merciless spinsters'. Revisiting England in 1947, two years after hostilities had ceased, he still found it 'a nation of queue-formers', of people who are 'a little too docile in their attitude toward official regulations'. At Westminster Abbey during a visit nine years later, Isherwood's hostility and bitterness turned to ridicule and scorn: he describes the Abbey as 'very funny—a charmingly absurd little antique shop, full of ridiculous statues'.[93]

One of the attractions of California, by contrast, is that its 'untamed, undomesticated' landscape gives its inhabitants a stronger 'sense of impermanence', so that social institutions and manners seem to be less set in stone. Isherwood talked in 1970 of how the 'fundamentally desert country' of the American West always has 'a mirage about it', a quality he welcomed since it makes 'the great, noble, traditional buildings of Europe seem rather too solid in comparison'. In an ironic way, it is this very sense of detachment that can be seen as the strongest sign of Isherwood's affiliation with what in 1955 he called an 'American-way-of-living kind of happiness': like the migrants of old, he writes of how he loves America 'just because I *don't* belong. Because I'm not involved in its traditions, not born under the curse of its history. I feel free here. I'm on my own. My life will be what I make of it.'[94] In *A Single Man*, the hero associates his sense of American

[91] W. H. Auden and Christopher Isherwood, *Plays and Other Dramatic Writings by W. H. Auden, 1928–1938*, ed. Edward Mendelson (London: Faber, 1989), 398.

[92] Charles Osborne, *W. H. Auden: The Life of a Poet* (London: Eyre Methuen, 1980), 180; Parker, *Isherwood*, 406, 445.

[93] Isherwood, *Diaries*, 84, 588, and *idem*, 'Coming to London', 155.

[94] Christopher Isherwood, 'Los Angeles', in *Exhumations*, 162, and *idem*, 'The Shore', ibid. 165; Derek Hart, 'A Fortunate, Happy Life', in *Conversations with Christopher Isherwood*, 55; Isherwood, *Diaries*, 482, 94.

national identity with a pride in being able to negotiate the freeways of Los Angeles: 'George feels a kind of patriotism for the freeways ... the fact that he can cope proves his claim to be a functioning member of society.' Other signs of Isherwood's assimilation into American life manifest themselves in his diaries of the late 1940s and early 1950s: in 1949, as a concerned cold war citizen, he describes the Soviet Union as the 'greatest police state on earth' and complains about the build-up of 'Soviet militarism and aggression'.[95] He is particularly exercised here about the repressive attitudes of the Soviet government towards homosexuals, and for Isherwood in this postwar period the United States crucially allowed not only the freedom to practise his art but also a relative freedom of sexual orientation. Whereas England in the austere post-1945 decade tended to associate homosexuality with Nazi decadence, with the narcissistic posturing of men in uniform, southern California at this time offered an environment that was considerably less censorious.

The doubleness of the national allegiances that Isherwood experienced in his personal life is systematically extended throughout his work into an analysis of Britain and America as alternative domains divided by, in Eliot's terms, a perpetual civil war. In *Kathleen and Frank*, Isherwood tells of how his ancestor, John Bradshaw, a strong supporter of the anti-royalist forces during the English Civil War, was the judge who condemned King Charles I to death; and though he describes himself as loathing 'puritanism and puritans, which made it impossible for him to side wholeheartedly with the Parliament', he nevertheless says that he 'hated nearly all monarchs' and 'seldom misses a chance to boast of being descended from The Regicide'. In his *Diaries*, Isherwood records a visit in 1940 to Charlie Chaplin, who entertained a similarly low opinion of British royalty—' "How can they possibly go on with all that nonsense," he kept repeating'—and in this light the United States appears to function still for British-born republicans as the land that their native country might have become if Cromwell's regime had managed to establish itself on a permanent basis.[96] (This, of course, contrasts markedly with Wodehouse, whose *Ring for Jeeves* celebrates the Earl of Rowcester's 'debonair ancestor ... who in the days of the Restoration had by his dash and gallantry won from the ladies of King Charles the Second's court the affectionate soubriquet of Tabasco Rowcester'.[97]) In a 1948 essay 'The Gita and War', Isherwood writes of the *Bhagavad gītā*'s perception of 'life itself' as 'double-faced', where 'any attempt at simplification will only bring us to ultimate confusion'; and as an allegory of this 'duality of attitude' he cites the conflict in the *Bhagavad gītā* between Arjuna and Krishna, where 'Two

<hr>

[95] Isherwood, *A Single Man*, 25; Christopher Isherwood, *Lost Years: A Memoir 1945–1951*, ed. Katherine Bucknell (London: Chatto & Windus, 2000), 189. Despite his cold war patriotism, Isherwood was also by instinct a liberal, voting (for instance) for George McGovern in the 1972 presidential election. Fleming, 'Christopher Isherwood', 92.
[96] Christopher Isherwood, *Kathleen and Frank* (Random House–Vintage, 2000), 218; *idem, Diaries*, 86.   [97] Wodehouse, *Ring for Jeeves*, 132.

factions, closely bound to each other by ties of blood and friendship, are about to engage in a civil war'.[98]

All of Isherwood's work, at some level, is about this condition of civil war, a duality which becomes for him metaphysical as well as existential. Recalling his youth in a 1965 interview, he remarked: 'What amazes me ... is why we all didn't have far more curiosity about America much earlier in our lives, because it is for English-speaking people so very much the other half of the coin. And really, what do you know until you have seen America?' Amidst the locked-in world of *Lions and Shadows* (1938), Yarmouth appears as a harbinger of this kind of alterity, as the narrator recalls watching 'a great liner vanishing in a smudge of smoke, towards America', while in *Down there on a Visit* Christopher recounts a trip to Germany in 1952 when he crosses 'into the through-the-looking-glass world' of East Berlin.[99] The transpositions in Isherwood's work between East and West, Europe and America, all have this 'through-the-looking-glass' quality, since they turn upon transformations predicated on essential forms of similarity as well as difference. His characters shuttle back and forth between past and present lives, between a repressive England and an emancipated America, with their guise at any given moment incorporating implicitly those other facets of personality which might be revealed through other sets of political and cultural circumstances. Isherwood's narrative landscapes, that is to say, are shot through with the trajectories of civil war, with a kind of ontological doubleness, so that the temporal aspects of his characters only ever manifest themselves in a series of fractions and fragments.

All of this has significant implications for Isherwood's portrayal of prewar Germany and for its subsequent relationship both with American modernism and with British nationalism. In *Christopher and his Kind* (1976), the narrator recalls telling the German passport official in March 1929 that he was 'looking for my homeland', while in that same year he described Germany with romantic enthusiasm 'as the country where all the obstructions and complexities of this life were cut through', a welcome antidote to the world of English middle-class values.[100] Isherwood later claimed that he could easily have lived in Germany on a permanent basis had it not been for the rise of Hitler, since he found the Germans, like the Americans, 'simple and natural' about sex. Berlin in the era of the Weimar Republic was heavily Americanized, as Daniel T. Rodgers has observed, so Isherwood's understanding of a continuity between Germany and America as domains of erotic freedom comes as no great surprise; but of course the more problematic question is the extent to which his fiction of

---

[98] Isherwood, 'The Gita and War', in *Exhumations*, 104.

[99] George Wickes, 'An Interview with Christopher Isherwood', in *Conversations with Christopher Isherwood*, 31; Christopher Isherwood, *Lions and Shadows: An Education in the Twenties* (London: Mandarin—Minerva, 1996), 142; Isherwood, *Down there on a Visit*, 341.

[100] Christopher Isherwood, *Christopher and his Kind, 1929–1939* (London: Methuen—Magnum, 1978), 17; Parker, *Isherwood*, 193.

this era also engages in dialogue with fascist values.[101] Politically he finds Nazi authoritarianism in its early years too reminiscent of his English public-school education—'The newspapers are becoming more and more like copies of a school magazine,' he writes in his Berlin diary for the winter of 1932–3: 'There is nothing in them but new rules, new punishments, and lists of people who have been "kept in." This morning, Göring has invented three fresh varieties of high treason'—and by the mid-1930s he considered himself to be 'a liberal, a supporter of the Popular Front and an advocate of armed resistance to fascism, in Spain and everywhere else'.[102] But just as his later exile from England could not conceal a primordial attachment to that country, so Isherwood finds himself becoming covertly attracted to a disciplinarian ethos that he consciously scorns. *Down there on a Visit* adduces 'a relation between the "cruel" ladies in boots who used to ply their trade outside the Kaufhaus des Westens and the young thugs in Nazi uniforms who are out there nowadays, pushing the Jews around', thereby parodying and emptying out the legitimacy of the Nazi drive for power by representing it as a form of libidinal investment and unacknowledged psychopathological fetishism. In *Lions and Shadows*, the narrator addresses the psychosexual implications of authoritarianism directly, writing of how 'the rulers of Fascist states ... profoundly understand and make use of' the 'phantasies and longings' associated with 'homosexual romanticism', leading him to 'wonder how, at this period, I should have reacted to the preaching of an English Fascist leader clever enough to serve up his "message" in a suitably disguised and palatable form?'[103] This is not, of course, to validate the practice of fascism, but just the opposite: to suggest how its compulsive systems of authority and violence can be understood as literalizations of 'phantasies and longings' that could be reflected more self-consciously and worked through in a politically neutral sphere.

Valentine Cunningham has chronicled how the aesthetics of fascism, with their emphasis on psychological toughness and a hard-edged quest for order, became quite common in England during the 1930s, and Isherwood's interest in new technologies, including the camera and the cinema, speaks to a steely quality which can be seen as antipathetic to what he regarded as the more provincial virtues of English culture.[104] In *Prater Violet* (1946), written in America but offering a retrospective view of England in the years leading up to the Second World War, the world of film production is described as 'a sort

---

[101] Winston Leyland, 'Christopher Isherwood Interview', in *Conversations with Christopher Isherwood*, 103; Daniel T. Rodgers, *Atlantic Crossings: Social Politics in a Progressive Age* (Cambridge, Mass.: Harvard University Press, 1998), 371.

[102] Christopher Isherwood, *Goodbye to Berlin*, in *The Berlin of Sally Bowles* (London: Hogarth Press, 1978), 577, and *idem, Exhumations*, 97.

[103] Isherwood, *Down there on a Visit*, 73, and *idem, Lions and Shadows*, 48.

[104] Valentine Cunningham, *British Writers of the Thirties* (Oxford: Oxford University Press, 1988), 64–5.

of infernal machine' which becomes complicit with the dehumanized nature of
fascist ideology and with anti-Semitism. This association is made explicit in an
exchange between the hero, still finding his feet as a screenwriter, and Lawrence
Dwight, a 'head cutter' with the Imperial Bulldog film company:

'The incentive is to fight anarchy. That's all man lives for. Reclaiming life from its natural
muddle. Making patterns.'
'Patterns for what?'
'For the sake of patterns. To create meaning. What else is there?'
'And what about the things that won't fit into your patterns?'
'Discard them.'
'You mean kill Jews?'
'Don't try to shock me with your bloody sentimental, false analogies ... technicians are
the only real artists, anyway.'[105]

The 'I am a camera' style of the Berlin novels, with its reliance upon an
impersonal and assiduously unsentimental narrative perspective, relies upon a
similar transposition of the human author into a fabricator of artistic 'patterns',
and *Prater Violet* interrogates the implications of this technical expertise in terms
of the wider politics of the 1930s.

One inference to be drawn from this again is what Andrew Hewitt calls the
'ideological continuum' between fascism and various forms of modernism.[106]
Italian fascists in the 1920s tended to idealize America as a land of 'endless possibilities' and a kind of technological sublime, while the widespread enthusiasm
for Mussolini in Italy was reciprocated in many quarters in the United States.
Mussolini was famously admired by Ezra Pound, whose *Jefferson and/or Mussolini*
(1935) praised the way in which ideas appeared to lead an active functional life
in Italy; the Italian fascist leader also excited the enthusiasm of Wallace Stevens
('pro-Mussolini personally', in 1935), Henry Miller (who preferred Mussolini's
bravado to the 'pussy footers and stinking hypocrites' of the British Empire), and
many others, including some prominent American Jews.[107] Nazi Germany was
in many ways a more complicated case, since its leaders condemned modernism
in the arts and demanded a return to Germanic national traditions; nevertheless,
as Hannah Arendt has argued, there was a contradiction at the heart of the Nazi
ideology since, while idealizing an expression of racial purity and eliminating
those who failed to conform to its perfect ideal, it also expressed a 'contempt

[105] Christopher Isherwood, *Prater Violet* (London: Methuen, 1984), 25, 55–6.

[106] Andrew Hewitt, 'Fascist Modernism, Futurism, and Post-Modernity', in *Fascism, Aesthetics,
and Culture*, ed. Richard J. Goslan (Hanover, NH: University Press of New England, 1992), 41.

[107] Roberto Maria Dainotto, 'The Bolshevik in the Garden: The Invention of America in Fascist
Italy', in *American and European National Identities: Faces in the Mirror*, ed. Stephen Fender (Keele,
Staffs.: Keele University Press, 1996), 58; John P. Diggins, *Mussolini and Fascism: The View from
America* (Princeton: Princeton University Press, 1972), 248. On the popularity of Mussolini among
American Jews, see Herbert S. Schneidau, *Waking Giants: The Presence of the Past in Modernism*
(New York: Oxford University Press, 1991), 251–2.

for the narrowness of nationalism, the provincialism of the nation-state', and consequently attempted to develop the conception of a national body capable of expanding to international, imperial dimensions.[108]

In this sense, the Nazis were attempting to mediate between the national and the transnational, to anchor and indeed reify the contours of national identity in an increasingly globalized environment where the very foundations of indigenous culture and national allegory seemed increasingly under threat. It is chastening to recall that when in 1937 the Nazis staged *Entartete Kunst*, their now notorious exhibition of the degenerate follies of avant-garde art, this political gesture was endorsed by such mainstream liberal journals as the *New Statesman*, which indicated its approval of Hitler's attempt to eradicate bohemian self-indulgence by demonstrating how art might instead endorse images of the cohesiveness and respectability of society. The exhibition itself was enormously popular in Germany, far more so than a parallel exhibition of 'pure' German art which had opened the day before, and, as Laura Frost has written, this suggests how 'antifascist, democratic culture has substantial, unacknowledged libidinal investments in fascism that need to be explored'.[109] Just as the Nazis needed the demonic image of the Jews to fuel their reactive, paranoid sense of national identity, as Adorno and Horkheimer argued in 1947, so the politics of anti-fascism found itself engaging inescapably with an aesthetic modernism to which it could never be implacably opposed. Richard Burt has suggested that the Nazis were not altogether opposed to modernism, they just provided a very different account of it, and the symmetrical twinning of *Entartete Kunst* with *Grosse Deutsche Kunstausstellung* implies this uneasy juxtaposition between the aesthetics of the Bauhaus and more traditionalist Old Teutonic styles. Some of this sense of ambiguity was captured by the American Jewish cultural critic Waldo Frank, in a 1940 essay for the *New Republic* entitled 'Our Guilt in Fascism', where he described fascism as a corrupt 'modern religion' which was, nevertheless, a national symptom of the modern crisis of 'empirical rationalism'. To respond to fascism, argued Frank, mankind should return to the 'pre-rational' world where it could sense the spirit of God within, where its 'primordial intuitions' would be at one with nature and society, thus rendering it less vulnerable to the false messiahs of the Right.[110]

---

[108] Hannah Arendt, *The Origins of Totalitarianism*, 2nd edn. (London: Allen & Unwin, 1958), 3–4.

[109] Frost, *Sex Drives*, 15; George L. Mosse, 'Beauty without Sensuality: The Exhibition Entartete Kunst', in *'Degenerate Art': The Fate of the Avant-Garde in Nazi Germany*, ed. Stephanie Barron (Los Angeles: Los Angeles County Museum of Art, 1991), 30–1.

[110] Theodor W. Adorno and Max Horkheimer, *Dialectic of Enlightenment*, trans. John Cumming (London: Verso, 1979), 185; Richard Burt, 'Degenerate "Art": Public Aesthetics and the Simulation of Censorship in Postliberal Los Angeles and Berlin', in *The Administration of Aesthetics: Censorship, Political Criticism, and the Public Sphere*, ed. Richard Burt (for the *Social Text* Collective) (Minneapolis: University. of Minnesota Press, 1994), 231–2; Diggins, *Mussolini and Fascism*, 445.

As Frank implies, modern man's 'guilt' with respect to fascism in 1940 lay in the way it shared many of the ideals of that political enterprise, a symbiosis that elucidates the covert links between fascism's quasi-mystical synthesis and modernism's quest to overcome contemporary states of alienation. Herbert S. Schneidau describes the great modernist writers as 'all atavists in some way', since they were attempting to redeem the new by rediscovering the old: D. H. Lawrence's exploration of Teutonic archetypes or Yeats's celebrations of feudal Ireland bear uncomfortable parallels with fascist Italy's mythologization of itself as the heir to Augustan Rome or the Nazis' Wagnerian invocation of medieval Germany.[111] In Huxley's interwar writings, as we have seen, such modernist utopianism is systematically connected to the expanding corporate and international power of the United States: in *Point Counter Point* (1928), Mark Rampton says, 'Bolsheviks and Fascists' are basically the same, since 'They all believe in industrialism in one form or another, they all believe in Americanization'. Thus, when Isherwood emigrates to America in 1939 he is not, as Cunningham suggested, merely retreating from the world of European politics and seeking 'metaphysical consolations in America'; instead, he is exploring an alternative site of modernity, another sexual and spiritual homeland which might operate as a counterpart to the exhausted state of England.[112] Isherwood maps out a new cultural environment which might incorporate those aspects of fascist modernism to which he was attracted in Berlin, but which were ultimately rendered out of bounds for him by the rise of the Nazis.

Isherwood's Californian narratives thus seek to reconstitute an English literary tradition within an alternative but parallel context. Just as he remarks on the English Civil War of the 1640s in *Kathleen and Frank*, so in *Goodbye to Berlin* he reports how the 'milkman says we'll have civil war in a fortnight'; and it is a fatalistic sense of being always caught up in internecine struggles that not only haunts Isherwood's books but also, at some level, provides their *raison d'être*. From California, one of his objectives is constantly to revisit and revise his heritage, to re-examine the institutions of English culture from an estranged, oppositional perspective, and his spiritual sense from Vedanta that there was an overall pattern in life, that 'some kind of intention is behind the whole thing, and that this intention has gradually fulfilled itself', would doubtless have encouraged him to seek out echoes and correspondences in his life and work.[113] In *Christopher and his Kind*, for example, the author ruminates on the difference between the German *Tisch* and the English 'table', concluding that the 'two things are essentially different, because they've been thought about differently by two nations with different cultures'. This might be construed as a

---

[111] Schneidau, *Waking Giants*, p. vii.

[112] Aldous Huxley, *Point Counter Point* (London: HarperCollins–Flamingo, 1994), 301; Cunningham, *British Writers of the Thirties*, 464.

[113] Isherwood, *Goodbye to Berlin*, 368; Parker, *Isherwood*, 730.

form of Neoplatonism, even though, struck with 'his own mystique about the German language', the narrator attributes his 'metaphysical' outlook partly to his psychosexual desires: 'For him, the entire German language—all the way from the keep off the grass signs in the park to Goethe's stanza on the wall—was irradiated with sex.' This type of philosophical idealism can also be correlated with an equivalent Neoplatonism in *A Single Man*, where George sees a Californian motel room as not just 'a room in a hotel' but '*the* Room, definitively, period ... a symbol ... an advertisement in three dimensions'. America is said here to be more advanced than Europe because it has achieved a greater degree of abstraction: 'we've renounced their world of individual differences, and romantic inefficiency, and objects-for-the-sake-of-objects.' *A Single Man* thus signals its affiliation with modernist utopias, where empirical objects are idealistically transfigured into abstract shapes; Isherwood's hero finds it admirable that Americans 'sleep in symbolic bedrooms, eat symbolic meals, are symbolically entertained', whereas the European, by contrast, is said to have 'a horror of symbols because he's such a grovelling little materialist'.

California in this sense can be seen as a mirror image of Berlin in the 1930s. Just as Isherwood found 'sadistic play' to be 'characteristic of German sensuality', so the landscapes of the American West offer vistas of sublimation, where corporeal discipline goes together with a purifying transcendence. America, declares the narrator of *A Single Man* in a bizarre echo of the imagined chronology of the Third Reich, is 'a far far more advanced culture—five hundred, maybe a thousand years ahead of Europe'.[114] Indeed, one of the things that *A Single Man* finds most attractive about the American West is its sense of impersonality, its non-human sense of scale. Isherwood wrote in a journal entry for May 1939 of how such 'distances', 'prodigality', and 'barrenness' are said to be hard for 'the European mind' to 'grasp'; Europeans more accustomed to a liberal humanist tradition cannot easily come to terms with the vast scale of this apparently inhumane landscape. For George in *A Single Man*, however, it is the stark impersonality of this environment that justifies the anonymous, interchangeable nature of his sexual encounters: characters are reduced to 'rock pools', where 'each pool is separate and different, and you can, if you are fanciful, give them names—such as George, Charlotte, Kenny, Mrs Strunk'. The human body is simply a machine which functions or not; the reduction of the authorial self to a camera in the Berlin stories is taken further here, so that human characters themselves modulate into machines, as George discovers when he merges into his automobile on the freeway: 'There is nothing to fear, as long as you let yourself go with it.' Auden considered *A Single Man* to be Isherwood's best work, and the narrative has a radical, clinical edge which sets it apart from the more traditional humanist conventions of English fiction at this time.[115]

---

[114] Isherwood, *Christopher and his Kind*, 23, 31; *idem, A Single Man*, 76–7.
[115] Isherwood, *Diaries*, 20, and *idem, A Single Man*, 155, 27; Parker, *Isherwood*, 725.

This erasure of personality is also inextricably interwoven with Isherwood's involvement in Hindu thought, which began shortly after he arrived in California and which led to his religious initiation by Swami Prabhavanandra in 1940. In *My Guru and his Disciple* (1980), Isherwood describes being introduced to the ideas of Eastern mysticism by Gerald Heard, another displaced Londoner, while in *A Meeting by the River* (1967) he integrates these religious concerns into another fictional narrative of doubles: two brothers, Patrick and Oliver, negotiate a series of dualities, sex against spirit, Los Angeles against the banks of the Ganges, immersion in the world against detachment from it. Isherwood's commitment to Hinduism induced what he called some 'predictable sneers ... from the English and the Eastern Americans alike' about the supposedly anti-intellectual atmosphere of southern California. Again, though, we see how Isherwood's thoroughgoing rejection of philosophical empiricism leads him imaginatively to extend the tradition of transatlantic modernism developed by T. S. Eliot and D. H. Lawrence, to offer a sense of the directions in which English literature and culture might have gone had the Second World War never happened. He cites *Ash Wednesday* in *My Guru and his Disciple*—'I began to understand what Eliot means in *Ash Wednesday*: "Teach us to care and not to care"'—and, as a great admirer of Lawrence's 'revelation that you could write about nature in a purely subjective way', his representations of a primordial American innocence remain unencumbered by the cautions about violence and incivility with which the English moralist sensibility customarily hedged them around in the post-1945 period.[116]

It was this principle of 'absolute interchangeability, that extinguishes man as an individual being' to which Adorno objected in relation to *Brave New World*, and Adorno's distaste for what he saw as an unholy collusion between totalitarianism and technology was, as we have seen, shared by other commentators in Britain, notably George Orwell.[117] However, one strain of English modernism which his American residence enabled Isherwood to explore is precisely this utopian dimension that was crushed out of English culture in the late 1940s, with Orwell's professed contempt for the principles of anti-humanism in *Nineteen Eighty-Four* (1949) becoming the classic statement of this position. In Isherwood, however, such utopianism is linked not only to an idyll of sexual freedom but also to a more general capacity to think the unthinkable, to dissolve the solidity of the institutions he found so wearisome in Europe by incorporating those aspects of 'impermanence' that he cherished in California. Michael Uebel has associated this utopian dissidence with a form of masochism, suggesting how the very failure to adjust to existing realities serves to 'redefine politics as *an art of the impossible* by altering the parameters of what is considered "possible"

---

[116] Christopher Isherwood, *My Guru and his Disciple* (London: Eyre Methuen, 1980), 252, 56; Carolyn G. Heilbrun, 'Christopher Isherwood: An Interview', *Conversations with Christopher Isherwood*, 147.   [117] Adorno, 'Aldous Huxley and Utopia', 104–5.

within the status quo ... Masochism has precisely this effect: it opens up the gap between what is and what is possible, clearing the space necessary for genuine critique.' Isherwood himself always loathed the term 'gay', preferring the older word 'queer', which he believed more accurately defined his generation's understanding of homosexuality, and in this sense Isherwood's utopianism might accurately be said to offer a queer critique of postwar British culture, to illuminate from the other side of the Atlantic the contracted nature of Britain's intellectual and psychological horizons in this post-1945 period.[118]

One aspect of fascist modernism which Isherwood does not avoid is its congenital anti-Semitism. He acknowledges 'anti-Semitic feelings' in a 1950 entry in his diaries and was still making overtly anti-Semitic remarks as late as the 1970s, while his conceptual emphasis on the mutual communality of all things made him no less uncomfortable with the idea of Jewish distinctiveness than was Eliot in his writings on the idea of a Christian community.[119] In *A Single Man*, George, in his role as professor, vigorously puts down a student who raises a question in class about whether Aldous Huxley might be anti-Semitic: 'The Nazis were *not* right to hate the Jews,' replies George, 'But their hating the Jews was *not* without a cause.' George goes on to express impatience with this 'organized' ethnic minority that, he says, has 'committees to defend it'.[120] Such an uncritical equation between cultural homogeneity and imperial power exemplifies a point made in 1944 by Orwell, about how the 'interconnexion between sadism, masochism, success-worship, power-worship, nationalism and totalitarianism is a huge subject whose edges have barely been scratched'. The modernist utopianism of Isherwood, in other words, exists concomitantly and in collusion with an American state of cultural imperialism; by contrast, Orwell, cherishing the ethical sanctity of his embattled island community, seeks to preserve its moral freedom from the 'power and successful cruelty' that he sees as endemic within 'totalitarian' states.[121] This again explains why for many British intellectuals in the 1940s the United States was beginning to succeed Nazi Germany as the symbol of a threatening, internationalizing modernism. America, from this perspective, was associating itself with brute power, a power expressed in troublingly abstract and, from an English point of view, potentially dehumanizing forms.

Despite the many disconcerting aspects to his post-1939 work, then, the notion prevalent among many British critics that Isherwood's major works were produced before his emigration and that nothing he 'wrote in the second half of his life was as good' is unconvincing.[122] It is an idea commonly applied also to transatlantic exiles of this era such as Thom Gunn and, as we shall see,

118 Isherwood, 'Los Angeles', 165; Michael Uebel, 'Masochism in America', *American Literary History*, 14 (2002), 402; Joseph Bristow, '"I am With You, Little Minority Sister": Isherwood's Queer Sixties', in *The Queer Sixties*, ed. Patricia Juliana Smith (New York: Routledge, 1999), 150.
119 Isherwood, *Lost Years*, 262; Parker, *Isherwood*, 143.   120 Isherwood, *A Single Man*, 57.
121 Orwell, 'Raffles and Miss Blandish', 222–3.
122 Peter Conrad, 'Tom, Dick and Christopher', *Observer Review*, 2 July 2000, 13.

17. David Hockney, 'Christopher Isherwood and Don Bachardy' (1976).

W. H. Auden, but it speaks more to the critic's expectations of and familiarity
with a certain style of English social realism than to the artistic achievements
of these writers themselves. If there is one British artist whom Isherwood
most resembles, it is perhaps not a literary figure at all, but the painter David
Hockney, who emigrated from the north of England to southern California in
the 1960s and who has similarly used the landscapes and natural environment
of his adopted home to mount an implicit critique of the social and aesthetic
assumptions informing his native land. Hockney came to know Isherwood well,
sketching his likeness several times (see Plate 17) and also painting in 1968 and
1984 two large-scale portraits of him and his partner Don Bachardy, presenting
them as a comfortable bohemian couple at home amidst their books and easels.
Hockney's early work was perhaps best known for its homoerotic imagery and
sexual iconoclasm, subjects naturally dear to Isherwood's heart, but the artist
(again like Isherwood) has also commented over the years on a range of legislative
restrictions associated with what he has called the 'hideous perversity' of 'Nanny
England': censorship, licensing, and animal quarantine laws, for example. And
just as Isherwood's later works re-envisage English manners from an estranged
perspective, so Hockney, in some of his later paintings such as *Garrowby Hill*
(1998), has applied the bright pastel colours characteristic of his California work

8. David Hockney, *Garrowby Hill* (1998). Photograph © 2006, Museum of Fine Arts, Boston.

to representations of his native Yorkshire dales, thereby defamiliarizing a country more normally framed in sombre colours and suggesting how it might be pictured differently (see Plate 18).[123]

Isherwood's American works similarly deploy a transatlantic perspective to defamiliarize naturalized English customs and modes of representation. They strive to peel away layers of aesthetic convention, to use journals and diaries to subvert those traditional processes of artistic selectivity which, in his eyes, systematically distort the actuality of events. This is why his later work aspires, in a kind of Zen-like fashion, to provide something like a transparent window on his own experiences of the world. *Christopher and his Kind*, for example, covers the same ground as *Goodbye to Berlin*, but it approaches the subject in a completely different way, striving austerely to substitute authenticity for conscious artifice

---

[123] Simon Watney, 'Portrait of an Artist', *Marxism Today*, Oct. 1988, 44; David Hockney and Paul Joyce, *Hockney on 'Art': Conversations with Paul Joyce* (London: Little, Brown and Company (UK), 1999), 235.

and endeavouring to make the strange familiar. In this sense Isherwood is the very opposite of a surrealist, since he takes what might be seen as peculiar or heterodox situations—sexual fetishism in Berlin, exuberant orgies in the Pacific Ocean, and so on—and, by a determinedly neutral tone, makes them seem bland, ordinary, psychologically and socially unexceptional. It is this capacity to transvalue the boundaries of the 'normal' that constitutes the strength and value of Isherwood's queer interrogation of English society.

In a paradoxical sense the widespread institutional investments in American studies as a form of area studies after the Second World War served to deflect attention away from the more disconcerting ways in which the American realm operated as an alternative conceptual landscape for English writers as well. Rather than subscribing to the myths of American exceptionalism that categorized US national identity as a world set distinctively apart, Wodehouse, Huxley, and Isherwood all sought to recontextualize their native culture within a transnational, transatlantic framework.[124] In their different ways, they all created an abstract, Americanized world of imaginative violence and utopian horizons that stands as a counterpoint to the assumed decencies of postwar British culture. Transatlantic displacement for these authors involved not merely a form of self-indulgent escapism, but a way of gaining alternative perspectives on English culture and reabsorbing it within the larger structures of international modernism. For Wodehouse, this internationalism involved primarily the culture of the global marketplace; for Huxley, the abstract trajectories of science and theocentrism; for Isherwood, particularly towards the end of his life, queer politics. In each case, however, the accusations of treason and betrayal that were levelled against these authors in Britain around the time of the Second World War can be seen in retrospect to signify their larger demurral from the domestic ideologies of Britain in the 1940s and 1950s, their refusal to be conscripted into the austere, repressive communalism that governed British culture and society in the aftermath of its victory in Europe. It is precisely the edgy, disquieting aspects of their work that illuminate what became forcibly omitted from narratives of English literature and culture in the middle years of the twentieth century.

---

[124] On the development of American studies in Britain in the post-1945 period, see Giles, *Virtual Americas*, 184–7.

8

Postwar Poetry and the Purifications of Exile

THE JUST CITY: W. H. AUDEN

In 1973, Philip Larkin produced his edition of the *Oxford Book of Twentieth-Century English Verse*, seeking to identify a native literary tradition organized around a colloquial idiom whose precursors were Wordsworth, Thomas Hardy, and the Georgian poets. In order to emphasize this lineage, Larkin chose to omit altogether from his anthology the works of Ezra Pound and to minimize the contributions of T. S. Eliot, on the grounds that it was not within the editor's remit to 'include poems by American or Commonwealth writers, nor poems requiring a glossary for their full understanding'.[1] The constellation of poets discussed in this chapter, however, set their face directly against Larkin's insular assumptions, since the concern of W. H. Auden, Denise Levertov, and Donald Davie was with ways in which the aesthetics of a transatlantic modernism might be incorporated into postwar English poetry. All three of these poets were born in England but spent the greater part of their later life in the United States, and they all appropriated American culture to construct an alternative, revisionist version of the English intellectual tradition, one grounded not on pastoral continuities but on a legacy of Reformation and Dissent. In this sense, Auden, Levertov, and Davie self-consciously aligned themselves with English reformers of earlier centuries who saw transatlantic displacement and exile as strategies for the purification and regeneration of their native country. Their work, like that of Wodehouse and Isherwood, was haunted by the traumatic conditions and divisions of war, and they all chose deliberately in the mid-twentieth century to alienate themselves from an England which had, so they believed, become belligerently antipathetic to the spirit of modernism in all of its guises. In a curiously heterodox fashion, Auden, Levertov, and Davie all elected to affiliate their work with the American tradition as a means of recuperating a purified version of that modernist impulse which had, so they believed, been fatally suppressed by the reactionary mood brought about in Britain by the exigencies of war.

Auden arrived in the United States with Isherwood in 1939, having already made his name as a chronicler of industrial Britain in the 1930s, and, like

---

[1] Philip Larkin, preface, in *The Oxford Book of Twentieth-Century English Verse*, ed. Larkin (Oxford: University Press, 1973), p. v.

Isherwood, he took American citizenship in 1946. As with Isherwood again, there has been a long critical tradition of regarding the work Auden produced after his move to the United States as inferior to his earlier writing. Delmore Schwartz, in a negative review of *The Age of Anxiety* in 1947, asserted that Auden's 'genius depends upon England, upon the English scene, upon perceptions and emotions inspired by being English', while Larkin in 1960 similarly argued of Auden's work that 'almost all we value is still confined to its first ten years', the decade of the 1930s, when he was 'a tremendously exciting English social poet' with a 'unique lucidity of phrase'. Larkin's perspective, in particular, is tinged with a cantankerous anti-Americanism: he talks of how Auden after 1939 turned into a 'bookish, American talent, too verbose to be memorable and too intellectual to be moving', and describes his later verse as a 'wilful jumble of Age-of-Plastic nursery rhyme' and 'Hollywood lemprière'. John Lemprière was a nineteenth-century compiler of classical dictionaries, and Larkin's point here is that by retreating into a scholastic, fustian world, Auden was abandoning his earlier 'neo-Wordsworthianism', through which he understood poetry simply as a form of 'natural speech', the articulation of the common voice of the people. Writing of Auden in 1997, Tom Paulin reiterated this view that 'in leaving England he lost touch with the deep structures of British English'.[2]

Auden, however, never liked this Wordsworthian tradition of English literature consistently championed by Larkin. His 'Letter to Lord Byron' (1936) sides with Byron in 'finding Wordsworth a most bleak old bore', and it mocks his 'followers' who 'come in train-loads to the Lakes' in search of an indigenous pastoral spirit.[3] In his first long American poem, *New Year Letter* (1940), Auden represents Wordsworth as having been ensnared by the 'platonic dream' of liberty projected by the French Revolution, and then, in reaction, turning into a crusty old Tory, supporting the 'Established Church' and 'The Squire's paternalistic hand' (p. 173). In his first few years in the United States, Auden marked his retreat from the Wordsworth inheritance by interesting himself in the technical and institutional aspects of the American literary scene, writing his 1939 poem 'In Memory of Sigmund Freud' in a syllabic form influenced by Marianne Moore, an idiom he subsequently described, in an essay on Moore, as 'very difficult for an English ear to grasp'. (As Nicholas Jenkins has observed, many of Auden's most important later works—'Music is International', 'Ischia', 'Prime'—were also written in syllabics.)[4] He also became acquainted with F. O. Matthiessen,

---

[2] John Haffenden, ed., *W. H. Auden: The Critical Heritage* (London: Routledge, 1983), 370, 414–18; Tom Paulin, 'Auden Never Got the Hang of Writing Prose, but at least he Saw Gossip as an Art Form', *Observer Review*, 16 March 1997, 15.
    [3] W. H. Auden, *Collected Poems*, ed. Edward Mendelson (London: Faber, 1976), 89. Subsequent page references to this edition are cited in parentheses in the text.
    [4] W. H. Auden, 'Marianne Moore', in *The Dyer's Hand*, 297; Nicholas Jenkins, 'Auden in America', in *The Cambridge Companion to W. H. Auden*, ed. Stan Smith (Cambridge: Cambridge University Press, 2005), 43.

whose monumental work *American Renaissance*, which established a rationale for the academic study of American literature, was published in 1941. Matthiessen included a selection of Auden's poems in his *Oxford Book of American Verse* as early as 1950, arguing in his introduction to this volume that in the way Auden 'writes about the problem of being a refugee and an exile ... he belongs to his adopted country as well as to Europe'.[5] For Matthiessen, a key figure in this reinscription of American literature within a comparative context was Henry James, on whom he published a critical book in 1944, and Auden similarly saw James as a 'guiding star' in the years immediately after his emigration, writing several essays applauding James's devotion to his craft, what he called 'the consistent integrity displayed both in the work and in the man'.[6] Auden's poem 'At the Grave of Henry James' was also published in a 1941 issue of the *Partisan Review*, the New York journal in which many of Matthiessen's critical essays on American literature were appearing, while Auden's 1946 introduction to James's *The American Scene* considers specifically the relationship between James's 'critical literary sense' and a politics of national identity.[7]

What has perhaps not been sufficiently recognized, though, is the extent to which Auden's work after his move to America continued crucially to be shaped by his wartime encounters with fascism. One reason why Auden was widely perceived in Britain as having betrayed his native land was not simply because he had left the country but because he seemed to become more ambiguous about the politics of fascism once in the United States. Auden had, of course, risen to fame in the 1930s as an anti-Fascist poet; in 1934, he described his old headmaster as imitating the role of a 'modern dictator' and wrote, only half-flippantly, that the 'best reason I have for opposing Fascism is that at school I lived in a Fascist state', while his partisan poem 'Spain 1937' took sides against Franco's Nationalist army in the Spanish Civil War.[8] In the United States, however, Auden's critique of fascism became more detached and academic in its orientation. He taught a class at Swarthmore College in 1942 on 'Romantic Literature from Rousseau to Hitler', following on from his suggestion in an address at Yale the previous year that Hitler's worldly prominence constituted the first time that 'Rousseau's reasoned accusation that Reason was the arch enemy of unity and happiness has been taken seriously and has attained political power'. As we have seen from the work of Siegfried Kracauer, such a tendency clinically to intellectualize the Hitler phenomenon was quite common in the United States in the 1940s: the American

5 F. O. Matthiessen, introduction, in *The Oxford Book of American Verse*, ed. Matthiessen (New York: Oxford University Press, 1950), p. xvi.

6 W. H. Auden, 'Henry James and the Dedicated', in *Prose*, ii: *1939–1948*, ed. Edward Mendelson (London: Faber, 2002), 242, and *idem*, 'Address on Henry James', in *Prose*, ii. 297.

7 W. H. Auden, 'At the Grave of Henry James', *Partisan Review*, 8/4 (July–Aug. 1941), 266–70, and *idem*, 'Introduction to *The American Scene*, by Henry James', in *Prose*, ii. 270.

8 W. H. Auden, 'The Liberal Fascist', in *The English Auden: Poems, Essays and Dramatic Writings, 1927–1939* (London: Faber, 1977), 325.

academic Peter Viereck published in 1941 *Metapolitics: From the Romantics to Hitler*, which similarly placed Hitler in a tradition of German romanticism extending back to Nietzsche and Wagner.[9] Having been taken aback by viewing the film *Sieg in Polen* at a German-language cinema in New York in December 1939, where apparently unexceptionable Germans in the audience began shouting 'Kill the Poles!', Auden became increasingly drawn to theoretical explanations of ways in which the Nazis were effectively holding up a mirror to dark places in the human soul. He remarked in 1940 that Hitler 'comes uncomfortably near being the unconscious of most of us', and in a review of Reinhold Niebuhr's *The Nature and Destiny of Man* the following year, he commented: 'It has taken Hitler to show us that liberalism is not self-supporting.' Hitler, like Rousseau, demonstrated for Auden the deleterious consequences of an ideology of human perfectionism predicated upon an absence of 'the doctrine of Original Sin', a doctrine that was, he argued, so 'unwelcome to the modern liberal'.[10] Although he admired much of D. H. Lawrence's writing, it was not accidental, Auden observed in 1947, that *The Plumed Serpent* 'should emit such an unpleasant whiff of fascism', since fascism was responding to 'the same Cartesian errors' as Lawrence in its belief that primitivist instincts must hold sway over 'the corrupt mind'. Rather than seeing spirit and body as paradoxically conjoined, fascism, like Lawrentian modernism, sought to eliminate the necessarily ironic mode of human incarnation, which held all terrestrial systems in abeyance.[11]

Such a long-sighted theoretical perspective was, of course, not immediately compatible with the more one-dimensional wartime slogans circulating in England in the early 1940s. Auden held a more abstract, intellectualized view of fascism than was common in Britain at this time, recognizing its affinities with a larger tradition of Western thought and culture. He was accordingly unwilling to attribute the outbreak of the Second World War 'to the sudden appearance of some unusually wicked men', saying that such an explanation was 'too simple'. He also declined to endorse the Manichaean allegory of good against evil being propagated by the British wartime government, arguing in 1940 that an 'open society' needed to interrogate the spaces between propositions and presuppositions, and that those who failed to engage in such radical questioning were 'as much the enemies of democracy as those who speak of German science or Fascist justice'. This principled refusal to identify with a Britain caught up in the turmoil of war would naturally have alienated him from his readership in a country where the rhetoric of sacrifice on behalf of the nation was still dominant; in what can only have been a deliberately provocative gesture, Auden wrote in

---

[9] Osborne, *W. H. Auden*, 212; Auden, '*Yale Daily News* Banquet Address', in *Prose*, ii. 119; Blake Morrison, *The Movement: English Poetry and Fiction of the 1950s* (Oxford: Oxford University Press, 1980), 173.

[10] Edward Mendelson, *Later Auden* (New York: Farrar, Straus & Giroux, 1999), 89; Stan Smith, *W. H. Auden* (Oxford: Blackwell, 1985), 13; Auden, 'The Means of Grace', in *Prose*, ii. 131, 134.

[11] Auden, 'Some Notes on D. H. Lawrence', in *Prose*, ii. 320.

the *Nation* in 1944 that 'to regard national statehood as anything more than a technical convenience of social organization ... is idolatry'.[12]

Although he accused fascism of typically seeking to suppress the contingency of its own values by coercing the masses into accepting as facts what were no more than manufactured myths, Auden also feared how the pressure of wartime propaganda would induce democracies such as Britain to 'construct an anti-fascist political religion'. In this sense, both Britain and the United States, no less than Germany and Italy, could become liable to the charge of collectivist coercion, and it is noticeable how one of the few really scathing reviews that Auden wrote after his move across the Atlantic was a 1942 notice of a paper by Van Wyck Brooks, 'Primary Literature and Coterie Literature'. Here Brooks, in a familiar American nativist argument, argues against 'coterie' writers whom he sees as excessively sceptical and highbrow—Henry James, Proust, T. S. Eliot—and he champions instead the virtues of the 'primary' writer 'who bespeaks the collective life of the people'. For Auden, this is 'amazing rubbish', implying a requirement for art to 'act as a State Religion', so that Brooks's cultural policy might be seen as a 'minor' embodiment of the policy which Hitler pursues in a 'major' way:

we are all too ready to accuse others of being Fascists, Reds, Bourgeois, or what-have-you, but all too reluctant to admit the sinister presence of a Fifth Column within our own personal mind and heart. Yet, unless we realise that a collective political victory over Germany and Japan, and a personal victory over ourselves are mutually interdependent aspects of the same problem, our chances of winning either battle are small.

Auden observes the irony of making these remarks on the first day of America's entry into the war, but he ends his review by cautioning against the potential moral equivalence of fascism and its opposite: 'The late Huey Long, when asked if Fascism could ever come to America, replied: "Sure. Only it will be called Anti-fascism." '[13]

This refusal of binary oppositions and Manichaean contraries is one of the presiding ideas in *New Year Letter*, where 'The Devil' himself is cast as 'the great schismatic who/First split creation into two' (p. 171). The burden of this complex poem is to preserve a sense of '*civitas*', of 'ideal order' (p. 162), and not to allow society to become fractured into a dualism determined by competing polarities of perfectionism and demonization. The notes to this poem describe the artist *qua* artist as 'the only person who is really a dictator', since the artist can tyrannize over his own closed society: 'It is not surprising', writes Auden, 'that Hitler began as a painter and has derived such inspiration from Wagner.' Nevertheless, the genuine poet, in Auden's universe, is the one who acknowledges the provisional nature of his own creation by preserving 'the gift of double focus':

---

[12] Auden, 'Romantic or Free?', in *Prose*, ii. 68, and *idem*, 'Children of Abraham', in *Prose*, ii. 224–5.

[13] Edward Mendelson, introduction, in *Prose*, ii. by W. H. Auden, p. xxiv; Auden, 'La Trahison d'un Clerc', in *Prose*, ii. 148–51.

That magic lamp which looks so dull
And utterly impractical
Yet, if Aladdin use it right,
Can be a sesame to light.

(p.176)

In its 1941 printing, the poem was retitled *The Double Man*, with an epigraph from Montaigne: 'We are, I know not how, double in ourselves, so that what we believe we disbelieve, and cannot rid ourselves of what we condemn.'[14] The poem's deliberate projection of truth as duplex and self-contradictory cuts against what is represented here as the diabolic impulse of polarity and absolutism:

O how the devil who controls
The moral asymmetric souls
The either-ors, the mongrel halves
Who find truth in a mirror, laughs.

(p. 176)

New Year Letter is dated on its title-page January 1, 1940 (p. 159), even though it was not actually completed until later in the year, and the use of this symbolic date clearly indicates how Auden was seeking deliberately to open a new chapter in his poetic career. The emphasis is upon an austere sense of freedom in this 'fully alienated land' (p. 183), with 'Retrenchment, Sacrifice, Reform' being the cornerstones of the enterprise (p. 161). This reformist agenda is underlined by a reference in the third part of the poem to Martin Luther helping to bring about 'a new *Anthropos*, an/Empiric Economic Man' (p. 184), and by the invocation of 'The Saints in Massachusetts Bay', seventeenth-century exiles from England such as John Winthrop, John Cotton, and Ann Hutchinson, whose journey westward across the Atlantic anticipated Auden's own quest for 'the Just City' (pp. 189–90). In this earlier age of Reformation, members of the Massachusetts Bay community exiled themselves in an attempt to introduce a spirit of regeneration and renewal into the corrupt English Church, and in the middle of the twentieth century Auden sees himself as charged with a similar mission.

Auden had previously used this phrase 'the Just City' in 'Spain 1937' to signify the 'proposal' of the Spanish Loyalists to construct a republican utopia. But *New Year Letter*'s revised notion of a 'Just City' is crucially inflected by Charles Williams's *The Descent of the Dove: A History of the Holy Spirit in the Church*, which Auden read in February 1940, shortly after the book was published.[15] Williams traced representations of the city in Christian thought, from Augustine's *City of God* onwards, arguing that a fundamental principle of 'the City of Christendom' was 'that all men must be capable of inclusion'. The *ecclesia*, said Williams,

---

[14] W. H. Auden, *The Double Man* (Westport, Conn.: Greenwood Press, 1979), 79–80, 3.
[15] Auden, 'Spain 1937', in *The English Auden*, 211; Mendelson, *Later Auden*, 124.

held each individual point of view to be necessarily imperfect, so that schism was considered 'the worst sin, for schism was bound to nullify the justice from which it might arise. However right a man's ideas, they were bound to go wrong if he nourished them by himself.' In Williams's interpretation of Church history, therefore, the Reformation should be understood as a mere struggle for temporal power, since Calvin's theological ideas were essentially the same as, indeed largely derived from, those of Augustine. For Williams, Montaigne's belief 'in the religion of custom, of good tradition' thus took on an exemplary status, since such ritualistic customs were predicated upon the insufficiency of individual human reason and made allowances for error within the larger body of the whole. Montaigne's observations on the 'double man', for whom any singular perspective is by definition inadequate, is cited here by Williams, and this is the phrase that was incorporated directly by Auden as his epigraph to the 1941 version of the poem.[16]

Williams also commented in *The Descent of the Dove* on what he called 'the new movement ... in middle Europe', which is 'not distinguished, even theoretically, by an image of universal humanity'. He differentiated Christianity, communism, and National Socialism according to their relationship to universal values: 'The Body and Blood of Christendom had been declared to be divine, human, and common; the body and blood of Communism were thought to be human and common; the body and blood of the new myth were merely German. It set itself against the very idea of the City; it raised against the world the fatalistic cry of Race.'[17] These remarks on fascism suggest how Auden's appropriations of Williams's religious thought, in *New Year Letter* and his later poems, arise out of a Christian response to the specific incidence of Nazi Germany. The fatal flaws in Nazi doctrine, according to Williams, were its rejection of Christian universal order and its blinkered insistence upon its own racial exceptionalism, its belief that German eschatology was validated simply by being German. Much of the theology that Auden absorbed during his early years in America, from Reinhold Niebuhr and others, looked back to 'the Protestantism of the Reformation' in its emphasis on how human freedom exists as the correlative to an age of anxiety, when reassuring old social customs have been superseded by the burdens of existential choice.[18] Auden himself edited a collection of Søren Kierkegaard's writings in 1952, and he was influenced strongly by what he called the 'via negativa' of Protestant theology in the early 1940s. But this was the Protestant spirit with an Anglican twist: Auden described himself in 1941 as 'Liturgically ... Anglo-Catholic', and he began attending church services again soon after his move to New York, where he formalized his affiliation by

---

[16] Charles Williams, *The Descent of the Dove: A Short History of the Holy Spirit in the Church* (London: Longmans, Green and Co., 1939), 230, 38, 174, 192–3.   [17] Ibid. 230.
[18] George Cotkin, *Existential America* (Baltimore: Johns Hopkins University Press, 2003), 47. On Auden and Niebuhr, see also Peter Conrad, *Imagining America* (London Routledge & Kegan Paul, 1980), 195–7.

rejoining the Anglican fold as an Episcopalian in October 1940. Consequently, Kierkegaard's maxim of how 'Before God we are always in the wrong', which Auden cited in a 1940 letter to Stephen Spender, was assimilated in his eyes into another version of Williams's ecclesiastical heterogeneity, through which any form of epistemological certainty became displaced into the radically unstable category of 'either/or'.[19] Whereas for the more inward Kierkegaard human anguish derives from the impossibility of definitive judgement, for the Anglican Williams the presence of doubt and dissent were integral components of any apostolic body.

It is, however, this traditional Anglican admission of toleration and difference that Auden finds to be lacking in the dismal conditions of England in the 1940s. The corruption of England derives not only from its incarceration within a rhetoric of wartime propaganda but also from the misconception of itself as an organic, idealized state. In a deliberate inversion of Eliot's use of Jessie L. Weston's work on the myth of the Fisher King in *The Waste Land*, Auden in *New Year Letter* reads the figure of the quester as necessarily isolated, an existential hero rather than a socially representative being: 'Each biggie in the Canning Ring / An unrobust lone FISHER-KING' (p. 190). In another specific rejection of Eliot's organicist nostalgia, he sees the forces of international abstraction and exchange supplanting the traditional autonomy of national communities:

> However we decide to act,
> Decision must accept the fact
> That the machine has now destroyed
> The local customs we enjoyed,
> Replaced the bonds of blood and nation
> By personal confederation.
>
> (p. 190)

Auden had earlier taken issue with 'modernism's ideologies of national rootedness' in 'In Memory of Sigmund Freud', which refers to Freud as an 'important Jew who died in exile' from Hitler's Germany (p. 216).[20] Auden had written to Eliot in 1934 of being 'rather shocked' by *After Strange Gods*, where Eliot notoriously declared that for reasons of 'race and religion' the presence of 'any large number of free-thinking Jews' was 'undesirable', and much of Auden's work in America was designed deliberately to counter the kind of organicist mystique which Eliot's work was promoting. After his move to New York, Auden became more overtly hostile to what he called the 'pernicious influence ... exerted by the Action Française movement' over writers such as Eliot, Pound, and Chesterton, and

---

[19] Osborne, *W. H. Auden*, 202–3; Mendelson, *Later Auden*, 174, 132.
[20] Nicholas Jenkins, 'Writing "Without Roots": Auden, Eliot, and Post-National Poetry', in *Something We Have That They Don't: British and American Poetic Relations since 1925*, ed. Steve Clark and Mark Ford (Iowa City: University of Iowa Press, 2004), 90.

more openly sympathetic to Judaism, impelled partly by the fact that Chester Kallman, his new American lover, was himself Jewish.[21] Auden returns to his barbed dialogue with Eliot in 'For the Time Being', a 'Christmas Oratorio' written in 1941–2. Here the narrator, speaking on behalf of the local government at the time of Christ's birth, reports how 'the recent restrictions / Upon aliens and free-thinking Jews are beginning / To have a salutary effect upon public morale' (p. 289). This is, of course, a direct response to Eliot's advocacy of a communitarian culture in *After Strange Gods*, and it is no coincidence that Auden's narrator in 'For the Time Being', with his studied tone of impersonality masking an obsequious attitude towards the temporal government, is curiously reminiscent of a voice on the BBC, with which Eliot enjoyed such a cordial relationship:

> You have been listening to the voice of Caesar
> Who overcame implacable Necessity
> By His endurance and by His skill has subdued the Welter of Fortune.
>
> (p. 287)

Auden is negotiating the same issues as Eliot—questions of social cohesion and religious redemption—but he approaches them from quite a different direction. In keeping with his transatlantic journey west rather than east, Auden prioritizes individual freedom, and he regards as tyrannical that version of social order idealized by Eliot. In his 1962 essay 'The Poet and the City', Auden specifically rejects the organicist, hierarchical system that was, for Eliot, the basis of all good order: 'A society which was really like a good poem,' writes Auden, 'embodying the aesthetic virtues of beauty, order, economy and subordination of detail to the whole, would be a nightmare of horror.'[22]

By using his adopted American scene to problematize both the racial exceptionalism of fascism and the coercive communal solidarity of Britain, Auden succeeded in engineering strategic dialogues among these various discursive locations, a triangulating process that enabled him to reintegrate German thought and culture within the larger body of the cosmopolitan *ecclesia*. 'Memorial for the City' (1949), dedicated to the memory of Charles Williams, is set in a postwar landscape, 'Among the ruins of the Post-Vergilian City / Where our past is a chaos of graves and the barbed-wire stretches ahead / Into our future till it is lost to sight' (p. 450). Auden himself had been disturbed by the three months he spent in Germany in the summer of 1945 on behalf of the US government to study the psychological effects of bombing (see Plate 19), but this poem, with its deliberately emblematic and non-particularistic quality, its vaguely ominous 'huts of some Emergency Committee' (p. 452), represents war as a common fate rather than a narrative embedded with a specific moral or nationalistic teleology. Its abstract, universal tone is commensurate with the reversed perspective in 'Josef

---

21 Mendelson, *Later Auden*, 150, 57; Eliot, *After Strange Gods*, 20.
22 Auden, 'The Poet and the City', in *The Dyer's Hand*, 85.

19. W. H. Auden in Nuremberg, May 1945. Photograph by Frank Lyell.

Weinheber', his 1965 tribute to the poet who lived in Kirchstetten, Austria, whence Auden himself had moved in 1958. Weinheber had collaborated with the Nazis before committing suicide at the end of the war, but Auden's tone here is more ruminative than accusatory:

> Categorised enemies
> twenty years ago,
> now next-door neighbors, we might
> have become good friends,
> sharing a common ambit
> and love of the Word
> over a golden *Kremser* ...
> To-day we smile at weddings
> where bride and bridegroom
> were both born since the Shadow
> lifted, or rather
> moved elsewhere: never as yet
> has Earth been without
> her bad patch, some unplace with
> jobs for torturers. ...
>
>   (pp. 568–70)

Auden's integration of various German phrases within this poem serves to emphasize not ethical relativism—the poem reminds Weinheber how 'men of great damage / and malengine took you up' (p. 569)—but, more generally, the impossibility of moral perfectionism. This is the Anglican view of evil as an inevitable privation, something that can never entirely disappear but will simply move 'elsewhere'.

'Josef Weinheber' shows Auden attempting to reclaim the irreducibly human capacities of its Nazi protagonist, just as in 1943, at the height of the conflict, he continued to insist that 'it is a German Age, and the chances are, I have a suspicion, that after the war it will continue to be'. Citing 'Rilke-Kafka-Berg-Strauss-Barlach-Klee-Husserl-Heidegger-Scheler-Barth' and others, Auden indicated how for him the idea of national culture was not an entirely redundant phenomenon; it was, instead, something which needed to be understood not in unilateral or exceptionalist terms but within the broader framework of a cosmopolitan *ecclesia*.[23] Rather than inculcating a utopian form of post-nationalism which would seek ideally to eliminate the nation as a source of value, Auden's poetry after 1939 increasingly takes on the characteristics of transnationalism, as it interrogates the parameters of different cultures by setting them dialectically in opposition to each other. His description of himself in 'The Cave of Making' (1964) as 'a minor Atlantic Goethe' (p. 522), an honorary German, suggests how the poet imagined himself bringing German and American modernism into dialogue with British culture in these difficult postwar years.

This is why Edmund Wilson was correct in 1956 to say that, although Auden's 'genius' remained 'basically English', the experience of America had served to eradicate some of his merely personal 'eccentricity' and had 'given him a point of view that is inter- or super-national'. As Wilson recognized, the heightened abstraction of Auden's style had enabled him to find a poetic manner—'his extraordinary new language, a brilliant international English'—that could appropriately reflect his theme of dissociation from place.[24] Auden's 'Bucolics', written in the early 1950s, start off with a promise of traditional romantic iconography—winds, woods, mountains, lakes, islands, plains, streams—but then subvert those expectations by reworking these landscapes in terms of their more human, metaphorical implications. Lakes, for example, are depicted as a useful ancillary to a political summit:

> Sly Foreign Ministers should always meet beside one,
> For, whether they walk widdershins or deasil,
> The path will yoke their shoulders to one liquid centre
> Like two old donkeys pumping as they plod ...
>
> (p. 430)

[23] Mendelson, *Later Auden*, 419.
[24] Haffenden, ed., *W. H. Auden: The Critical Heritage*, 406, 408.

Implicit in this comic demystification is a deliberate refusal of immanent value, a rejection of the pastoral tradition which would grant an integral spirit to the natural world. Auden's complaint against Wordsworth was the way he attempted to define moral virtue and national identity as inhering within particular landscapes, a romantic assumption with which Auden's postwar writing takes issue. Whereas Wordsworth's *Prelude* roots its 'British theme' in the 'holy ground' of place and custom, Auden's great poem 'In Praise of Limestone' (1948) intertextually argues with this conception of the egotistical sublime by invoking a landscape of inconstancy and dissolution: 'this land is not the sweet home that it looks, / Nor its peace the historical calm of a site / Where something was settled once and for all' (p. 415).[25] Auden's fallible, hesitant narrative voice evokes here a condition of impermanence, whose aesthetic and moral ideals cannot be expounded in terms of the enduring physical properties of any given country. This is also why, unlike Isherwood, Auden refused to respond intellectually to his new American environment of open space and transcendental vastness. While Isherwood in California relished the metamorphic qualities of the southwestern landscape, Auden, ensconced firmly within the protective civic milieu of New York, developed an aesthetic style that became increasingly deracinated and abstract. For him, as he said in 'In Praise of Limestone', the greatest artistic 'comfort is music/Which can be made anywhere, is invisible, / And does not smell' (p. 415). His 1947 Phi Beta Kappa poem at Columbia University, 'Music is International', even more clearly expresses this idea of how art's 'universal language' should preserve a scrupulous distance from the charms of local colour. One American poet who was significantly influenced by the garrulous, reflective qualities of Auden's later style was John Ashbery, who wrote his senior thesis at Harvard in 1949 on 'The Poetic Medium of W. H. Auden', while in 1956, as an editor of the Yale Series of Younger Poets, Auden himself helped Ashbery to publish his first book, *Some Trees*.[26]

In 'American Poetry', an essay originally published as the introduction to the *Faber Book of Modern American Verse* (1956), Auden contrasts the representation of 'personal' relationships between nature and man in the works of Wordsworth, Tennyson, and Hardy—a society in 'race and religion more or less homogeneous and in which most people lived and died in the locality where they were born'—to the greater emphasis on 'social fluidity' and 'breaking social and personal ties' which he finds exemplified in the work of American poets. In this essay, Auden goes on to relate the dissolution of social bonds in the United States to the 'separation of Church and State' that he sees as 'the most revolutionary feature of the Constitution':

---

[25] Wordsworth, *The Prelude*, 44, 502.
[26] Ashbery subsequently acknowledged how his *Three Poems* (1972) was heavily influenced by Auden's *The Sea and the Mirror* (1944). Mark Ford, *John Ashbery in Conversation with Mark Ford* (London: Between the Lines, 2003), 56.

Between 1533 and 1688 the English went through a succession of revolutions in which a Church was imposed on them by the engines of the State, one king was executed and another deposed, yet they prefer to forget it and pretend that the social structure of England is the product of organic peaceful growth. The Americans, on the other hand, like to pretend that what was only a successful war of secession was a genuine revolution.

Auden again takes issue with Eliot as he emphasizes how the English conception of organic continuity is no more than an illusion of coherence within a culture riven perpetually by civil strife: 'From the beginning,' he adds, 'America had been a pluralist state and pluralism is incompatible with an Established Church'.[27] This is why, as Auden continually remarks in the 1940s, the United States is a 'protestant society' in that it refuses these institutional orthodoxies while insisting that 'the truth is best arrived at by free controversy'.[28] At the same time, Auden's perception that American independence was the product of 'secession' rather than 'revolution' indicates how, in his eyes, these two discrete national cultures were sundered from a single body. This positions them as alter egos, counterpoised forces which subvert each other's assumptions, rather than simply as implacable opponents. Like the 'theocratic COTTON' and 'legal WINTHROP' whom he salutes in *New Year Letter* (p. 189), Auden was not a schismatic but a reformer, someone who sought to regenerate English poetry, as Winthrop had hoped to regenerate the Anglican body, from within.

In this sense, Auden's work after 1940 has something in common with English metaphysical poetry of the seventeenth century, since it is concerned to bring the Established Church into dialogue with reformist movements rather than seeing them as altogether separate entities. In a review of Lionel Trilling's *Matthew Arnold* published in *Common Sense* just a few months after he arrived in the United States in 1939, Auden argued that neither Arnold not Whitman could be seen as artistically self-sufficient: Arnold, with his 'disciplined and fastidious abstractions', had too much 'aloofness', while Whitman, with his 'formless originality', suffered from a 'lack of discrimination'. What Auden seeks ideally is a kind of transatlantic balance, so that British poetry could become more Americanized, and vice versa. He says that a British poet 'is in much greater danger of becoming lazy, or academic, or irresponsible', but that, conversely, 'for a "serious" poet to write light verse is frowned on in America', where the dominant aesthetic tends towards 'strain and overearnestness'.[29] Auden consequently sets himself to compose metaphysical poetry that confounds both British amateurishness and American sententiousness by becoming a kind of deadly serious game, establishing for itself a tone of ludic iconoclasm which brings English stylistic mannerisms into juxtaposition with American thematic impulses. One example of this kind of transatlantic aesthetic can be seen in

---

[27] Auden, 'American Poetry', in *The Dyer's Hand*, 357–8, 361–2.
[28] Auden, 'Romantic or Free?', 67.
[29] Auden, 'Whitman and Arnold', in *Prose*, ii. 12, and *idem*, 'American Poetry', 366.

'Under Which Lyre', the Phi Beta Kappa poem which Auden read at Harvard in 1946, immediately before a speech by the Harvard University Orator, who had recently served as wartime director of censorship for the US government.[30] Auden's poem is written in an American vernacular idiom, full of observations about 'co-eds' and 'quizzes', 'freshman' and 'sophomoric' culture (pp. 259–62); yet its final injunction to its graduating audience is to scorn the conventional paraphernalia of American academic life by pursuing a greater sense of individual idiosyncrasy:

> Thou shalt not do as the dean pleases,
> Thou shalt not write thy doctor's thesis
>   On education,
> Thou shalt not worship projects nor
> Shalt thou or thine bow down before
>   Administration.
>
> .   .   .   .
>
>   If thou must choose
> Between the chances, choose the odd. ...
>
> (pp. 262–3)

The ideas in 'Under Which Lyre' are, as the poem puts it, 'Related by antithesis' (p. 260). There is a conscious sense of turning established social conceptions on their head, of taking pleasure in a state of inversion.

This kind of interruption of the commonplace is also linked particularly in Auden's poems of the 1940s to a Kierkegaardian agnosticism, what the character of Malin in *The Age of Anxiety* (1946) calls 'the flash / Of negative knowledge ... That Always-Opposite which is the whole subject / Of our not-knowing' (p. 408). Displacement from the habits of his home culture, that is to say, operated for the American Auden as an analogue of displacement from worldly conditions more generally. 'The Dark Years', written in 1940, focuses in a highly wrought, metaphysical fashion on paradoxical points of intersection between the timeless and time, with the phrase 'nutritive chain of determined being' oscillating punningly between an existential and a Calvinist significance, indicating either a being 'determined' in the sense of self-willed or a being whose fate is predetermined. The poem's final stanza similarly cuts savagely in opposite directions:

> let ... the shabby structure of indolent flesh
> give a resonant echo to the Word which was
>   from the beginning, and the shining
> Light be comprehended by the darkness.
>
> (p. 223)

'Comprehended' here could mean either understood by or embraced within, as if the 'darkness' might either relinquish itself to light or, alternatively, engulf it.

---

[30] Mendelson, *Later Auden*, 263.

This mode of metaphysical conundrum re-echoes throughout Auden's poems in the decade after his move to America. 'At the Grave of Henry James' (1941) addresses a similarly mordant conflict between corporeal mutability and artistic immortality, while in numerous other poems of this era the imagery of time, clocks, and decay is set within a framework of alienation from the past. In 'A Walk after Dark' (1948), the poet ruminates on reaching middle age—'unready to die / But already at the stage / When one starts to resent the young' (p. 267)—and he links his sense of an unforeseeable personal destiny to the deracinating circumstances of his adopted country, a land outside the predictability of historical custom where the future is constitutionally uncertain:

> Asking what judgment waits
> My person, all my friends,
> And these United States.

(p. 268)

The climactic self-consciousness of the national affiliation in the last line of this poem reveals the critical inadequacy of Barbara Everett's argument that the division of Auden's career into 'English' and 'American' phases is simply a biographical convenience which bears little relationship to 'the fabric of Auden's real life', his creative life.[31] On the contrary, it is apparent that Auden represents his exile from England and his continuing alienation from the common culture of the United States as vehicles to turn against each other, so that he tries to infuse into the American scene an Anglican spirit of High Church frivolity while simultaneously undertaking a New World reformation of the principles of English literary culture.

Isherwood, in *My Guru and his Disciple*, suggested that it was Auden's 'Christian values which he had learned from his mother, as a child, and which he had never entirely abandoned' that allowed him to adapt more easily to life as an exile.[32] However this may be, it is clear that, like Isherwood, Auden sought in America to reinscribe his past within a different conceptual framework rather than simply to leave it behind. In their mutual concern for forms of Christian regeneration, there are clearly some similarities between the later works of Eliot and Auden, and the latter's poem 'Memorial for the City' carries an epigraph from Juliana of Norwich, the fourteenth-century mystic also quoted extensively by Eliot in 'Little Gidding'. Auden, however, always remained more sceptical than Eliot about the institutionalization of theological conceptions within the ideological state apparatus of the nation. In a 1966 essay, he said that as an Episcopalian he considered 'the adoption of Christianity as the official state religion, backed by the coercive powers of

---

[31] Barbara Everett, 'Auden Askew', *London Review of Books*, 19 Nov. 1981, 5.
[32] Isherwood, *My Guru and his Disciple*, 5.

the State, however desirable it may have seemed at the time, to have been a "bad," that is to say, an un-Christian thing'.[33] Such a forceful emphasis on disestablishment can be traced back to his writings of the 1940s, after his move to America: in a 1948 lecture at the University of Virginia on 'Poetry and Freedom', Auden stressed the function of art as a 'means of transforming closed communities into open ones', emphasized the significance of personal responsibility and the dangers of state censorship, and associated these principles of liberty with the Reformation, one of the 'four major revolutions' of the Christian era, which disseminated 'the assertion that every individual has a right to choose the society to which he is qualified to belong'. Auden went on to promulgate the continuing relevance of this doctrinal conflict to the modern era, claiming: 'Every time that the state assigns people to jobs, the Reformation is betrayed.'[34]

It is obvious enough how this commitment to an ideal of negative freedom can be seen as commensurate with the cold war culture of the United States, with its rejection of the spectre of totalitarian bureaucracy and its assumption, as Auden himself wrote in 1941, that a civilized society is 'one in which a common faith is combined with a skepticism about its finality'. What is unusual about Auden, though, is that he seeks the intellectual genealogy of this scepticism not in domestic versions of American philosophy such as pragmatism but in English metaphysical poetry. The restoration of a 'civilized social order', he writes in this same essay, involves a 'recognition in every field of intellectual and social activity of the importance of metaphysics', and his mature work is conducted in spirited dialogue with the secular ethos of American social science, looking back instead to the English Civil War and the Reformation as crucial sites for an understanding of American culture within a longer perspective of transatlantic history.[35] Rather than merely turning himself into an American pragmatist, Auden in America takes on the role of a cultural theologian seeking to reconstitute the secular strains of postwar history within a metaphysical framework. The second part of *The Age of Anxiety* takes its epigraph from George Herbert's poem 'Miserie'—'A sick toss'd vessel, dashing on each thing; / Nay, his own shelf: / My God, I mean myself'—and all of Auden's work in exile contains traces of this Protestant mysticism, being designed to regenerate an exhausted English tradition as well as to resituate American culture within a less dogmatically nationalistic framework (p. 357). The Luther depicted in *New Year Letter* as introducing 'a new *Anthropos*' (p. 184) consequently becomes for Auden a harbinger of transatlantic division, through whose aegis alternative Anglophone literary and intellectual traditions are mapped out.

---

[33] Auden, 'Heresies', in *Forewords and Afterwords*, ed. Edward Mendelson (London: Faber, 1973), 41.   [34] Auden, 'Poetry and Freedom', in *Prose*, ii. 493–5.
[35] Auden, 'A Note on Order', in *Prose*, ii. 101–3.

THE DOUBLE IMAGE: DENISE LEVERTOV

In 1942, Auden began writing religious commentaries for the Catholic magazine *Commonweal* under the soubriquet 'Didymus', the surname of the apostle Thomas who first doubted and then believed.[36] Didymus is also a significant figure for Denise Levertov, a poet born in Essex, England, in 1923 who married an American serviceman and emigrated to the United States in 1948. Her Russian father, a Hasidic Jew, had converted to Christianity while attending university in Germany, and he subsequently moved to England, establishing himself there as an Anglican parson. In her essay 'The Sense of Pilgrimage' (1967), Levertov wrote that the myth of a 'life-pilgrimage' had informed her poetry from the beginning, an idea she said was linked in her mind with John Bunyan, a strong influence from her own childhood reading, as well as with the various experiences of exile in her own family. Levertov discussed in this essay her early desire 'to become a world traveler, and discoverer, and explorer', and various tropes of traversal permeate her poetry: for example, the image of 'The Jacob's Ladder', which she uses as the title of a 1961 collection, is a metaphor borrowed from Hasidic literature signifying a means of access between earth and heaven, the human and the divine.[37] All of Levertov's poetry, in fact, revolves around questions of thresholds, borders, transpositions between different states of being. There is clearly an autobiographical aspect to this theme in terms of her own displacement to the United States after the Second World War, and in her 1967 poem 'Stepping Westward' she plays intertextually with Wordsworth's title by imitating his metaphors of transformation and renewal:

> What is green in me
> darkens, muscadine ...
>
> I fall
> in season and now
> is a time of ripening.[38]

Yet for Levertov, as for Auden, her personal exile becomes symptomatic of larger conceptual dislocations, particularly the movement between religious belief and agnosticism that becomes more prevalent in her later poetry. This is why, in 'Mass for the Day of St Thomas Didymus' (1982), she finds herself unable to encounter

---

[36] Osborne, *W. H. Auden*, 212.

[37] Denise Levertov, 'The Sense of Pilgrimage', in *The Poet in the World* (New York: New Directions, 1973), 64, 66.

[38] Denise Levertov, 'Stepping Westward', in *Poems, 1960–1967* (New York: New Directions, 1983), 165.

any state of radiant epiphany, and so is thrown back upon the doubter's familiar
Pascalian wager: 'O deep, remote unknown, / O deep unknown, / Have mercy
upon us.'[39]

Levertov was also influenced as a young woman in England by the work
of T. S. Eliot, with whom she corresponded briefly, though after her move
to America she found herself becoming increasingly unsympathetic to his
conservative critical ideas.[40] Nevertheless, like Eliot and Auden, Levertov was
much taken with the medieval visionary Juliana of Norwich, whom she cites in
her 1987 collection *Breathing the Water*, and her representation of transatlantic
displacement from the 1950s through until her death in 1997 involves similar
questions to those Eliot and Auden were asking about relationships between
artistic modernism and cultural reformation within a transnational context.
Levertov recalled how when she was growing up, 'people in England were really
very ignorant of American poetry', and her early work, culminating in her first
book *The Double Image* (1946), emerged from the intellectual framework of
English neo-Romanticism, spearheaded by David Gascoyne and Dylan Thomas,
that Levertov later explained as a deliberate reaction against the 'drabness and
grayness' of wartime England.[41] Gascoyne and Thomas specialized in verbal
hyperbole and in a luxuriant imagery driven by surreal dream worlds of desire,
and shades of this kind of conflict between the worlds of night and day, inner
fantasy and outer reality, pervade the doubled-up idiom of Levertov's early verse,
as in 'Durgan':

> ... looking
> into the pools as enigmatic eyes
> peer into mirrors, or music echoes
> out of a wood the waking dream of day,
> blind eyelids lifting to a coloured world.[42]

Given this vision of a private world protecting itself against a hostile external
environment, the landscapes of war tend to appear in *The Double Image*
only obliquely and phantasmagorially. In 'Christmas 1944', for example, the
narrator talks of lying awake and 'dreaming of Europe', where there is 'a plague
on many houses, fear knocking on the doors'. From the early 1930s, when
Hitler came to power, Levertov's family had been involved in helping Jewish

---

[39] Denise Levertov, 'Mass for the Day of St Thomas Didymus', in *Poems, 1972–1982* (New
York: New Directions, 2001), 267.

[40] Walter Sutton, 'Conversation with Denise Levertov', in *Denise Levertov: In Her Own Province*,
ed. Linda Welshimer Wagner (New York: New Directions, 1979), 40.

[41] William Packard, 'Interview with Denise Levertov', in *Denise Levertov*, 1; 'Denise Levertov,
interviewed by Sybil Estess', in *American Poetry Observed: Poets on Their Work*, ed. Joe David
Bellamy (Urbana, Ill.: University of Illinois Press, 1984), 157.

[42] Denise Levertov, 'Durgan', in *Collected Earlier Poems 1940–1960* (New York: New Directions,
1979), 21.

refugees from Germany and Austria; although her father had converted to Anglicanism, he still identified himself as 'a "Jewish" Christian' who 'emphasized the fact that Jesus and the disciples were Jews'. 'Christmas 1944' accordingly combines its evocation of an enclosed family circle with hints of malice and menace:

> Though we are safe
> in a flickering circle of winter festival
> we dare not laugh; or if we laugh, we lie,
> hearing hatred crackle in the coal,
> the voice of treason, the voice of love.[43]

This is the basis of the double image in Levertov's early English poetry: a responsiveness to shifting perspectives, an implicit awareness of worlds beyond the poet's purview which are glimpsed, if not fully embodied.

In a 1971 interview, Levertov said that if she had remained in England she probably 'would not have developed very far because it was not a good time for English poetry. It was really in the doldrums, and I think I might have found it stultifying.'[44] After her move in 1948, Levertov wholeheartedly embraced her new homeland and took American citizenship in 1956, though it was not until 1957 that her first collection of poems written in the United States, *Here and Now*, was published. The obvious thing to say about the American idiom developed by Levertov in the 1950s is that it is attracted by a metaphysics of presence, an idea of encompassing the world within its processes of flux and change. The philosophical influences on this radiant language are Emerson and Heidegger; the poetic influences are Charles Olson and the Black Mountain group and, especially, William Carlos Williams, to whom Levertov became a close friend during the final decade of his life. A poem such as 'Zest', from *Here and Now*, signals a radical simplification of Levertov's earlier neo-Romantic style, a movement away from staid iambics and an intense focus instead on attending to the physical world 'here and now', a concentration which is seen as the means towards renewal:

> DISPOSE YOUR ENERGIES
> PRACTISE ECONOMIES
> GO INDOORS, REFUSING
> TO ATTEND THE EVENING LANGUORS OF SPRING
>
> WORK BY A STRONG LIGHT
> SCOUR THE POTS
> DESTROY OLD LETTERS[45]

---

[43] Levertov, 'Christmas 1944', in *Collected Earlier Poems*, 25; Bellamy, ed., *American Poetry Observed*, 158.

[44] Packard, 'Interview with Denise Levertov', 8.

[45] Levertov, 'Zest', in *Collected Earlier Poems*, 40.

20. Denise Levertov in America, photographed by Dante Levi in 1962.

Paying tribute to Olson in a 1968 lecture, Levertov cited in particular his notion of how a human being 'fills his given space', and, as Kenneth Rexroth said in 1956, Levertov's American poems are 'alive to all the life of speech in the country' in a way that Auden's work never was. Auden, complained Rexroth, 'spent years in America and never learned to use a single phrase of American slang without sounding like a British music-hall Yank comic', whereas Levertov, with 'a kind of animal grace of the word', more readily assimilated American dialects.[46] This, of course, was also the basis for the profound influence on her work of Williams, who, she said in 1965, 'gave me the use of the American language. He showed me how it and the American idiom could be used'.[47] While Auden attempted consciously to fuse British formalism and the American vernacular into a hybrid transatlantic style, Levertov worked self-consciously to refashion herself as an American poet.

At the same time, Levertov's poetry always retains an element of strategic detachment from its American surroundings. Whereas Williams tried chauvinist-ically to insist on the dominance of 'the American idiom' in her work, Levertov herself preferred to emphasize her mixed, multicultural heritage. She tried to explain this dilemma to a recalcitrant Williams in a letter of 21 September 1960:

For me personally, I cannot put the idea of 'American idiom' *first* ... You must take into consideration that I grew up not in an American, and not in an *English*, but a *European* atmosphere; my father was naturalized in Eng. only around the time I was born—his background was Jewish, Russian, Central European—and my mother, herself proudly Welsh; had lived in Poland, Germany, and Denmark etc. all the years between 1910 & (?) 1923. And then, when I came to the U.S., I was already 24 years old—so tho' I was very impressionable, good melting-pot material, the American idiom is an acquired language for me. Certainly I am an American poet, if anything—I know I am not an English one ... but in speaking to Mitch or *to myself* my vocabulary is a mixture of different elements—more American than anything else but still not standard American so to speak ... [48]

In 'Alienation in Silicon Valley', one of the poems in her last collection, *This Great Unknowing* (1999), Levertov talks about being 'inside' the world 'but not at home' within it. Though this is not a landscape which is 'mine by right', such an awareness of alienation can turn into a positive faculty of perception: 'it's only by virtue of being outside those worlds / I can perceive them'. This poem cites de Tocqueville, the most famous chronicler of the United States from a perspective of outsiderhood, and Levertov here uses the Williams language of an 'American idiom' but refracts it through a consciousness of alienation—structural alienation, so to speak—so that the links forged between mind and landscape remain arbitrary rather than natural:

> I can cast
> on my mind's screen an orchard,

---

[46] Denise Levertov, 'Origins of a Poem', in *Poet in the World*, 51; Kenneth Rexroth, 'The Poetry of Denise Levertov', in *Denise Levertov: Selected Criticism*, ed. Albert Gelpi (Ann Arbor: University of Michigan Press, 1993), 13–14.   [47] Sutton, 'Conversation with Denise Levertov', 37.
[48] Levertov, *The Letters of Denise Levertov and William Carlos Williams*, ed. Christopher MacGowan (New York: New Directions, 1998), pp. viii, 99–100.

acres of orchards—but I never
touched their earth.[49]

This spectre of alienation serves to compromise the ideology of organicism expounded by Levertov in her most famous critical essay, 'Some Notes on Organic Form', published in 1965. 'For me', she wrote there, 'back of the idea of organic form is the concept that there is a form in all things (and in our experience) which the poet can discover and reveal.' This 'religious devotion to the truth, to the splendor of the authentic' is differentiated by her from the 'analogies, resemblances, natural allegories' which are the product of 'man's creative works' and which are validated by their proximity to this 'form beyond forms', in which the life of art partakes.[50] What increasingly happens in Levertov's later poetry, however, is that this confidence in organic form is supplanted by a reluctant recognition of how aesthetic analogies and resemblances have only a provisional purchase upon what is ultimately an unknowable world. Levertov said in 1971 that gradually she came to realize how her move to the United States and her assumption of an American poetic language had not involved such a 'dramatic break' as she first thought, and especially in her later work, she moves, as she put it, 'back and forth between English and American usage', with the organic form of the Olson tradition being hedged around by the kind of surrealist doubling and duplicity more characteristic of her first English poems. In the 1950s, during a period of enthusiastic American cultural nationalism, Levertov was widely hailed as an author who had seen the error of old European ways and reversed the trajectories of James, Eliot, and Pound by abandoning England for America. By the 1970s, though, Levertov was describing herself as 'genuinely of both places', and she had developed a more theoretically sophisticated conception of herself as a transnational poet.[51]

In 'Great Possessions', an essay from 1970, Levertov wrote of how 'banal poetry' is often associated with 'a fake surrealism', and how she was seeking something more akin to 'a supernatural poetry … a penetration by the imaginative faculty through to the meaning of appearances'. Nevertheless, her emphasis here on '*the artist as translator*', empowered not just to change one language into another but to modulate experience into other dimensions, strongly influences what Levertov called the 'magical' qualities of her own writing. James E. B. Breslin actually used the phrase 'a poetics of magical realism' to describe the appearance in Levertov's work of parallel worlds, mental universes, which become associated through a process of reflexive mirroring with the primal scenes of their origin.[52] In many of

[49] Denise Levertov, 'Alienation in Silicon Valley', in *This Great Unknowing: Last Poems* (Newcastle: Bloodaxe, 2001), 56.
[50] Levertov, 'Some Notes on Organic Form', in *Poet in the World*, 7, 13.
[51] Packard, 'Interview with Denise Levertov', 8–9.
[52] Levertov, 'Great Possessions', in *Poet in the World*, 98, 93, 95; James E. B. Breslin, *From Modern to Contemporary: American Poetry, 1945–1965* (Chicago: University of Chicago Press, 1984), 146.

her later poems about her native English county of Essex, in particular, Levertov invokes an image of the mind as a landscape within whose internal labyrinths trapdoors open between the present and the past. We see this for example in 'Olga Poems', written in memory of her sister:

> In Valentines
> a root protrudes from the greensward several yards from its tree
>
> we might raise like a trapdoor's handle, you said,
> and descend long steps to another country
>
> where we would live without father or mother
> and without longing for the upper world. *The birds*
> *sang sweet, O song, in the midst of the daye ....*

Levertov spoke later about how she found her diction becoming 'quite British' in this sequence of elegies for her sister, but the poems work themselves out within what is described here as a 'cavern of transformation', where the process of artistic metamorphosis is set within a framework of estrangement and loss.[53]

One of Levertov's relatively early poems about her childhood, 'A Map of the Western Part of the County of Essex in England' (1961), depicts the narrator puzzling over a geographical map as she attempts mentally to re-create the physical dimensions of her former home. In her subsequent work, though, Levertov often attempts to remap time rather than space, to portray the dimension of past history as a sedimented construct that might be extracted in dreams, as in the 1982 poem 'Winter Afternoons in the V.& A., pre-W.W.II':

> Here was history
> as I desired it: magical, specific,
> jumbled, unstinting,
>
> a world for the mind to sift
> in its hourglass—now, while I was twelve,
> or forever[54]

Again, as she recalls the Victoria and Albert Museum in London, there is an emphasis on the 'magical' transposition between past and present. What is evoked is not an American world bound together by the natural lineaments of organic form but a transnational circuit linked by the disjunctive juxtapositions of surrealism.

Levertov's poetic narratives thus create a series of parallel but separate worlds, just as in her last religious poems alternative dimensions of worldly matter and unknowable spirit are set alongside each other within a continuum whose

---

[53] Denise Levertov, 'Olga Poems', in *Poems, 1968–1972* (New York: New Directions, 1987), 115–17; Packard, 'Interview with Denise Levertov', 8.

[54] Levertov, 'Winter Afternoons in the V. & A., pre-W.W.II', in *Poems, 1972–1982*, 221.

points of intersection appear irregular and fragmentary. As Albert Gelpi has noted, the idea of seeing double, first broached in *The Double Image*, in fact pervades all of Levertov's work. Her 1960 collection is entitled *With Eyes at the Back of Our Heads*, and in 'Janus', a reminiscence from *Tesserae* (1995), Levertov recalls climbing over the brick wall of a seemingly enchanted garden and being disturbed to come across a tramp: 'a revelation of how intimately opposites live, their mysterious simultaneity, their knife-edge union: the Janus face of human experience'. In this same volume, she recalls as a child absconding and wandering through the streets of Clacton, an Essex seaside resort, without her absence being noticed, so that she 'witnessed, in conscious solitude, that magical transformation, *entre chien et loup*, which Magritte has evoked in certain paintings'.[55] The reference to Magritte exemplifies how there is in Levertov's later work a lingering spirit of surrealism, through which organic form is displaced into arbitrary forms of connection as the different shapes and habits of England and America are brought paradoxically into dialogue. This is a landscape of eerie transformation, as in a Magritte painting, where dreams and realities have become enigmatically interchangeable.

If her English legacy of surrealism tended to reconstitute the Black Mountain metaphysics of presence within a more ironic and reflexive setting, Olson's aesthetics of organic form also opened up a framework for Levertov, like Auden, to reconceptualize her experience of war within a less Manichaean framework. As we have seen, the Second World War marked an epochal event for Levertov not only in her encounters with the Jewish refugees assisted by her parents—Levertov later said that she 'knew what went on in concentration camps more than most people did until the war was over'—but also, indirectly, in the way it led to her own emigration.[56] As with Auden's exile, however, Levertov's move away from England enabled her to avoid the retrospective mythologies of good against evil, common decency against *uebermensch* utopianism, that impelled English literary culture towards a conservative rejection of modernist idealism after 1945. In her 1961 poem 'During the Eichmann Trial', Levertov subtly explores the interconnections between the Nazi criminal who had recently been recaptured and the more mundane postwar world:

> He had not looked,
> pitiful man whom none
>
> pity, whom all
> must pity if they look
> into their own face. ...

[55] Albert Gelpi, 'Introduction: Centering the Double Image', in *Denise Levertov*, ed. Gelpi, 3; Denise Levertov, *Tesserae: Memories and Suppositions* (Newcastle: Bloodaxe, 1997), 56, 37.
[56] Bellamy, ed., *American Poetry Observed*, 157.

With its epigraph from Robert Duncan—'When we look up / each from his being'—Levertov's poem reconceives Eichmann within a context of mutual interdependency where guilt becomes generalized rather than localized. The awful truth about Eichmann, suggests this poem, is precisely that it is impossible to demonize him, to eradicate a sense of common guilt by projecting evil on to another:

> He stands
> isolate in a bulletproof
> witness-stand of glass,
>
> a cage, where we may view
> ourselves, an apparition
>
> telling us something he
> does not know: we are members
>
> one of another.[57]

It is this principled refusal of polarity that also led Levertov to campaign vigorously against US involvement in the Vietnam War. In 'A Vision' (1967), she envisages two angels facing each other within a Neoplatonic circle of 'intellectual love':

> so that each angel was iridescent with the strange newly-seen
> hues he watched; and their discovering pause
> and the speech their silent interchange of perfection was
>
> never became a shrinking to opposites,
>
> and they remained free in the heavenly chasm,
> remained angels, but dreaming angels,
> each imbued with the mysteries of the other.

This might be described as Blakeian in its radical projection of apparent opposites as mutually dependent: 'Without Contraries', proclaimed Blake, 'is no progression.'[58] And just as Blake's visionary poem *America* sees the United States as Britain's counterpart rather than its nemesis, as we saw in Chapter 2, so Levertov refuses the dialectics of exclusion and represents wars of all kinds as based upon the collective repression of essential homogeneities and the false reification of political difference.

By seeking to reunite the idiom of postwar English poetry with the less insular spirit of American modernism, then, Levertov worked not only to transcend the local empiricism of British culture but also to reimagine its historical

---

[57] Denise Levertov, 'During the Eichmann Trial', in *Poems, 1960–1967*, 63, 65. Levertov's implicit critique here of the premises of exceptionalism anticipates the argument in Hannah Arendt's *Eichmann in Jerusalem*, published in 1963.

[58] Denise Levertov, 'A Vision', in *Poems, 1960–1967*, 224; William Blake, *The Marriage of Heaven and Hell*, in *Complete Poems*, 181.

burdens within a more expansive metaphysical circumference. Levertov's Vietnam poetry was widely criticized by American scholars such as Charles Altieri, who complained about its 'loose propagandistic phrases' and its tendency to oversimplify complicated political situations by representing evil as a mere 'privation' of good.[59] What is especially provocative about this work, however, is not simply its anti-war viewpoint but its concern to place the United States in relation to a wider world without insisting upon an antithetical polarity between home and abroad. In this sense, the intuitive assimilation of analogies and resemblances across a transnational field becomes, for Levertov, a means not only of critiquing the old ghosts of American exceptionalism but also of repositioning American literature as a global rather than a purely domestic concern. By explicitly opposing US military involvement overseas, Levertov was implicitly commenting on a broader American cultural willingness to partition the world in Manichaean terms, to impose categorical divisions between the values of the United States and those of other nations. In this way, despite its creative appropriations of the Olson tradition, her work also succeeds in breaking out of the charmed circle of American cultural Transcendentalism, where the metaphysics of presence is deployed to celebrate local circumstances.

A GATHERED CHURCH: DONALD DAVIE

The alternative, transatlantic tradition of English modernist poetry promoted by Auden was carried through in curmudgeonly fashion during the latter part of the twentieth century by Donald Davie, whose work, like that of Auden, was crucially scarred by the legacy of fascism. Davie came from the same generation of English writers as Levertov, having been born one year before her in 1922, though his exile to the United States took place at a relatively later stage of his career: he left the University of Essex in 1968 to work at Stanford and then, from 1978, at Vanderbilt, returning permanently in 1988 to England, where he died in 1995. Davie's early English writing is, like Levertov's, heavily shadowed by memories of the Second World War, during which he saw five years' active service in the navy. Along with other poets in Britain involved with the 'Movement', Davie turned in the decade after the war to pointedly anti-romantic attitudes, associating an ethic of rational control and demystification with a rejection of the more grandiose, self-indulgent designs of modernist fantasy:

> If too much daring brought (he thought) the war,
> When that was over nothing else would serve

[59] Charles Altieri, *Enlarging the Temple: New Directions in American Poetry during the 1960s* (Lewisburg, Pa.: Bucknell University Press, 1979), 234–5.

But no one must be daring any more,
A self-induced and stubborn loss of nerve.

('Creon's Mouse' (1955))[60]

Objecting to the poetics of symbolism which, like fascism, seemed to offer too much scope for an evasion of personal responsibility, Davie campaigned for a postwar 'poetry of decency' which would consciously exclude the uglier aspects of the irrational. This led him, as Blake Morrison has argued, towards a deliberate forgetfulness, an implicit belief that to represent the effects of fascism directly would be somehow to diminish or domesticate their traumatic force: 'horrors named make exorcisms fail', Davie declares in 'Eight Years After' (p. 36), written in 1955.[61] Such a strategy of evasion led to most of Davie's writing about fascism in the 1950s approaching its subject by an indirect, circuitous route, as in his critical work *Purity of Diction in English Verse* (1952), where he argues for a conceptual link between the fractured syntax of modernism and a fascist politics of power and spectacle:

[Ezra Pound] pins his faith on individual words, grunts, broken phrases, half-uttered exclamations (as we find them in the Cantos), on speech atomized, all syllogistic and syntactical forms broken down. Hence his own esteem of the definite lands him at last in yawning vagueness, the 'intuitive' welcome to Mussolini ...

It would be too much to say that this is the logical end of abandoning prose syntax. But at least the development from imagism in poetry to fascism in politics is clear and unbroken.[62]

Davie's attitude towards Pound changed fundamentally, however, in the late 1950s. Returning to England after spending the academic year 1957–8 teaching at the University of California, Santa Barbara, Davie became more enthusiastic about the virtues of literary modernism, positively reappraising the hard-edged qualities of Pound's art in *Ezra Pound: Poet as Sculptor* (1964) and subsequently writing of Pound as a necessary bulwark against what he called, quoting Auden, the 'suffocating insular coziness' of England. Though Davie admits in 1991 that he had 'as often been exasperated by Pound as exalted and delighted by him', he nevertheless admires Pound's resistance to British 'tolerance of the amateurish' and he complains of how British academia tended to be unduly obsessed with Pound's fascism, thereby imprisoning his work in an 'ideological straitjacket'.[63] In his 1973 book *Thomas Hardy and British Poetry*, in which he argues that the limited provincial objectives of Hardy have, 'for good and

[60] Donald Davie, *Collected Poems*, ed. Neil Powell (Manchester: Carcanet, 2002), 17. All subsequent page references to Davie's poems are taken from this edition and are cited in parentheses in the text.

[61] Chris Miller, 'The Pope and the Canon: Eliot, Johnson, Davie and the Movement', *PN Review*, 23/6 (July–Aug. 1997), 49; Morrison, *The Movement*, 88–9.

[62] Donald Davie, *Purity of Diction in English Verse* (London: Routledge & Kegan Paul, 1967), 99.

[63] Donald Davie, *Studies in Ezra Pound* (Manchester: Carcanet, 1991), 269, 7, 227, 365.

ill', influenced the trajectory of twentieth-century British poetry more than the development of international modernism, Davie similarly suggests that Pound was attracted not by thin, nostalgic sentimentality but by 'a liking and a need for the rigid, for what he calls "the hard" '. This hardness is linked here with Pound's 'authoritarian politics', which is understood implicitly as an analogue to Davie's own increasingly reactionary politics in his later years.[64]

Whereas Davie's poetry of the 1950s is suspicious of modernism, then, his work in the 1960s attempts more constructively to reintegrate it within the dynamics of English literature and culture. 'Barnsley and District' (1961), which revisits his own hometown landscape, ruminates uneasily on how little this scene has changed, while considering simultaneously how it might have altered had the outcome of the war been different:

> Judy Sugden! Judy, I made you caper
> With rage when I said that the British Fascist
> Sheet your father sold was a jolly good paper
>
> And you agreed and I said, Yes, it holds
> Vinegar, and everyone laughed...
>
> If your father's friends had succeeded, or if I
> Had canvassed harder for the Peace Pledge Union
> A world of difference might have leapt to the eye
>
> In a scene like this which shows in fact no change.
> That must have been the summer of '39.
>
> (p. 156)

In a discussion of this poem, Robert von Hallberg suggested how Davie's perception of Barnsley remaining unchanged over a quarter of a century furnishes an 'optimistic' view of human history, the notion that all ideological disputes will naturally pass in time.[65] But this is, I think, too emollient a reading; the poem ends with a sense of inertia, of mere habit and custom proving more durable than political ideas, so that the longevity of this childhood environment appears to undermine any prospect of radical transformation:

> And politics has no landscape. The Silesian
> Seam crops out in prospects felt as deeply
> As any of these, with as much or as little reason.
>
> (p. 157)

In his book on Hardy, Davie says that the Nazis are our experience 'of what a right-wing alternative to parliamentary democracy is like', so that 'the shabby

[64] Donald Davie, *Thomas Hardy and British Poetry* (London: Routledge & Kegan Paul, 1973), 3, 174.
[65] Robert von Hallberg, 'Donald Davie and the Moral Shape of Politics', in *Donald Davie and the Responsibilities of Literature*, ed. George Dekker (Manchester: Carcanet, 1983), 90.

second-best we have is indeed unavoidably our choice, the alternative having turned out so much worse'.[66] Nevertheless, there is a note of regret both here and in 'Barnsley and District' at the apparent failure of modernist ideals to embody themselves successfully within the world and a consequent sense of frustration and disappointment at the need to acquiesce in a culture of the 'shabby second-best'.

In his critical writings after 1960, especially, Davie appears to take the values of close reading for granted and to regard literary modernism itself as a *donnée*. Although he assiduously investigates the relationships between literary modernism and wider cultural concerns—the other arts, the social and political implications of poetry, and so on—he always does so from a position where textual analysis is paramount, with other concerns following on from that. Modernism's emphasis on the formal autonomy of the well-wrought urn becomes in this sense Davie's intellectual home, his secure castle, which is why he came down so hard on the theory of postmodernism which attempted radically to interrogate the whole process of formalist separatism and canon formation. Shortly before his death in 1995, Davie attacked Terry Eagleton's inaugural lecture at Oxford for denying truth value to poetry, calling it 'a present danger, to any of us who care about "Value and Heritage"'.[67] For similar reasons, he always had trouble with T. S. Eliot's poetry, lambasting 'The Dry Salvages' in 1956 as 'simply *rather a bad poem*', with 'stumbling trundling rhythms' and 'reach-me-down phrases', and complaining again in 1991 about the 'fissures' in *Four Quartets*, a poem he consequently regarded as not the 'monumental edifice that some of Eliot's adulators pretend'.[68] *Four Quartets* does indeed contain many kinds of 'fissures'—stylistic oscillations between heightened symbolist and colloquial verse, for instance—but this testifies to Eliot's conscious effort to embrace diversity, to weave together high and low cultures into the fabric of a unified national consciousness. Such integration is something towards which the sharp dissentient voice of Davie was consistently antipathetic. Whereas Eliot was always trying to heal the civil war, Davie was more interested in opening it up again; his concern was to propagate a reformist zeal capable of regenerating what he saw as the flaccid conditions of English literature and culture.

Rather than looking back to the Civil War of the seventeenth century, though, Davie returned constantly to the eighteenth century as the locus of an alternative cultural heritage. In his 1976 Clark Lectures at Cambridge, he argued that Marxist historians such as Christopher Hill had attributed disproportionate kudos to John Bunyan and other proselytizers for the short-lived Cromwellian

---

[66] Davie, *Thomas Hardy and British Poetry*, 74.

[67] Donald Davie, 'The Canon, Values and Heritage', *PN Review*, 21/5 (May–June 1995), 13–14.

[68] Donald Davie, 'T. S. Eliot: The End of an Era', in *The Poet in the Imaginary Museum: Essays of Two Decades*, ed. Barry Alpert (Manchester: Carcanet, 1977), 32–4; *idem*, ' "The Dry Salvages": A Reconsideration', *PN Review*, 17/5 (May–June 1991), 25.

republic. Instead, he proposed that a more valuable intellectual heritage of dissent could be traced back to the loyalist traditions of the eighteenth century, with their rationalist emphasis on 'measure', 'exclusion', 'simplicity (hard-earned)', and 'sobriety'.[69] Davie's interest in neoclassical aesthetics goes back to his early poems in strict iambic pentameters: in 'Homage to William Cowper' he describes himself as 'A pasticheur of late-Augustan styles' (p. 8), and much of his work over the following decades sets an equivalent sense of order and measure against the disorder that, in his eyes, threatens to overwhelm his native country. Being what Bernard Bergonzi describes as 'emphatically a moralist, imbued with the rigorous spirit of the Cambridge English school of the forties and fifties', Davie abhorred what he perceived as the licentious climate of the 1960s—for him, 'a terrible decade in British culture'. He expressed an equal loathing for the 'squalid tastelessness' of the Profumo affair and other sexual scandals in the political world, as well as for the lack of respect for old codes of practice among students on British university campuses; indeed, the latter caused him such grief as a senior administrator at the University of Essex that he decided to ship out to Stanford in 1968.[70] The late 1960s have been described by Andrew Shelley as an 'equivalent' for Davie to the time 'of Eliot's Civil War and the ensuing dissociation of sensibility', another period in English history when the nation was divided by what its protagonists took to be systematic splits between apparently irreconcilable factions.[71]

Many of Davie's most acerbic critiques of England appeared after his move to California. Even when he was working in the States, he kept a house in England, where he spent between three and six months every year; and, as his former colleague at Essex and Stanford George Dekker noted, Davie tended to keep aloof from American politics and to focus most of his rebarbative energy upon the state of England.[72] *The Shires*, a collection of poems published in 1974, offers an ironic bird's-eye view of each English county, while *Thomas Hardy and British Poetry*, published the previous year, lurches at times into a manic Leavisite jeremiad, complaining of how in Britain 'virtually all the sanctuaries have been violated, all the pieties blasphemed', so that even 'the bread we eat—chemically blanched, ready-sliced, untouched by human hand—bears no perceivable relation to the wheat-ear'. This is an angry, almost deliberately unbalanced book which uses a hectoring tone of outrage to unsettle what it takes to be the moribund state of British culture: thus, 'the distinguishing mark of the British Left' is its 'readiness to opt in the last resort for solidarity at all costs', while 'moral fastidiousness' certainly finds 'no home in the British Conservative

[69] Davie, *Essays in Dissent*, 23.

[70] Bernard Bergonzi, 'Davie, Larkin, and the State of England', *Contemporary Literature*, 18 (1977), 346; Nicolas Tredell, 'In Conversation with Donald Davie', *PN Review*, 19/2 (Nov.-Dec. 1992), 67; Davie, *Thomas Hardy and British Poetry*, 71.

[71] Andrew Shelley, 'Donald Davie and the Canon', *Essays in Criticism*, 42 (1992), 16.

[72] George Dekker, introduction, in *Donald Davie and the Responsibilities of Literature*, 2.

Party', so that those seeking such distinction 'must look further to the Right'. Davie cites the example of D. H. Lawrence as a justification for this position, and in fact Davie's whole political stance here becomes reminiscent of the organicist movements in the early 1930s, a parallel reinforced by his invocation of J. R. R. Tolkien's medievalist fantasy *Lord of the Rings* as 'one of the most serious' products of English literature since 1945, a 'parable' about the systematic failure of 'authority in public matters', a warning of how power should always be 'resisted and refused by anyone who wants to live humanely'.[73] In this context, it is not difficult to see why Labour government minister Jon Silkin should have described Davie's attitudes to socialism in 1978 as 'hostile to the point of sadistic hysteria', nor indeed why *PN Review*, the journal co-edited by Davie during the 1980s, was sometimes described as being controlled by 'proto-fascists and anti-semites'.[74]

Davie's spirit of reaction, however, was dictated less by any specific political programme than by what comes through in his writing as a bewildered sense of loss, the seemingly incomprehensible lack of interest on the part of the common world in any idea of moral transformation. In 'Revulsion' (1968), he acknowledges that 'My strongest feeling all / My life has been, / I recognize, revulsion / From the obscene' (p. 204); and the poems of this era collected in *Essex Poems* (1969) chronicle scenes of desolation, depicting a brutally material world from which any promise of poetic or political regeneration appears to have been evacuated:

> Landscapes of supertax
> Record a deathful failure
> As clearly as the lack
> Of a grand or expansively human
> Scale to the buildings of Ilford.
>
> The scale of that deprivation
> Goes down in no statistics.

('Thanks to Industrial Essex' (1969); p. 188)

Davie's critical work of this time similarly indicts English letters for their parochialism and complacency, sounding the familiar refrain that the cultural establishment is too willing to champion the 'suburban' poetic perspectives of Hardy and Larkin rather than engage with the modernist complexities of Charles Tomlinson and J. H. Prynne. Larkin's *Oxford Book of Twentieth-Century English Verse* is roundly accused of 'cynicism', of shirking its 'responsibilities quite shamefully' in its supposedly philistine refusal to make serious 'critical discrimination among poems'. This is akin to Davie's earlier dismissal of Eliot's

---

[73] Davie, *Thomas Hardy and British Poetry*, 70–3, 94.
[74] Jon Silkin, 'Which England Shall We Labour For? A Reply to Donald Davie's Conservative England', *Parnassus: Poetry in Review*, 7/1 (1978), 283; Donald Davie, editorial, *PN Review*, 9/2 (1982), 1.

Old Possum's Book of Practical Cats as a 'collection of whimsical fireside charades in verse', pandering to the typically English notion of poetry as a 'superior parlour game', and also to his rebuke of Auden for the way in which he 'generalizes about English life too much on the basis of his own late-Edwardian childhood in a comfortable rentier household'.[75]

This indictment of Auden in class terms is particularly significant because Davie's view of England after 1960 can be seen as a highly sectarian affair, where the social and religious heritage of Dissent is locked into, and becomes commensurate with, the political imperative of Augustan rationalism and moral order. The lower-class culture of Dissent, in other words, becomes a patriotic imperative which stands as an intellectual rebuke to the complacent Anglican ruling classes. His poems pursue the same agenda by extolling eighteenth-century figures such as Edmund Burke, George Crabbe, and, in 'Homage to George Whitefield', the preacher born in Gloucester who became a central figure in the Connecticut River Valley during the 'Great Awakening' of the 1730s and 1740s. Davie also wrote in 'Summer Lightning' (1982) of how 'I fear God, fear the Crown, the Law' (p. 429); and it was this respect for traditional conservative values that led him in 1992 to nominate Samuel Johnson as the epitome of the 'responsible eighteenth-century critic'. Such respect for the rule of law also manifests itself in 'Reminded of Bougainville' (1990), which links the 'brave' enterprise of the 1982 Falklands War with memories of the Second World War (p. 492). Davie recorded around this time how he had sympathized initially with the bellicose political outlook of Margaret Thatcher, who came to power in 1979, although his enthusiasm cooled when he saw the 'highly selective' manner in which she exercised her authority.[76]

Davie's intellectual engagement with, and twenty-year exile in, America acted as a counterpoint to these frustrations with Britain in several ways. Davie had been introduced to Ed Dorn by J. H. Prynne during his days in Cambridge, and the Black Mountain aesthetics represented by Dorn, Olson, and others helped make him not only more sympathetic to the legacy of Poundian modernism but also more responsive to what Olson recognized as the prime differentiating category of American culture, that of space. 'Space', Davie reiterated in 1992, 'is the first thing about America that strikes anybody from Europe ... The entire ratio between the human being and the non-human creation is totally different from Europe, and this is both frightening and extraordinarily exhilarating.'[77] Davie asserted in 1970 that one of the reasons why English poetry of this time seemed 'impoverished' was that 'it cannot respond to poetry such as his [Dorn's] and Olson's', though one way in which his own poetry negotiated these vast spatial vectors, particularly around the time of his own emigration, was through a

[75] Davie, *Thomas Hardy and British Poetry*, 75; *idem*, 'Larkin's Choice', *Listener*, 29 March 1973, 421; *idem*, *Studies in Ezra Pound*, 264–5.
[76] Tredell, 'In Conversation with Donald Davie', 65, 68.   [77] Ibid. 69–70.

21. Donald Davie with Janet Lewis (Mrs Yvor Winters) in the orchard next to her house in Los Altos, California, 1978.

renewed interest in the British explorers of previous centuries who had sought to map out North American territories.[78] Thus, 'Vancouver', written in California, focuses upon the anti-heroic figure of George Vancouver, 'Weird revenant to North Pacific air' (p. 245), who explored the coast of the Pacific Northwest in the wake of Captain Cook and who gave his name to the present-day Canadian city, while 'England', from the same period, aligns the 'eleven hours flying time' between twentieth-century London and California with the similar terrestrial arcs plotted by navigators of earlier eras (p. 216). The second section of the latter poem considers the involvement of Sir George Simpson in the Hudson's Bay Company, and this suggests Davie's recognition of a continuity between himself and nineteenth-century British adventurers, who, as we saw in Chapter 3, were keen to appropriate the Pacific Northwest as part of a British imperial heritage. Like George Ruxton, indeed, Davie perceives the loss of these Western territories as fatal to the long-term interests of British culture, as he plays off in the mind the 'superannuated' gestures of the 'impeccably evenly-toned / social comedies' coming out of England (p. 225) against the 'breakthrough into spaciousness' which he seeks (p. 298). In 'Seeing Her Leave', a poem about his

---

[78] Davie, 'The Black Mountain Poets: Charles Olson and Edward Dorn', in *Poet in the Imaginary Museum*, 190.

own daughter's flight back to England, Davie contrasts 'the civic, the moralistic' codes of London with the pristine pastoral splendours of California: 'The bare / Beaches, the stony creek / That no human affair / Has soiled' (p. 331). It is noticeable here that the poet does not seek simply to reproduce an idiom of organic form in the manner of the American Black Mountain poets; instead, he retains a deliberate duality of perspective, approaching this condition of organicism through a ratiocinating measure, like those old British explorers who sought to impose at least a hypothetical order on the currents of the Pacific Northwest through their elaborate systems of cartography.

One corollary of this reconsideration of British involvement with America is its restoration of a missing historical dimension to the landscapes of the United States which have tended to be represented within typologies of the atemporal, allegorical, or prophetic. If 'diluted Marxism' has been characteristic of recent British intellectual culture, he argues in *Thomas Hardy and British Poetry*, so a 'diluted Freudianism has been characteristic of America', resulting in an obsession with identity politics, with depicting the other as a mere projection of the self, a move which has tended to exclude more amorphous and variegated historical perspectives.[79] Davie's own interest in American culture, as in British culture, tended towards the eighteenth rather than the nineteenth century: with its emphasis on latitudes and longitudes and its attention to the specific characteristics of various American geographical regions, Davie's America is positioned on a curved rather than a flat earth, with Cook, Vancouver, and his other explorers locating America spatially and culturally within an imaginary eighteenth century which becomes, as Howard Erskine-Hill observed, 'the medium for a modern internationalism'.[80] Davie admired eighteenth-century America because it concerned itself with the country's position in relation to the rest of the world, and he was correspondingly wary of nineteenth-century American culture, with its emphasis on national independence and self-reliance. In a 1980 lecture, 'American Literature: The Canon', Davie argued that our modern assumptions about the shape of American literature derive too unquestioningly from Blake, with his prophetic vision of America as a sign of apocalyptic renewal: 'whether we know it or not,' said Davie, 'we approach literature with Romantic assumptions and Romantic expectations.' Instead, he called for a study of American literature which paid attention to history as well as genre, substituting for the perennial emphasis on originality of expression more attention to work by earlier writers such as John Fiske, Cotton Mather, and Edward Taylor, writers who cannot easily be brought into alignment with the dominant critical trajectory of romanticism. Davie criticized scholars of nineteenth-century American literature in particular for disregarding

[79] Davie, *Thomas Hardy and British Poetry*, 186.
[80] Howard Erskine-Hill, 'Two Hundred Years Since: Davie, the Eighteenth Century and the Image of England', in *Donald Davie and the Responsibilities of Literature*, ed. Dekker, 116.

historiography and political oratory as valid literary genres; he pointed not only to Washington Irving but also to George Bancroft, John Lothrop Motley, William Hickling Prescott, and Francis Parkman, asking: 'If Gibbon and Macaulay are glories of English literature, are not Prescott and Parkman among the glories of the American?'[81]

Clearly, there is a self-consciously transatlantic dimension to this argument. By seeking to reunite the teleology of American literature with writers who flourished in North America before the War of Independence, Davie seeks to redefine the subject as something more than a narrowly nationalistic phenomenon. He also makes the case here for the importance of narratives emerging from the Hudson's Bay Company, citing in particular *Adventures of the First Settlers on the Oregon or Columbia River*, published in 1849 by Alexander Ross, who had emigrated from Scotland to North America in 1805. At the same time, he explicitly disagrees with the view that the shared language makes cultural differentiations between English and American national identities redundant: he argues that it is impossible for literature to be 'quite unaffected by the political and social and physical dimensions of the regions where it is produced and responded to', and in this sense he agrees with Eliot's view that the English and American traditions represent 'two literatures in the same language'.[82] As with Eliot, the sense of duality and friction is important; in one of his late poems, 'Meteorologist, September', Davie observes that events such as the American Revolution are not the seamless, triumphal events that retrospective mythologies have often made them out to be:

> The year goes round,
> yes, but with what ructions!
> The violence of the turns!
> Why else are Revolutions always bloody
> except that seasonal change is the type of them,
> calamitous though foreseen? ...
> God does not make His changes
> without some pother.
>
> (p. 443)

Such scenes of conflict imply one of the main attractions of America so far as Davie is concerned, the way it introduces elements of violence and contradiction into sheltered, restrictive cultural forms. In his *Sequence for Francis Parkman* (1961), Davie shows nineteenth-century western pioneers becoming lost amidst the unmapped territories along the Des Moines River; chronicling the disjunctions between theory and fact, place name and natural object, he evokes the bracing sense of dispossession that goes with this movement into

---

[81] Donald Davie, 'American Literature: The Canon', in *Two Ways Out of Whitman: American Essays* (Manchester: Carcanet, 2000), 11, 7–8.

[82] Ibid. 2; Eliot, 'American Literature and the American Language', 51.

uncharted territory. In a poem dedicated to another British exile, 'To Thom Gunn in Los Altos, California' (1977), Davie similarly praises Gunn for his refusal to be confined intellectually within this 'Garden of Eden', the manner in which he seeks instead to explore every frontier and transgress against every given boundary:

> Conquistador! Live dangerously, my Byron,
> In this metropolis
> Of Finistère. Drop off
> The edge repeatedly, and come
> Back to tell us!

(p. 346)

The invocation here of Byron, patron saint of the English transnational poetic tradition, is telling. Davie, however, is fascinated by Gunn's example partly because of the threat it appears to pose to his own more traditional poetics:

> What are we doing here?
> What am I doing, I who am scared of edges?

(p. 347)

From this point of view, the authority and authenticity of Davie's American poetry derive precisely from the way it turns back upon itself, the way it undermines its own rationalist premises. America consequently emerges in Davie's work as a site of illuminating contradiction, a milieu in which conventional structures are splintered apart, irradiated by an enigmatic light that cannot ultimately be confined to worldly categories. In 'Or, Solitude', written as a coda to *Essex Poems* just before he left for Stanford, Davie imagines American landscapes of 'Iowan snows' or 'Out West' and associates them with a 'metaphysicality' which he feels has been lacking within his more materialistic English milieu:

> The metaphysicality
> Of poetry, how I need it!
> And yet it was for years
> What I refused to credit.

(p. 199)

As Gareth Reeves has observed, it is noticeable how frequently 'the word "metaphysical" crops up in the poetry, often in an American context'.[83] The sense of dispossession that Davie associates with America becomes, in other words, a parallel to a Christian ethic of dematerialization, through whose auspices his poetry aspires towards an incomprehensible world of spirit.

---

[83] Gareth Reeves, 'Beyond the New World: Donald Davie's Anglo-American Confessions', *PN Review*, 25/3 (Jan–Feb. 1999), 55.

The method here is not unlike that of Davie's transatlantic forerunner, the seventeenth-century exile from Leicestershire, Edward Taylor, to whose metaphysical style Davie pays tribute in 'Having No Ear' (1982):

> Having no ear, I hear
> And do not hear the piano-tuner ping,
> Ping, ping one string beneath me here, where I
> Ping-ping one string of Caroline English to
> Tell if Edward Taylor tells
> The truth, or no.

(p. 407)

Just as Taylor's poems self-consciously deploy bizarre metaphors to evoke the insuperable disjunctions between human and divine epistemologies—describing the universe as a 'Bowling Alley' in *God's Determinations*: 'Who in this Bowling Alley bowld the sun?'—so Davie here uses his own unreceptiveness to music to indicate the way in which Taylor's verse is attuned not to harmony but to truth.[84] Indeed, the ugly repetitions in this poem—'Ping-ping', and so on—seem to suggest a harsh aesthetic mode where euphony itself has become a seductive, misleading form. This emphasis on aesthetic disjunction is taken to a further extreme in Davie's 1988 collection *To Scorch or Freeze*, a rewriting of biblical psalms which, in the manner of Taylor, scathingly castigates the presumptions of anthropomorphism and the frivolities of metaphorical analogy:

> To justify God's ways to man
> like Eliphaz the Temanite
> is a presumptuous folly;
> it cannot be done.

('Just You Wait!'; p. 456)

Davie chooses here to experiment with a radical breach between the conventional notion of psalms as mellifluous artefacts and the rough, colloquial reality which his concentration upon their theological content addresses. The title of the poem 'Their Rectitude Their Beauty' indicates clearly enough how Davie conceives the integrity of these works to lie in their inner meaning, not in their formal surfaces (p. 450). *To Scorch or Freeze* is, as Jeremy Hooker noted, a curious mixture of religious language and slangy colloquialism, and it may not be coincidental that Davie wrote most of these poems in the Bible Belt, shortly before his return to England from Tennessee.[85] In 'The Garden of the Savoy' (1990), he finds it apposite to be 'fetching up here, in the tetchy unreconciled / South' (p. 528); and Davie's last American poems are set within a landscape of rupture, riven by

---

[84] Edward Taylor, *The Poems of Edward Taylor*, ed. Donald E. Stanford (New Haven: Yale University Press, 1960), 387.
[85] Jeremy Hooker, 'Donald Davie's "Poems about the Sacred"', *PN Review*, 19/2 (Nov.–Dec. 1992), 34.

fracture and division, whose very irreconcilability provides the impetus for the poet's fretful metaphysical scrutinies.

Davie, then, looks to America in order to recover an intellectual tradition of Dissent which he sees as having been effectively written out of English culture by the nation's Anglican hegemony. Born a Baptist in Yorkshire, Davie lost his religious faith altogether in his early twenties, but in 1969, while at Stanford, he began attending Episcopalian services in Los Altos Hills, and, following in the footsteps of Auden thirty-two years earlier, was duly baptized into the American Episcopalian Church in 1972. Davie claimed, however, that the one religious doctrine he always held to, even during his years of unbelief, was that of man's innate depravity and Original Sin, and it could justly be said of him, as of Eliot, that his work attends as much to the cultural as to the metaphysical implications of Christian traditions.[86] His 1976 Clark Lectures, published as *A Gathered Church*—taking its title from the idea of a community gathered from the world but in tension with it—forcefully repudiates the popular *canard*, fostered by the Church of England and by the High Anglican sensibility of Matthew Arnold, which systematically linked Dissent to an ugly philistinism. On the contrary, Davie stresses the 'multivocal' sensibility apparent in the paradoxical verses of the eighteenth-century writer Isaac Watts, whose intellectual strictness and sense of himself as an internal émigré are compared to those of Edward Taylor.[87] Davie also features Watts prominently in his *New Oxford Book of Christian Verse* (1981), where he chastises the 'elitism' of previous Oxford editors such as Lord David Cecil in excluding hymns from the literary canon and argues that Watts's texts work both as hymns and as poems in the way they translate theological rigour into a plain style accessible to large numbers of people. Davie chooses to exalt here 'a language stripped of fripperies and seductive indulgences', preferring instead 'the most direct and unswerving English'; besides Watts, the authors most heavily represented in this anthology include George Herbert, Charles Wesley, Christopher Smart, and William Cowper. As a work of reparation, this collection is fascinating, though it is hardly unbiased or ideologically neutral; in particular, the way in which Davie dismisses the concept of ambiguity as 'unseemly' and gives short shrift to Catholic poets such as John Donne and Gerard Manley Hopkins suggests a cultural hostility grounded upon theological differences of which he can hardly have been unaware.[88] In an example of his self-consciousness about ways in which religious and literary judgements are knitted together, Davie's critical work *The Eighteenth-Century Hymn in England* (1993) claims that the greatness of Dryden's poetry has too often

---

[86] Gregory A. Schirmer, ' "This That I Am Heir To": Donald Davie and Religion', in *Donald Davie and the Responsibilities of Literature*, ed. Dekker, 129, 138.

[87] Davie, *Essays in Dissent*, 47, 64–7, 74; Gareth Reeves, 'Hearing Davie', *PN Review*, 19/2 (Nov.–Dec. 1992), 49.

[88] Donald Davie, ed., *The New Oxford Book of Christian Verse* (Oxford: Oxford University Press, 1981), pp. xx, xxiv.

been 'obscured for many readers because he characteristically (not universally) pitches his tone of address too high for their comfort'; but, again, Davie's own preferred focus in this book is not on the 'high' but the 'plain style', as epitomized by the work of William Cowper. In Cowper, Davie finds the Church's 'doctrines lock together in an intellectual structure' without resorting to the flashy transubstantiations of Catholic wordplay or the idiosyncratic systems of Blakeian prophecy.[89]

Davie, then, revises Eliot's Anglican attempt to bind together the two halves of English culture sundered through civil war. Whereas Eliot journeyed eastwards, both literally and metaphorically, Davie's journey was westwards, as he sought to imitate the seventeenth-century Pilgrim Fathers by regenerating his native culture through the infusion of a rigorous dissenting spirit. He accordingly begins 'Wild Boar Clough' (1981) by deliberately parodying Eliot's *Four Quartets*:

> A poet's lie!
>   The boarhound and the boar
> Do not pursue their pattern as before…
> Extinct, the English boar; he leaves a lack.
> Hearts of the disinherited grow black.
>
>   (p. 368)

Eliot had written in 'Burnt Norton' of how 'the boarhound and the boar / Pursue their pattern as before/But reconciled among the stars' (p. 172). But for Davie there can be within his native culture no ultimate reconciliation or apostolic inheritance; instead, he illuminates what he sees as the continuing sources of antagonism between Establishment quietism and Reformation rupture. Despite his antipathy towards Eliot's outlook, both literary and social, Davie acknowledged in 1974 that 'Eliot has been a presence in my life more insistently influential than any other writer whatever'. Although Davie found this discovery of kinship 'surprising', the overt antagonism clearly bespeaks a sense of intertwinement: he and Eliot were, in many ways, alter egos, poet-critics who were attempting to bring the English literary tradition into alignment with their own sense of the country's authentic theological tradition.[90] America functions as a focal point for both writers: Eliot leaves the United States but translates its populist dimensions into his revisionist version of English hierarchical culture, while Davie exiles himself from England but seeks to relocate his version of its literary culture within a transatlantic context.

Like Auden and Levertov, and indeed like Wodehouse and Isherwood, Eliot and Davie were also deeply troubled throughout their work by the Second World War. This disturbance was related as much to the anti-modernist reactions

---

[89] Donald Davie, *The Eighteenth-Century Hymn in England* (Cambridge: Cambridge University Press, 1993), 31, 137, 157.   [90] Reeves, 'Beyond the New World', 56.

disseminated in Britain after 1945 as to the wartime events themselves. Many of these English authors who sought refuge in the United States were widely accused in their native land of betrayal, but their own sense of discomfort with, and eventual dissociation from, British culture arose from a recognition of how it had been forced by the political circumstances of the time to become fascism's antithesis: anti-utopian, anti-organicist, keen to enforce an ultimately repressive notion of common decency. This is not, of course, to wish the course of history different, but it is to suggest that these writers in American exile sought the space to work out an alternative conception of modernism after the English version had been more or less stopped dead in its tracks by the traumatic experiences of 1939–45. While the extent of general sympathy for Nazi Germany in Britain during the 1930s, including among intellectuals and other public figures, is still a highly sensitive and in some cases censored topic, what is apparent is that American culture began to become visible in the 1940s as a parallel strand running alongside and operating as a counterpart to more traditional English conceptions of community. This strand was, of course, impelled partly by postwar economics and the increasing dominance of the United States in the global marketplace, but it also came increasingly to be influenced during the subsequent decade by the intellectual attractions of America, whose horizons seemed to offer a promise of modernity and the aesthetic avant-garde which, as Davie and others recognized, had been ideologically squeezed out from the domestic parameters of the British homeland.

In this sense, the idea of a 'special relationship' between Britain and the United States, heavily promoted for their own ends by politicians and diplomats both during and after the War, offered only a sanitized, anodyne version of a transatlantic face-off which was, across a broad cultural spectrum, much more disturbing. By exiling themselves from England to the United States to produce a counternarrative of mid-twentieth-century modernism, Auden, Levertov, and Davie effectively interrogated the triumphalist mythology that pitted traditional virtue against fascist barbarism, a mythology which glossed over the repressive, regressive attitudes towards racial identity within the English domain itself. These poets sought deliberately to explore ways in which the English poetic tradition might creatively be reconceived within an alternative matrix of radical modernity, one infused with a purified metaphysical dimension. Just as the nineteenth-century English radicals looked to America to recover a spirit of republicanism that had been frozen out of English public discourse by the wars with France, so these twentieth-century dissidents looked to America to recover an idiom of modernity forcibly excluded from England by the wars with Germany.[91] In both cases America operated for these British-born writers as a point of triangulation, a means of refracting the disturbingly alien, foreign

---

[91] On the legacy of the wars with Germany, see Gilroy, *After Empire*, 97–8; on the legacy of the wars with France, see D. Simpson, *Romanticism, Nationalism, and the Revolt against Theory*, 4–17.

aspects of European culture in a more amenable and recognizable form. This is why transatlantic modernism still enjoys an uncomfortable relationship with the English poetic tradition: after 1940, Auden committed the heresy of reinscribing his local versions of English 'natural speech' within a more stylistically expansive and ethically uncommitted framework, and many critics, even today, remain disconcerted by his refusal to take sides.

9

Postmodernist Fiction and the Inversion
of History

PERVERSE REFORMATIONS: J. G. BALLARD

'Americanization', Jonathan Zeitlin has written, 'should be understood not as a neutral analytical concept but rather as a contested historical project.' As we have seen, there have been many different versions of Americanization within English cultural history since the 1780s, ranging from Wordsworth's fear that the Great Reform Act would transform sturdily independent MPs into 'slavish Delegates' to Gissing's concern that American commerce would overwhelm the local markets of late Victorian London.[1] In the post-1945 period, America became more frequently associated with industrial processes of mass production and consumption, and this in turn fostered a new series of transatlantic tensions around the status of popular culture and its relationship to more traditional forms of high art. Although these cultural antagonisms go back to the 1920s, when some thought that T. S. Eliot was trying to corrupt English letters by incorporating into his poetry the rhythms of jazz, they became much more widespread in the second half of the twentieth century, as outlets for the products of American entertainment systems became more diffuse. In this respect, postmodernism, with its more ambivalent attitude towards the marketplace, its characteristic emphasis on commodification and 'dispersal' rather than more hermetic forms of modernist 'centering' or 'design', was often understood as, in Andreas Huyssen's phrase, a 'specifically American' idea. In the eyes of some, this more democratic, or vulgarizing, invocation of 'the imagery of everyday life' appeared as an all-pervading threat to the more enclosed social and aesthetic hierarchies still prevalent in Europe.[2]

---

[1] Jonathan Zeitlin, 'Introduction: Americanization and its Limits: Reworking U.S. Technology and Management in Post-War Europe and Japan', in *Americanization and its Limits: Reworking U.S. Technology and Management in Post-War Europe and Japan*, ed. Jonathan Zeitlin and Gary Herrigel (Oxford: Oxford University Press, 2000), 18; *Letters of William and Dorothy Wordsworth*, v. 468.

[2] Marjorie Perloff, 'Modernist Studies', in *Redrawing the Boundaries: The Transformation of English and American Literary Studies*, ed. Stephen Greenblatt and Giles Gunn (New York: Modern Language Association of America, 1992), 169–70; Andreas Huyssen, *After the Great Divide: Modernism, Mass Culture, Postmodernism* (Bloomington, Ind.: Indiana University Press, 1986), 190.

22. J. G. Ballard, photo portrait by Steve Double (1987).

Conversely, the responsiveness to America among British writers of postmodernist fiction such as J. G. Ballard, Angela Carter, and Martin Amis testifies to an openness on their part to cultures of the demotic, a willingness to exploit transatlantic perspectives as a counterpoint to what they take to be the ossified condition of the middlebrow English novel. Carter, like Amis, was a great admirer of Ballard, counting him among the 'seers, or prophets' of English fiction in the way his science fiction narratives helped introduce alternative dimensions into the genre during the second half of the twentieth century.[3] As with Auden and

---

[3] Angela Carter, introduction, in *Expletives Deleted: Selected Writings* (London: Chatto & Windus, 1992), 4.

Davie, the transnational dimensions of these novelists also served to expose their narratives to dark refractions of the recent wartime past, thereby effectively disrupting the more insular moral assumptions of British culture. While Isherwood reflected upon the legacy of the Second World War from his distant vantage point in southern California, Ballard dissected the repercussions of the War for English society from amidst the heart of 'Swinging London', suggesting ways in which the emollient liberalism of what was ostensibly a socially and politically consensual state could barely conceal a mournful, traumatized attachment to the aftershocks of apocalyptic violence. Ballard himself was born in Shanghai in 1930 and lived in a comfortable English expatriate community until the outbreak of the Second World War, when he and his family were interned by the Japanese; in 1946 they returned to England, where the author has lived ever since. Ballard's writing, drawing on pastiche versions of mass culture and influenced by the aesthetics of surrealism, has positioned itself in a self-consciously oblique relationship to English literary traditions, and through the long-standing fascination with the United States which runs through his work, he effectively repositions English culture within an Atlantic framework.

As Emily Apter has observed, the institutionalization of comparative literature as an academic field in the middle years of the twentieth century was impelled partly by a deliberate reaction against what Erich Auerbach, Leo Spitzer, and others took to be the dangerously nationalistic basis of Nazi culture. From their Istanbul exile, Auerbach and Spitzer prided themselves on a cosmopolitan dissociation of linguistic scholarship from the intellectually petty concerns of local tyrants. Apter described Spitzer as 'a figure of transnational humanism *avant la lettre*'; yet Ballard's style of transnationalism is different and in many ways more troubling, since his work refuses the moral polarity that would clearly separate off humanism from fascism.[4] Instead, Ballard evokes a world in which the legacy of war is more amorphous, where the psychopathologies of everyday life are disconcertingly liable to switch positions across national spectrums. As they traverse geographical frontiers, Ballard's narratives simultaneously move across boundaries conventionally demarcating the realms of normality and deviance. In particular, America in his texts operates not as a site of ethical exceptionalism but as a figure of aesthetic disruption and potential reversibility, a way of running the world backwards. For Ballard, accordingly, transnationalism betokens not a humanist transcendence of politics or location but, rather, a way of inverting history, of illuminating those more opaque, deterritorialized forces which traditional national narratives have glossed over or suppressed.

Deterritorialization as a theoretical idea was developed in the wake of poststructuralism by Gilles Deleuze and Félix Guattari to signify 'decoded flows'

---

[4] Emily Apter, 'Global *Translatio*: The "Invention" of Comparative Literature, Istanbul, 1933', *Critical Inquiry*, 29 (2003), 272.

that might undermine bureaucratic mechanisms of imposing legal and moral restrictions according to a principle of 'territoriality', a principle naturally cherished by nation-states. Ballard's work shows a similar propensity for, in the phrase of Deleuze and Guattari, 'dismantling the face' of territorial authority, for implying ways in which the hierarchical order of spatial location and differentiation can be turned on its head.[5] *Empire of the Sun* (1984), an account of a boy's life in a Shanghai internment camp which is presented as fiction although based on fact, magnifies the strangeness of English behaviour by refracting its bizarre quality through the defamiliarized environment brought about by a process of forced deterritorialization. The internment camp functions in this sense like a miniature version of England, keeping many of its social virtues intact: despite his imprisonment by the Japanese, the hero of this novel, Jim, finds the world of the camp 'familiar and reassuring', and he continues to hoard 'his Cathedral School blazer' and diligently to produce 'his Latin homework for Dr Ransome'.[6] As the narrator remarks, 'the homework helped the physician to sustain the illusion that even in Lunghua Camp the values of a vanished England still survived' (*E* 147). There is clearly an incongruity here between the macabre landscape of world war and the manners of middle-class England, with its Edwardian fantasies of 'sunlit lawns that seemed to cover the entire country' (*E* 133); but the brilliance of *Empire of the Sun* lies in the way it constructs a 'landscape of hallucination' (*E* 188) where these English rituals are hollowed out by being framed within a radically discontinuous, aberrant context. At one point Jim is reading Lewis Carroll's *Through the Looking Glass*, which he finds 'a comforting world less strange than his own' (*E* 59), and all of Ballard's work at some level turns upon *Alice-in-Wonderland*-like shifts in perspective designed to invert the epistemological premises of the local and familiar. Towards the end of *Empire of the Sun*, Jim moves across his dormitory and stretches out on the bunk of Mrs Vincent, with whom he has been sharing a room in the camp: 'Seen from Mrs Vincent's vantage-point, the past three years appeared subtly different; even a few steps across a small room generated a separate war' (*E* 237).

This displacement of perspective, though apparently trivial, is typical of *Empire of the Sun*, which plays with such spatial remappings in the same way as Jim himself likes to play with globes, finding points of cross-over between proximate and distant. Roger Luckhurst has astutely remarked that *Empire* and its sequel, *The Kindness of Women* (1991), should be seen not so much as plain autobiographies that might 'decode' the general 'enigmatic crypticness of Ballard's work' but as texts which treat 'the impossibility of determining a clear boundary between

---

[5] Gilles Deleuze and Félix Guattari, *Anti-Oedipus: Capitalism and Schizophrenia,* i, trans. Robert Hurley, Mark Seem, and Helen R. Lane (London: Athlone Press, 1984), 196–7, and *idem, A Thousand Plateaus: Capitalism and Schizophrenia,* ii, trans. Brian Massumi (London: Athlone Press, 1988), 509, 188.

[6] J. G. Ballard, *Empire of the Sun* (London: Victor Gollancz, 1984), 143, 136. Subsequent page references to this edition are cited as '*E*' in the text.

beginnings and ends, ends and re-beginnings'.[7] Such confusion of boundaries is endemic to *Empire of the Sun*: war becomes for Jim a mental rather than a physical event, the stuff of dreams; and in another conceptual inversion he talks of how after the dropping of atom bombs on Nagasaki and Hiroshima 'the confusions of the arbitrary peace' have been 'imposed on the settled and secure landscape of the war' (*E* 233). A little later, he mentions how the light of the atom bomb heralds 'the end of one war and the beginning of the next' (*E* 256), and of how the former Lunghua prisoners, after years of trying to escape from the camp, 'were now back at its gates, ready to take up their stations for World War III' (*E* 243). The state of war becomes here a psychological compulsion which subverts the sentimental affinities customarily associated with a child's-eye view of the world, with the novel's flattened tone deliberately underplaying scenes of parental separation and reconciliation which in another narrative would have been presented more melodramatically. (There is a marked difference in this respect between Ballard's novel and the subsequent film version made by Steven Spielberg.)

This decathected narrative idiom is carried over into *The Kindness of Women*, where the sudden death of the narrator's wife while on holiday in Spain is conveyed with laconic military understatement. *Kindness* deals with the aftermath of the war against fascism, yet it is clear that England in the 1940s and 1950s is 'still trapped by its memories of the Second World War', with the narrator finding himself in a situation where the 'English talked as if they had won the war, but behaved as if they had lost it'.[8] In this way, Ballard picks up on a theme also addressed in different ways by Auden, Isherwood, and other English writers with transatlantic horizons: the awkwardness of the categorical distinction between the virtue of home and the corruption of an enemy abroad, the surreptitious complicity of Britain itself with the dynamics of fascism. The narrator, recalling his culture shock on arriving in England in 1946, reminds himself how '[t]he British had known their own war, a conflict with clear military and political goals, so unlike the war in China', and he describes how '[o]ver the rubble of bombed streets and the deflated hopes of a better world they had imposed a mythology of slogans, a parade of patriotic flags that sealed the past away forever, far from any searching eye' (*K* 78–9). But the implication here is that the narrator's memories of distant Shanghai serve to unmask these domestic mythologies of triumphalism that were propagated in Britain during the 1940s. In an essay on George Orwell's *Nineteen Eighty-Four*, a novel published four years after the end of the War, Thomas Pynchon suggested that Orwell's targets may have been not so much Stalin and Trotsky as 'Churchill's war cabinet', which 'had behaved no

[7] Roger Luckhurst, 'Petition, Repetition, and "Autobiography": J. G. Ballard's *Empire of the Sun* and *The Kindness of Women*', *Contemporary Literature*, 35 (1994), 706, 697.

[8] J. G. Ballard, *The Kindness of Women* (London: HarperCollins, 1991), 68. Subsequent page references to this edition are cited as '*K*' in the text.

differently than a fascist regime, censoring news, controlling wages and prices, restricting travel, subordinating civil liberties to self-defined wartime necessity'; and certainly in Ballard's world the legacy of the Second World War is associated with various forms of false consciousness.[9] He has remarked how little English fiction there has been about the war in the Far East, 'perhaps because the British lost it', and he also commented in a 1995 essay on how the victories of Japanese forces killed off the 'myth of European invincibility', revealing instead how the 'British Empire was based on bluff, in many ways a brilliant one, but that bluff had been called'.[10]

In this light, the boyish character of Jim in *Empire*, who 'accepted without question the stern morality of the *Chums Annuals*' (*E* 56), functions as another kind of displacement, representing metonymically the *naïveté* of an English view of the world as it struggled to come to terms with a disorienting new global environment. This contrary motion of tunnel and global vision, insularity and demystification, also emerges in *The Kindness of Women*, where the narrator comments on how the 'fake gothic pageant' (*K* 68) of Cambridge is sustained, unbeknownst to its academic inhabitants, by American nuclear bombers stationed at an airbase just north of the city, 'guarantors of the civilised order upon which the university so preened itself' (*K* 233). Repression, then, becomes a keynote of English life: Ballard subsequently described postwar England as 'the most repressed society I'd ever known', and this repression relates not just to sex but also to wider areas of knowledge, with the English preferring to preserve their ignorance of how the atom bomb had 'in some way split the sky, and reversed the direction of everything' (*K* 43).[11] England thus becomes for Ballard's persona not so much a rooted landscape but a 'zone of transit' (*K* 67), a derealized realm whose inhabitants appear like 'actors playing parts' (*K* 54), going through their rituals of gentility under the shadow of a looming apocalypse that threatens to render their charades redundant.

Much of Ballard's other writing circles back obsessively to this condition of war, which is represented not as a discrete historical event but as a collective trauma from which the English have never fully recovered. In 'First Impressions of London' (1993), he recalls how when he arrived in 1946 he found 'an exhausted ferret-like people defeated by war and still deluded by Churchillian rhetoric, hobbling around a wasteland of poverty, ration books and grotesque social division'. Even after half a century, he contends, this state of siege still endures:

---

[9] Thomas Pynchon, introduction, in *Nineteen Eighty-Four*, by George Orwell (London: Penguin, 2003), p. viii.

[10] Angela Carter, 'J. G. Ballard: *Empire of the Sun*', in *Expletives Deleted*, 48; J. G. Ballard, 'The End of My War', in *A User's Guide to the Millennium: Essays and Reviews* (London: HarperCollins, 1996), 289.

[11] V. Vale and Andrea Juno, eds., *Re/Search: J. G. Ballard* (San Francisco: Re/Search Publications, 1984), 115.

To understand London now one has to grasp the fact that in this city, as nowhere else in the world, World War II is still going on. The spivs are running delis and restaurants, and an occupying army of international bankers and platinum-card tourists has taken the places of the American servicemen. The people are stoical and underpaid, with a lower standard of living and tackier services than in any comparable western capital. The weary camaraderie of the Blitz holds everything together. Bombs should fall tonight but probably won't, but one senses that people would welcome them.[12]

There are many mementoes of war in Ballard's fiction. In *Concrete Island* (1974), Jane Sheppard lives in an old air-raid shelter on a traffic island beside an arterial road. In *High-Rise* (1975), the broken windowpane in a tower block reminds the hero of 'some kind of cryptic notation, a transfer on the fuselage of a wartime aircraft marking a kill'. In line with the anthropological, atavistic propensities of this latter narrative, the 'clan leader' of this embattled high-rise—with the apposite surname 'Royal'—takes to wearing a white safari jacket like 'an eccentric camp-commander', while another regresses from being a television newsreader to being a primitive 'clan chief', coming back to the apartment building every evening 'like a returning bomber pilot'. Ballard's point here is that the class divisions within English society eventually create a 'civil war within the high-rise', where a ruthless and aggressive commitment to the arts of survival naturally supersedes more polite social conventions, so that the inhabitants of this London tower block find themselves at the end 'like the tenants of a crowded beach visited by a sudden holocaust'.[13]

As these conjectures about civil war would suggest, Ballard's stylistic preference is to write thesis novels, geometric equations where hypotheses are adduced and resolutions predicted accordingly. Rather like Edgar Allan Poe, he is much less interested in the unpredictable nature of human character or in what he calls the 'social novel' than in 'the individual's relationship with the technological landscape'.[14] This helps to explain his frequently voiced contempt for the tradition of English 'naturalistic' and 'middlebrow' fiction: Anthony Powell, John Le Carré, John Fowles, and the 'so-called "Hampstead novels"'. 'Parochialism seems to me to be the besetting sin of contemporary English fiction,' wrote Ballard in 1978, and he went on to criticize the 'obsession' of native writers 'with obscure social nuances, with the minutiae of everyday language and behaviour' and their 'moralizing concern for the limited world of their own parish that would do credit to an elderly spinster peering down at her suburban side-street'.[15] Conversely, this also explains his great admiration for American author William Burroughs, whom he called in 1997 'the most important writer in the English language to

[12] Ballard, 'First Impressions of London', in *User's Guide*, 185.
[13] J. G. Ballard, *High-Rise* (London: Flamingo–HarperCollins, 2003), 45, 105, 73, 107, 131, 195.   [14] J. G. Ballard, 'Fictions of Every Kind', in *User's Guide*, 205.
[15] Vale and Juno, eds., *Re/Search*, 6; Richard Kadrey and Suzanne Stefanac, 'J. G. Ballard on William S. Burroughs' Naked Truth', *Salon*, 2 Sept. 1997; online: www.salon.com, accessed 1 June 2003; J. G. Ballard, 'Memories of Greeneland', in *User's Guide*, 137.

have appeared since the Second World War'. Burroughs's concern to imbricate human consciousness with the soft machines of modern technology finds an echo in Ballard, and the association with Burroughs also helps to elucidate his understanding of fascism's dehumanizing qualities as a latent potential within Western civilization: 'Hitler tapped into all kinds of ... buried layers of psychopathy,' remarked Ballard in a 2000 interview; 'it's an example of what *could* happen.'[16] This sinister pattern of doubling is worked out most fully in the short story 'One Afternoon at Utah Beach' (1978), set in the French location where the United States First Army came ashore on D-Day. After becoming aware that his wife is having an affair, Ogden discovers on the beach a corpse of a German soldier 'in some way preserved by the freezing air'; he then proceeds to become the dead soldier's alter ego, dressing in the Nazi uniform and planning to avenge himself violently on his wife and her lover, an act described here as 'the last war crime committed during World War II'.[17] Although Ballard has affirmed his contempt for 'Fascist infatuation with power and brute force', he also remarked in a review of Hitler's *Mein Kampf* that he found the 'whole apparatus of the Nazi superstate', with 'its nightmare uniforms and propaganda', its 'maximizing of violence and sensation', to be 'strangely prophetic of our own'.[18] Again, the division between humane values and fascist forms of violence becomes in Ballard's work a disturbingly grey area.

For all of Ballard's proselytizing on behalf of science fiction, then, and for all of his assertions that 'the future provides a better key to the present than does the past', his own fiction is in fact immersed in history. As he acknowledged in a 1983 interview, 'we don't arrive at every moment of consciousness completely free of the past. The past is enshrined in us, of course.'[19] Within this context, the fabled domain of America functions not as a purely abstract realm, but as an alternative to British society in quite specific historical and political instances. Ballard's own personal acquaintance with the United States has, in fact, not been particularly extensive: when he was 9, shortly before the outbreak of war, his parents took him on 'a trip across the Pacific states', and in 1955 the RAF sent him to Canada for a month's 'acclimatisation' to North American life.[20] Ballard was then stationed with the Royal Canadian Air Force in London, Ontario, and he made 'a number of trips across the border into the States—went to Detroit, Buffalo, Niagara Falls, and around there', although 'these were short trips, overnight in the case of Detroit'. Ballard found the United States at this time 'unbelievably different from

---

[16] Kadrey and Stefanac, 'J. G. Ballard'; Chris Hall, 'Flight and Imagination', *Spike Magazine*, 2000; online: www.spikemagazine.com, accessed 1 June 2003.

[17] J. G. Ballard, 'One Afternoon at Utah Beach', in *The Complete Short Stories* (London: Flamingo–HarperCollins, 2001), 976, 980.

[18] Vale and Juno, eds., *Re/Search*, 47; J. G. Ballard, 'Alphabets of Unreason', in *User's Guide*, 221.

[19] J. G. Ballard, 'The Innocent as Paranoid', in *User's Guide*, 93; Vale and Juno, eds., *Re/Search*, 45.

[20] Vale and Juno, eds., *Re/Search*, 35. Ballard confirmed the dates of his RAF experiences in Canada in a letter to the author, 19 Aug. 2003.

life in austerity England', and he wrote subsequently of how 'all the optimism of Eisenhower's post-war America was expressed in the baroque vehicles that soared along its highways, as if an advanced interstellar race had touched down on a recreational visit'. But after 1955 he did not visit the States again until 1986, and in December 1987 he paid his first ever visit to Los Angeles for the film première of *Empire of the Sun*. Ballard records how on this visit he 'was struck by the total familiarity of the urban landscape, accurately presented in thousands of films and TV episodes', and consequently he says that he feels he 'didn't need to' acquaint himself with American culture any more closely. He has frequently expressed admiration for Jean Baudrillard's 'brilliant' *America* (1986), though he believes Baudrillard's account 'would have been even better had he never gone there', since the 'real America doesn't quite live up to' his spectacular view of it. 'I sense that too whenever I'm there,' commented Ballard: 'I keep waiting for the movie to start.'[21]

What this suggests, of course, is the way in which Ballard's understanding of America is driven by a multimedia version of the myth and symbol iconography that empowered the classic phase of American studies in the 1950s. Just as R. W. B. Lewis, Henry Nash Smith, and other scholars sublimated the material of US culture into a series of archetypal topoi that supposedly gave special meaning to the American experience, so Ballard projects America within a mythic dimension where historical complexity and contingency would seem like tiresome distractions from these grand symbolic narratives. There is no doubt that Ballard's reverence for the 'psychological' power of the 'American Dream' was shaped by typical postwar idealizations of US social and economic power, of the kind that fuelled the American studies movement in its early phases: in the introduction to *Myths of the Near Future* (1982), the author writes of how after the Second World War 'we all became Americans, turning our backs on the past and confident that we could shape our world in any way we wished, dream any dream and see it come to life'.[22] But this utopian strain, so frequently associated in Ballard's work with the New World, can be seen as framed within an ironic structure of estrangement which locks it into a perpetual dialogue with the confining forces of history. Ballard has compared Baudrillard's *America* to the writing of Jonathan Swift; and if the more striking images in Baudrillard's treatise—how in California, for instance, culture, politics, and sexuality 'are seen exclusively in terms of the desert, which here assumes the status of a primal scene', with an 'astral quality'—are understood not in documentary terms but as lyrical meditations on what Ballard has called 'the peculiar latent psychology waiting to emerge into the daylight', then the dialectic between transcendence and desublimation in both Baudrillard and Ballard becomes easier to understand. (In a 2000 interview, Chris Hall quoted Ballard as saying: 'That's what I'm trying to do. Look at the world and see its latent content.')[23] This condition of psychological latency consequently becomes analogous to a form of aesthetic sublimation: just as Swift's 'Modest Proposal', with its outrageous suggestion that the problems of the Irish famine might be solved by eating children, effectively twists political questions into an aesthetic realm which reflects back on current events the more powerfully because of the treatise's seemingly detached position, so Ballard advances the idea of America as an ulterior realm in order to reflect back on the legitimacy of British culture. Both sides of the equation, the displacement of the event and also its unravelling, are necessary to the peculiar dynamic of his work. Working within the spirit of transatlantic alterity that we have seen in nineteenth-century writers such as Mary Shelley—another enthusiast for science fiction, of course—Ballard appropriates America aesthetically to create a virtual history of what England might have been like in an alternative cosmos, had events taken a different turn.

The Alice-in-Wonderland logic of Ballard's writing, then, is especially pertinent to his representations of America. At the end of *The Kindness of Women*, witnessing the re-creation of scenes from his Shanghai childhood in Hollywood, he notes: 'The puzzle had solved itself; the mirror, as I had promised, had been broken from within' (*K* 284). As *Empire of the Sun* suggests, Ballard's perceptions of America were shaped by his childhood in Shanghai, where he first saw American films and cars, and by his experiences in Lunghua Camp, where he made friends with US servicemen and came to believe that the 'huge, streamlined bombers summed up all the power and grace of America' (*E* 173). Like Isherwood and Wodehouse, Ballard finds that his attraction to America as a hard-edged, technologically ruthless culture sits uneasily with the nostalgic, sentimental sense of decency that became an established part of English culture after 1945. Indeed, part of Ballard's attraction to the world of science fiction arose from an impatience with this quietist gentility that was institutionalized in England during the postwar period as a deliberate reaction against ideologies of fascist brutality. *Hello America* (1981), which projects an apocalyptic vision of an American continent in the year 2030 overcome by climate change and an all-encompassing desert, insists in the introduction that it is 'strongly on the side of the U.S.A., and a celebration of its optimism and self-confidence, qualities that we Europeans so conspicuously lack'. This futuristic fantasy presents a derealized version of US history in which former presidents—and other cultural icons such as Huckleberry Finn, Humphrey Bogart, and Joe Di Maggio—have been resuscitated as robots, and where the English protagonist, after his voyage from Plymouth, feels confident

---

[23] Bradley Butterfield, 'Ethical Value and Negative Aesthetics: Reconsidering the Baudrillard-Ballard Connection', *PMLA*, 114 (1999), 65; Jean Baudrillard, *America*, trans. Chris Turner (London: Verso, 1988), 28; C. Hall, 'Flight and Imagination'.

that he will still 'find the El Dorado he had dreamed of for so long ... that vision of the United States enshrined in the pages of *Time* and *Look*, and which still existed somewhere'.[24]

Ballard's line in *Hello America*, then, is to take familiar American myths about westward exploration and to flip them over, so that they mirror inversely his dystopian vision of a parched twenty-first-century future. From these barren conditions, 'virtually the entire population of the United States migrated back to its original ethnic departure points in Europe and Africa, Asia and South America, a vast reverse migration duplicating the original westward passage two hundred years earlier'. What this enables Ballard to do is to illuminate, like Baudrillard, what he takes to be America's mythic infrastructure: when Paco travels to a deserted California, he seeks out an abandoned automobile in order to visit 'the old freeway system', which he believes 'should last as long as the Pyramids'.[25] By transposing his characters into sightseers, who look over the West Coast as though they were inspecting the monuments of ancient Egypt, Ballard displaces quotidian American landscapes into another dimension through a strategy reminiscent of Emerson's celebrated move, in his 1844 essay 'The Poet', to bridge familiar and transcendent, 'newspaper and caucus' with 'the town of Troy, and the temple of Delphi'.[26] Indeed, in a curious echo of the Emersonian style, Ballard in *The Kindness of Women* describes Los Angeles as 'the oldest city of the 20th century, the Troy of its collective imagination' (*K* 279). The utopian strain in Ballard's writing is, as in Emerson, intimately connected with a rhetoric of apocalypse through which mere 'clock time' gives way to what W. Warren Wagar has called a 'kairotic moment', an instant of authenticity and revelation that, as Ballard himself describes it in 'Myths of the Near Future', brings 'separated elements into a single whole again'.[27] Time, consequently, is a major theme in Ballard's fiction, with the idea of a 'simultaneity' linking past, present, and future allowing for the possibility of people being 'woken from the present into the infinite realm of their time-filled selves'. In Ballard, 'nostalgia for the future' becomes a legitimate response to the recursive cycle wherein 'we try to repeat those significant events which have already taken place in the future', and this kind of circular structure also underpins the collapse of distinct temporal categories that we see in a text such as *Hello America*.[28]

There is, nevertheless, a sense in which this transcendent simultaneity of *Hello America* is hedged around by the historically specific circumstances of its provenance, the oil shortages of the late 1970s: 'All around them ... was ample

[24] J. G. Ballard, *Hello America* (London: Vintage–Random House, 1994), 5, 49.

[25] Ibid. 47, 140.   [26] Emerson, 'The Poet', 21–2.

[27] W. Warren Wagar, 'J. G. Ballard and the Transvaluation of Utopia', *Science-Fiction Studies*, 18/1 (March 1991), 63; J. G. Ballard, 'Myths of the Near Future', in *Complete Short Stories*, 1076.

[28] Ballard, 'Myths of the Near Future', 1084, and *idem*, 'News from the Sun', in *Complete Short Stories*, 1025–6.

evidence of the desperate attempts by the last Americans to beat the energy crisis.' The ensuing sequence of future fictional events is extrapolated from this crisis which dogged Jimmy Carter's presidency, with the narrator recording how 'By the mid-1990s the automotive giants of the United States, Europe and Japan had cut car production by a third', and how in 2000 'the operation of private gasoline-driven vehicles' was made illegal.[29] Neither of these predictions of the future came true, of course, and Ballard's science fiction, like other works in this genre, always runs the risk of seeming simply to be overtaken by events. Yet the author's own description of science fiction as creating 'a paradoxical universe where dream and reality become fused together' links it more firmly with the aesthetics of surrealism, a movement described by Ballard as 'the most important imaginative enterprise this century has embarked on', despite the long-standing moral disapproval of it by 'the critical bureaucracy' in England.[30] For Ballard, science fiction, like surrealism, unveils a hallucinatory world whose cogency derives not so much from the accuracy of its predictions as from its capacity to evoke interference and alterity within the domain of the real. Ballard wrote in 1974 about how one of the features of science fiction was 'its attempt, now more or less abandoned by the so-called mainstream novel, to place some kind of metaphysical and philosophical framework around man's place in the universe', and in this light the prophetic displacements of *Hello America* should be understood as a way of subverting the restrictive boundaries of the familiar.[31] As Roger Luckhurst has observed, Ballard's writing positions itself on the hinge, the Derridean *brisure*, between transcendence and simulation, and the shock effect of his work (like that of the surrealists) arises from his capacity continually to change the reader's angle of perception, to switch perspectives—between time and timelessness, history and myth, England and America.[32] Ballard thus reproduces a legendary version of the American experience not simply in order to critique England but to expose the gaps in England's comprehension of itself, to hypothesize a parallel universe in which events might be ordered differently.

For Ballard, this narrative estrangement from domestic landscapes carries political as well as psychological resonance, as he extends his perception of temporal simultaneity to reinscribe the Reformation within contemporary English culture, thus outlining ways in which civil war and transatlantic insurrection recur in unremitting cycles. Ballard's story 'The Waiting Grounds' contrasts 'the total unifying time of the cosmos ... the great cosmic round' with the brief parallel world of 'private times'; and at the end of *The Kindness of Women*, when the narrator sees the Hollywood production company deploying a house near his current residence in the London Home Counties as a 'virtual replica' of his

---

[29] Ballard, *Hello America*, 41, 44–5.

[30] J. G. Ballard, 'Time, Memory and Inner Space', in *User's Guide*, 200; Vale and Juno, eds., *Re/Search*, 23, 116.   [31] J. G. Ballard, 'The Cosmic Cabaret', in *User's Guide*, 204.

[32] Roger Luckhurst, *'The Angle Between Two Walls': The Fiction of J. G. Ballard* (Liverpool: Liverpool University Press, 1997), p. xiii.

childhood family home in Shanghai, he muses on how 'Deep assignments ran through our lives; there were no coincidences' (*K* 274–5).[33] Extended into the public realm, this emphasis on structural repetition implies a continual mirror play between past and present, as, for instance, in the story 'Theatre of War', which deduces from the class divisions of postwar Britain a renewed prospect of internecine conflict: 'After three hundred years, could civil war again divide the United Kingdom?' This in turn exemplifies an aside in 'News from the Sun', the previous story in *Myths of the Near Future*, about the significance of interpenetration between past, present, and future: 'Simultaneity? It's possible to imagine that everything is happening at once, all the events "past" and "future" which constitute the universe are taking place together. Perhaps our sense of time is a primitive mental structure that we inherited from our less intelligent forebears.'[34] In his 1993 annotations to *The Atrocity Exhibition*, the author talks of how major museums all over the world have bowed to the influence of Disney and become 'theme parks in their own right. The past, whether Renaissance Italy or ancient Egypt, is reassimilated and homogenized into its most digestible form.'[35] For Ballard, the negative aspect of such commodification is its potential erasure of the alterity of history, the way in which the present can be crucially reconfigured in the light of shadows from other temporal dimensions.

Both past and future, then, are represented in Ballard's writing not just as a one-dimensional simulacrum but as the physical force field through which his version of British culture is energized. The narrator in *The Kindness of Women* recalls how as an undergraduate at Cambridge he 'had prayed for a new Thomas Cromwell who would launch the dissolution of the universities', though he gratefully acknowledges how 'mass tourism had accomplished this, overwhelming the older European universities as it would soon destroy Rome, Florence and Venice' (*K* 232–3). This reference to Thomas Cromwell, an administrator with Lutheran leanings who was the architect of Henry VIII's Reformation and who dissolved the monasteries in 1536, indicates Ballard's conscious affiliation of himself with Puritan iconoclasts; just as Henry VIII sought to dismantle the monastic order, so Ballard's narrator expresses impatience with what he takes to be the complacent, self-enclosed world of the university establishment. *Cocaine Nights* (1996) similarly enacts a perverse version of a Reformation narrative, being set in a small Spanish resort, Estrella de Mar, full of slothful exiles from Britain who spend their time watching soccer on satellite television. In an attempt to regenerate the community, the 'new Messiah', Bobby Crawford, aims to organize a programme of 'civic renewal' around a stringent devotion to drugs, gambling, and pornography. Estrella de Mar is subsequently described as becoming 'as serious in its pleasures as a seventeenth-century New England settlement', but

[33] J. G. Ballard, 'The Waiting Grounds', in *Complete Short Stories*, 93.
[34] Ballard, 'Theatre of War', in *Complete Short Stories*, 953, and *idem*, 'News from the Sun', 1025.
[35] Ballard, *Atrocity Exhibition*, 56.

whereas John Winthrop's city on a hill committed itself austerely to Christian improvement, Ballard's community dedicates itself to a life of deviance. The thesis of this 'reversed world' is that crime can appear as a humanizing endeavour, an outburst of energy enabling Estrella de Mar to slough off its collective torpor, to escape from its obsession with 'security grilles' and 'surveillance cameras'; the psychiatrist Dr Sanger declares that 'the arts and criminality have always flourished side by side', and he pronounces pompously on how 'transgressive behaviour is for the public good'.[36] Part of the paradox in *Cocaine Nights* is that all these recipes for heterodoxy are presented in a formal, buttoned-down prose style as conservative in its own way as the sermonizing mode of Winthrop's 'A Model of Christian Charity', so that the novel's scheme for social regeneration and renewal might be seen ironically to be just as moralistic as the American Puritan campaign to reform England in the 1630s.

Winthrop makes another cameo appearance in *Super-Cannes* (2000), where the narrator complains that another psychiatrist, Dr Penrose, makes the high-tech community known as 'Eden II ... sound like Winthrop's City on a Hill'. The very name of this business park, of course, evokes an idea of paradise regained; Penrose in fact describes it as 'a suburb of paradise' as well as 'an ideas laboratory for the new millennium', though the narrator wonders sceptically if it is not simply a commercial venue with luxurious facilities for multinational companies. Again, though, the landscape of this novel suggests a deliberate move away from the old territorial restrictions of Europe towards an Americanized model organized around the transnational mobility of scientific and financial data, one with 'no ground already staked out, no title deeds going back to bloody Magna Carta'. Ballard has elsewhere described his vision of the future as 'a kind of California spreading across the globe', while an Australian expatriate in *Super-Cannes* similarly describes the Côte d'Azur as 'Europe's California. High-tech industries, an army of people programming the future, billions surfing on a silicon chip'. In addition, what the narrator reluctantly admires about Penrose and acknowledges as 'the core truth of his bold but deranged vision' involves the engineering at Eden–Olympia of a new model of freedom in which 'psychopathy was being rehabilitated, returned like a socialized criminal to everyday life'. Penrose says of his clinical subjects that 'Only their psychopathies can set them free', and again Winthrop's legacy of transatlantic reformation has here been turned on its head, with the New World no longer offering a promise of spiritual redemption but, equally prophetically, the prospect of salvation through mass deviance.[37]

A more rhetorical aspect of Ballard's perverse logic of reformation involves his displacement of organic metaphor into arbitrary simile. In *Crash* (1973),

---

[36] J. G. Ballard, *Cocaine Nights* (London: Flamingo–HarperCollins, 1996), 181, 254, 116, 280, 219.

[37] J. G. Ballard, *Super-Cannes* (London: Flamingo–HarperCollins, 2000), 357, 20, 16, 79, 128, 360, 365; Vale and Juno, eds., *Re/Search*, 163.

the victims of the car crash are described as 'like two minor royalties at a levée', with their 'chromium and cellulosed bodies gleaming like the coronation armour of an archangelic host'. Rather than enjoying a natural position within a hierarchical environment, like kings and archangels in days of old, Ballard's heroes are exiled linguistically into mere replicas of that divine order. As in the work of seventeenth-century Puritan writers, the loss here of a naturalized world of common reference demands a stylistic movement towards allegory, where the emphasis falls upon figurative rather than literal or transparent forms of meaning. Although the passengers in *Crash* 'had the blank and unresponsive look of a madonna in an early Renaissance icon', in this post-Reformation landscape the religious emblem has lost its supernatural aura and become merely another flattened image within a world where 'angular control surfaces and rounded sections of human bodies' come together 'in unfamiliar junctions'. This shift of organic into mechanic is matched by a modulation of the human into the technological: the narrator talks of an 'engineering structure' supporting the frame of the human body, linking this again to memories of 'fighter aircraft' during the Second World War. More generally, as Paul Youngquist has suggested, *Crash* can be seen to work as a parody of Christian myths of resurrection, as it displays bodies being mangled without the prospect of celestial transfiguration. In this light, the unremittingly hypothetical conception of Ballard's similes—'My body glowed from these points, *like* a resurrected man basking in the healed injuries that had brought about his first death' (my emphasis)—serves only to re-emphasize the structural demystification at work here: resurrection takes place in a parallel universe conjoined to this narrative world only by the empty figure of similitude. In his introduction to the French edition of the novel, Ballard claimed that 'the past itself, in social and psychological terms, became a casualty of Hiroshima and the nuclear age'; but in *Crash* we see him metaphorically revisiting the past only to turn it inside out, just as he suggests in this introduction that Stanley Kubrick's film *2001: A Space Odyssey* was a 'scientific pageant that became a kind of historical romance in reverse'.[38]

Ballard's manifesto for reforming England, then, involves the need 'to dismantle that *smothering conventionalized reality* that wraps itself around us' by more openness to representations of sex and violence and by a wider dissemination of pornography; he describes pornography, in fact, as 'a powerful catalyst for social change', whose 'periods of greatest availability have frequently coincided with times of greatest economic and scientific advance'.[39] Ballard especially deplores the 'all-powerful media scene' in Britain, whose capacity to sanitize and trivialize, so he said in 1982, is all the more distasteful because of its intellectual pretensions:

---

[38] J. G. Ballard, *Crash* (New York: Vintage–Random House, 1985), 154, 174, 21, 80, 68, 157, 4; Paul Youngquist, 'Ballard's Crash-Body', *Postmodern Culture*, 11/1 (Sept. 2000), 26.

[39] Vale and Juno, eds., *Re/Search*, 47; Ballard, *Atrocity Exhibition*, 36.

I loathe the 'cultural' side of British TV—it's sinister. It creates the impression that some of the greatest works of the human imagination in music, literature, or the visual arts can be reduced somehow to a kind of *panel game* ... The British imagine that it's the *Americans* who've always lived in a society dominated by advertising and media values, but I don't think that's true. I think *we* are the people most dominated by the media landscape; the most dominated the world has ever known ... This is due to the huge network of national newspapers and magazines that everybody reads in great numbers. The output of daily papers with huge circulations is unequaled anywhere in the world. TV dominates everything and is watched by everyone all the damned time. Advertising is very powerful here. Given the size of the country, the volume and turnover of images—the constant bombardment—is enormous ... It's a great mistake to imagine the British are terribly literary—they're not. They watch TV. Their familiarity with their great literature is strictly in terms of TV adaptations—people know all about Lord Byron not because they've read his poetry, but because they've seen a TV drama-documentary on him. That's no exaggeration, it's literally true ... shocking.[40]

Again, the tone of jeremiad here is not too dissimilar from that of a seventeenth-century church minister in New England chastising his congregation for its lack of religious purity. Indeed, in *Millennium People* (2003) a vengeful 'apocalypse' is wreaked upon the national state of complacency, with the BBC forming a prime target in the terrorists' project to destroy the old world of 'C20 trash' and 'build a saner England'. As he joins a demonstration outside Broadcasting House, the narrator comments on how 'for more than sixty years the BBC had played a leading role in brainwashing the middle classes', how in fact it had 'defined the national culture'; accordingly, the protesters, imagining themselves to be like 'a revolutionary rabble breaking into an *ancien régime* drawing room and confronting the effigies of a corrupt aristocracy', take by storm a Council Chamber lined with portraits of BBC director-generals and daub their faces 'with a series of Hitler moustaches'. One of the themes of *Millennium People* is how 'the educated middle classes', with their blinkered determination to preserve their material comforts and guard their own power, 'were turning towards fascism'; but, as in the Reformation climate of the seventeenth century, the outbreak of 'a primitive religion' reacts iconoclastically against this sense of impending 'brain-death'. One of the rebels here tells the narrator that he appears to be regenerated by the prospect of violence—'you were like Columbus sighting the New World'—and, once again, the impetus of Ballard's narrative is geared towards shaking England out of its condition of spiritual torpor.[41]

For Ballard, then, the cultural values perpetuated by the British media are a middlebrow phenomenon, concerned more with promoting social respectability than with any genuine interest in intellectual exploration. There is a complementary symmetry here with T. S. Eliot's view of the BBC in the middle of

---

[40] Vale and Juno, eds., *Re/Search*. 18, 31–32.
[41] J. G. Ballard, *Millennium People* (London: Flamingo–HarperCollins, 2003), 67, 81, 118, 149–50, 156, 181, 38, 63, 163.

the twentieth century: whereas Eliot admired the BBC for its ability to bind the country into a renewed sense of national fellowship, Ballard excoriates it for the bland, homogenized assumptions it perpetuates. Such an antithesis suggests how debates about disestablishment have not gone away, but have simply been deflected into new social and political arenas. Eliot, an American who transplanted himself to London, defended the BBC as a twentieth-century corollary to the Church of England, an arm of state that would work to preserve the organic idea of the nation as a cohesive unit, even within an increasingly disparate and fractured environment; Ballard, by contrast, living in England but taking his intellectual directions more from American culture, sees the centralized state and its media apparatus as forms of institutional repression. Ballard loathes the 'seductive authority' and silent censorship that he finds to be an integral part of British culture, and he rejects entirely the association of English language and literature with forms of collective pedagogy and national citizenship, moral and political agendas that, as we saw at the beginning of this book, were endorsed enthusiastically by Establishment figures such as Sir Arthur Quiller-Couch and Henry Newbolt at the beginning of the twentieth century.[42]

In this sense, Ballard's fascination with corporeal dismemberment, most evident in *Crash*, might also be seen as a comment on how the body politic itself is rent asunder by the collision of what the novel describes as 'hemispherical and rectilinear geometries'.[43] Just as in Ballard's fiction the organic nature of the human body is superseded by its technological replica, so the censorship controversies around David Cronenberg's film version of *Crash* in 1996 were related not so much to its simple depiction of violence as to its apparent abandonment of any notion of a shared social state or sense of communal responsibility. Robert L. Caserio has compared *Crash* to the work of Leo Bersani and Ulysse Dutoit in the way its 'dismembering, immobilizing process' threatens to hollow out civic agendas, of the kind traditionally associated with what John Gray, in an anti-globalization polemic, called the 'settled continent of diverse historic communities' in Europe. Whereas Gray at the turn of the twenty-first century fiercely opposed ways in which American propulsions of 'late modern capitalism' were producing 'a life of fragments and a proliferation of senseless choices', Ballard, by contrast, welcomes such fragmentation as a way of eroding the ossified structures of feudal centralization and control.[44] This again links him to the reformation impulse we have seen in Clough, Gissing, Davie, and other British writers over the past two centuries, and it re-enacts the impulse to dissolve the centralizing power of the Establishment that can be traced within English culture back to the schismatic movements of the sixteenth and seventeenth centuries.

---

[42] Ballard, *Atrocity Exhibition*, 103.   [43] Ballard, *Crash*, 178.
[44] Robert L. Caserio, 'Mobility and Masochism: Christine Brooke-Rose and J. G. Ballard', *Novel*, 21 (1988), 295; John Gray, *False Dawn: The Delusions of Global Capitalism*, rev. edn. (London: Granta Books, 2002), 231, 38.

At the heart of the British Establishment is of course the monarchy, and it is the status of monarchy, and in particular the way it is interwoven with the extended *ecclesia* of the nation, that perturbs many of the writers in this Atlantic republican tradition. It is no coincidence that Ballard should have nominated Byron as his example of a writer whose radical work has been vitiated by British television, since, as we have seen, Byron's satirical impulse in the early nineteenth century was specifically anti-monarchical and sympathetic to the newly emerging United States. Ballard stated explicitly in 2002 his belief that Britain 'should be a republic and the royal family and all inherited titles should be abolished', going on to describe the monarchy as 'a complete anachronism, a Ruritanian kind of fantasy that helps to anchor Britain in the past, and also plays on our weakness for nostalgia'.[45] In 1982, he expressed his admiration for Marcus Serjeant, who fired six blank shots at the Queen during the annual Trooping the Colour ceremony; Ballard described this as a 'wonderful conceptual act', something which brought out the simulated condition of the monarchy itself: 'there was the Queen in a fantasy/fancy dress uniform, followed by all these real soldiers dressed up in costume to look like 17th-century soldiers, being fired on by a man with a replica pistol! Wonderful piece of street theater.' The authorities, of course, did not regard it so humorously and incarcerated the pseudo-assassin for two years, as if to rebuff Ballard's thesis on the 'death of affect' by indicating their continuing allegiance to the sanctity of these royal rituals.[46] Elsewhere, Ballard has linked the monarchy with vacuous cults of celebrity, comparing Princess Margaret to Ronald Reagan and envisaging Buckingham Palace being sold off by the middle of the twenty-first century to 'EuroDisney management'. At the end of *Millennium People*, the popular rebellion against the state that begins in a London housing complex is described as having turned Chelsea Marina into 'a unique republic'.[47]

Republicanism is, of course, an old theme in English literature and culture, manifesting itself as far back as John Milton and being shaped around the turn of the nineteenth century by the events of the American and French Revolutions, as we see in the writings of Tom Paine and William Hazlitt. David Norbrook has argued, though, that the actual period of a republican administration in England, between 1649 and 1660, has been more or less written out of the national history and that 'literary history in the twentieth century has often had a strongly monarchist bias'.[48] It is likely, though, that this bias is more implicit than explicit, arising out of a series of assumptions about the relationship between literature and society that have remained largely unexamined. The attempts of Cromwell's

---

[45] J. G. Ballard, 'It's About Being a Citizen, Not a Subject', *Guardian*, 1 June 2002, 13.
[46] Vale and Juno, eds., *Re/Search*, 7; Ballard, introduction, in *Crash*, 1.
[47] J. G. Ballard, 'In Search of the Last Emperor', in *User's Guide*, 248; *idem*, *Millennium People*, 294.
[48] David Norbrook, *Writing the English Republic: Poetry, Rhetoric and Politics, 1627–1660* (Cambridge: Cambridge University Press, 1999), 4, 7.

regime to institute a written constitution and to separate the executive from the legislative branches of state governance were pushed intellectually into the background by the subsequent prestige of romantic conceptions of national culture, epitomized by Coleridge's model of an Anglican community centred upon the organic coherence of church, monarchy, and countryside. To follow the aesthetic line promulgated by Coleridge, Arnold, or Eliot, which postulates symbiotic interpenetrations between English literature and the world of English nature, is inevitably to marginalize more consciously discursive forms as 'not natural' or as lacking 'sensuousness', as Arnold complained of Clough's work, and so to relegate the voice of Clough, Byron, or Davie to a position on the cultural margins.[49] In this sense, Ballard's invocation of a republican inheritance, his realignment of English culture on a transatlantic axis, carries a distinct political charge in its adumbration of a parallel universe, its projection of ways in which British cultural history might have worked itself out in a different dimension.

AMERICAN GHOSTS: ANGELA CARTER

Ballard's inversion of history can be seen as commensurate with the historicist reconfiguration of England's past in the writings of Angela Carter, who was born ten years after Ballard, in 1940, but who died young, in 1992. Carter's emergence as a writer was facilitated by the American novelist Robert Coover, who as fiction editor of the *Iowa Review* helped to make her work more generally visible by featuring it in a double issue of the journal in 1975. The two writers subsequently became lifelong friends, and Carter went to Brown University in Rhode Island, where Coover taught, as a visiting professor in the Writing Program for the 1980–1 academic year. Like Coover, Carter greatly admired the Columbian novelist Gabriel García Márquez and the Spanish film-maker Luis Buñuel, both of whom exploited techniques of 'magic realism' to disturb more conventional forms of mimesis, and her attempts to introduce this kind of aesthetic innovation into the sheltered domain of English fiction were assisted by important sociological changes in the book-publishing industry that began in the 1980s. In his introduction to a special issue of *Granta* in 1980 entitled 'The End of the English Novel', Bill Buford lamented the limited and 'self-protected' nature of the British book trade that reinforced a sense of provincialism and hindered the appearance of more experimental writing.[50] Buford blamed this on the unchallenged hegemony of high street chains such as W. H. Smith, along with the general absence in England at that time of specialized campus bookstores, all of which meant that popular realist fiction dominated the marketplace as surely as cheap imports from Britain had exercised a stranglehold on the American

---

[49] Arnold, *Letters of Matthew Arnold to Arthur Hugh Clough*, 98–9.
[50] Bill Buford, 'Introduction: The End of the English Novel', *Granta*, 3 (1980), 12.

literary marketplace before the passage of the international copyright law in 1891. During the 1980s, however, the expansion of higher education outlets in Britain and the development of 'new production technologies [which] made it possible to print fewer copies at a realistic price' helped to ensure that more titles were produced and that book publishing gradually became more diverse.[51] Buford's special issue of *Granta* in 1980 featured an excerpt from Salman Rushdie's forthcoming novel *Midnight's Children* as well as new writing by Carter, Emma Tennant, and Russell Hoban, while a critical piece by Lorna Sage anticipated what was to become by the end of that decade almost a critical cliché, 'the importance of the alien perspective' and the value of English fiction 'written from elsewhere'.[52]

If transatlantic postmodernism reconfigured domestic landscapes with respect to geographical space, situating the native culture in relation to its overseas counterparts, it also reordered the co-ordinates of English fiction in relation to time. Huyssen has written of the obsession with imagery of the past in 'the postmodern 1980s', the ways in which emblems of cultural memory were stored nostalgically in the forms of museum artefacts or computer data banks, and he has associated this 'memorial or museal sensibility' with a crisis of temporality as perceptions of 'historical continuity' and sequence fell into abeyance and the past became something to be evoked only through the realm of the simulacrum. This self-conscious rendering of a fictitious narrative of the past, which was also promoted academically by Stephen Greenblatt and other 'new historicists' of this era, spoke to a dwindling of faith in the efficacy of collective national memory and ancestral bonding, of the kind that had inspired the organicist patternings of T. S. Eliot forty years earlier, and a corresponding recognition that notions of history and tradition could be projected only partially and reflexively. Consequently, the idea of America as it circulates in British postmodern narratives functions not merely as an alternative cultural domain but also as an emblem of difference, a realm that signifies the loss of epistemological certainty and foregrounds the theoretical limits of representation. Greenblatt in *Marvelous Possessions* associates the 'wonder' of the New World for Europeans of the Renaissance era with an intimation of 'striking indeterminacy', with a landscape of the marvellous that comprised 'part of a renunciation of possession', and this experience of displacement on many different levels is a common thread that binds together these transatlantic postmodernists.[53]

The writing of Carter, born in Sussex and brought up in Yorkshire, is suffused with what seems at times like an oppressive weight of English local detail, particularly from the world of south London, where the author spent most

---

[51] John Feather, *A History of British Publishing* (London: Routledge, 1988), 224.

[52] Lorna Sage, 'Invasion from Outsiders', *Granta*, 3 (1980), 136.

[53] Andreas Huyssen, *Twilight Memories: Marking Time in a Culture of Amnesia* (New York: Routledge, 1995), 253; Stephen Greenblatt, *Marvelous Possessions: The Wonder of the New World* (Oxford: Clarendon Press, 1991), 24.

of the last fifteen years of her life. However, she claimed that '[l]ike most Europeans of my generation, I have North America in my bloodstream', and, as Linden Peach suggested, Carter's compulsive interest in America stemmed partly from a desire to interrogate the pertinence of local myths, to 'deconstruct the processes that produce social structures and shared meanings'. By transposing various scenarios within her fictional world overseas—most notably in *The Infernal Desire Machines of Doctor Hoffman* (1972), set in weirdly deracinated landscapes of the Americas and Africa—Carter effectively reconceptualizes her own native culture as equivalently 'foreign'.[54] Besides her stints as a visiting professor of creative writing in the United States—with Coover at Brown, then at the University of Texas, Austin (1985), the University of Iowa (1986), and the State University of New York, Albany (1988)—Carter also lived for three years between 1969 and 1972 in Japan, and all of these experiences would have helped to sharpen the aesthetics of estrangement in her writings. The protagonist of her short story 'Flesh and the Mirror' says that she welcomes the collapse of her normal safety structures and 'being at the mercy of events'—'That is why I like to be a foreigner; I only travel for the insecurity'—and in the afterword to her collection *Fireworks* (1974), where this story was first published, the author recalls how to come back from Japan to England in 1972 was to return to 'a new country. It was like waking up, it was a rude awakening.'[55]

Carter admitted in a 1977 interview, however, that she had 'always felt foreign in England', and even in her early work of the 1960s there is a marked tendency to stake out America as a site of alterity.[56] *The Magic Toyshop* (1967) cites in its first paragraph John Donne's Elegy XIX, 'Going to Bed'—'O, my America, my new found land'—as it associates the beginning of 15-year-old Melanie's menstrual cycle with the development of a sexuality that will stand in a transgressive relationship to the repressive social climate of provincial England in the 1960s. America in this context functions as a glamorous shadow land, a distant realm of myth: the family dog is said to have 'an uncanny quality of whiteness, like Moby Dick', while Melanie finds it easier 'to face the fact of Uncle Philip if she saw him as a character in a film, possibly played by Orson Welles'.[57] This notion of America as a scene of imaginative fantasy or psychological escape also manifests itself in *Several Perceptions* (1968), where Joseph rebels against his suburban family environment, garishly illustrated by its 'plaster ducks' in the sitting room along with the 'tooled leather *TV Times* cover', and turns for emancipation to a

[54] Carter, introduction, in *Expletives Deleted*, 4; Linden Peach, *Angela Carter* (Basingstoke: Macmillan, 1998), 4.

[55] Angela Carter, 'Flesh and the Mirror', in *Burning Your Boats: Collected Short Stories* (London: Chatto & Windus, 1995), 72, and *idem*, 'Appendix: Afterward to *Fireworks*', ibid. 459–60. All subsequent page references to Carter's stories are taken from this edition and are cited as *SS* in the text.

[56] Lorna Sage, 'The Savage Sideshow: A Profile of Angela Carter', *New Review*, 4/39–40 (June–July 1977), 53.

[57] Angela Carter, *The Magic Toyshop* (London: Virago, 1981), 1, 83, 76.

world of American culture, represented here by comic books, an American girl 'full of gaiety' with a 'high-school cheerleader laugh', and the Gothic romances of Edgar Allan Poe (of which Joseph says he 'used to be very fond'). Joseph consequently rejects his girlfriend Charlotte, a student of English literature and a devotee of F. R. Leavis who spends her time composing 'endless essays concerning Jane Austen's moral universe', and he takes his cue instead from David Hume, cited in the epigraph to the novel, for whom ideas of selfhood, ethical continuity, and 'the laws of cause and effect' were much more problematical; Joseph says that his 'actual physical self...often seemed to him no more than an arbitrary piece of theorizing, a random collection of impulses hurtling through a void'.[58] Carter herself read English at the University of Bristol between 1962 and 1965, a time when the influence of Leavis was at its height, though she managed to avoid his more moralistic assertions about the degradations of modern culture by specializing in the medieval period. Indeed, she subsequently attributed the self-conscious use of allegory in her fiction to the fact that 'as a medievalist, I was trained to read books as having many layers'.[59]

In her early novels, then, Carter represents America largely in mythic terms, as a potential site of Gothic romance or pastoral transformation: in *Love* (1971), for example, the character of Buzz goes round in a black suit looking 'fresh from a visit to the tomb of Edgar Allan Poe'.[60] Like Ballard, she was strongly influenced in these early works by the exceptionalist notion, common in the mid-twentieth century, of America as a domain set fabulously apart. An important figure for her at this time was Leslie Fiedler, whose *Love and Death in the American Novel* (1960) attempted critically to valorize a popular, melodramatic fictional tradition full of Freudian psychosexual resonance. Carter's 'post-apocalyptic' novel *Heroes and Villains* (1969), set in a 'hypothetical landscape of ruin and forest', takes one of its epigraphs directly from Fiedler's *Love and Death*: 'The Gothic mode is essentially a form of parody, a way of assailing clichés by exaggerating them to the limit of grotesqueness.'[61] Fiedler himself was one of the influential 'myth and symbol' critics of American literature who emerged in the mid-1950s, for whom the special circumstances and cultural identity of the nation were bound up with a certain controlling idea: in his case, the Gothic as a scene of radical psychological transformation, driven by a masculine flight from sexuality and domesticity. Carter's works of the 1960s tend to reproduce this mythology in order to highlight what she takes to be the similarly claustrophobic aspects of English cultural traditions: just as Fiedler understood American literature to be an extended disquisition on sexual phobias, so Carter in the 1960s represents England synchronically as a landscape of petty repressions. In the 1970s,

58 Angela Carter, *Several Perceptions* (London: Virago, 1995), 105, 7, 140, 114, 4, 21, 5.
59 John Haffenden, *Novelists in Interview* (London: Methuen, 1985), 87.
60 Angela Carter, *Love*, rev. edn. (London: Random House–Vintage, 1997), 36.
61 Angela Carter, *Heroes and Villains* (London: Heinemann, 1969), pp. 177, 132, v.

though, after her return from Japan, Carter's work became more self-consciously historicist in its orientation; she shared in the general enthusiasm among radical British intellectuals of that decade for Gramsci's theory of hegemony, Foucault's equation of power with sexuality, and, especially, Roland Barthes's interrogation of myth as 'depoliticized speech' in *Mythologies*, a key text of this era. In a 1983 essay on gender politics, Carter echoes Barthes by stating overtly her belief that 'all myths are products of the human mind and reflect only aspects of material human practice', concluding that she is 'in the demythologising business'.[62] Her frequent articles on cultural topics for *New Society*, many of them subsequently collected under the title *Nothing Sacred*, reinforce this image of a writer determined to approach her subjects in a secular, political fashion. In a 1977 interview, Carter claimed that to be against God was as important as being a feminist: 'you have to keep the flag flying. Atheism is a very rigorous system of disbelief, and one should keep proclaiming it.' Similarly, her polemical work *The Sadeian Woman* (1979) takes its epigraphs from Foucault and from Frantz Fanon as it assiduously critiques 'the fictions of romantic love' that deny women the prospect of sexual agency by erroneously conflating cultural stereotypes with natural law: 'Myth deals in false universals', she writes, 'to dull the pain of particular circumstances.'[63]

It is this more precise focus upon 'particular circumstances' that directs Carter in her later work to approach America more knowingly, to regard it less in purely lyrical terms as a romantic alternative to English domesticity and rather to adumbrate particular historical moments when the American scene can be appropriated as an analogue or antidote to the trajectory of British culture. *The Passion of New Eve* (1977) starts off in the 'alchemical city' of New York, described as being rent by a racial civil war—'The blacks had burned down Grand Central Station'—which functions here explicitly as a magnification of the racial strife besetting England: the English narrator, Evelyn, reports on how 'the first National Front members had just taken their seats in the House; there were riots in Birmingham and Wolverhampton; the power workers had been on strike for months'. This represents only a small exaggeration of facts about English life in the early 1970s: Enoch Powell, the openly racist Conservative Member of Parliament who attempted to reverse government immigration policies, served as MP for Wolverhampton until 1974, while, following a miners' strike and resultant shortages of fuel, a three-day working week and state of national emergency were declared by Edward Heath's government in December 1973. *The Passion of New Eve* thus plays with the idea of doubles and reversals, switching the gender of the narrator from male to female, Evelyn to Eve, and constructing

---

[62] Barthes, 'Myth Today', 142; Angela Carter, 'Notes from the Front Line', in *On Gender and Writing*, ed. Michelene Wandor (London: Pandora, 1983), 71.
[63] Sage, 'Savage Sideshow', 57; Angela Carter, *The Sadeian Woman: An Exercise in Cultural History* (London: Virago, 1979), 12, 5.

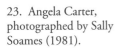

23. Angela Carter,
photographed by Sally
Soames (1981).

a landscape of multiple fissures where the narrator sees 'the desolation of the entire megapolis' and calls it 'a mirror of my own'. California here has declared itself to be an independent republic, and within California there is a '[c]ivil war within the civil war', with Los Angeles and the San Francisco Bay Area pointing missiles at each other. This aesthetic depiction of a 'post-apocalyptic' world works to transform alchemically the fractured state of England, to set its political divisions of the 1970s within the form of an 'arid pastoral' encompassing a more expansive mythological circumference.[64] Unlike the earlier novels, whose mythic resonances gesture more towards an archetypal or fairy-tale significance, *The Passion of New Eve* uses myth reflexively and ties it into particular historical circumstances.

Many of Carter's short stories engage in similar dialectics between Old World and New World, reorienting British history through an explicitly transatlantic framework while at the same time interrupting American spiritual horizons with the shadows of a murkier Gothic past. 'The Cabinet of Edgar Allan Poe',

---

[64] Angela Carter, *The Passion of New Eve* (London: Arrow, 1978), 16, 32–3, 38, 166, 178, 132.

from *Black Venus* (1985), pays homage to Poe, another laureate of borders and liminal states, for the way in which he fails to conform to the morals of the American republic and 'possesses none of its virtues' (*SS* 262). This theme is developed more fully in several stories collected under the title *American Ghosts and Old World Wonders* (1993): for example, in 'John Ford's *'Tis Pity She's a Whore'* the English Jacobean dramatist is conflated with the twentieth-century American film-maker of the same name, as the story imagines how Ford's seventeenth-century play might be reframed through the lens of the modern director. This produces a composite scenario wherein two apparently quite different artists are brought into parallel, as if to highlight points of convergence and divergence between cultures that used to be symbiotically intertwined but are now politically sundered. Again, 'The Ghost Ships' specifically looks back to the schisms of the seventeenth century, describing how the pagan survivals of Christmas are received frostily in Puritan New England—'The very thought of Cotton Mather, with blossom in his hair, dancing round the Maypole makes the imagination reel' (*SS* 377)—and implicitly critiquing the moral fervour of the separatists for their hostility towards the ghosts of Christmas past: 'New England is the new leaf they have just turned over; Old England is the dirty linen their brethren at home have just—did they not recently win the English Civil War?—washed in public' (*SS* 376). It is noticeable that many of Carter's later works return compulsively to points at which these two Anglophone cultures divide, as if to suggest how the erasure of metaphysical idealism from an English milieu was matched by a suppression of the corporeal and carnivalesque on the American side. In 'The Merchant of Shadows', contemporary California is associated with a metaphysics of light, a land where 'Light was made Flesh' (*SS* 363), and this is linked not only to the Hollywood film industry but also to the work of seventeenth-century alchemists; this mood of apotheosis, however, proves ultimately too intense for the British film student narrating this story, who longs at the end 'to go home' to 'rain … and television, that secular medium' (*SS* 375). Alchemy appears again in 'Alice in Prague' in the shape of John Dee (1527–1608), sometime astrologer to Queen Elizabeth I and a devotee of witchcraft and the occult: 'For Dr Dee', we are told, 'the invisible is only another unexplored country, a brave new world' (*SS* 398). As an expatriate in Prague, Dee is said to share with Archduke Rudolph an 'enthusiasm for the newly discovered Americas' (*SS* 402), and Carter's story eulogizes him as someone who 'truly believed that nothing was unknowable. That is what makes him modern' (*SS* 405). It is this iconoclastic willingness to refuse the limitations of traditional knowledge and to envision new worlds that links Dee here with the utopian horizons of America and that makes him a characteristic Carter character.

'Alice in Prague' talks of how '[t]he hinge of the sixteenth century, where it joins with the seventeenth century, is as creaky and judders open as reluctantly as the door in a haunted house'; but it is precisely that hinge, at the moment when the Renaissance was 'guttering out' and the 'Age of Reason' no more than a 'distant light' on the horizon (*SS* 398), to which Carter's texts constantly return. This is also, of course, the historical moment at which America was first beginning to impinge upon the British consciousness, and Carter fictionally recapitulates ways in which the shadows of America become associated with magical spheres of transformation and transgression. 'Our Lady of the Massacre', published in *Black Venus*, furnishes a more proletarian perspective on this transatlantic bifurcation by relating the story of a woman transported in the seventeenth century from Lancashire to Virginia, where she cuts off her master's ears, throws in her lot with the Indians, and sets off to walk towards Florida; she is determined to get 'to where the English have no dominion' (*SS* 250), and proudly asserts that she walks 'now, where no person of my country ever trod before' (*SS* 251–2). Like the eponymous heroine of Daniel Defoe's *Moll Flanders* (1722), Carter's protagonist finds that her fortunes improve radically in this new environment; despite the scathing disapproval of the governor of Virginia, who denounces her as a 'heathen' (*SS* 258), she is regarded here as 'a good man's wife' even though she was cast as 'a bad woman in my own country' (*SS* 255). On one level, this can be seen as a typical tale of displacement and immigration, where the host country provides a new environment that offers a form of moral regeneration by rendering old social categories obsolete; it is the world not only of Defoe but also of Crèvecoeur and Jefferson. What is significant here, however, is that through this pastiche of Defoe—hailed by Carter as 'father of the bourgeois novel in England' (*SS* 460)—we infer what she takes to be the necessarily transatlantic genealogy of the English novel. Rather than following the path laid out by English critic Ian Watt, who saw Defoe as the precursor of a middle-class fictional tradition concerned above all with social and economic respectability, Carter, like American critics Nancy Armstrong and Leonard Tennenhouse, understands Defoe to be part of a bilateral world whose values derive from American captivity narratives and other transatlantic cross-currents and influences. This significantly reconceives the 'great tradition' of English literature to be a hybrid phenomenon, predicated not so much upon forms of moral continuity, as Leavis and Watt imagined, but upon a dynamic of dislocation and traversal.[65]

Particularly in her later fiction, then, Carter is more self-consciously theoretical and historicist than Ballard in the way she foregrounds both the science and the limitations of representation. *Nights at the Circus* (1984) describes its heroine, Fevvers, from what is called on the first page a 'steatopygous perspective': 'The artist had chosen to depict her ascent from behind—bums aloft, you might

[65] Nancy Armstrong and Leonard Tennenhouse, 'The American Origins of the English Novel', *American Literary History*, 4 (1992), 386–410, and *idem, The Imaginary Puritan: Literature, Intellectual Labor, and the Origins of Personal Life* (Berkeley: University of California Press, 1992). See also Watt, *Rise of the Novel*, and Leavis, *Great Tradition*.

say.'[66] This about-face epitomizes the novel's structure of inversion, through which opposites are brought paradoxically into conjunction. In the same vein, Carter's rhetoric in this novel consciously aspires to a condition of liminality and doubleness, as the narrator observes: 'It could be said that, for all of the peoples of the region, there existed no difference between fact and fiction; instead, a sort of magic realism' (p. 260). Fevvers herself is a 'Cockney Venus' (p. 7), a 'fabulous bird-woman' (p. 15) endowed with the power of flight who straddles human and divine worlds: 'Queen of ambiguities, goddess of in-between states, being on the borderline of species' (p. 81). Part of this 'in-between' quality of Carter's fiction involves an interruption of the idea of reason through mechanisms of burlesque, so that the oxymorons built into this narrative—'innocent beasts and wise children' (p. 155)—betoken a traditional state of pastoral transformation and reconciliation, signified here by the final marriage of Fevvers to Californian adventurer Jack Walser. *Nights at the Circus* gestures at the end towards 'the customary endings of the old comedies' (p. 280), and it is true that there is a consummation of a kind here, though whether this 'attraction of opposites' actually 'exorcises ... the sado-masochistic tenor of sexual relations in Carter's earlier fictions', as Ann Massa and Alistair Stead suggest, is more doubtful.[67] Although Fevvers is described as the 'reconciler of fundament and firmament' (p. 81), this novel, like Carter's other work, takes its primary impetus from an interpenetration of opposites rather than their easy harmonization, and the careful dating of events in the book also works as a counterpoint to the putatively timeless world of old comedy. The novel is set in 1899, and it refers back briefly to the nineteenth-century war between Britain and the United States in the passage where Colonel Kearney passes out while trying to seduce Fevvers: 'Couldn't get' is star-spangled banner up', she remarks, 'Britannia's revenge for the War of 1812' (p. 171). The novel's explicit feminist theme—symbolized by Fevvers's capacity for flight, which anticipates a 'New Age in which no women will be bound down to the ground' (p. 25)—also serves to circumscribe the utopian mythology with a more hard-edged materialist dimension, through which Carter's visionary capacities are given a distinct political edge. As she herself wrote in *The Sadeian Woman*, 'There is no way out of time.'[68]

It is a politicized version of pastoral that also underpins Carter's last novel, *Wise Children* (1991), the one nominated by Salman Rushdie as her finest.[69] The story is plotted around the production of a film version of Shakespeare's *A Midsummer Night's Dream* directed in Hollywood by venerable English actor

        [66] Angela Carter, *Nights at the Circus* (London: Chatto & Windus–Hogarth Press, 1984), 7. Subsequent page references to this edition are cited in the text.
        [67] Ann Massa and Alistair Stead, foreword, in *Forked Tongues: Comparing Twentieth-Century British and American Literature*, ed. Ann Massa and Alistair Stead (London: Longman, 1994), 13.
        [68] Carter, *Sadeian Woman*, 110.
        [69] Salman Rushdie, 'Angela Carter, 1940–1992: A Very Good Wizard, a Very Dear Friend', *New York Times Book Review*, 8 March 1992, 5.

Sir Melchior Hazard, and it is narrated by Dora Chance, an illegitimate twin daughter of Melchior who is 'Cockney to the core' and rooted in the world of south London.[70] The novel turns upon a series of polarities—tragedy versus comedy, England versus America, high culture versus low culture, Melchior as 'a pillar of the legit. theatre' versus his daughters who 'are illegitimate in every way' (p. 11)—but the progressive effect of the narrative is to problematize these binary oppositions, to suggest how they can ultimately be seen as mutually constitutive. In this sense, America fulfils its traditional role in Carter's fiction as a scene of pastoral transformation: when Dora goes to Hollywood to play a part in Melchior's film, she talks of how the California sun 'shone on everyone, whether they had a contract or not' and describes it as '[t]he most democratic thing I'd ever seen … And, tell the truth, it changed me. It changed me for good and all' (p. 121). Carmen Callil thought *Wise Children* to be 'a novel of Thatcher's Britain, as Britain split in two', and certainly many of the class divisions apparent in this text speak to the condition of a nation riven between voices of the Establishment and those planted firmly on the social margins. Steven Connor read the book more optimistically, seeing in the creative transfer of Shakespeare to the silver screen a 'mutual contamination' of high and low cultures; but such interpenetrations within the novel are specifically associated with its transatlantic dimension, which becomes at times oddly patriotic in the way it seeks to revalidate Shakespeare as a cultural monument within an Anglo-American context.[71] Thus, Melchior dreams of taking over Hollywood, describing the success of his film as 'Shakespeare's revenge for the War of Independence' (p. 148), while Dora joins in with an insistent bout of patriotic fervour on Shakespeare's birthday: 'Cry God for England, Harry and St George' (p. 197). They stay in California at a hotel called the Forest of Arden, with 'replicas of Anne Hathaway's cottage' nearby (p. 120), and the burden of this allegory appears to indicate that the expansive world of Elizabethan England is being re-created within a West Coast environment.

Through these proposed transatlantic reconciliations, *Wise Children* furnishes a utopian image of an undivided England, the country as it was before the great schism of the seventeenth century divided the English-speaking world in two. Like Byron 170 years earlier, Carter attributes the class hierarchies and other forms of social exclusion to the loss of a democratic impulse which was, in Shakespeare's day, an integral part of the social fabric, but which subsequently cut itself off and migrated to America. This is why the burlesque version of Shakespeare acted out on this transatlantic stage becomes for Carter an emblem of pastoral reconciliation, of the kind of heterogeneous English culture to which

---

[70] Angela Carter, *Wise Children* (London: Chatto & Windus, 1991), 143. Subsequent page references to this edition are cited in parentheses in the text.

[71] Carmen Callil, 'Flying Jewellery', *Sunday Times*, 23 Feb. 1992, sec. 7, 6; Steven Connor, *The English Novel in History, 1950–1995* (London: Routledge, 1996), 37.

her work aspires; moreover, the bizarre connections and puns that permeate this narrative provide a formal correlative to its vision of binding together disparate materials into a state of unity. As its title suggests, *Wise Children* yokes together contraries, assimilating youth and age into a continuous circle while making England and America appear as benign cultural extensions of each other. In a 1980 essay on Grace Paley, Carter described 'the unique quality of the greatest American art' as not 'optimism' but '*inexhaustibility*', and it is this kind of resourcefulness that she wishes above all to recuperate for British culture. The allure of America's more diffuse radical tradition became particularly attractive to Carter during the Thatcher years, and in 1988 she wrote of her admiration for Edmund White's novel *The Beautiful Room is Empty*, recommending it as a text with which to counter the Conservative government's promotion of Section 28, which prohibited schools from disseminating information about homosexuality.[72]

Like Ballard, Carter tended, particularly in the latter part of her career, to write thesis novels, propositions evolving out of cultural and political concerns which are subsequently worked out in fictional terms. In a 1985 interview, she admitted that 'my fiction is very often a kind of literary criticism, which is something I've started to worry about quite a lot'.[73] This theoretical awareness certainly ensured a measure of consistency between Carter's fiction and her cultural journalism, though it also means that individual characters within her novels are usually less significant than the abstract ideas they embody. Carter's self-conscious use of allegory works something like Brecht's alienation technique in drama, estranging the reader from any comfortable feeling of empathy with the dramatis personae and directing them instead towards political issues raised by the text. In her essay 'Notes on the Gothic Mode', Carter said that she thought it was 'immoral to read simply for pleasure' and declared 'art's singular moral function' to be 'that of provoking unease'. She also asserted here that '[a]ll art, of any kind, is part of politics—it either expresses or criticizes an ideology'. Nevertheless, Carter's work also incorporates an art of paradoxical transformation, through which the proximate circumstances of her English environment are rendered radically mutable. 'I like all paradoxes,' wrote Carter in this same essay, and her scabrous depiction before the 1983 General Election of Margaret Thatcher as a 'nanny' catering to 'the joys of masochism', speaks to a Sadeian view of politics whereby the supposedly disinterested structures of bureaucratic reason are actually driven by a furious libidinal instinct, with the art of burlesque negotiating a radical demystification of dualistic abstraction, a dissolution of spirit into matter.[74] Carter thus reconceives the past reflexively, in a self-consciously fictional manner,

---

[72] Angela Carter, 'Grace Paley: *The Little Disturbances of Man* and *Enormous Changes at the Last Minute*', in *Expletives Deleted*, 158, and *idem*, 'Edmund White: *The Beautiful Room is Empty*', ibid. 139–42.   [73] Haffenden, *Novelists in Interview*, 79.
[74] Angela Carter, 'Notes on the Gothic Mode', *Iowa Review*, 6/3–4 (Summer–Fall 1975), 133–4; *idem*, 'Masochism for the Masses', *New Statesman*, 3 June 1983, 8.

as she rewrites the history of insurrection and schism to postulate a utopian state in which the transatlantic divide might once again be resolved into a continuum. Rather than regarding postmodern America merely as an infinitely malleable site of simulations, Carter looks at the idea of the New World from a more knowing historical perspective and repositions it in relation to her home culture through time as well as space.[75]

PARALLEL UNIVERSES: MARTIN AMIS

As Carter's comments before the 1983 election imply, Anglo-American post-modernism in the 1980s developed both within the shadow of, and as an oppositional response to, the political momentum of Margaret Thatcher and Ronald Reagan. Thatcher became British Prime Minister on 4 May 1979 and resigned eleven and a half years later, on 27 November 1990; Reagan's American presidency ran from 20 January 1981 until 20 January 1989. It would probably be true to say that many of the key social and economic developments of the 1980s—the growth of information technology, the consequent new mobility of global finance, the shift from a corporate to a market economy and from labour-intensive to capital-intensive industry—would have happened whoever had been in control of these countries politically. Nevertheless, the personalities of Thatcher and Reagan made them particularly easy to caricature and demonize, and in the work of Carter, Rushdie, Martin Amis, and others we see attempts to criticize the state of the nations through an intense focus on their political figure-heads. The particularly mordant aspect of Amis's comic perspective, though, is linked to a collapse of the satiric impulse, a failure to gain the moral plateau that would enable his works effectively to critique the shortcomings of Thatcherite British culture. Amis's transatlantic narratives consequently revolve in a kind of dark circle, where humanist reactions against the all-encompassing logic of capitalist corruption remain ironically incarcerated within a structural double bind, through which America comes to appear, as Amis himself put it, 'more like a world than a country', not a territory positioned antithetically to Britain but its inescapable corollary.[76]

Amis has a personal history which links him strongly with the United States. As a 10-year-old, he spent the 1959–60 academic year in New Jersey while his father was a visiting professor at Princeton, and both his wives have been American; 'I feel fractionally American myself', said Amis in his introduction to a collection of non-fiction pieces about America, *The Moronic Inferno*.[77] Like

[75] For a more Baudrillardian view of Carter's engagement with America as simulacrum, see Richard Brown, 'Postmodern Americas in the Fiction of Angela Carter, Martin Amis and Ian McEwan', in *Forked Tongues*, ed. Massa and Stead, 92–110.

[76] Stefano De Luigi and Martin Amis, *Pornoland* (London: Thames & Hudson, 2004), n.p.

[77] Martin Amis, *The Moronic Inferno and Other Visits to America* (London: Penguin, 1987), p. ix.

Carter, Amis is a militant atheist, scathing about Ronald Reagan's proclivity to harmonize his political policies with his reading of the Book of Revelation—'a forgetful old actor with a head full of Armageddon theology and Manichaean adversarialism, interspliced with war movies and scraps of *Reader's Digest*'—and since 9/11 he has been equally critical about the 'intellectually null' George W. Bush's 'theological' invocation of an 'axis of evil'. This has led Amis to be especially critical of what he sees as the imperial aspects of US foreign policy and of the general blindness to overseas affairs of Americans, with their 'assiduous geographical incuriosity' and 'deficit of empathy for the sufferings of people far away'. He indicted particularly in this regard the cataclysm wrought by American forces when they wiped out as much as 5 per cent of the Iraqi population during the war of 1991.[78]

Amis wrote a profile of Rushdie for *Vanity Fair* in 1990, at the height of *The Satanic Verses* controversy, in which he attempted to exonerate the persecuted author by proclaiming: 'he is neither a god nor a devil: he is just a *writer*—comical and protean, ironical and ardent.' But in suggesting that Rushdie's fiction might be understood according to a 'purity of literary response' and the book's own qualities of 'passionate invention', Amis was highlighting that lack of critical self-awareness endemic to his own writing.[79] To discuss Rushdie's novel as though its artistic genius could simply transcend cultural politics is manifestly absurd; the novelist Will Self, a friend of Amis's, has called this theoretical illiteracy a kind of 'calculated stupidity' on his part, and it may well be that the latter's work is stronger precisely because of its lack of reflective capacities.[80] Whereas Rushdie's narratives juggle knowingly with ideas, the force of Amis's best writing is more brutal and emotive, arising out of an almost visceral sense of disgust. As a corollary to this, though, Amis's fiction, unlike Rushdie's, varies wildly in quality. His best works, *Money* (1984) and *London Fields* (1989), are major novels by any standards; Saul Bellow was even moved in 1990 to associate Amis with Joyce and Flaubert, saying that he detected in him 'signs of a very large outline'.[81] The less successful novels, though, are much thinner and more proselytizing, and it is as though the poignancy and zest of *Money* and *London Fields* derive from powerful textual contradictions, from a sense that the author is not fully in control of his material.

Money is one of the emblematic texts of the 1980s, a novel which brilliantly encapsulates how the capitalist chain reactions of Thatcher and Reagan worked themselves out through a transatlantic vortex. One of the strengths of the book,

[78] Martin Amis, 'Nuclear City: The Megadeath Intellectuals', in *Visiting Mrs Nabokov and Other Excursions* (London: Jonathan Cape, 1993), 22; *idem*, 'The Palace of the End', *Guardian*, 4 March 2003, 23; *idem*, 'Fear and Loathing', *Guardian*, 18 Sept. 2001, sec. 2, 5.

[79] Martin Amis, 'Salman Rushdie', in *Visiting Mrs Nabokov*, 170, 177.

[80] Stephen Moss, 'After the Storm: Profile of Martin Amis', *Guardian Weekend*, 3 Oct. 1998, 24.

[81] Mira Stout, 'Martin Amis: Down London's Mean Streets', *New York Times Magazine*, 4 Feb. 1990, 35.

though, is precisely that it takes no fixed position on this world of 'supply and demand': the transnational circulations of finance are here presented as a disturbing, overwhelming phenomenon which simply sweeps away the old refuges of liberal humanism and consequently disqualifies the potential of satire.[82] Or, to put this another way, *Money* constitutes a kind of negative satire, a satire without any concomitant sense of moral outrage. Whereas the novels of Kingsley Amis, Martin's father, tend more towards a style of classical satire influenced by Samuel Johnson and inflected by traditional conservative values, *Money* preserves a cutting edge of black humour but denies the possibility of any stable point of comparison against which the grotesque events portrayed might be judged. In interviews, Amis has openly expressed what he calls 'strong moral views', castigating money as 'the central deformity in life' and denouncing television as 'the greatest source of crime now'.[83] In his best fiction, however, this authorial voice is melded into a more complex series of textual and social networks where the safe haven of a singular perspective becomes impossible to find.

Money is dated very precisely, unfolding against a backdrop of the Charles–Diana royal wedding and the urban riots in England during the summer of 1981, and it concludes in January 1982, a few months before victory in the Falklands War had helped to consolidate the fortunes of what had appeared until that time a rather insecure Thatcher government. Monetarism in the early 1980s was a shock to the system as far as Britain was concerned, the unleashing of free market forces upon what had previously been a rather somnolent social and economic culture, and *Money* is suffused with a sense of the harshness and rawness of this political experiment. Amis later said that '*Money* needed Margaret Thatcher in its subliminal background', and the entire landscape of this book is metaphorically commodified, as though the whole country were for sale: the narrator refers, for instance, to a 'standard-issue British pigeon' (p. 203).[84] This supersession of nature by commerce ushers in an England newly overwhelmed by the products of 'market forces' (p. 72), where television, pornography, and fast food outlets are quickly usurping the place of bookstores. America is of course represented here as the home of money—in New York, reports the hero John Self, there are 'taxi-meters, money-clocks, on the ambulances in this city: that's the sort of place I'm dealing with' (p. 10)—and Self, who is said to have an American mother and to have spent seven of his childhood years living in New Jersey, shuttles back and forth between London and Manhattan in a circular motion that reflects the ideology of exchange upon which the rhetoric of this book is predicated. The language of *Money* is highly charged and slightly manic, and it signifies a world in which natural, corporeal entities have been weirdly anthropomorphized and thus turned into artificial constructions: Self talks about a toothache 'on

---

[82] Martin Amis, *Money: A Suicide Note* (London: Jonathan Cape, 1984), 34. Subsequent page references to this edition are cited in parentheses in the text.
[83] Haffenden, *Novelists in Interview*, 10, 22.   [84] Moss, 'After the Storm', 26.

my upper west side' (p. 10), punks are referred to as 'parrot-crested blankies' (p. 147), film actor Lorne Guyland is said to have 'that tan-and-silver sheen of the all-American robot kings' (p. 176), a cloud in the sky is metamorphosed by Self's mind into 'a pussy' as he wonders: 'can pornography now shape the clouds and hold all sway in the middle air?' (p. 235). Within this sinister process of reversal and exchange, humans have become automatized as machines are actively personified: Self remarks towards the end of how 'A fat bus snorted in astonishment' (p. 356).

This all-consuming process of linguistic metamorphosis, which reconstructs the world according to the principles of metaphor such that one side of a figurative equation is held in balance against another, acts as a correlative to the commercial processes of exchange which also pervade the novel and which preclude for the narrator any possibility of transcendence. Self is said to be reading a book about Hitler (p. 300), and indeed it is a kind of imperial structure which is being described here, where money is 'the great conspiracy ... [t]he great addiction' (p. 359). Financial values form an all-encompassing infrastructure within the novel: the 'streets are full of movement but hardly anybody goes where they go through thought or choice, free of money motive. Only people with money do that' (p. 254). Self's point here is both paradoxical and recursive, suggesting how money becomes a redundant idea only for those who already have it in excess. This implies not only the ideological circumference of this particular text, enclosed in a capitalist world of no exit, but also indicates how these fictional characters, impelled automatically by the 'money motive', are deprived of choice and therefore of moral free will. Indeed, the authorial figure of Martin Amis, when he makes an appearance in the final section of the book, declares that 'as a controlling force in human affairs, motivation is pretty well shagged out by now' (p. 335). The idea of fiction centred upon psychologically consistent and ethically responsible characters, so beloved of earlier generations of English novelists, has been frozen out by Amis's monetarist environment.

All of this ensured that *Money* came in for some fairly predictable disapproval from British journalists: John Carey criticized it for an 'absence of human beings and the studious avoidance of anything resembling geniality', while Andrew Marr dismissed Amis as merely a 'brilliant stylist' and his books as 'all surface glitter'.[85] One of the strengths of *Money*, though, lies precisely in the way it iconoclastically dismantles false institutional profundities and repackages them as 'surface glitter', emptying out the iconography of the conventional world and exposing its complicity with hollow forms of simulacra. One aspect of this denaturalization is the appropriation for commercial buildings in Manhattan of famous names from American literary history: the Walden Center (p. 207), the Carraway foyer (p. 328), the Ashbery Hotel (p. 327). Another involves

---

[85] John Carey, 'Two Englishmen Abroad', *Sunday Times*, 30 Sept. 1984, 42; Jason Cowley, 'Portrait: Martin Amis', *Prospect*, Aug.–Sept. 1997, 22.

the repeated allusions in the narrative to the royal wedding: the description of Princess Diana as someone whose complexion is softened by 'the colour of money' (p. 248) emphasizes how the class system of Britain is also inextricably interwoven with economic advantage and how the monarchy projects itself within an expensive culture of public spectacle. Similarly, the references here to unemployment and urban unrest indicate a world from which old paternalistic assumptions have been unceremoniously evacuated and where the brutal pressures of monetarism now reign unchecked: 'the whole of England has been scalded by tumult and mutiny,' reports Self (p. 68), '[t]he dole-queue starts at the exit to the playground' (p. 147). In London, the 'talk is all of royalty and riots' (p. 219), and this epitomizes the fractured condition of England in 1981 when the economic autonomy of the nation-state itself was first coming under serious threat from transnational corporations. Although there are gestures in the last part of *Money* towards various forms of pastoral regeneration—environmentalism, health, feminism—they appear here as merely tenuous or hypothetical possibilities, presented much less compellingly than the market cycles and exchanges that drive the narrative.

Like Ballard, then, Amis runs transnational worlds in parallel, though his primary concern is not so much to disturb local pieties as to suggest areas of congruence between Britain and the United States, ways in which the British state might be seen as morphing into an extension of the American empire. Whereas in *Money* a London executive visits New York, in *London Fields* this perspective is reversed by having an American narrator on the first page fly into England. The image of parallel universes is made explicit here—'I hope there are parallel universes,' says narrator Samson Young, 'I hope alternatives exist'—and one function of this transatlantic narrative is to cast an eye on 'slum-and-plutocrat Great Britain', where, 'against all the historical odds', the social and economic structures of class reveal '[t]errific staying power'.[86] Although set in 1999, *London Fields* was published in 1989, and the rigidity of the class divisions portrayed here reflect the merciless climate of the Thatcher decade. Class is shown to limit the options of Amis's characters in unconscious ways and to eliminate their powers of rational choice: 'It would surprise Keith a lot if you told him it was *class* that poisoned his every waking moment' (p. 24). The immobility of the English class system works here as a synecdoche of the more general sense of fatalism that broods over this novel, set in a country that is 'all burgled out' (p. 248), where time seems literally to run backwards: the heroine, Nicola Six, has experienced a premonition of her own murder, and the book builds inevitably towards its grisly climax.

Setting this novel on the eve of the millennium allows it to exist in two temporal spheres at once: in apocalyptic as well as historical time. The images of eclipse and 'perfect parallax', when 'two white balls conjoined … and the moon

---

[86] Martin Amis, *London Fields* (New York: Harmony Books, 1989), 239, 137–8, 24. Subsequent page references to this edition are cited in parentheses in the text.

began to burn like a little sun' (p. 444), exemplify the novel's sense of entropy and inversion, its reversal of pastoralism into a cold scientific determinism: 'this is London; and there are no fields. Only fields of operation and observation, only fields of electromagnetic attraction and repulsion, only fields of hatred and coercion' (p. 134). As one English review pointed out, the novel is more effective in its treatment of 'the texture of poverty' in London than in its more 'ostensible concern with the horrors of global warfare'; yet, as the *New York Times* also noted, *London Fields* is 'not a safe book', but one 'controlled and moved ... by the density of its language', which is 'demonically alive'.[87] The images associated with the Black Cross pub where Nicola is eventually murdered reverberate ominously and evoke a country dominated, unbeknownst to itself, by spectres of the irrational and barbaric. As in *Money*, Hitler makes a cameo appearance in this novel—he is said to be 'still running the century' (p. 395)—while one of the characters, Guy Clinch, has been reading Martin Gilbert's work *The Holocaust* (p. 418). Nicola's faculty of foresight is also associated metaphorically with the Second World War, in so far as she explains her capacity to herself when young by inventing a friend called Enola Gay, who 'had the knack or gift of always knowing how things would unfold' (p. 66). Enola Gay was, of course, the name of the plane that flew the mission to Hiroshima in 1945, and so the novel's sense of fatalism, of things unfolding according to an inexorable design, is aligned specifically with the legacy of this war and with the atomic bomb. This is the same kind of point that we saw being made in Donald Davie's poetry, that post-1945 mythologies celebrating the triumph of British decency over imperial fascism represented too simplistic an antithesis. In *London Fields*, national exceptionalisms of every kind are undermined: just as England is enmeshed within 'gross fantasies of enslavement, humiliation, appetite, murder' (p. 342), so America can no longer offer the prospect of utopian renewal. America, says Samson Young, wanted to be 'good', 'better', and '*special*', but 'in reality she was sleeping, and deep-dreaming' (p. 367). When Clinch travels to the twin town of New London in Connecticut, he stays at an airport hotel called the Founding Fathers, but all the echoes of the Mayflower now seem merely ironic: 'He had a sense, as you were bound to have in America now, of how a whole continent had been devoured, used up, chewed up' (p. 422).

The parallels rather than differences between America and Europe are also worked through in *Time's Arrow* (1991), a story told chronologically in reverse which traces the life of surgeon Tod Friendly back from his elderly years in 'washing-line and mailbox America, innocuous America' to his earlier incarnation as Odilo Unverdorben in an Auschwitz concentration camp.[88] The reversal of time here is commensurate with the moral reversals of the narrative, although in

---

[87] Christina Koning, 'Death by Request', *Guardian*, 21 Sept. 1989, 26; Bette Pesetsky, 'Lust Among the Ruins', *New York Times Book Review*, 4 March 1990, 42.

[88] Martin Amis, *Time's Arrow; or, The Nature of the Offense* (New York: Harmony Books, 1991), 6.

technical terms the ingenuities of the book are applied inconsistently. Amis said that he took the idea of the plot's reverse movement from Kurt Vonnegut's war novel *Slaughterhouse Five*, in which the main character watches films of bombing raids over Germany running backwards, but in Amis's novel this conceit is developed into a more extensive structural principle.[89] At some moments everything seems to be happening back to front—during a cancer operation, for example, we see Friendly 'spooning tumor into the human body'—but the fact that the sentences are necessarily designed to be read forwards ensures the overall effect here is not like that of a film in reverse, and indeed Friendly's thought processes are represented in a relatively orthodox sequential manner. Nevertheless, the book does encapsulate several of Amis's persistent themes: the dominance of the past over the present, and the sense of fatalism this engenders; the insufficiency of the idea of American exceptionalism and the inevitable incorporation of the United States into cycles of human corruption; and the haunting memory of the Nazi project as the central, defining event in the twentieth century. For Amis, the Second World War epitomized a human instinct for large-scale destruction which remains unchecked even after the elimination of National Socialism: 'Probably human cruelty is fixed and eternal,' says the narrator in *Time's Arrow*. 'Only styles change.'[90]

Amis's stylistic genius, then, works most effectively in its delineation of what John Updike called, in a review of *Night Train* (1997), a 'post-human' landscape. For all his ethical protestations about nuclear weapons—'the worst thing that has ever happened to the planet', he claims in *Einstein's Monsters* (1987)—and for all his genuine outrage at authoritarianism and cruelty, Amis's fiction thrives paradoxically off points of cross-over between a traditional liberal humanism and this 'post-human' scenario.[91] *Night Train*, a murder mystery set in the United States, situates itself in a liminal position between human and cosmic time—the dead woman, Jennifer Rockwell, had worked as an academic cosmologist, studying 'questions having to do with the age of the universe'—and this intrusion of astronomical perspectives seems to render the issue of one human death moot. The novel's designation of what it calls 'relative states. Popularly known as "parallel universes"' can therefore be understood in a number of overlapping ways.[92] Amis's parallel universes involve alignments between human and extra-human spatial and temporal dimensions; his fictional narratives work through points of cross-over and intersection which function as a corollary to his stylistic interpenetration between liberal humanism and scientific automatism and, by extension, between the cultures of Britain and America. This is not to claim that Britain should be understood simply as liberal and America as

---

[89] Nicolas Tredell, ed., *The Fiction of Martin Amis: A Reader's Guide to Essential Criticism* (Duxford, Cambridge: Icon, 2000), 132. [90] Amis, *Time's Arrow*, 87, 40.
[91] Tredell, ed., *Fiction of Martin Amis*, 174; Martin Amis, *Einstein's Monsters* (London: Penguin, 1988), 2. [92] Martin Amis, *Night Train* (London: Jonathan Cape, 1997), 90, 47.

scientific; it is, though, to suggest that the frisson of Amis's style emerges from the way it conceptualizes disparate categories in parallel terms, playing them off against each other. His black comedy derives not simply from a substitution of American contexts for their British counterparts, but from that process of transformation whereby a certain set of aesthetic and cultural values is confronted with a foreign agent, an agent that twists the domestic landscape into sinister new shapes. This stylistic hybridity, therefore, does not involve simply the inclusion of 'a great deal of American writing' alongside 'sharply observed work of English social comedy', as Bernard Bergonzi suggested; more specifically, it demands the metamorphosis of English into Americanized forms, so that native scenes are defamiliarized and threatened with conscription into a potentially alarming new universe.[93] The 1997 short story 'The Janitor on Mars' is one of the most successful of his science fiction pieces, because it combines radically alien perspectives—the idea of a Martian civilization that rose and fell long before the development of Earth—with the comically dehumanized idea of a robot as 'janitor'. This serves not simply to transcend social comedy but literally to translate it into another dimension, with Amis's construction of parallel worlds here owing much to the example of Ballard's ambidextrous science fiction, part realism and part fantasy.[94]

For all this fictional ambivalence, Amis never moves away entirely from a conservative moral perspective, something he inherits partly from his father and partly from Saul Bellow, whose views on the corruption of life in America he frequently cites and whom he embraces in his memoir *Experience* (2001) as a surrogate 'father' after Kingsley's death.[95] The non-fictional *Moronic Inferno* takes its title from Bellow's 1975 novel *Humboldt's Gift*—'Now the moronic inferno had caught up with me'—and Amis's volume could hardly have been more censorious in tone had it been written by Bellow himself or Bellow's friend Allan Bloom, well known for his diatribe *The Closing of the American Mind*, published in 1987, just one year after *The Moronic Inferno*; indeed, Amis cites Bloom's work with approbation in *Experience*.[96] In *The Moronic Inferno*, Amis disapproves of nearly every American public figure he meets, on the grounds that they have failed to do justice to 'human complexity'. Thus, Truman Capote lacks 'moral imagination, moral artistry'; Philip Roth's novels 'have no plot and little patterning'; Norman Mailer, 'like America ... went too far in all directions'; William Burroughs's work is 'trash, and lazily obsessive trash too'. Only Bellow himself, who 'really is a great American writer', is exempted from this inferno, since he understands that 'being human' is 'not a given but a gift,

---

[93] Tredell, ed., *Fiction of Martin Amis*, 61.

[94] Martin Amis, 'The Janitor on Mars', in *Heavy Water and Other Stories* (London: Jonathan Cape, 1998), 154–93. For Amis's view of Ballard, see *The War Against Cliché: Essays and Reviews, 1971–2000* (London: Jonathan Cape, 2001), 95–112.

[95] Martin Amis, *Experience* (London: Jonathan Cape, 2000), 360.

[96] Amis, *Moronic Inferno*, p. x, and *idem*, *Experience*, 202.

a talent, an accomplishment, an objective'. The premiss of *The Moronic Inferno* is thus an American exceptionalism in reverse, the notion that the country itself represents an insult to human decency, the same sense of moralistic outrage that inspired Samuel Johnson to pamphleteer against American insurrectionists in the eighteenth century. At times, indeed, Amis's tone veers towards the Johnsonian in its capacity to give offence: 'As soon as you leave New York you see how monstrously various, how humanly balkanized, America really is,' he writes in a piece on Gloria Steinem. 'Do all these people actually *have* a human potential? Don't we need the norms? How much variety can a society contain? How much can it stand?' This is troubling not only in its contempt for diversity—exemplified here by the phrase 'monstrously various'—but also in its reification of an unexamined idea of 'human potential' as a universal value. This is also consistent with the author's reactionary assumption that the institutional 'norms' of any given society should 'contain' and thus preclude the dangerous possibility of excessive 'variety'.[97]

Throughout Amis's more recent work, there is a curious obsession with patrilineal inheritance, with the genealogies of established traditions. This concern appears in another guise in *The Information* (1995), in which there is an extended disquisition on how the 'four seasons are meant to correspond to the four principal literary genres. That is to say, summer, autumn, winter and spring are meant to correspond (and here I list them hierarchically) to tragedy, romance, comedy and satire.'[98] The phrase 'meant to' is perhaps misleading in this context, implying that such an arrangement is a fact of nature, whereas actually these mythic archetypes derive from the influential theories proposed by Northrop Frye in his *Anatomy of Criticism* (1957). Frye's structuralist formulas appeared intellectually somewhat dated by 1995, and the confusion of genres adumbrated by *The Information*, 'the undermining of innocence and Eden' (p. 62) by unregenerate urban landscapes such as the 'verdant world' of a park called 'Dogshit' (p. 446), speak to a sense of hybridity inherent not only in Amis's fiction but within the postmodern condition in general. What is anomalous, though, is the nostalgia for generic purity which this intellectual deference to Frye implies, a retrospective mood reinforced by the direct citation early in *The Information* of T. S. Eliot's theory of the dissociation of sensibility: 'Richard hurriedly wondered whether this had been a natural resource of men and women—passionate speech—before 1700 or whenever Eliot said it was, before thought and feeling got dissociated' (p. 26). It is, however, precisely the way in which these twinnings exist alongside nostalgia for a prelapsarian state of unity that fires Amis's creative imagination. *The Information* is organized around such pairings, with oscillations between England and America and between Richard

---

[97] Amis, *Moronic Inferno*, 87, 39, 47, 73, 144, 200, 208, 142.
[98] Martin Amis, *The Information* (London: Flamingo–HarperCollins, 1995), 53. Subsequent page references to this edition are cited in parentheses in the text.

Tull and Gwyn Barry being replicated in Richard's twin sons, Marco and Marius, who are also, like Richard and Gwyn, one day apart in age. Yet this 'possibility of additional or parallel universes', explicitly addressed here by the narrator, seemingly 'presents the writer with something new to worry about. Shakespeare is the universal. That is to say, he plays well enough in *this* universe ... But how would he go down in all the others?' (p. 253).

The Information, then, puzzles intellectually over an awareness of its own narrative decentring, positioning itself at a juncture in history when an excess of information—through media, computers, and other outlets—is threatening to invalidate the whole concept of universal values. In this sense, the world of the 1990s is linked with earlier periods of overload and schism: with the seventeenth century, as signalled by the Eliot quotation, when England and America first divided; and with the early nineteenth century, when, amidst the exponential growth of commercial publishing, Coleridge allegedly became 'the last man to have read everything' (p. 242). At the same time, there is a residual attachment here to the exposition of knowledge in clearly demarcated categories and a powerful feeling of regret for the loss of this epistemological coherence. It is a pattern foreshadowed in Amis's early novel *Other People* (1981), whose amnesiac heroine at the end is planning to read Robert Burton's *Anatomy of Melancholy* (1621), a classic text of parallel universes in which an inherited sense of humanist order finds itself being usurped by the sprawling new worlds opened up by geographic discovery; not coincidentally, these 'barabarous, uncivill' lands are associated by Burton explicitly with Virginia, California, and other parts of America.[99] As always, then, Amis's fiction is more multidimensional than his cultural journalism, more open to the ways in which elements of the amorphous or the irrational compromise the self-righteous stance of the columnist, and from this perspective it is easier to see how his non-fiction writing expounds a conservative ideology endorsed only ambiguously by his major novels.

Amis has always entertained the notion that 'literature' and 'ideology' are mutually incompatible, that aesthetic style is a phenomenon which simply transcends political categories.[100] This is, of course, to understand the concept of ideology in a narrow Marxist sense, rather than to see it as a term with broad cultural implications. Such an emphasis on the autotelic quality of literature derives from a variety of sources: from his study of English literature at Oxford in the late 1960s, when a strictly apolitical critical formalism reigned unchallenged; as a reaction against his subsequent stint as literary editor of the London periodical the *New Statesman* during the 1970s, at a time when Gramscian approaches to the arts predominated in radical circles; and from his immersion during the

---

[99] Martin Amis, *Other People: A Mystery Story* (London: Jonathan Cape, 1981), 212; Robert Burton, *The Anatomy of Melancholy*, ed. Thomas C. Faulkner, Nicolas K. Kiessling, and Rhonda L. Blair, i (Oxford: Clarendon Press, 1989), 74.
[100] Martin Amis, 'The Ending: Don Juan in Hull', in *The War Against Cliché*, 153.

1980s and 1990s in a postmodern celebrity culture, with its stylized ontology of depthlessness. But to claim for himself 'the ideology of no ideology' is to be blind to the complex, shifting relationship between ideology and aesthetics that permeates his own narratives, a relationship that varies widely from one piece of work to another.[101] The cultural implications of his fiction and non-fiction are by no means the same, as we have seen, and the complex layers of defamiliarization in his best novels—*Money, London Fields*, and, more unevenly, *The Information* and *Yellow Dog* (2003)—are very different in kind from the thinner, one-dimensional perspectives that constrain his less ambitious writing. Whereas Rushdie as a journalist has specialized in short, polemical 'op-ed' pieces which have only a tangential relationship to his fiction, Amis has generally preferred the longer celebrity profile, with some elements of this genre—deference to the idea of fame, hostility to overintellectualization, moral precepts shared with an English middle-class readership—also haunting some of Amis's literary output. Rushdie, in other words, has tended to dissociate his careers as a celebrity and as an author, but Amis frequently conflates them, so that the parochial assumptions informing the world of London high journalism work their way at times into his fiction.

Yellow Dog attempts to confront directly such assumptions through its coruscating satire of London 'yellow' journalism, epitomized in this novel by Clint Smoker and his tabloid newspaper, the *Morning Lark*. The narrative also implicates royalty within this vacuous world of celebrity culture, sardonically contrasting the present King Henry IX, who likes watching snooker on television, with 'his numerical predecessor, that glittering Renaissance prince, who was interested in astronomy, theology, mathematics, military science, navigation, oratory, modern and ancient languages, cartography and poetry'.[102] Again, the emphasis of Amis here is on declension, on the fall of the British monarchy from its illustrious position in history to a situation where the King's 15-year-old daughter has been caught up within a farrago of pornographic videos and tabloid exposures. The novel's pointed citation of Victorian constitutional historian Walter Bagehot on how 'a princely marriage ... was the most brilliant edition of a universal fact' (p. 80) reinforces this sense of the monarchy's fatal decline from its position at the apex of cosmic order. 'When Henry came to the throne,' we are told, 'about a quarter of the population still believed that he had been personally appointed by God' (p. 150), but the redundancy of such common beliefs is revealed by the end of this story, when the King instructs his equerry to 'Procure for me the Instrument of Abdication', suggesting how he believes that the monarchy no longer has the imprimatur to act as head of state. 'The people will have to grow up,' admits the empty-headed potentate: 'I'll have to grow up' (p. 325).

---

[101] Martin Amis, 'The Voice of the Lonely Crowd', *Guardian Review*, 1 June 2002, 6.
[102] Martin Amis, *Yellow Dog* (London: Jonathan Cape, 2003), 53. Subsequent page references to this edition are cited in parentheses in the text.

As so often in Amis, though, this iconoclastic gesture is hemmed in by reactionary counter-currents, by a tone of censorious retrospection which appears to undermine in advance the legitimacy of anything new or different. On one hand, *Yellow Dog* uses a transatlantic dimension to hollow out Bagehot's traditionalist notion of the English constitution, representing the pornographic industry of southern California as a radically demystifying enterprise, even one with potentially revolutionary implications. The royal equerry, seeing his beloved Victoria in a 'Princess Lolita' sex video (p. 203), muses on how 'pornography turned the world upside down' (p. 257), thereby making reference back to the tune played according to legend by the British army when General Cornwallis brought the American War of Independence to an end by surrendering at Yorktown in 1781. This motif of inversion, of up-ending the Establishment, is taken up also by Joseph Andrews, an East End gangster in exile in California who blackmails the monarchy over the pornographic film of Princess Victoria and talks lugubriously of returning to his old drinking haunt, 'the World Upside Down' (p. 312). But just as the book's central character, Xan Meo, regresses from 'rational contemporary attitudes' to 'primitive beliefs' (p. 209) when he suffers severe head injuries after being attacked in a London pub, so the structure of Amis's novel harks back nostalgically to a state of primordial innocence and pastoral order. Xan is said at one point to be 'sharing Adam's agony, after the Fall: "... cover me, ye pines, Ye cedars with innumerable boughs, Hide me. ..."' Both the literary reference here to Milton's *Paradise Lost* and the elegiac emphasis on how Xan himself 'had fallen' imply a landscape in which violation is entangled inextricably with a sense of loss (p. 212). America is described with disapprobation as a country where 'pornography is heading for the mainstream' (p. 237) and 'where old men dressed like children' (p. 179), and there is a hankering throughout this novel to counter what one character calls 'the end of normalcy' (p. 236) by retreating to an imaginary prelapsarian condition, a world of natural order, like the mythic landscape of 'innocence and Eden' hypothesized in *The Information* (p. 62).

Given the fact that violence, incest, and the 'obscenification of everyday life' (p. 335) all appear to be rife throughout *Yellow Dog*, the only alternative to this myth of innocence would appear to be apocalyptic destruction, duly heralded here by the imminent air disaster threaded through the narrative and, on a macrocosmic scale, by the impending visit of a comet to planet Earth. Amis's work, in other words, alternates between a retrospective moral conservatism and a more exuberant nihilism. Although *Yellow Dog* takes stylistic pleasure in its portrayal of the corrupt state of England, the book is so riven by aesthetic and ideological contradictions that its only option at the end is to implode catastrophically upon itself. In this light, it is easy to see why the author is so opposed to what he sees as the intrusive procedures of critical analysis, for the rhetorical finesse and power of this book emanate from an atavistic, regressive mood of comic disgust whose strength is precisely that it remains intellectually inchoate. Amis's eye for the darker alleyways of urban life has been likened to that of Dickens, and the comparison is not entirely inappropriate; but his work also resembles that of Dickens in its ultimately sentimental attachment to the gods of hearth, home, and childhood to which the novel circles back in its final pages.[103] Like Dickens in *Martin Chuzzlewit*, Amis in *Yellow Dog* visits America only to disapprove of that country's proclivity for abstraction and its elimination of a humanist centre of gravity.

This attachment to domesticity manifests itself most overtly in *Experience*, a form of 'higher autobiography' which explicitly promotes the values of family loyalty, filial generation, and lived 'experience' over the distractions of academic theory, and which ends by positing a conservative notion of organic continuity, of genes and generations. Amis records here how he recognizes his own 'Englishness ... most acutely' during conversations with his American wife, and if the considerable strength of his best work derives from a subversion of safe moral positions, it is nevertheless easy enough to understand why both he and many of his readers continue to be attached to a reassuring sense of English identity which still comes through in much of his work.[104] It is ultimately not surprising to find that Amis was among the great and the good who attended the festivities at the Millennium Dome in London on New Year's Eve 1999, or that he was also among the famous figures from the British world of arts and media invited to the Queen's Golden Jubilee party at the Royal Academy of Arts in 2002. Such recognition by the Establishment is symptomatic of the ways in which, for all Amis's satire of the monarchy and his protestations of how English 'genteelism' can be 'inhibiting', his work can be seen to be largely complicit with traditional English values. In a 1998 interview with the *Paris Review*, Amis confirmed that 'writers I like and trust have at the base of their prose something called the English sentence', and he cited as a major influence on his work the novels of Jane Austen. However, the variations in the quality of Amis's output, probably larger than those for any other writer of comparable stature—particularly one who is self-conscious about his place in the literary canon—correspondingly ensure that the cultural and ideological implications of his work also fluctuate considerably.[105] Indeed, it is a reluctant structure of inversion that mediates Amis's most compelling narratives, and in this sense the transatlantic dimensions in his work open up parallel worlds which serve to displace the idea of authorial autonomy upon which his own idealizations of literary style as an end in itself are predicated.

This structural displacement of humanist centres of gravity is, of course, characteristic of postmodernism in general; but within the British context such

---

[103] Robert Douglas-Fairhurst, 'Dickens with a Snarl', *Observer Review*, 24 Aug. 2003, 15.

[104] Amis, *Experience*, 176, 6, 326.

[105] Moss, 'After the Storm', 26; Francesca Riviere, 'The Art of Fiction: CLI, Martin Amis', *Paris Review*, no. 146 (Spring 1998), 119. For Amis's declared ambition of making a 'contribution' to the canon, see Cowley, 'Portrait: Martin Amis', 23.

dislocations seemed particularly contentious in the second half of the twentieth century, because of the ethical imperatives and strong sense of national identity associated with the outcome of the Second World War. It is no coincidence that Amis, in *Time's Arrow* and other works, circles back to the memory of war, as if attempting to reclaim a distinct moral vantage point which would put postmodern excesses of information into more orderly relief. Yet, as we see from Ballard's post-traumatic narratives, one of the consequences of war was to institutionalize in Britain smothering notions about the responsibilities of collective life, and Ballard's own fiction works almost like a form of psychoanalysis in the way it diagnoses the repressions and exclusions underpinning conventional representations of the social state. Just as Carter declared overtly that she was 'in the demythologizing business', so Ballard and Amis in different ways interrogate the cultural narratives by which postwar Britain explained the world to itself.[106] All of these writers create fictional narratives which recast history in a different light, offering alternative ways of interpreting the English past: Carter's reconstitution of Elizabethan pastoral posits a continuum, rather than an antithesis, between the radical popular culture of America and traditional English social hierarchies; Ballard's symbolic engagement with the Reformation advocates a perverse kind of moral rearmament, through which sex and violence would become a battering-ram against Establishment complacency; Amis's representation of the 1981 royal wedding incorporates the monarchy within a corrupt cycle of international finance and celebrity culture, as if the public icons of Charles and Diana had no more legitimacy than hucksters in the Hollywood firmament.

For all of these writers, it is no longer simply a question of Britain being touched from a distance by the romantic glamour and commercial muscle of America; for better or worse, their native country has itself become culturally and economically an integral part of a wider transatlantic dynamic. In Ballard, Carter, and Amis we see the postwar moral compass of the nation thrown out of kilter by its exposure to the turbulent currents of an invasive postmodernity, but we also read this process as effectively reconstituting the larger trajectories of British history, which, in these iconoclastic fictional excavations, are shown to be imaginatively embedded within the *longue durée* of Atlantic republicanism. Just as the academic new historicists sought reflexively to appropriate different aspects of a memorialized past, so Ballard, Carter, and Amis displaced the English novel in the late twentieth century on to a transatlantic axis in order to produce revisionist accounts of the British institutional realm. Ballard's reclamation of the spirit of the Reformation, Carter's invocation of Elizabethan carnival, and Amis's lament for the seventeenth-century dissociation of sensibility all point to an imaginative desire to superimpose the past upon the present, to reinterpret the established narrative of British history contrariwise. By invoking a parallel

---

[106] Carter, 'Notes from the Front Line', 71.

American dimension to reposition the enclosed vistas of the English scene within a more expansive framework, all of these writers, in their different ways, pose uncomfortable questions about how the nation's territorial, hierarchical, and ethical boundaries came to be consolidated, for what purposes, and in whose interests.

10

Global English and the Politics of Traversal

THE ART OF BLASPHEMY: SALMAN RUSHDIE

Although questions about the pertinence of universal values go back far into history, the last quarter of the twentieth century, and particularly the 1990s, saw the emergence of a quite distinctive discourse around the issue of globalization. This was impelled by various factors, the most conspicuous of which were revolutions in communications technology which made the transfer of ideas and commodities across national frontiers much easier, and which in turn left the economies of nation-states more exposed to rapid transfers of global capital by transnational corporations and others.[1] The increasing prominence of English as a global language—not, usually, as a replacement for local languages, but as something to run alongside them, a lingua franca—also owed much to the exponential growth of satellite television and Internet networks at this time. As David Crystal has explained, the 'world status' of the English language was primarily the result of two factors: 'the expansion of British colonial power, which peaked towards the end of the nineteenth century, and the emergence of the United States as the leading economic power of the twentieth century'.[2] This increasing viability of English as a world language helped to create a new, international version of it as an agent of communication, most obvious perhaps in the truncated codes used by air traffic control systems and the like. In its more elaborate and sophisticated manifestations, though, this circulation of global English has crucially influenced the work of writers such as Salman Rushdie, who was born in Bombay in 1947 and whose native tongue was Urdu. This realization of English as a double or parallel phenomenon not only undermines the conventional practice of translation, which depends upon a clear distinction between primary and secondary languages, but also problematizes the Wordsworthian understanding of English as an expression of indigenous experience, the 'real language of men' in 'common life'.[3] For the global writers of Rushdie's generation, English did not necessarily comprise a local idiom in any recognizable form at all.

---

[1] For a classic account of these developments, see Arjun Appadurai, *Modernity at Large: Cultural Dimensions of Globalization* (Minneapolis: University of Minnesota Press, 1996).

[2] David Crystal, *English as a Global Language*, 2nd edn. (Cambridge: Cambridge University Press, 2003), 59. [3] Wordsworth, 'Preface to *Lyrical Ballads*', 431, 456.

The purpose of this chapter is to examine how this internationalization of English has provided the discursive framework for the fiction of Rushdie and Caryl Phillips. In particular, I will argue that the prevalence of a transatlantic dynamic in their work effectively reorganizes the territorial boundaries and categories on which traditional understandings of English literature have been predicated. When the idea of 'a global society' began to be widely discussed at the beginning of the 1990s, its emergence was frequently understood in progressive terms as a 'clash between traditionalism, manifesting itself in nationalism, and cultural holism, manifesting itself in globalism'. Cultural holism, as defined by American scholar Betty Jean Craige, involved 'a widespread appreciation of diversity, which multicultural education fosters' and a capacity for 'appreciating ... the world's variety of human expression'.[4] This emollient liberal thesis was taken up and adjusted by Francis Fukuyama, whose book *The End of History* (1992) identified not environmentalism or multiculturalism but the 'spread of a universal consumer culture'—along with the natural ally of a free market, 'prosperous and stable liberal democracies'—as the benevolent agency whose global dissemination would eventually put paid to the jealously guarded interests of local tyrants.[5] This triumphal march of liberal capitalism coincided in Tony Blair's Britain with the country's image of itself in the late 1990s as a tolerant, multicultural society, where diversity was welcomed and where ethnic or religious intolerance was thought to involve regrettable lapses on the part of particular individuals rather than any structural incompatibilities within the established order. The enormous commercial success in 2000 of Zadie Smith's *White Teeth*, with its good-natured evocation of racially diverse communities in north London, epitomized this optimistic vision of social integration, making *White Teeth*, in Bruce King's words, 'the desired multicultural novel of a new multiracial England'.[6] Smith herself read English at King's College, Cambridge—Rushdie's own Alma Mater, a college with a strong liberal tradition—and her work is clearly influenced heavily by the comic exuberance and compulsive hybridity of Rushdie's style.

But in Rushdie's own work, as in that of Phillips, the conceptual edges are much harder, the frictions between national pieties and a demystifying transnational impulse more awkward to negotiate. Rushdie, in particular, has been a difficult figure for English literature to assimilate, in part because the strong presence particularly in his later writings of an American cultural imaginary gives his work a different centre of gravity, an alternative source of power, which throws the domestic mythologies of English society into uncomfortable relief. Although Rushdie is a major figure in the annals of English literature, then, he represents an altogether different kind of English literature. In a riposte to George Steiner's

[4] Betty Jean Craige, 'Literature in a Global Society', *PMLA*, 106 (1991), 395–9.
[5] Francis Fukuyama, *The End of History and the Last Man* (London: Hamish Hamilton, 1992), pp. xv, 12.
[6] King, *The Internationalization of English Literature*, 290. *White Teeth* quickly sold nearly a million copies in paperback.

Eurocentric thesis on the death of the novel, the author himself argued in 2000 that 'a new novel is emerging, a post-colonial novel, a de-centred, transnational, inter-lingual, cross-cultural novel'; and he regarded this as a counterbalance to what he called in 1993 'the devastating effect of the Thatcher years', when many English writers 'had lost all ambition, all desire to wrestle with the world' and had retreated instead into aesthetic territory dealing 'with tiny patches of the world, tiny pieces of human experience'.[7] By contrast, Rushdie has compared himself linguistically to Vladimir Nabokov, another writer who 'crossed a language frontier', and his work uses England, as Nabokov's work used America, not as a *donnée* but as a kind of laboratory for linguistic and cultural experiments.[8]

Rushdie himself was educated in England, at Rugby School, and he became a British subject at the age of 17 before going to Cambridge University to read history; he then moved to London, though since 2000 he has lived in New York. In an early essay published in 1982, Rushdie argues that Britain should begin to create 'great literature out of the phenomenon of cultural transplantation', as America had done previously through its immigrant writing.[9] In another essay a year later, in which he ridicules the academic notion of 'Commonwealth literature' for the way 'it places Eng. Lit. at the centre and the rest of the world at the periphery', Rushdie also confirms his interest in linguistic politics by suggesting that the current 'pre-eminence' of English as a 'world language' is attributable not so much to 'the British legacy' as to 'the effect of the primacy of the United States of America in the affairs of the world'. Rushdie's non-fiction writing also shows an easy familiarity with theorists of nationalism, from Benedict Anderson to Edward Said: indeed, Rushdie was using the word 'transnational' as early as 1983.[10] His essay 'Is Nothing Sacred?' (1990) also cites Rorty's *Philosophy and the Mirror of Nature*, Lyotard's *Postmodern Condition*, and Foucault's work on authorship, and it goes on explicitly to defend the genre of the novel in intellectual terms, as 'the crucial art form of what I can no longer avoid calling the post-modern age'.[11] Furthermore, his 1995 novel *The Moor's Last Sigh* jokes with Homi Bhabha's theories of hybridity, parodying the title of one of Bhabha's essays through Dr Zeenant Vahil's critical work, 'Imperso-Nation and Dis/Semi/Nation: Dialogics of Eclecticism and Interrogation of Authenticity in A.Z'.[12] All of this testifies to Rushdie's own fluency in the theoretical language of international English, his self-consciousness about how his own fiction relates

[7] Salman Rushdie, 'In Defence of the Novel, Yet Again', in *Step Across This Line: Collected Non-Fiction 1992–2002* (London: Jonathan Cape, 2002), 57, and *idem*, 'The Best of Young British Novelists', in *Step Across This Line*, 38.

[8] Salman Rushdie, 'Step Across This Line: The Tanner Lectures on Human Values, Yale, 2002', in *Step Across This Line*, 434.

[9] Salman Rushdie, 'Imaginary Homelands', in *Imaginary Homelands: Essays and Criticism, 1981–91* (London: Granta–Penguin, 1991), 20.

[10] Salman Rushdie, '"Commonwealth Literature" Does Not Exist', in *Imaginary Homelands*, 66, 64, 69.   [11] Salman Rushdie, 'Is Nothing Sacred?', in *Imaginary Homelands*, 424.

[12] Salman Rushdie, *The Moor's Last Sigh* (London: Jonathan Cape, 1995), 329.

to discursive constructions of national identity. Whereas Martin Amis is entirely dismissive of what he takes to be academic jargon, Rushdie is much more conversant with its idiosyncrasies; this is yet another language that Rushdie can speak, even if he does so, characteristically, in an oblique and sardonic fashion.

Rushdie first met Angela Carter at a London dinner party in 1976, before either of them was widely known, and he subsequently recalled describing Carter to another guest at this party as 'the most brilliant writer in England'.[13] Like Carter, Rushdie has always taken pleasure in assuming an overtly provocative stance towards public authorities, with his fictionalization of the historical events surrounding Indian independence in *Midnight's Children* (1981), and in particular his allegedly defamatory representation of Sanjay, son of Indian Prime Minister Indira Gandhi, embroiling the author in political controversy early in his career. In 1984, the London High Court ruled in favour of Mrs Gandhi's libel suit, forcing Rushdie to read out a public apology and to remove the offending passage from subsequent editions of the novel.[14] In this sense, Rushdie's version of magic realism, with its uneasy conjunction of fact and fiction, has always involved him in fraught relationships with civil and religious bodies; like Carter, he is a great admirer of Gabriel García Márquez, but his style tends to be more openly offensive and interventionist than that of the Colombian writer. The most obvious example of this is Rushdie's non-fiction work *The Jaguar Smile* (1987), which seeks to make a direct political statement by its analysis of social conditions in Nicaragua, a country that was described by President Reagan in the early 1980s as a totalitarian state in order to justify the clandestine US war against the Sandinista government. Rushdie here defends the Sandinistas, declaring that they came to power through the ballot box and were therefore legitimate rulers, though he pointedly opposes their censorship of the press, recalling his own 'outrage at the British government's manipulation of the news media during the Falklands/Malvinas war'.[15]

It is clear then, even before the diplomatic controversy over *The Satanic Verses* blew up in 1989, that Rushdie prized above all freedom of expression. In 1988, he was part of the 20 June group founded by London literary intellectuals to oppose Thatcher—Angela Carter, Harold Pinter, Ian McEwan, and John Mortimer were other prominent members—and in the same year he also signed Charter 88, which sought to exert pressure on the British government by demanding a bill of rights and a written constitution. Rushdie subsequently recalled how Charter 88 'initially attracted media derision and met with political apathy', with one obvious reason for this being that such an emphasis on constitutional reform and personal liberty was more commonly associated with the United States and

[13] Rushdie, 'Angela Carter, 1940–1992', 5.
[14] Margareta Petersson, *Unending Metamorphoses: Myth, Satire and Religion in Salman Rushdie's Novels* (Lund: Lund University Press, 1996), 22.
[15] Salman Rushdie, *The Jaguar Smile: A Nicaraguan Journey* (London: Vintage, 2000), 33.

sat uneasily with the traditions of class solidarity which still predominated within British socialism of the 1980s.[16] In his own 'Charter 88' essay, Rushdie castigated Labour politician Roy Hattersley for asserting, 'in authentically Orwellian tones', that 'true liberty requires action from the government'; instead, Rushdie cited as his preferred model the US Constitution, whose Fifth Amendment 'makes it impossible for an American Thatcher to remove a defendant's right to silence in a court of law'. This 1988 article argues that 'the true conservatives in Britain are now in the Labour Party', and it is philosophically consistent with the essay 'In Good Faith' published two years later, after the infamous fatwa had been declared, where Rushdie avers how he has 'fought against communal politics all my adult life'.[17] Indeed, 'the Rushdie affair' was cited by Stuart Hall and David Held, in the 'New Times' debate within British Marxist circles of the late 1980s, as epitomizing an urgent need to rethink the 'politics of citizenship' as something distinct from older models of a 'culturally homogeneous population' acting 'within the framework of a strong and unitary national state'.[18] Rushdie's move in 1987 from his British agent and publisher to an American agent, Andrew Wylie, for *The Satanic Verses* is another indication of the author's gradual shift westward across the Atlantic, mentally if not physically, in the late 1980s.

In this sense, the fatwa proclaimed on 14 February 1989 by the Ayatollah Khomeini and his fundamentalist acolytes in response to alleged blasphemies in *The Satanic Verses* served merely to consolidate what was already a growing affinity between Rushdie and the United States. The reaction in Britain to 'the Rushdie affair' was mixed: the government found itself with little option other than to protect one of its citizens and to uphold the idea of free speech, but public support for the author was less than wholehearted, with, according to a BBC poll in July 1990, 42 per cent of British Muslims actually supporting the fatwa.[19] There was, accordingly, much discussion in Britain of whether the blasphemy laws, originally designed in medieval times to protect the Christian Church from heresy, might usefully be extended by the logic of multiculturalism to embrace other faiths, a policy endorsed by the Archbishop of Canterbury, Robert Runcie. Prince Charles, meanwhile, publicly dismissed Rushdie as 'a bad writer' and complained about the cost to the Crown of protecting him; Rushdie returned this particular favour in a 1997 piece after Princess Diana's death, when he argued that Britain might be a 'happier' place if it 'learned to live without kings

---

[16] Salman Rushdie, 'The Human Rights Act', in *Step Across This Line*, 354.

[17] Salman Rushdie, 'Charter 88', in *Imaginary Homelands*, 163–5, and *idem*, 'In Good Faith', in *Imaginary Homelands*, 404.

[18] Stuart Hall and David Held, 'Citizens and Citizenship', in *New Times: The Changing Face of Politics in the 1990s*, ed. Stuart Hall and Martin Jacques (London: Lawrence and Wishart, 1989), 187–8. Hall and Held here explicitly give their support to Charter 88, which they describe as 'an immediate and practical intervention ... to be welcomed and endorsed' (p. 187). This debate was initiated by a special issue of *Marxism Today* in October 1988 on the theme of 'New Times'.

[19] Petersson, *Unending Metamorphoses*, 201.

and queens'.[20] What made much less impact in these British debates about *The Satanic Verses*, though, was any emphasis on freedom of expression as a principle that could not be abridged; Rushdie's own view that the 'British blasphemy law is an outdated relic of the past ... and ought to be abolished' carried relatively little weight within a political framework in which the interests of church and state, religious and secular governance, have always been closely intertwined. 'Britain's vaunted "unwritten constitution" ', declared Rushdie acerbically in 2000, 'wasn't worth the paper it wasn't written on.'[21]

This is, of course, quite different in kind from the American republican tradition, where the legal separation of church and state makes the right to dissent a fundamental axiom of the constitutionally free society. However strong conservatism might periodically be as a political force in America, the Rushdie affair clearly illuminated ways in which the relationship between church and state in Britain and the United States remains structurally different. It is, then, not surprising that most of the unambiguous support for Rushdie's position came from the States, support for which the author was increasingly grateful as the long years of his internal exile dragged on; Rushdie observed plangently in 1993 that while the American press was generally 'sympathetic and positive' towards his case, considering it to be 'about freedom of expression, and state terrorism', in Britain, by contrast, 'it seems to be about a man who has to be saved from the consequences of his own actions'. It was, perhaps, partly Rushdie's supercilious demeanour and apparent delight in the role of devil's advocate which failed to endear him to the British public: an avowed atheist since the age of 15, he propounded the view that 'blasphemy and heresy, far from being the greatest evils, are the methods by which human thought has made its most vital advances'.[22] Nevertheless, this conscious attempt to affiliate himself with traditions of 'heresy' links Rushdie to a transatlantic intellectual inheritance of disestablishment extending back through Tom Paine to the radical reformers of the seventeenth century. His 1990 essay 'In God We Trust' advocates for Islam the 'willingness to separate Church and State' that developed earlier within certain branches of Christianity, and, in an article shortly after the attacks on the United States by Al-Qaeda in 2001, Rushdie called similarly for 'a Reformation in the Muslim world'. He also spoke here of the need for Islam both to 'take on board ... secular-humanist principles' and to displace religion from a theocratic public arena 'to the sphere of the personal ... in order to become modern'.[23]

[20] Nick Cohen, 'A Windsor in the Soup', *Observer*, 29 Sept. 2002, 31; Salman Rushdie, 'Crash: The Death of Princess Diana', in *Step Across This Line*, 121.

[21] Salman Rushdie, 'Islam and the West', in *Step Across This Line*, 324–5, and *idem*, 'The Human Rights Act', 353.

[22] Salman Rushdie, 'Messages from the Plague Years', in *Step Across This Line*, 242–3, 232, and *idem*, 'In God We Trust', in *Imaginary Homelands*, 377.

[23] Rushdie, 'In God We Trust', 380, and *idem*, 'Not About Islam?', in *Step Across This Line*, 396–7.

As a literary text, of course, *The Satanic Verses* is much more complicated and ambivalent than the subsequent slogans made it out to be. The novel is immersed in British culture, with the hero, Saladin Chamcha, proclaiming that he prefers the 'faded splendours' of London to 'the hot certainties of that transatlantic New Rome with its Nazified architectural gigantism, which employed the oppressions of size to make its human occupants feel like worms'.[24] For Saladin, American culture appears to be potentially dehumanizing: on one of his frequent plane journeys he unhappily encounters an American 'creationist scientist', Eugene Dumsday (p. 79), who cautions the 'young people of America' against the pernicious influence of 'Mr Darwin and his works' (p. 76), while the Marxist film-maker George Miranda austerely describes 'Amrika' as 'Power in its purest form, disembodied, invisible. We can't see it but it screws us totally, no escape' (p. 56). What Saladin seems to cherish in the London portrayed in this novel is its more random, human aspects: he marries an English woman, Pamela, and though he comments acerbically on the social revolution in Britain during the 1980s—'Maggie the Bitch' is again a totemic hate figure here (p. 269)—nevertheless the narrative takes a certain wry pleasure in the familiarity of its civic landscapes: 'Wren's dome, the high metallic spark-plug of the Telecom Tower, crumbling in the wind like sandcastles' (p. 327), even 'the Angel Underground' (p. 328), a London tube station which becomes a comically appropriate point of departure for Gibreel Farishta, the novel's 'archangel in human form' (p. 315). Though the book is empathetically attached to the physical architecture of London, it is less friendly towards the idea of Britain itself, 'that coffin of an island' as Rosa Diamond calls it (p. 146), no longer a 'moderate and common-sensical land' (p. 158) but one watched over by brutal, racist policemen. There is a passing reference here to 'Ignatius Sancho, who became in 1782 the first African writer to be published in England' (p. 292), and one theme of this novel is the mutual reciprocity between Britain and the rest of the world over many centuries: the trouble with the English, says Indian film producer Mr Sisodia, is that their 'history happened overseas', so they 'don't know what it means' (p. 343).

Technically, the issue of blasphemy in the novel involves Rushdie's aesthetic characterization of 'the Prophet, Mahound' (p. 393), or Muhammad, a form of representation forbidden under Islamic law. At a talk in Cambridge in 1993, Rushdie recalled that it was during his final year of reading history there, while studying for a special paper on Muhammad, the rise of Islam, and the Caliphate, that he 'came across the story of the so-called "satanic verses" or temptation of the Prophet Muhammad, and of his rejection of that temptation'. There is, then, an important sense in which *The Satanic Verses* speaks knowledgeably, even in some ways academically, about the object of its inquiry. The author

---

[24] Salman Rushdie, *The Satanic Verses* (London: Viking Penguin, 1988), 399. Subsequent page references to this edition are cited in parentheses in the text.

himself described his novel as 'a committedly secular text that deals in part with the material of religious faith', but in fact *The Satanic Verses* is saturated in the culture of Islam in the same way as James Joyce's *Ulysses* is saturated in Catholicism, and within this kind of framework the question of any single authorial perspective becomes much more difficult to determine.[25] The most obvious examples of deference towards religion in *The Satanic Verses* are the episodes involving Ayesha, who divines Mishal's terminal cancer through palm reading and subsequently leads her on a pilgrimage towards Mecca. Whether or not the waters of the Arabian Sea miraculously part to let them pass on this journey is left ambiguous; questioned by detectives about the mass drownings, Osman the bullock-boy replies: 'And just at the last, I saw it happen, the marvellous thing. The water opened, and I saw them go along the ocean-floor, among the dying fish' (p. 504). Rushdie described himself in 1984 as being in 'exactly the position of the lapsed Catholic. I am a lapsed Muslim, which is to say you still define yourself by the thing you've lapsed from'; and, as Sara Suleri has observed, *The Satanic Verses* is in fact 'a deeply Islamic book', arranged in a classic double bind whereby 'the desacralizing of religion can simultaneously constitute a resacralizing of history'.[26] 'Genuine blasphemy', as Eliot famously declared in his essay on Baudelaire, 'is a way of affirming belief', and in this sense Rushdie's strategic defence of *The Satanic Verses* in the wake of threats to his life—'where there is no belief, there is no blasphemy ... I have never in my adult life affirmed any belief, and what one has not affirmed one cannot be said to have apostasized from'—is directly contradicted by the structural duplicities of his fictional narrative.[27]

There is, then, a misleading discontinuity between Rushdie as a public figure—an energetic polemicist in newspaper columns—and Rushdie as a novelist, whose works tend to be much more complex and multifaceted. *The Satanic Verses* is organized structurally around the idea of displacement and transposition between parallel universes: Saladin's return to India to visit his dying father at the end of the novel is of a piece with the continual traversals between spirit and matter, religious prototype and secular comedy, that inspire this magic realist mode. Often this takes burlesque forms, as when the pilgrims walking to Mecca think they hear a 'doom-trumpet', which turns out to be 'in point of fact, the horn of Mirza Saeed's Mercedes-Benz station wagon' (p. 491). The point, though, is that *The Satanic Verses* is predicated upon an idea of metamorphosis wherein categories slide into their opposite, and this is why any attempt to circumscribe the novel as radically secular must be reductive. That Rushdie should have wished in public to take up such an

---

[25] Rushdie, 'Messages from the Plague Years', 249, 252.

[26] Peter Craven, 'An Interview with Salman Rushdie', *Scripsi*, 3/2–3 (1985), 125; Sara Suleri, *The Rhetoric of English India* (Chicago: University of Chicago Press, 1992), 190–1.

[27] T. S. Eliot, 'Baudelaire', in *Selected Essays*, 3rd edn., 421; Rushdie, 'In Good Faith', 405.

uncompromising position is itself interesting, of course: as Michael Trussler has suggested, Rushdie's narratives tend to be worked out 'from within a society dominated utterly by the spectacle', and there is a sense in which the fatwa was itself a global media event, a way to disseminate the values of Islam through the channels of electronic news outlets. At some level, perhaps, *The Satanic Verses* sought deliberately to spark something like the response it got: the book itself is manifestly aware of institutional implications of religious discourse—Zeenat Vahil talks in the final section about trying to avoid 'schisms' (p. 537)—and the provocative nature of the work clearly signals what Nico Israel calls Rushdie's 'spectacularity', his penchant for worldwide fame and self-promotion.[28] Other examples of Rushdie's globalizing instincts would include meeting President Clinton at the White House, singing on stage with the rock band U2 (see Plate 24), and appearing on the American television chat show hosted by David Letterman.

All of this suggests the extent to which Rushdie is a creature of what he calls 'the post-modern age', at home within its media networks and celebrity

24. Salman Rushdie emerging briefly from hiding to appear on stage with Bono at a U2 concert, Wembley Arena, 1993.

---

[28] Michael Trussler, 'Literary Artifacts: Ekphrasis in the Short Fiction of Donald Barthelme, Salman Rushdie, and John Edgar Wideman', *Contemporary Literature*, 41 (2000), 266; Nico Israel, *Outlandish: Writing Between Exile and Diaspora* (Stanford, Calif.: Stanford University Press, 2000), 125.

culture; one could hardly imagine an exponent of high modernism, Joyce for instance, appearing on television chat shows with equal enthusiasm to defend the qualities of *Ulysses*. The ferocity of the reaction against Rushdie both from Muslims and from the British Establishment thus served paradoxically to vouch for the pertinence of one of his book's main themes, the powerful cultural legacy of religious ideas within the contemporary world, the efficacy of what Bhabha has called 'hybrid articulations of the sacred-in-the-secular, psychic fantasy as part of social rationality, the archaic within the contemporaneous'.[29] The reconfiguration of national territories in Rushdie's work, in other words, operates alongside parallel transpositions whereby religious iconography is transferred into forms of metaphorical play or psychological compulsion, so that it functions as what Raymond Williams would have called a 'residual' impulse, a force enjoying a significant afterlife in political and aesthetic terms without being understood as any kind of theological truth.[30] Rushdie's version of postmodernism, then, is far from a weightless concept; instead, it turns upon a structure of traversal, whereby a mythological point of origin is crossed over, reinscribed within an alternative conceptual space. Consequently, Aijaz Ahmad's dismissal of Rushdie as a deracinated elitist, someone who appears to 'float, effortlessly, through a supermarket of packaged and commodified cultures, ready to be consumed', depends on erroneously extrapolating simplified ideas from Rushdie's journalism and then reading them back into his novels.[31] Whatever Rushdie's public image may be, in his fictional narratives we see postmodern comedies of displacement coming into harsh, tortuous conflict with the strictures of locality, so that his fractured texts do not simply lampoon Indian or Islamic or Thatcherite cultures but reveal ways in which they intersect awkwardly with the forces of globalization.

The Moor's Last Sigh is a good example of this cross-cultural heterogeneity, organized as it is around a kind of structural pun, whereby Indian culture finds itself miscegenated within a sprawling global mix. In this novel, an Indian singer has become 'well known in Bombay's nightclubs, as the purveyor, under the stage name of "Jimmy Cash," of what he liked to call "Country and Eastern" music, a set of twangy songs about ranches and trains and cows with an idiosyncratic Indian twist'. Meanwhile the narrator, Moraes Zogoiby, traduces the whole concept of ethnicity and identity politics as he meditates upon the notion of 'Indian country', cross-hatching the Asian country of his birth with memories of John Wayne shooting Indians in Hollywood westerns: 'Not even an Indian was safe in Indian country; not if he was the wrong kind of Indian, anyway.' Surrealism forms an aesthetic subtext in *The Moor's Last Sigh*—Chirico's paintings are

---

[29] Rushdie, 'Is Nothing Sacred?', 424; Homi Bhabha and John Comaroff, 'Speaking of Postcoloniality, in the Continuous Present: A Conversation', in *Relocating Postcolonialism*, ed. David Theo Goldberg and Ato Quayson (Oxford: Blackwell, 2002), 24.

[30] Raymond Williams, 'Base and Superstructure in Marxist Cultural Theory', *New Left Review*, no. 82 (Nov.–Dec. 1973), 10.

[31] Aijaz Ahmad, *In Theory: Classes, Nations, Literatures* (London: Verso, 1992), 128.

mentioned in the context of a 'surreal foreignness' which hovers over the entire narrative—and this sense of discordance reinforces Rushdie's observation, in a 1982 essay, that the idea of 'multiculturalism', like those of 'integration' and 'racial harmony', is nothing more than a 'sham'.[32] Rushdie's work affords a distinctly uncomfortable prospect for liberal pedagogues because it says more about the intractable nature of conflict and opposition than about possibilities of reconciliation. This is also why Rushdie likes to give his work a provocative, blasphemous edge: he points out the implicit limits of particular cultures by deliberately pushing his work beyond the boundaries of accepted custom.

The Ground Beneath Her Feet (1999), another masterful work in an extraordinary series of novels throughout the 1980s and 1990s, foregrounds this theme of displacement by taking as its focus rock music, described by Rushdie in a 1999 essay as something that crossed 'all frontiers and barriers of language and culture to become only the third globalized phenomenon in history after the two World Wars'.[33] Again, India, Britain, and America are lined up in transnational parallels: one of the older Indians, Sir Darius Xerxes Cama, a student of Aryan myths, hankers after all things British, cherishing a nostalgic image of England 'as a pure, white Palladian mansion set upon a hill above a silver winding river', while his son's lover, Vina Apsara, growing up as 'Nissy Poe' in the United States, hypothesizes a link between herself and Christopher Columbus, who 'went looking for Indians and found America'.[34] The triangulations between India, Britain, and America are worked out here in an extremely intricate fashion: for instance, Queen Catherine of Braganza, wife of the English king Charles II, is said to be 'the secret link between the cities of Bombay and New York. Bombay came to England in her dowry; but she was also the Queen in the N.Y. borough of Queens' (p. 79). But the dominant motifs in this book involve dividing, slicing, fracturing. America is said by the Indian narrator Rai to have 'got rid of the British long before we did' (p. 59), and the transatlantic sundering of the British Empire in 1782 is seen to foreshadow Britain's relinquishment of India and its partition of India and Pakistan in 1947: 'Everything starts shifting, changing, getting partitioned, separated by frontiers, splitting, re-splitting, coming apart' (p. 164). Hence the novel's central metaphor of earthquake, where 'the self-contradictory earth' (p. 327) opens up so as to undermine the stability of the ground beneath our feet. Indians, says Rai, are 'obsessed by place, belonging-to-your-place, knowing-your-place' (p. 55); but the narrative invalidates the possibility of such social or philosophical stability, substituting instead Rushdie's typical world where frontiers exist for the negative purpose of being a provocation to transgression: 'don't take that chance don't step across that line don't ruffle my sensitivities' (p. 177).

---

[32] Rushdie, *The Moor's Last Sigh*, 209, 414, 383, and *idem*, 'The New Empire within Britain', in *Imaginary Homelands*, 137.   [33] Salman Rushdie, 'Rock Music', in *Step Across This Line*, 300.
[34] Salman Rushdie, *The Ground Beneath Her Feet* (London: Jonathan Cape, 1999), 86, 122. Subsequent page references to this edition are cited in parentheses in the text.

America functions within this global milieu partly as an occasion for trans-formation. Observing how '[o]ur lives tear us in half', the narrator in *The Ground Beneath Her Feet* associates 'the dream America everyone carries round in his head' with one side of this equation (p. 419), the virtual image which always offers a prospect of alterity on domestic soil. In keeping with this sense of himself as 'a discontinuous being', he subsequently moves to America in order to pursue the successful rock singer Vina: 'in this I have truly become an American, inventing myself anew to make a new world in the company of other altered lives' (p. 441). There are oblique references in this novel to *The Great Gatsby*—Nick Carraway and Jay Gatsby are said to be 'two young turks' on a rock music critics' panel (p. 484), while Dr T. J. Eckleburg, who in *Gatsby* appears in an oculist's advertisement overlooking the Valley of Ashes, has here become an 'ocular couturier *par excellence*' (p. 186)—and it is a Gatsbyesque projection of the American ethic of self-transformation into surrogate forms of divinity that fires the imaginations of Rushdie's hubristic characters. It is important to note, though, how this American world is always defined in this novel through parallelisms; the American Mull Standish comes to England to set up a pirate music radio station, Radio Freddie, as a direct challenge to the state-sponsored BBC Light Programme, and, in a comic inversion of the terms of the American Renaissance, the disc jockeys he selects to perpetrate this transatlantic coup are 'Mr. Nathaniel Hawthorne Crossley and Mr. Waldo Emerson Crossley' (p. 271). The famous declaration of American cultural independence by Emerson and Hawthorne in the nineteenth century is accordingly refurbished within the icon-oclastic climate of the 1960s, with maverick American outsiders setting out once again to challenge the institutional complacency and social conformity of British culture. Standish himself plays reflexively off the seventeenth-century Pilgrim Father, whose adventures were made famous in Henry Wadsworth Longfellow's 1858 poem 'The Courtship of Miles Standish', while Rushdie's Standish pays homage to his provenance by nicknaming the plane on which he travels to England 'the Mayflower' (p. 258). In this way, all the historical reduplications proposed by the text are echoed in its formal mirrorings, which reinscribe English and American literary culture within a global framework of pastiche. To take just one other example of this, two pompous Indian policemen are given the names Detective Inspector Sohrab and Detective Constable Rustam (p. 170), intertex-tually trading off Matthew Arnold's poem 'Sohrab and Rustum', a melancholy meditation on fatherhood and patriarchy published in 1853.

The saturnine comic brilliance of this novel, then, lies in the way in which it sets up a series of self-mirroring intertextual frameworks and uses these in order radically to destabilize the epistemological premises of the narrative, so that reading the book becomes akin to feeling the ground constantly shaking beneath our feet. The story unfolds in a parallel world of virtual history, where John F. Kennedy narrowly escapes assassination in Dallas and fictional characters—Sal Paradise, Nathan Zuckerman, Charlie Citrine—have become famous authors;

and all of this underlines the idea of characters living in two worlds at once, of the novel being organized around structural alternatives which intersect with each other in disorienting ways. The narrator talks about 'the outsideness of what we're inside', of finding a 'technique for jumping the points, from one track to the other' (p. 350), and the transnational dimension within *The Ground Beneath Her Feet* offers a formula for achieving exactly this. Sir Darius talks in chapter 2 about how 'The only people who see the whole picture ... are the ones who step out of the frame' (p. 43)—words re-echoed in chapter 7 (p. 203)—and he associates this sense of 'outsideness' with 'outcastes, lepers, pariahs, exiles, enemies, spooks, paradoxes' (p. 43). Just as Rushdie's early fiction turns on an 'east, west' axis, inscribing India and Britain as each other's other, so his later work appropriates the transatlantic dividing line to hollow out national mythologies and to present the parallel, virtual world of America as that which remains tantalizingly latent, a kind of absent presence, in other cultural formations.[35]

Rushdie justified his departure for New York early in 2000 by saying that 'for somebody who lived in England for as long as I did, relatively little of my work has dealt with it'. His enthusiastic embrace of the New York social scene raised hackles among many British observers, however, with Fay Weldon for one complaining of how 'Salman has made his home among the posers'.[36] *Fury* (2001) offers a fictionalized version of this transatlantic emigration through its story of Professor Malik Solanka, a historian of ideas and a doll-maker with expertise in remaking the 'world in inanimate miniature', who 'had come to America as so many before him to receive the benison of being Ellis Islanded, of starting over'.[37] While *Fury* addresses issues of globalization, it places the United States firmly at the centre of the circulation of multinational capital: 'Everyone was an American now, or at least Americanized: Indians, Iranians, Uzbeks, Japanese, Lilliputians, all. America was the world's playing field, its rule book, umpire and ball. Even anti-Americanism was Americanism in disguise, conceding, as it did, that America was the only game in town and the matter of America the only business at hand' (p. 87). Published in America by Random House on 4 September 2001, one week before 9/11, the novel portrays in retrospect a particular moment in American history, the time of peace and 'plenty' (p. 6) at the end of the Clinton era, when stock market values were high, when the 'future was a casino, and everyone was gambling, and everyone expected to win' (p. 4). There are, however, prescient rumblings of the catastrophe that was shortly to be visited upon New York. Solanka hears a New York taxi driver shouting that 'Islam will cleanse this street of godless motherfucker bad drivers' and prophesying how 'the victorious jihad will crush your balls in its unforgiving fist' (p. 65), while Solanka himself fears that this 'golden age' must

---

[35] Salman Rushdie, *East, West* (London: Jonathan Cape, 1994).
[36] D. T. Max, 'Manhattan Transfer', *Observer Review*, 24 Sept. 2000, 2.
[37] Salman Rushdie, *Fury* (London: Jonathan Cape, 2001), 30, 51. Subsequent page references to this edition are cited in parentheses in the text.

end: 'America, because of its omnipotence, is full of fear; it fears the fury of the world and renames it envy' (p. 114). One part of the 'fury' of the novel's title, then, refers to the prospect of revenge, while another part points to the power of the artistic furies: 'Out of *furia* comes creation, inspiration, originality, passion, but also violence, pain, pure unafraid destruction, the giving and receiving of blows from which we never recover' (pp. 30–1). A further aspect of this 'fury', though, involves Rushdie's anger towards England in the wake of his experiences there after the fatwa. Solanka has willingly exchanged the 'country of reserve, of the understatement and the unsaid' (p. 35) for a more extravagant culture epitomized here again by the figure of 'Jay Gatsby, the highest bouncer of them all, [who] failed too in the end, but lived out, before he crashed, that brilliant, brittle, gold-hatted, exemplary American life' (p. 82). This image of bouncing, which recurs on the novel's last page, suggests, in typical Gatsby fashion, something that simultaneously goes high, like a bouncing ball, but is also liable to be empty or hollow, like a bouncing cheque.

Rushdie's willingness to make use of such 'exemplary' narratives of American culture suggests the indebtedness in his later works to traditional 'myth and symbol' versions of American national identity. Just as Leo Marx in *The Machine in the Garden* characterized Gatsby as 'an archetypal American' who typifies the reconciliation of pastoralism and technology in US culture, so Rushdie invokes Scott Fitzgerald's hero as a symbol of American wealth and modernity, of the high-tech paradise which America presents to the rest of the world.[38] *Fury* thus offers not so much a portrait of the internal complexities of American society as a projection of what the USA signifies beyond its own borders. In keeping with the computer hyperlinks and web pages with which the novel's miniaturist hero experiments, *Fury* presents a simulated, digitalized version of American nationalism designed to reflect back on the exhausted condition of England—the narrative does indeed recoil upon itself, ending up back in London, on Hampstead Heath—as well as on the fundamentalist rhetoric of Islam; indeed, in an essay that first appeared in April 2001, a few months before *Fury* was published, Rushdie remarked approvingly on 'what a difference the internet has made to press freedoms in India'.[39] Rushdie's willingness after his move to the United States to refer back to legendary narratives such as *The Great Gatsby* in order to explain contemporary American culture suggests his readiness to embrace some of the theoretical tenets of American exceptionalism, the belief that American civilization should be seen as qualitatively different from that of other places. He reinforced this view in his Tanner Lectures on Human Values at Yale in 2002, in which he celebrated Columbus as an avatar of visionary displacement and equated Frederick Jackson Turner's 'frontier-crossing' ethic

[38] Leo Marx, *The Machine in the Garden: Technology and the Pastoral Ideal in America* (New York: Oxford University Press, 1964), 356.
[39] Salman Rushdie, 'It Wasn't Me', in *Step Across This Line*, 374.

with patterns of mobility that he claimed were endemic in 'American literature from Twain to Bellow'.[40] Rushdie's love for Victor Fleming's film *The Wizard of Oz*, on which he wrote a commentary in 1992, also testifies to his reverence for these mythic dimensions in American popular culture.

It is possible, in fact, that Rushdie's experiences with the fatwa and his subsequent removal from England have confirmed him in a cultural attachment to American values infused with the typical fervour of an immigrant or convert. It is noticeable that Rushdie's journalistic pieces for the *New York Times* became more belligerently pro-American after 9/11: he strongly supported US military action in Afghanistan and berated 'the depth of anti-American feeling among large segments of the population, as well as the news media' in Britain and Europe for what he took to be the 'hypocrisy' of their belief that somehow the United States had deserved what had happened to it.[41] He also specifically rejected Samuel P. Huntington's pessimistic thesis about a 'clash of civilizations': Huntington, in a 1993 *Foreign Affairs* article, argued that the polarities of the cold war were being superseded by 'fault lines between civilizations' driven by cultural and religious difference, but Rushdie responded that such clashes were not merely between but within civilizations, with 'the Islamists' project ... not only turned against the West and "the Jews," but also against their fellow-Islamists'. Whereas Huntington cautioned that the 'very phrase "the world community" has become the euphemistic collective noun (replacing "the Free World") to give global legitimacy to actions reflecting the interests of the United States and other Western powers', Rushdie, by contrast, sided with opponents of Huntington who regarded values of freedom and secular modernity as universal human rights.[42] This is commensurate with the way in which his narratives treat Islam not as a homogeneous entity but as a body riven with scepticism and schism; it is also why, for all their stylistic immersion in pastiche and hybridity, his novels are in many ways indebted less to a spirit of postmodernist multiculturalism than to the more reflexive, self-interrogative dimensions of modernism. The sense of ironic textual estrangement from religious dogma in *The Satanic Verses* is of the same order as one finds in Joyce's *Ulysses*, and, for all of the contradictions in Rushdie's book, its status as an artistic event evokes the kind of cerebral utopianism outlined in a 1989 interview by the rationalist political philosopher Jürgen Habermas: 'We cannot pick and choose our own traditions, but we can be aware that it is up to us *how* we continue them ... every continuation of tradition is selective, and precisely this selectivity must pass today through the filter of critique, of a self-conscious appropriation of history.'[43] It is precisely

---

[40] Rushdie, 'Step Across This Line', 408, 424.

[41] Salman Rushdie, 'Anti-Americanism', in *Step Across This Line*, 399–400.

[42] Samuel P. Huntington, 'The Clash of Civilizations?', *Foreign Affairs*, 72/3 (Summer 1993), 22, 39; Rushdie, 'Not About Islam?', 395.

[43] Jürgen Habermas, 'The Limits of Neo-Historicism', in *Autonomy and Solidarity: Interviews with Jürgen Habermas*, ed. Peter Dews, rev. edn. (London: Verso, 1992), 243.

such 'self-conscious appropriation of history' that characterizes the way in which this fictional work relates to the author's own Islamic heritage, but this kind of 'selectivity' also implies how Rushdie's identification of himself with the United States enables him to gain a certain intellectual distance and power over local forms of tyranny. By affiliating itself with American values of universal freedom, Rushdie's work uproots national icons and patriarchal figureheads in the cultural sphere as clinically as US military forces have dispatched troublesome leaders in the political arena.

There is, then, a touch of intellectual imperialism in Rushdie's writing, a fierce disregard for what it denigrates as foolish parochial customs. It is this tone of disdain that surely helped to account for some of the hostility towards Rushdie's work in Britain that became explicit around the time of his emigration. Despite being, as University of London professor John Sutherland observed in 2001, 'a very great novelist', England's 'greatest', someone whose work is comparable to that of Thomas Mann or D. H. Lawrence, both Rushdie and his work have frequently come under attack from English newspapers. The *Independent on Sunday*, for instance, denounced *Fury* as 'gibberish', a novel without 'a coherent plot' which 'fails on every single level', leading the reviewer to conclude that Rushdie 'has long been over-rated as a novelist'.[44] The intemperance of this invective is itself interesting, and in part it exemplifies, banally enough, the impatience felt by journalists towards literary styles that appear to them excessively complicated or self-indulgent. It is striking, though, that Rushdie, through his frequent newspaper columns and his willing participation in celebrity culture, should render himself especially vulnerable to this kind of populist attack in a way that someone like Joyce never did. Such controversies speak also to the deliberate worldliness of Rushdie's texts, their provocative courting of the offensive: *Fury* embraces America as a land of 'broken English' (p. 51), just as *The Ground Beneath Her Feet* asserts that 'England can no longer lay exclusive claim to the English language' (p. 378), and such an uncompromising idiom of perpetual decentring and fragmentation is disconcerting to those, Americanists as well as Anglophiles, who would prefer fiction with a more accustomed epistemological and ethical circumference.

As Malik Solanka in *Fury* recognizes, one of the ironies of his position is that, although he 'loathed Margaret Thatcher' personally, he shared the instincts of Thatcherite conservatism 'to destroy the old power-blocs' (p. 23), to undermine the corporate models predicated upon the inviolability of the bureaucratic state that dominated British politics in the era of 'Butskellite' consensus between 1945 and 1979.[45] For all of the negative portrayals of Thatcher's Britain, particularly

---

[44] John Sutherland, 'The Sound and the Fury', *Guardian*, 25 Aug. 2001, 8; Matt Thorne, 'Rich Man's Blues', *Independent on Sunday*, 26 Aug. 2001, 15.

[45] 'Butskellite', a composite term derived from the names of Conservative politician R. A. Butler and Labour party leader Hugh Gaitskell, was a word used frequently to describe a general

in *The Satanic Verses*, there is an obvious complicity between Rushdie's pre-disposition towards American ideologies of freedom and his rejection of what he has described as a pusillanimous English communal culture. Like Thatcher, Rushdie openly values money, success, personal mobility, and the subversion of established institutions; indeed, disestablishment, the severing of links between enterprise and tradition, has become an intellectual necessity for him in the cultural sphere no less than it was for Thatcher in the political sphere. It would hardly be appropriate to call Rushdie's texts Thatcherite, and certainly their resol-utely iconoclastic features were viewed askance by the Conservative governments of the 1980s and early 1990s. What his fiction does embody, however, is the kind of pressure on the nation-state as a unit of social and economic cohesion that coincided with Thatcher's time in Downing Street, since Rushdie's work reflects the manifold stresses and tensions involved in the emergence of globalization dur-ing this era. The transnational dimensions of Rushdie's fiction, in other words, speak to a situation in which the cultural autonomy of the British nation was itself coming increasingly under erasure; but, rather than comfortingly papering over the cracks, his work chooses gleefully to expose the ways in which these crevices were opening up, how the ground was shaking beneath the country's feet. Rushdie's narratives therefore seek not to transcend national or ethnic identity but to hollow it out, to reposition it within a transnational framework wherein the idea of cultural heritage becomes inverted. Disavowing the familiar notion of postcolonialism as what Nico Israel has called a 'cordoned-off subdiscipline', Rushdie's work intimates that all forms of literature, not just its postcolonial variants, emerge through power plays across national and religious divides.[46] As a declared non-believer in relation to nationalism as well as religion, Rushdie's blasphemous temper has naturally failed to endear him to the keepers of vari-ous sacred flames, but his structures of traversal and travesty brilliantly rewrite national history in the light of globalization to reveal the cross-currents, frictions, and absences occluded by more conventional forms of identity politics.

A NEW WORLD ORDER: CARYL PHILLIPS

One general inference to be drawn from Rushdie's work, then, is the decentring of 'English' itself as a natural standard-bearer for Anglophone writing. The pressures of globalization have uncoupled the idea of 'English literature' from the wider notion of literature in English and have consequently repositioned the home-grown English literary canon as one of many competing discourses within

convergence of policies between the two main political parties around the need for strong central planning and a welfare state. This consensus started to unravel in the changed economic conditions of the 1970s, and ended abruptly when Margaret Thatcher came to power in 1979.

[46] Israel, *Outlandish*, 127.

a post-imperial framework. Michael Bérubé, in fact, argues that the orthodox academic distinction between modernism and postmodernism will finally be of less intellectual significance than the division of twentieth-century literature into periods before and after the global expansion of literature in the English language, a temporal and ideological break for which he uses the Second World War as a convenient marker.[47] One of the most striking features of Rushdie's work, exemplified by the seemingly casual reference to Ignatius Sancho in *The Satanic Verses*, is its explicit theoretical awareness of how a country's historical narratives are retrospectively fabricated, and its literary canons reconstructed accordingly. Indeed, the provocative contention of Rushdie and Caryl Phillips is that such contemporary revisions of the English canon alter our perspectives on the past, so that the historical relationship of British to American culture emerges as a precursor and analogue to more recent debates about national identity that have manifested themselves within the intellectual framework of postcolonialism. By arranging English, American, and postcolonial literatures in

25. Caryl Phillips, photographed by Jillian Edelstein (1992).

[47] Michael Bérubé, 'Introduction: Worldly English', *Modern Fiction Studies*, 48 (2002), 3.

parallel and subjecting them systematically to a politics of traversal, Rushdie and Phillips suggest how American and postcolonial writing have long been integral to the formation of English. They also imply how the academically demarcated boundaries of American and postcolonial studies in recent times have typically been predicated upon rigid assumptions about binary oppositions between centre and margin, oppositions into which the more fluid, variegated dimensions of transnationalism have been uncomfortably shoehorned. By seeking overtly to participate in theoretical discourses about the institutionalization of English, Rushdie and Phillips raise questions about the present, the past, and, most crucially, the problematic relationship of present to past.

Phillips himself was born on the Caribbean island of St Kitts in 1958 and was brought to England when only a few months old, in the large wave of immigration from the West Indies to Britain during the 1950s. Like Martin Amis, Phillips read English at Oxford, but he then took up a series of visiting academic positions overseas (in India, Singapore, and Barbados as well as the United States), before being appointed in 1998 as a professor at Barnard College in New York, where he renewed his social acquaintance with Salman Rushdie; in 2005, he moved to Yale. Like Rushdie, Phillips found his patriotic allegiance to the United States becoming stronger after 9/11; he took US citizenship in 2002, telling an American audience two years later that it was the terrorist attacks which had convinced him finally to identify formally with the country.[48] Intellectually, though, Phillips remains equally focused on Britain; as a black writer who experienced an English educational system in the 1960s and 1970s that was 'inflexible and not readily open to change', Phillips's central project is to restore to the heritage of English literature and culture its occluded history of slavery and race. In this sense, his work seeks to realign the British cultural domain within a transnational system whose other nodes are the United States and the Caribbean. He thus envisages English literature as being involved in a more complex situation than what he called the 'woefully narrow idea of national identity' prevalent in his youth would imply, and, after winning the Commonwealth Writers prize in 2005, Phillips created a stir in Britain by persistently declining an invitation to meet the Queen, describing the idea of a hereditary head of state as 'simply nonsense'. Justifying his refusal further, Phillips explained: 'I'm trying to interrogate British history and mythologies and duplicities, and one of the enduring myths is the royal family, which is white and Christian and "pure-blooded," and on which the sun never sets.'[49]

---

[48] Phillips made this remark at an awards ceremony for the 2004 Pen/Faulkner Fiction Award, for which *A Distant Shore* was a finalist. Bob Hoover, 'Updike "Pleased and Moved" to Accept American Fiction's Most Prestigious Honor', *Pittsburgh Post-Gazette*, Arts and Entertainment, 10 May 2004; online: http://www.post-gazette.com, accessed 29 April 2005.

[49] Caryl Phillips, 'Confessions of a True Believer', *Guardian Review*, 4 Jan. 2003, 5; Maya Jaggi, 'No Thanks, Ma'am', *Guardian 2*, 15 June 2005, 4.

It is clear from his non-fiction works such as *The European Tribe* (1987) and the essays collected in *A New World Order* (2001) that Phillips is intensely concerned with the institutional imperatives of cultural history, with the retrospective reconfiguration of the past into canonical forms. This revisionist impulse is shown also by his anthology *Extravagant Strangers: A Literature of Belonging* (1997), which attempts to redescribe the circumference of English literature by bringing into conjunction black writers who escaped from slavery and subsequently settled in eighteenth-century London (Olaudah Equiano, Ignatius Sancho), writers born in the colonies (William Thackeray, George Orwell), colonial subjects (C. L. R. James, V. S. Naipaul), descendants of colonizers (Doris Lessing), descendants of the colonized (Rushdie), immigrants (T. S. Eliot, Joseph Conrad, Wyndham Lewis), and many others. Phillips explains in the preface that the anthology developed after he was invited to lecture at a university in Singapore on how a recent wave of writing by 'outsiders' to Britain was 'reinvigorating' the canon: 'I bristled at the implication that before this "recent wave" there was a "pure" English literature, untainted by the influence of outsiders. To my way of thinking, English literature has, for at least 200 years, been shaped and influenced by outsiders.'[50] Phillips thus places himself in something like the position of T. S. Eliot in 'Tradition and the Individual Talent', seeking to revise and reconstitute the past in order to elucidate the pressing concerns of the present. All of this might be understood in one way as an attempt to rework his experience of the Oxford English course of the late 1970s, covering an arc from *Beowulf* to Ted Hughes, which Phillips has described as being almost entirely blind to issues of race. American literature was Phillips's route into these issues of racial difference: he first discovered the work of Richard Wright and Ralph Ellison on a trip to the United States in the summer of 1978, immediately prior to his third year at Oxford, and then wrote about these authors on the American Literature paper available as a special option to finalists. However, Phillips subsequently recalled how, despite Britain at this time 'being torn apart by "race riots"… there was no discourse about race in British society and certainly no black writers' included at that time on the established syllabus of English literature at Oxford.[51]

Phillips's first novel, *The Final Passage* (1985), is a semi-autobiographical novel addressing his parents' emigration from the Caribbean to Britain, but its epigraph is taken from Eliot's 'Little Gidding'—the famous lines about how 'A people without history / Is not redeemed from time, for history is a pattern / Of timeless moments'—and this foreshadows the recursive theme both in this novel and in Phillips's work generally: he is concerned to place particular events within a larger pattern, where journeys take on typological overtones and history repeats itself.[52] Phillips's interest is not so much in individual experience as in

[50] Caryl Phillips, ed., *Extravagant Strangers: A Literature of Belonging* (London: Faber, 1997), p. x.
[51] Caryl Phillips, 'Marvin Gaye', in *A New World Order: Selected Essays* (London: Secker & Warburg, 2001), 35.   [52] Caryl Phillips, *The Final Passage* (London: Picador, 1995), 3.

recording how the fate of individuals is encompassed by wider cultural forces, and this is why so many of his novels—*Higher Ground* (1989), *Crossing the River* (1993), *The Nature of Blood* (1997)—move backwards and forwards in space and time, adducing parallels and analogies between historical situations that might otherwise seem quite disparate. This, again, is the kind of theoretical impulse that informs Eliot's revisions of the literary canon, bringing different writers into juxtaposition so that a tradition is understood retrospectively in a new way, and it suggests how, for all his overt indifference to critical theory, there is a conscious continuum between Phillips's fictional and non-fictional narratives.

We see this self-conscious relationship to the English tradition in the novel *Cambridge* (1992), which re-creates the life of Emily Cartwright, an English spinster dispatched by her father to visit his sugar estate in the West Indies. The plot reveals British complicity in the nineteenth-century slave trade, with its second part being narrated by a slave who is given the name of Cambridge by his new master, Mr Wilson, described by Cambridge himself as 'but one of a large multitude of contented plunderers happily accommodated in the bosom of English society'. In light of his given name, Cambridge's own 'polite English' works as an ironic inversion of the kind of discourse sanctioned by the country's social and educational establishment; Cambridge refers to himself as a 'virtual Englishman' and says he is outraged 'to be treated as base African cargo'.[53] Phillips has spoken about his great admiration for nineteenth-century novelists such as Hardy, Tolstoy, and Dickens, writers whose work 'I love', and Paul Sharrad has suggested a specific intertextual relationship to Dickens in *Cambridge*, with Phillips giving his slave an active voice in order to avoid the 'spurious comfort', the 'reductive enclosure of gentility and good feelings', into which Dickens's narratives finally lapse.[54] This attempt to produce a revisionist version of British cultural history is consistent with the concerns of the non-fiction work *The Atlantic Sound* (2000), in which Phillips discusses the architectural and economic links in the eighteenth and nineteenth centuries between Liverpool, 'the most important slave port in Europe', and Charleston, South Carolina, which 'occupied the same position in North America'. He talks of how Charleston House in Abercromby Square, Liverpool, 'effectively served as the confederate embassy during the American Civil War', and he says that it 'greatly concerns' him that Liverpudlians 'do not know the true story of how and why these buildings came to be built'. Many of Phillips's essays call specifically for what *The European Tribe* calls a 'historical striptease' on Britain's part, a recognition of the extent to which the country's mercantile wealth developed out of slaveholding interests.[55] Wandering around late twentieth-century Liverpool,

---

[53] Caryl Phillips, *Cambridge* (New York: Knopf, 1992), 141, 112, 156.

[54] Renée Schattemann, 'An Interview with Caryl Phillips', *Commonwealth Essays and Studies*, 23/2 (Spring 2001), 105; Paul Sharrad, 'Speaking the Unspeakable: London, Cambridge and the Caribbean', in *De-Scribing Empire: Post-Colonialism and Textuality*, ed. Chris Tiffin and Alan Lawson (London: Routledge, 1994), 211.

[55] Caryl Phillips, *The Atlantic Sound* (London: Faber, 2000), 86–7, and *idem, The European Tribe* (London: Faber, 1999), 127.

Phillips encounters simply a loutish, depressive historical amnesia which represses such knowledge as too uncomfortable to face.

In recent years, as Bénédicte Ledent has observed, the theme of imperialism has received far more critical attention in discussions of English literature than the issue of slavery, so in this sense Phillips's writing acts also as a corrective to what are now familiar notions about the hegemonic designs of the British Empire.[56] The essays in *A New World Order* draw heavily on Edouard Glissant's 'theory of Relation' as 'a synthesising space in which opposites can live comfortably together', and for Phillips, as for Glissant, the 'creolising' geography of the Caribbean provides a 'perfect model' for an 'age in which migrations across boundaries are an increasingly familiar part of our individual lives as national borders collapse and are redrawn'.[57] Seeing his own work as traversing the Caribbean Sea as well as the Atlantic, Phillips looks to the United States 'to aid me in my attempts to understand contemporary Britain', while his movements around the Atlantic rim engender a 'restlessness of form', a constant shifting of focus, through which the values of each country are refracted through the perspectives of others; hence he talks of wishing his ashes 'to be scattered in the middle of the Atlantic Ocean at a point equidistant between Britain, Africa and North America'. Like Rushdie and other postmodernist writers who experienced the atmosphere of England in the 1980s, Phillips has tended to demonize the figure of Margaret Thatcher, and he says that he first felt the desire to emigrate from Britain to the United States most powerfully in 1987, after Thatcher had won her third successive election victory with a 'discordant, neo-imperial, rhetoric of exclusion'.[58] But he has by no means simply left behind the cultural assumptions of England: in his 1997 review of the *Norton Anthology of African-American Literature*, edited by Henry Louis Gates and Nellie Y. McKay, he criticized the selection of writers such as Sojourner Truth and Maria W. Stewart, arguing that their work 'would seem to belong more to the realm of speech-making and religio-political agitation than literature', and even suggesting that 'the shadowy hand of political correctness' might have been responsible for their inclusion in this anthology.[59]

This is, as it were, the Oxford side of Phillips, the side committed to traditional literary values. He started his career as a writer and director for the theatre, and the structuring of novels such as *Crossing the River* around multiple first-person narratives is a technique owing much to the dramatic monologue, with the author rendering himself anonymous and allowing his characters to do the talking for

---

[56] Bénédicte Ledent, *Caryl Phillips* (Manchester: Manchester University Press, 2002), 130.

[57] Caryl Phillips, 'Edouard Glissant: Promiscuities', in *New World Order*, 182–3, and *idem*, 'The Gift of Displacement', in *New World Order*, 132.

[58] Phillips, 'Marvin Gaye', 35, 'Gift of Displacement', 130, and *idem*, 'The "High Anxiety" of Belonging', in *New World Order*, 304.

[59] Caryl Phillips, 'Literature: The New Jazz for Black America?', *Observer Review*, 6 April 1997, 17.

him. Phillips himself has said in interviews that whereas Rushdie is 'like a puppet master' who manipulates his characters in order to write 'novels of ideas', he himself wants 'to be invisible behind my people because it's as though I feel entrusted with their lives'.[60] To put this another way, whereas in Rushdie's novels 'the central character is him and his consciousness', for Phillips the complexity of human character antecedes the abstract authorial idea: 'By placing character at the heart of these events, then you immediately have tension because characters resist sloganeering. They just won't behave themselves.' This again presupposes a more traditional, liberal humanist style of fiction in which idiosyncratic individuality resists the reductive enclosures of philosophical conditioning. Phillips has said that he is interested not in proselytizing but in focusing on 'ambiguity', on 'the grey area', and in this sense he endorses the humanist literary model promoted by Iris Murdoch in her famous 1961 essay 'Against Dryness', very influential in the Oxford English faculty during Phillips's era, which argued that theoretical abstractions tended to obscure the complex nature of 'the real impenetrable human person'.[61] At the same time, the elaborate eighteenth-century journals and monologues in *Crossing the River* and other works are not, of course, authentic documents but brilliantly contrived forms of pastiche. There is, consequently, a sense in which, like Greenblatt and the academic new historicists, Phillips's reconstructions of the past are predicated upon something like a structural oxymoron, whereby the attempt to reconstitute the past is matched by an implicit recognition that such plenitude can never be fully achieved. Another model for this kind of self-reflexive consciousness is Brechtian drama, which always seeks to disrupt the aesthetic frame, to disturb the luxuries of empathy, so as to force the audience into an intellectual recognition of how their own situation relates to that being portrayed on the stage. Phillips's narratives are thus organized strategically around loss and absence, around a paradoxical failure to represent their own subject-matter, just as naming a slave 'Cambridge' points implicitly to the gap between inscription and embodiment: a Cantabrigian, Cambridge is not.

From this point of view, Phillips's re-creations of history are always retrospectively projected from, in the title of his 2003 novel, 'a distant shore'. It is an austere, abstract England that emerges in this latter novel, one looked at from a distance rather than comfortably from within. The story is told by a series of narrators—the retired schoolteacher Dorothy, the African asylum seeker Solomon—who are themselves alienated from modern English society, and this tone of isolation, of a picaresque self enjoying little sense of communal affiliation,

[60] Schattemann, 'Interview with Caryl Phillips', 95; Lars Eckstein, 'The Insistence of Voices: An Interview with Caryl Phillips', *ARIEL: A Review of International English Literature*, 32/2 (April 2001), 37.

[61] Schattemann, 'Interview with Caryl Phillips', 95, 103; Iris Murdoch, 'Against Dryness: A Polemical Sketch', *Encounter*, 16/1 (Jan. 1961), 16–20. Murdoch was married to John Bayley, author of *The Characters of Love: A Study in the Literature of Personality* (1960) and other critical works, who was Thomas Warton Professor of English at Oxford during Phillips's time there.

haunts most of Phillips's writing. There are some fairly obvious links here with black American writers who were interested in existentialism: he always felt a special affinity with his friend James Baldwin, and he has cited Ellison as 'the outstanding writer and intellectual that the [African-American] tradition has so far produced'.[62] But Phillips's own emphasis on the isolated subject altogether lacks the ebullience with which it is endowed in Ellison's writing. In *A Distant Shore*, estrangement develops as a reaction of disgust against the environment, with racism appearing not so much as vicious prejudice but rather as a form of stupidity: Dorothy thinks despairingly of how her friend Mahmood, when running an Indian restaurant, had to put up with 'fat-bellied Englishmen and their slatterns rolling into The Khyber Pass after the pubs had closed, calling him Ranjit or Baboo or Swamp Boy, and using poppadoms as frisbees'.[63] English racism is presented by Phillips as a form of incivility and atavism, but the way in which the narrative of *A Distant Shore* moves backwards and forwards in time conveys a sense that such attitudes are somehow inevitable; unlike in Ellison, there is often in Phillips a fatalistic sense of entrapment, of being unable ultimately to avoid the depressing weight of the social environment.

For Phillips, then, racism is not so much an individual aberration as something associated inextricably with the communitarian instincts of British society. Reviewing *The Atlantic Sound*, the black British writer Gary Younge accused Phillips during his foreign travels of appearing 'socially conservative' in his fastidious avoidance of contact with 'strangers' and with other aspects of the vulgar world; and certainly, unlike Rushdie, Phillips has little interest in the gregarious spirit of human comedy.[64] *A Distant Shore* frequently uses the word 'tribe' to describe groupings of people, and this picks up on a theme in *The European Tribe*, which talks of how the 'tribes of Europe are forever suspicious of each other … anxious to protect national identities'. In this sense, Europe appears to be 'a continent … sadly wedded to the ugly conceit of racialism': the bigotry in Northern Ireland is of a piece with French xenophobia and with the hostility of Norwegian immigration officials to those who are not white. This again traps the narrator within a landscape of alienation and depression, and it also forces him to rationalize the Nazi regime not as 'the grandiose dream of a lunatic fringe' but as consistent with the fear of the foreign that pervades Europe.[65] Like C. L. R. James, whom Phillips acknowledges as 'the outstanding Caribbean mind of the twentieth century', Phillips regards Hitler and Stalin as logical corollaries to the idea of a European nation-state based implicitly around racial doctrines, rather than as macabre exceptions to this rule.[66]

---

[62] Phillips, 'Literature: The New Jazz for Black America?', 17.
[63] Caryl Phillips, *A Distant Shore* (London: Secker & Warburg, 2003), 202.
[64] Gary Younge, 'Home Run', *Guardian*, 27 May 2000, 8.
[65] Phillips, *A Distant Shore*, 137, and *idem, The European Tribe*, pp. xii–xiii.
[66] Caryl Phillips, 'C. L. R. James: Mariner, Renegade and Castaway', in *New World Order*, 152.

This in turn leads Phillips frequently to return to the shadow of Nazism as a dark epitome of the racial compulsions that haunt his narratives. The final part of *Higher Ground* focuses upon Jewish refugees in the 1940s fleeing from the Nazis and hoping to settle in Palestine, and it juxtaposes this Jewish diaspora with earlier slave migrations from Africa, as described in the first section of the book. The second part of the novel is set in 1967 and is narrated by a black American, Rudi, serving six years in prison for attempted robbery. Rudi spends his enforced leisure studying American history, which he chronicles through the fictional device of letters home to his relatives, and this effectively links the African-American racial experience with political issues of national identity: among the stories Rudi relates is that of Crispus Attucks, a black man shot by a British soldier in Boston in March 1770 in an incident which helped to spark off the American War of Independence. The final section of *Crossing the River* is also set 'somewhere in England' in the early 1940s, and it parallels the jingoistic rhetoric of wartime England both with the journal of an eighteenth-century English slave-trader and with the efforts of the American Colonization Society in the nineteenth century to repatriate former slaves to the west coast of Africa on the grounds that this would remove a cause of increasing social stress in the United States. These parallel narratives create something like a nest of Chinese boxes, a self-mirroring structure whose common thread is the desire for racial and national purity. This pattern testifies again to the inherent pessimism of Phillips's work, his sense that cultural systems of exclusion are rooted in tribal loyalties and that the fundamental instincts of societies change only very gradually, if at all. Phillips has expressed his admiration for the Japanese novelist Shusaku Endo who writes about similar forms of social immobility, admitting how 'the inflexible rigidity of the Japanese society that Endo portrays does, in fact, strike a familiar chord in me'.[67]

A Distant Shore includes another glancing reference to anti-Semitism, with the northern English village 'folks' making the life of a Jewish doctor 'a misery' and driving her out of the community.[68] Phillips's most extended treatment of anti-Semitism is, however, in *The Nature of Blood*. Described by the author as a kind of 'prequel' to Shakespeare's *Othello*, *The Nature of Blood* re-creates the resentment felt among sixteenth-century Venetian aristocrats—who feel that it is 'important to keep the bloodlines pure'—towards the Doge, who has hired an African general to command his armies.[69] *Othello* was the Shakespeare play designated for special study when Phillips sat his final examinations at Oxford in 1979, and *The Nature of Blood* might be seen as another attempt to revise the Oxford English syllabus in order to atone for its occluded racial dimension, to reread the play as turning crucially on racial difference rather than, as in the

---

[67] Caryl Phillips, *Crossing the River* (London: Bloomsbury, 1993), 125, and *idem*, 'Confessions of a True Believer', 5.   [68] Phillips, *A Distant Shore*, 9.
[69] Schattemann, 'An Interview with Caryl Phillips', 97; Caryl Phillips, *The Nature of Blood* (London: Faber, 1997), 112.

liberal humanist interpretation, jealousy.[70] The novel adduces analogies among different types of racial persecution, comparing the ritualistic Jewish killing of Christian children in order to drain their blood at Portobuffole in 1480 with the Nazi extermination of the Jews in pursuit of similar motives of racial cleansing. Phillips remarked in a 2001 interview on what he took to be the common features of institutional torture: 'Somebody who dies in the bottom of a slave ship is suffering in the same way as somebody who dies in Auschwitz. It's the same thing as far as I am concerned.'[71] This inclines Phillips against understanding the Holocaust in exceptionalist terms, as a unique event within human history, and it moves him closer to the controversial position expounded by Zygmunt Bauman, who opposed the idea of the Holocaust as a phenomenon with a 'uniquely Jewish character' by claiming that in its instrumental rationality it tended rather to embody 'the hidden possibilities of modern society'. For Paul Gilroy, similarly, the most sinister aspect of Hitler was not that he represented 'supernatural evil' but that he promoted a populist version of the racial science that was used all too often in the twentieth century to underwrite national formations of all kinds.[72]

One of the effects of Phillips's work, then, is to offer a revisionist account of the Second World War. He recalls how when he was at school in England during the 1960s and 1970s 'all the focus was on European history, where Britain could pat herself on the back and say "we won two World Wars"'; but his own fiction problematizes such moral triumphalism through its inscription of parallel narratives which suggest how various forms of racial prejudice and exploitation are embedded also within the fabric of the British nation.[73] Phillips's own manifesto for a 'new world order' as described in his critical essays involves 'travelling furiously across borders and boundaries', a collapse of the old hierarchical 'colonial, or postcolonial, model', and its replacement by 'one global conversation with limited participation open to all, and full participation available to none'; however, the more reactive force of his fiction suggests the difficulty of realizing such utopian designs.[74] Although his work willingly appropriates the radical genius of American writers such as Baldwin, Wright, and Ellison in order to highlight the more moribund contours of English culture, it also resists what he calls 'the essentializing politics of race which plague the United States' and, in particular, the association of any given form of racial identity with some kind of redemptive spirit. Phillips thus uses his 'creolising Caribbean consciousness' not only to illuminate the racial dimensions suppressed by British national traditions,

---

[70] Paper 2(b) of the Final Honour School in English at Oxford in 1979 required a two-hour essay on either *Othello* or *As You Like It*. In a letter to the author on 10 Aug. 2004, Phillips confirmed that he had opted for *Othello*, a play he had also studied previously at secondary school for A level.

[71] Eckstein, 'Insistence of Voices', 37.

[72] Zygmunt Bauman, *Modernity and the Holocaust* (Cambridge: Polity, 1989), pp. ix, 12; Paul Gilroy, *Between Camps: Race, Identity and Nationalism at the End of the Colour Line* (London: Allen Lane–Penguin, 2000), 147. [73] Eckstein, 'Insistence of Voices', 40.

[74] Phillips, 'Introduction: A New World Order', in *New World Order*, 5.

but also to disseminate a secular, sceptical mode of traversal which cuts against what he takes to be an American tendency to reify race into a fixed, putatively metaphysical conception.[75] As someone with roots in an intellectual tradition of liberalism, Phillips finds that academic 'black studies departments ... don't necessarily make a lot of sense to me', and he is hostile to what he calls 'Race posturing' in the United States: 'There is money to be made from the race dozens, from declaring "I am somebody" as opposed to wondering who the other person is.'[76] Like Gilroy in *Between Camps*, Phillips concludes that the category of race can have strategic importance in a political sense, but that as a philosophical idea it has little intellectual substance: 'Race matters ... but not that much.'[77]

According to Werner Sollors, the 'new emphasis on ethnic identity and on cultural pluralism in modern democratic societies' emerged after the Second World War in direct reaction 'against the fascist trajectory from racist stereotype to genocide'.[78] What the work of Phillips and Rushdie suggests, though, is the relative theoretical weakness of these postwar liberal models and of the extent to which racial assumptions cannot readily be dissociated from ideas of ethnic identity. Walter Benn Michaels has shown how a conception of race as nativity played a formative part in the development of American national identity in the modernist period—in Hemingway, William Carlos Williams, and other supposedly enlightened writers—and, despite his evocation of a 'new world order', Phillips's emphasis on the 'tribe' as a foundational principle of modern societies works pessimistically to endorse Michaels's idea of the fundamental intractability of racial difference.[79] What this means as a corollary is that the Nazi project appears to be a crystallization of tendencies already implicit in Western civilization rather than merely a gross moral anomaly. This in turn undermines the premises of exceptionalism of every kind, and one of the most notable characteristics of Phillips's work is the way it draws analogies between Jewish history and the racial experiences of other 'tribes'.

One of the functions of the transatlantic model of postmodernism, then, is to respond indirectly to the historical trauma of the Second World War by problematizing the various binary oppositions that would separate off the democratic triumphalism of Britain or America from the iniquities of fascism. Just as Phillips's novels illuminate the different forms of fascism endemic to British culture, so Amis's fictional narratives rotate upon a transatlantic axis of dehumanization wherein the modern United States is linked uncomfortably to Nazi Germany, as is most evident in *Time's Arrow*. This doppelgänger effect develops specifically out of a process of triangulation, through which Britain, the United States, and Germany switch their commonly accepted positions on

---

[75] Caryl Phillips, 'The Burden of Race', in *New World Order*, 15, and *idem*, 'The Gift of Displacement', 133.   [76] Schattemann, 'Interview with Caryl Phillips', 104.
[77] Phillips, 'The Burden of Race', 16–17.
[78] Werner Sollors, 'Ethnic Modernism, 1910–1950', *American Literary History*, 15 (2003), 75.
[79] See Michaels, *Our America*, 1–16.

the ethical map of twentieth-century culture. It is reminiscent of the twinnings and shifts in perspective that we saw in the novels of Christopher Isherwood, which draw parallels between prewar Berlin and postwar Los Angeles. Analogies are not equivalences, of course, and there is no implication in Isherwood, Amis, or Phillips that the state of English culture in any way mitigates the Nazi evil; but there is an important sense in which these transatlantic exchanges serve to bring back into an intellectual framework the larger ramifications of the Second World War, represented in Amis's fiction as the pivotal event of the twentieth century, but whose continuing significance within contemporary global culture has perhaps been undervalued. One reason for this comparative neglect may be the thesis concerning the exceptionalist nature of the Holocaust, which can be traced back to Adorno's argument in *Negative Dialectics* (1966) that Auschwitz marked a radical break with the capacities of human experience, a phenomenon not only beyond representation but also sectioned off from other forms of atrocity. This line is pursued by Anthony Julius's study *Transgressions* (2002), which asserts that the Holocaust should be regarded as morally sacrosanct and therefore as forming a limit to aesthetic theories of transgression, the place where there is a clear distinction between darkness and light and where boundaries cannot be crossed.[80] However, Julius's work was subjected to a respectful demurral by Rushdie in his Tanner Lectures at Yale—'I am not sure he is right'—and it is a systematic traversal of parameters, both geographical and ideological, which impels the fiction of Phillips and Amis as well as Rushdie.[81] The spectre of racial hatred and religious hatred haunts all of their narratives, suggesting the amorphous, ubiquitous qualities of human intolerance and casting shadows over more benign liberal beliefs in the 'end' of history.

In this sense, the Caribbean geography of 'relation', less a distinct locale than a matrix of mediation or traversal, might be said to exemplify the mobile condition of contemporary writing in English. More generally, as we see from Rushdie and Phillips, the second half of the twentieth century witnessed a shift towards American culture as a focal point for literature in English within the new global system. Whereas at the beginning of the twentieth century it was English literature that provided the common frame of reference, by the end of the century it was US culture that had become the default model for anglophone discourse, the refractive nexus or channel through which other currents had to pass. American literature in the new millennium encompassed Rushdie, Phillips, and many other writers not born within the territory of the United States who looked to America as a means of relating their own indigenous culture to wider aspects of the world system. This ensured that, by the turn of the twenty-first century, the old mythic conception of American literature as a world elsewhere, a site of pastoral regeneration and self-affirmation, had become an idea of only historical interest.

---

[80] Theodor W. Adorno, *Negative Dialectics*, trans. E. B. Ashton (London: Routledge & Kegan Paul, 1973), 361–8; Julius, *Transgressions*, 197.   [81] Rushdie, 'Step Across This Line', 441.

Conclusion: The Transnationalization
of English Literature

In his General Editor's Preface to the Oxford English Literary History, which he describes as 'the twenty-first-century successor to the Oxford History of English Literature', Jonathan Bate makes clear that there is no place in this multi-volume big tent for American literature. 'Most of the writing of other English-speaking countries, notably the United States of America, is excluded,' he writes: 'We are not offering a world history of writing in the English language. Those Americans who lived and worked in England are, however, included.'[1] What this means, in effect, is that the identifying principle of English literature becomes neither race nor language but location, the dwelling place where particular writers 'lived and worked'. This is entirely compatible with the theory of environmentalism expounded by Bate in his earlier work, *Romantic Ecology*, with its emphasis on a 'theology of place', where meaning is held to be immanent within local situations.[2] A theoretical idiosyncrasy of this Oxford English Literary History, in other words, is the way it seeks to expand and institutionalize this kind of critical Wordsworthianism as an explanatory framework for English literature as a whole.

Such an emphasis on what Ian Baucom has called a 'redemptive localism', predicated upon 'the identity-endowing properties of place', has not been unusual in relation to the emphasis on national bonds of affiliation that has dominated literary categories for the past 100 years.[3] In this context, however, it produces another example of how these national categories can skew critical perspectives, since Bate's choice serves not only to exclude American literature but also to marginalize writers born in England who either emigrated to America or who were powerfully influenced by America as a cultural idea. The number of British writers who have actually become US citizens is relatively small: Auden and Isherwood in 1946, Wodehouse in 1955, Levertov in 1956, Phillips in 2002. To these might be added Susanna Rowson, who lived the last thirty-one years of her life in the new United States at a time when the legal protocols of citizenship

---

[1] Jonathan Bate, 'General Editor's Preface', in *The Victorians*, by Philip Davis, *Oxford English Literary History*, viii: 1830–1880, p. viii.
[2] Jonathan Bate, *Romantic Ecology: Wordsworth and the Environmental Tradition* (London: Routledge, 1991), 92.   [3] Baucom, *Out of Place*, 32, 4.

had not yet been so formalized and, from a reverse perspective, Henry James and T. S. Eliot, who by becoming British subjects—James in 1915, Eliot in 1927—brought their inheritance of American customs and traditions into a proper English domain. But many other English writers spent longer or shorter periods in the United States without changing their legal identification: Thom Gunn lived for nearly fifty years in San Francisco as a resident alien, while Aldous Huxley spent twenty-five years in southern California even though debarred from American citizenship because he would not declare his pacifism to be a matter of his religion, a compromise which might have made him acceptable to the authorities as a conscientious objector. Rushdie in 2002 said that he had 'no plans to take citizenship', though he added how he had 'now moved into understanding the world from the kind of position Americans think about things', so that when he returns to London he finds himself 'constantly shocked by the relatively alien mindset with which I'm confronted and with which I used to be completely at home'.[4] Ruxton, Clough, Lawrence, and Davie also lived for spells in the United States without seeking citizenship, while Gissing, Wilde, Carter, and Amis visited for shorter periods. Other English writers, such as Dickens, Anthony Trollope, and J. G. Ballard, spent relatively little time themselves in the United States but nevertheless found America emerging as a shaping, constitutive force within their work.[5] Still others—Price, Byron, Wordsworth, the Shelleys—never set foot in America at all, but found themselves impelled to respond, either positively or reactively, to the looming spectre of an alternative Western republic.

If the fluid, amorphous aspects of this relationship between literature and national identity create obvious problems of academic classification, they also suggest the manifold ways in which English and American literature have been intertwined since the eighteenth century. They also highlight ways in which literary histories written from nationalist standpoints, either explicitly or implicitly, remain locked into teleological structures that necessarily remain blind to anything which would radically traverse or obstruct their nativist agenda. It is not difficult to see why, in this formulation, the transnational qualities of Susanna Rowson should appear anomalous, why early Isherwood should be rated more highly than late Isherwood, why the fiction produced by Rushdie after his move to New York would be dismissed as self-indulgent. In this sense, Bate's principle of a rooted Englishness, for all of its gestures towards naturalization and inclusiveness, appears to be as much of an ideological construction as were those models of national identity on which Sir Arthur Quiller-Couch based his anthologies of English verse and prose at the beginning of the twentieth century. As Etienne Balibar has observed, any scheme of genealogy or kinship needs a

---

[4] Dave Welch, 'Salman Rushdie, Out and About', Powells.com Interviews, 25 Sept. 2002; online: http://www.powells.com/authors/rushdie.html, accessed 30 April 2005.
[5] For a discussion of the representation of America in Trollope's fiction, see Giles, *Transatlantic Insurrections*, 181–6.

principle of closure and exclusion in order to verify its family values, and in the Oxford English Literary History it is the United States which is positioned outside the 'symbolic kernel' of its imagined English community.[6]

This attribution to English literature of a discrete if diverse identity forms a mirror image of the old separatist model of American exceptionalism, through which certain types of differential conditions were mythologized in relation to America and then simply read back into critiques of its culture. The method here became entirely circular, with ideas of regeneration, the frontier, the elect nation, and so on being extrapolated from cultural narratives and then deployed as a theoretical matrix in order to rediscover those very same ideas, which were then triumphantly understood to authenticate the exceptionalist nature of American culture as a whole. As with Sir Arthur Quiller-Couch, the methodological mistake here was to imagine that conceptions projected retrospectively upon cultural landscapes might somehow be immanent within them. In his highly sophisticated treatment of this question in 'Tradition and the Individual Talent', T. S. Eliot noted how such epistemological dilemmas form at some level an inevitable part of how literary criticism and other academic disciplines operate: the scholar, according to Eliot, is confronted with the problem of reflexivity, 'a perception, not only of the pastness of the past, but of its presence', of ways in which the past is 'altered by the present as much as the present is directed by the past'.[7] The contemporary critic or historian, in other words, relates a story of the past which appears to be unfolding chronologically, from beginning to end, but whose trajectory has in fact been apportioned backwards, from end to beginning; the sequences of cause and effect thus represent, as in one of Edgar Allan Poe's detective stories, a kind of optical illusion. The fact that scholars can never recover the plenitude of the past does not, of course, mean that they can or should avoid reinterpreting it, since, as Eliot also noted, the utility of tradition lies always in its relationship to the present, to the ways in which particular cultures construct imagined histories in the light of their contemporary concerns. But just as work in the field of American literature in the twenty-first century has begun to move away overtly from exceptionalist paradigms, so the study of English literature in the new millennium will need self-consciously to confront the hydra-headed aspects of its own historical provenance.

In this regard, the canonical traditions of English outlined by Quiller-Couch, Bate, and Eliot himself, all equally partial in their own distinct ways, have recently been challenged by a revisionist impulse to set English literature in a global context, an impulse which has been particularly prevalent in the

---

[6] Etienne Balibar, 'The Nation Form: History and Ideology', in *Race, Nation, Class: Ambiguous Identities*, ed. Etienne Balibar and Immanuel Wallerstein, trans. Chris Turner (London: Verso, 1991), 99.   [7] Eliot, 'Tradition and the Individual Talent', in *Selected Essays*, 14–15.

United States.[8] Claudia Sadowski-Smith, in fact, has suggested that 'cultural work on globalization … has lagged somewhat behind comparable discourses in economics, political science, and sociology', although English historians such as Linda Colley have affiliated themselves explicitly with this impetus of globalization, with Colley's *Captives* positioning itself deliberately in opposition to the 'segregation of British domestic history from the history of varieties of Britons overseas'.[9] The visibility of postcolonial and post-imperial discourses, to which Colley's work makes extensive reference, should be one of the factors driving a reconsideration of interactions between British and US culture since the American Revolution. Just as black figures have remained mysteriously invisible in the annals of English literature, as Caryl Phillips has complained, so America has been understood by conventional English literary critics as a distant and separate sphere, a marginalized phenomenon, rather than one that has been integral to the formation of English as a subject over the past 250 years. To move American culture out of its foreign ghetto and to reintroduce it within the body of English literature is consequently to be made aware of a wide-ranging Atlantic republican tradition which has, through the ages, shed an oblique, interrogative light on the royalist assumptions that have silently structured the English cultural landscape.

Given current academic concerns with postcolonialism and power relations, it should not be forgotten that America itself formed part of the British Empire for many years, or that the relationship between English literature and America goes back to the days of Thomas More's *Utopia* (1516) and Shakespeare's *Tempest* 100 years later.[10] One of the aims of this book has been to give some indication of the broad historical scope within which these transatlantic dynamics have developed, their links with older issues of Reformation and disestablishment as well as with twentieth-century debates about the status of modernism. If the fraught Anglo-American dialectic in the nineteenth century tended to be focused on conceptions of the national body and its relation to the legitimacy of individual dissent, this dialectic in the twentieth century turned more on questions of global empire, with the exhausting defeat of Nazi Germany making Britain subsequently less comfortable with the growth of the United States into a technologically sophisticated superpower. The familiar nostrum of a 'special relationship' between Britain and the United States, promoted so heavily by

[8] See e.g. 'Special Topic: Globalizing Literary Studies', co-ordinated by Giles Gunn, with contributions from Paul Jay, Stephen Greenblatt, Edward W. Said, and Rey Chow, *PMLA*, 116 (2001), 16–74.

[9] Claudia Sadowski-Smith, 'Contesting Globalisms: The Transnationalization of U.S. Cultural Studies', *Postmodern Culture*, 10/1 (Sept. 1999), 2; Linda Colley, *Captives: Britain, Empire and the World, 1600–1850* (London: Jonathan Cape, 2002), 18.

[10] On the significance of America for More, Spenser, and other sixteenth-century English writers, see Jeffrey Knapp, *An Empire Nowhere: England, America, and Literature from* Utopia *to* The Tempest (Berkeley: University of California Press, 1992).

Churchill in the 1940s and 1950s, involved a particular response to a pressing political situation; it should not be expanded into a sentimental narrative about undying bonds of friendship between the two peoples, since, as we have seen, conflict as much as co-operation has characterized their interactions ever since the American War of Independence. Synchronous with this putative special relationship was the emergence of American studies as a professional field, but one of the unfortunate aspects of the way in which this subject has evolved academically over the last fifty years has been the way it typically truncates narratives in time as well as compressing them in space, a pattern which has had an inhibiting effect on broader historical considerations of the United States within a transnational framework. Besides circumscribing its theoretical scope by focusing exclusively on the site of the nation, American studies has tended to foreshorten temporal perspectives by implying that debates about the transmission and circulation of American culture are a recent phenomenon. According to this reading, the *locus classicus* for studies of 'Americanization' becomes the years immediately after the Second World War, a time commensurate with the emergence of American studies itself, with the chief emblems of this invasion of US mass culture being Hollywood films, popular music, and, later, McDonalds restaurants. In fact, though, over the past three centuries transnational pressures of many different kinds—religious, economic, political—have threatened the 'integrity or autonomy' of the nation-state, so that what one might call the established version of English culture, the High Anglican version promulgated by Matthew Arnold, could be said to have flourished in part only through the systematic repression of its transatlantic axis.[11]

It is no coincidence that it should have been an American by birth, T. S. Eliot, who commented most astutely in 'Tradition and the Individual Talent' on how these canonical narratives in English literature have been institutionalized. 'Every nation', said Eliot, 'has not only its own creative, but its own critical turn of mind; and is even more oblivious of the shortcomings and limitations of its critical habits than those of its creative genius.'[12] Within Britain itself, however, there has been a long-standing reluctance to take fully into account the institutional networks within which literature is necessarily mediated. There are several compelling reasons for this: the incorporation within critical culture itself of an ingrained Wordsworthian sensibility, with its view of analytical frameworks as intrusive and demeaning; the continuing popularity of a Leavisite belief in close, passionate engagement with sacred texts; and, since about 1980, the relative loss of social and economic status by British universities and their supplantation as principal disseminators of cultural information, material, and value by the greatly expanded power of television and print media. In the United States, however, such a shift in cultural power from higher education to the

---

[11] Michael Geyer and Charles Bright, 'World History in a Global Age', *American Historical Review*, 100 (1995), 1056.   [12] Eliot, 'Tradition and the Individual Talent', 13.

media has not been so apparent; in a situation where university libraries have richer resources and the mass media are less culturally ambitious, the institutional contexts of literature and literary study have continued to be much more an object of concern and debate. In part, as John Guillory has observed, these debates have involved a set of largely predictable questions about who should be included in or excluded from the canon, framed according to the demands of 'identity politics' within a liberal agenda of multiculturalism. As Guillory goes on to argue, however, more crucial than any specific 'question of who is in or out of the canon' is an awareness of 'canonical *form*' itself as a shaping factor in social and institutional settings, a recognition of how 'the effects of ideology are generated around the conceptualization of literature itself'. In this sense, to fetishize the 'aesthetic' as though it could ever be isolated from the pressures of ideology is nonsensical.[13] As we saw when comparing Arnold and Clough, assumptions about what constitutes art and aesthetics crucially shaped not only the reception of these poets in their own time but also their subsequent assimilation into (or, in Clough's case, exclusion from) the 'great tradition' of English literature.

One of the most valuable qualities of a counterpointed Atlantic republican tradition is to make visible these suppressed institutional networks and relations that customarily remain merely latent within the English cultural and academic domain. All literary traditions depend upon embedded intertextual assumptions, and by making this intertextuality explicit, it becomes easier to challenge inherited perspectives and to open up new horizons. How, for example, might English literature appear differently if it were seen in relation to Byron rather than Wordsworth, Clough rather than Arnold, the later Auden rather than the earlier Auden? Many of the writers considered here have been linked with the legacy of dissent, in either its lower-case, maverick aspect or its upper-case, religious variant: Price, Clough, Gissing, Lawrence, and Davie would fall into the latter category. Sometimes this spirit of nonconformity was associated with heterodox interpretations of sexuality, as in Clough, Lawrence, Isherwood, and Carter. Frequently, as in the work of Mary Shelley, Huxley, and Ballard, the prospect of America was bound up with fears or expectations about scientific and technological progress. On occasions, as with Levertov and Rushdie, writers moved from Britain to the United States in the hope of giving their work the kind of radical, oppositional edge they had found more difficulty in sustaining amidst the smothering circumstances of English social life. But several others, such as Ruxton, Wodehouse, and Davie, had explicitly conservative political views, and it would be wrong to conflate this Atlantic republican tradition with political republicanism in the more specific sense. As the historical trajectory of this book suggests, transactions between English and American culture have been significant within a wide variety of very different situations—the American Revolution,

---

[13] Guillory, *Cultural Capital*, pp. 13, xiii, 135, 335.

the Great Reform Bill, the stand-off over Oregon, the exponential growth of American economic power at the end of the nineteenth century, the Second World War—and rather than trying to reduce these relations to any mythical opposition of national types, this account has tried to allow for their complex, multifaceted configurations. Ultimately what this Atlantic inheritance restores to English literature is not a political republic but an alternative realm, a parallel universe both spatially and intellectually. The American tradition in English literature illuminates the anamorphic dimensions associated with conventional representations of the subject, revealing ways in which its appearance of orthodoxy depends upon the way it is viewed from one particular perspective. It is this constantly shifting, deviating form of conceptual parallax that serves to throw the more insular contours of English native culture into relief.

Works Cited

Abrams, M. H. *Natural Supernaturalism: Tradition and Revolution in Romantic Literature*. New York: Norton, 1971.

_____ and Greenblatt, Stephen. Preface to *The Norton Anthology of English Literature*, 7th edn., vol. ii, New York: Norton, 2000, pp. xxxiii–xlii.

Ackroyd, Peter. *T. S. Eliot*. London: Hamish Hamilton, 1984.

Adorno, Theodor W. *Negative Dialectics* (1966), trans. E. B. Ashton. London: Routledge & Kegan Paul, 1973.

_____ 'Aldous Huxley and Utopia', *Prisms* (1967), trans. Samuel and Shierry Weber. Cambridge, Mass.: MIT Press, 1981, 95–117.

_____ and Horkheimer, Max. *Dialectic of Enlightenment* (1947), trans. John Cumming, 1972. Repr. London: Verso, 1979.

Ahmad, Aijaz. *In Theory: Classes, Nations, Literatures*. London: Verso, 1992.

Albanese, Catherine L. *Sons of the Fathers: The Civil Religion of the American Revolution*. Philadelphia: Temple University Press, 1976.

Altieri, Charles. *Enlarging the Temple: New Directions in American Poetry during the 1960s*. Lewisburg, Pa.: Bucknell University Press, 1979.

Amis, Martin. *Other People: A Mystery Story*. London: Jonathan Cape, 1981.

_____ *Money: A Suicide Note*. London: Jonathan Cape, 1984.

_____ *The Moronic Inferno and Other Visits to America* (1986). Repr. Harmondsworth: Penguin, 1987.

_____ *Einstein's Monsters* (1987). Repr. London: Penguin, 1988.

_____ 'Nuclear City: The Megadeath Intellectuals' (1987). In *Visiting Mrs Nabokov*, 13–33.

_____ *London Fields*. New York: Harmony Books, 1989.

_____ 'Salman Rushdie' (1990). In *Visiting Mrs Nabokov*, 170–8.

_____ *Time's Arrow; or, The Nature of the Offense*. New York: Harmony Books, 1991.

_____ 'The Ending: Don Juan in Hull' (1993). In *The War Against Cliché*, 153–72.

_____ *Visiting Mrs Nabokov and Other Excursions*. London: Jonathan Cape, 1993.

_____ *The Information*. London: Flamingo–HarperCollins, 1995.

_____ *Night Train*. London: Jonathan Cape, 1997.

_____ 'The Janitor on Mars.' In *Heavy Water and Other Stories*, London: Jonathan Cape, 1998, 154–93.

_____ *Experience*. London: Jonathan Cape, 2000.

_____ 'Fear and Loathing.' *Guardian*, 18 Sept. 2001, sec. 2, 2–5.

_____ *The War Against Cliché: Essays and Reviews, 1971–2000*. London: Jonathan Cape, 2001.

Amis, Martin. 'The Voice of the Lonely Crowd.' *Guardian Review*, 1 June 2002, 4–6.

—— 'The Palace of the End.' *Guardian*, 4 March 2003, 23.

—— *Yellow Dog*. London: Jonathan Cape, 2003.

Anderson, Amanda. *The Powers of Distance: Cosmopolitanism and the Cultivation of Detachment*. Princeton: Princeton University Press, 2001.

Anderson, Benedict. *Imagined Communities: Reflections on the Origin and Spread of Nationalism*. London: Verso, 1983.

Antelyes, Peter. *Tales of Adventurous Enterprise: Washington Irving and the Poetics of Western Expansion*. New York: Columbia University Press, 1990.

Appadurai, Arjun. *Modernity at Large: Cultural Dimensions of Globalization*. Minneapolis: University of Minnesota Press, 1996.

Apter, Emily. 'Global *Translatio*: The "Invention" of Comparative Literature, Istanbul, 1933.' *Critical Inquiry*, 29 (2003), 253–81.

Arac, Jonathan. 'Narrative Forms.' In *Cambridge History of American Literature*, ii. Ed. Bercovitch, 605–777.

Arendt, Hannah. *The Origins of Totalitarianism*, 2nd edn. London: Allen & Unwin, 1958.

—— *Eichmann in Jerusalem: A Report on the Banality of Evil*. London: Faber, 1963.

Armstrong, Isobel. *Victorian Poetry: Poetry, Poetics and Politics*. London: Routledge, 1993.

Armstrong, Nancy, and Tennenhouse, Leonard. 'The American Origins of the English Novel.' *American Literary History*, 4 (1992), 386–410.

—— *The Imaginary Puritan: Literature, Intellectual Labor, and the Origins of Personal Life*. Berkeley: University of California Press, 1992.

Arnold, Matthew. 'Byron' (1881). In *English Literature and Irish Politics*, ed. R. H. Super, in *The Complete Prose Works*, ix. 217–37. Ann Arbor: University of Michigan Press, 1973.

—— 'A Word about America' (1882). In *Philistinism in England and America*, 1–23.

—— 'A Word More about America' (1885). In *Philistinism in England and America*, 194–217.

—— 'Civilisation in the United States' (1888). In *The Last Word*, 350–69.

—— *The Letters of Matthew Arnold to Arthur Hugh Clough*, ed. Howard Foster Lowry. London: Oxford University Press, 1932.

—— *The Poems of Matthew Arnold*, ed. Kenneth Allott. London: Longmans, 1965.

—— *Culture and Anarchy, with Friendship's Garland and Some Literary Essays* (1869). *The Complete Prose Works*, ed. R. H. Super, v. Ann Arbor: University of Michigan Press, 1965.

—— *Philistinism in England and America*. In *The Complete Prose Works*, ed. R. H. Super, x. Ann Arbor: University of Michigan Press, 1974.

Arnold, Mathew. *The Last Word*. In *The Complete Prose Works*, ed. R. H. Super, xi. Ann Arbor: University of Michigan Press, 1977.

Ashberry, John. *Three Poems*. New York: Viking Press, 1972.

Asher, Kenneth. *T. S. Eliot and Ideology*. Cambridge: Cambridge University Press, 1995.

Ashton, Rosemary. *The Life of Samuel Taylor Coleridge: A Critical Biography*. Oxford: Blackwell, 1996.

Auden, W. H. 'The Liberal Fascist' (1934). In *The English Auden*, 321–7.

_____ 'Spain 1937' (1937). In *The English Auden*, 210–12.

_____ 'Whitman and Arnold.' Review of *Matthew Arnold*, by Lionel Trilling (1939). In *Prose*, ii. 11–13.

_____ 'Romantic or Free?' (1940). In *Prose, ii.* 63–72.

_____ 'At the Grave of Henry James.' *Partisan Review*, 8/4 (July–Aug. 1941), 266–70.

_____ *The Double Man* (1941). Repr. Westport, Conn.: Greenwood Press, 1979.

_____ 'The Means of Grace.' Review of *The Nature and Destiny of Man*, by Reinhold Niebuhr (1941). In *Prose*, ii. 131–4.

_____ *New Year Letter*(1941). In *Collected Poems*, 159–93.

_____ 'A Note on Order' (1941). In *Prose*, ii. 100–3.

_____ '*Yale Daily News* Banquet Address' (1941). In *Prose*, ii. 119–25.

_____ 'La Trahison d'un Clerc.' Review of 'Primary Literature and Coterie Literature', by Van Wyck Brooks (1942). In *Prose*, ii. 148–51.

_____ 'Children of Abraham' (1944). Review of *The Jew in Our Day*, by Waldo Frank. In *Prose*, ii. 224–6.

_____ 'Henry James and the Dedicated' (1944). In *Prose*, ii. 242–4.

_____ *The Sea and the Mirror* (1944). In *Collected Poems*, 309–41.

_____ 'Address on Henry James' (1946). In *Prose*, ii. 296–303.

_____ 'Introduction to *The American Scene*, by Henry James' (1946). In *Prose*, ii. 296–303.

_____ *The Age of Anxiety: A Baroque Elegy* (1947). In *Collected Poems*, 343–409.

_____ 'Some Notes on D. H. Lawrence' (1947). In *Prose*, ii. 317–22.

_____ 'Dingley Dell and the Fleet' (1948). In *The Dyer's Hand*, 407–28.

_____ 'Poetry and Freedom' (1948). In *Prose*, ii. 487–97.

_____ 'American Poetry' (1956). In *The Dyer's Hand*, 354–68.

_____ 'Marianne Moore' (1959). In *The Dyer's Hand*, 296–305.

_____ 'The Poet and the City' (1962). In *The Dyer's Hand*, 72–89.

_____ *The Dyer's Hand and Other Essays* (1963). Repr. London: Faber, 1975.

_____ 'Heresies' (1966). In *Forewords and Afterwords*, ed. Edward Mendelson. London: Faber, 1973, 40–8.

_____ *Collected Poems*, ed. Edward Mendelson. London: Faber, 1976.

_____ *The English Auden: Poems, Essays and Dramatic Writings, 1927–1939*. London: Faber, 1977.

Auden, W. H. *Prose*, ii: *1939–1948*, ed. Edward Mendelson. London: Faber, 2002.

——, and Isherwood, Christopher. *Plays and Other Dramatic Writings by W. H. Auden, 1928–1938*, ed. Edward Mendelson. London: Faber, 1989.

Bagehot, Walter. *The English Constitution, 1865–67*, ed. Paul Smith. Cambridge: Cambridge University Press, 2001.

Baguley, David. *Naturalist Fiction: The Entropic Vision.* Cambridge: Cambridge University Press, 1990.

Bailyn, Bernard. *The Ideological Origins of the American Revolution.* Cambridge, Mass.: Harvard University Press, 1967.

Baker, Herschel. *William Hazlitt.* Cambridge, Mass.: Harvard University Press, 1962.

Baker, Paul R. 'Lord Byron and the Americans in Italy.' *Keats–Shelley Journal*, 13 (1964), 61–75.

Baker, Robert S. Introduction. In Aldous Huxley, *Complete Essays*, vi: *1956–1963*, pp. xi–xviii.

Baldick, Chris. *The Social Mission of English Criticism, 1848–1932.* Oxford: Clarendon Press, 1983.

—— In *Frankenstein's Shadow: Myth, Monstrosity, and Nineteenth-Century Writing.* Oxford: Clarendon Press, 1987.

Balibar, Etienne. 'The Nation Form: History and Ideology.' In *Race, Nation, Class: Ambiguous Identities*, ed. Etienne Balibar and Immanuel Wallerstein (1988), trans. Chris Turner, 86–106, London: Verso, 1991.

Ballard, J. G. 'The Waiting Grounds' (1959). In *Complete Short Stories*, 72–95.

—— 'Time, Memory and Inner Space' (1963). In *User's Guide*, 199–201.

—— 'Alphabets of Unreason' (1969). In *User's Guide*, 221–3.

—— 'The Innocent as Paranoid' (1969). In *User's Guide*, 91–8.

—— 'Fictions of Every Kind' (1971). In *User's Guide*, 205–7.

—— *Crash* (1973). Repr. New York: Vintage-Random House, 1985.

—— *Concrete Island.* London: Jonathan Cape, 1974.

—— 'The Cosmic Cabaret' (1974). In *User's Guide*, 202–4.

—— *High-Rise* (1975). Repr. London: Flamingo–HarperCollins, 2003.

—— 'Theatre of War' (1977). In *Complete Short Stories*, 953–67.

—— 'Memories of Greeneland' 1978. In *User's Guide*, 137–9.

—— 'One Afternoon at Utah Beach' (1978). In *Complete Short Stories*, 972–81.

—— *Hello America* (1981). Repr. London: Vintage–Random House, 1994.

—— 'News from the Sun' (1981). In *Complete Short Stories*, 1010–36.

—— 'Myths of the Near Future' (1982). In *Complete Short Stories*, 1061–84.

—— *Empire of the Sun.* London: Victor Gollancz, 1984.

—— *The Kindness of Women.* London: HarperCollins, 1991.

—— *The Atrocity Exhibition*, rev. edn. London: Flamingo–HarperCollins, 1993.

—— 'First Impressions of London' (1993). In *User's Guide*, 185.

—— 'In Search of the Last Emperor' (1993). In *User's Guide*, 248–50.

_____ 'The End of My War' (1995). In *User's Guide*, 283–94.

_____ *Cocaine Nights*. London: Flamingo–HarperCollins, 1996.

_____ *A User's Guide to the Millennium: Essays and Reviews*. London: Harper-Collins, 1996.

_____ *Super-Cannes*. London: Flamingo–HarperCollins, 2000.

_____ *The Complete Short Stories*. London: Flamingo–HarperCollins, 2001.

_____ 'It's About Being a Citizen, Not a Subject.' *Guardian*, 1 June 2002, 13.

_____ *Millennium People*. London: Flamingo–HarperCollins, 2003.

Barrell, John. *English Literature in History, 1730–80: An Equal, Wide Survey*. London: Hutchinson, 1983.

Barrish, Phillip. *American Literary Realism, Critical Theory, and Intellectual Prestige, 1880–1995*. Cambridge: Cambridge University Press, 2001.

Barthes, Roland. 'Myth Today.' In *Mythologies* (1957), trans. Annette Lavers, 107–59. St. Albans, Herts.: Paladin-Granada, 1973.

Bate, Jonathan. *Romantic Ecology: Wordsworth and the Environmental Tradition*. London: Routledge, 1991.

_____ 'General Editor's Preface.' In Philip Davis, *The Victorians*, pp. vii-ix. *Oxford English Literary History*, viii.

Baucom, Ian. *Out of Place: Englishness, Empire, and the Locations of Identity*. Princeton: Princeton University Press, 1999.

Baudrillard, Jean. *America* (1986), trans. Chris Turner. London: Verso, 1988.

Bauman, Zygmunt. *Modernity and the Holocaust*. Cambridge: Polity, 1989.

Bayley, John. *The Characters of Love: A Study in the Literature of Personality*. London: Constable, 1960.

Bellamy, Joe David, ed. *American Poetry Observed: Poets on their Work*. Urbana, Ill.: University of Illinois Press, 1984.

Belloc, Hilaire. Introduction. In *Weekend Wodehouse* (1939), 5–7. Repr. London: Hutchinson, 1986.

Bercovitch, Sacvan. *The Rites of Assent: Transformations in the Symbolic Construction of America*. New York: Routledge, 1993.

_____ ed. *The Cambridge History of American Literature*, ii: *Prose Writing, 1820–1865*. Cambridge: Cambridge University Press, 1995.

Berger, Max. *The British Traveller in America, 1836–1860*. New York: Columbia University Press, 1943.

Bergonzi, Bernard. 'Davie, Larkin, and the State of England.' *Contemporary Literature*, 18 (1977), 343–60.

Bersani, Leo. *A Future for Astyanax: Character and Desire in Literature*. London: Marion and Boyars, 1978.

_____ *The Culture of Redemption*. Cambridge, Mass.: Harvard University Press, 1990.

Bérubé, Michael. 'Introduction: Worldly English.' *Modern Fiction Studies*, 48 (2002), 1–17.

Bhabha, Homi. 'DissemiNation: Time, Narrative, and the Margins of the Modern Nation.' In *Nation and Narration*, ed. Homi Bhabha, 291–322. London: Routledge, 1990.

——and Comaroff, John. 'Speaking of Postcoloniality, in the Continuous Present: A Conversation.' In *Relocating Postcolonialism*, ed. David Theo Goldberg and Ato Quayson, 15–46. Oxford: Blackwell, 2002.

Billington, Ray Allen. *The Far Western Frontier, 1830–1860*. New York: Harper and Brothers, 1956.

Birkbeck, Morris. *Notes on a Journey in America: From the Coast of Virginia to the Territory of Illinois: With Proposals for the Establishment of a Colony of English*. Philadelphia, 1817.

Biswas, Robindra Kumar. *Arthur Hugh Clough: Towards a Reconsideration*. Oxford: Clarendon Press, 1972.

Blake, William. *The Marriage of Heaven and Hell* (1790–3). In *Complete Poems*, 180–95.

——*America* (1793). In *Complete Poems*, 208–24.

—— *The Complete Poems*, ed. Alicia Ostriker. London: Penguin, 1977.

Blanchard, Mary Warner. *Oscar Wilde's America: Counterculture in the Gilded Age*. New Haven: Yale University Press, 1998.

Bloch, Ruth H. *Visionary Republic: Millennial Themes in American Thought, 1756–1800*. Cambridge: Cambridge University Press, 1985.

Bloom, Allan. *The Closing of the American Mind*. New York: Simon & Schuster, 1987.

Blunden, Edmund. 'Ourselves and Germany: A Retrospect.' *Anglo-German Review*, 3/7 (July 1939), 210.

Boehmer, Elleke, ed. *Empire Writing: An Anthology of Colonial Writing, 1870–1918*. Oxford: Oxford University Press, 1998.

Bolt, Christine. *Victorian Attitudes to Race*. London: Routledge & Kegan Paul, 1971.

Booth, Howard J. 'Male Sexuality, Religion and the Problem of Action: John Addington Symonds on Arthur Hugh Clough.' In *Masculinity and Spirituality in Victorian Culture*, ed. Andrew Bradstock, Sean Gill, Anne Hogan, and Sue Morgan, 116–33. Basingstoke: Macmillan, 2000.

Boswell, James. *The Life of Johnson*, ed. Christopher Hibbert. London: Penguin, 1979.

—— *The Journal of a Tour to the Hebrides* (1775), ed. Peter Levi. London: Penguin, 1984.

Boulting, John, dir. *Brighton Rock*. Screenplay by Graham Greene and Terence Rattigan. Associated British Picture Corporation, 1947.

Bowlby, Rachel. Review of *The Whirlpool*, by George Gissing, ed. Patrick Parrinder. *Gissing Newsletter*, 21/2 (April 1985), 22–9.

Bradbury, Malcolm. 'How I Invented America.' *Journal of American Studies*, 14 (1980), 115–35.

_____ *Dangerous Pilgrimages: Trans-Atlantic Mythologies and the Novel.* London: Secker & Warburg, 1995.

Brantlinger, Patrick. *Rule of Darkness: British Literature and Imperialism, 1830–1914.* Ithaca, NY: Cornell University Press, 1988.

Breslin, James E. B. *From Modern to Contemporary: American Poetry, 1945–1965.* Chicago: University of Chicago Press, 1984.

Bristow, Joseph. ' "Love, let us be true to one another": Matthew Arnold, Arthur Hugh Clough, and "our Aqueous Ages." ' *Literature and History*, 3rd ser., 4/1 (Spring 1995), 27–49.

_____ ' "I am With You, Little Minority Sister": Isherwood's Queer Sixties.' In *The Queer Sixties*, ed. Patricia Juliana Smith, 145–63. New York: Routledge, 1999.

Brody, Jennifer DeVere. *Impossible Purities: Blackness, Femininity, and Victorian Culture.* Durham, NC: Duke University Press, 1998.

Brooke, Stopford A. *Four Poets: A Study of Clough, Arnold, Rossetti and Morris.* London: Pitman, 1908.

Brooks, Peter. *Body Work: Objects of Desire in Modern Narrative.* Cambridge, Mass.: Harvard University Press, 1993.

Brown, Charles Brockden. *Wieland; or, The Transformation* (1798), ed. Emory Elliott. Oxford: Oxford University Press, 1994.

_____ *Edgar Huntly; or, Memoirs of a Sleepwalker* (1799), ed. Norman S. Grabo. New York: Penguin, 1988.

_____ *Arthur Mervyn; or, Memoirs of the Year 1793* (1799–1800), ed. Warner Berthoff. New York: Holt, Rinehart and Winston, 1962.

Brown, Christopher. 'Empire without Slaves: British Concepts of Emancipation in the Age of the American Revolution.' *William and Mary Quarterly*, 3rd ser., 56 (1999), 273–306.

Brown, Gillian. *The Consent of the Governed: The Lockean Legacy in Early American Culture.* Cambridge, Mass.: Harvard University Press, 2001.

Brown, Richard. 'Postmodern Americas in the Fiction of Angela Carter, Martin Amis and Ian McEwan.' In *Forked Tongues*, ed. Massa and Stead, 92–110.

Buford, Bill. 'Introduction: The End of the English Novel.' *Granta*, 3 (1980), 7–16.

Burke, Edmund. *Reflections on the Revolution in France* (1790), ed. J. C. D. Clark. Stanford, Calif.: Stanford University Press, 2001.

Burt, Richard. 'Degenerate "Art": Public Aesthetics and the Simulation of Censorship in Postliberal Los Angeles and Berlin.' In *The Administration of Aesthetics: Censorship, Political Criticism, and the Public Sphere*, ed. Richard Burt (for the *Social Text* Collective), 216–59. Minneapolis: University of Minnesota Press, 1994.

Burton, Robert. *The Anatomy of Melancholy*, 3 vols. (1621), ed. Thomas C. Faulkner, Nicolas K. Kiessling, and Rhonda L. Blair. Oxford: Clarendon Press, 1989–94.

Bush, Ronald. 'T. S. Eliot: Singing the Emerson Blues.' In *Emerson: Prospect and Retrospect*, ed. Joel Porte, 179–97. Cambridge, Mass.: Harvard University Press, 1982.

Butler, Marilyn. *Romantics, Rebels and Reactionaries: English Literature and its Background, 1760–1830*. Oxford: Oxford University Press, 1981.

—— 'Byron and the Empire in the East.' In *Byron: Augustan and Romantic*, ed. Rutherford, 63–81.

Butterfield, Bradley. 'Ethical Value and Negative Aesthetics: Reconsidering the Baudrillard–Ballard Connection.' *PMLA*, 114 (1999), 64–77.

Butterfield, Herbert. *George III and the Historians*. London: Collins, 1957.

Byron, Lord. *Beppo: A Venetian Story* (1817). In *Poetical Works*, iv. 129–60.

—— *Don Juan* (1819–24). In *Poetical Works*, v.

—— *The Vision of Judgement, by Quevedo Redivivus* (1822). In *Poetical Works*, vi. 309–45.

—— *The Age of Bronze; Or, Carmen Seculare et Annus Haud Mirabilis* (1823). In *Poetical Works*, vii. 1–25.

—— *The Complete Poetical Works*, 7 vols, ed. Jerome J. McGann. Oxford: Oxford University Press, 1980–93.

—— *Letters and Journals*, v, ed. Leslie A. Marchand. London: John Murray, 1976.

Callil, Carmen. 'Flying Jewellery.' *Sunday Times* (London), 23 Feb. 1992, sec. 7, 6.

Cannadine, David. *Ornamentalism: How the British Saw their Empire*. London: Allen Lane–Penguin, 2001.

Carey, John. 'Two Englishmen Abroad.' *Sunday Times* (London), 30 Sept. 1984, 42.

—— *The Intellectuals and the Masses: Pride and Prejudice among the Literary Intelligentsia, 1880–1939*. London: Faber, 1992.

Carroll, David. *French Literary Fascism: Nationalism, Anti-Semitism, and the Ideology of Culture*. Princeton: Princeton University Press, 1995.

Carter, Angela. *The Magic Toyshop* (1967). Repr. London: Virago, 1981.

—— *Several Perceptions* (1968). Repr. London: Virago, 1995.

—— *Heroes and Villains*. London: Heinemann, 1969.

—— *The Infernal Desire Machines of Doctor Hoffman: A Novel*. London: Hart-Davis, 1972.

—— *Fireworks: Nine Profane Pieces* (1974). In *Collected Short Stories*, 25–107.

—— 'Appendix: Afterword to *Fireworks*' (1974). In *Collected Short Stories*, 459–60.

—— 'Notes on the Gothic Mode.' *Iowa Review*, 6/3–4 (Summer–Fall 1975), 132–4.

—— *The Passion of New Eve* (1977). Repr. London: Arrow, 1978.

—— *The Sadeian Woman: An Exercise in Cultural History*. London: Virago, 1979.

—— 'Our Lady of the Massacre' (1979). In *Collected Short Stories*, 248–61.

—— 'The Cabinet of Edgar Allan Poe' (1982). In *Collected Short Stories*, 262–72.

____ 'Grace Paley: *The Little Disturbances of Man* and *Enormous Changes at the Last Minute*' (1980). In *Expletives Deleted*, 155–8.

____ *Nothing Sacred: Selected Writings*. London: Virago, 1982.

____ 'Masochism for the Masses.' *New Statesman*, 3 June 1983, 8–10.

____ 'Notes from the Front Line' (1983). In *On Gender and Writing*, ed. Michelene Wandor, 69–77. London: Pandora, 1983.

____ 'J. G. Ballard: *Empire of the Sun*' (1984). In *Expletives Deleted*, 44–50.

____ *Nights at the Circus*. London: Chatto & Windus–Hogarth Press, 1984.

____ *Black Venus* (1985). In *Collected Short Stories*, 229–317.

____ *Love*, rev. edn. (1987). Repr. London: Random House–Vintage, 1997.

____ 'Edmund White: *The Beautiful Room is Empty*' (1988). In *Expletives Deleted*, 139–420.

____ 'John Ford's *'Tis Pity She's a Whore*' (1988). In *Collected Short Stories*, 332–48.

____ 'The Merchant of Shadows' (1989). In *Collected Short Stories*, 363–75.

____ 'Alice in Prague *or* The Curious Room'(1990). In *Collected Short Stories*, 397–408.

____ *Wise Children*. London: Chatto & Windus, 1991.

____ *Expletives Deleted: Selected Writings*. London: Chatto & Windus, 1992.

____ *American Ghosts and Old World Wonders* (1993). In *Collected Short Stories*, 319–413.

____ 'The Ghost Ships' (1993). In *Collected Short Stories*, 376–81.

____ *Burning Your Boats: Collected Short Stories*. London: Chatto & Windus, 1995.

Caserio, Robert L. 'Mobility and Masochism: Christine Brooke-Rose and J. G. Ballard.' *Novel*, 21 (1988), 292–310.

Castronovo, Russ. *Necro Citizenship: Death, Eroticism, and the Public Sphere in the Nineteenth-Century United States*. Durham, NC: Duke University Press, 2001.

Chandler, James. *England in 1819: The Politics of Literary Culture and the Case of Romantic Historicism*. Chicago: University of Chicago Press, 1998.

Chesnutt, Charles Waddell. *Tales of Conjure and the Color Line: Ten Stories*, ed. Joan R. Sherman. Mineola, NY: Dover Publications, 1998.

Chibnall, Steve, and Murphy, Robert. eds. *British Crime Cinema*. London: Routledge, 1999.

____ 'Parole Overdue: Releasing the British Crime Film into the Critical Community.' In *British Crime Cinema*, ed. Chibnall and Murphy, 1–15.

Chinitz, David. 'T. S. Eliot and the Cultural Divide.' *PMLA*, 110 (1995), 236–47.

Chorley, Katharine. *Arthur Hugh Clough: The Uncommitted Mind, A Study of his Life and Poetry*. Oxford: Clarendon Press, 1962.

Chow, Rey. 'How (the) Inscrutable Chinese Led to Globalized Theory.' *PMLA*, 116 (2001), 69–74.

Christophersen, Bill. 'Picking Up the Knife: A Psycho-Historical Reading of *Wieland.' American Studies*, 27/1 (Spring 1986), 115–26.

Clark, J. C. D. *The Language of Liberty, 1660–1832: Political Discourse and Social Dynamics in the Anglo-American World*. Cambridge: Cambridge University Press, 1984.

——— *English Society, 1660–1832: Religion, Ideology and Politics during the Ancien Regime*, 2nd edn. Cambridge: Cambridge University Press, 2000.

Clough, Arthur Hugh. *The Bothie of Tober-na-Vuolich* (1848). In *Poems*, 44–93.

——— *Amours de Voyage* (1858). In *Poems*, 94–133.

——— *Mari Magno, or Tales on Board* (1863). In *Poems*, 374–439.

——— *Dipsychus* (1865). In *Poems*, 218–99.

——— *The Correspondence of Arthur Hugh Clough*, ed. Frederick L. Mulhauser, 2 vols. Oxford: Clarendon Press, 1957.

——— *Selected Prose Works of Arthur Hugh Clough*, ed. Buckner B. Trawick. University, Ala.: University of Alabama Press, 1964.

——— *The Poems of Arthur Hugh Clough*, 2nd edn., ed. F. L. Mulhauser. Oxford: Clarendon Press, 1974.

——— *The Oxford Diaries of Arthur Hugh Clough*, ed. Anthony Kenny. Oxford: Clarendon Press, 1990.

Clowes, St. John L., dir. *No Orchids for Miss Blandish*. RKO Pictures, 1948.

Cobbett, William. *A History of the Protestant Reformation in England and Ireland: Showing how that Event has Impoverished the Main Body of the People in Those Countries* (1826), 2 vols. Repr. London, 1857.

——— *Rural Rides* (1830), ed. Ian Dyck. London: Penguin, 2001.

Cochrane, J. G. *Catalogue of the Abbotsford Library*. Edinburgh, 1838.

Cohen, Nick. 'A Windsor in the Soup.' *Observer* (London), 29 Sept. 2002, 31.

Cohen, Scott A. ' "Get Out!": Empire Migration and Human Traffic in *Lord Jim.' Novel*, 36 (2003), 374–97.

Coleridge, Samuel Taylor. 'Lecture on the Slave Trade.' In *Lectures 1795: On Politics and Religion*, ed. Lewis Patton and Peter Mann, *Collected Works*, i. 231–51. Princeton: Princeton University Press, 1971.

——— *On the Constitution of the Church and State* (1829), ed. John Colmer, in *Collected Works*, x. Princeton: Princeton University Press, 1976.

——— *Poetical Works, I (Part One)*, ed. J. C. C. Mays, in *Collected Works*, xvi. Princeton: Princeton University Press, 2001.

Colley, Linda. *Britons: Forging the Nation, 1707–1837*. New Haven: Yale University Press, 1992.

——— *Captives: Britain, Empire and the World, 1600–1850*. London: Jonathan Cape, 2002.

Colligan, Collette. 'Anti-Abolition Writes Obscenity: The English Vice, Transatlantic Slavery, and England's Obscene Print Culture.' In *International Exposure: Perspectives on Modern European Pornography, 1800–2000*, ed. Lisa Z. Sigel, 67–99. New Brunswick, NJ: Rutgers University Press, 2005.

Collini, Stefan. *Public Moralists: Political Thought and Intellectual Life in Britain, 1850–1930*. Oxford: Clarendon Press, 1991.

Collinson, Patrick. 'From Iconoclasm to Iconophobia: The Cultural Impact of the Second English Reformation.' In *The Impact of the English Reformation, 1500–1640*, ed. Peter Marshall, 278–308. London: Arnold, 1997.

Connor, Steven. *The English Novel in History, 1950–1995*. London: Routledge, 1996.

Conrad, Peter. *Imagining America*. London: Routledge & Kegan Paul, 1980.

_____ 'Tom, Dick and Christopher.' Review of *Lost Years: A Memoir*, by Christopher Isherwood. *Observer Review* (London), 2 July 2000, 13.

Cooper, James Fenimore. *The Spy: A Tale of the Neutral Ground*, (1821), ed. Wayne Franklin. London: Penguin, 1997.

_____ *The Pioneers* (1823), ed. James D. Wallace. Oxford: Oxford University Press, 1991.

_____ *Gleanings in Europe: England* (1837), ed. Donald A. Ringe and Kenneth W. Staggs. Albany, NY: State University of New York Press, 1982.

Cooper, John Xiros. *T. S. Eliot and the Ideology of* Four Quartets. Cambridge: Cambridge University Press, 1995.

Cotkin, George. *Existential America*. Baltimore: Johns Hopkins University Press, 2003.

Coustillas, Pierre. Introduction. In *Workers in the Dawn*, by George Gissing, pp. xi–xxxii.

_____ and Partridge, Colin, eds. *Gissing: The Critical Heritage*. London: Routledge and Kegan Paul, 1972.

Cowley, Jason. 'Portrait: Martin Amis.' *Prospect*, Aug.–Sept. 1997, 19–23.

Cracroft, Richard H. ' "Half Froze for Mountain Doins": The Influence and Significance of George F. Ruxton's *Life in the Far West*.' *Western American Literature*, 10 (1975), 29–43.

Craige, Betty Jean. 'Literature in a Global Society.' *PMLA*, 106 (1991), 395–401.

Crane, Stephen. *Maggie: A Girl of the Streets* (1893). In *Bowery Tales*, ed. Fredson Bowers, 1–77. Charlottesville: University Press of Virginia, 1969.

Craven, Peter. 'An Interview with Salman Rushdie.' *Scripsi*, 3/2–3 (1985), 107–26.

Crawford, Robert. *Devolving English Literature*. Oxford: Oxford University Press, 1992.

_____ *The Modern Poet: Poetry, Academia, and Knowledge since the 1750s*. Oxford: Oxford University Press, 2001.

Crèvecoeur, J. Hector St John de. *Letters from an American Farmer and Sketches of Eighteenth-Century America* (1782), ed. Albert E. Stone. New York: Viking Penguin, 1981.

Crumpton, Philip. Introduction. In *Movements in European History*, by D. H. Lawrence, pp. xv-xlvi.

Crystal, David. *English as a Global Language*, 2nd edn. Cambridge: Cambridge University Press, 2003.

Cunningham, Valentine. *British Writers of the Thirties*. Oxford: Oxford University Press, 1988.

Dainotto, Roberto Maria. 'The Bolshevik in the Garden: The Invention of America in Fascist Italy.' In *American and European National Identities: Faces in the Mirror*, ed. Stephen Fender, 57–72. Keele, Staffs.: Keele University Press, 1996.

Damrosch, David. *What is World Literature?* Princeton: Princeton University Press, 2003.

Daubeny, Charles. *A Guide to the Church in Several Discourses*. London, 1798.

David, Deirdre. *Rule Britannia: Women, Empire, and Victorian Writing*. Ithaca, NY: Cornell University Press, 1995.

Davidson, Cathy N. *Revolution and the Word: The Rise of the Novel in America*. New York: Oxford University Press, 1986.

Davie, Donald. *Purity of Diction in English Verse* (1952). Repr. London: Routledge & Kegan Paul, 1967.

—— 'T. S. Eliot: The End of an Era' (1956). In *Poet in the Imaginary Museum*, 32–41.

——*A Sequence for Francis Parkman* (1961). In *Collected Poems*, 127–36.

——*Ezra Pound: Poet as Sculptor* (1964). In *Studies in Ezra Pound*, 11–209.

——*Essex Poems* (1969). In *Collected Poems*, 178–99.

—— 'The Black Mountain Poets: Charles Olson and Edward Dorn' (1970). In *Poet in the Imaginary Museum*, 177–90.

—— 'Anglican Eliot.' *Southern Review*, NS 9, no. 1 (1973), 93–104.

—— 'Larkin's Choice.' Review of *The Oxford Book of Twentieth-Century English Verse*, ed. Philip Larkin. *Listener*, 29 March 1973, 420–1.

——*Thomas Hardy and British Poetry*. London: Routledge & Kegan Paul, 1973.

——*The Shires* (1974). In *Collected Poems*, 299–324.

——*The Poet in the Imaginary Museum: Essays of Two Decades*, ed. Barry Alpert. Manchester: Carcanet, 1977.

—— 'American Literature: The Canon' (1980). In *Two Ways Out of Whitman: American Essays*, 1–13. Manchester: Carcanet, 2000.

—— 'Editorial.' *PN Review*, 9/2 (1982), 1.

——*To Scorch or Freeze: Poems about the Sacred* (1988). In *Collected Poems*, 438–75.

—— ' "The Dry Salvages": A Reconsideration.' *PN Review*, 17/5 (May–June 1991), 21–6.

——*Studies in Ezra Pound*. Manchester: Carcanet, 1991.

——*The Eighteenth-Century Hymn in England*. Cambridge: Cambridge University Press, 1993.

—— 'The Canon, Values and Heritage.' *PN Review*, 21/5 (May–June 1995), 12–15.

_____ *Essays in Dissent: Church, Chapel, and the Unitarian Conspiracy.* Manchester: Carcanet, 1995.

_____ *Collected Poems*, ed. Neil Powell. Manchester: Carcanet, 2002.

_____ ed. *The New Oxford Book of Christian Verse.* Oxford: Oxford University Press, 1981.

Davies, Kate. *Catherine Macaulay and Mercy Otis Warren: The Revolutionary Atlantic and the Politics of Gender.* Oxford: Oxford University Press, 2005.

Davis, Douglas. 'M15: Wodehouse was Nazi Collaborator.' *Jerusalem Post*, 19 Sept. 1999; <http://www.jpost.com/com/Archive/19.Sep.1999/News/Article/-9.html>, accessed 28 July 2002.

Davis, Philip. *The Victorians. Oxford English Literary History*, viii: *1830–1880.* Oxford: Oxford University Press, 2002.

Dawson, Graham. *Soldier Heroes: British Adventure, Empire and the Imagining of Masculinity.* London: Routledge, 1994.

Deering, Dorothy. 'The Antithetical Poetics of Arnold and Clough.' *Victorian Poetry* (1978), 16–31.

Defoe, Daniel. *The Fortunes and Misfortunes of the Famous Moll Flanders* (1722), ed. G. A. Starr. London: Oxford University Press, 1971.

Dekker, George. *The American Historical Romance.* Cambridge: Cambridge University Press, 1987.

_____ ed. *Donald Davie and the Responsibilities of Literature.* Manchester: Carcanet, 1983.

Delavenay, Emile, and Keith, W. J. 'Mr. Rolf Gardiner, "The English Neo-Nazi": An Exchange.' *D. H. Lawrence Review*, 7 (1974), 291–4.

Deleuze, Gilles, and Guattari, Félix. *Anti-Oedipus: Capitalism and Schizophrenia*, i, trans. Robert Hurley, Mark Seem, and Helen R. Lane. London: Athlone Press, 1984.

_____ *A Thousand Plateaus: Capitalism and Schizophrenia*, ii (1980), trans. Brian Massumi. London: Athlone Press, 1988.

Delfiner, Rita. 'The Camera Speaks.' *New York Post*, 17 Feb. 1972, n.p.

Dellamora, Richard. *Masculine Desire: The Sexual Politics of Victorian Aestheticism.* Chapel Hill, NC: University of North Carolina Press, 1990.

De Luigi, Stefano, and Amis, Martin. *Pornoland.* London: Thames & Hudson, 2004.

Denisoff, Dennis. *Aestheticism and Sexual Parody, 1840–1940.* Cambridge: Cambridge University Press, 2001.

Denning, Michael. *The Cultural Front: The Laboring of American Culture in the Twentieth Century.* London: Verso, 1996.

De Tocqueville, Alexis. *Democracy in America* (1835), trans. Gerald E. Bevan. London: Penguin, 2003.

De Voto, Bernard. *The Year of Decision: 1846.* Boston: Little, Brown and Company, 1943.

Dickens, Charles. *American Notes for General Circulation* (1842), ed. John S. Whitley and Arnold Goldman. Harmondsworth: Penguin, 1972.

—— *The Life and Adventures of Martin Chuzzlewit* (1843–4), ed. Patricia Ingham. London: Penguin, 1999.

—— *The Letters of Charles Dickens*, iii: *1842–1843*, ed. Madeleine House, Graham Storey, and Kathleen Tillotson. Oxford: Clarendon Press, 1974.

—— *The Letters of Charles Dickens*, IV: *1844–1846*, ed. Kathleen Tillotson. Oxford: Clarendon Press, 1977.

Dickstein, Morris. *Double Agent: The Critic and Society*. New York: Oxford University Press, 1992.

Diggins, John P. *Mussolini and Fascism: The View from America*. Princeton: Princeton University Press, 1972.

Dimbleby, David, and Reynolds, David. *An Ocean Apart: The Relationship between Britain and America in the Twentieth Century*. London: Hodder & Stoughton and the BBC, 1988.

Dollimore, Jonathan. *Sex, Literature and Censorship*. Malden, Mass.: Polity, 2001.

Donaldson, Frances. *P. G. Wodehouse: A Biography*. London: Weidenfeld & Nicolson, 1982.

Douglas, Ann. *Terrible Honesty: Mongrel Manhattan in the 1920s*. New York: Farrar, Straus & Giroux, 1995.

Douglas-Fairhurst, Robert. 'Dickens with a Snarl.' Review of *Yellow Dog*, by Martin Amis. *Observer Review* (London), 24 Aug. 2003, 15.

Dowling, Linda. *The Vulgarization of Art: The Victorians and Aesthetic Democracy*. Charlottesville, Va.: University Press of Virginia, 1996.

Dowling, William C. *Literary Federalism in the Age of Jefferson: Joseph Dennie and The Port Folio, 1801–1812*. Columbia, SC: University of South Carolina Press, 1999.

Doyle, Brian. *English and Englishness*. London: Routledge, 1989.

Dunkerley, James. *Americana: The Americas in the World around 1850*. London: Verso, 2000.

Dunlap, William. *Memoirs of C. B. Brown, the American Novelist*. London, 1822.

Duyckinck, Evert A., and Duyckinck, George L. *Cyclopaedia of American Literature*, 2 vols. New York: Scribner, 1855.

Eagleton, Terry. *Heathcliff and the Great Hunger: Studies in Irish Culture*. London: Verso, 1995.

Echeverria, Durand. *Mirage in the West: A History of the French Image of American Society to 1815*. Princeton: Princeton University Press, 1957.

Eckstein, Lars. 'The Insistence of Voices: An Interview with Caryl Phillips.' *ARIEL: A Review of International English Literature*, 32/2 (April 2001), 33–43.

Edwards, Owen Dudley. *P. G. Wodehouse: A Critical and Historical Essay*. London: Martin Brian and O'Keefe, 1977.

Eliot, T. S. 'Tradition and the Individual Talent' (1919). In *Selected Essays*, 13–22.

_____ Review of *A History of American Literature*, ii, ed. William P. Trent, John Erskine, Stuart P. Sherman, and Carl van Doren. *Athenaeum*, 25 April 1919, 236.

_____ 'The Metaphysical Poets' (1921). In *Selected Essays*, 281–91.

_____ *The Waste Land* (1922). In *Complete Poems*, 59–80.

_____ 'Lancelot Andrewes' (1926). In *Selected Essays*, 341–53.

_____ 'John Bramhall' (1927). In *Selected Essays*, 354–62.

_____ 'The Literature of Fascism.' *Criterion*, 8 (Dec. 1928), 280–90.

_____ 'Dante' (1929). In *Selected Essays*, 237–77.

_____ 'Baudelaire' (1930). In *Selected Essays*, 419–30.

_____ 'Thoughts after Lambeth' (1931). In *Selected Essays*. 363–87.

_____ 'Catholicism and International Order.' *Christendom*, 3 (1933), 171–84.

_____ *After Strange Gods: A Primer of Modern Heresy*. London: Faber, 1934.

_____ 'Milton I' (1936). In *On Poetry and Poets*, 138–45.

_____ 'Byron' (1937). In *On Poetry and Poets*, 193–206.

_____ *The Idea of a Christian Society*. London: Faber, 1939.

_____ *Old Possum's Book of Practical Cats* (1939). In *Complete Poems*, 207–36.

_____ *Four Quartets* (1944). In *Complete Poems*, 169–98.

_____ 'Milton II' (1947). In *On Poetry and Poets*, 146–61.

_____ *Selected Essays*, 3rd edn. London: Faber, 1951.

_____ 'American Literature and the American Language' (1953). In *To Criticize the Critic and Other Writings*, rev. edn., 43–60. London: Faber, 1978.

_____ *On Poetry and Poets*. London: Faber, 1957.

_____ 'The Influence of Landscape upon the Poet.' *Daedalus*, 89 (Spring 1960), 419–28.

_____ *The Complete Poems and Plays*. London: Faber, 1969.

Ellis, David. *D. H. Lawrence: Dying Game, 1922–1930*. Cambridge: Cambridge University Press, 1998.

Emerson, Ralph Waldo. 'Nature' (1836). In *Nature, Addresses, and Lectures*, 1–45.

_____ 'The American Scholar' (1837). In *Nature, Addresses, and Lectures*, 49–70.

_____ 'Human Culture' (1837). In *The Early Lectures of Ralph Waldo Emerson*, ii: *1836–1838*, ed. Stephen E. Whicher, Robert E. Spiller, and Wallace E. Williams, 205–364. Cambridge, Mass.: Harvard University Press, 1964.

_____ 'Man the Reformer' (1841). In *Nature, Addresses, and Lectures*, 145–60.

_____ 'Circles' (1841). In *Essays: First Series*. In *The Collected Works*, ii, ed. Alfred R. Ferguson and Jean Ferguson Carr, 177–90. Cambridge, Mass.: Harvard University Press, 1979.

_____ 'The Poet' (1844). In *Essays, Second Series*, 1–24.

_____ 'New England Reformers: Lecture at Amory Hall' (1844). In *Essays, Second Series*, 147–67.

Emerson, Ralph Waldo. *English Traits* (1856). In *The Collected Works*, v, ed. Douglas Emory Wilson. Cambridge, Mass.: Harvard University Press, 1994.

―― 'Thoreau' (1862). In *Selected Essays*, ed. Larzer Ziff, 393–415. New York: Viking Penguin, 1982.

―― *The Journals and Miscellaneous Notebooks*, iii: *1826–1832*, ed. William H. Gilpin and Alfred R. Ferguson. Cambridge, Mass.: Harvard University Press, 1963.

―― *The Journals and Miscellaneous Notebooks*, ix: *1843–1847*, ed. Ralph H. Orth and Alfred R. Ferguson. Cambridge, Mass.: Harvard University Press, 1971.

―― *Nature, Addresses, and Lectures. The Collected Works*, i, ed. Robert E. Spiller and Alfred R. Ferguson. Cambridge, Mass.: Harvard University Press, 1971.

―― *The Journals and Miscellaneous Notebooks*, x: *1847–1848*, ed. Merton M. Sealts jun. Cambridge, Mass.: Harvard University Press, 1973.

―― *The Journals and Miscellaneous Notebooks*, xi: *1848–1851*, ed. A. W. Plumstead and William H. Gilman. Cambridge, Mass.: Harvard University Press, 1975.

―― *Essays, First Series. The Collected Works*, ii, ed. Alfred R. Ferguson and Jean Ferguson Carr. Cambridge, Mass.: Harvard University Press, 1979.

―― *Essays, Second Series. The Collected Works*, iii, ed. Alfred R. Ferguson and Jean Ferguson Carr. Cambridge, Mass.: Harvard University Press,1983.

―― *The Letters of Ralph Waldo Emerson*, viii: *1845–1849*, ed. Eleanor M. Tilton. New York: Columbia University Press, 1991.

Erskine-Hill, Howard. 'Two Hundred Years Since: Davie, the Eighteenth Century and the Image of England.' In *Donald Davie and the Responsibilities of Literature*, ed. Dekker, 112–28.

Evans, Eric J. *The Great Reform Act of 1832*, 2nd edn. London: Routledge, 1994.

'Fascist Meeting.' *Picture Post*, 29 July 1939, 32–4.

Everett, Barbara. 'Auden Askew.' *London Review of Books*, 19 Nov. 1981, 3–6.

Feather, John. *A History of British Publishing*. London: Routledge, 1988.

Ferguson, Niall, ed. *Virtual History: Alternatives and Counterfactuals*. London: Picador, 1997.

Fernihough, Anne. *D. H. Lawrence: Aesthetics and Ideology*. Oxford: Clarendon Press, 1993.

―― ed. *The Cambridge Companion to D. H. Lawrence*. Cambridge: Cambridge University Press, 2001.

Fiedler, Leslie A. *Love and Death in the American Novel*. New York: Criterion Books, 1960.

Fisher, Philip. 'Introduction: The New American Studies.' In *The New American Studies: Essays from* Representations, pp. vii-xxii. Berkeley: University of California Press, 1991.

Fleming, Anne Taylor. 'Christopher Isherwood: He Is a Camera' (1972). In *Conversations with Christopher Isherwood*, ed. Berg and Freeman, 90–7.

Fleming, Victor, dir. *The Wizard of Oz*. Metro-Goldwyn-Mayer, 1939.

Fletcher, Ian, ed. *Decadence and the 1890s*. Stratford-upon-Avon Studies, 17. London: Edward Arnold, 1979.

—— and Bradbury, Malcolm. Preface. In *Decadence and the 1890s*, ed. Fletcher, 7–13.

Forbes, Duncan. *The Liberal Anglican Idea of History*. Cambridge: Cambridge University Press, 1952.

Ford, Mark. *John Ashbery in Conversation with Mark Ford*. London: Between the Lines, 2003.

Forster, E. M. *Howards End*. London: Arnold, 1910.

Forsyth, R. A. ' "The Buried Life"—The Contrasting Views of Arnold and Clough in the Context of Dr. Arnold's Historiography.' *ELH*, 35 (1968), 218–53.

Frank, Waldo. 'Our Guilt in Fascism.' *New Republic*, 6 May 1940, 603–8.

Frost, Laura. *Sex Drives: Fantasies of Fascism in Literary Modernism*. Ithaca, NY: Cornell University Press, 2002.

Froude, James Anthony. *The Nemesis of Faith*. London, 1849.

—— *History of England from the Fall of Wolsey to the Death of Elizabeth*, 12 vols. London, 1856–70.

Frye, Northrop. *Anatomy of Criticism: Four Essays*. Princeton: Princeton University Press, 1957.

Fukuyama, Francis. *The End of History and the Last Man*. London: Hamish Hamilton, 1992.

Fuller, Margaret. *Summer on the Lakes* (1844). In *Portable Margaret Fuller*, 69–227.

—— 'Woman in the Nineteenth Century.' 1845. In *Portable Margaret Fuller*, 228–362.

—— *The Portable Margaret Fuller*, ed. Mary Kelley. New York: Penguin, 1994.

Gagnier, Regenia. *Idylls of the Marketplace: Oscar Wilde and the Victorian Public*. Stanford, Calif.: Stanford University Press, 1986.

Gannon, Franklin Reid. *The British Press and Germany, 1936–1939*. Oxford: Clarendon Press, 1971.

Gardner, Helen. *The Composition of* Four Quartets. London: Faber, 1978.

Gash, Norman, ed. *Documents of Modern History: The Age of Peel*. London: Edward Arnold, 1968.

Gatrell, Simon. 'England, Europe, and Empire: Hardy, Meredith, and Gissing.' In *The Ends of the Earth*, ed. Simon Gatrell, 67–82. London: Ashfield Press, 1992.

Gellhorn, Martha. 'Is There a New Germany?' *Atlantic*, 213/2 (Feb. 1964), 69–76.

Gelpi, Albert, ed. *Denise Levertov: Selected Criticism*. Ann Arbor: University of Michigan Press, 1993.

Gelpi, Albert, 'Introduction: Centering the Double Image.' In *Denise Levertov*, ed. Gelpi, 1–8.

Geyer, Michael, and Bright, Charles. 'World History in a Global Age.' *American Historical Review*, 100 (1995), 1034–60.

Gilbert, Martin. *The Holocaust: The Jewish Tragedy*. London: Collins, 1986.

Giles, Paul. *Transatlantic Insurrections: British Culture and the Formation of American Literature, 1730–1860*. Philadelphia: University of Pennsylvania Press, 2001.

—— *Virtual Americas: Transnational Fictions and the Transatlantic Imaginary*. Durham, NC: Duke University Press, 2002.

Gilroy, Paul. *Between Camps: Race, Identity and Nationalism at the End of the Colour Line*. London: Allen Lane-Penguin, 2000.

—— *After Empire: Melancholia or Convivial Culture?* Abingdon: Routledge, 2004.

Gissing, A. C., ed. *Selections, Autobiographical and Imaginative from the Works of George Gissing*. London: Cape, 1929.

Gissing, George. *Workers in the Dawn* (1880). Repr. Brighton: Harvester Press, 1985.

—— *The Unclassed* (1884), ed. Jacob Korg. Brighton: Harvester Press, 1976.

—— *Thyrza: A Tale* (1887), ed. Jacob Korg. Brighton: Harvester Press, 1974.

—— *The Nether World* (1889), ed. John Goode. Brighton: Harvester Press, 1974.

—— *New Grub Street* (1891), ed. Bernard Bergonzi. London: Penguin, 1968.

—— *Born in Exile* (1892), ed. Pierre Coustillas. Brighton: Harvester Press, 1978.

—— *The Odd Women* (1893), ed. Elaine Showalter. New York: New American Library–Penguin, 1983.

—— *In the Year of Jubilee* (1895). Repr. Brighton: Harvester Press, 1976.

—— 'The Place of Realism in Fiction' (1895). In *Selections*, ed. A. C. Gissing, 217–21.

—— *The Whirlpool* (1897), ed. Patrick Parrinder. Brighton: Harvester Press, 1977.

—— *Lost Stories from America: Five Signed Stories Never Before Reprinted, a Sixth Signed Story, and Seven Recent Attributions*, ed. Robert L. Selig. Lewiston, NY: Edwin Mellen Press, 1992.

—— *The Collected Letters, 1863–1903*, 9 vols., ed. Paul F. Mattheisen, Arthur C. Young, and Pierre Coustillas. Athens, Oh.: Ohio University Press, 1990–7.

Godechot, Jacques. *France and the Atlantic Revolutions of the Eighteenth Century, 1770–1799*, trans. Herbert H. Rowen. New York: Free Press, 1965.

Godwin, William. *Enquiry Concerning Political Justice and its Influence on Morals and Happiness*, (1793), ed. F. E. L. Priestley. Toronto: University of Toronto Press, 1946.

—— *Things as They Are; or, The Adventures of Caleb Williams* (1794), ed. Maurice Hindle. London: Penguin, 1988.

—— *Mandeville: A Tale of the Seventeenth Century in England*. Edinburgh, 1817.

Gordon, Jan B. ' "Decadent Spaces": Notes for a Phenomenology of the *Fin de Siècle.*' In *Decadence and the 1890s,* ed. Fletcher, 31–58.

Gosse, Edmund. *Books on the Table.* London: Heinemann, 1921.

Gougeon, Len. *Virtue's Hero: Emerson, Antislavery, and Reform.* Athens, Ga.: University of Georgia Press, 1990.

Grant, Michael, ed. *T. S. Eliot: The Critical Heritage,* 2 vols. London: Routledge & Kegan Paul, 1982.

Gravil, Richard. *Romantic Dialogues: Anglo-American Continuities, 1776–1862.* Basingstoke: Macmillan, 2000.

Gray, John. *False Dawn: The Delusions of Global Capitalism,* rev. edn. London: Granta Books, 2002.

Green, Martin. *The Problem of Boston: Some Readings in Cultural History.* New York: Norton, 1966.

Greenblatt, Stephen. *Marvelous Possessions: The Wonder of the New World.* Oxford: Clarendon Press, 1991.

_____ 'Racial Memory and Literary History.' *PMLA,* 116 (2001), 48–63.

Greenfield, Bruce. *Narrating Discovery: The Romantic Explorer in American Literature, 1790–1855.* New York: Columbia University Press, 1992.

Griffiths, Richard. *Fellow Travellers of the Right: British Enthusiasts for Nazi Germany, 1933–9.* London: Constable, 1980.

Grosser, Alfred. *The Western Alliance: European–American Relations since 1945* (1978), trans. Michael Shaw. London: Macmillan, 1980.

Guillory, John. *Cultural Capital: The Problem of Literary Canon Formation.* Chicago: University of Chicago Press, 1993.

Gunn, Giles. 'Introduction: Globalizing Literary Studies.' *PMLA* 116 (2001), 16–31.

Habermas, Jürgen. 'The Limits of Neo-Historicism.' In *Autonomy and Solidarity: Interviews with Jürgen Habermas,* ed. Peter Dews, rev. edn., 237–43. London: Verso, 1992.

Haffenden, John. *Novelists in Interview.* London: Methuen, 1985.

_____ ed. *W. H. Auden: The Critical Heritage.* London: Routledge, 1983.

Haigh, Christopher. *English Reformations: Religion, Politics, and Society under the Tudors.* Oxford: Oxford University Press, 1993.

Hall, Chris. 'Flight and Imagination.' *Spike Magazine,* 2000. Online: <www.spikemagazine.com>, accessed 1 June 2003.

Hall, Robert A., jun. *The Comic Style of P. G. Wodehouse.* Hamden, Conn.: Archon, 1974.

Hall, Stuart, and Held, David. 'Citizens and Citizenship.' In *New Times: The Changing Face of Politics in the 1990s,* ed. Stuart Hall and Martin Jacques, 173–88. London: Lawrence and Wishart, 1989.

Halperin, John. *Gissing: A Life in Books.* Oxford: Oxford University Press, 1982.

Hamilton, Paul. *Metaromanticism: Aesthetics, Literature, Theory.* Chicago: University of Chicago Press, 2003.

Hardy, Thomas. *Tess of the d'Urbervilles* (1891). Repr. London: Macmillan, 1974.

Harper, Francis E. W. *Iola Leroy* (1892), ed. Frances Smith Foster. New York: Oxford University Press, 1988.

Harris, Wendell V. *Arthur Hugh Clough*. New York: Twayne, 1970.

Harrison, Anthony H. *Christina Rossetti in Context*. Brighton: Harvester Press, 1988.

Hart, Derek. 'A Fortunate, Happy Life' (1970). In *Conversations with Christopher Isherwood*, ed. Berg and Freeman, 52–6.

Hawes, Clement. 'Johnson and Imperialism.' In *The Cambridge Companion to Samuel Johnson*, ed. Greg Clingham, 114–26. Cambridge: Cambridge University Press, 1997.

Haynes, Sam W. 'Anglophobia and the Annexation of Texas: The Quest for National Security.' In *Manifest Destiny and Empire*, ed. Haynes and Morris, 115–45.

——and Morris, Christopher, eds. *Manifest Destiny and Empire: American Antebellum Expansionism*. College Station, Tex.: University of Texas at Arlington–Texas A & M Press, 1997.

Hazlitt, William. 'What is the People?' (1817). In *The Fight*, 364–90.

—— 'Character of Cobbett' (1822). In *Table Talk*, 43–51.

—— 'On the Spirit of Monarchy' (1823). In *The Fight*, 339–53.

—— 'Lord Byron.' In *Spirit of the Age*, 157–81.

—— *The Spirit of the Age* (1825). Repr. Oxford: Woodstock Books, 1989.

—— *Selected Writings: Table Talk*, ed. Duncan Wu. London: Pickering & Chatto, 1998.

—— *The Fight and Other Writings*, ed. Tom Paulin and David Chandler. London: Penguin, 2000.

Heilbrun, Carolyn G. 'Christopher Isherwood: An Interview' (1976). In *Conversations with Christopher Isherwood*, ed. Berg and Freeman, 141–51.

Hewitt, Andrew. 'Fascist Modernism, Futurism, and "Post-Modernity."' In *Fascism, Aesthetics, and Culture*, ed. Richard J. Golsan, 38–55. Hanover, NH: University Press of New England, 1992.

—— *Fascist Modernism: Aesthetics, Politics, and the Avant-Garde*. Stanford, Calif.: Stanford University Press, 1993.

Hietala, Thomas R. ' "This Splendid Juggernaut": Westward a Nation and its People.' In *Manifest Destiny and Empire*, ed. Haynes and Morris, 48–67.

Hitchens, Christopher. 'Something about the Poems: Larkin and Sensitivity.' *New Left Review*, no. 200 (July–Aug. 1993), 161–72.

—— Introduction. In *The Mating Season*, by P. G. Wodehouse, pp. v–xi.

Hockney, David, and Joyce, Paul. *Hockney on 'Art': Conversations with Paul Joyce*. London: Little, Brown and Company (UK), 1999.

Holderness, Graham. *D. H. Lawrence: History, Ideology and Fiction*. Dublin: Gill and Macmillan, 1982.

Holmes, Richard. *Shelley: The Pursuit* (1974). Repr. London: Harper-Collins, 1994.

Hooker, Jeremy. 'Donald Davie's "Poems about the Sacred."' *PN Review*, 19/2 (Nov.–Dec. 1992), 33–5.

Hoover, Bob. 'Updike "Pleased and Moved" to Accept American Fiction's Most Prestigious Honor.' *Pittsburgh Post-Gazette*, Arts and Entertainment, 10 May 2004. Online:<http://www.post-gazette.com>, accessed 29 April 2005.

Horsman, Reginald. *Race and Manifest Destiny: The Origins of American Racial Anglo-Saxonism.* Cambridge, Mass.: Harvard University Press, 1981.

Howe, Anthony. *Free Trade and Liberal England, 1846–1946.* Oxford: Clarendon Press, 1997.

Huntington, Samuel P. 'The Clash of Civilizations?' In *Foreign Affairs*, 72/3 (Summer 1993), 22–49.

Huxley, Aldous. *Antic Hay.* London: Chatto & Windus, 1923.

——*Jesting Pilate* (1926). Repr. London: Chatto & Windus, 1930.

—— 'The Outlook for American Culture: Some Reflections in a Machine Age' (1927). In *Complete Essays*, iii. 185–94.

——*Point Counter Point* (1928). Repr. London: HarperCollins–Flamingo, 1994.

—— 'Wordsworth in the Tropics' (1929). In *Complete Essays*, ii. 334–42.

——*Brave New World* (1932). Repr. London: Grafton, 1977.

—— 'Ballyhoo for Nations' (1935). In *Complete Essays*, iii. 426–38.

—— 'D. H. Lawrence' (1936). In *Complete Essays*, iv. 71–91.

——*After Many a Summer* (1939). Repr. London: Chatto & Windus, 1962.

—— 'Politics and Religion' (1941). In *Complete Essays*, v. 5–21.

——*Ape and Essence.* New York: Harper, 1948.

—— 'The Doors of Perception' (1954). In *Complete Essays*, v. 157–91.

—— 'The Education of an Amphibian' (1956). In *Complete Essays*, v. 191–209.

—— 'Gesualdo: Variations on a Musical Theme' (1956). In *Complete Essays*, v. 436–49.

—— 'Knowledge and Understanding' (1956). In *Complete Essays*, v. 209–29.

——*Brave New World Revisited.* London: Chatto & Windus, 1959.

——*Literature and Science.* London: Chatto & Windus, 1963.

——*Letters of Aldous Huxley*, ed. Grover Smith. London: Chatto & Windus, 1969.

——*Complete Essays*, ii: *1926–1929*, ed. Robert S. Baker and James Sexton. Chicago: Dee, 2000.

——*Complete Essays*, iii: *1930–1935*, ed. Robert S. Baker and James Sexton. Chicago: Dee, 2001.

——*Complete Essays*, iv: *1936–1938*, ed. Robert S. Baker and James Sexton. Chicago, Dee, 2001.

——*Complete Essays*, v: *1939–1956*, ed. Robert S. Baker and James Sexton. Chicago: Dee, 2002.

Huxley, Aldous. *Complete Essays*, vi: *1956–1963*, ed. Robert S. Baker and James Sexton. Chicago: Dee, 2002.

Huxley, Julian, ed. *Aldous Huxley, 1894–1963: A Memorial Volume*. London: Chatto & Windus, 1965.

Huysmans, J. K. *Against Nature*, (1884), trans. Robert Baldick. London: Penguin, 1959.

Huyssen, Andreas. *After the Great Divide: Modernism, Mass Culture, Postmodernism*. Bloomington, Ind.: Indiana University Press, 1986.

—— *Twilight Memories: Marking Time in a Culture of Amnesia*. New York: Routledge, 1995.

Ickstadt, Heinz. 'Globalization and the National Paradigm; or, can English (and American) Studies be Globalised?' *European English Messenger*, 9/2 (Autumn 2000), 19–21.

Irving, Washington. 'Lord Byron' (1814). In *Miscellaneous Writings, 1803–1859*, i. *Complete Works*, xxviii, ed. Wayne R. Kime, 114–17. Boston: Twayne, 1981.

—— *A History of New York* (1818). *Complete Works*, vii, ed. Michael L. Black and Nancy B. Black. Boston: Twayne, 1983.

—— *The Alhambra* (1832). In *Complete Works*, xiv, ed. William T. Lenehan and Andrew B. Myers. Boston: Twayne, 1983.

—— 'An Unwritten Drama of Lord Byron' (1835). In *Miscellaneous Writings, 1803–1859*, ii. *Complete Works*, xxix, ed. Wayne R. Kime, 88–90. Boston: Twayne, 1981.

—— *Astoria, or Anecdotes of an Enterprize beyond the Rocky Mountains* (1836). In *Complete Works*, xv, ed. Richard Dilworth Rust. Boston: Twayne, 1976.

—— *The Western Journals of Washington Irving*, ed. John Francis McDermott. Norman, Okla.: University of Oklahoma Press, 1944.

Isherwood, Christopher. *All the Conspirators* (1928). Repr. London: Random House–Vintage, 2000.

—— *Lions and Shadows: An Education in the Twenties* (1938). Repr. London: Mandarin–Minerva, 1996.

—— *Goodbye to Berlin* (1939). In *The Berlin of Sally Bowles*, 281–583. London: Hogarth Press, 1978.

—— *Prater Violet* (1946). Repr. London: Methuen, 1984.

—— 'Coming to London' (1947). In *Exhumations*, 150–6.

—— 'Los Angeles' (1947). In *Exhumations*, 156–62.

—— 'The Gita and War' (1948). In *Exhumations*, 103–11.

—— 'The Shore'(1952). In *Exhumations*, 162–6.

—— *Down There on a Visit* (1962). Repr. London: White Lion, 1974.

—— *A Single Man*. London: Methuen, 1964.

—— *Exhumations: Stories, Articles, Verse*. London: Methuen, 1966.

—— *A Meeting by the River*. London: Methuen, 1967.

—— *Kathleen and Frank* (1971). Repr. Random House–Vintage, 2000.

_____ *Christopher and his Kind, 1929–1939* (1976). Repr. London: Methuen–Magnum, 1978.

_____ *My Guru and his Disciple.* London: Eyre Methuen, 1980.

_____ *Diaries*, i: *1939–1960*, ed. Katherine Bucknell. London: Random House-Vintage, 1997.

_____ *Lost Years: A Memoir 1945–1951*, ed. Katherine Bucknell. London: Chatto & Windus, 2000.

_____ *Conversations with Christopher Isherwood*, ed. James J. Berg and Chris Freeman. Jackson, Miss.: University Press of Mississippi, 2001.

Israel, Nico. *Outlandish: Writing Between Exile and Diaspora.* Stanford, Calif.: Stanford University Press, 2000.

Jaggi, Maya. 'No Thanks, Ma'am.' *Guardian* (London), 15 June 2005, sec. 2, 4.

Jain, Manju. *T. S. Eliot and American Philosophy: The Harvard Years.* Cambridge: Cambridge University Press, 1992.

James, Henry. 'Middlemarch.' In *The Art of Criticism: Henry James on the Theory and Practice of Fiction*, ed. William Veeder and Susan M. Griffin, 48–58. Chicago: University of Chicago Press, 1986.

Jameson, Fredric. *Fables of Aggression: Wyndham Lewis, the Modernist as Fascist.* Berkeley: University of California Press, 1979.

_____ *The Political Unconscious: Narrative as a Socially Symbolic Act.* Ithaca, NY: Cornell University Press, 1981.

_____ *A Singular Modernity: Essays on the Ontology of the Present.* London: Verso, 2002.

Jay, Paul. 'Beyond Discipline? Globalization and the Future of English.' *PMLA*, 116 (2001), 32–47.

Jenkins, Nicholas. 'Auden in America.' In *The Cambridge Companion to W. H. Auden*, ed. Stan Smith, 39–54. Cambridge: Cambridge University Press, 2005.

_____ 'Writing "Without Roots": Auden, Eliot, and Post-National Poetry.' In *Something We Have That They Don't: British and American Poetic Relations since 1925*, ed. Steve Clark and Mark Ford, 75–97. Iowa City: University of Iowa Press, 2004.

Jenkins, Roy. *Churchill.* London: Macmillan, 2001.

Johannsen, Robert W. 'Introduction.' In *Manifest Destiny and Empire*, ed. Haynes and Morris, 1–6.

Johnson, Samuel. *The History of Rasselas, Prince of Abyssinia.* 1759. In *Rasselas and Other Tales*, ed. Gwin J. Kolb, The Yale Edition of the Works of Samuel Johnson, xvi. 1–176. New Haven: Yale University Press, 1990.

_____ *The Patriot* (1774). In *Political Writings*, 387–400.

_____ *Taxation No Tyranny: An Answer to the Resolution and Address of the American Congress* (1775). In *Political Writings*, 401–55.

Johnson, Samuel. *A Journey to the Western Islands of Scotland* (1775), ed. Mary Lascelles. The Yale Edition of the Works of Samuel Johnson, ix. New Haven: Yale University Press, 1971.

—— *Political Writings*, ed. Donald J. Greene. The Yale Edition of the Works of Samuel Johnson, x. New Haven: Yale University Press, 1977.

Jordanova, Ludmilla. 'The Authoritarian Response.' In *The Enlightenment and its Shadows*, ed. Peter Hulme and Ludmilla Jordanova, 200–16. London: Routledge, 1990.

Joseph, Gerhard. 'Construing the Inimitable's Silence: Pecksniff's Grammar School and International Copyright.' *Dickens Studies Annual*, 22 (1993), 121–35.

Joyce, James. *Ulysses*. Paris: Shakespeare and Co., 1922.

Julius, Anthony. *T. S. Eliot, Anti-Semitism, and Literary Form*. Cambridge: Cambridge University Press, 1995.

—— *Transgressions: The Offences of Art*. London: Thames & Hudson, 2002.

Kadrey, Richard, and Stefanac, Suzanne. 'J. G. Ballard on William S. Burroughs' Naked Truth.' *Salon*, 2 Sept. 1997. Online:<www.salon.com>, accessed 1 June 2003.

Kaiser, David Aram. *Romanticism, Aesthetics, and Nationalism*. Cambridge: Cambridge University Press, 1999.

Karle, Deepika. 'A Reader's Guide to P. G. Wodehouse's America.' *Studies in American Humor*, NS 7 (1989), 32–44.

Keane, John. *Tom Paine: A Political Life*. London: Bloomsbury, 1995.

Keats, John. *The Letters of John Keats, 1814–1821*, ed. Hyder Edward Rollins, 2 vols. Cambridge: Cambridge University Press, 1958.

Keenan, Joe. Introduction. In *The Code of the Woosters*, by P. G. Wodehouse, pp. v–xiii.

Keith, W. J. 'Spirit of Place and *Genius Loci*: D. H. Lawrence and Rolf Gardiner.' *D. H. Lawrence Review*, 7 (1974), 127–38.

Kelsall, Malcolm. *Byron's Politics*. Brighton: Harvester Press, 1987.

Kenner, Hugh. *The Invisible Poet: T. S. Eliot* (1960). Repr. London: Methuen, 1965.

—— *A Sinking Island: The Modern English Writers*. London: Barrie & Jenkins, 1988.

Kenny, Anthony. *God and Two Poets: Arthur Hugh Clough and Gerard Manley Hopkins*. London: Sidgwick & Jackson, 1988.

—— Biographical Introduction. In *The Oxford Diaries of Arthur Hugh Clough*, pp. ix–lxiv. Oxford: Clarendon Press, 1990.

—— *Arthur Hugh Clough: A Poet's Life*. London: Continuum, 2005.

Kermode, Frank. 'Apocalypse and the Modern.' In *Visions of Apocalypse: End or Rebirth?*, ed. Saul Friedländer *et al.*, 84–106. New York: Holmes and Meier, 1985.

Kiernan, Robert F. *Frivolity Unbound: Six Masters of the Camp Novel*. New York: Continuum–Frederick Ungar, 1990.

Kimball, Roger. 'The Genius of Wodehouse.' *New Criterion*, 19/2 (Oct. 2000), 5–12.

Kincaid-Weekes, Mark. 'Decolonising Imagination: Lawrence in the 1920s.' In *Cambridge Companion to D. H. Lawrence*, ed. Fernihough, 67–85.

King, Bruce. *The Internationalization of English Literature. Oxford English Literary History*, xiii: *1948–2000*. Oxford: Oxford University Press, 2004.

Knapp, Jeffrey. *An Empire Nowhere: England, America, and Literature from* Utopia *to* The Tempest. Berkeley: University of California Press, 1992.

Kojecký, Roger. *T. S. Eliot's Social Criticism*. London: Faber, 1971.

Koning, Christina. 'Death by Request.' Review of *London Fields*, by Martin Amis. *Guardian* (London), 21 Sept. 1989, 26.

Kracauer, Siegfried. *From Caligari to Hitler: A Psychological History of the German Film* (1947), rev. edn., ed. Leonardo Quaresima. Princeton: Princeton University Press, 2004.

Kristeva, Julia. *Nations without Nationalism* (1990), trans. Leon S. Roudiez. New York: Columbia University Press, 1993.

Kumar, Krishan. *The Making of English National Identity*. Cambridge: Cambridge University Press, 2003.

Lang, Fritz, dir. *Die Niebelungen*. UFA Studio, 1924.

———— *The Last Will of Dr. Mabuse*. Nero Film—Deutsche Universal, 1933.

———— *Scarlet Street*. Universal Pictures, 1945.

———— *While the City Sleeps*. RKO, 1956.

Langford, Paul. 'The English Clergy and the American Revolution.' In *The Transformation of Political Culture: England and Germany in the Late Eighteenth Century*, ed. Eckhart Hellmuth, 275–307. Oxford: Oxford University Press; London: German Historical Institute, 1990.

———— *Englishness Identified: Manners and Character, 1650–1850*. Oxford: Oxford University Press, 2000.

Larkin, Philip. *Selected Letters of Philip Larkin, 1940–1985*, ed. Anthony Thwaite (1992). Repr. New York: Farrar, Straus & Giroux, 1993.

———— ed. *The Oxford Book of Twentieth-Century English Verse*. Oxford: Oxford University Press, 1973.

Lauter, Paul. 'To the Reader': Preface to the First Edition. In *Heath Anthology of American Literature*, 2 vols., pp. xxxiii–xliii. Lexington, Mass.: D. C. Heath, 1990.

Lawrence, D. H. *Sons and Lovers* (1913), ed. Helen Baron and Carl Baron. Cambridge: Cambridge University Press, 1992.

———— *The Rainbow* (1915), ed. Mark Kinkead-Weekes. Cambridge: Cambridge University Press, 1989.

———— 'Democracy' (1919). In *Reflections on the Death of a Porcupine*, 61–83.

Lawrence, D. H. 'Blessed Are the Powerful.' In *Reflections on the Death of a Porcupine*, 319–28.

—— *Women in Love* (1920), ed. David Bradshaw. Oxford: Oxford University Press, 1998.

—— *Movements in European History* (1921), ed. Philip Crumpton. Cambridge: Cambridge University Press, 1989.

—— 'America, Listen to Your Own' (1922). In *Phoenix*, 87–91.

—— 'Indians and an Englishman' (1922). In *Phoenix*, 92–9.

—— 'Taos' (1922). In *Phoenix*, 100–3.

—— 'Au Revoir, U.S.A.' (1923). In *Phoenix*, 104–6.

—— *Studies in Classic American Literature* (1923), ed. Ezra Greenspan, Lindeth Vasey, and John Worthen. Cambridge: Cambridge University Press, 2003.

—— 'A Letter from Germany' (1924). In *Phoenix*, 107–10.

—— 'St Mawr' (1925). In *The Short Novels*, ii. 1–147. London: Heinemann, 1956.

—— *The Plumed Serpent*, (1926), ed. L. D. Clark. Cambridge: Cambridge University Press, 1987.

—— '[Return to Bestwood]' (1926). In *Late Essays*, 15–24.

—— 'Which Class I Belong To' (1927). In *Late Essays*, 33–40.

—— 'Hymns in a Man's Life' (1928). In *Late Essays*, 128–34.

—— 'New Mexico' (1928). In *Phoenix*, 141–7.

—— 'Things' (1928). In *The Complete Short Stories*, 3 vols., iii. 844–53. London: Heinemann, 1955.

—— 'Myself Revealed' (1929). In *Late Essays*, 175–81.

—— 'Nottingham and the Mining Countryside' (1930). In *Late Essays*, 285–94.

—— *Phoenix: The Posthumous Papers of D. H. Lawrence*, ed. Edward D. McDonald. London: Heinemann, 1936.

—— *The First Lady Chatterley*. New York: Dial Press, 1944.

—— *Mornings in Mexico and Etruscan Places*. London: Heinemann, 1956.

—— *The Short Novels*, ii. London: Heinemann, 1956.

—— *The Complete Poems*, ed. Vivian de Sola Pinto and Warren Roberts, 2 vols. London: Heinemann, 1964.

—— *The Letters of D. H. Lawrence*, i, ed. James T. Boulton. Cambridge: Cambridge University Press, 1979.

—— *Apocalypse and the Writings on Revelation*, ed. Mara Kalnins. Cambridge: Cambridge University Press, 1980.

—— *The Letters of D. H. Lawrence*, ii, ed. George J. Zytaruk and James T. Boulton. Cambridge: Cambridge University Press, 1981.

—— *The Letters of D. H. Lawrence*, iv, ed. Warren Roberts, James T. Boulton, and Elizabeth Mansfield. Cambridge: Cambridge University Press, 1987.

—— *Reflections on the Death of a Porcupine and Other Essays*, ed. Michael Herbert. Cambridge: Cambridge University Press, 1988.

_____ *Late Essays and Articles*, ed. James T. Boulton. Cambridge: Cambridge University Press, 2004.

Lears, T. J. Jackson. *No Place of Grace: Antimodernism and the Transformation of American Culture, 1880–1920*. New York: Pantheon Books, 1981.

Leavis, F. R. *Mass Civilisation and Minority Culture*. Cambridge: Minority Press, 1930.

_____ *The Great Tradition: George Eliot, Henry James, Joseph Conrad*. London: Chatto & Windus, 1948.

_____ *D. H. Lawrence: Novelist* (1955). Repr. London: Chatto & Windus, 1967.

_____ *Anna Karenina and Other Essays*. London: Chatto & Windus, 1967.

_____ 'The Complex Fate' (1952). In *Anna Karenina*, 152–60.

_____ 'The Americanness of American Literature' (1952). In *Anna Karenina*, 138–51.

_____ ' "Lawrence Scholarship" and Lawrence' (1963). In *Anna Karenina*, 167–76.

Ledent, Bénédicte. *Caryl Phillips*. Manchester: Manchester University Press, 2002.

Leonard, William Ellery. *Byron and Byronism in America*. Boston: Columbia University Studies in English, 1905.

Levertov, Denise. *The Double Image* (1946). In *Collected Earlier Poems*, 19–26.

_____ *Here and Now* (1957). In *Collected Earlier Poems*, 27–52.

_____ *With Eyes at the Back of Our Heads* (1960). In *Collected Earlier Poems*, 83–131.

_____ *The Jacob's Ladder* (1961). In *Poems, 1960–1967*, 1–72.

_____ 'Some Notes on Organic Form' (1965). In *Poet in the World*, 7–13.

_____ 'The Sense of Pilgrimage' (1967). In *Poet in the World*, 62–86.

_____ 'Origins of a Poem' (1968). In *Poet in the World*, 43–56.

_____ 'Great Possessions' (1970). In *Poet in the World*, 89–106.

_____ *The Poet in the World*. New York: New Directions, 1973.

_____ *Collected Earlier Poems 1940–1960*. New York: New Directions, 1979.

_____ *Poems, 1960–1967*. New York: New Directions, 1983.

_____ *Poems, 1968–1972*. New York: New Directions, 1987.

_____ *Breathing the Water*. Newcastle: Bloodaxe, 1988.

_____ *Tesserae: Memories and Suppositions* (1995). Repr. Newcastle: Bloodaxe, 1997.

_____ *The Letters of Denise Levertov and William Carlos Williams*, ed. Christopher MacGowan. New York: New Directions, 1998.

_____ *This Great Unknowing: Last Poems* (1999). Repr. Newcastle: Bloodaxe, 2001.

_____ *Poems, 1972–1982*. New York: New Directions, 2001.

Levine, George. 'The Ambiguous Heritage of *Frankenstein*.' In *The Endurance of* Frankenstein: *Essays on Mary Shelley's Novel*, ed. George Levine and U. C. Knoepflmacher, 3–30. Berkeley: University of California Press, 1979.

Levine, Lawrence. *Highbrow/Lowbrow: The Emergence of Cultural Hierarchy in America*. Cambridge, Mass.: Harvard University Press, 1988.

Levine, Robert S. *Conspiracy and Romance: Studies in Brockden Brown, Cooper, Hawthorne, and Melville*. Cambridge: Cambridge University Press, 1989.

Lewis, Meriwether, and Clark, William. *The Journals of Lewis and Clark*, ed. Frank Bergeron. New York: Penguin, 1989.

Leyland, Winston. 'Christopher Isherwood Interview' (1973). In *Conversations with Christopher Isherwood*, ed. Berg and Freeman, 98–109.

Limerick, Patricia Nelson. *The Legacy of Conquest: The Unbroken Past of the American West*. New York: Norton, 1987.

Lincoln, Abraham. ' "House Divided" Speech at Springfield, Illinois' (1858). In *The Portable Abraham Lincoln*, ed. Andrew Delbanco, 88–97. New York: Viking Penguin, 1992.

Liu, Alan. *Wordsworth: The Sense of History*. Stanford, Calif.: Stanford University Press, 1989.

Lowell, J. R. *Poems of James Russell Lowell*. London: Oxford University Press, 1912.

Lowry, Malcolm. *Under the Volcano* (1947). Repr. London: Picador, 1993.

Lucas, John. *England and Englishness: Ideas of Nationhood in English Poetry*. London: Hogarth Press, 1990.

Luckhurst, Roger. 'Petition, Repetition, and "Autobiography": J. G. Ballard's *Empire of the Sun* and *The Kindness of Women*.' *Contemporary Literature*, 35 (1994), 688–708.

—— '*The Angle Between Two Walls': The Fiction of J. G. Ballard*. Liverpool: Liverpool University Press, 1997.

Lukács, Georg. *The Historical Novel* (1937), trans. Hannah and Stanley Mitchell. London: Merlin Press, 1962.

Lynch, Tom. 'Re: Rocky Mtn Writers.' 19 May 1997. Online: <http://www.earthsystems.org/gopher/asle>, accessed 22 Feb. 2001.

Lyotard, Jean-François. *The Postmodern Condition: A Report on Knowledge* (1979), trans. Geoff Bennington and Brian Massumi. Minneapolis: University of Minnesota Press, 1984.

McAfee, Robert Breckinridge. *History of the Late War in the Western Country*. Lexington, Ky., 1816.

McCord, Norman. *The Anti-Corn Law League, 1838–1846*. London: Allen & Unwin, 1958.

McCrum, Robert. *Wodehouse: A Life*. London: Viking–Penguin, 2004.

MacCulloch, Diarmaid. *Reformation: Europe's House Divided, 1490–1700*. London: Allen Lane, 2003.

MacDermott, Kathy. 'Light Humor and the Dark Underside of Wish Fulfillment: Conservative Anti-realism.' *Studies in Popular Culture*, 10/2 (1987), 37–53.

McFarlane, Brian. 'Outrage: *No Orchids for Miss Blandish*.' In *British Crime Cinema*, ed. Chibnall and Murphy, 37–50.

Mackay, Alexander. *The Western World; or, Travels in the United States in 1846–47*, 3 vols. London, 1849.

Mackenzie, John M. *Propaganda and Empire: The Manipulation of British Public Opinion, 1880–1960*. Manchester: Manchester University Press, 1984.

Malchow, H. L. *Gothic Images of Race in Nineteenth-Century Britain*. Stanford, Calif.: Stanford University Press, 1996.

Maltz, Diana. 'Practical Aesthetics and Decadent Rationale in George Gissing.' *Victorian Literature and Culture*, 28 (2000), 55–71.

——— 'Bohemia's Bo(a)rders: Queer-Friendly Gissing.' *Gissing Journal*, 37/4 (Oct. 2001), 7–28.

Margolis, John D. *T. S. Eliot's Intellectual Development, 1922–1939*. Chicago: University of Chicago Press, 1972.

Markovits, Stefanie. 'Arthur Hugh Clough, *Amours de Voyage*, and the Victorian Crisis of Action.' *Nineteenth-Century Literature*, 55 (2001), 445–78.

Martin, Robert K. *The Homosexual Tradition in American Poetry*. Austin, Tex.: University of Texas Press, 1979.

Martineau, James. *Types of Ethical Theory*, 2 vols. Oxford: Clarendon Press, 1885.

Marx, Leo. *The Machine in the Garden: Technology and the Pastoral Ideal in America*. New York: Oxford University Press, 1964.

Massa, Ann, and Stead, Alistair, eds. *Forked Tongues: Comparing Twentieth-Century British and American Literature*. London: Longmans, 1994.

Matthiessen, F. O. *American Renaissance: Art and Expression in the Age of Emerson and Whitman*. New York: Oxford University Press. 1941.

——— ed. *The Oxford Book of American Verse*. New York: Oxford University Press, 1950.

Max, D. T. 'Manhattan Transfer.' *Observer Review* (London), 24 Sept. 2000, 2.

Meckier, Jerome. *Innocent Abroad: Charles Dickens's American Engagements*. Lexington, Ky.: University Press of Kentucky, 1990.

——— 'Aldous Huxley's Americanization of the *Brave New World* Typescript.' *Twentieth Century Literature*, 48 (2002), 427–60.

Mendelson, Edward. *Later Auden*. New York: Farrar, Straus & Giroux, 1999.

——— Introduction. In *Prose*, ii, by W. H. Auden, pp. xlii–xxxi.

Merk, Frederick. *The Oregon Question: Essays in Anglo-American Diplomacy and Politics*. Cambridge, Mass.: Harvard University Press, 1967.

Michaels, Walter Benn. 'Philosophy in Kinkanja: Eliot's Pragmatism.' *Glyph*, 8 (1981), 170–202.

——— *The Gold Standard and the Logic of Naturalism*. Berkeley: University of California Press, 1987.

——— *Our America: Nativism, Modernism and Pluralism*. Durham, NC: Duke University Press, 1995.

Michelson, Peter. *Speaking the Unspeakable: A Poetics of Obscenity*. Albany, NY: State University of New York Press, 1993.

Micklus, Robert. 'A Voyage of Juxtapositions: The Dynamic World of *Amours de Voyage.' Victorian Poetry*, 18 (1980), 407–14.

Milder, Robert. 'The Radical Emerson?' In *Cambridge Companion to Emerson*, ed. Porte, 49–75.

Miller, Chris. 'The Pope and the Canon: Eliot, Johnson, Davie and the Movement.' *PN Review*, 23/6 (July–Aug. 1997), 45–50.

Miller, Perry. 'Errand into the Wilderness' (1952). In *Errand into the Wilderness*, 1–15. Cambridge, Mass.: Harvard University Press, 1956.

Miyoshi, Masao. 'Clough's Poems of Self-Irony.' *Studies in English Literature*, 5 (1965), 691–704.

Mizejewski, Linda. *Divine Decadence: Fascism, Female Spectacle, and the Making of Sally Bowles*. Princeton: Princeton University Press, 1992.

Moody, A. D. *Tracing T. S. Eliot's Spirit: Essays on his Poetry and Thought*. Cambridge: Cambridge University Press, 1996.

Moon, Michael. *Disseminating Whitman: Revision and Corporeality in* Leaves of Grass. Cambridge, Mass.: Harvard University Press, 1991.

Mooneyham, Laura. 'Comedy among the Modernists: P. G. Wodehouse and the Anachronism of Comic Form.' *Twentieth Century Literature*, 40 (1994), 114–38.

Moretti, Franco. *Signs Taken for Wonders: Essays in the Sociology of Literary Forms*, rev. edn., trans. Susan Fischer, David Forgacs, and David Miller. London: Verso, 1988.

Morrison, Blake. *The Movement: English Poetry and Fiction of the 1950s*. Oxford: Oxford University Press, 1980.

Moss, Stephen. 'After the Storm: Profile of Martin Amis.' *Guardian Weekend* (London), 3 Oct. 1998, 22–6.

Mosse, George L. *Nationalism and Sexuality: Respectability and Abnormal Sexuality in Modern Europe*. New York: Howard Fertig, 1985.

——— 'Beauty without Sensuality: The Exhibition Entartete Kunst.' In *'Degenerate Art': The Fate of the Avant-Garde in Nazi Germany*, ed. Stephanie Barron, 24–31. Los Angeles: Los Angeles County Museum of Art, 1991.

Mulvey, Christopher. *Transatlantic Manners: Social Patterns in Nineteenth-Century Anglo-American Travel Literature*. Cambridge: Cambridge University Press, 1990.

Murdoch, Iris. 'Against Dryness: A Polemical Sketch.' *Encounter*, 16/1 (Jan. 1961), 16–20.

Nalbantian, Suzanne. *Seeds of Decadence in the Late Nineteenth-Century Novel: A Crisis in Values*. New York: St Martin's Press, 1983.

Namier, Sir Lewis. *England in the Age of the American Revolution*, 2nd edn. London: Macmillan, 1961.

Naremore, James. *More Than Night: Film Noir in its Contexts*. Berkeley: University of California Press, 1998.

Nattrass, Leonora. *William Cobbett: The Politics of Style*. Cambridge: Cambridge University Press, 1995.

Neville-Sington, Pamela. Introduction. In *Domestic Manners of the Americans*, by Fanny Trollope, pp. vii–xli. London: Penguin, 1997.

Nicoloff, Philip L. *Emerson on Race and History: An Examination of* English Traits. New York: Columbia University Press, 1961.

Norbrook, David. *Writing the English Republic: Poetry, Rhetoric and Politics, 1627–1660*. Cambridge: Cambridge University Press, 1999.

North, Michael. *Reading 1922: A Return to the Scene of the Modern*. New York: Oxford University Press, 1999.

Olson, Kirby. 'Bertie and Jeeves at the End of History: P. G. Wodehouse as Political Scientist.' *Humor: International Journal of Humor Research*, 9/1 (1996), 73–88.

Orwell, George. 'Charles Dickens' (1940). In *Collected Essays*, i. 413–60.

_____ Review of *Burnt Norton, East Coker, The Dry Salvages*, by T. S. Eliot (1942). In *Collected Essays*, ii. 236–42.

_____ 'Raffles and Miss Blandish' (1944). In *Collected Essays*, iii. 212–24.

_____ 'In Defence of P. G. Wodehouse' (1945). In *Collected Essays*, iii. 341–55.

_____ 'The Decline of the English Murder' (1946). In *Collected Essays*, iv. 98–101.

_____ 'As I Please' (6 Dec. 1946). In *Collected Essays*, iv. 251–4.

_____ 'George Gissing' (1948). In *Collected Essays*, iv. 428–36.

_____ *Nineteen Eighty-Four* (1949). Introduction by Thomas Pynchon. London: Penguin, 2003.

_____ *Collected Essays, Journalism and Letters of George Orwell*, i: *An Age Like This, 1920–1940*, ed. Sonia Orwell and Ian Angus. London: Secker & Warburg, 1968.

_____ *Collected Essays, Journalism and Letters of George Orwell*, ii: *My Country Right or Left, 1940–1943*, ed. Sonia Orwell and Ian Angus. London: Secker & Warburg, 1968.

_____ *Collected Essays, Journalism and Letters*, iii: *As I Please, 1943–1945*, ed. Sonia Orwell and Ian Angus. London: Secker & Warburg, 1968.

_____ *Collected Essays, Journalism and Letters*, iv: *In Front of Your Nose, 1945–1950*, ed. Sonia Orwell and Ian Angus. London: Secker & Warburg, 1968.

Osborne, Charles. *W. H. Auden: The Life of a Poet*. London: Eyre Methuen, 1980.

Pace, Joel. 'Wordsworth in America: Publication, Reception, and Literary Influence, 1802–1850.' D. Phil. thesis, University of Oxford, 1999.

Packard, William. 'Interview with Denise Levertov' (1971). In *Denise Levertov*, ed. Wagner, 1–21.

Packer, Barbara L. 'The Transcendentalists.' In *Cambridge History of American Literature*, ii, ed. Bercovitch, 331–61.

Paine, Thomas. *Rights of Man* (1791–2), ed. Henry Collins. London: Penguin, 1969.

Parker, Peter. *Isherwood: A Life.* London: Picador, 2004.

Parkman, Francis, jun. *The Oregon Trail* (1849), ed. David Levin. New York: Viking Penguin, 1982.

Paulin, Tom. *Minotaur: Poetry and the Nation State.* London: Faber, 1992.

―――― 'Auden Never Got the Hang of Writing Prose, but at least he Saw Gossip as an Art Form.' Review of *Essays and Reviews and Travel Books in Prose and Verse, Volume One: Prose, 1926–1938,* by W. H. Auden. *Observer Review* (London), 16 March 1997, 15.

Paulson, Ronald. *Representations of Revolution (1789–1820).* New Haven: Yale University Press, 1983.

Peach, Linden. *Angela Carter.* Basingstoke: Macmillan, 1998.

Peacock, Thomas Love. *Memoirs, Essays, and Reviews,* ed. Howard Mills. London: Rupert Hart-Davis, 1970.

Pells, Richard. *Not Like Us: How Europeans Loved, Hated, and Transformed American Culture since World War II.* New York: Basic Books, 1997.

Perloff, Marjorie. 'Modernist Studies.' In *Redrawing the Boundaries: The Transformation of English and American Literary Studies,* ed. Stephen Greenblatt and Giles Gunn, 154–78. New York: Modern Language Association of America, 1992.

Pesetsky, Bette. 'Lust Among the Ruins.' Review of *London Fields,* by Martin Amis. *New York Times Book Review,* 4 March 1990, 1, 42.

Petersson, Margareta. *Unending Metamorphoses: Myth, Satire and Religion in Salman Rushdie's Novels.* Lund: Lund University Press, 1996.

Phelps, Barry. *P. G. Wodehouse: Man and Myth.* London: Constable, 1992.

Phillips, Caryl. *The Final Passage* (1985). Repr. London: Picador, 1995.

―――― *The European Tribe* (1987). Repr. London: Faber, 1999.

―――― *Higher Ground: A Novel in Three Parts.* London: Viking, 1989.

―――― *Cambridge.* New York: Knopf, 1992.

―――― *Crossing the River.* London: Bloomsbury, 1993.

―――― 'C. L. R. James: Mariner, Renegade and Castaway' (1996). In *New World Order,* 152–71.

―――― 'Literature: The New Jazz for Black America?' Review of *Norton Anthology of African-American Literature,* ed. Henry Louis Gates and Nellie Y. McKay. *Observer Review* (London), 6 April 1997, 17.

―――― *The Nature of Blood.* London: Faber, 1997.

―――― 'Edouard Glissant: Promiscuities' (1999). In *New World Order,* 172–86.

―――― *The Atlantic Sound.* London: Faber, 2000.

―――― 'The "High Anxiety" of Belonging' (2000). In *New World Order,* 303–9.

―――― 'Marvin Gaye' (2000). In *New World Order,* 35–59.

―――― *A New World Order: Selected Essays.* London: Secker & Warburg, 2001.

―――― 'Introduction: A New World Order'. In *New World Order,* 1–6.

―――― 'The Burden of Race.' In *New World Order,* 9–17.

―――― 'A New World Order.' In *New World Order,* 1–6.

_____ 'The Gift of Displacement.' In *New World Order*, 129–34.

_____ 'Confessions of a True Believer.' *Guardian Review* (London), 4 Jan. 2003.

_____ *A Distant Shore*. London: Secker & Warburg, 2003.

_____ , ed. *Extravagant Strangers: A Literature of Belonging*. London: Faber, 1997.

Pickering, Paul A., and Tyrrell, Alex. *The People's Bread: A History of the Anti-Corn Law League*. London: Leicester University Press, 2000.

Pittock, Murray. 'Dowson and Clough.' *Notes and Queries*, NS 34 (1987), 501–2.

Pletcher, David M. *The Diplomacy of Annexation: Texas, Oregon, and the Mexican War*. Columbia, Mo.: University of Missouri Press, 1973.

Plimpton, George, ed. *Poets at Work: The* Paris Review *Interviews*. London: Penguin, 1989.

Plumb, J. H. 'British Attitudes to the American Revolution.' In *The American Experience: The Collected Essays*, ii, 61–73. New York: Harvester Wheatsheaf, 1989.

Pocock, J. G. A. *The Machiavellian Moment: Florentine Political Thought and the Atlantic Republican Tradition*. Princeton: Princeton University Press, 1975.

_____ '1776: The Revolution Against Parliament.' In *Three British Revolutions: 1641, 1688, 1776*, ed. J. G. A. Pocock, 265–88. Princeton: Princeton University Press, 1980.

Pool, James. *Hitler and his Secret Partners: Contributions, Loot and Rewards, 1933–1945*. New York: Pocket-Simon & Schuster, 1997.

Poole, Adrian. *Gissing in Context*. London: Macmillan, 1975.

Poovey, Mary. *Making a Social Body: British Cultural Formation, 1830–1864*. Chicago: University of Chicago Press, 1995.

Porte, Joel, ed. *The Cambridge Companion to Emerson*. Cambridge: Cambridge University Press, 1999.

Porter, Clyde and Reed, Mae. *Ruxton of the Rockies*, ed. LeRoy R. Hafen. Norman, Okla.: University of Oklahoma Press, 1950.

Porter, Roy. 'The Enlightenment in England.' In *The Enlightenment in National Context*, ed. Roy Porter and Mikuláš Teich, 1–18. Cambridge: Cambridge University Press, 1981.

_____ *Enlightenment: Britain and the Creation of the Modern World*. London: Penguin, 2000.

Pound, Ezra. *Jefferson and/or Mussolini: L'Idea Statale; Fascism, as I Have Seen It*. London: Nott, 1935.

Price, Richard. *Britain's Happiness, and the Proper Improvement of it* (1759). In *Political Writings*, 1–13.

_____ *Two Tracts on Civil Liberty, the War with America, and the Debts and Finances of the Kingdom* (1778). In *Political Writings*, 14–100.

_____ *Observations on the Importance of the American Revolution* (1785). In *Political Writings*, 116–51.

_____ *A Discourse on the Love of Our Country* (1789). In *Political Writings*, 176–96.

Price, Richard. *Political Writings*, ed. D. O. Thomas. Cambridge: Cambridge University Press, 1991.

Priestley, J. B. *Literature and Western Man*. New York: Harper & Row, 1960.

Pynchon, Thomas. Introduction. In *Nineteen Eighty-Four*, by George Orwell, pp. v–xxv. London: Penguin, 2003.

Quiller-Couch, Sir Arthur, ed. *The Oxford Book of English Verse, 1250–1900*. Oxford: Oxford University Press, 1900.

——— ed. *The Oxford Book of English Prose*. London: Oxford University Press, 1925.

Quinn, Revd Edward. 'Christian Politics.' *Criterion*, 17 (July 1938), 626–44.

Quinton, Anthony. 'Wodehouse and the Tradition of Comedy.' In *From Wodehouse to Wittgenstein: Essays*, 318–34. Manchester: Carcanet, 1998.

Rawson, Claude. 'Byron Augustan: Mutations of the Mock-Heroic in *Don Juan* and Shelley's *Peter Bell the Third*.' In *Byron: Augustan and Romantic*, ed. Rutherford, 82–116.

Reed, Carol, dir. *The Third Man*. British Lion Films Ltd., 1949.

Reeves, Gareth. 'Hearing Davie.' *PN Review*, 19/2 (Nov.–Dec. 1992), 48–51.

——— 'Beyond the New World: Donald Davie's Anglo-American Confessions.' *PN Review*, 25/3 (Jan.–Feb. 1999), 53–7.

Reeves, John. *Thoughts on the English Government*. London, 1795.

Rexroth, Kenneth. 'The Poetry of Denise Levertov' (1956). In *Denise Levertov*, ed. Gelpi, 11–14.

Reynolds, David. *Rich Relations: The American Occupation of Britain, 1942–1945* (1996). Repr. London: Phoenix Press, 2000.

Reynolds, Matthew. *The Realms of Verse: English Poetry in a Time of Nation-Building*. Oxford: Oxford University Press, 2001.

Richey, William. ' "The Lion & Wolf shall cease": Blake's America as a Critique of Counter-Revolutionary Violence.' In *Blake, Politics, and History*, ed. Jackie DiSalvo, G. A. Rosso, and Christopher Z. Hobson, 196–211. New York: Garland, 1998.

Ricks, Christopher. *T. S. Eliot and Prejudice*. London: Faber, 1988.

Riviere, Francesca. 'The Art of Fiction: CLI, Martin Amis.' *Paris Review*, no. 146 (Spring 1998), 108–35.

Rodgers, Daniel T. *Atlantic Crossings: Social Politics in a Progressive Age*. Cambridge, Mass.: Harvard University Press, 1998.

Rogin, Michael Paul. *Subversive Genealogy: The Politics and Art of Herman Melville*. New York: Knopf, 1983.

Rorty, Richard. *Philosophy and the Mirror of Nature*. Oxford: Blackwell, 1980.

Ross, Alexander. *Adventures of the First Settlers on the Oregon or Columbia River*. London, 1849.

Ross, Andrew. *The Failure of Modernism: Symptoms of American Poetry*. New York: Columbia University Press, 1986.

Rothschild, Emma. *Economic Sentiments: Adam Smith, Condorcet, and the Enlightenment.* Cambridge, Mass.: Harvard University Press, 2001.

Rowson, Susanna. *Charlotte Temple* (1791), ed. Cathy N. Davidson. New York: Oxford University Press, 1986.

——— *Reuben and Rachel; or, Tales of Old Times.* Boston, 1798.

Rushdie, Salman. *Midnight's Children.* London: Jonathan Cape, 1981.

——— 'Imaginary Homelands' (1982). In *Imaginary Homelands*, 9–21.

——— 'The New Empire within Britain' (1982). In *Imaginary Homelands*, 129–38.

——— ' "Commonwealth Literature" Does Not Exist' (1983). In *Imaginary Homelands*, 61–70.

——— *The Jaguar Smile: A Nicaraguan Journey* (1987). Repr. London: Vintage, 2000.

——— 'Charter 88' (1988). In *Imaginary Homelands*, 163–5.

——— *The Satanic Verses.* London: Viking Penguin, 1988.

——— 'In God We Trust' (1990). In *Imaginary Homelands*, 376–92.

——— 'In Good Faith' (1990). In *Imaginary Homelands*, 393–414.

——— 'Is Nothing Sacred?' (1990). In *Imaginary Homelands*, 415–29.

——— *Imaginary Homelands: Essays and Criticism, 1981–91.* London: Granta–Penguin, 1991.

——— 'Angela Carter, 1940–1992: A Very Good Wizard, a Very Dear Friend.' *New York Times Book Review*, 8 March 1992, 5.

——— 'Messages from the Plague Years' (1992–7). In *Step Across This Line*, 229–83.

——— 'The Best of Young British Novelists' (1993). In *Step Across This Line*, 34–9.

——— *East, West.* London: Jonathan Cape, 1994.

——— *The Moor's Last Sigh.* London: Jonathan Cape, 1995.

——— 'Crash: The Death of Princess Diana' (1997). In *Step Across This Line*, 118–21.

——— *The Ground Beneath Her Feet.* London: Jonathan Cape, 1999.

——— 'Islam and the West' (1999). In *Step Across This Line*, 323–5.

——— 'Rock Music' (1999). In *Step Across This Line*, 299–301.

——— 'The Human Rights Act' (2000). In *Step Across This Line*, 353–5.

——— 'In Defence of the Novel, Yet Again' (2000). In *Step Across This Line*, 54–63.

——— *Fury.* London: Jonathan Cape, 2001.

——— 'Not About Islam?' (2001). In In *Step Across This Line*, 394–7.

——— 'It Wasn't Me' (2001). In *Step Across This Line*, 372–4.

——— 'Anti-Americanism' (2002). In *Step Across This Line*, 398–400.

——— 'Step Across This Line: The Tanner Lectures on Human Values, Yale, 2002.' In *Step Across This Line*, 405–42.

Rushdie, Salman. *Step Across This Line: Collected Non-Fiction 1992–2002.* London: Jonathan Cape, 2002.

Russell, Bertrand. 'Portraits from Memory, III: D. H. Lawrence.' *Harper's Magazine*, Feb. 1953, 93–5.

Rutherford, Andrew, ed. *Lord Byron: The Critical Heritage.* London: Routledge, 1970.

——— ed. *Byron: Augustan and Romantic.* Basingstoke: Macmillan and the British Council, 1990.

Ruxton, George F. *The Oregon Question: A Glance at the Respective Claims of Great Britain and the United States to the Territory in Dispute.* London: John Ollivier, 1846.

———*Adventures in Mexico and the Rocky Mountains.* London: John Murray, 1847.

——— *Life in the Far West* (1848), ed. LeRoy R. Hafen. Norman, Okla.: University of Oklahoma Press, 1951.

Ryan, Robert M. *The Romantic Reformation: Religious Politics in English Literature, 1789–1824.* Cambridge: Cambridge University Press, 1997.

Sack, James J. *From Jacobite to Conservative: Reaction and Orthodoxy in Britain, c. 1760–1832.* Cambridge: Cambridge University Press, 1993.

Sadoff, Dianne L. *Monsters of Affection: Dickens, Eliot, and Bronte on Fatherhood.* Baltimore: Johns Hopkins University Press, 1982.

Sadowski-Smith, Claudia. 'Contesting Globalisms: The Transnationalization of U.S. Cultural Studies.' *Postmodern Culture*, 10/1 (Sept. 1999), 1–20.

Sage, Lorna. 'The Savage Sideshow: A Profile of Angela Carter.' *New Review*, 4, 39–40 (June–July 1977), 51–7.

——— 'Invasion from Outsiders.' *Granta*, 3 (1980), 131–6.

Said, Edward. 'Globalizing Literary Study.' *PMLA*, 116 (2001), 64–8.

Sartre, Jean-Paul. *What Is Literature?* (1948), trans. Bernard Frechtman. London: Methuen, 1950.

Schattemann, Renée. 'An Interview with Caryl Phillips.' *Commonwealth Essays and Studies,* 23/2 (Spring 2001), 93–106.

Schirmer, Gregory A. '"This That I Am Heir To": Donald Davie and Religion.' In *Donald Davie and the Responsibilities of Literature*, ed. Dekker, 129–42.

Schneidau, Herbert S. *Waking Giants: The Presence of the Past in Modernism.* New York: Oxford University Press, 1991.

Schonhardt-Bailey, Cheryl, ed. *Free Trade: The Repeal of the Corn Laws.* Bristol: Thoemmes Press, 1996.

Schuchard, Ronald. *Eliot's Dark Angel: Intersections of Life and Art.* Oxford: Oxford University Press, 1999.

Scott, P. G. 'A. H. Clough's *Poems* (1862): The English and American Editions.' *Harvard Library Bulletin*, 20/3 (July 1972), 320–36.

Scott, Walter. *Waverley* (1814), ed. Andrew Hook. London: Penguin, 1972.

——— *Guy Mannering* (1815). London: Nelson, 1938.

_____ *Ivanhoe: A Romance* (1819), ed. Graham Tulloch. London: Penguin, 2000.

_____ *The Life of Napoleon Buonaparte, Emperor of the French, with a Preliminary View of the French Revolution*, 9 vols. Paris, 1827.

Sedgwick, Ellery. *The* Atlantic Monthly, *1857–1909: Yankee Humanism and High Tide and Ebb*. Amherst, Mass.: University of Massachusetts Press, 1994.

Seeley, Sir John. *The Expansion of England: Lectures*. London, 1883.

Seldes, Gilbert. *The Seven Lively Arts*. New York: Harper, 1924.

Seldon, M. H. 'First Sight of Germany.' *Anglo-German Review*, 1/4 (Feb. 1937), 192.

Shand-Tucci, Douglas. *Boston Bohemia, 1881–1900. Ralph Adams Cram: Life and Architecture*. Amherst, Mass.: University of Massachusetts Press, 1995.

Sharrad, Paul. 'Speaking the Unspeakable: London, Cambridge and the Caribbean.' In *De-Scribing Empire: Post-Colonialism and Textuality*, ed. Chris Tiffin and Alan Lawson, 201–17. London: Routledge, 1994.

Shelley, Andrew. 'Donald Davie and the Canon.' *Essays in Criticism*, 42 (1992), 1–23.

Shelley, Mary Wollstonecraft. *Frankenstein, or The Modern Prometheus* (1818). *The Novels and Selected Works*, i, ed. Nora Crook. London: William Pickering, 1996.

_____ *The Last Man* (1826). *The Novels and Selected Works*, iv, ed. Jane Blumberg and Nora Crook. London: William Pickering, 1996.

_____ *Lodore* (1835). *The Novels and Selected Works*, vi, ed. Fiona Stafford. London: William Pickering, 1996.

_____ *Rambles in Germany and Italy*, 2 vol. (1844). In *Travel Writing*, 49–296.

_____ *Travel Writing. The Novels and Selected Works*, viii, ed. Jeanne Moskal. London: William Pickering, 1996.

_____ *The Letters of Mary Wollstonecraft Shelley*, iii, ed. Betty T. Bennett. Baltimore: Johns Hopkins University Press, 1988.

Shelley, P. B. *A Philosophical View of Reform* (1819). In *Shelley's Prose*, 229–61.

_____ *The Complete Poetical Works of Percy Bysshe Shelley*, ed. Neville Rogers, 2 vols. Oxford: Oxford University Press, 1972–5.

_____ *Shelley's Prose; or, The Trumpet of a Prophecy*, ed. David Lee Clark (1966). Repr. London: Fourth Estate, 1988.

Showalter, Elaine. *Sexual Anarchy: Gender and Culture at the Fin de Siècle*. New York: Viking, 1990.

Sigg, Eric. 'Eliot as Product of America.' In *The Cambridge Companion to T. S. Eliot*, ed. A. David Moody, 14–30. Cambridge: Cambridge University Press, 1994.

Silkin, Jon. 'Which England Shall We Labour For? A Reply to Donald Davie's Conservative England.' *Parnassus: Poetry in Review*, 7/1 (1978), 280–7.

Simmons, James C. *Star-Spangled Eden: Nineteenth-Century America through the Eyes of Dickens, Wilde, Frances Trollope, Frank Harris, and Other British Travellers*. New York: Carroll and Graf, 2000.

Simpson, Alexander. *The Oregon Territory: Claims Thereto of England and America Considered; Its Condition and Prospects.* London, 1846.

Simpson, David. *Romanticism, Nationalism, and the Revolt against Theory.* Chicago: University of Chicago Press, 1993.

Slater, Michael, ed. *Dickens on America and the Americans.* Brighton: Harvester Press, 1979.

Slinn, E. Warwick. *Victorian Poetry as Cultural Critique: The Politics of Performative Language.* Charlottesville, Va.: University Press of Virginia, 2003.

Smith, Adam. *The Wealth of Nations, Books IV–V* (1776), ed. Andrew Skinner. London: Penguin, 1999.

Smith, Anthony D. *Nationalism and Modernism: A Critical Survey of Recent Theories of Nations and Nationalism.* London: Routledge, 1998.

Smith, Barbara Clark. 'The Adequate Revolution.' Review of *The Radicalism of the American Revolution*, by Gordon S. Wood. *William and Mary Quarterly*, 3rd ser., 51 (1994), 684–92.

Smith, Goldwin. 'The Schism in the Anglo-Saxon Race.' In *Canadian Leaves: History, Art, Science, Literature, Commerce. A Series of Papers Read before the Candian Club of New York*, ed. G. M. Fairchild Jun., 19–57. New York, 1887.

Smith, Jad. 'Völkisch Organicism and the Uses of Primitivism in Lawrence's *The Plumed Serpent*.' *D. H. Lawrence Review*, 30/3 (2002), 7–24.

Smith, Stan. *W. H. Auden.* Oxford: Blackwell, 1985.

Smith, Zadie. *White Teeth.* London: Hamish Hamilton, 2000.

Smith-Rosenberg, Carroll. 'Subject Female: Authorizing American Identity.' *American Literary History*, 5 (1993), 481–511.

Snow, C. P. *The Light and the Dark.* London: Faber, 1947.

—— *The Conscience of the Rich* (1958). Repr. London: Penguin, 1961.

—— *The Sleep of Reason.* London: World Books, 1968.

Sollors, Werner. 'Introduction: After the Culture Wars; or, From "English Only" to "English Plus." ' In *Multilingual America: Transnationalism, Ethnicity, and the Languages of American Literature*, ed. Werner Sollors, 1–13. New York: New York University Press and Longfellow Institute, 1998.

—— 'Ethnic Modernism, 1910–1950.' *American Literary History*, 15 (2003), 70–77.

Sontag, Susan. 'Fascinating Fascism' (1974). In *A Susan Sontag Reader*, 305–25. New York: Random House–Vintage, 1983.

Spanos, William V. 'Hermeneutics and Meaning: Destroying T. S. Eliot's *Four Quartets*.' *Genre*, 11 (1978), 523–73.

Spater, George. *William Cobbett: The Poor Man's Friend*, 2 vols. Cambridge: Cambridge University Press, 1982.

Spender, Stephen. 'Cats and Dog' (1939). In *T. S. Eliot: The Critical Heritage*, ed. Grant, ii. 406–8.

Spengemann, William C. 'American Writers and English Literature.' *ELH*, 52 (1985), 209–38.

____*A Mirror for Americanists: Reflections on the Idea of American Literature*. Hanover, NH: University Press of New England, 1989.

Spicer, Andrew. 'The Emergence of the British Tough Guy: Stanley Baker, Masculinity and the Crime Thriller.' In *British Crime Cinema*, ed. Chibnall and Murphy, 81–93.

Sproat, Iain. *Wodehouse at War*. London: Milner and Company, 1981.

Stafford, Fiona. J. *The Last of the Race: The Growth of a Myth from Milton to Darwin*. Oxford: Clarendon Press, 1994.

Stanley, Arthur Penrhyn. *The Life and Correspondence of Thomas Arnold, D.D.*, 6th edn. London, 1846.

Sterrenburg, Lee. '*The Last Man*: Anatomy of Failed Revolutions.' *Nineteenth-Century Fiction*, 33 (1978), 324–47.

Stonehouse, J. H. *Catalogue of the Library of Charles Dickens from Gadshill*. London: Piccadilly Fountain Press, 1935.

Stout, Mira. 'Martin Amis: Down London's Mean Streets.' *New York Times Magazine*, 4 Feb. 1990, 32–48.

Stowe, Harriet Beecher. 'The True Story of Lady Byron's Life' (1870). In *The Oxford Harriet Beecher Stowe Reader*, ed. Joan D. Hedrick, 531–58. New York: Oxford University Press, 1999.

Strachey, Lytton. *Eminent Victorians: Cardinal Manning, Florence Nightingale, Dr. Arnold, General Gordon* (1918). Repr. London: Collins, 1959.

Streeby, Shelley. 'Joaquín Murrieta and the American 1848.' In *Post-Nationalist American Studies*, ed. John Carlos Rowe, 166–99. Berkeley: University of California Press, 2000.

Sulcer, Robert, jun. 'Ten Percent: Poetry and Pathology.' In *Victorian Sexual Dissidence*, ed. Richard Dellamora, 235–52. Chicago: University of Chicago Press, 1999.

Suleri, Sara. *The Rhetoric of English India*. Chicago: University of Chicago Press, 1992.

Sutherland, Bruce. 'George Frederick Ruxton in North America.' *Southwest Review*, 30/1 (Autumn 1944), 86–91.

Sutherland, John. 'The Sound and the Fury.' Review of *Fury*, by Salman Rushdie. *Guardian* (London), 25 Aug. 2001, 8.

Sutton, Walter. 'Conversation with Denise Levertov' (1965). In *Denise Levertov*, ed. Wagner, 22–40.

Swinburne, A. C. *Songs before Sunrise*. London, 1871.

Symons, Arthur. 'The Decadent Movement in Literature' (1893). In *Dramatis Personae*, 92–117. London: Faber and Gwyer, 1925.

Tanner, Tony. *The Reign of Wonder: Naivety and Reality in American Literature*. Cambridge: Cambridge University Press, 1965.

——*Adultery in the Novel: Contract and Transgression.* Baltimore: Johns Hopkins University Press, 1979.

Taylor, Edward. *The Poems of Edward Taylor,* ed. Donald E. Stanford. New Haven: Yale University Press, 1960.

Tennyson, Alfred, Lord. *The Poems of Tennyson,* ii, 2nd edn., ed. Christopher Ricks. Harlow: Longman, 1987.

Terkel, Studs. 'Christopher Isherwood' (1977). In *Conversations with Christopher Isherwood,* ed. Berg and Freeman, 166–80.

Tharoor, Shashi. 'How the Woosters Captured Delhi.' *Guardian Review* (London), 20 July 2002, 4–6.

Thomas, Helen. *Romanticism and Slave Narratives: Transatlantic Testimonies.* Cambridge: Cambridge University Press, 2000.

Thoreau, Henry David. 'Advantages and Disadvantages of Foreign Influences on American Literature' (1836). In *Early Essays and Miscellanies,* ed. Joseph J. Moldenhauer and Edwin Moser, with Alexander C. Kern, 38–41. Princeton: Princeton University Press, 1975.

——*A Week on the Concord and Merrimack Rivers* (1849), ed. Carl F. Hovde, William L. Howarth, and Elizabeth Hall Witherell. Princeton: Princeton University Press, 1980.

——'A Yankee in Canada' (1853). In *Collected Essays and Poems,* 256–323.

——*Walden* (1854), ed. J. Lyndon Shanley. Princeton: Princeton University Press, 1971.

——'Walking' (1862). In *Collected Essays and Poems,* 225–55.

——*The Maine Woods* (1864), ed. Joseph J. Moldenhauer. Princeton: Princeton University Press, 1972.

——*Collected Essays and Poems,* ed. Elizabeth Hall Witherell. New York: Library of America, 2001.

Thorne, Matt. 'Rich Man's Blues.' Review of *Fury,* by Salman Rushdie. *Independent on Sunday* (London), 26 Aug. 2001, 15.

Thorpe, Michael, ed. *Clough: The Critical Heritage.* London: Routledge & Kegan Paul, 1972.

Tillotson, Kathleen. *Novels of the Eighteen-Forties,* 2nd edn. Oxford: Clarendon Press, 1956.

Tolkien, J. R. R. *The Lord of the Rings,* 3 vols. London: Allen & Unwin, 1954–5.

Torgovnick, Marianna. *Gone Primitive: Savage Intellects, Modern Lives.* Chicago: University of Chicago Press, 1990.

Tredell, Nicolas. 'In Conversation with Donald Davie.' *PN Review,* 19, 2 (Nov.–Dec. 1992), 61–71.

——ed. *The Fiction of Martin Amis: A Reader's Guide to Essential Criticism.* Duxford, Cambridge: Icon, 2000.

Trollope, Fanny. *Domestic Manners of the Americans* (1832), ed. Pamela Neville-Sington. London: Penguin, 1997.

Trotter, David. 'The Avoidance of Naturalism: Gissing, Moore, Grand, Bennett, and Others.' In *The Columbia History of the British Novel*, ed. John Richetti, 608–30. New York: Columbia University Press, 1994.

Trudgill, Eric. *Madonnas and Magdalens: The Origins and Development of Victorian Sexual Attitudes*. London: Heinemann, 1976.

Trumpener, Katie. *Bardic Nationalism: The Romantic Novel and the British Empire*. Princeton: Princeton University Press, 1997.

Trussler, Michael. 'Literary Artifacts: Ekphrasis in the Short Fiction of Donald Barthelme, Salman Rushdie, and John Edgar Wideman.' *Contemporary Literature*, 41 (2000), 252–90.

Twain, Mark. *Life on the Mississippi* (1883). Repr. New York: Oxford University Press, 1996.

—— *The Tragedy of Pudd'nhead Wilson and the Comedy of Those Extraordinary Twins* (1894). Repr. New York: Oxford University Press, 1996.

Uebel, Michael. 'Masochism in America.' *American Literary History*, 14 (2002), 389–411.

Vale, V., and Juno, Andrea, eds. *Re/Search: J. G. Ballard*. San Francisco: Re/Search Publications, 1984.

Viereck, Peter. *Metapolitics: From the Romantics to Hitler*. New York: Knopf, 1941.

Voelker, Frederic E. 'Ruxton of the Rocky Mountains.' *Missouri Historical Society Bulletin*, 5/2 (Jan. 1949), 79–90.

Von Hallberg, Robert. 'Donald Davie and the Moral Shape of Politics.' In *Donald Davie and the Moral Responsibilities of Literature*, ed. Dekker, 74–94.

Vonnegut, Kurt. *Slaughterhouse Five, or, The Children's Crusade: A Duty-Dance with Death*. New York: Delacorte Press, 1969.

Wagar, W. Warren. 'J. G. Ballard and the Transvaluation of Utopia.' *Science-Fiction Studies*, 18/1 (March 1991), 53–70.

Wagner, Linda Welshimer, ed. *Denise Levertov: In Her Own Province*. New York: New Directions, 1979.

Waldstreicher, David. *In the Midst of Perpetual Fêtes: The Making of American Nationalism, 1776–1820*. Williamsburg, Va.: Omohundro Institute of Early American History and Culture; Chapel Hill, NC: University of North Carolina Press, 1997.

Walkowitz, Judith R. *City of Dreadful Delight: Narratives of Sexual Danger in Late-Victorian London* (1992). Repr. London: Virago Press, 1994.

Wallace, Edward J. *The Oregon Question Determined by the Rule of International Law*. London, 1846.

Ward, Geoff. *The Writing of America: Literature and Cultural Identity from the Puritans to the Present*. Cambridge: Polity, 2002.

Warre, Captain H. [Henry]. *Sketches in North America and the Oregon Territory*. London, 1849.

Waters, Frank. *Book of the Hopi* (1963). Repr. London: Penguin, 1977.

Watney, Simon. 'Portrait of an Artist.' *Marxism Today*, Oct. 1988, 44–5.

Watt, Donald, ed. *Aldous Huxley: The Critical Heritage*. London: Routledge & Kegan Paul, 1975.

Watt, Ian. *The Rise of the Novel: Studies in Defoe, Richardson and Fielding*. London: Chatto & Windus, 1957.

Waugh, Evelyn. *The Loved One: An Anglo-American Tragedy*. London: Chapman & Hall, 1948.

——— 'An Act of Homage and Reparation to P. G. Wodehouse' (1961). In *The Essays, Articles and Reviews of Evelyn Waugh*, ed. Donat Gallagher, 561–8. London: Methuen, 1983.

——— *The Letters of Evelyn Waugh*, ed. Mark Amory. London: Weidenfeld & Nicolson, 1980.

Webster, Len. 'A Very Individualistic Old Liberal' (1971). In *Conversations with Christopher Isherwood*, ed. Berg and Freeman, 57–71.

Weisbuch, Robert. *Atlantic Double-Cross: American Literature and British Influence in the Age of Emerson*. Chicago: University of Chicago Press, 1986.

——— 'Post-colonial Emerson and the Erasure of History.' In *Cambridge Companion to Emerson*, ed. Porte, 192–217.

Welch, Dave. 'Salman Rushdie, Out and About.' Powells.com Interviews, 25 Sept. 2002. Online:<http://www.powells.com/authors/rushdie.html>, accessed 30 April 2005.

Welles, Orson, dir. *The Stranger*. RKO Pictures, 1946.

Whale, John. *Imagination under Pressure, 1789–1832: Aesthetics, Politics and Utility*. Cambridge: Cambridge University Press, 2000.

Whistler, James McNeill. *The Gentle Art of Making Enemies*. London: Heinemann, 1890.

White, Edmund. *The Beautiful Room is Empty*. London: Picador, 1988.

Whitehead, Kate. *The Third Programme: A Literary History*. Oxford: Clarendon Press, 1989.

Whitman, Walt. 'Democratic Vistas' (1871). In *Complete Poetry and Collected Prose*, 929–94.

——— 'Emerson's Books, (the Shadows of Them)' (1892). In *Complete Poetry and Collected Prose*, 1052–5.

——— *Complete Poetry and Collected Prose*, ed. Justin Kaplan. New York: Library of America, 1982.

Wickes, George. 'An Interview with Christopher Isherwood' (1965). In *Conversations with Christopher Isherwood*, ed. Berg and Freeman, 24–44.

Wickwire, Franklin, and Wickwire, Mary. *Cornwallis: The Imperial Years*. Chapel Hill, NC: University of North Carolina Press, 1980.

Widmer, Edward L. *Young America: The Flowering of Democracy in New York City*. New York: Oxford University Press, 1999.

Wilde, Oscar. 'Impressions of America' (1883). In *The Artist as Critic*, 6–12.

——— 'Mr. Whistler's Ten O'Clock' (1885). In *The Artist as Critic*, 13–16.

____ 'The Gospel According to Walt Whitman' (1889). In *The Artist as Critic*, 121–5.

____ 'The Decay of Lying' (1891). In *The Artist as Critic*, 290–320.

____ *The Artist as Critic: Critical Writings of Oscar Wilde*, ed. Richard Ellmann. London: W. H. Allen, 1970.

____ *The Complete Illustrated Stories, Plays and Poems*. London: Chancellor Press, 1986.

Williams, Charles. *The Descent of the Dove: A Short History of the Holy Spirit in the Church*. London: Longmans, Green and Co., 1939.

Williams, Ernest. 'Get Out!' *Outlook* (London), 19 Feb. 1898, 76–7.

Williams, Raymond. *Culture and Society, 1780–1950*. London: Chatto & Windus, 1958.

____ *The Long Revolution*. London: Chatto & Windus, 1961.

____ *The English Novel from Dickens to Lawrence*. London: Chatto & Windus, 1970.

____ 'Base and Superstructure in Marxist Cultural Theory.' *New Left Review*, no. 82 (Nov.–Dec. 1973), 3–16.

Williams, William Carlos. *In the American Grain*. New York: Boni, 1925.

Willis, Frederick. *101 Jubilee Road: A Book of London Yesterdays*. London: Phoenix House, 1948.

Wilson, Rob. 'Exporting Christian Transcendentalism, Importing Hawaiian Sugar: The Trans-Americanization of Hawai'i.' *American Literature*, 72 (2000), 521–52.

Winthrop, John. 'A Model of Christian Charity' (1630). In *The American Puritans: Their Prose and Poetry*, ed. Perry Miller, 78–84. New York: Doubleday Anchor, 1956.

Wodehouse, P. G. 'Jeeves and the Unbidden Guest' (1925). In *Carry On, Jeeves*, 51–71.

____ 'Jeeves Takes Charge' (1925). In *Carry On, Jeeves*, 9–32.

____ *Carry On, Jeeves* (1925). Repr. London: Penguin, 1957.

____ *Meet Mr. Mulliner*. London: Herbert Jenkins, 1927.

____ *Thank You, Jeeves* (1934). Repr. London: Penguin, 1999.

____ 'Archibald and the Masses.' *Hearst's International combined with Cosmopolitanism*, 99/2 (Aug. 1935), 34–8.

____ *The Code of the Woosters* (1938). Introduction by Joe Keenan. London: Penguin, 1999.

____ *Joy in the Morning* (1946). Repr. London: Barrie & Jenkins, 1974.

____ *The Mating Season* (1949). Introduction by Christopher Hitchens. London: Penguin, 1999.

____ *Ring for Jeeves* (1953). Repr. London: Coronet, 1983.

____ *Plum Pie* (1966). Repr. London: Pan, 1968.

____ 'A Note on Humour.' In *Plum Pie*, 248–51.

____ 'Jeeves and the Greasy Bird.' In *Plum Pie*, 7–47.

Wodehouse, P. G. *Much Obliged, Jeeves* (1971). Repr. London: Sphere, 1972.

―――*Aunts Aren't Gentlemen* (1974). Repr. London: Penguin, 1977.

―――*Yours, Plum: The Letters of P. G. Wodehouse*, ed. Frances Donaldson. London: Hutchinson, 1990.

Wood, Gordon S. *The Radicalism of the American Revolution*. New York: Knopf, 1992.

Wood, Marcus. *Blind Memory: Visual Representations of Slavery in England and America, 1780–1865*. Manchester: Manchester University Press, 2000.

―――*Slavery, Empathy, and Pornography*. Oxford: Oxford University Press, 2002.

Woodcock, George. *Dawn and the Darkest Hour: A Study of Aldous Huxley*. London: Faber, 1972.

Wordsworth, William. 'Preface to *Lyrical Ballads with Pastoral and Other Poems*' (1802). In *Selected Poems*, ed. John O. Hayden, 431–59. London: Penguin, 1994.

―――*The Prose Works of William Wordsworth*, ed. W. J. B. Owen and Jane Worthington Smyser, 3 vols. Oxford: Clarendon Press, 1974.

―――*The Prelude: The Four Texts*, ed. Jonathan Wordsworth. London: Penguin, 1995.

―――*The Letters of William and Dorothy Wordsworth*, 2nd edn., v: *The Later Years. Part II: 1829–1834*, ed. Alan G. Hill. Oxford: Clarendon Press, 1979.

Younge, Gary. 'Home Run.' *Guardian* (London), 27 May 2000, 8.

Youngquist, Paul. 'Ballard's Crash-Body.' *Postmodern Culture*, 11/1 (Sept. 2000), 1–28.

Zeitlin, Jonathan. 'Introduction: Americanization and its Limits: Reworking U.S. Technology and Management in Post-War Europe and Japan.' In *Americanization and its Limits: Reworking U.S. Technology and Management in Post-War Europe and Japan*, ed. Jonathan Zeitlin and Gary Herrigel, 1–50. Oxford: Oxford University Press, 2000.

Zuckerman, Michael. 'Rhetoric, Reality, and the Revolution: The Genteel Radicalism of Gordon Wood.' *William and Mary Quarterly*, 3rd ser., 51 (1994), 693–702.

Index